# UNITED STATES DIPLOMATIC HISTORY

## *The Age of Ascendancy*

*Volume 2*
*Since 1900*

### GERARD CLARFIELD
University of Missouri-Columbia

PRENTICE HALL   Englewood Cliffs, New Jersey 07632

*Library of Congress Cataloging-in-Publication Data*

Clarfield, Gerard H.
    United States diplomatic history : the age of ascendancy /
  Gerard Clarfield.
      p.   cm.
    Includes bibliographical references and indexes.
    Contents: v. 1 to 1914 — v. 2. Since 1900
      1. United States—Foreign relations.   I. Title.
  E183.7.C59   1992        327.73        91-20218
  ISBN 0-13-029190-0 (v. 1)
  ISBN 0-13-029232-x (v. 2)

E
183.7
.C59
1992
v.2

Acquisitions editor: Stephen Dalphin
Editorial/production supervision and
    interior design: Barbara Reilly
Copy editor: Ann Hofstra Grogg
Cover design: Wanda Lubelska Design
Prepress buyer: Debra Kesar/Kelly Behr
Manufacturing buyer: Mary Ann Gloriande
Editorial assistant: Caffie Risher

*For Leslie and Joe,*
*who fully appreciate what W. C. Fields*
*had in mind when he said, "On the*
*whole, I'd rather be in Philadelphia."*

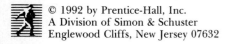 © 1992 by Prentice-Hall, Inc.
A Division of Simon & Schuster
Englewood Cliffs, New Jersey 07632

Printed in the United States of America
10  9  8  7  6  5  4  3  2  1

ISBN    0-13-029232-X

Prentice-Hall International (UK) Limited, *London*
Prentice-Hall of Australia Pty. Limited, *Sydney*
Prentice-Hall Canada Inc., *Toronto*
Prentice-Hall Hispanoamericana, S.A., *Mexico*
Prentice-Hall of India Private Limited, *New Delhi*
Prentice-Hall of Japan, Inc., *Tokyo*
Simon & Schuster Asia Pte. Ltd., *Singapore*
Editora Prentice-Hall do Brasil, Ltda., *Rio de Janeiro*

# CONTENTS

# *PREFACE*

It wasn't too long ago (before the proliferation of good, relatively inexpensive paperback books) that students were required to depend upon a textbook as their main source of information in history courses. These books were by and large extremely thorough, and of course, students received a solid grounding in the major issues. But they also spent a good deal of time unraveling the mysteries surrounding obscure boundary disputes, quarrels over fishing rights, and pelagic sealing controversies, all matters of less than earth-shaking consequence.

As teachers I think we are more sensitive today. We know that a good teaching tool does not need to be, indeed probably should not be, encyclopedic. At the same time I think we are also wise enough to know what should be remembered. My hope is that this book lives up to that standard.

Like all syntheses, this book is based in large part on an extensive reading of the work of others. I have, through the use of notes and the section on supplementary reading, acknowledged many but by no means all of my debts. I would therefore like to take this opportunity to thank those whose names do not appear in these pages but whose work has nevertheless contributed so much to my understanding of our diplomatic history. I would also like to express my profound appreciation to Michael Barnhart of the

State University of New York at Stony Brook, Lawrence Gelfand of the University of Iowa, and Burton Kaufman of Virginia Polytechnic Institute and State University for their careful reading of this work in manuscript and the many helpful suggestions they have offered. I am also deeply grateful to Mrs. Patty Eggleston for her help in preparing the manuscript for publication. Last, but by no means least, I thank my editors, Barbara Reilly who has been a joy to work with, and Ann Hofstra Grogg whose extraordinary labors on my behalf have been an enormous asset.

# INTRODUCTION

At the dawn of the twentieth century, the United States was already an imperial power with island outposts in the Caribbean and the Pacific, economic interests that stretched far beyond its borders, and a burgeoning foreign trade that was important to the continued health and well-being of its domestic economy. At the same time, however, Americans were profoundly ambivalent about the political role their country should play in world affairs. Policy makers and the public at large agreed that the United States should establish and maintain hegemony over the Western Hemisphere. Repeated interventions in the internal affairs of Latin American countries generated little in the way of domestic opposition. Moreover, so long as Washington confined itself to diplomatic initiatives, the public was generally supportive of efforts by a succession of administrations to play an important role in China even when that meant becoming entangled in a Far Eastern version of great power politics.

At the same time the tradition of non-entanglement in Europe's political affairs and wars remained a powerful force in American life. Of all the presidents prior to World War I, only the ebullient Theodore Roosevelt presumed to play any sort of role on the European stage. And even Roosevelt confined himself to a bit part. By the same token, the country refused to support a large peacetime military establishment. To be sure, there were those such as the naval strategist, Captain Alfred Thayer Mahan, who in the late nineteenth century described the oceans not as barriers but as highways connecting the Old and New Worlds. Still, the prevailing sentiment was that the oceans would insulate the United States from Old World conflicts, and that the country could carry on in the tradition of the founding fathers by pursuing its own global interests while avoiding entanglement in European wars.

In a sense then, the first four decades of this century may be viewed as the period during which Americans finally resolved a dilemma that was as old as the country itself. It took the Great War of 1914–1918, the failure of Woodrow Wilson's effort to create a lasting peace through the instrumentality of the League of Nations, and the coming of another even more devastating war to form a new national consensus. But well before the end of World War II it was generally assumed that the country would play a leading role in global political affairs after the war.

During World War II, most Americans imagined that once Fascism, Nazism, and Japanese militarism had been smashed, a lasting peace would result. Some placed their faith in the old Wilsonian concept of collective security and looked to the newly created United Nations to do the job. More realistic observers, including President Franklin D. Roosevelt, recognized that the United Nations could not maintain a stable new order without great power agreement, and therefore placed heavy reliance on continued postwar inter-allied cooperation as the real key to peace. All were to be grievously disappointed, for the rivalry between the United States and the Soviet Union that began as a result of conflicting war aims quickly developed into a cold war that dominated international affairs for the next four decades.

The confrontation with the Soviet Union and the struggle against the expansion of international communism became key features of American foreign policy in the postwar era. In pursuit of victory in the cold war, American presidents financed the reconstruction of Western Europe and encouraged the resuscitation of America's wartime enemies, Germany and Japan. They also fought two major land wars in Asia, mounted covert actions to thwart revolutionary movements throughout the Third World, repeatedly interfered in the internal affairs of other nations, sanctioned political assassinations, and distorted the constitutional system to create what historian Arthur Schlesinger Jr. dubbed "The Imperial Presidency." In the name of national security, the United States, a country with a long anti-military tradition, also proclaimed itself the policeman for the world and lavished trillions of dollars on the defense establishment, thus creating a dangerous military-industrial complex and the "national security state" in which we still live.

When the first atomic bomb was exploded near Alamagordo, New Mexico in July 1945, civilization entered a new era. For the first time in history, political leaders commanded the power to destroy humankind and perhaps all life on the planet. That fact alone should have produced a powerful incentive for "putting the genie" of nuclear power "back in the bottle." But this was the era of the cold war and so instead of a serious cooperative effort at controlling the atom, the superpowers treated the world to the nuclear arms race, an ever-increasing level of insecurity, and a number of unimpressive and often insincere attempts at arms control.

For a quarter of a century, from the end of World War II until the early 1970s, few dared to challenge the assumptions on which cold war foreign policy was founded. It took the catastrophe of the Vietnam War before some began to raise questions. And it took the collapse of the Soviet empire as well as a new, more forthcoming attitude on the part of Soviet leaders before it was generally accepted that the cold war was in fact a thing of the past.

As it became apparent that the old system was dying, some in the American diplomatic community mourned its passing. They pointed out that the Soviet–American confrontation had created stability and a high level of predictability in international affairs. Such a view is of course extraordinarily myopic. The evils produced by the cold war far outweighed the good.

We live during a particularly exciting moment in world affairs. Eastern Europe and the Soviet Union are suffering from grave economic and political problems that have produced serious instability; a united Germany, also suffering from internal stress, is predominant in Europe; and Japan has become a global economic power. The Middle East and Africa are aflame. And as I write, the war in the Persian Gulf has just come to a close, leaving in its wake widespread instability throughout the region.

The American people and their leaders have emerged from this most recent conflict exultant, filled with hubris, and confident, as they have not been since the days of Vietnam, that this country can shape the course of world history and create what President George Bush describes as "a new world order." Whether that is true or not is problematic. Notwithstanding the United States's impressive showing in the Gulf War, Washington's position in the world has eroded—along with its once overwhelming economic strength. One thing, however, seems certain. We are at another of those moments in world affairs that bears the earmarks of a watershed. All in all, it is a fine moment to take stock, to look back. I hope that students will want to do that and that this volume will be helpful.

In 1900, 140,000 Boxers, like the man pictured above, rose up in a desperate attempt to drive foreign exploiters from China.

# WORLD POWER, 1899–1913

At the end of the Spanish-American War, the United States controlled a Pacific empire as well as Cuba and Puerto Rico. But that was only the beginning of a pattern of imperialism practiced first by President William McKinley and after his assassination by President Theodore Roosevelt. Before the new century was too far advanced the United States had fought a costly war to quell a rebellion in the Philippines, asserted its claim to free access to the China market, transformed Cuba into a protectorate, gained control of the Isthmus of Panama, and begun construction of the canal that earlier policy makers had only dreamed about. It was an extraordinary epoch in the history of American expansion.

On July 25, 1894, a clash between Chinese and Japanese naval forces signaled the beginning of a war in which Japan won not only major concessions from her adversary but also the respect of many in the West, who realized that it had, as Secretary of the Navy Hilary Herbert observed, "leaped, almost at one bound, to a place among the great nations of the earth."[1] The Treaty of Shimonoseki, signed on April 17, 1895, reflected the enormity of Japan's victory. China was driven from Korea and forced to cede Formosa, the Pescadores, and the Liaotung peninsula in southern Manchuria together with the ports of Dalian (Dairen) and Lüshun (Port Arthur).

Japan had taken a giant step toward great power status. But in moving into Manchuria, it went too far for the Russians, who had their own ambitions in that part of the world. Supported by France and Germany, St. Petersburg forced Japan to return the Manchurian plumb to China. Even so, Japan had clearly emerged on the world stage, a power to be reckoned with in the Far East.

The end of the Sino-Japanese War marked only the beginning of China's difficulties. In the next few years the great European powers moved in on "the sick man of Asia," securing leaseholds and spheres of influence over large areas of the country. The Russians took a leasehold over Lüshun (Port Arthur) and Lüda (Dairen) on the Liaodong (Liaotung) Penninsula (the area they had only recently forced the Japanese to surrender) and expanded their influence throughout Manchuria. The Germans acquired a leasehold over the port city of Quingdao (Tsingtao) on Kiaochow Bay as well as economic privileges on the Shantung Peninsula. And Britain took the port of Weihaiwei while bolstering its sphere of influence in the vast Yanhzi (Yangtse) River Valley. By 1898, China seemed well on the way toward dismemberment, a victim of European colonialism.

These developments were viewed with alarm by a number of special interest groups in the United States, who urged the McKinley administration to adopt a more assertive China policy. The missionary societies that sent men and women to labor in God's Chinese vineyard demanded that the government protect their people from Chinese xenophobes and, just as important, that it save China from dismemberment.

Elements of the business community also called on the government to take a greater interest in China. American cotton manufacturers and the Standard Oil Company of New York, which had developed a large market for kerosene in China, led the fight. They were supported by the American China Development Company as well as other important bankers and capitalists interested in investment opportunities there. In 1898 concerned businessmen organized the American Asiatic Association and the Committee on American Interests in China to lobby for a more aggressive Far Eastern policy. Soon the periodical press began to feature articles on America's growing need for Asian markets, while Congress and the administration received an increasing volume of mail calling for action.

## HAY'S OPEN DOOR NOTES

After the Spanish-American War, and in many ways because of it, President McKinley showed a new sensitivity to Far Eastern developments. The president was reacting to the growing domestic pressure, his own imperialistic ambitions, and the fact that other powers seemed on the verge of dismembering the Celestial Empire. He had not acquired Hawaii, Guam, and the Philippines only to be left on the outside looking in while other nations divided the China market among themselves. The president and Secretary of State John Hay both relied heavily on William W. Rockhill, chief of the

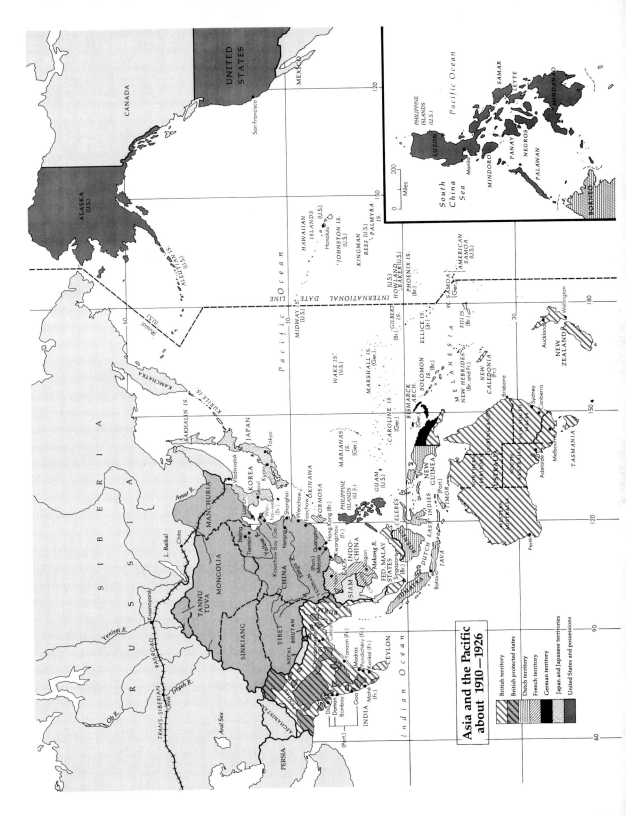

## Asia and the Pacific about 1910–1926

British territory
British protected states
Dutch territory
French territory
German territory
Japan and Japanese territories
United States and possessions

State Department's Latin American Division and a leading expert on Far Eastern affairs, to develop a new China policy. As a dedicated Sinophile, Rockhill was naturally appalled at the prospect of China's destruction at the hands of the industrialized nations. But as a policy maker he was primarily concerned because he believed that the dismemberment of China would close the China market, undermine the balance of power in Asia, fuel the already intense competition among the imperialist powers operating there, and perhaps lead to a general war.

It seemed to Rockhill that the United States ought to take whatever steps were necessary to forestall these portentious developments by preserving an independent and sovereign China. He was so convinced that the breakup of China would prove catastrophic that he even believed Washington ought to intervene with force if necessary to preserve a sovereign China. But he realized that there was no domestic support for anything beyond peaceful interposition on China's behalf. Words unsupported by deeds would have to suffice.

Rockhill fashioned a statement that, slightly edited in the State Department and signed by Secretary Hay, was sent as a circular message to St. Petersburg, Rome, London, Paris, Berlin, and Tokyo. This first "open door" note, which was issued on September 6, 1899, did not directly challenge the legitimacy of foreign leaseholds or spheres of influence (an area in which a single power exercises near-exclusive influence) in China. To have done so would have been to invite a speedy rebuff. Instead it asked only that the powers agree to provide equality of commercial opportunity for citizens of all nations in leaseholds and spheres, that the Chinese tariff in treaty ports under foreign control should continue in force, that the Chinese government be allowed to collect these duties, and that they cooperate to support the open door principle.

The powers differed in their reaction to Hay's note. The Italians, who had no sphere of influence or leasehold in China at the time, quickly endorsed the open door policy. The British and Japanese responded ambivalently. And the Russians, Germans, and French were evasive, determined to keep competitors out of areas they controlled. One can hardly blame them. After all, a major reason for acquiring a privileged position in China was to lay the foundation for monopolistic trade and investment practices.

In spite of the fact that aside from the clear and unqualified support for the open door offered by the Italians, the other interested powers, responded evasively, Hay interpreted their replies positively, announcing in March 1900 that they had given his proposal "final and definitive" acceptance.[2] Even though this was clearly not the case, Hay felt certain that none of the nations with ambitions in China would admit publicly that they were unwilling to accept a set of principles so eminently fair. He was right. None of the nations involved ever did challenge his interpretation of what they had done. But that did not mean that they were prepared to live by the open door principle either.

Considering that he confined himself to mere note writing, Hay was

The Boxer uprising and the siege of Beijing led a number of foreign nations, including the United States, to send troops to quell the rebellion. Here members of the multinational force are on parade inside the Forbidden City.

probably not too disappointed with what he had accomplished. He had quieted those business and missionary groups that were then calling for a more assertive China policy. He had also managed to make the American position regarding China clear while establishing the parameters for the international debate over China that was to follow. The open door policy did not protect China from international preditors. But it did serve to embarrass those who ignored it and to caution them, too, that their policy ran contrary to the stated interests of the United States, a nation to be reckoned with as the new century dawned.

Hay was aware that the status quo in China was fragile and that, open door or no, the more ambitious of the powers, Russia in particular, would seize any opportunity for further expansion at China's expense. Such an opportunity presented itself in June 1900, when the Boxer uprising broke out. The Boxers (in Chinese, I Ho Ch'uan, or Righteous, Harmonious Fists), 140,000 strong, were members of a secret society committed to the forceful expulsion of foreigners and foreign influences from China. Encouraged by the Dowager Empress Cixi (Tz'u-Hsi), and at first supported by elements of

A group of American cavalrymen, part of the multi-national force sent to put down the Boxer uprising, patrol along the Great Wall of China.

the Chinese army, the Boxers began their attacks on foreigners and Chinese Christian converts in 1898. This rising tide of officially sanctioned antiforeignism culminated in the summer of 1900, when the Boxers, supported by units of the Chinese army, besieged the diplomatic quarter in Beijing (Peking). The siege lasted for two months, until at length an international force of some twenty thousand, including British, French, German, Japanese, Russian, and American troops, marched into Beijing and rescued the besieged westerners.

At the time only a few prescient observers like Sir Robert Hart, head of the Chinese customs service, recognized the true significance of the Boxer uprising. Hart realized that the Boxers' purpose had been "to free China from the . . . corroding influence of a foreign cult and . . . from foreign troops, contamination, and humiliation." Though they had failed, Hart was convinced that the Boxers represented "today's hint to the future."[3]

Sensitive Western observers such as Hart were few and far between. Certainly Hay was not among them. Utterly contemptuous of the Chinese, he saw the Boxer uprising as significant only because it provided an opening for ambitious powers to make new encroachments on the already tottering Manchu dynasty, thus threatening America's interests in China as well as the Far Eastern balance of power.

Hay managed to block a proposal to use the international force assembled in Beijing to suppress the Boxers elsewhere in China. But he believed that further action was essential if the country was to be saved from partition. In July 1900, after a series of hurried consultations, he sent a second open door note to the powers, this time emphasizing the importance of preserving Chinese sovereignty and independence. Basing his argument on the fiction that the Beijing government had nothing to do with the Boxer uprising, the secretary of state insisted that the powers could have no legitimate objective in China beyond restoring order. China, he argued, should be preserved as a "territorial and administrative entity."[4]

Hay's second open door note had been a shot in the dark based on a desperate hope. And in fact it had no significant impact on the other nations involved in the China intervention. It is true that China was not partitioned, but other interested nations had recognized that taking control of large portions of China would be very costly. Moreover, they agreed with Hay's basic point, that a sovereign China was vital to the Far Eastern balance of power.

Although this second note had no real effect on the other interested powers, it is nevertheless important in that it broadened the meaning of the open door policy. At the beginning of the new century, Washington sought equality of commercial opportunity in China as well as the preservation of China as a sovereign entity. Still, the question remained, How would the United States go about achieving these aims? Hay himself was pessimistic, complaining that "not a single power" could be relied upon to support "our policy of abstention from plunder and the Open Door." The Russians, who were so obviously anxious to absorb Manchuria, were Hay's special concern. "Dealing with a government with whom mendacity was a science is an extremely difficult and delicate matter," he said.[5]

## ROOSEVELT AND THE OPEN DOOR

After the siege of Beijing had been raised, the powers agreed to remove their forces from China proper. But St. Petersburg saw the vast province of Manchuria, an area rich in natural resources that had never been entirely under Chinese control, in a different light. The czar's government used the opportunity created by the Boxer uprising to station troops there and extend its influence throughout the region.

As the Russians tightened their control over Manchuria, American businessmen, especially cotton manufacturers who traded extensively there, urged Washington to do something. They feared, no doubt correctly, that once St. Petersburg had consolidated its position, American manufactured goods would be shut out of that growing market.

Theodore Roosevelt, who became president in 1901 after McKinley's assassination, responded with appropriate diplomatic protests but went no further. Even assuming that he was personally anxious to defend the open door against the Russians in Manchuria, he was in no position to do so. As the human and material costs of putting down the long and bloody Philippine insurrection grew, public enthusiasm for imperialism waned, making an aggressive Far Eastern policy impossible. And so Roosevelt interpreted the open door policy in a minimalist way. "All we ask," he told St. Petersburg, "is that our great and growing trade shall not be interrupted and that Russia shall keep its solemn promises. . . . We have always recognized the exceptional position of Russia in relation to Manchuria."[6] The Russians, however, were unwilling to concede even that much.

If Roosevelt felt constrained to allow St. Petersburg to close the door in Manchuria, the same was not true of Japan's leaders, who viewed Russian adventurism there as a great threat. As part of its quest for economic power and international respectability, Japan was committed to an expansionist policy. It set out first to expand its already established position in Korea. In 1910 the Hermit Kingdom was fully integrated into the Japanese empire. It is not surprising, then, that Japan viewed the Russian presence in neighboring Manchuria as a threat to its vital interests.

Aware that the United States was having no luck in securing equality of commercial opportunity in Russian-dominated Manchuria, Japan first turned to Washington, hoping for support in its efforts to check the Russian advance there. But Roosevelt was unable to help. Rebuffed by the United States, the Japanese turned to London, where they found a willing partner against a mutual adversary. The Anglo-Japanese Alliance of 1902 gave the Russians a temporary fright. Chastened by this threatening combination, they agreed to withdraw their military forces from Manchuria.

In Washington, Roosevelt and Secretary of State Hay tried to take advantage of the leverage provided by the Anglo-Japanese accord, increasing the diplomatic pressure on the Russians. A frustrated Roosevelt even told Hay, "I wish in Manchuria to go to the very limit the people will stand. If only we were sure neither France nor Germany would join in, I should not in the least mind going to 'extremes' with Russia."[7] But Roosevelt was blowing smoke. He knew there was insufficient domestic support for an aggressive China policy.

In 1903 the Russians reneged on their promise to withdraw their forces from Manchuria and rejected a Japanese proposal for a diplomatic resolution to the Manchurian question. Tokyo reacted on February 4, 1904, by breaking relations with St. Petersburg. Two days later the Japanese launched a surprise attack on Russian naval forces at Lüshun and then declared war. By May of the following year most of southern Manchuria was in Japanese hands. The final blow for the Russians fell on May 27–28, 1905, when, in the two-day battle of Tsushima Strait, a Japanese fleet sank thirty-two Russian war vessels in one of the most celebrated naval battles of all time.

When news of the Japanese attack on Port Arthur reached Washington, the president was delighted. He told his son, "I was thoroughly pleased with the Japanese victory, for Japan is playing our game." When Roosevelt made that remark he was only echoing the views of most informed Americans. Prior to the war Japan had shown no interest in China proper. It appeared that it would be satisfied with a secure sphere of interest in Korea and a guarantee for her "existing rights in Manchuria." But once the fighting began, Prime Minister Katsura Tarō later explained, Tokyo expanded its objectives to include a Manchurian "sphere of influence where our rights and interests could be maintained and expanded."[8]

As this change in Japanese policy became apparent, Roosevelt's thinking changed, too. Where once he saw Tokyo as a check on Russian expansionism and a champion of the open door, now he began to think in terms of using Russia to balance Japan's growing power in the region. He told his friend Senator Henry Cabot Lodge that while he believed a Russian victory in the war would have been "a blow to civilization," it was equally true that its "destruction as an eastern Asiatic power would also" have been "unfortunate." Russia, he thought, "should be left face to face with Japan so that each may have a moderating action on the other."[9]

In May 1905 a nearly bankrupt Japanese government asked Roosevelt to arrange a mediated settlement to the war. The president jumped at the chance, arranging a peace conference that met at Portsmouth, New Hampshire. Roosevelt relished the opportunity to be at the center of events, for he was by nature a performer. But he also had two very practical reasons for wanting to play the role of mediator. First, he could encourage the sort of balance of forces in the Far East that he had described to Lodge. But more important, Roosevelt knew that Japan had only two directions in which to expand. If it did not focus its energies on the Asian mainland, it would certainly move into the Pacific, where America had the Philippines and other territories to protect. Roosevelt used his position as peacemaker to direct Japanese energies toward Manchuria, where he hoped it would be occupied both by the economic opportunities the area offered and by the threat of a still-powerful Russia.

As a mediator Roosevelt had only limited influence over the outcome of the peace conference. Nevertheless, the Treaty of Portsmouth served his purposes very well indeed. Japan took over the Russian leasehold on the Liaodong (Liaotung) Peninsula, including Lüshun (Port Arthur) and Lüda (Dairen) and won control of the South Manchurian Railroad. The Russians also ceded the southern half of Sakhalin Island and recognized Japan's paramount interests in Korea. But Russia remained predominant in northern Manchuria, with control over the Chinese Eastern Railroad. It was still a power to be contended with in the Far East.

## ROOSEVELT'S PACIFIC DIPLOMACY

The Russo-Japanese War left China in a worse position than before. Whereas once it had only to worry about Russian imperialism on its Manchurian frontier, now it had to concern itself with the Japanese as well. Unable to protect Manchuria from foreign imperialism, policy makers in Beijing, especially the very influential Yüan Shikai (Shih-k'ai), tried to entice the United States into a large-scale economic involvement there. In this way they hoped to provide Washington with an incentive for defending not only American investments but China's sovereignty there as well. America seemed the logical choice for such a role, since it had no allies among the more rapacious imperialist powers, had shown no real interest in acquiring Chinese territory, advocated the commercial open door in China, and in its second open door note had publicly stated its concern for the preservation of Chinese sovereignty.

In 1906, at Yüan's urging, the Chinese government began a vigorous public relations campaign in the United States that was designed to reignite lagging American interest in the China market. At the same time Beijing tried to interest American capitalists in Manchuria as a field for investment. They attempted to convince E. H. Harriman, the railroad mogul, to build a railroad in southern Manchuria, an area then dominated by Japan's South Manchurian line. Later they tried to interest a number of influencial Americans, including Secretary of War William Howard Taft and the American consul in Shenyang (Mukden), Manchuria, Willard Straight, in using American capital to create a development bank for Manchuria. They even broached the subject of a Sino-American alliance that would "guarantee China against the ambitions of Japan, and at the same time safeguard American commercial interests."[10]

But all of China's efforts were to no avail, since they ran directly contrary to Roosevelt's purposes. In the aftermath of the Russo-Japanese War, the president became increasingly concerned over the possibility that Japan and the United States might come to blows in the Pacific. His fears may have been exaggerated, but they were not without foundation, for just as the Spanish-American War had stimulated popular support for imperialism in the United States, so the war with Russia had kindled the same sort of enthusiasm in the minds of many in Japan. Thus one Japanese expansionist, sounding for all the world like some nineteenth-century prophet of America's "Manifest Destiny," proclaimed:

> From the ice-bound northern Siberian plains to the continental expanses of China, Korea, and East Asia; farther south, to the Philippines, the Australian continent and other South Sea islands; then eastward to the western coasts of North and South America, washed by the waves of the Pacific Ocean-there is none in these regions which cannot be an object of our nation's expansion. If our people succeed in constructing new Japans everywhere in these areas and engage in vigorous activities throughout the Pacific, then our country's predominance over the Pacific will have been ensured.[11]

To discourage the eastward and southward tendency of Japan's expansionism, which would lead it into conflict with the United States, Roosevelt persisted in his efforts to use diplomacy to focus its expansive energies on Korea and Manchuria while securing the Philippines and America's other Pacific holdings against the possibility of Japanese aggression. Toward this end Roosevelt sent his affable secretary of war, William Howard Taft, to Tokyo for conversations with Japan's Prime Minister, Katsura Tarō.

By this time China, Russia, Britain, and France had all recognized that Korea had become part of the Japanese empire. Now, under terms of the Taft-Katsura agreement, Roosevelt, too, recognized Japan's suzerainty there. In return Japan "confirmed in the strongest terms" that it had no "aggressive designs" on the Philippines.[12] The president had what he wanted—a guarantee from the only real power the United States faced in the western Pacific that it did not covet the islands. And he had achieved this goal without surrendering anything tangible.

Roosevelt's attempt to secure America's Pacific holdings through diplomacy was almost immediately threatened by events over which he hadn't the least control. After 1870 perhaps as many as 100,000 Japanese immigrants settled in California and the other Pacific Coast states. Anti-Japanese sentiment in California grew in proportion to this population, but it became hysterical after Japan demonstrated its military strength during the Russo-Japanese War. This fear of the "yellow peril" first led to demands for the exclusion of all Japanese immigrants. Then, in October 1906, the San Francisco School Board carried Pacific Coast racism one step further, segregating some ninety-three Japanese children (twenty-five of whom were American citizens) in special schools.

Some Japanese reacted furiously to San Francisco's segregationist policy. Thus *Shinsekai*, a Japanese-language daily published in San Francisco, predicted that sooner or later Japan and the United States must fight. An editorial in the same paper urged those Japanese then living in California to resist white persecution.

> Japan is not China. Behind you stand the navy of five hundred thousand tons and the Army of one million men. Above all you have the support of forty-five million countrymen. Struggle, endeavor, and overwhelm the white race. Never use cunning means as the whites do. The struggle between races is not only a problem involving interests but is a problem of life and death.[13]

There was plenty of war talk in Japan, too. But the ruling elite there took a much different view of the matter. Convinced that the United States was fundamentally friendly and anxious to preserve the lucrative trade with America, Japan's leaders had no intention of allowing the immigration question to build to a crisis and were confident that the president would act expeditiously to correct the situation.

Tokyo may have been calm, but in Washington Roosevelt and Secretary of State Elihu Root, who had come to the Department after John Hay's death in 1905, were worried. Root thought the Japanese a "proud, sensitive, warlike" people who could take the Philippines, Hawaii and even the Pacific Coast from an unprepared United States. He believed that the anti-Japanese movement in California had created "an immediate and present danger to be considered and averted now, today."[14] Root's fears were no doubt exaggerated. But there can be no question that administration leaders believed that war over the immigration issue was a distinct possibility. Roosevelt even warned the governor general of the Philippines to prepare for an attack that, recalling Port Arthur, he thought might come with dramatic suddenness.

To extricate himself from what appeared to be a dangerous situation, Roosevelt brought the mayor of San Francisco and the entire city school board to Washington for some earnest persuasion. Out of this meeting came an agreement. If the president could secure an end to Japanese immigration, San Francisco would abandon its policy of school segregation.

Subsequent negotiations with Tokyo resulted in an exchange of notes, sometimes called the Gentlemen's Agreement that brought an immediate reduction in tension. Under terms of this unofficial accord, Japanese immigration from Hawaii to the mainland was halted, and Japan agreed to issue new passports only to relatives of those already in the United States or former residents of the United States. By mid-1908 the number of Japanese entering the United States had been reduced to a trickle.

## THE GREAT WHITE FLEET

It was in June 1907, during this period of crisis in Japanese-American relations, that Roosevelt decided to send "the Great White Fleet"—sixteen battleships and auxiliaries all painted white—on a global cruise that included a three-day stop in Yokohama. At the time, the Japanese naval attaché in Washington informed his superiors that he had no doubt the sailing of the fleet was intended to impress Japan with America's naval might. It is likely the crisis with Japan did influence Roosevelt's thinking regarding the navy. But Roosevelt did not believe in making threats he could not carry out, and he knew that in the western and perhaps even the central Pacific the Imperial Japanese Navy ruled the waves.

In fact, Roosevelt's original motives for sponsoring this grand naval event had as much to do with domestic as with international affairs. By the summer of 1907 he had concluded that the long-range strategic interests of the United States required a larger navy—for two reasons. First, though negotiations which would lead to the Gentlemen's Agreement had reduced tensions, the president could not discount the possibility of a war with Japan at some time in the future. In such a war, he believed, America's Pacific holdings, even the Pacific Coast, would be hostage to Japanese naval power unless the United States had a much enlarged navy. Second, in 1906 the British commissioned the first of a new class of battleship, the HMS *Dreadnaught*, a ship destined to revolutionize naval warfare.

The development of this new *Dreadnaught* class of battleships and the naval armaments race that followed between England and Germany convinced Roosevelt that the United States would have to build four battleships a year to keep pace. The problem was how to win the support of an indifferent public and a downright hostile Congress to such a building program. The answer was "the Great White Fleet," a floating photo opportunity designed to attract media attention, arouse public support for American naval power, and thus influence Congress. It is true that before the fleet actually sailed Roosevelt came to believe that its presence in Pacific waters might have a calming effect on those in Japan who dreamed of Pacific conquest. But the real purpose of the scheme was to impress Americans, not the Japanese.

Roosevelt had a terrific knack for public relations, there is no getting around it. The fleet's sailing, and its visits to exotic ports of call around the world, had precisely the effect he hoped for. The public was entranced. And while Congress proved unwilling to fund the entire naval package Roosevelt proposed, it did agree to fund the construction of two battleships a year for an indefinite period.

When, on October 18, 1908, the American fleet dropped anchor in the harbor at Yokohama, the Japanese government viewed it not as a threat but as an opportunity, for they thought it of vital importance to establish a new basis for mutual understanding with Washington. Anxious to convince Roosevelt that the United States had nothing to fear from Japan in the Pacific, they treated the officers and men of the American fleet to a warm welcome.

Behind this fine reception for the American fleet lay the fact that during the summer of 1908 the Japanese government had at last developed some very clearly defined ideas about the course Japanese expansionism ought to take. Where once Japan's policy makers had debated the advantages of Asian expansion as opposed to expansion across the Pacific, Prime Minister Katsura Tarō turned Japan's complete attention toward Korea and Manchuria, areas where commercial and investment opportunities beckoned and where Japanese colonists were settling in increasing numbers. The Katsura ministry also decided that improved commercial relations with the United States should have a higher priority than the rights of overseas emigrants and clamped down hard on immigration to the United States, so that by the end of the year more Japanese were leaving American shores than were arriving.

Having thus set the stage, the Katsura government then opened negotiations in Washington, hoping to win Roosevelt's endorsement for an expanded Japanese presence in Manchuria. The result was the Root-Takahira Agreement of 1908. Under the terms of this accord, the two nations agreed to "respect the territorial possessions belonging to each other" in the Pacific, affirmed "the independence and integrity of China and the principle of equal opportunity for the commerce and industry of all nations in the Empire"; and agreed to maintain the status quo in the Pacific area.[15] In secret conversations the two sides clarified the vague understanding regarding Japan's interests on the Asian mainland. It was understood that Japan agreed to keep the door open for commerce in southern Manchuria but that because the area was vital, China should not exercise sovereignty there. For its part, Japan agreed to halt all emigration to the United States.

Root-Takahira was the capstone of Roosevelt's Pacific diplomacy. He had been convinced from the start that there was no genuine reason that Japan and the United States could not solve their differences peacefully. And between them he and Prime Minister Katsura had managed to do so. Roosevelt encouraged the Japanese to look to the continent of Asia and not to the Pacific as an area for expansion, thus securing America's Pacific possessions and blunting the threat of a contest for control of the Pacific basin. Toward that end he recognized Japan's suzerainty over Korea and its preeminent position in southern Manchuria. In return, the Japanese helped Roosevelt resolve the question of Japanese emigration into the United States and guaranteed continued United States control of the Philippines and her other Pacific holdings. Of course in the process Roosevelt had been forced to narrow (some have argued virtually abandon) the open door policy. But since the United States had neither the power nor the inclination to defend the open door, he felt he had lost very little.

## CARIBBEAN ADVENTURE

At the same time that they were becoming increasingly involved in Asia, Washington's policy makers sought to transform the dream of an interoceanic canal into a reality. As President McKinley explained in his 1898 annual message to Congress, "The annexation of the Hawaiian islands and the prospective expansion of our influence and commerce in the Pacific" made an American-controlled canal indispensable. And even before he became president, Theodore Roosevelt, a "Mahonite" through and through, said:

> [I]f we are to hold our own in the struggle for naval and commercial supremacy . . . we must build the Isthmian canal, and we must grasp the points of vantage which will enable us to have our say in the destiny of the oceans of the east and west.[16]

One major obstacle standing between Washington and the achievement of this goal remained, as before, the Clayton-Bulwer Treaty of 1850. The agreement had served a purpose at mid-century, but in 1898 the restraints it imposed on America's ambitions proved intolerable. Thus even before the Senate had ratified the treaty ending the war with Spain, Secretary of State Hay opened talks with the British minister in Washington, Sir Julian Pauncefote, aimed at abrogating the old treaty

The first Hay-Pauncefote Treaty, which was signed on February 5, 1900, was in some ways similar to the agreement it was designed to replace. The United States gained the right to build and control a canal. But it would still be bound to keep the waterway open to the commercial and naval vessels of all nations in war as well as in peacetime. Nor would Washington be allowed to fortify it against attack.

The agreement ran into stiff legislative opposition. Even Henry Cabot Lodge, a leading Senate Republican, refused to support it. Hay, who had little respect and less tolerance for most senators, was furious. To a friend he raged, "I have never seen such an exhibition of craven cowardice, ignorance, and prejudice." It had, he continued, "never entered into my mind that anyone out of a madhouse could have objected to the Canal

Convention." When a New York newspaper quoted Andrew Carnegie as saying that, if the treaty passed, it would be the death of the Republican party, Hay sneered, "the frantic little lunatic."[17]

But the last straw for Hay came when Theodore Roosevelt, then the Republican governor of New York, jumped into the fray, publicly criticizing the secretary's handiwork. "Et tu" Hay raged in what one historian has described as "a scorching" letter to his erstwhile friend. "Cannot you leave a few things to the President and the Senate, who are charged with them by the Constitution?"[18]

Hay's ranting notwithstanding, Lodge, Roosevelt, and the majority in the Senate had every right to be concerned. It is debatable whether the national interest would have been served by fortifying a canal. But there can be no doubt that a completely neutral canal open to America's enemies in wartime would have been enormously disadvantageous. After long debate, the Senate approved an amended version of the Hay-Pauncefote Treaty that would have allowed Washington to close the waterway to enemy shipping in the event of war.

When the British rejected the treaty as amended, a frustrated John Hay offered to resign. But McKinley would not hear of it. Instead he sent Hay back into the fray, no doubt with some sound advice on how important it was to keep in touch with Senate opinion when negotiating a treaty. On April 25, 1901, a new draft treaty, which authorized Washington to build, control, and fortify a canal, was forwarded to London. Though it was no more favorable to British interests than its predecessor, London reversed itself, approving the new pact. And so on November 18, Hay and Pauncefote met in the secretary's office in the old State, War, and Navy Building to sign the agreement. A few weeks later the Senate gave its assent.

## PANAMA OR NICARAGUA?

At one time or another at least five different locations had been under consideration as possible sites for a canal. But by the early part of this century only two remained in contention. One, which crossed the Isthmus of Panama, had already been the scene of a failed attempt at canal construction by the defunct, De Lesseps Company. The other was the river and lake route that ran through Nicaragua.

The Nicaraguan route seemed an odds-on choice to be selected. The reports of various commissions dating back to President Ulysses S. Grant's time indicated that it was preferable from an engineering standpoint. Moreover, the Panama route was under lease to the New Panama Canal Company. This offspring of the De Lesseps Company was asking $109 million for its Panama holdings.

These considerations no doubt explain why, following the ratification of the Hay-Pauncefote Treaty, Secretary Hay undertook preliminary negotiations with Managua, and the House of Representatives passed a resolution by a vote of 308–2 calling for the construction of a Nicaraguan canal.

Critics of the New Panama Canal Company were right about many things, among them that the company's owners had no intention of actually building a canal. Their sole purpose was to sell the company's assets to the United States. To achieve this end they took into their employ one William N. Cromwell, partner in the New York law firm of Sullivan and Cromwell. A skilled lobbyist who reveled in his reputation as a mystery man about Washington—someone who brought people together and got things done—Cromwell worked for almost a decade to overcome official sentiment favoring the Nicaraguan route. He developed immense quantities of information to prove that Panama was the superior choice and spent lavishly to befriend and influence important political figures.

Cromwell's work paid off in a number of ways. He convinced Mark Hanna, the Ohio senator and confidant of President William McKinley, that the Panama route was the better of the two choices. And it was Hanna who turned out to be the most effective spokesperson for Panama during the Senate debate on the question. Cromwell was also instrumental in convincing President McKinley to appoint another commission of experts to report on the relative merits of each of the proposed canal routes. Moreover, it was Cromwell who convinced the commission members that they could learn most about the Panama route not in Central America's steaming, yellow fever–infested jungles, but in Paris, where the company had its records. And when the commission, headed by Admiral John G. Walker, arrived in the French capital, Cromwell was there to greet them. He remained with the commissioners throughout their long stay, providing information and of course lavish entertainment in that magnificent city.

While in Paris, the Walker Commission also came under the influence of Philippe Bunau-Varilla, the former chief engineer of the De Lesseps Company and once the director general of its successor. This charismatic Frenchman was driven by two parallel ambitions. First, he wanted to achieve the fulfillment of a dream he had entertained for two decades—the completion of a canal across the isthmus. Second, he wanted the New Panama Canal Company to net as much as was conceivable for its assets.

Between them, Cromwell and Bunau-Varilla put intense pressure on the Walker Commission, hoping for a report that would recommend building a Panama canal. Their best efforts notwithstanding, the commission's recommendation favored Nicaragua. The report did differ from earlier studies in one significant way, however. It made a strong case for the Panama route on engineering grounds. Only the fact that the New Panama Canal Company was asking $109 million for its assets made the Nicaraguan site more attractive. Admiral Walker explained to Bunau-Varilla that he believed the company's assets worth no more than $40 million and that at that price the Panama route would be more attractive.

On November 16, 1901, the commission made its recommendation public. With a bill authorizing the construction of a Nicaraguan canal already before Congress, all that remained, it seemed, was for Congress to return from its Christmas holiday and vote. At this point, however, the situation began to change. First, on January 4, 1902, following a stormy meeting of the stockholders, the New Panama Canal Company lowered the asking price for its lease and other assets to $40 million. Admiral Walker then told Congress that this change in the company's position changed things considerably. Finally, President Roosevelt jumped into the fray. After extensive discussions with the engineers on the Walker Commission, he became convinced that Panama was the superior route. At his suggestion the commission then issued a new report reversing its earlier recommendation. There ensued a battle royal in the Senate, where the Democrats, led by Senator John T. Morgan of Alabama, suspected that Roosevelt's sudden interest in the canal question had more to do with certain large political contributions made to the Republican party by Cromwell than with any engineering considerations.

All these developments notwithstanding, it still appeared that the Senate would endorse a Nicaraguan canal when the vote came. But that all changed just before eight in the morning on May 8, 1902, when a dormant volcano, Mount Pelée, on the island of Martinique exploded. In about two minutes the city of St. Pierre and its more than thirty thousand inhabitants perished.

The disaster came as wonderful news to Philippe Bunau-Varilla, who had come to the United States to lobby for the Panama site. For weeks he had been warning anyone interested in listening that Nicaragua, which was alive with volcanoes, was no place to put a canal. Now here was an example of what one could do. Aware that Nicaragua had issued a postage stamp with a picture of Mount Momotombo happily belching clouds of smoke, he rushed to a stamp dealer and purchased one of these little beauties for each senator. Bunau-Varilla's little gambit was hardly necessary. The catastrophe that had befallen Martinique was far too graphic a warning for the Senate to ignore. The Walker Commission's changed report, presidential pressure, and the explosion of Mount Pelée combined to change Senate opinion. By a vote of 42–34 the upper house voted in favor of a Panama site for the canal. A few days later the House fell into line, voting for Panama by the lopsided majority of 259–8.

## REVOLUTION IN PANAMA

Bogotá had promised that, if Panama was selected as the site for the canal, there would be no trouble arranging an agreement transferring control of a canal zone to the United States. In fact, however, the negotiations turned into a nightmarish succession of frustrations for both sides. Two issues divided Washington and Colombia. The first was the question of sovereignty over the area in question. Washington wanted something akin to extraterritorial privileges, while President Marroquín, fighting for his political life, could ill-afford to make such a concession. The second issue had to do with the fact that the United States was prepared to pay $40 million to the New Panama Canal Company for its lease but only $10 million to Colombia for rights to the land.

After months of wrangling John Hay broke this deadlock by warning Dr. Tomás Herrán, the Colombian chargé in Washington, that if he refused to sign a treaty the administration would turn to the Nicaraguans. Hay was bluffing. Theodore Roosevelt was determined to have the Panama site. But the bluff worked. The Hay-Herrán Treaty signed early in 1903 authorized the United States to buy the French company's lease and granted Washington wide-ranging legal and administrative authority over a canal zone six miles wide. In return the United States agreed to pay Bogotá $10 million in cash and an annuity of $250 thousand. The agreement was to remain in effect for one hundred years and could be renewed at Washington's request.

Not long afterward rumors of Colombia's discontent began reverberating in Washington. When Roosevelt learned that the Colombian Senate might reject the treaty, he wrote that "those contemptible little creatures in Bogotá ought to understand how much they are jeopardizing things and imperiling their own future." As the moment of truth arrived, Hay, who had himself described the Colombians as "greedy little anthropoids," warned President Marroquín directly that if Colombia either rejected the treaty or delayed its ratification, the United States would take this as a breach of faith and that "action might be taken . . . which every friend of Colombia would regret."[19]

All of this bluster did no good. The Colombian Senate voted unanimously to reject the treaty. When Roosevelt learned of the rejection, he exploded in wrathful indignation. He was not going to allow "that Bogotá lot of jack rabbits . . . to bar one of the future highways of civilization." Hay agreed. The "poor creatures" in Colombia "had their spree," he wrote. "But now Blue Monday has come." Roosevelt and Hay now agreed that by hook or crook the United States would have the Panama route. Still, the secretary advised against moving too quickly. "Our intervention," he thought, "should not be haphazard."[20] Roosevelt, who agreed on the importance of moving carefully, ordered two army officers to Panama to assess the possibility of a revolution there. But before Roosevelt's agents could report, the president learned of a Panamanian revolutionary movement nearer at hand, one that promised to separate Panama from Colombia and provide the canal site the United States wanted with a minimum of direct American involvement.

This movement was headquartered in a very curious place, room 1162 of the Waldorf-Astoria Hotel, Philippe Bunau-Varilla's favorite haunt when in New York. Bunau-Varilla had come to New York for a meeting with Dr. Manuel Guerrero Amador, agent for a group of Panamanian revolutionaries. Almost from the moment of their meeting, Bunau-Varilla took charge of planning the revolution. With $40 million at stake, he wanted nothing to go wrong.

The Frenchman moved quickly, using a State Department go-between to arrange a meeting with the president. At this conference Roosevelt was careful to say nothing that could tie him directly to the revolutionaries. At the same time, however, he made his position clear. "I have no doubt," he later wrote, "that he was able to make a very accurate guess [as to how Roosevelt would react to a revolution] and to advise his people accordingly. In fact, he would have been a very dull man had he been unable to make such a guess."[21] A few days later, at a conference in the State Department, the Frenchman learned even more about what he might expect from the United States should Panama break from Colombia. When he remarked that Colombia's decision to reject the Hay-Herrán Treaty had made a Panamanian revolution more or less certain, John Hay said that the United States would not be caught napping in such an event. American naval forces, Hay pointedly explained, had already been ordered to sail for the isthmus.

Confident that he knew exactly what to expect from Washington, Bunau-Varilla provided Amador, who was to head Panama's provisional government, with the draft of a declaration of independence, a constitution, and a national flag that his wife and daughter had thoughtfully sewn for the revolutionaries. Most important he provided the $100,000 the revolutionaries needed to purchase the loyalty of the local Colombian garrison. On November 3, 1903, the day after the USS *Nashville* arrived in Colón on the Atlantic side of the isthmus, the conspirators in Panama City on the Pacific side declared Panamanian independence.

The revolution came off with only one hitch. Purely by chance a force of four hundred Colombian soldiers landed in Colón just before the rebels declared their intentions. Had this force been allowed to use the railroad that spanned the isthmus, it might have been able to crush the rebellion. But that possibility was blocked by Commander John Hubbard of the *Nashville*, who, acting on secret orders, forbade the use of the railroad to all military forces. There followed some tense negotiations involving Commander Hubbard, the officer in command of the Colombian force, and local railroad officials who were working in collusion with the revolutionaries. At length, however, with the *Nashville*, now close in shore, its decks cleared and its guns ready for action, the Colombians were persuaded to board a British steamer then docked at Colón and sail away. That was on November 5, the same day that the USS *Dixie*, the first of nine American warships to converge on Panama in the next several days, put four hundred marines ashore at Colón. On November 6, Washington extended de facto recognition to the republic of Panama.

The final stage in the rather tawdry story took place in Washington, where Bunau-Varilla had become Panama's first diplomatic representative. With the revolution an accomplished fact, he produced a revision of the Hay-Herrán Treaty that was so favorable to the United States there could be no doubt the Senate would give its blessings. Under terms of the revised agreement, sovereignty over the canal zone was transferred to Washington in everything but name. Second, the canal zone was to be controlled by

An American-controlled canal across Central America became a reality after Theodore Roosevelt and John Hay resorted to some blatant international skullduggery. Here the battleship USS *Utah* sails through the Gaillard Cut.

Washington "in perpetuity." Other articles of the treaty in fact turned Panama into a protectorate.

The first president to think seriously about constructing an interoceanic canal had been James K. Polk. Fifty years later the dream became a reality. And, although many criticized the president for this blatant act of international piracy, Roosevelt himself never doubted that he had acted correctly. In 1911, during a speech at the University of California's Greek Theater, he told eight thousand listeners, "I took the Isthmus, started the canal, and then left Congress not to debate the canal, but to debate me."[22] That was a view that never entirely lost its popularity. Seventy years later, when the Senate debated another Panama Treaty, this time one intended to return the Canal Zone to Panama, one senator who opposed the agreement remarked that the canal was ours, "we stole it fair and square."

## CUBA, EVER ELUSIVE ISLE

Throughout the nineteenth century it had been a forgone conclusion among expansionists that one day the United States would annex Cuba. But when at last the opportunity came, the Teller Amendment—a pledge that the United States would not take the island—stood in the way.

The Spanish-American War left President McKinley in a dilemma. He was not prepared to violate the Teller Amendment. But neither was he willing to turn the island over to the insurgents, since no one of any stature in Washington believed the Cuban separatists were capable of creating a stable government. This judgment was founded on a set of interrelated considerations. First, the insurgents had thus far been unable to create anything resembling a functioning government. More important, American policy makers believed that to succeed, a government must have the support of its educated and propertied classes. But in Cuba this group had been almost solidly behind the Spanish during the war. Finally, there was the question of race. The Americans who went to Cuba were appalled by the character of the insurgent army. The guerrilla force that had fought the Spanish to a standstill was half-starved, poorly clothed, and undisciplined—and it was largely made up of illiterate Afro-Cuban peasants.

Many Americans who served in Cuba quickly concluded that civilization would not be served by turning Cuba over to the insurgents. "The Cubans are utterly irresponsible," one officer wrote. They are "partly savage, and have no idea of what good government means." Another thought that "Providence" had "reserved a fairer future for this noble country than to be possessed by this horde of tatterdemalions." Under American control Cuba would no doubt "blossom as the rose." And "in the course of three or four generations," he thought, "even the Cubans may be brought to appreciate the virtues of cleanliness, temperance, industry, and honesty." Welcomed by the Spanish and the propertied class of Cubans as though he had come to save the island from the insurgents, the American commander, General William Shafter wrote: "As I see it we have taken Spain's war upon ourselves."[23]

In a very short while such views came to dominate thinking in Washington, where policy makers agreed that the army should remain in Cuba until a stable, responsible, and friendly government had been established there. This arrangement, they believed, would prove mutually advantageous. For the United States it would mean increased trade, expanded investment opportunities, greater security for the canal that was soon to be built, and an end to European intervention in the region. For the indigenous population it would mean peace, prosperity, and a higher living standard. General Leonard Wood, who became governor general of Cuba in 1899, was quite specific in defining what he thought stability entailed: "When money can be borrowed at a reasonable rate of interest and when capital is willing to invest in the Island, a condition of stability will have been reached."[24]

As governor general, Wood worked to achieve two separate but related objectives—economic growth and the creation of a conservative, stable political order. His economic policies were a spectacular success. This growth, however, came at a price to the Cubans. The island was transformed into a virtual economic colony of the United States. Within three years American investments in Cuba had doubled. Over the next two decades Americans, who invested more than $1 billion in the island's economy, came to control a large share of the sugar and tobacco industries and were firmly entrenched in utilities, mining, banking, railroads, and communications.

As Roosevelt's secretary of war, Elihu Root drafted the Platt Amendment, which transformed Cuba into a protectorate of the United States and set the stage for American domination of the Caribbean region.

Unhappily for Wood, his efforts in the political realm did not work out nearly so well. He set out to create a Cuban-run administration for the island, recruiting upper-class Cubans to fill administrative positions wherever possible. By early 1900 the job was complete, and while he had been forced to employ some devoted Cuban nationalists who were less than enthusiastic about the American occupation, he still thought it "safe to say that eight out of ten people" in positions of authority "are our friends; by our friends I mean the friends of good government and of what we are doing."[25]

Creating a conservative administration for Cuba was one thing. But keeping it in power turned out to be quite another. Wood's instructions required him to hold an election to select delegates for a Constitutional Convention and to hold national elections as soon as possible. Aware that the great majority of the Cuban people had no use for those he was banking on to control Cuban political life, Wood disenfranchised about two-thirds of the Cuban electorate (males over the age of twenty-one) by establishing property and literacy requirements for voting.

These draconian measures notwithstanding, Wood's efforts to control the elections proved a dismal failure. The voting for delegates to the Constitutional Convention made it clear that Cuba's upper classes, too many of whom had supported Spain during the revolution, had no mandate to rule. "I am disappointed in the composition of the Convention," Wood explained to Secretary of War Elihu Root. It was controlled by the "worst agitators and political radicals in Cuba."[26] Under the circumstances, he warned, it would be a disastrous error for the United States to leave the island.

Satisfied that Cuba's future could not be left in the hands of the nationalists who controlled the convention, Secretary Root laid down harsh conditions that Cuba was required to meet before Washington would end the military occupation. The most important of Root's demands, which Congress enacted as the Platt Amendment to the Army Appropriations Act of 1901, gave the United States the right to intervene in Cuba to preserve the island's independence and to maintain a stable and responsible government on the island. It also guaranteed the United States rights to a naval base and stipulated that Cuba would not enter into arrangements with foreign powers tending to limit or impair the island's independence. Finally, it forbade the Cubans from leasing or in any other way alienating territory to a foreign government and required that they contract no debts that normal island revenues would be inadequate to repay.

The delegates to the convention at first resisted this obvious attempt to limit the new nation's sovereignty. But when it became clear that the alternative was continued military occupation, they very reluctantly incorporated the terms of the Platt Amendment in the new constitution. Cuba's leaders understood just how much they had surrendered, as did General Wood, who later observed, "There is, of course little or no independence left in Cuba under the Platt Amendment."[27] Cuba had become an American protectorate.

With the aid of General Wood, whose management of the election made the outcome a forgone conclusion, Tomás Estrada Palma was elected the first president of Cuba. The sixty-six-year-old patriot and former president of the Cuban Revolutionary party was, from the American point of view, a perfect choice. A naturalized American citizen who endorsed the Platt Amendment and advocated close economic ties with the United States, he viewed independence as a temporary condition, a way station on the road toward annexation to the United States. But the very same qualities that made him acceptable to the United States finally disqualified him to be president of a truly independent Cuba.

In 1906, following a corrupt election in which the opposition was systematically counted out at the polls by Estrada's Moderate party, a revolution broke out. This rebellion was in part a reaction to the crooked election. But it was also a reflection of the anger felt by Cuban nationalists who wanted more than the quasi-independence granted them by the United States.

President Estrada's government proved unable to put down the rebellion but was also unwilling to agree on a compromise that would have resulted in some sharing of power with the nationalist opposition. In fact

An American sentry stands guard at the Guantánamo naval base in Cuba, outpost of America's Caribbean empire.

the president and his supporters saw no reason to compromise. Instead they relied on the United States to crush the rebellion for them. Estrada resigned and informed Washington that he could no longer preserve order or protect life and property on the island. Under the terms of the Platt Amendment, this step should have triggered an American intervention to restore order and shore up the government.

Unhappily for Estrada's Moderates, things did not develop this way. Theodore Roosevelt, who had already gained an unsavory reputation in Latin America for earlier interventions, was furious. He had no desire to intervene in Cuba, especially to preserve a corrupt government. "I earnestly hope I can persuade the Cubans to act decently and go on governing themselves," he wrote. "I shall make every effort to this end and intervene only when it is evident that no other course is open."[28]

True to his word, Roosevelt sent not the marines but his premier troubleshooter, William Howard Taft, to look into the situation. Taft had hardly arrived in Cuba before he realized that the government Washington had so painstakingly created was "nothing but a house of cards."[29] That judgment was more accurate than even Taft guessed. Estrada Palma's government served Washington's interests very well indeed. But its pro-American policies meant that it could never claim the support of true Cuban nationalists. It had no mandate to rule save that conferred upon it by Washington.

Acting on Taft's advice and very much against his own inclinations, Roosevelt finally landed six thousand marines in Cuba and established a new provisional government for the island. Three years later, in 1909, a new Cuban government under General José Miguel Gomez took power. But the political realities remained unchanged. In years to come Cuban leaders often mouthed anti-American rhetoric when in search of political support at home. At the same time only a very few ever even considered throwing off the constraints imposed on Cuban independence by Washington. The Platt Amendment and Cuba's status as a virtual economic colony of the United States in a sense made real politics on the island impossible.

## POLICING THE CARIBBEAN

When Theodore Roosevelt came to the presidency, he had no clear-cut policy for the Caribbean region. Within three years, however, a chain of events that began with a crisis in Venezuela and ended with another in the Dominican Republic led him to originate a new and revolutionary Caribbean policy that involved a major reinterpretation of the Monroe Doctrine.

Cipriano Castro, "the Lion of the Andes" and the dictator of Venezuela, provoked a crisis with England and Germany by refusing to repay debts owed to bondholders from those as well as certain other countries. After diplomatic efforts failed, Berlin and London agreed that, unless the United States objected, they would force Castro to pay up. The Roosevelt administration had no objections so long as no territory changed hands. On the contrary, as the president himself explained to a German acquaintance, "If any South American state misbehaves toward any European country, let the European country spank it."[30] In early December 1902, a joint Anglo-German naval force, taking TR at his word, destroyed or seized a number of Venezuelan gunboats, landed troops at La Guayra, and bombarded Puerto Cabello.

That was enough persuasion for Venezuela's Castro, who quickly suggested arbitration. Roosevelt, surprised by the strong negative reaction in the United States to the Anglo-German intervention, urged Berlin and London to agree, and they did so.

With Herbert Bowen, the American minister to Venezuela representing Castro, a settlement was hammered out that called for the repayment of Venezuela's debts to all bondholders regardless of their nationality. Only one issue remained unresolved. England and Germany insisted that their bondholders should be paid first since they had gone to the trouble and expense of forcing the Venezuelans to behave responsibly. This question was taken to the Permanent Court of International Justice at the Hague, where the justices upheld the claim of the blockading powers.

The court's decision, which placed a premium on the use of force, left Theodore Roosevelt in a quandary. Venezuela was not the only Caribbean nation to act irresponsibly toward foreign bondholders. On the contrary, such behavior was common practice in those southerly climes. It was unthinkable that the United States should protect Latin American countries attempting to repudiate their debts. But neither could the United States have the warships of foreign nations charging about an area as strategically and economically important as the Caribbean. Such thoughts led the president to only one conclusion. "If we are willing to let Germany or England act as the policemen of the Caribbean, then we can afford not to interfere when gross wrongdoing occurs. But if we intend to say 'Hands off' to the powers of Europe, then sooner or later we must keep order ourselves." In his December 1904 message to Congress, Roosevelt transformed that idea into a corollary to the Monroe Doctrine. Western hemispheric nations that behaved responsibly, he said, "need fear no interference from the United States." On the other hand,

> Chronic wrongdoing, or an impotence which results in a general loosening of the ties of civilized society, may in America, as elsewhere, ultimately require intervention by some civilized nation, and in the Western Hemisphere the adherence of the United States to the Monroe Doctrine may force the United States, however reluctantly, in flagrant cases of such wrongdoing or impotence, to the exercise of an international police power.[31]

In asserting America's role as the police of the Western Hemisphere, Roosevelt had a specific situation in mind. Between 1900 and 1903 the Dominican Republic had been under increasing pressure from European as well as American creditors. As if threats of foreign intervention to collect debts were not enough to trouble the government of President Carlos Morales, in 1903 civil war broke out on the island. To save himself, Morales proposed that the United States take the republic as a protectorate. But by this time Samaná Bay had lost its appeal. Roosevelt, who had enough foreign troubles without borrowing more, wanted no part of such an arrangement, telling a friend that he had "about the same desire to annex" the Dominican Republic "as a gorged boa constrictor might have to swallow a porcupine wrong-end-to."[32] Still, something had to be done to head off what appeared to be a carbon copy of the Venezuelan crisis. Though there was no immediate threat of European intervention, the situation inside the Dominican Republic was so chaotic, the chances that the Morales government would be able to pay its debts so remote, that Roosevelt felt compelled to head off that possibility.

The solution that Roosevelt settled upon was in effect a modified version of the Platt Amendment. President Morales agreed to negotiate a $20 million loan from American bankers to be used to refund the republic's debt and to allow Roosevelt to select a receiver general of customs. This official was to turn over 45 percent of the customs receipts to Morales for his country. The rest would go to pay the island nation's debts. To further ensure stability, order, and the continued rule of a cooperative government,

Activities of the U.S.
in the Caribbean, 1898-1917

Legend:
- U.S. protectorates
- U.S. military expeditions
- *PUERTO RICO* U.S. possessions

Map labels: Columbus / Villas raid March, 1916; UNITED STATES; Pershing's expedition 1916-1917; Parral Skirmish with Carranza's troops; GULF OF MEXICO; BAHAMAS (Br.); Bahia Honda Leased, 1903-1912; Havana; DOMINICAN REPUBLIC; MEXICO; Tampico American sailors arrested April, 1914; 1914; U.S. occupation 1889-1902, 1906-1909, 1912, 1917; CUBA; U.S. occupation 1916-1924; PUERTO RICO; VIRGIN IS. (Br.); PACIFIC OCEAN; Guantanamo Bay U.S. naval base leased, 1903; Vera Cruz Seized by U.S. navy April, 1914; GUATEMALA; BRITISH HONDURAS; JAMAICA (Br.); HAITI U.S. occupation 1915-1934; VIRGIN IS. Purchased from Denmark, 1917; CARIBBEAN SEA; HONDURAS U.S. occupation 1924-1925; EL SALVADOR; NICARAGUA U.S. occupation 1912-1925 1927-1933; CANAL ZONE Leased, 1903; Proposed canal; Panama Canal; COSTA RICA; PANAMA; COLOMBIA; VENEZUELA; ATLANTIC OCEAN

Scale: 0 — 500 Miles; 0 — 500 Kilometers

Roosevelt also ordered the navy to aid President Morales in his war against the rebels. Happy to oblige, the navy played a major role in bringing the war to a satisfactory conclusion. In fact the commander of the USS *Detroit* later claimed that he was "entirely responsible for the placing of Morales in power."[33]

Roosevelt, who was fond of the African proverb: "Speak softly and carry a big stick, you will go far," fundamentally altered the meaning of the Monroe Doctrine, transforming it into a justification for intervention in the internal affairs of nations throughout the hemisphere. Like those who succeeded him, he no doubt felt justified in taking this position. But repeated interventions have embittered Washington's relations with all of Latin America while making it abundantly clear that, so far as the United States is concerned, the sovereignty of almost all of the nations to the south has its limits. And those limits will be determined by policy makers on the Potomac.

## TAFT, KNOX, AND DOLLAR DIPLOMACY

Theodore Roosevelt left the White House in 1909 satisfied that the country was in safe hands and that the policies he had established would be continued. But President William Howard Taft had very different ideas about a number of things, among them the sort of Far Eastern policy he hoped to pursue.

In the first place, Taft disagreed with Roosevelt's general assessment

When William Howard Taft entered the White House, he reversed Theodore Roosevelt's Far Eastern policy much to the disadvantage of the United States.

of both China and Japan. Roosevelt was disdainful of the Chinese, whom he viewed as a senile, untrustworthy, and despicable people. On the other hand, he had great admiration and respect for the Japanese, who had succeeded so well in superimposing a veneer of modernism over their traditional feudal culture. Taft, more sensitive than Roosevelt to the revolutionary stirrings then taking place in China, took a more sentimental position, arguing that the United States had a responsibility to guide and protect the Chinese as they went through the modernizing process.

Taft complemented his sympathy for China with an ingrained prejudice against Japan. In 1905 on a trip to the Far East he remarked, "A Jap is first of all a Jap and would be glad to aggrandize himself at the expense of anybody."[34] The anti-Japanese bias that Taft brought with him to the White House also had a powerful influence on his Far Eastern policies.

Taft chose as his secretary of state Philander Knox, a Wall Street attorney without previous diplomatic experience who shared his prejudices. Knox, who was given a free hand at the State Department, quickly abandoned Roosevelt's policy of accommodation with Japan in favor of one designed to challenge its position in Manchuria. The open door was once again in favor in Washington. But with a difference. John Hay had confined himself to note writing and what in those days passed for diplomatic finesse. Knox was short on finesse but determined to act on behalf of China and America's economic future there.

Where Roosevelt refused to be taken in by the delicious fantasy of the China market, both Knox and Taft spoke frequently of China's "almost boundless commercial possibilities" and saw their role at least in one sense as advance men for American commerce. "Today diplomacy works for trade," Knox said. "And the Foreign Offices of the world are powerful engines for the promotion of the commerce of each country."[35] If America was to achieve its commercial ends, China had to remain an independent and sovereign nation. Chinese integrity and America's commercial interests, therefore, were two sides of the same coin.

It was one thing to argue that the United States had a vital interest in defending the open door in China but quite another to develop a policy that had any chance of achieving that end. Russia and Japan were firmly entrenched in Manchuria, and the other imperialist powers continued to cling to their leaseholds and spheres of influence. Lacking domestic support for the forceful defense of the open door, how, then, was the United States to convince China's exploiters to change their ways?

The State Department's solution to this knotty problem was called "dollar diplomacy," a policy that aimed at creating an expanded American influence in China by economic means. This policy called for the government to take the lead in encouraging large-scale American investment in China's economic development with particular emphasis on railroad projects. Knox assumed that these investments would, as they had in the American West, begin a cycle of economic growth, creating vast new opportunities for further American investment. And just as the West had once formed an expanding market for eastern manufactured goods, so China would play a similar role for American producers in the decades to come. In this way the long-dreamed-of China market would become a reality, while China itself grew strong.

The political component of Knox's dream was as important as the economic side. As America's investment in China grew, Knox assumed that Washington's voice would necessarily carry more weight in deciding China's future. And the United States would exercise that influence to save China from dismemberment.

As a first step toward transforming dollar diplomacy from a theoretical possibility into a reality, Knox spearheaded a drive to organize the American Group, a consortium of powerful banking institutions. Members of the group, including representatives from Kuhn Loeb & Company, J. P. Morgan and Company, and National City Bank, agreed to work with the administration to develop investment opportunities in China. This partnership of government and business was never entirely cordial, however. The bankers were always interested in profits first, while the government often hoped to use the economic clout wielded through the American Group to achieve political aims regardless of profits.

Once the bankers had been organized, Knox pressed the Chinese, who were at first unenthusiastic, to allow American representation in a consortium of British, German, and French bankers then preparing to finance the construction of a railroad to run from Beijing (Peking) to Canton with a branch into Sichuan (Szechuan). At length, and much to the irritation of the European partners, Beijing granted the American Group a one-fourth share in the approximately £ 6 million loan.

In November 1909, encouraged by this early success, Knox undertook a much more ambitious initiative, this time trying for nothing less than the destruction of the Japanese sphere of influence in Manchuria. Knox advanced into the tangled thicket of Manchurian affairs ignorant and unprepared. The secretary's proposal was simplicity itself. He recommended that an international consortium of bankers purchase the Japanese and Russian railroads in Manchuria. In theory, once Manchuria's rail system had been internationalized, it was to be returned to China. In fact, however, the railroads would be supervised by the interested powers.

Had it succeeded, this "neutralization scheme" as it was called, would have destroyed the Russian and Japanese spheres of influence in Manchuria and opened the area to broadly based international investment that, Knox believed, would lead to rapid economic development, strengthen China's hold on the region, and create expanded opportunities for trade.

Knox seems to have assumed that the Russians would cooperate. He was just as convinced that the Japanese would not. But if Tokyo refused to sell, he proposed to build a railroad parallel to her South Manchurian line and engage in cutthroat competition to drive Japan from its sphere in southern Manchuria.

Seldom has a diplomatic initiative been more poorly conceived. Knox assumed, without consulting the Foreign Office, that he could count on British support for the plan. It is true that at this time London was trying to cultivate improved relations with the United States. But England could not afford to antagonize Russia or its ally Japan over Manchuria and so refused to support Knox. The secretary had also incorrectly assumed that the Russians were anxious to disentangle themselves from Manchuria and would happily sell the Chinese Eastern Railroad to an American-backed international consortium. Instead, the Russians categorically refused to play ball. As for the Japanese, they assumed, correctly, that Taft and Knox had aimed this initiative primarily at them. Their reaction was to draw closer to Russia. In January 1910, the two nations issued a joint statement denouncing the American plan. Six months later they announced a formal agreement recognizing each other's sphere of influence in Manchuria and agreeing to maintain the status quo there against the threat of foreign intervention.

Knox's scheme, designed to weaken the Russo-Japanese stranglehold over Manchuria, had instead strengthened it. China's control over the region had been further eroded, and the open door was less a reality than ever. Knox gained only one thing for his trouble—the enmity of Japan and Russia.

Criticism of administration blundering came from many quarters. But it was Roosevelt's personal criticism that stung Taft and Knox the most.

In attempting to put the administration back on the correct course, Roosevelt pointed out in a letter to Taft that "our vital interest" was to keep Japanese immigration at an absolute minimum while preserving Japan's "good will." On the other hand, the "vital interest of the Japanese is in Manchuria and Korea. It is therefore peculiarly our interest not to take any steps as regards Manchuria which will give the Japanese cause to feel, with or without reason, that we are hostile to them, or a menace—in however slight a degree—to their interests." Roosevelt thought the open door policy "an excellent thing," and he hoped that at some point in the future it could be "maintained by diplomatic agreement." But, he continued, "the whole history of Manchuria alike under Russia and . . . Japan" proves that the open door is closed "as soon as a powerful nation determines to disregard it, and is willing to run the risk of war rather than forgo its intention."[36]

Philander Knox defended his policies in a weakly argued reply to Roosevelt. But in the aftermath of the neutralization fiasco, he nevertheless changed his approach to Far Eastern affairs and moderated his hopes for what might be achieved in China. There would be no more spirited initiatives aimed at eliminating the Japanese and Russian spheres of influence in Manchuria. Instead, Knox tried to foster cooperation between the United States, Britain, Germany, and France. His hope was to work with these powers to moderate the more extreme behavior of Russia and Japan and win international support for the open door.

Toward that end Knox and Taft lent their support to the American Group, which was then negotiating an agreement under which American capitalists joined their European confreres in the Hukuang Railroad loan. Having failed to check the despoilers by direct action, Knox and Taft concluded that their only real choice was to join with them and to use the leverage created by economic cooperation to mitigate the worst aspects of imperialism in China. It was a forlorn hope based on the illogical assumption that one can be in league with a set of exploiters and yet not of them. The futility of this approach was brought home to American policy makers in 1911, when Japanese and Russian interests became part of the international consortium that Knox hoped to use to moderate their behavior.

Taft and Knox left office in March 1913, with their Far Eastern policy in a shambles. They had set out to establish the open door in China while at the same time protecting that unfortunate nation from exploitation and possible dismemberment. But they showed little understanding of international politics, adopting strategies that had no chance of succeeding. As a result of their efforts, Japan was transformed into a suspecious adversary, commercial opportunities in Manchuria were further limited, and China's hold over that important province was further undermined.

## DOLLARS AND BULLETS IN THE CARIBBEAN

Taft and Knox viewed the Roosevelt administration's Dominican experiment as a great success. The country had a stable government; America's trade with the island republic was growing; and the country was paying its foreign debt promptly, thus reducing the danger of foreign intervention. Most important, all of this had been accomplished without a resort to force. Here, truly, it appeared that the United States had achieved its purposes by "substituting dollars for bullets." In the State Department, where dollar diplomacy was in vogue, they called it a "brilliant" achievement, a model for handling similar problems throughout the Caribbean and Central America.[37]

The Taft administration applied this remedy wherever instability reared its ugly head in Central America and the Caribbean, but always with disappointing results. The reason is clear. The premise that economic reforms alone could guarantee internal peace and stability in the region was a gross oversimplification based on an inadequate analysis of regional problems.

After 1905, for example, the Dominican Republic enjoyed a period of internal peace not because of the customs receivership but because it was ruled by President Ramón Cáceres, a strong and popular leader. Cáceres's assassination in November 1911 ushered in a long period of political unrest. A new government headed by General Alfredo Victoria quickly alienated other political leaders, who soon entered into armed opposition.

The Taft administration pressed the Victoria regime for economic and political reforms, hoping in this way to restore order. Failing that, Washington forced Victoria from power and arranged the election of a new government more completely under its control. But not even these efforts could end the chaos. When Taft left office in 1913, "the Dominican showcase" lay shattered, a monument to the illusion that dollars alone could bring stability to the region.

In 1907 the Roosevelt administration joined with Mexico in sponsoring a conference of Central American countries that met in Washington, D.C. Out of that conference came a treaty of peace and amity signed by all of the nations of the region. But Nicaragua's dictator, José Santos Zelaya, was more interested in consolidating Central America by conquest than in good relations with his neighbors. At the time Taft and Knox took power in Washington he was making threatening gestures toward Honduras and El Salvador. He was also encouraging revolutionary groups inside El Salvador and was interfering in Costa Rica's election. From Washington's perspective, he was the prime troublemaker in all of Central America and openly anti-American to boot.

In 1909, General Juan J. Estrada led a revolution against Zelaya. Though in fact Washington was delighted by this development, Taft and Knox, anxious to avoid arousing anti-American sentiment in Latin America, adopted a policy of strict neutrality in the early stages of the conflict. Then, however, Zelaya made a serious mistake, ordering the execution of Lee Roy Cannon and Leonard Groce, two American soldiers of fortune serving with the rebels. In Washington, where tears were seldom shed for the likes of Cannon and Groce, policy makers decided to make the most of the incident. The United States made a formal protest and demanded reparations. When Zelaya didn't move quickly enough, they gave serious consideration to military action but stopped short of that, breaking off diplomatic relations.

The purpose of this American pressure was to force Zelaya from power. And it succeeded. The dictator resigned and went into exile. But Washington was not pleased with José Madriz, who succeeded to the presidency. He had been too close to Zelaya, too much a part of the old governing elite. President Taft therefore decided to withhold recognition from the new regime, hoping that General Estrada's rebels would win the ongoing civil war. For a time that seemed unlikely. Early in 1910 government forces had Estrada's army pinned down in Bluefields, their last stronghold, and were preparing to deliver the decisive blow, when the United States Navy interceded to save him.

Once it became clear that the United States was prepared to use force on behalf of General Estrada, the Madriz government fell to pieces. Estrada became the provisional president on August 31, 1910.

With all of the pieces at last in place, Washington then attempted to apply the Dominican solution in Nicaragua. Secretary of State Knox withheld American recognition, something Estrada desperately needed, until Nicaragua agreed to negotiate a loan with American bankers for the purpose of reorganizing Nicaragua's finances. To secure the loan, Estrada was forced to appoint an American expert with control over Nicaragua's customs houses as well as the power to reorganize the country's finances. Only then did Washington extend recognition to his government.

Administration hopes notwithstanding, political instability continued in Nicaragua, and General Estrada was driven from power to be replaced by his vice-president, Adolfo Díaz. Still the instability continued.

In July 1912, the minister of war, General Luis Meña, led the army into open rebellion. Meña's rebellion posed an especially serious problem for Washington because it was accompanied by a virulent brand of anti-Americanism. With Nicaragua now heavily in debt to those American bankers who had only recently financed the refunding of the national debt, the American minister in Managua asked the Díaz regime to guarantee that it could protect American lives and property. The embattled Díaz, who saw this as an opportunity to save his tottering government, replied that such a guarantee was impossible and asked Washington to land troops not only to protect American lives and property but to protect "all the inhabitants of the republic."[38]

In the summer of 1912 the United States landed two thousand marines and bluejackets in Nicaragua. In earlier such ventures, troop landings had been enough to quell a rebellion. But in Nicaragua anti-Americanism was so strong that the American forces had to join in the fighting. By September the rebellion was virtually over and most of the marines had been withdrawn. But a large legation guard remained, a warning that the United States would not tolerate further revolutionary activity.

In Santo Domingo and Nicaragua, and in Honduras and Guatamala, too, dollar diplomacy failed. It failed because it was founded on the false assumption that the Caribbean and Central American elitists who struggled for power wanted one thing only—control of national revenues. In most instances this meant the customs houses. Policy makers concluded, therefore, that by establishing customs receiverships the United States could create a disincentive for revolution and encourage internal peace and stability. This hopelessly inadequate analysis failed to take into account the fact that political instability is often the result of cultural considerations, personal ambition, and other noneconomic factors. It also neglected the possibility that some governments provoked revolution simply by being needlessly repressive.

## ENDNOTES

1. Hilary Herbert, quoted in Charles E. Neu, *The Troubled Encounter: The United States and Japan* (John Wiley and Sons, N.Y., 1975), p. 33.

2. John Hay, quoted in A. Whitney Griswold, *The Far Eastern Policy of the United States* (Harcourt Brace and Co., N.Y., 1938), p. 78.

3. Robert Hart, quoted in Michael Hunt, *The Making of a Special Relationship: The United States and China to 1914* (Columbia University Press, N.Y., 1983), p. 187.

4. John Hay, Circular Telegram, July 3, 1900, *Foreign Relations of the United States, 1900* (Washington, 1901), p. 299.

5. Hay, quoted in Howard K. Beale, *Theodore Roosevelt and the Rise of America to World Power* (Johns Hopkins University Press, Baltimore, Md., 1956) p. 195.

6. Theodore Roosevelt, quoted in Michael Hunt, *Frontier Defense and the Open Door: Manchuria in Chinese-American Relations, 1895–1911* (Yale University Press, New Haven, Ct., 1973), pp. 77–78.

7. Roosevelt to Hay, July 18, 1903, *The Letters of Theodore Roosevelt*, ed. Elting E. Morison (Harvard University Press, Cambridge, Mass., 1951), III, p. 638; see also Warren I. Cohen, *America's Response to China* (Columbia University Press, N.Y., 3rd ed., 1990) pp. 26–54.

8. Theodore Roosevelt to Theodore Roosevelt Jr., Feb. 10, 1904, *ibid.*, IV, p. 724; Prime Minister Katsura Tarō, quoted in Akira Iriye, *Pacific Estrangement, Japanese and American Expansion, 1897–1911* (Harvard University Press, Cambridge, Mass., 1972), p. 93.

9. Roosevelt, quoted in Beale, *Theodore Roosevelt*, p. 314.

10. Quoted in Hunt, *Frontier Defense*, p. 166.

11. Tōgō Minoru's *Nihon, Shokumin-ron*, translated and quoted in Akira Iriye, *Pacific Estrangement: Japanese and American Expansion, 1897–1911* (Harvard University Press, Cambridge, 1972), p. 132.

12. Taft Katsura Agreement, quoted in Tyler Dennett, *Roosevelt and the Russo-Japanese War*, (Doubleday and Page, N.Y., 1922), pp. 112–14.

13. *Shinsekai*, November 16, 28, 1906, translated and quoted in Iriye, *Pacific Estrangement*, pp. 140–41.

14. Elihu Root, quoted in Charles E. Neu, *The Troubled Encounter*, pp. 49–50.

15. Japanese Ambassador to the Secretary of State, November 30, 1908, *Foreign Relations of the United States, 1908*, (Washington, 1912), pp. 510–11; see also Raymond Esthus, *Theodore Roosevelt and Japan* (University of Washington Press, Seattle, Wash., 1967), pp. 266–87.

16. William McKinley, quoted in Lewis Gould, *The Presidency of William McKinley* (University of Kansas Press, Lawrence, Ks., 1980), p. 196; Roosevelt, quoted in David McCulloch, *The Path Between the Seas* (Simon and Schuster, N.Y., 1977), p. 254.

17. Hay, quoted in Beale, *Theodore Roosevelt*, pp. 102–3.

18. John Hay, quoted in *ibid.*, p. 103.

19. Hay, quoted in Henry F. Pringle, *Theodore Roosevelt, A Biography* (Harcourt Brace and Co., N.Y., 1931), pp. 311–12.

20. Hay, quoted in Kenton Clymer, *John Hay: The Gentleman as Diplomat* (Ann Arbor, 1975), pp. 205–7.

21. Roosevelt, quoted in Pringle, *Theodore Roosevelt*, p. 325.

22. Roosevelt, quoted *ibid.*, p. 330.

23. William Shafter and others, quoted in Louis A. Perez Jr., *Cuba Between Empires, 1878–1902* (University of Pittsburgh Press, Pittsburgh, Pa., 1983), pp. 215, 218.

24. Leonard Wood, quoted in David F. Healy, *The United States in Cuba, 1898–1902* (University of Wisconsin Press, Madison, Wis., 1963), p. 133.

25. Wood, quoted in Perez, *Cuba Between Empires*, p. 292.

26. Wood, quoted in *ibid.*, p. 310.

27. Wood, quoted in *ibid.*, p. 349.

28. Roosevelt, quoted in Dana G. Munro, *Intervention and Dollar Diplomacy in the Caribbean, 1900–1921* (Princeton University Press, Princeton, N.J., 1964), p. 129.

29. William Howard Taft, quoted in Henry F. Pringle, *The Life and Times of William Howard Taft* (Farrar and Rinehart, N.Y., 1939), II, p. 307.

30. Roosevelt, quoted in Dexter Perkins, *The Monroe Doctrine, 1869–1907* (Johns Hopkins University Press, Baltimore, Md., 1937), p. 333; see also Beale, *Theodore Roosevelt*, pp. 396–98, 406.

31. Roosevelt, quoted in Pringle, *Roosevelt*, p. 295; Roosevelt, quoted in Perkins, *A History of the Monroe Doctrine* (Little, Brown and Co., Boston, 1941), pp. 240–41.

32. Roosevelt, quoted in Dana G. Munro, *Intervention and Dollar Diplomacy in the Caribbean*, p. 91.

33. Quoted in *ibid.*, p. 94.

34. William Howard Taft, quoted in Hunt, *The Making of a Special Relationship*, p. 210.

35. Philander Knox, quoted in Michael Hunt, *The Making of a Special Relationship* (Columbia University Press, N.Y., 1983), p. 209.

36. Theodore Roosevelt, quoted in A. Whitney Griswold, *The Far Eastern Policy of the United States* (Yale University Press, New Haven, Conn., 1938), pp. 131–32.

37. Knox, quoted in Walter V. and Marie V. Scholes, *The Foreign Policies of the Taft Administration* (University of Missouri Press, Columbia, Mo., 1970), p. 40.

38. Alfredo Díaz, quoted in *ibid.*, p. 65.

# 16

# WILSON AND MORAL DIPLOMACY, 1913–1917

Woodrow Wilson practiced a form of moral imperialism that led to repeated interventions in the internal affairs of America's Latin American neighbors.

In March 1913, Woodrow Wilson became the first Democrat since Cleveland and the first southerner since Zachary Taylor to take the oath of office as president of the United States. A Virginian and the son of a Presbyterian minister, Wilson was a true "scholar in politics." After receiving his Ph.D. in 1886, he taught history and political science at Bryn Mawr and then at Wesleyan University before returning to his alma mater, Princeton. A popular teacher and a fine scholar—his study *Congressional Government* (1885) was a highly respected work—he was elected president of the university in 1902. In 1910, after fighting a losing battle over plans for a graduate school he left the university to run for governor of New Jersey and won. Two years later, thanks in part to a bitter split in the Republican party, he was elected president.

Wilson was an eloquent speaker and a brilliant man. But he was not likable. Arrogant, self-righteous, and cursed with a stubbornness that did not serve him well, he tried to dominate others and compromised only when he felt he had to. His schoolmaster's demeanor did not sit well with many, especially on the Republican side of the aisle in Congress, who bridled at his condescending ways.

The inheritor of Taft's failed Far Eastern policy, Wilson came to power at a critical moment in Chinese history. By 1913 the Manchu dynasty had collapsed and been replaced by a shaky government headed by Yüan Shihkai. Predictably, the various foreign powers with Chinese interests used the opportunity created by China's increasingly chaotic political situation to penetrate further into Manchuria, Xinjiang (Sinkiang), Tibet, Mongolia, and elsewhere.

In considering the Far Eastern situation, Wilson was moved less by his concern for China as a market or an area of political and strategic importance than by a sense of moral outrage. The president learned most of what little he knew about China from missionary accounts of the situation there. These were overwhelmingly critical of the exploitative imperialist powers and supportive of Yüan Shihkai's (Shih-k'ai's) republic. Moved by these accounts as well as his own sympathy for Yüan, whom he mistakenly believed to be struggling to establish a democratic political system, Wilson explained early in his administration that he felt "keenly the desire to help China."[1]

Given these attitudes, it is not surprising that shortly after taking office the new president executed a dramatic shift in America's Far Eastern policy. He described it as a return to the principles first enunciated by John Hay, which he mistakenly believed had been abandoned by Taft and Knox. But there was a difference, for where Hay's policy sprang from a combination of commercial ambition and geopolitical concerns, Wilson's purposes were fundamentally moralistic.

Not a week after his inauguration President Wilson was approached by representatives of the American Group, who were anxious to know his attitude toward future investment in China. During the last months of the Taft administration the six-nation banking consortium had been approached by Yüan's government, which was seeking a loan to help reorganize China's finances and stabilize the regime. As the talks progressed, the American members of the consortium lost interest in the deal. They doubted that a large issue of Chinese bonds would appeal to American investors and were jittery about how the Wilson administration would react to the loan. The bankers told Wilson that they had never been enthusiastic about investing in China. And now, with that nation in chaos, they were even less inclined to do so. They were willing to continue as active participants in the consortium only if Wilson requested their cooperation and guaranteed that the government would stand behind them.

Wilson, who had campaigned against the "special interests," misunderstood the nature of the relationship that had existed between the bankers and the Taft administration. He assumed that the State Department had been fronting for a group of exploitative capitalists anxious to profit at China's expense. Without consulting State Department officials, whom he distrusted, the president withdrew the government's support from the American Group. In a statement to the press he explained that he found the terms of the loan agreement then being negotiated unacceptably exploitative, dangerously close to threatening "the administrative independence of China itself."[2] Wilson thus ended the group's involvement in the consortium and, not incidentally, destroyed the only vehicle at hand for influencing developments in China.

Not long after this Wilson took another dramatic but misguided step, extending diplomatic recognition to Yüan Shihkai's (Shih-K'ai's) government. Tokyo objected that the decision was premature, since China was in a state of political chaos with Sun Yat-sen's Guomindang (Kuomintang) party challenging Yüan and that recognition would "practically amount to inter-ference in favor of Mr Yüan."[3] Others noted that Yuan's was not the sort of government the United States ought to support. It was a republic in name only. Moreover, there was strong reason to believe that Yüan himself had been involved in at least one recent political assassination. But Wilson, anxious to take the moral high ground, ignored all such arguments.

It was one thing to stand on the side of truth, justice, and the open door, a moral exemplar for the Chinese to follow, but quite another to organize a policy that promised positive results. When it came to developing an effective policy, Wilson had nothing to offer. He was strong on rhetoric and moral posturing but weak on performance. In fact, he was not even inclined to pay close attention to Far Eastern developments unless literally forced by circumstances to do so.

## THE RETURN OF THE YELLOW PERIL

The spring of 1913, when racial tensions in California produced a renewed crisis with Japan, was one of those moments. Japanese immigration into the Golden State had ended before this. But California's established Japanese population was fifty thousand and growing. The mere existence of a thriving Japanese community, even this relatively small one, was too much for the state's Japanophobes.

The fact that many of California's Japanese residents were acquiring agricultural land seemed particularly threatening to some. Thus Senator James D. Phelan warned that if something was not done his state would soon become nothing more than a "Japanese plantation." The California legislature responded by enacting the Webb Alien Land Act, which forbade those "unqualified for citizenship" from owning land in California.[4]

Wilson, who shared Taft's antipathy for the Japanese and opposed their immigration on racial grounds, did nothing to discourage California's lawmakers from passing the Webb Act. A few days after its passage, however, he was jolted by a strong note from Tokyo objecting to the Webb Act and asking that Japanese immigrants living in the United States be guaranteed the same rights as resident aliens from other countries.

The Japanese protest was firmly stated, but there was nothing in it that should have caused a panic. Yet the military jumped to the conclusion that war was imminent. The Army and Navy Joint Board urged Wilson to redeploy ships from Chinese waters to the Philippines and to strengthen American land forces there as well as in Hawaii. Admiral Bradley Fiske, who seems to have believed that Hawaii and the Philippines were in immediate danger, warned the president that "war was not only possible but even probable."[5]

Wilson refused to make any military preparations on the ground that such movements would promote hysteria at home and might be viewed as provocative in Tokyo. The president's decision should have been final. But the Joint Board leaked its views to the press, setting off a minor panic. The members of the board may have assumed that the public hysteria would force Wilson to follow their advice. But they had badly misjudged their man. Infuriated, he dissolved the board and pursued a diplomatic settlement with Japan.

By the end of May 1913, tensions had eased, and the war scare was over. But kind words and conciliatory gestures had not resolved the basic problem. The Webb Act was still the law in California, and Tokyo remained displeased that Japanese citizens were not accorded the same rights as other resident aliens in the United States.

World War I came as a heaven-sent opportunity to the Japanese. With Europe in turmoil, Tokyo moved quickly first to strengthen its position on the Asian continent and then to establish itself as the paramount power in China. Japan began by joining the Allies and seizing Germany's holdings in Micronesia, at Qingdao (Tsingtao) on Kiaochow Bay, and on the Shandong (Shantung) Peninsula. Next, to assure hegemony in China, Tokyo forwarded to Beijing (Peking) a peremptory note listing twenty-one demands separated into five groups. The first four of these groups were intended to secure Japan's position on the Shandong Peninsula and in other areas it claimed as spheres of influence. These were rough equivalents to the sort of concessions that European imperialists had claimed elsewhere in China. But the fifth group was quite different. The concessions Tokyo demanded here were clearly aimed at transforming China into a Japanese protectorate.

Though the Japanese warned Beijing not to reveal the nature of these demands, Chinese officials leaked them to Western diplomats, hoping to win support. Paul Reinsch, the American minister in China who was very pro-Chinese, urged the administration to take a strong stand against Japan. Under ordinary circumstances Wilson would no doubt have taken the diplomat's advice. But the president, who was then preoccupied by a deepening crisis with Mexico and the dangerous European situation, had no time for China. He left the issue in the hands of Secretary of State William Jennings Bryan.

Bryan, who unlike the president admired and trusted the Japanese, sent a note objecting to Tokyo's fifth category of demands. At the same time, however, in a remark that seemed to indicate the United States was backing away from the open door, he admitted that "territorial contiguity" created "special relations" between Japan and China.[6] When the Japanese assured the secretary that their differences with Beijing were in fact not very great, he backed still further away, leaving both Tokyo and Beijing with the impression that the United States had no quarrel with Japan's China policy.

After receiving strident complaints from Paul Reinsch in Beijing about Bryan's bungling, Wilson himself took over the direction of Far Eastern policy. In a move that no doubt puzzled and confused the Japanese, who on the basis of their dealings with Bryan could only have concluded that the United States was willing to acquiesce in their China policy, he sent a firm warning to Tokyo in the form of a strong reiteration of the open door policy with special reference to maintaining the territorial integrity as well as the sovereignty of China.

Not long after receiving Wilson's warning, Tokyo in fact did abandon its claims under the fifth group of the twenty-one demands. Japan did so, however, not because of American objections but in response to a strong protest from its British ally and as a result of opposition from elder statesmen inside the Japanese power structure who believed that the attempt to turn China into a protectorate went too far.

At this point, with little hope of any further help from Britain and nothing more substantive than rhetoric coming out of Washington, Beijing came to terms with Japan. An agreement signed by the two Asian nations confirmed Japan's claims to its spheres of influence in Manchuria and China proper and tightened the economic ties that bound China to Japan's growing empire.

Aware of the importance of gaining great power approval for its expanded position in China, Tokyo next launched a carefully orchestrated diplomatic offensive that netted it most of the support it required. In 1916, Britain, Russia, and France all recognized Japan's paramount position in China. Only one important power with Far Eastern interests refused to go along. The last word from Washington on this subject came in identical notes sent to Beijing and Tokyo, in which the president refused to recognize any agreements that either violated the principles of the open door or limited American treaty rights in China.

Wilson thus identified the United States as the sole obstacle standing between Japan and the achievement of its aims in China. Such a policy might have been acceptable if Wilson had been willing to back up his words with force. But he wasn't. Since Japan viewed its interests on the Asian continent as vital and worth fighting for, Wilson's policy left the United States frustrated and, some argued, humiliated. Theodore Roosevelt once explained that an old cowboy saying, "Never draw unless you mean to shoot," was sound advice in diplomacy. [7] Wilson followed another line of reasoning—that the United States ought always to stand for moral principles. Unhappily, however, to take a moral stand, as he did in this case, did China no good and contributed to the worsening relationship between Japan and America.

In April 1917, the United States entered World War I against the Central Powers and became in effect Japan's ally. Nevertheless, relations between the two countries remained in a state of disarray. Suspicions were rife. Some inside Japan's ruling elite believed that Japan and the United States were headed for a showdown over control of the western Pacific and China. They argued that Washington would use the war as a pretext to strengthen its military and naval forces in the Pacific in preparation for war with Japan.

A number of American policy makers in the State Department and the military were thinking along similar lines. Convinced that Japan and the United States were destined someday to clash, the Navy's General Board concluded that the United States should develop a naval force capable of controlling the western Pacific, an area that was, in a manner of speaking, Japan's backyard. To achieve that end, the board recommended the construction of a fleet no less than twice the size of Japan's.

All the war talk notwithstanding, Washington and Tokyo were both anxious to improve relations. With that in mind, Viscount Kikujiro Ishii and Secretary of State Robert Lansing, who had replaced Bryan at the State Department, opened negotiations in August 1917. But the talks hit a snag almost immediately. Both sides wanted better relations. But neither Washington nor Tokyo was prepared to make the necessary concessions. Wilson's most trusted adviser, Colonel Edward House, urged the president to recognize Japan as more or less preeminent in China. Otherwise, he thought, trouble was certain. "Japan is barred from all the undeveloped places of the earth, and if her influence in the East is not recognized as in some degree superior to that of the Western powers, there will be a reckoning."[8] But Wilson, who remained sympathetic to China and committed to a rigid interpretation of the open door policy, was unprepared to make any such concession. Nor could he, for domestic political reasons, satisfy the Japanese on the questions of immigration and land ownership in California. As for the Japanese, they wanted nothing less than an American recognition of their "paramount interests" in China.

Though it soon became clear that no basis existed for a substantive agreement, neither side wanted to admit this publicly. And so the diplomats drafted a deliberately vague, ambiguous accord. Under the terms of the Lansing-Ishii Agreement of 1917 the United States and Japan reaffirmed their joint commitment to the open door in China and to China's territorial integrity and independence. At the same time, however, the United States recognized that Japan had certain unspecified "special interests" in China.[9] Because the meaning of this phrase went unexplained, each side was able to interpret the agreement quite differently. Secretary Lansing understood that the agreement settled nothing. He and Viscount Ishii made that clear in a secret protocol to the agreement in which they agreed to maintain the status quo in China until after the war, when, presumably, further negotiations would take place. The two nations had merely agreed to put off until another time their contest over the future of China and the Pacific.

## WILSON'S CARIBBEAN INTERVENTIONS

During the presidential election campaign, Latin Americans thrilled to Woodrow Wilson's rhetoric, to his denunciation of dollar diplomacy and Republican imperialism. But Wilson behaved in much the same way as his predecessors. Nor was he averse to using force to achieve his ends. On the contrary, his criticism of Republican tactics notwithstanding, he intervened in the Caribbean more frequently than either Roosevelt or Taft.

Nicaragua's problems had by no means been resolved by the time Wilson assumed office. The Díaz government, which, it will be recalled, came to power with more than a little help from Taft and Knox, was virtually bankrupt. The salaries of government employees had not been paid in months, and the government's creditors were demanding payment of long-standing debts. The government's problems, of course, encouraged rival political factions to think in terms of a coup.

Wilson and Bryan believed that financial aid was the key to internal peace in Nicaragua and did just what Taft and Knox would have done. The secretary worked with the Díaz regime and a group of New York bankers to arrange the necessary loan. Though the bankers did finally agree to extend a loan, it was not nearly enough to resolve Nicaragua's ongoing problems. Bryan then tried another approach. The Taft administration had earlier negotiated a treaty with Nicaragua that granted the United States control over Nicaragua's canal route, a naval base in the Gulf of Fonseca and a lease on the Corn Islands. In return the United States had agreed to pay Nicaragua $3 million. This 1911 agreement had been rejected by the Senate. But Bryan now revived the project in the form of the Bryan-Chamorro Treaty of 1914. He wasn't so much interested in the strategic advantages it offered the United States as the economic aid it could provide to the Nicaraguans. The Bryan-Chamorro Treaty as finally ratified by the Senate was a major disappointment to the Wilson administration. The $3 million it produced did next to nothing to resolve Nicaragua's financial problems. Political instability there remained a serious problem as well.

Just how much of a problem this was, and how determined the Wilson administration was to maintain order in Central America, became clear in 1916 when Nicaragua was scheduled to hold presidential elections. Wilson's commitment to democratic principles notwithstanding, the State Department interceded to block the efforts of antigovernment candidates and secure the election of General Emiliano Chamorro, a man who was popular in Washington because of his pro-American views and his willingness to cooperate closely with the administration. To make certain that no further revolutionary activity followed Chamorro's election, the United States retained an unusually large legation guard in Managua as a symbol of American power and a warning to potential revolutionaries.

In the Dominican Republic, where an American-controlled customs receivership remained in place, Wilson was again confronted by an unstable, not to say chaotic, political situation. He concluded that greater control was needed and that the United States would have to intervene to put all the nation's financial affairs on a sound footing and end internal corruption as well. He pressed the Dominican government for control not only of the customs houses but of all aspects of national finance. This pressure was, of

American marines on patrol in Santo Domingo.

course, an unacceptable intrusion on Dominican sovereignty and was for that reason resisted. Even the Platt Amendment had not gone so far.

After the First World War began, Washington's demands grew more strident. For years American policy makers had been concerned over the possibility that Germany, the only major naval power without a base in the Western Hemisphere, might seek one in the Caribbean. Continued instability in the Dominican Republic seemed an open invitation to German intervention.

By the autumn of 1915 the State Department was no longer asking but demanding that the Dominican government turn control of customs, government finance, and the military over to Washington. Finally, in 1916, an exasperated Wilson landed troops to enforce his demands. His original plan was to disarm the various factions on the island and hold democratic elections—at the point of a gun. The new government would then be required to make all the concessions demanded earlier by the State Department.

This fantastic scheme, clearly a reflection of the president's frustration, led to a complete fiasco. The intervention produced a tidal wave of anti-Americanism in the Dominican Republic that made anything other than continued military occupation of the country impossible. And so the United States Navy ruled there until 1921. Not until 1924 did Washington think it safe to allow real elections.

The republic of Haiti shares the island of Hispaniola with the Dominican Republic. There, revolution had been a way of life as one revolutionary dictatorship followed another in monotonous succession. Elections were farcical and governments uniformly corrupt. A rebellion in early 1914 marked the beginning of an unusually prolonged period of political unrest, during which the Haitian government failed to make the required payments on its foreign debt, much of which was owned by German and French bondholders.

Wilson and Secretary of State Bryan felt they had to take steps to end disorder inside Haiti in order to ensure the continued payment of the republic's foreign debt and eliminate the possibility of foreign intervention there. While they were considering how best to achieve these ends, General Guillaume Sam, the latest Haitian dictator, was overthrown in a coup and fled to the French legation in Port-au-Prince. Before his flight General Sam made one very serious mistake. He ordered the execution of 167 political prisoners. The next day an organized mob broke into the French legation, dragged General Sam into the street, and literally hacked him to pieces. This was in July 1915, by which time the war in Europe was eleven months old. Unwilling to give either France or Germany an opportunity to intervene and perhaps remain in Haiti, President Wilson sent in the marines.

After order had been restored, the United States Navy supervised presidential elections and forced the newly created Haitian government to agree to a treaty that granted Washington control of its customs houses, its finances, and the military. The treaty also gave the United States the Platt Amendment right to intervene militarily in Haitian affairs to defend the terms of the treaty and Haitian independence and to protect lives and property on the island. This 1915 agreement marked the beginning of a fifteen-year period during which American forces remained in Haiti, a constant reminder that Haitian independence was more myth than reality.

Following the acquisition of the site for the Panama canal, the purpose of three successive administrations was to forge a policy that would be beneficial not only to the United States but to Caribbean and Central American states as well. Had they succeeded, the United States would have profited from an expanding regional trade, improved investment opportunities, an end to European intervention, and greater security for the Panama Canal. The Caribbean peoples would have benefited from peace and improved economic and social conditions.

Though in the short run it appeared that dollar diplomacy had succeeded in the Dominican Republic, it soon became clear that stability could not be achieved by economic means alone. And when the United States was confronted with the choice of leaving the peoples of Central America and the Caribbean free to fight things out among themselves or intervening with military force to establish order, policy makers in Washington invariably chose the latter course. There was always a good reason for this. Sometimes American economic interests seemed threatened. On other occasions intervention was considered a strategic necessity. But no matter how the United States justified its behavior, it was clear that the peoples of Central America and the Caribbean were free only in a nominal sense and that their sovereignty was limited by the strategic and economic needs of the United States.

## MEXICO, THE FORGOTTEN REVOLUTION

For more than three decades, from 1876 until 1910, Mexico was governed by Porfirio Díaz. It was a period of relative stability and economic progress for the country. But it was not a time that the great mass of the Mexican people remember fondly. Foreigners and a small group of elitists controlled Mexico's land and resources, while most of its fifteen million people lived as landless peasants in a feudal condition.

By 1910, the Díaz dictatorship was on its last legs, threatened by an accumulation of discontents at all levels of Mexican society. As the presidential elections of that year approached, Díaz found himself on the defensive, challenged by a number of opposition leaders. These men had emerged from the shadows of Mexican politics after the dictator himself thoughtlessly suggested in an interview with an American newspaperman that he believed Mexico was ready for democracy.

Among those hoping to bring down the dictator, none was more prominent than Francisco de Madero. Idealist, dreamer, and mystic, Madero headed the Anti-Reelection party. A practicing spiritualist who believed that he was in contact with the great minds of the past, this slight, frail-looking man thought he had been chosen to bring about a major revolution not only in Mexico but perhaps throughout the world.

When it became clear during the election campaign that Madero was attracting support, Díaz had him arrested, tried on charges of sedition, convicted, and imprisoned. With Madero out of the way, the old man himself went on to an overwhelming victory at the polls. But Díaz paid a high price for having made a mockery of the elections. Once it became clear that honest elections were impossible, revolution became inevitable.

The spark that kindled this astonishing event came when Madero escaped from his prison cell and fled to San Antonio, Texas, where he took control of a revolutionary junta headquartered there. Safe on the American side of the Rio Grande, he issued a revolutionary manifesto and announced that November 20, 1910, was to be the day on which the Mexican people would rise and destroy the Díaz tyranny.

On the appointed day uprisings against the government did take place in numerous parts of the country. The movement, which gained momentum in the months that followed, was never very large. But the men who led it, Francisco Villa and Emiliano Zapata among them, were skillful guerrilla fighters who kept the government on the defensive while draining its strength. Díaz, now nearly eighty, was too old to lead. And the government, lacking strength and substance, collapsed like a house of cards. On May 25, 1911, Díaz resigned and went into exile.

Madero was an easy winner in the presidential elections that followed.

But it soon became clear that though he had been an appealing symbol in the struggle against Díaz, he was ineffective as a national leader.

Along the road to power, Madero promised labor reforms, a free system of education, judicial and agrarian reform, and the creation of a truly democratic political order. In fact, however, he seems to have been primarily interested in implementing political reforms. On the other hand, many of those who backed his cause including Emiliano Zapata in Morelos, Francisco Villa in Chihuahua, Alvaro Obregón in Sonora, and to a lesser extent Venustiano Carranza, were leaders of a social revolution that had attracted the support of workers, peasants, and a large number of middle-class Mexicans as well. Madero was unprepared to lead this genuinely revolutionary movement. But neither could he contain it. Mexico therefore continued in a revolutionary condition.

## THE AMERICAN REACTION TO REVOLUTION

The Taft administration, like other foreign governments with interests in Mexico, at first greeted the Mexican Revolution calmly. From a distance Madero's movement appeared to be nothing more than an attempt by one elite to seize political power from another. Foreign economic holdings did not seem to be threatened. But as it became clear that Madero could not control the forces he had helped set in motion, that attitude changed. During the Díaz years, Americans had invested in excess of $1 billion in the country. Now that investment was at risk, as were the lives of some fifty thousand Americans resident in Mexico. Taft reacted to the escalating danger by urging those Americans who could to leave Mexico immediately. He also mobilized a force of twenty thousand, deploying it near the border. Naval forces cruised in Mexican waters, their marine contingents ready for action in the event that a landing should prove necessary. But Taft hoped to avoid intervention. Mexico was a large country, and the violence was widespread. Intervention would be expensive and probably ineffective.

The president's fondest hope was that Madero would be able to create a stable government without American interference. To aid in the endeavor, he declared an embargo on the sale of weapons to Mexico, a policy that substantially reduced the flow of arms to rebel forces and favored Madero. In the months that followed Madero did strengthen his hold over parts of his sprawling country. But still the revolution continued, with American lives and property increasingly at risk.

By the autumn of 1912, Taft was clearly out of patience. He explained to Secretary of State Philander Knox that he thought "we ought to put a little dynamite in" a note about to be sent to Mexico City "for the purpose of stirring up that dreamer who seems unfitted to meet the crisis in the country of which he is President." In December, State Department officials threatened the Mexican foreign minister with military intervention "if the ongoing killing of Americans and the destruction of American property did not stop."[10]

Henry Lane Wilson, the American minister in Mexico, urged the president to topple the Madero regime. Wilson was not the only one thinking such thoughts. By this time Britain and Germany, the other powers with important economic interests in Mexico, also believed that Madero would have to go. Still, Taft delayed. He was a cautious man, made more so by warnings from Secretary Knox that Wilson was apparently exaggerating the danger in order "to force this government's hands in its dealings with the Mexican situation."[11]

On February 10, 1913, the final crisis of the Madero regime came when fighting broke out between government forces and a rebel force led by Felix Díaz and General Bernardo Reyes. Mexico City became a war zone, and the diplomatic quarter was caught in the cross-fire. In the midst of the battle, Minister Wilson decided that the time had come to seek Madero's resignation. He told a group of diplomats meeting with him in the American legation that "Madero is crazy, a fool, a lunatic, and must be declared legally incapable of exercising his duties."[12] Though uninstructed, Wilson went to the Presidential Palace and, speaking for himself as well as the German, British, and Spanish ministers, demanded that Madero step down. But the president refused, and the battle for Mexico City continued.

A week after the fighting in the city began, the government's fate was sealed when General Victoriano Huerta, who commanded the government's forces, informed Henry Lane Wilson that he was going to overthrow Madero. Wilson, acting without instructions as he would throughout the crisis, made no objection. Thus it was with Wilson's tacit approval that Madero and his cabinet were taken prisoner. Huerta's next objective was to end the fighting in the city. Again he turned to Wilson, and again the minister did not disappoint him. At Wilson's invitation Huerta and the rebel leader, Felix Díaz, met in the American embassy, where a compromise was hammered out that left Huerta as the provisional president of Mexico. By mediating between Huerta and the rebels, Wilson in effect sanctioned the agreement. Thereafter Huerta must have believed that he was acting with American support.

Among Huerta's remaining problems was the question of what to do about his prisoner, the former president. As before, he asked Wilson's advice. The envoy's enigmatic response, which has sometimes been interpreted as authorization for Madero's assassination, was that Huerta "ought to do that which was best for the peace of the country."[13] Two days later, in the dark of night, while ostensibly being transferred from one prison to another, Madero was murdered.

Unmoved by this bloody business, Minister Wilson urged the administration to extend immediate recognition to the new government. Mexico's internal affairs, he believed, even when they involved the assassination of a deposed president, were none of America's business. The United States wanted a government in Mexico that was able to protect American lives and property, and Huerta had a better chance of accomplishing this than anyone else.

If Wilson was indifferent to Madero's fate, the American people were shocked and outraged by his murder. For the Taft administration to recognize Huerta even before he had washed the blood from his hands would not serve Republican party purposes. With little time remaining before Woodrow Wilson took the oath of office, Taft and Knox preferred to leave this messy business unresolved.

## WILSON AND HUERTA

Victoriano Huerta was an affront to everything Woodrow Wilson held sacred. The self-righteous American president made it clear from the beginning that he would "never recognize a government of butchers."[14] More significant, he became obsessed by the idea that Huerta must be driven from power.

Practical men, including those with Mexican interests, leaders of the American colony in Mexico, and even Wilson's closest personal adviser, Colonel Edward M. House, argued that Huerta should be recognized because he stood the best chance of establishing a stable government in Mexico. But Wilson rejected that view, arguing that there were times when in order to do what was morally correct the United States might have to sacrifice its interests. Thus he told an audience in Mobile, Alabama, "We must show ourselves friends by comprehending their [Latin America's] interests whether it squares with our own interest or not."[15]

Wilson did not believe that it was enough to be against Huerta. He hoped to guide Mexico toward the creation of a democratically elected government that would operate on constitutional principles. The president's purpose, he once explained to an English visitor, was to "teach the Latin American Republics to elect good men."[16]

Wilson also believed that it was the duty of the United States to spread the gospel of free enterprise to Mexico as well as other underdeveloped lands. Because of his beliefs, he had little use for Venustiano Carranza's Constitutionalists or others such as Villa and Zapata, who represented the real revolutionary force at work in Mexico. Huerta would have to go. But Wilson hoped to replace him with a moderate who was committed to democratic rule and free enterprise, someone who would accept guidance from Washington and protect American propertied interests.

In August 1913, Wilson began a diplomatic offensive intended to bring Huerta down. He sent the former governor of Minnesota, John Lind, as his special emissary to Mexico with an offer to mediate between Huerta and Carranza. But what Wilson called mediation was in fact an invitation for Huerta to resign. The president proposed a military truce to be followed by free elections in which Huerta would not be a candidate. Wilson had a warning for the Constitutionalists, too. He demanded that Carranza fight "with a ballot and not with the gun" and made it clear that he would refuse to recognize any government produced by a revolution.[17]

Huerta not only rejected Wilson's proposal; he held fraudulent elections, after which he had himself proclaimed president of Mexico. The old general, who understood that his action would infuriate Wilson, did not take this step lightly. He was being strongly backed by London and the British minister in Mexico City, Sir Lionel Carden. British companies had vital interests in Mexico, especially in oil. From the Foreign Office's point of view, Huerta seemed more likely to protect those interests than the revolutionaries who opposed him.

Like Huerta, Carranza also rejected Wilson's proposal for mediation and free elections. The Constitutionalist leader suspected, no doubt correctly, that Wilson wanted to be rid of him, too. Certain that Wilson's ultimate ambition was the creation of a satellite government in Mexico City, he did not intend to be played like a pawn on Washington's chessboard.

Wilson's failed effort at "mediation" had one unexpected result: it strengthened Huerta's position inside Mexico, where anti-Americanism was rife. This development had no effect on Wilson, however, who stubbornly persisted in seeking the dictator's removal. He implemented an embargo on the sale of arms to Mexico and sought to convince the European powers to join him in isolating Huerta by withholding recognition.

Berlin quickly agreed to follow Wilson's lead in Mexico. Downing Street, on the other hand, hung back. The Royal Navy, which was then converting from coal to oil, was becoming more dependent on Mexican oil. Moreover, other British investments in Mexico had to be protected. At length, however, after tapping into alternative sources of petroleum and winning assurances from Wilson that the United States would "protect all foreign property in Mexico during the civil war," Britain's foreign secretary, Sir Edward Grey, agreed to follow Washington's lead in Mexico.[18] Given the tense European situation, at the time American friendship meant far more to London than its connection with General Huerta.

Wilson complemented his attempts to isolate Huerta diplomatically with secret offers of support to the Constitutionalists. But in return, he demanded that following Huerta's departure the Constitutionalists agree to the creation of a provisional government, to be followed swiftly by democratic elections.

Carranza wanted no part of such an arrangement. He informed Wilson's emissary that he would use force against any American incursions into Mexico and would make no commitments regarding Mexico's political future. He wanted diplomatic recognition and renewed access to American arms and ammunition, nothing more. Stunned by this peremptory rebuff, Wilson refused to extend recognition to Carranza's provisional government. He did, however, raise the arms embargo. It was a marriage of convenience. The Constitutionalists, after all, were the only force inside Mexico capable of driving Huerta from power.

Wilson expected that as a result of his exertions Huerta would soon have no choice but to resign. But, though the Constitutionalists were stronger than before, their advance south was slow. Meanwhile Wilson's interference in Mexico's internal affairs had done much to strengthen Huerta, who, as winter gave way to spring, 1914, showed no signs of running for cover. The president now awakened to the unhappy truth. His blustering and pressure tactics had placed his and his country's credibility on the line. Now Huerta *had* to go. But the only way left to accomplish that seemed armed intervention. And Wilson was emotionally unprepared to take that last drastic step.

## THE MARINES TAKE VERACRUZ

In April 1914, Tampico, an oil refining center on the Pánuco River just a few miles from the Gulf of Mexico, was tense and excited. A battle seemed certain to take place there between a garrison loyal to Huerta and a Constitutionalist force massing near the town. Tampico was also the port of call of an American naval squadron commanded by Admiral Henry T. Mayo, whose job it was to protect American lives and property there.

On the morning of April 9, 1914, the crew of a U.S. Navy whaleboat put in at a dock that had been declared off limits by the commander of the Tampico garrison. The American sailors were loading drums of gasoline on to their boat, when they were arrested by a Mexican patrol and marched to a nearby prison. There, a ranking officer freed the men, who were returned to the wharf with his apologies. They finished their work and returned to their ship. The whole affair took less than an hour.

That would have been that but for Admiral Mayo's insistence that this insult to the Stars and Stripes—the whaleboat was flying a flag fore and aft—should not go unnoticed. He demanded that General Morelos Zaragosa, who commanded at Tampico, discipline the officer who arrested his men, forward a written apology, and "hoist the American flag on a prominent position on shore and salute it with twenty one guns."[19] Zaragosa, no fool, asked Mexico City for instructions.

General Huerta was willing to court martial the officer who made the arrests and forward a written apology to Mayo. But he could not under duress fire a salute to the American flag without undermining his political strength at home. His nationalist credentials would have been down the drain.

Huerta's refusal to fire that salute gave President Wilson an opportunity to increase the pressure. With Congress and the public firmly behind him, he ordered the entire Atlantic fleet to Tampico. The navy was ordered to blockade Mexican ports, cutting Huerta off from much-needed military supplies being shipped in from Europe, until he fired those twenty-one guns in honor of Old Glory.

The president was forced to change his plans at the last minute when the State Department informed him that because an official state of war did not exist it would be a violation of international law to interdict the arms traffic between Mexico and Europe. An illegal blockade would undoubtedly produce serious problems for the administration with a number of Huerta's arms suppliers, including Britain and Germany. At the same time, Wilson learned of the imminent arrival at Veracruz of the German merchant ship *Ypiranga* carrying a cargo of arms and ammunition. The only way to deny Huerta these weapons while avoiding difficulties with the Germans was to seize the *Ypiranga*'s cargo after it had been unloaded and before it could be shipped to Huerta's forces. It was for this purpose that Wilson ordered the marines ashore at Veracruz.

On April 20, 1914, several hundred marines and naval personnel went ashore in the Mexican port city. The initial landing went without incident because the Huertista commander there agreed not to resist. But as the Americans moved outward from the wharf area, they encountered small-arms fire from civilians and a number of overzealous naval cadets in the city. The fighting continued throughout the day, until Veracruz had been secured. When it ended eighty Americans had been killed or wounded. The Mexicans suffered more than three hundred casualties.

Wilson was shocked. Convinced of the righteousness of his cause, he had expected that the American invaders would be treated as liberators. He became even more flustered when not only Huerta but Carranza, too, denounced the invasion and demanded an immediate troop withdrawal. It is not surprising, then, that when Argentina, Brazil, and Chile offered to mediate between Mexico and the United States, he leapt at the opportunity while insisting that American troops would remain in Veracruz until an agreement was signed.

The so-called ABC Mediation, for the initials of the three countries that served as mediators, began on May 20, 1914, at Niagara Falls, New York, and settled nothing. Wilson continued to insist that the purpose of the talks should be to end Huerta's rule and lay the groundwork for free elections in Mexico. But Huerta didn't want free elections. Neither, for that matter, did Carranza, who was winning the war and seemed likely to achieve power by the sword. "The First Chief," as Carranza called himself, was in fact so uninterested in what happened at the conference that he at first refused to send a delegation. When he relented, it was only to hold secret talks with the American delegates there. But nothing came of these discussions either. Carranza steadfastly denied Wilson what he most wanted—control over the Mexican Revolution. In the end the delegates to the conference framed some face-saving protocols and adjourned having achieved nothing.

While the talks went on, the war did, too. And with some unexpected (and unwanted) help from the Americans, the Constitutionalists finally drove Huerta from power. The cost of the war and General Huerta's dependence on printing press money to meet his growing financial needs had placed the Mexican economy in jeopardy even before the landing at Veracruz. The continued American control of the customs houses there cut Huerta off from an important source of scarce revenues. The result was even more paper money. By July, government issued currency was worthless, and the economy was in a tailspin. Beset by overwhelming problems both on the battlefield and in the counting house, the old general at last resigned and went into European exile.

Wilson imagined that once Huerta was out of the way he would be able to play honest broker in Mexico, arranging for the creation of a new government based on democratic principles, committed to the free enterprise system, and willing to protect foreign property. When Mexico continued in a revolutionary condition, with the various factions fighting each other, the president, anxious to keep Carranza from attaining complete control of Mexico, called for the creation of a coalition government and warned that continued instability would leave the United States no choice but to "decide" for itself "what means should be employed to help Mexico save herself."[20]

This threat of intervention netted the president little save the anger and resentment of Zapata and Carranza, both of whom wasted no time throwing the president's warning back in his face. Zapata's brother, Eufemio, was particularly vehement: "We are not afraid to defend our country . . . even if they [the Americans] send millions of soldiers. We will fight them, one against hundreds."[21]

Of the major Mexican revolutionary leaders, only Francisco Villa responded affirmatively to the president's call for a coalition government and an end to the fighting. But by this time he had failed in an attempt to seize power, been outmaneuvered politically by the Constitutionalists, and been outgeneraled by Alvaro Obregón. Villa was at the time penned up in northern Mexico, an irritant but no longer a threat to Carranza's leadership.

Though Woodrow Wilson had no strong positive feelings for Francisco Villa, he liked Carranza even less. "We do not wish the Carranza faction to be the only one to deal with in Mexico," Secretary Lansing wrote. "Carranza seems so impossible that an appearance, at least, of opposition to him will give us the opportunity to invite a compromise of factions."[22] For this reason the Wilson administration lent its support to Villa while continuing to insist on the creation of a broadly based coalition government for Mexico.

Unhappily for Wilson, compromise was not in the cards. Before the end of 1915, Villa, with fewer than five hundred soldiers left in his command, was reduced to fighting a guerrilla war against Carrancista forces. Under these circumstances Wilson finally and reluctantly extended de facto recognition to Carranza's government.

## A SECOND INTERVENTION

Washington's decision to recognize the Carranza regime came as a shock to Francisco Villa, who charged that in return for recognition and a $500 million loan, Carranza had sold out to the United States. "The price of these favors," he alleged, "was simply the sale of our country by the traitor Carranza."[23] Convinced of this, Villa redirected his guerrilla activities away from Carrancista forces and against Americans. In January 1916, his men

General Francisco Villa (second from the left) provoked an American military intervention in Mexico by a raid on Columbus, New Mexico, in which several Americans were killed. The intervention led to a crisis between President Woodrow Wilson and President Venustiano Carranza of Mexico that almost resulted in war.

slaughtered sixteen American mining engineers working in Sonora. Then, on March 9, four hundred of his raiders crossed the border into New Mexico. They rampaged through the streets of the town of Columbus, shooting anyone in sight until they were driven off by a cavalry unit stationed there.

Villa's was a clever strategy. He assumed that the Columbus raid would result in an American intervention in Mexico. If Carranza allowed American forces to enter the country unopposed (which Villa thought he might feel compelled to do to maintain his secret arrangement with Washington), he would be proven to be a traitor to the revolution. If he resisted, it would mean a war with the United States that would destroy his power.

With the American public and the Republican opposition demanding action, Wilson had no choice but to intervene. He promised to send troops into Mexico but temporarily held off, hoping that Carranza could be convinced to request American aid against Villa. But that was a forlorn hope. At length Wilson acted without Carranza's consent. And so, for the second time in two years an American force, this time six thousand strong under the command of General John J. ("Black Jack") Pershing, invaded Mexico, bent on trapping Villa.

The American intervention proved to be an enormous bonus for Villa, whose popularity soared in 1916. Whereas his force had been reduced almost to the vanishing point not long before, by the end of the year he commanded an army of ten thousand men. Meanwhile Carrancista troops grew restless, more ready to join Villa than to aid the Americans in hunting him down. As one observer wrote: "The general sentiment among the rank and file of the revolutionary (Carrancista) forces is one of sympathy with Villa. They openly express their admiration for his adventure and their regret for not having been with him."[24]

With six thousand American soldiers racing about in a country where anti-Americanism was rampant, incidents were bound to occur. Not a month after Pershing's troops crossed the border, an American patrol was attacked by a mob that included a number of Mexican government soldiers. Two Americans and forty Mexicans were killed in the fray. Carranza, reacting to growing internal pressures, demanded that Pershing's force withdraw immediately. But Wilson, who was under similar pressure, refused to budge until Villa was brought to justice. Two months later in June 1916, the situation took an even more dangerous turn when a small American force clashed with a larger body of Mexican troops. Twelve Americans were killed in this affray, and twenty-three were taken prisoner.

With the two nations poised on the brink of war, Wilson demanded the return of the prisoners and, to make certain that Carranza understood the gravity of the situation, mobilized the national guard. He even drafted a message to Congress asking for the authority to occupy northern Mexico. But he soon thought better of it and never delivered that message. There was little popular support for a full-scale war with Mexico. Moreover, it seemed very likely that the United States might soon be dragged into the European conflict. Under the circumstances, a war with Mexico had to be avoided. When Carranza made a friendly gesture, releasing the American prisoners and proposing a negotiated settlement to the crisis, Wilson quickly agreed.

The Mexican-American conference, which convened in September 1916 in Atlantic City, only served to accentuate the chasm dividing Mexico and the United States. Washington, continuing to treat Mexico as if it were simply another banana republic, insisted that Carranza guarantee to protect the lives and property of Americans doing business in Mexico and recognize America's right to intervene militarily if the Mexican government should fail or be unable to do so. Carranza rejected this astonishing demand out of hand and refused to discuss any political issues until all American forces had been withdrawn from Mexican territory.

The Mexican-American talks reached total deadlock in late December 1916. What happened next was largely dictated by European developments. In mid-January 1917, the Imperial German government announced the resumption of unrestricted submarine warfare. This decision made American intervention in the European war inevitable. Wilson then had little choice but to withdraw General Pershing's force from Mexican soil. The last troops left on February 5, 1917. But Mexican-American relations remained in a state of disarray. The adoption of the Mexican constitution of 1917, which asserted the government's right to expropriate foreign holdings, only exacerbated tensions.

General John J. ("Black Jack") Pershing led the American force that entered Mexico to track down Francisco Villa and his men. They failed and were subsequently withdrawn in 1917, when it became clear that the United States would soon become involved in the European war.

The year 1917 was epochal in Mexican history. Not only did the country receive a new reform constitution, but Carranza won an overwhelming victory in the first free elections since Madero's time. Of course, none of this was the result of Woodrow Wilson's repeated interferences in Mexico's internal affairs. When all was said and done, "moral imperialism" had not influenced in any positive way the course of Mexican history.

## ENDNOTES

1. *The Cabinet Diaries of Josephus Daniels, 1913–1921*, ed. E. David Cronan (University of Nebraska Press, Lincoln, Neb., 1963), p. 17.

2. Woodrow Wilson, quoted in Arthur Link, *Woodrow Wilson and the Progressive Era* (Harper and Row, N.Y., 1954), p. 83.

3. Quoted in Warren I. Cohen, *America's Response to China: A History of Sino-American Relations* (Columbia University Press, N.Y., 3rd ed., 1990), p. 73.

4. James D. Phelan, quoted in Arthur Link, *Woodrow Wilson, The New Freedom* (Princeton University Press, Princeton, N.J., 1956), p. 289.

5. Admiral Bradley Fiske, quoted in *ibid.*, p. 297.

6. Secretary of State William Jennings Bryan to the Japanese Ambassador, March 13, 1915, *Foreign Relations of the United States, 1915* (Washington, 1924), pp. 105–11.

7. Theodore Roosevelt to William Howard Taft, December 22, 1910, *The Letters of Theodore Roosevelt*, ed. Elting E. Morison (Harvard University Press, Cambridge, Mass., 1951), VII, p. 190.

8. Edward M. House, quoted in Charles E. Neu, *The Troubled Encounter, The United States and Japan* (John Wiley and Sons, N.Y., 1975), p. 92.

9. Lansing-Ishii Agreement, quoted in A. Whitney Griswold, *The Far Eastern Policy of the United States* (Harcourt Brace and Co., N.Y., 1938), p. 216.

10. Quoted in Walter V. and Marie Scholes, *The Foreign Policies of the Taft Administration* (University of Missouri Press, Columbia Missouri, 1970), p. 95.

11. Philander Knox, quoted in *ibid.*, p. 96.

12. Henry Lane Wilson, quoted in Kenneth Grieb, *The United States and Huerta* (Lincoln, Nebraska, 1969), p. 16.

13. Scholes, *Foreign Policies of the Taft Administration*, p. 101.

14. Wilson, quoted in Arthur Link, *Woodrow Wilson and the Progressive Era*, p. 109.

15. Woodrow Wilson, quoted in *ibid.*, pp. 117–18.

16. Wilson, quoted in *ibid.*, p. 119.

17. Wilson, quoted in Friedrich Katz, *The Secret War in Mexico: Europe and the U.S. and the Mexican Revolution* (University of Chicago Press, Chicago, Ill., 1981), pp. 168–69.

18. Quoted in *ibid.*, pp. 189–90.

19. Admiral Mayo, quoted in Howard F. Cline, *The United States and Mexico* (Harvard University Press, Cambridge, Mass., 1953), p. 156.

20. Wilson, quoted in Robert E. Quirk, *The Mexican Revolution, 1914–1915* (University of Indiana Press, Bloomington, Ind., 1960), pp. 256–57.

21. Eufemio Zapata, quoted in Katz, *The Secret War in Mexico*, p. 299.

22. Robert Lansing, quoted in *ibid.*, p. 300.

23. Francisco Villa, quoted in *ibid.*, p. 306.

24. Anonymous, quoted in *ibid.*, p. 308.

The war wasn't entirely popular in 1917. Here the navy tries a little unsubtle psychology to encourage men to enlist.

# 17

# *THE STRUGGLE FOR NEUTRALITY, 1914–1917*

In August 1914, the great European powers tumbled one after another into the abyss of war, taking much of the rest of the continent and then the world with them. When the fighting stopped four years later, the Russian, German, Turkish, and Austro-Hungarian empires lay in ruins. Britain and France, though victorious on the battlefield, were so broken they never again attained the levels of power and influence they had enjoyed in earlier times. Nineteenth-century Europe and the civilization it created had been destroyed. The world would never be the same.

During the summer of 1914 Americans reacted to the growing threat of a general European war with stunned disbelief. The early twentieth century had been the heyday of the peace movement. Two international conferences held at the Hague, the first in 1899 and the second in 1907, had produced a number of declarations and conventions codifying many of the rules of war. The 1899 conference had also established the Hague Tribunal for the arbitration of international disputes. There had been frequent European crises, to be sure, but Americans by and large retained a sunny confidence that peace would be preserved. Hadn't Andrew Carnegie established a $10,000,000 endowment to abolish war? And hadn't the economist Norman Angell proven in *The Great Illusion* (1911) that war had become obsolete as a result of the interconnectedness of modern industrial economies? In 1913 Dr. David Starr Jordan, director of the World Peace Foundation, stated flatly: What shall we say of the Great War of Europe, ever threatening, ever impending, and which never comes? We shall say that it will never come. Humanly speaking it is impossible.[1] Even after the war began Americans had difficulty dealing with the facts of the mass slaughter taking place across the Atlantic. "This dreadful conflict . . . came to most of us as lightning out of a clear sky," wrote one observer. "The horror of it kept me awake for weeks, nor has the awfulness of it all deserted me."[2]

President Woodrow Wilson responded to the European war by immediately declaring America's neutrality. Two weeks later, perhaps concerned by the obvious anti-German, pro-Allied sentiments being expressed in much of the Eastern press, he appealed for calm. "Every man who really loves America will act and speak in the true spirit of neutrality, which is the spirit of impartiality and fairness, and friendliness to all concerned." Whether or not the country could remain neutral, he thought, would be determined largely by "what newspapers and magazines contain, what ministers utter in their pulpits, and men proclaim as their opinion in the street." He warned against "passionately taking sides." The country, he said, "must be neutral in fact as well as in name during these days that are to try men's souls. We must be impartial in thought as well as in action, must put a curb upon our sentiments as well as upon every transaction that might be construed as a preference of one party to the struggle before another."[3]

The *New York Sun* applauded the president's policy. "There is nothing reasonable in such a war . . . and it would be folly for the country to sacrifice itself to the frenzy of dynastic policies and the clash of ancient hatreds which is urging the Old World to destruction." Another more prescient editorial in the *St. Louis Globe Democrat* pointed out that though desirable, it would not be easy to remain at peace. America's only security, the paper warned, would be in maintaining "absolute, strict neutrality which is what the public opinion of this country will demand."[4]

Presidential statements and press opinion notwithstanding, absolute impartiality proved impossible. German Americans, for obvious reasons, tended to favor the Central Powers (Germany, Austria-Hungary, Bulgaria, and Turkey). Irish Americans, who by and large hated the British, felt similarly. But on the whole the great majority tended to support the Allies (France, England, Russia, Japan, and later Italy) from the start.

The generally pro-Allied stand taken by most Americans was rooted in a shared cultural tradition and strengthened by the fact that in recent years Anglo-American relations had been reasonably cordial, while Berlin and Washington had frequently been at odds in the international arena. Americans were also reacting to Germany's ruthless prosecution of the war. When the German army invaded neutral Belgium in violation of Berlin's solemn guarantees, Americans were shocked. But it was German brutality that truly aroused popular fury. The execution of innocent civilians and the burning of the ancient city of Louvain outraged American sensibilities.

The celebrated American newspaper reporter, Richard Harding

Davis, was on a train near Louvain when the city with its cathedral, its magnificent library, and its many art treasures was put to the torch. The story he filed told it all.

> For two hours on Thursday night I was in what for six hundred years had been the city of Louvain. The Germans were burning it, and to hide their work kept us locked in the railroad carriages. But the story was written against the sky, was told to us by German soldiers incoherent with excesses; and we could read it in the faces of women and children being led to concentration camps and of citizens on their way to be shot.

"Louvain, poor Louvain," lamented another American observer. With it had been destroyed more art treasures "than Prussia had produced in its entire history.[5]

Official Washington was no less pro-Allied than the general population. With the exception of Secretary of State William Jennings Bryan, who resigned in 1915, top American policy makers all shared a pro-Allied orientation. Bryan's successor in the State Department, the dapper conservative, Robert Lansing, viewed the war in Europe as a struggle between German autocracy and Western democracy and believed that the United States ought to join the Allies in their struggle. The president's close personal adviser, Colonel Edward M. House, did not share Lansing's view that German power ought to be utterly destroyed. He saw a place for Germany in Central Europe as a check on Russian expansionism and an element in the balance of power. But he did believe that Germany ought to be reduced in stature. He too, therefore, inclined toward the Allies and supported American intervention in the war.

Like his advisers, Woodrow Wilson sympathized with the Allies. Yet it is also true that Wilson's most deeply held desire was to remain neutral. He viewed Americans as "the champions of peace and concord" and insisted that he would not allow the country to be "thrown . . . off balance by a war with which we have nothing to do" and "whose causes cannot touch us."[6] Wilson never allowed his or his advisers' pro-Allied feelings to interfere with this greater purpose. In this sense he accurately reflected the feelings of most Americans, pro-Allied or not, who also believed that the United States ought not to become involved in Europe's madness.

During the summer of 1914, while Europe moved toward war, the American economy drifted into a recession. Once the fighting began, however, Americans quickly sensed new opportunities at hand. Thus the *Detroit Free Press* predicted that the war would create increased demands for American agricultural products and the "prospect of much money for American farmers in this year when we are to have a great crop." The *New York Mail* agreed, arguing that "such a war could hardly be otherwise than materially profitable to us." At the very least, opined still another New York paper, it would create "a supreme opportunity for American manufacturers to gain world-wide markets."[7]

The war's immediate effect was not what these optimistic forecasters had predicted. A panic gripped Wall Street, and commodity prices collapsed. But confidence soon returned as Britain and France flooded the American marketplace with orders for vast quantities of food, raw materials, and munitions.

This salient fact highlights the dilemma that Woodrow Wilson confronted as he sought to keep America out of the war. Americans wanted to remain neutral—it was true. But they also wanted prosperity, and prosperity was increasingly dependent on an expanded trade with the Allies. As time wore on, it became more and more difficult to have both peace and prosperity. In the end it proved impossible.

## DEBATING THE DECLARATION OF LONDON

At the beginning of the war the State Department proposed that the belligerents abide by rules of conduct laid down in the Declaration of London, a nonbinding document drafted at an international conference in 1909 that claimed wide freedoms for neutral trading nations and sharply restricted belligerent rights. Had all sides agreed, this would have enabled the United States to trade with the Central Powers in essentials, such as food and raw materials, through neutral ports in the Netherlands and Denmark. Germany and Austria-Hungary, with nothing to lose since the British controlled the seas, promptly agreed, contingent upon acceptance by the Allies. London, however, refused. To have done otherwise would have vastly diminished the Royal Navy's ability to enforce a tight naval blockade of the Central Powers.

Although Britain's foreign secretary, Sir Edward Grey, refused to be bound by the Declaration of London, which he considered anachronistic in an age of total war, neither was he prepared to go too far in a restrictive direction. He believed it was vital to preserve harmony with Washington even at some cost to the effectiveness of Britain's naval blockade. During the first several months of the war, then, Grey threaded his way between the demands of the Admiralty for a more effective blockade and his own view that too much pressure might lead to a break with America. He explained to his ambassador in Washington, "We wish in all our conduct of the war to do nothing which will be a cause of complaint or dispute as regards the United States Government; such a dispute would indeed be a crowning calamity . . . and probably fatal to our chances of success."[8] In this spirit he refused to interdict America's trade in raw cotton with Germany while at the same time approving the Royal Navy's mine blockade of the North Sea. When American ships were seized, he frequently interceded to speed judicial proceedings and sometimes arranged for the purchase of sequestered cargoes to keep friction to a minimum.

Grey's cautious policies paid dividends. The Wilson administration soon dropped its request that the belligerents adhere to the Declaration of London. It also reversed an early prohibition on loans and credits to the belligerents, opening the way for an expanded war trade, the lion's share of which was with the Allies. Nor did the president protest Britain's mining of the North Sea, which, though a violation of international law, had little effect on American interests.

Wilson's policy of benevolent neutrality sent an important message reverberating through the American business community. Put simply, it meant that the United States would do little beyond issuing formal protests when the Royal Navy seized ships and cargoes destined for the Central Powers. Since Britain controlled the seas and there were ample profits to be made in trade with the Allies, commerce with the Central Powers literally dried up while trade with the Allies rose from a peacetime figure of $825 million annually to more than four times that amount. In this way the vast power of the American economy was linked to the Allied cause.

The policies that produced this outcome were the result of considerations that had nothing to do with the president's pro-allied sentiments. First, Wilson knew that the war trade had brought the country from the brink of depression back to prosperity. It only made sense then to do what was necessary to advance America's trading interests. Moreover, during the first half-year of the war, when Wilson was developing his neutral policy, it did not appear that the Germans could do anything about the burgeoning trade with the Allies. The German battle fleet was bottled up, and Wilson was as yet unaware of the danger to American commerce posed by the submarine. Wilson thought the United States could safely exploit a burgeoning neutral trade that had become vital to the domestic economy.

## STRICT ACCOUNTABILITY

World War I was, for the most part, a long and frustrating experience for the officers of the German High Seas Fleet. During the early years of the century, under the stewardship of Grand Admiral Alfred von Tirpitz, the German navy had grown into a first-class fighting organization. But in 1914 it was still not powerful enough to contest with the British Grand Fleet for control of the seas. And so Germany's frowning battleships remained bottled up behind minefields in the North Sea ports, unable to contribute to the war effort.

At the beginning of the war, the German navy's High Command gave little thought to the potential of the twenty-one boats that constituted its submarine fleet. The navy's attitude toward the submarine changed drastically late in September 1914, however, when the obsolete U-9 sank three British cruisers in a single day. Impressed by this achievement, Admiral von Tirpitz convinced the kaiser to authorize a submarine campaign against all shipping in British waters. Some weeks in advance of the date, Berlin announced that after February 18, 1915, the waters around Great Britain would be considered "war zones" and that ships found in these areas, no matter what flag they flew, would be sunk on sight, without warning.

The German announcement flew in the face of the long-established

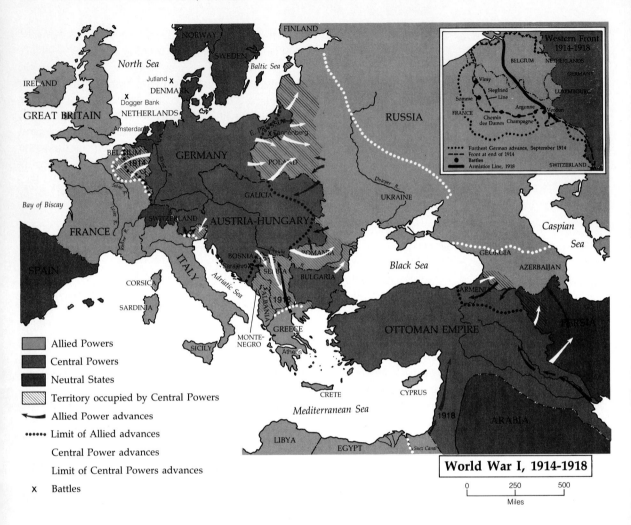

Allied Powers

Central Powers

Neutral States

Territory occupied by Central Powers

Allied Power advances

Limit of Allied advances

Central Power advances

Limit of Central Powers advances

x   Battles

**World War I, 1914-1918**

0        250        500

Miles

precedent that belligerent warships could not attack a merchant or passenger ship without first stopping it, making certain of its nationality, and guaranteeing the safety of its passengers and crew. The decision to abandon this traditional form of cruiser warfare was dictated by two considerations. First, the German Admiralty had few U-boats and hoped to rely on the fear of attack to keep neutrals from trading with the Allies. Second, slow-moving, thin-skinned submarines could not surface to carry out "visit and search" procedures without making themselves vulnerable to attack by warships or armed merchant vessels.

The German announcement provoked widespread outrage in the United States. *The New York Tribune* called "Germany's threat of lynch law against neutral shipping" the "crowning blunder of German diplomacy." And the *St. Louis Post Dispatch* warned that "the sinking by a German submarine of an American or other neutral ship carrying American goods, without search and without precautions for the safety of those aboard would be intolerable; it would be equivalent to an act of war."[9]

Berlin's new policy shocked official Washington, too. The war trade with the Allies was integral to the American economy and had to be protected. Moreover, Wilson believed that what the Germans threatened was a clear violation of international law. The nation's honor and interest, it seemed, were both at stake. On February 10, 1915, the president therefore warned Berlin that he would hold Germany "strictly accountable" for attacks on American ships by German submarines.[10]

The German Admiralty was inclined to ignore Wilson's warning. But the head of Germany's civilian government, Chancellor Theobald von Bethmann-Hollweg, was deeply concerned. He was convinced that the German navy both overestimated the importance of submarine warfare and underestimated the effect American intervention would have on the course of the war.

In the first of several encounters, Bethmann was able to extract only a small concession from the German navy. Submarine commanders were ordered to spare American vessels in the war zones "when they are recognizable as such."[11] When one takes into account the difficulty submarine commanders had identifying ships through primitive periscopes under adverse weather conditions, and the fact that they were unlikely to pay much attention to such vague orders in any event, it is clear that mistakes were going to be made.

Official Washington did not protest when the British passenger liner *Falaba* was sunk with the loss of one American life. They overlooked the attack on the American tanker *Gulflight* as well, even though three Americans were killed. Then, however, came an event that could not be ignored. On May 7, 1915, the U-20 was cruising in the Irish Sea near the St. George's Channel, when its captain, Lieutenant Commander Walther Schwieger, sighted a large passenger liner traveling at about fourteen knots. At 3:10 in the afternoon Commander Schwieger launched a torpedo that struck the giant liner dead center. A terrible explosion followed. In a little more than fifteen minutes, the British liner *Lusitania* sank carrying 1,198 of her 1,959 passengers and crew, including 128 Americans, to their deaths.

News of the *Lusitania*'s fate created a wave of outrage that spread across the United States. Theodore Roosevelt, roused from his bed by an inquiring reporter, called the sinking "not merely piracy, but piracy on a vaster scale of murder than old time pirates ever practiced." He thought it "inconceivable that we refrain from taking action in this matter." The *New York Tribune* opined, "The nation which remembered the sailors of the *Maine* will not forget the civilians of the *Lusitania*." And the *Nation* raged: It is a deed for which a Hun would blush, a Turk be ashamed, and a Barbary Pirate apologize. To speak of technicalities and the rules of war in the face of such wholesale murder on the high seas, is a waste of time. The law of nations and the law of God have been alike trampled upon. . . . The torpedo that sank the *Lusitania* also sank Germany in the opinion of mankind. . . . It is at once a crime and a monumental folly. . . . She has affronted the moral sense of the world and sacrificed her standing among the nations.[12]

From London, Ambassador Walter Hines Page cabled the president, urging an immediate declaration of war. Colonel House offered the same advice. But Wilson, perhaps sensing that the public was not ready for war, refused to go so far. Instead, he sent a strong protest to Berlin in which he called for an end to the submarine campaign and demanded that Germany return to the practice of traditional cruiser warfare. But he made no direct threats and thus kept his options open.

On the surface the German government seemed unwilling to give ground in the face of Wilson's protest. The Foreign Ministry expressed regret at the loss of American life but defended Commander Schwieger's action by pointing out that the *Lusitania* was carrying contraband (4,200 crates of munitions), that the German ambassador had placed an advertisement in the New York papers warning potential travelers not to sail on the great liner, and that England was carrying out its own ruthless war at sea in an effort to starve Germany into submission.

While the Foreign Ministry publicly defended the sinking of the *Lusitania*, behind the scenes a battle royal took place between the German Admiralty and Chancellor Bethmann-Hollweg, who found a powerful ally in the person of General Erich von Falkenhayn, chief of the general staff. Supported by Falkenhayn, Bethmann won an important victory. In June 1915, the kaiser instructed the navy not to torpedo any ship without warning unless absolutely certain that it was of belligerent registry and not to attack passenger liners no matter what flag they flew. Admiral Tirpitz and the navy won only a single point in the dispute with Bethmann-Hollweg. These new regulations were to remain secret so that neutrals might be discouraged from trading with the Allies out of fear of a submarine attack.

In Washington, where these developments remained unknown, the administration split over what to do in the face of Germany's apparent unwillingness to change its policy. Wilson felt he had no choice but to increase the pressure. But Secretary William Jennings Bryan, a near-pacifist, was convinced that to go further would mean war. Rather than send a second *Lusitania* note, he resigned and was replaced by Robert Lansing. But of course there was no war. Instead, Washington and Berlin continued to exchange notes while the German Foreign Ministry persisted in its evasive tactics. At length, in July 1915, the exasperated Wilson ended the correspondence by warning that he would view further sinkings as "deliberately unfriendly."[13]

A month later, with German-American relations very tense, the U-24, cruising in waters not far from where the *Lusitania* was attacked, sent the White Star liner *Arabic* to the bottom. Two Americans died in the attack. This sinking, which was clearly contrary to the secret orders previously issued to the submarine fleet, never should have happened. The youthful commander of the U-24 acted in panic, fearing that the *Arabic* was attempting to ram his boat.

Accident or not, the *Arabic* affair brought the crisis in German-American relations to a head. Convinced from prior conversations with the new Secretary of State, Robert Lansing, that the sinking would mean war, the German ambassador, Count Johann Heinrich von Bernstorff, cabled Berlin at once. "I fear I cannot prevent rupture this time if our answer in *Arabic* matter is not conciliatory; I advise dispatch of instructions at once to negotiate whole question. Situation may thus perhaps be saved."[14]

Over the German navy's fierce objections, Bethmann convinced the kaiser to prohibit further unannounced attacks on passenger ships. On September 1, Count von Bernstorff was thus able to deliver the so called *Arabic* pledge, a public announcement of Germany's revised policy, to the State Department. Woodrow Wilson had won a major diplomatic victory. Still, the president realized that the *Arabic* pledge had been issued as a matter of expediency and that at some time in the not-too-distant future German submarines would probably once again go on the prowl. It was also clear that if there was another German-American crisis, the president would have to do more than make threats.

## HOUSE TRIES MEDIATION

From the beginning of the war the president saw himself in the role of peacemaker. He reveled in the idea, which appealed to his vanity and his sense of moral purpose alike. Early in 1916 he sent Colonel House on a tour of European capitals to assess possibilities for a mediated settlement. House had gone on a similar errand in 1915, only to discover that neither side was interested in anything short of total victory. Quick visits on the second trip to London, Paris, and Berlin convinced him that nothing had changed. But during his stopover in the German capital, House also seems to have concluded that the advocates of unrestricted submarine warfare were gaining political strength. He judged from this trend that full-scale U-boat warfare would soon be resumed and that American intervention was therefore inevitable.

Following his depressing stopover in Berlin, House returned to London more anxious than ever to bring about a settlement to the war. In a near-desperate effort to get the belligerents talking before America was dragged into the war, he told Sir Edward Grey that if the Allies asked Wilson to mediate and Berlin refused, "the United States would probably enter the war against Germany." On the other hand, he promised that, if Berlin agreed to talks, Wilson would either "secure peace on terms not unfavorable to the Allies" or, if Germany proved "unreasonable," the United States "would leave the conference as a belligerent on the side of the Allies."[15]

House left London for Washington convinced that at the appropriate moment the Allies would ask Wilson to provide his good offices. But that call never came. Either the terrible costs of the war made it impossible for the Allies to consider anything short of victory, or, like House, they, too, believed that a renewal of Germany's submarine campaign would force the United States into the war. In that case it would have been foolish to accept mediation when American intervention would put victory within reach.

While Colonel House was in Europe preaching mediation, Wilson and Secretary Lansing tried another method of forestalling a future German-American crisis. Lansing's "modus vivendi proposal" called on the Allies to disarm their merchant vessels. This action, he argued, would enable German submarine commanders to practice traditional cruiser warfare, which would be advantageous for all sides. Submariners would have no fear of being attacked while their boats were surfaced. Allied and American merchant and passenger ships, meanwhile, would no longer be threatened with unannounced attack.

Lansing's idea was widely applauded in the United States, where it was viewed as a simple, neat method of bringing international law into accord with "the new conditions of warfare." It is hardly necessary to add, however, that it did not enjoy the same popularity in Paris and London, where it was denounced as pro-German.

If the Allies were appalled by Lansing's proposal, Bethmann-Hollweg, who was under constant pressure to loosen the restrictions on submarine operations, considered it a godsend. He endorsed Lansing's idea and quickly announced that in the future only armed merchant ships would be subject to attack without warning. The modus vivendi proposal had turned into a nightmare for the Wilson administration. It is not surprising, then, that only days after Bethmann-Hollweg made his announcement an embarrassed Lansing told reporters that he was abandoning the idea. He said that while he continued to believe merchant ships should not be armed, so long as the Allies refused to cooperate the United States could not accept the German position as legitimate.

The confusing muddle caused by the modus vivendi proposal came at the same moment in 1916 that Wilson launched his military preparedness campaign. The juxtaposition of these two developments aroused concern in Congress, where some charged that the president was attempting to maneuver the United States into the war. Hadn't he literally invited the Germans to adopt a policy of unannounced attacks on armed merchant ships? And wasn't it true that many Americans traveled or served as crew members on such vessels? What would the president do if some of these Americans lost their lives in submarine attacks?

When Wilson told a congressional delegation that he would hold Germany "strictly accountable" for American lives lost in this way, Democrats in the House of Representatives rebelled, demanding the opportunity to vote on a resolution introduced by Representative Jeff McLemore of Texas that warned American citizens not to travel on belligerent merchant vessels. A similar resolution introduced by Senator Thomas P. Gore of Oklahoma was also before the Senate.

More was at issue than the substance of two nonbinding resolutions. Passage would have been the equivalent of a vote of no-confidence in the president that could have seriously hindered his ability to conduct foreign policy. Aware of this, Wilson threatened, cajoled, and wielded the patronage power to reassert his control over Congress. He also had the advantage of widespread support in the press. Reflecting a generally held view, the *St. Louis Globe Democrat* denounced the Gore-McLemore resolutions as "a retreat . . . . under fire," while the *New York Sun* praised Wilson for his opposition to "the sort of peace that can be bought only by national humiliation."[16] By the end of the first week in March, the McLemore resolution had been defeated in the House, and the Senate had defeated Senator Gore's original resolution and tabled a last-minute substitute motion offered by the Oklahoman.

The president had reasserted his control over the foreign policy process with little time to spare, for on March 25, 1916, another submarine attack threatening to American lives took place. The victim was a French channel steamer, the *Sussex*. Though the ship was not sunk, more than eighty persons, including several Americans, were injured in the attack.

In Washington, Secretary Lansing, Colonel House, and even Mrs. Edith Wilson urged the president to break relations with Germany. But Wilson demurred. Back and forth the correspondence went between the State Department and the White House as the president attempted to strike exactly the proper tone in the note he intended to forward to Berlin. At length he agreed to go further than ever before, threatening a break in relations unless Germany agreed to stop her submarine attacks on noncombatant ships. The German response to this, the most serious threat to German-American relations yet, was all Wilson could have hoped for. Bethmann-Hollweg took responsibility for the attack on the *Sussex* and informed Washington that the U-boat commander involved would be disciplined. The German note also promised that in the future submarines would practice only traditional cruiser warfare.

The president was elated by the outcome of the *Sussex* crisis. The Germans had again made significant concessions. Yet he was not inclined to overestimate the importance of the *Sussex* pledge, for Bethmann-Hollweg had left himself a way out of this seemingly blanket commitment. He informed Wilson that if the United States could not convince Britain to abide by international law (the British blockade that was strangling Germany economically was clearly illegal), Germany might at some future time be forced to reconsider its submarine policy.

## GROWING TENSION WITH THE ALLIES

During the earliest stages of the war, as we have seen, Anglo-American relations remained surprisingly friendly. Things began to change, however, in the spring of 1915. As fantasies of a short and glorious war died on the moonscape that was the western front, London concluded that it had to fight the war more vigorously. Sir Edward Grey warned of the danger a more effective blockade might pose for Anglo-American relations, but his voice was drowned out by a chorus of demands for a more complete blockade.

In May 1915, a new coalition government replaced the old ministry of Herbert Asquith. And although Asquith remained the prime minister and Grey stayed on as foreign secretary, real power fell to more militant cabinet ministers such as David Lloyd George, minister of war, who believed that America was so utterly committed to the Allied cause and so economically dependent on the war trade that Britain need expect nothing more threatening out of Washington than strong rhetoric. In the following months this new government tightened the blockade, imposing new restrictions on American trade.

In spite of this growing pressure, President Wilson took no action against the Allies. He behaved as policy makers in London hoped he would, but not for the reasons they believed. Until May 1916, the president was too deeply embroiled with Germany to quarrel with Britain. In a situation not unlike that faced by James Madison a century before, he realized that to contest with both major belligerents simultaneously would weaken his credibility with each. That was especially true in dealing with Germany, since the possibility that the United States might intervene on the Allied side provided Wilson with important leverage.

After the *Sussex* crisis, Wilson was free, at least in the near term, to concentrate on Allied behavior. And there was much to be concerned about. First and foremost came the question of Britain's increasingly high-handed, not to say illegal blockade practices. There was also the matter of the Irish rebellion of April 1916. The ruthlessness with which the British crushed the uprising and the subsequent execution of Sir Roger Casement and other leaders of the rebellion came as a shock to those Americans, who had grown accustomed to viewing the English as representing virtue in the war against "the Hun." The *New Republic* thought the executions had "done more to drive America back to isolation than any other event since the war began."[17] That may or may not have been true, but there can be no doubt that the largely Democratic Irish American community was outraged and that in an election year a Democratic president seeking another four years in the White House had to take cognizance of these developments.

Wilson was already angry with the British, then, when on July 18, 1916, the Foreign Office published a blacklist of eighty-seven American companies accused of doing business with the Central Powers. British firms were forbidden from doing any business with these concerns. But the blacklist's intended effect went further than that. Britain's allies, including the Commonwealth countries, were certain to respect it, as were those American bankers and businesspeople anxious to maintain good relations with their Allied trading partners.

In Wilson's view the blacklist was a blatant attempt to stop all American firms from engaging in commerce with the Central Powers on pain of being driven out of business. Not long after publication of the blacklist, he sent a blistering protest to London. At the same time he told Colonel House: "This blacklist business is the last straw. . . . I am seriously considering asking Congress to authorize me to prohibit loans and restrict exportations to the Allies."[18]

When the Foreign Office failed to change its policy, Wilson in fact did win from Congress the power to apply retaliatory trade sanctions. He also considered methods of preventing American bankers from continuing to finance the Allies and called his pro-Allied ambassador in London, Walter Hines Page, home "for consultations."

Wilson took no action against the British prior to the presidential election. To have done otherwise would have been politically suicidal in a country that, in spite of recent developments, remained predominantly pro-Allied. Nor is it possible to say what he might have done after the election, since Berlin then took new initiatives that distracted him. All that can be said is that Wilson was genuinely angry and had great economic power at his disposal. Whether he would have used that power to the disadvantage of the Allied war effort remains a matter of speculation.

## THE LAST CHANCE FOR PEACE

By the autumn of 1916, Chancellor Bethmann-Hollweg's ability to hold Germany's submarine enthusiasts in check had been reduced to the vanishing point. As the terrible costs of the war grew, so did the political power of those who believed that the submarine could bring the horrifying military impasse to an end. The German navy continued to make the same argument as in the past, claiming that it could strangle the Allies economically in six months. But the argument had increased appeal when made against the backdrop of a seemingly endless mass slaughter. When the new commanders of the army, Generals Paul von Hindenburg, and Erich Ludendorff, came out in support of unrestricted U-boat warfare, Bethmann-Hollweg realized that he had lost his leverage.

Convinced that American intervention in the war would spell disaster for Germany, Bethmann-Hollweg tried to forestall the U-boat enthusiasts by making a last bid for peace. In mid-October 1916, with the kaiser's approval, he asked Wilson to call for a peace conference. He encouraged the president to act quickly, hinting that unless a settlement was arranged soon Germany might be forced to reinstitute unrestricted submarine warfare.

Bethmann-Hollweg's urgent appeal notwithstanding, Wilson refused to take any action that might alienate any significant bloc of voters prior to the November elections. In December, however, after he had been safely reelected, he forwarded a peace proposal in identic notes to the Central Powers and the Allies, at the same time calling on them to reveal their war aims as a sign of good faith.

Bethmann-Hollweg was not prepared to admit publicly that Germany, which occupied a large portion of Europe militarily, would settle for nothing less than major territorial concessions in France and Belgium, Eastern Europe,

Africa, and the Pacific as well as a substantial financial indemnity. He therefore rejected the president's appeal, indicating that he would only reveal Germany's objectives in direct talks with the Allies. London and Paris, with expansive plans of their own for the postwar world, were no less discouraging.

The refusal of both sides to announce their war aims satisfied Wilson that the peace settlement that was to come should not be structured by the European powers alone but by "the organized major force of mankind." In an important Senate speech given on January 22, 1917, Wilson insisted that only a "peace without victory" would prove lasting. The future of humanity, he thought, depended not on "a balance of power, but a community of power: not organized rivalries, but an organized common peace." Presaging much that was to come, Wilson now for the first time publicly committed the United States to participation in a postwar "league for peace."[19]

The president's Senate speech came only eight days before Germany announced the resumption of unrestricted submarine warfare. Wilson was devastated by the news. During earlier crises he had moved from protests to warnings to threats. Now he had no choice but to break diplomatic relations. Still, he continued to hope that Berlin would alter course before it was too late.

On February 25, the president received a cable from Ambassador Walter Hines Page in London that seriously dampened those hopes. The British had intercepted and decoded a message from the German foreign minister, Arthur Zimmermann, to the German embassy in Mexico City. The Zimmermann telegram, enclosed in Page's cable, instructed the German ambassador in Mexico to approach President Venustiano Carranza about an alliance. If Mexico would join in a war against the United States, Germany would see to it that "the lost territory in Texas, New Mexico, and Arizona" was returned.[20] Zimmermann further suggested that Carranza contact the Japanese about prospects for a tripartite alliance.

Wilson reacted to the Zimmermann telegram by ordering the arming of American merchant ships. Still hoping to avoid war, however, he refrained from taking any further action until he quite literally had no choice.

Between March 16 and 18, 1917, three American merchant ships were sunk by German submarines. Two days later former President Theodore Roosevelt issued a call to arms: "Let us dare to look the truth in the face," he said. "Let us dare to use our own strength in our own defense and strike hard for our national interest and honor. There is no question about 'going to war.' Germany is already at war with us. The only question for us to decide is whether we shall make war nobly or ignobly."[21]

It was an awful week for the president, who was bombarded by calls for war and equally emphatic appeals for peace. Newspaper reports warned that the Allied armies on the western front were about to crack, that the U-boat campaign was driving Britain and France to the wall, and that England's fiscal structure was in a state of virtual collapse. Still the president hesitated. He held a cabinet meeting to give his advisers one more opportunity to offer their opinions. To a man they were agreed. The president had no choice

This photograph, taken in January 1917, shows General Paul von Hindenburg (left), Kaiser Wilhelm, and General Erich Ludendorff studying reconnaissance photographs.

but to fight. All through that meeting Wilson sat silent, giving no hint as to what he might do. But on the following day he scheduled a special session of Congress. After that no one had any doubt about what was to come.

On the evening of April 2, 1917, Wilson mounted the rostrum in the House of Representatives to address a joint session of Congress. He was, characteristically, unable to ask the American people to make the sacrifices war would require for anything less than a high moral purpose. Arguing that Germany's campaign of unrestricted submarine warfare constituted not simply "war against the Government and people of the United States," but "warfare against mankind," he insisted that there could "be no assured security for the democratic governments of the world" so long as powerful autocracies like Germany existed. He called on the nation to join him in a great international crusade. "The world must be made safe for democracy," he said. "Its peace must be planted upon the tested foundations of political liberty."

Wilson's speech elicited wild applause. But he took little solace in that. "My message today was a message of death for our young men," he remarked sadly. "How strange it seems to applaud that."[22] Wilson's struggle for neutrality had ended in failure. On April 4, the Senate voted 82–6 for war. Two days later the House approved a similar resolution by a vote of 373–50.

## WHY WE FOUGHT

It was the Germans who decided that the United States would intervene in World War I. The declaration of unrestricted submarine warfare was unquestionably the precipitating cause. And the German government understood when it made that decision that the Wilson administration would fight.

Here American troops parade through Perth, Scotland, on their way to the Western Front.

But if U-boat warfare was the proximate cause of American intervention, it is important to note that the German decision was based on two and one-half years of experience that led German naval and military leaders to the curious but not entirely unjustified conclusion that the entrance of the world's greatest economic power, a nation with vast military potential, would have no effect on the outcome of the war. How could that be?

Part of the answer lies in the fact that the German military calculated that an unrestricted submarine campaign would "bring England to her knees" in six months, long before the United States, which had no army to speak of, could deploy a significant military force on the Continent. But more important was the fact that France and Britain were hopelessly dependent on the United States for munitions, steel, foodstuffs, and a wide variety of raw materials including cotton and petroleum. A cutoff in American supplies, one British government report concluded, "would practically stop the war."[23] The Germans understood and hoped to take advantage of this all-too-obvious fact.

In effect, the United States had by 1915 become the nonbelligerent ally of Britain and France. One unfortunate result was that as Germany became more desperate—more willing to take a calculated risk—the idea of interrupting the war trade between America and the Allies became increasingly attractive. After all, it was inconceivable that in the six months the German military believed it would take to force England and France to collapse the United States could do more than it was already doing. On the contrary, with a hundred German submarines on the prowl, the United States would be able to do much less. Said Hindenburg: "We are counting on the possibility of war with the United States, and have made all preparations to meet it. Things cannot be worse than they are now."[24]

The United States entered World War I not as an ally but as an "associated power." That was entirely appropriate, since Wilson and the Allies differed widely over war aims. By 1917 Wilson had assumed the leadership of an international liberal movement that called for global disarmament, an end to balance-of-power politics, and an international organization of nations committed to preserving peace through a system of collective security. An important first step toward the achievement of a lasting peace, Wilson believed, was a settlement based on terms that would be just and equitable toward victor and vanquished alike.

Wilson's inability to convince either the Central Powers or the Allies to accept mediation or even to state their war aims convinced him that neither side shared his enthusiasm for a liberal peace. Any remaining doubts that he may have harbored on this score were erased in May 1917, when Arthur Balfour, Britain's foreign secretary, arrived in Washington carrying a briefcase bulging with plans for the future of the world. Balfour described for Wilson and Colonel House the terms of several agreements made for the division of the spoils at war's end. Italy was to have territory in the South Tirol, control of the Brenner Pass, Trieste, and a substantial portion of the Adriatic Coast as well as lesser concessions in Albania and the Middle East. Russia had been promised Istanbul and control of the Bosporus and the Dardanelles, key to the eastern Mediterranean. Rumania was to have concessions in Transylvania. And in the Pacific, Japan and Britain would divide Germany's island holdings while Tokyo took over Germany's leasehold on the Shandong (Shantung) Peninsula in China. Meanwhile France and Britain would take control of oil-rich Mesopotamia and Syria.

Wilson listened but said nothing. There was a war to be won. The contest over peace terms would begin later. And Wilson thought he had a strong hand to play. The economies of the Allied powers had been devastated. They were already deeply indebted to American creditors and would no doubt borrow more as the war progressed. The president intended to use the Allies' debt as well as their obvious need for capital to twist some arms. "When the war is over," he explained, "we can force them to our way of thinking, because by that time they will, among other things, be financially in our hands."[25]

## ENDNOTES

1. David Starr Jordan, quoted in Walter Millis, *The Road to War: America, 1914–1917* (Boston: Houghton Mifflin, 1935), p. 19.

2. Robert N. Page, quoted in Arthur Link, *Woodrow Wilson and the Progressive Era* (New York: Harper and Row, 1954), p. 145.

3. Woodrow Wilson, speech of August 19, 1914, *The Public Papers of Woodrow Wilson*, ed. Ray Stannard Baker and William E. Dodd (New York: Harper, 1925–27), III, p. 158.

4. *New York Sun* and *St. Louis Globe Democrat*, quoted in the *Literary Digest*, August 8, 1914, p. 215.

5. Richard Harding Davis and anonymous, quoted in *Literary Digest*, September 12, 1914, p. 459.

6. Wilson, quoted in Charles Seymour, *American Diplomacy during the World War* (Baltimore: Johns Hopkins University Press, 1942), pp. 7–8.

7. *Detroit Free Press* and *New York Mail*, quoted in the *Literary Digest*, August 8, 1914, p. 215.

8. Sir Edward Grey, quoted in Ernest R. May, *The World War and American Isolation, 1914–1917* (Cambridge, Mass.: Harvard University Press, 1959), p. 18.

9. *New York Tribune* and *St. Louis Post Dispatch*, quoted in *Literary Digest*, February 20, 1915, p. 358.

10. Robert Lansing to James W. Gerard, February 10, 1915, *Foreign Relations of the United States, 1915, Supplement, The World War* (Washington, D.C.: 1928), p. 99.

11. Orders to German submarine commanders, quoted in May, *World War and American Isolation*, p. 126.

12. *New York Tribune*, quoted in *Literary Digest*, May 15, 1915, pp. 1133–34; *Nation*, May 13, 1915.

13. Wilson, quoted in Ross Gregory, *The Origins of American Intervention in the First World War* (New York: W. W. Norton, 1971), p. 65.

14. Count Johann von Bernstorff, *My Three Years in America* (New York: Scribner's, 1920), p. 173.

15. Sir Edward Grey, *Twenty Five Years* (London: Stokes Publishers, 1925), II, 126–28.

16. *St. Louis Globe Democrat* and *New York Sun*, quoted in *Literary Digest*, March 11, 1916, p. 625.

17. *New Republic*, July 29, 1916, pp. 321–22, quoted in Arthur Link, *Woodrow Wilson and the Progressive Era*, p. 218.

18. Wilson, quoted in Gregory, *Origins of American Intervention*, p. 99.

19. Wilson, Peace without Victory speech, January 22, 1917, *Public Papers of Woodrow Wilson*, IV, 407–14.

20. Page to Lansing, February 24, 1917, *Foreign Relations of the United States, 1917, supplement*, (Washington, D.C., 1931), pp. 147–48.

21. Theodore Roosevelt, quoted in *Literary Digest*, March 31, 1917, p. 881.

22. Wilson speech of April 2, 1917, *Foreign Relations of the United States, 1917, supplement* I (Washington, D.C.: 1931), pp. 195–203; Wilson, quoted in William E. Leuchtenburg, *The Perils of Prosperity, 1914–1932* (Chicago: University of Chicago Press, 1958), p. 30.

23. "Minutes of the Interdepartmental Committee on the Dependence of the British Empire on the United States," October 4, 1916, quoted in Gregory, *Origins of American Intervention*, pp. 108–9.

24. Paul von Hindenburg, quoted in May, *World War and American Isolation*, p. 414.

25. Wilson, quoted in Seymour, *American Diplomacy during the World War*, p. 270.

In 1919 Johnny came marching home in a huge parade down New York's Fifth Avenue.

# 18

# *PEACE WITHOUT VICTORY, 1917–1919*

The American intervention was one of two major developments that affected the course of the war in 1917. The second was the Russian Revolution. In November, with the Russian army in a state of dissolution, the provisional government nearly paralyzed, and the economy in a state of collapse, the Bolshevik faction of the Russian Social Democratic party, led by Vladimir Ilyich Lenin, seized power. Echoing a call made earlier by Woodrow Wilson, Lenin challenged the belligerents to state their war aims and called for a just peace based on the principle of national self-determination. Because he could neither consolidate his power nor pursue his plans for the economic reorganization of Russia while the war continued, Lenin simultaneously sought a separate peace with Germany.

President Wilson was rocked by the announcement that Russia might leave the war and embarrassed by the fact that the Bolsheviks and not the Allies had come forward with a liberal peace proposal. He appealed to Britain and France to join in a public statement of war aims that would rebut the Bolsheviks. But the Allies had no intention of endorsing Wilson's liberal agenda. When they refused, he decided to go forward alone.

On January 8, 1918, Wilson delivered his famous Fourteen Points speech, an address best known for the liberal peace plan it advanced. Here Wilson outlined a settlement that would be just to victor and vanquished alike. The first five of his points called for an end to secret diplomacy, for "open covenants of peace, openly arrived at," freedom of the seas, the elimination to the extent possible of barriers to trade among nations, disarmament, and "an adjustment of colonial claims" with an eye to the interests of the colonial powers as well as the colonial peoples themselves. The next eight points were more specific, dealing with various territorial adjustments to be made in Europe and the Near East, all of which were to be based on the principle of national self-determination. The final point, the capstone to Wilson's vision for the postwar world, called for the creation of "a general association of nations . . . for the purpose of affording mutual guarantees of political independence and territorial integrity to great and small states alike."[1]

Wilson's speech, more than a statement of principle, was intended to serve certain pragmatic purposes as well. The entire first half of the address was an appeal to the Russian people to remain in the war against German imperialism. Wilson also put the Allies on notice that he understood their war aims were different from his and that he would not support a settlement that divided the spoils and sowed the seeds of future wars. Finally, Wilson hoped to reach a war-weary German population, to drive a wedge between Germany's established "political structure" and its many more liberal groups. "We have no jealousy of German greatness," he said. "We wish her only to accept a place of equality among the peoples of the world . . . instead of a place of mastery."[2]

The president's speech was greeted with great enthusiasm in the United States. The *New York Tribune*, a Republican paper, went so far as to compare Wilson with Lincoln. "There is nothing more admirable in American history than his address of yesterday," the paper said. "In a single speech he has transformed the whole character and broken with all the tradition of American policy. He has carried the United States back to Europe; he has established an American world policy and ideals of international policy throughout the civilized world." The Allies, on the other hand, adopted a tone of haughty intolerance toward the president. "God has given us Ten Commandments, and we broke them," remarked Premier Georges Clemenceau of France. "Wilson gives us the Fourteen Points. We shall see." The Bolsheviks sneered at Wilson's appeal, and the German foreign minister retorted in anger that "only a victor speaks to the vanquished in such language" and Germany was far from defeated.[3]

## THE RUSSIAN INTERVENTION

On March 3, 1918, Bolshevik and German delegates, meeting at Brest-Litovsk, signed a separate treaty of peace. Under the terms of this agreement Russia lost control of 1.3 million square miles of territory, 62 million people, one-quarter of the country's rail network, a third of its farmland, three-quarters of its coal and iron ore deposits, and one-third of its factories. It was a harsh settlement. But Lenin thought the sacrifices necessary if he was to consolidate the Bolshevik hold on power.

Early in 1918, even before the Treaty of Brest-Litovsk ended Russian involvement in the war, France and Great Britain agreed to support anti-German and anti-Bolshevik elements inside Russia for the dual purposes of reestablishing an eastern front and overthrowing the Bolsheviks. Wilson, who had no love for the Bolsheviks, nevertheless believed intervention would be a mistake. The president had a naive faith in the democratic instincts of the Russian people and was confident that if left to their own devices they would reject Bolshevism. To those who argued that Bolshevism should be forcibly crushed, he replied that "trying to stop a revolutionary movement with field armies is like using a broom to hold back a great ocean. The only way to act against Bolshevism is to destroy its causes."[4] Intervention, he insisted, would have only negative results, strengthening the Bolsheviks' hold on power and perhaps driving Lenin into the arms of the Germans.

For months Wilson resisted Allied pressure to support the intervention. In late June 1918, however, he changed his mind. A major German offensive on the western front was by this time more than two months old and had not yet spent its force. Everybody was jittery and prone to overestimate German capabilities. Even Colonel Edward M. House, who had earlier opposed intervention, warned that "something must be done immediately about Russia" if it were not to fall prey to the Germans.[5]

On July 6, 1918, the president announced that a small contingent of American troops—about five thousand—would be sent to Archangel and that some eight thousand more would go to revolution-torn Siberia. Hoping to head off a unilateral Japanese intervention, Wilson invited Tokyo to cooperate in the Siberian venture by sending a similar-size force to join the Americans. He was quite specific in explaining the purposes of the intervention. The troops were to guard storehouses of weapons, to help the Czech Legion (a force of forty-five thousand Czechs and Slovaks who had been fighting as part of the czarist army) leave Russian territory, and to disarm any former German and Austrian prisoners of war who might be free and operating inside Russia. Clearly, he wanted it understood that he would not sanction interference in Russia's internal affairs.

Historians have long debated the reasons behind Wilson's decision to intervene in Russia. Some contend that he intended from the start to support the Allied attempt to overthrow the Bolsheviks. Others believe that Wilson was either responding to what appeared to be a genuine German threat in Russia or that he felt compelled to act to preserve good relations with Britain and France. It may be that historians have had difficulties explaining the intervention because Wilson himself was ambivalent about what he hoped to accomplish. For example, only a few days after stating categorically that American forces were not in Russia to interfere in its internal affairs he explained in a memorandum to the Allies that he believed the American presence in Siberia would encourage the growth of non-Bolshevik self-governing groups there. He also authorized American forces

American troops sent to Vladivostok in 1918 parade past the headquarters building of the Czech Legion, while Japanese marines stand at attention.

to aid the Czech Legion, which, far from trying to get out of Russia, was supporting anti-Bolshevik elements in the Russian Civil War.

Whatever his reasons for intervening in the first place, there is strong evidence to suggest that Wilson quickly developed second thoughts about the interventions. As early as September 18, 1918, he rejected an Allied request for reinforcements in eastern Russia. When he learned that the British, who were in overall command around Archangel, were using American troops to support anti-Bolshevik forces, he sent a scorching protest to London and reiterated standing orders that American forces there were to confine themselves to guarding arms storehouses and securing port facilities, nothing more.

The president was equally dismayed by developments in Siberia. Japan's civilian government had agreed to participate in a small-scale joint intervention along the lines Wilson first described. Tokyo also promised not to interfere in Russia's internal affairs. But once the operation began, the Japanese army, which had its own expansionist ambitions in the region, took control, sending more than seventy-two thousand troops into Siberia. Japan's military also supported local anti-Bolshevik forces there, hoping to use them as the basis for a puppet government to be established later.

Wilson was infuriated by these developments. Distrusting the Japanese, he kept the American force in Siberia for the next seventeen months.

Whatever his original purpose had been, in Asiatic Russia the preservation of the open door became his principal objective.

In the end neither the United States nor Japan gained a solitary thing from the Siberian adventure. The American military presence there had no effect on Japan's expansionists. But neither did the Japanese succeed in their plans for establishing a puppet state in Russia's maritime provinces. Two years after the American withdrawal, the Japanese also left. By that time it was clear that Siberia's future was for the Bolsheviks to decide.

Wilson's Russian policy produced only negative results. By participating in the intervention, even halfheartedly, he became part of a coalition working to destroy the Bolshevik Revolution. Soviet leaders never forgot that fact. Ironically, the interventions also served to strengthen the Bolsheviks internally. And of course Wilson never intended that. The president's original instincts were sound. It would have been wiser to let the Russian people resolve their differences without foreign intervention.

**ARMISTICE**

Following the Treaty of Brest-Litovsk, the German High Command shifted forty divisions from Russia to the Western Front for another great offensive. The attack, which came on March 21, 1918, created a great bulge in Allied lines. But the Germans failed to break out into open country, and in August the Allies began a counteroffensive. While French, British, and American forces slugged it out with the Germans in the West, elsewhere Germany's allies began to collapse. In September, Bulgaria surrendered. In October the Austrians were routed by the Italians at the battle of Vittorio Veneto. In that same month an entire Turkish army surrendered to General Edmund Henry Allenby in Syria. Meanwhile the Austro-Hungarian empire began to disintegrate as Czech and Polish leaders established independent governments. In Germany, too, there were signs of popular discontent.

In late September 1918, General Erich Ludendorff, the German commander, panicked. Until then he had given not the slightest hint to anyone in Berlin that he expected anything short of victory. Then, suddenly, he announced that the army faced a catastrophe unless the government could arrange an armistice. When on October 2 he made it clear that an armistice must come within forty-eight hours, Prince Max of Baden, Germany's new head of government, cabled President Wilson proposing an armistice to be followed by peace "on the basis" of the Fourteen Points.

In the exchange of notes that followed, Wilson insisted that German forces would have to withdraw from France and Belgium immediately and that an armistice agreement would have to guarantee "the maintenance of the present military supremacy of the armies of the United States and the Allies in the field."[6] He also insisted that Berlin would have to accept the Fourteen Points and that negotiations would be confined to working out details necessary to implement those points.

American troops in action on the Western Front.

While discussing armistice terms with the Germans, Wilson sent Colonel House to Paris to arrange a prearmistice agreement with the Allies. For six days House and the Allied leaders wrangled before settling on terms. German forces would be required to withdraw to the right bank of the Rhine, leaving most of their heavy weapons and equipment behind them. Berlin would also be required to surrender the High Seas Fleet and 160 submarines. The Allies also insisted on occupying Germany to the Rhine, with bridgeheads across the river.

House and the Allied negotiators then turned to the more difficult political side of the equation. Convincing Britain and France to accept the Fourteen Points was no easy task. It was at this point that House cabled Wilson: "I am now busy bringing every force to bear to help win a people's victory." But he was obviously not having much success, for he advised the president to increase his leverage by reducing the number of troops sailing for Europe and cutting back on the money, food, and raw materials the United States was providing. "Unless we deal with these people with a firm hand," he wrote, "everything we have been fighting for will be lost."[7]

At length the Allies agreed, with certain reservations, to accept the Fourteen Points as "the basis" for a peace settlement. Convinced that "freedom of the seas" was a euphemism for a free trade policy that would leave England at a serious postwar economic disadvantage vis-à-vis the United

Members of the 369th Infantry return home in 1919. During the war, African-Americans were segregated in special units and relegated to menial tasks in the military.

States, the British refused to endorse that point, agreeing only to discuss the question at the peace conference. Other issues that remained unresolved were the future of the Central Powers' colonial holdings and the question of reparations, a cause célèbre in every Allied capital. House did not win even this limited victory easily. At one point he actually threatened to seek a separate peace if the Allies continued to be uncooperative.

At 11:00 A.M. on November 11, 1918, the German government having agreed to Allied armistice terms, four years of war came to an end. Europe was in chaos. The Continent was, according to the aging Czech patriot Tomás Masaryk, "a laboratory resting upon a vast cemetery." Not a single stable government was to be found in all of Central and Eastern Europe. Russia was in the throes of a social revolution and a civil war all at once. In Hungary, Mihály Károlyi's government collapsed in the spring of 1919 to be replaced by a soviet regime headed by Lenin's friend and fellow communist, Béla Kun. Kun was driven from power by the Allies, but the proto-fascist government of Admiral Miklós Horthy promised no good for the peace of Central Europe.

An unstable situation also developed in Germany, where in theory a new democracy had replaced the old imperial structure. Friedrich Ebert, a social democrat, headed the Weimar Republic. But at the local level other centers of power grew up to challenge the government's authority. In Kiel, for example, sailors and workers created a council similar to the local soviets that had emerged in Russia in the early days of the revolution there. The

Kiel example was followed in towns and seaports throughout Germany. As the movement gained momentum, it became clear that the Ebert government faced a serious challenge.

Conservatives, moderates, most social democrats, and the army rallied to the support of the Weimar authorities. But the independent socialists and the Marxian Spartacists led by Karl Liebknecht and Rosa Luxemburg, echoing Lenin's cry of "all power to the soviets," threw their support to the local councils. In January 1919, the Spartacists called a general strike. When rioting broke out in Berlin, the German army crushed the strike and the Spartacists. Liebknecht and Luxemburg, arrested during the fighting, were brutally murdered by soldiers.

The end of the Spartacist uprising in Germany was by no means the end of instability either there or elsewhere in Europe. The delegates who assembled in Paris in January 1919 to redraw the map of Europe and establish a lasting peace clearly had their work cut out for them. And they would have to work with the specter of revolution very much in view.

## WILSON GOES TO THE SUMMIT

As Woodrow Wilson prepared for the all-important Paris peace conference, he made a decision that unquestionably weakened him politically when later he submitted the completed Treaty of Versailles to the Senate. Since the Republicans enjoyed a two-vote majority in the upper house and controlled the Senate Foreign Relations Committee, he would have been well advised to include among the delegates who accompanied him to Paris an influential Republican, preferably a Republican senator. But driven by a powerful messianic impulse, Wilson wanted no one on the peace commission who approached him in stature. Nor did he want to negotiate bargaining positions inside his own delegation while at the same time dealing with the likes of France's Georges Clemenceau and Britain's David Lloyd George. Moreover he was convinced that it would be impossible to find an influential Republican who would support the revolution in foreign policy that he had in mind. And so the delegation he took with him to Paris was made up entirely of subordinates, including Secretary of State Robert Lansing, Colonel House, General Tasker Bliss, and Henry White, a career diplomat.

Even without Republican representation at Paris, the president was confident that when the time came he would be able to force the Senate to approve the treaty he was about to negotiate. Before leaving for the conference he told Jules Jusserand, the French ambassador, exactly that, remarking, "The Senate must take its medicine." Others were not so certain. Frank Cobb of the *New York World*, a journalist friendly to Wilson, noted with more than a little concern that the president took with him "a purely personal commission of excellent gentlemen . . . who have no political standing."[8]

The Paris peace conference opened amid wild confusion on January

At the Paris peace conference the Big Four made most of the key decisions. From left to right they are David Lloyd George, Vittorio Orlando, Georges Clemenceau, and Woodrow Wilson.

18, 1919. Twenty-seven nations and Britain's five dominions sent delegations. Because practically no time was spent establishing procedures or an appropriate agenda prior to the conference, it was from start to finish, as Britain's Arthur Balfour put it, "a rough and tumble affair."[9] As a result, certain issues, especially Germany's future, received less attention than they deserved. And the question of whether the defeated Central Powers should be represented at the conference was never even addressed.

Early in the conference, Wilson seized the initiative, calling for the establishment of a committee, which he would head, to draft the covenant of a new collective security organization, the League of Nations. He also insisted that the covenant should be made integral to the treaty. Wilson hoped to serve two purposes by tying the peace treaty and the League into a single package. First, because he believed that the Allies, especially France and Japan, were not exactly entranced by the idea of the league, it was a method of ensuring that the more "realistic" among the powers would either have to join the league or refuse to make peace. Second, Wilson, was convinced that the Senate would never work up the courage to reject a peace treaty, even if it did contain provisions for future international cooperation.

The conference quickly approved Wilson's proposal. A League of Nations committee dominated by the president, Britain's Lord Robert Cecil, and Jan Smuts of South Africa was immediately organized. Using draft proposals prepared prior to the conference, and working at night, Wilson and his colleagues produced the Covenant of the League of Nations, which they presented at a dramatic plenary session of the conference. Wilson had lived for the moment. It was the fulfillment of years of toil and hope. One can only imagine how he must have felt as he announced to the assembled delegates that "a living thing is born."[10]

While in the evenings Wilson worked to create the instrument he hoped would turn his liberal vision into a new international order, during the day he was often reminded just how difficult it was to change long-established international behavior. An early indication that the Fourteen Points might be in trouble at Paris came when the delegates considered what to do with Germany's overseas empire. Wilson wanted the German colonies in Africa and the Pacific parceled out among smaller nations to be administered as league mandates until such time as they were prepared for self-government. But the president had to contend with the ambitions of South Africa, Australia, New Zealand, and Japan. All of these countries had seized German colonies during the war and were determined to keep them.

The outcome of this tug of war was a substantive victory for imperialism. The delegates agreed to create a mandate system as Wilson wished. But Germany's colonies were turned over to the powers that had taken them during the war to be administered as integral parts of the mandating countries. The mandate system was in effect nothing more than imperialism by another name.

## A DEVELOPING OPPOSITION

Toward the end of February 1919, following the publication of the League Covenant in the press, a small number of senators including Miles Poindexter of Washington, William E. Borah of Idaho, and James Reed of Missouri went on record as opposing membership. They claimed, among other things, that the league would abridge national sovereignty, abrogate the Monroe Doctrine, and deny the United States control over internal issues such as tariffs and immigration policy.

In Wilson's absence, other members of the administration rushed to the league's defense. Thus Secretary of the Navy Josephus Daniels warned that "any man in this country who tries to stir up opposition to the League of Nations will be guilty of trying to pave the way for another world deluge of blood, and will be just as great a criminal as the ex-Kaiser." The League Covenant, he insisted, made "Magna Carta and the Declaration of Independence mere forerunners of an immortal instrument that blesses all the world for all generations."[11]

Even significant elements of the pro-Republican press came to Wilson's defense. Thus the *Springfield Daily Republican* charged that "the men who are now attempting to wreck the League of Nations are in reality attempting to wreck the peace of the world." The *Minneapolis Tribune* said, "We want a League of Nations to prevent war, and we ought to be able to get it." And the *Philadelphia Inquirer* asked, "Must we, for the absurd fear of 'entangling alliances' become a nation to be scorned and hissed?" It is "unthinkable" the *Inquirer* continued, that the United States "should be the one skulker among nations."[12]

Not long after the president presented the finished Covenant of the League of Nations to the delegates at Paris, he sailed for the United States. Congress was about to adjourn, and important legislative business awaited his attention. The long leisurely days on board the *George Washington* gave the president time to relax, to think, and to plan. The development of an opposition was not unexpected. But that did not make it any less infuriating to Wilson. As soon as the *George Washington* arrived in Boston, he declared war.

> We set this Nation up to make men free . . . and now we will make men free. If we did not do that all the fame of America would be gone and all her power would be dissipated. She would then have to keep her power for those narrow, selfish, provincial purposes which seem so dear to some minds that have no sweep beyond the nearest horizon. I should welcome no sweeter challenge than that. I have fighting blood in me.[13]

Wilson remained in the United States only briefly before returning to the conference table in Paris. But during those few weeks the opposition gained momentum. Henry Cabot Lodge, the Republican chair of the Senate Foreign Relations Committee, gave a number of speeches warning against an abandonment of America's traditional policy of nonentanglement. The league, he claimed, represented a movement away from true Americanism and "toward the other end of the line at which stands the sinister figure of Trotzky [*sic*], the champion of internationalism."[14] Coming from Lodge this was ironic, not to say shabby politics. He knew better than most that nonentanglement in European political affairs was no longer a viable policy. Twenty years before as a leading imperialist he had helped kill it.

Wilson invited members of the relevant House and Senate committees to the White House and tried to allay their concerns. He changed no minds, however. Said one Republican opponent of the League, "I feel as if I had been wandering with Alice in Wonderland and had tea with the Mad Hatter."[15]

On the last day of the congressional session, just before Wilson returned to Paris for the conclusion of the peace conference, Lodge unveiled the "Republican Round Robin," a statement signed by thirty-nine Senators— six more than were required to defeat the treaty—which stated that in its present form the League Covenant was unacceptable. The *New York Sun,* a Republican sheet, gleefully declared the League of Nations "dead," since Wilson clearly did not have the votes for passage. In a very clearheaded editorial, the *St. Louis Globe Democrat* blamed Wilson for this situation. He had transformed the league into a partisan issue "by the conspicuous, if not deliberate offensiveness of his attitude toward the Republican leaders in Congress, and, for that matter, toward Congress as a whole."[16]

Even the stubborn Wilson now recognized that he had a problem. Therefore, on his return to Paris he reconvened the committee that had drafted the League Covenant and made changes. Wording was added to make it clear that no government would be required to accept a mandate, that the league had no power to interfere in the internal affairs of member nations, and that the league and its members accepted the Monroe Doctrine as inviolable. Having satisfied at least some of his domestic critics, Wilson then turned to the many important issues the conference had not yet addressed.

## THE RUSSIAN PUZZLE, THE GERMAN SETTLEMENT

The armistice of November 1918, eliminated any wartime justification for the presence of foreign forces on Russian soil. Wilson, therefore, urged the Allies to withdraw their troops, arguing that their continued presence in Russia would only encourage the rest of the Russian left to rally behind the Bolsheviks. But all of the president's importuning netted him nothing. Clemenceau, Winston Churchill, and others on the right were determined to give all the aid and comfort in their power to Admiral Aleksandr Vasilyevich Kolchak and his White counterrevolutionaries.

Following a failed attempt to bring about a mediated settlement to the Russian Civil War, Wilson sent a young member of the American delegation, William C. Bullitt, on an unofficial fact-finding mission to Moscow. Bullitt, the journalist Lincoln Steffens, and two others journeyed to the Russian capital, where they spent a week ensconced in an abandoned palace negotiating with the Soviet foreign minister, Georgi Chicherin, and his deputy, Maxim Litvinov. The brilliant and mercurial Bullitt, who made more of his mission than Wilson seems to have intended, returned to Paris in mid-March 1917, with an armistice proposal that had the approval of Lenin himself. The plan called for a cease-fire in place with all factions holding the territory they then possessed, a general amnesty, the withdrawal of Allied forces, and an end to Allied aid to the Whites.

Bullitt, who was convinced that the Bolsheviks were in power to stay and that continued Allied support for Admiral Kolchak's counterrevolution-aries was foolish, had succeeded in arranging an easy way out of a difficult situation for the Allies. But neither the cease-fire proposal nor his extraor-dinarily perceptive report was ever seriously considered by any of the leaders at Paris. Anti-Bolshevik sentiment was so strong that it was politically impossible for Western European statesmen to support such a plan.

The decision to ignore Bullitt's proposal was a serious error. Optimistic reports then circulating in Paris about the White Army's recent successes were sheer fantasy. Only a large-scale troop commitment could have saved the Whites and Kolchak. And none of the Allies was prepared for that. When the Paris conference ended, the Allies were no closer to a solution to the Russian puzzle than they had been when they met. As for William Bullitt, he resigned from the American delegation and went into self-imposed exile in Europe where, from the sandy shores of the Mediterranean he intended to "watch the world go to hell."[17]

If the Russian question perplexed the conferees at Paris, Germany's future and the related question of French security loomed even more important. Clemenceau called for the permanent dismemberment of Germany. He wanted to separate the area west of the Rhine into two Rhenish states that would remain under French military occupation. He also sought permanent control of bridgeheads across the Rhine.

Wilson, who saw a clear analogy between what Clemenceau now proposed and the German seizure of Alsace-Lorraine in 1870, viewed this idea with horror. Together he and Britain's David Lloyd George, who agreed that the French plan would lay the foundation for another great war, set out to find a compromise.

Throughout March 1919, a titanic struggle raged in Paris between Wilson and Clemenceau, until on April 3 the president, never a robust man, fell dangerously ill and threatened to leave the conference unless the French agreed to a compromise. At this juncture, the French premier gave in. Under the terms of the agreement thus forged the Rhineland would remain an integral but permanently demilitarized part of Germany. The Saarland, however, would for fifteen years remain under French control. At the end of that time a plebescite would be held to determine whether the area would remain a permanent part of France or be returned to Germany. Finally—and this was crucial to the compromise—the United States and Britain agreed to sign a defensive treaty with France guaranteeing that they would come to its aid in the event it was ever attacked by Germany.

Wilson, Lloyd George, and Clemenceau had far less difficulty agreeing that Germany should never again be allowed to develop the ability to make aggressive war. They agreed that the German General Staff should be eliminated; that the German army, which was to have no tanks, artillery, or aircraft, was to be limited to 100,000 men; and that the German navy was to be reduced to token size, with no capital ships of more than ten thousand tons and no submarines whatsoever.

If the victors agreed on the importance of limiting Germany's future military potential, vast differences separated Wilson from the European Allies with regard to war reparations. The French, who argued that Germany ought to pay the entire cost of the war, which they calculated at about $100 billion, hoped by saddling the German economy with this huge burden to weaken a dangerous neighbor permanently. Britain's Lloyd George, on the other hand, recognized that the $100 billion figure was not only unrealistic but unwise. Yet in his recent political campaign his supporters had promised that if reelected he would squeeze Germany "till the pips squeak."[18] He, too, therefore, felt compelled to press this extravagant claim.

Wilson, who saw things quite differently, convinced the Allied powers that Germany could not pay such a vast sum, that if its economy was crippled in this way all of Europe would suffer, and that such an imposition would be a violation of the prearmistice agreement. At the president's insistence then, Article 231 of the treaty, which did hold the Germans morally responsible for the entire cost of the war—the so-called war guilt clause—nevertheless limited reparations to losses suffered by civilians at the hands of the Germans.

Wilson hoped that before the conference adjourned he would be able to establish a maximum reparations bill that would be well within Germany's capacity to pay. But during his illness Colonel House agreed to establish a special reparations commission that would set a final figure based on the claims it received. Wilson was appalled at what House had done, for he was certain the commission would set a far higher figure than he had in mind or than the Germans would willingly accept. And on that score he was entirely correct.

In 1921 the reparations commission announced that Germany owed $33 billion in reparations. Though large, this sum was not entirely beyond Germany's ability to pay. That was not the point. The war guilt clause and the reparations bill together turned "peace without victory" from a noble ambition into an empty slogan. Wilson recognized and was frustrated by that fact.

Nor was the president any more successful in defending liberal principles against the ambitions of the other Allied powers. For example, he knew when he arrived in Paris that because of Allied commitments made to Italy in 1915 he would have to accept Italian claims to Trieste, parts of the South Tirol, the Trentino, and the Adriatic Coast, even though these regions were not all inhabited by ethnic Italians. He drew the line, however, when Italy's Vittorio Orlando demanded control of the port city of Fiume on the Adriatic. The city itself was largely Italian, but the surrounding country was dominated by a Slavic population. What decided the issue for Wilson was the fact that Fiume was the only good seaport available to the new country of Yugoslavia then being created at the conference.

The rancorous struggle over Fiume, which was highlighted by a ten-day Italian walkout, ended in deadlock. The question was left for the infant League of Nations to resolve. But it was the Italians who settled the question by seizing the city in 1922.

Wilson lost still another skirmish at Paris, this one to the Japanese, who had come to the conference with three specific purposes in mind. They wanted the League Covenant to contain a statement on racial equality; they hoped to win recognition of their right to retain Germany's northern Pacific island colonies; and they wanted their claim to the old German leasehold on the Shandong Peninsula affirmed.

The Japanese lost the fight over racial equality but won on two other fronts, in both instances successfully challenging Wilsonian principles. Wilson's surrender on the Shandong question came as a shock to the Chinese delegates at the conference. But when the Japanese threatened a walkout he felt he had no choice. The French were clearly halfhearted in their endorsement of the league, the Italians too; the Germans and Russians were not even represented and would not be league members, at least for some time. Under the circumstances, Wilson could not afford a Japanese boycott.

## THE TREATY IN PERSPECTIVE

The treaty of Versailles was a far cry from the liberal vision that Wilson had offered the world. In the rough and tumble of the negotiations, the Fourteen Points were often sacrificed in the interest of compromise and consensus. In spite of Wilson's brave words about national self-determination, more than 10 percent of Germany's prewar population would in the future live as minorities in other European countries, 3 million of them in Czechoslovakia alone. Italians ruled over Austrians in the Tirol and over Slavic peoples on the Adriatic, and the Japanese controlled millions of Chinese on the Shandong Peninsula.

Wilson left Paris in some ways a bitter man. He had gone to the Continent arrogant and optimistic, only to discover that the problems of the Old World were more intractable than he had supposed. Yet if the treaty fell short of Wilson's liberal ambitions, it is important to note that but for Wilson the German settlement would have been even more harsh than it was and that in general the peacemakers did attempt to adhere to the principle of national self-determination in redrawing the map of Europe. Versailles was a compromise among Wilsonian principles, the French desire for revenge and security, and the ambitions of the other nations present at the conference.

No one was more aware of the inadequacies of the treaty than Wilson himself. Still, he remained hopeful, for in his judgment he had won the most important victory of the conference. The League of Nations was a reality. If the postwar world was to be an imperfect place, the instrument to improve it was at hand. In the years to come humankind could carry forward what had been begun in Paris.

## ENDNOTES

1. Woodrow Wilson, Fourteen Points speech, January 8, 1918, *The Public Papers of Woodrow Wilson*, ed. Ray Stannard Baker and William E. Dodd (New York: Harper, 1925–1927), V, pp. 155–62.

2. Ibid.

3. *New York Tribune*, January 9, 1918; Georges Clemenceau, quoted in Arnold A. Offner, *The Origins of the Second World War, American Foreign Policy and World Politics, 1917–1941* (New York: Praeger, 1975); p. 30; German foreign minister, quoted in *Literary Digest*, January 12, 1918, p. 15.

4. Wilson, quoted in Offner, *Origins of the Second World War*, p. 30.

5. Edward M. House, quoted in Arthur C. Walworth, *America's Moment, 1918: American Diplomacy at the End of World War I* (New York: W. W. Norton, 1977), p. 196.

6. Wilson, quoted in Charles Seymour, *American Diplomacy during the World War* (Baltimore: Johns Hopkins University Press, 1942), pp. 318–19.

7. House, quoted in Walworth, *America's Moment*, pp. 53, 61.

8. Wilson, quoted in Nicholas Murray Butler, *Across the Busy Years: Recollections and Reflections* (New York: Charles Scribner's Sons, 1939), II, pp. 197–200; Frank Cobb, quoted in Walworth, *America's Moment*, p. 130.

9. Arthur Balfour, quoted in David Thompson, *Europe since Napoleon* (New York: Alfred A. Knopf, 1957), p. 580.

10. Wilson, quoted in Thomas A. Bailey, *Woodrow Wilson and the Lost Peace* (Chicago: Quadrangle Books, 1963), p. 193.

11. Josephus Daniels, quoted in *Literary Digest*, March 1, 1919, p. 11.

12. *Springfield Daily Republican, Minneapolis Tribune*, and *Philadelphia Inquirer*, quoted in ibid., pp. 11–13.

13. Wilson, quoted in Daniel Smith, *The Great Departure: America and World War I, 1914–1920* (New York: John Wiley and Sons, 1965), p. 132.

14. Henry Cabot Lodge, quoted in *Literary Digest*, March 15, 1919, p. 15.

15. Quoted in Armin Rappaport, *A History of American Diplomacy* (New York: Macmillan, 1975), p. 273.

16. *New York Sun* and *St. Louis Globe Democrat*, quoted in *Literary Digest*, March 15, 1919, pp. 13–16.

17. William Bullitt, quoted in Edward Bennett, *Recognition of Russia: An American Foreign Policy Dilemma* (Waltham, Mass.: Blaisdell, 1969) p. 37. See also Beatrice Farnsworth, *William C. Bullitt and the Soviet Union* (Bloomington, Ind.: Indiana University Press, 1967).

18. Eric Geddes, quoted in Paul Birdsall, *Versailles Twenty Years After* (New York: Reynal and Hitchcock, 1941), p. 39.

# 19

# "LET LODGE COMPROMISE"
## Wilson and the League, 1919–1920

HE KEPT US OUT OF PEACE.

Those who supported the League of Nations blamed Henry Cabot Lodge for the defeat of the treaty in the Senate. But Lodge could not have done it without a good deal of help from Woodrow Wilson.

On July 8, 1919, the *George Washington* steamed into New York Harbor carrying the president toward his last and greatest political battle. While in Paris, Wilson had made more compromises than he cared to contemplate. But that was all behind him now. At home and in his own milieu, he would fight for the Treaty of Versailles and the League of Nations.

Wilson needed a two-thirds majority in the Senate, where the Republicans held a two-vote edge. It is not surprising, then, that as he prepared to submit the treaty to the upper house the press was filled with speculation on the possibility of a bipartisan deal in which the treaty would be approved with Republican-sponsored reservations. Wilson was asked about this possibility at a press conference. At first he tried to evade the question. Then he said with great emphasis, "The Senate is going to ratify the Treaty."[1] The reporters may have taken this as sound strategy on the president's part: not giving anything away until he had to. In fact, however, the president had no intention of compromising. He wanted the treaty as written or no treaty at all.

At first glance Wilson's confrontational strategy appeared to have a chance of success. Public opinion was solidly behind membership in the League of Nations. By the time Wilson returned to America more than thirty state governors and legislatures had come out in support of the treaty. And a *Literary Digest* survey taken at the time showed that the editors of most of the country's newspapers felt similarly. Out of 1,377 newspapers polled, 718 supported immediate ratification, 478 gave the treaty conditional approval, and only 181 were opposed.[2]

The treaty did, of course, run into some opposition. Many liberals, for example, felt that Wilson had betrayed his ideals at Paris. Here was no "peace without victory" but a traditional division of the spoils that seemed certain to produce another great war in the not-too-distant future. Thus a leading liberal journal, the *Nation*, attacked the treaty as "A Colossal Humbug," and the idealistic young William Bullitt, Wilson's onetime emissary to Lenin, testified before the Senate Foreign Relations Committee opposing ratification.[3]

Traditionalists feared the league as a superstate that would undermine American sovereignty and involve the nation in wars that were none of its business. "The abolition of war is like the abolition of slavery, a matter of education and civilization," wrote William Randolph Hearst. "But peace for our own country can be secured if we retire behind the greatest navy in the world and attend to our own business." Like others dubbed "isolationists," Hearst did not believe that the league would "establish peace." On the contrary, he thought "the real danger is that it will drag the United States into wars that it would otherwise have no connection with."[4]

A number of ethnic minorities also opposed the treaty. German Americans thought it unjust to the Fatherland. Italian Americans were angered over Wilson's handling of the Fiume question. And the Irish viewed the league, where Britain and the Commonwealth nations would have six votes, as an institution committed to the preservation of an unjust status quo, a barrier to Irish freedom.

## THE TREATY IN THE SENATE

As things turned out, the public debate over the treaty and the question of membership in the league, while intense, was largely irrelevant. This issue was decided in the Senate in one of the great political clashes of this century.

The chair of the Foreign Relations committee and the man who devised Republican strategy toward the treaty was Henry Cabot Lodge of Massachusetts. His attitude was shaped by a variety of considerations, not the least of which was the burning hatred he felt for Wilson. But Lodge was not motivated by personal animus alone. A Roosevelt-style imperialist and a believer in balance-of-power politics, he had no faith in the idea of collective security. Lodge believed that a perfectly sound "league" already existed between the United States, Britain, and France. Nothing more was needed, provided the great powers had the resolve to maintain the peace. If they lacked that resolve, no League of Nations could preserve it for them.

Lodge would happily have consigned the League of Nations to the scrap heap of history. But that was out of the question, since public opinion strongly favored the league. Moreover, his own Republican Party was badly divided over the treaty and league membership. Some, led by the former president, William Howard Taft, supported the treaty as written. At the other extreme stood a group of fourteen "irreconcilables" led by Idaho's William E. Borah and Hiram Johnson of California, who opposed league membership under any circumstances. The largest group of Republicans were willing to vote for the treaty with modifications. This group was divided between "mild" and "strong" reservationists.

To keep the Republican party united, Lodge adopted a compromise position by becoming the leader of the Senate's strong reservationists. The reservations to the treaty that he advocated were not so unreasonable that the mild reservationists would refuse to support them. At the same time the Taft group was willing to go along for partisan reasons and because Lodge argued persuasively that the reservations would do no harm and might even do some good. Lodge was even able to convince the irreconcilables to support his reservations during the Senate debate (though they intended to oppose the treaty when it came to a final vote) on the ground that should the treaty pass, the reservations would make league membership somewhat more acceptable.

Lodge knew that the president could only gain a two-thirds majority in favor of the treaty without reservations by keeping the votes for all forty-seven Democrats, winning over the dozen or so mild reservationists, and capturing a few votes from among the strong reservationists. Since that scenario seemed unlikely, it appeared that Wilson would have to accept a "Republicanized" version of the treaty or none at all. The president made no secret of his determination not to compromise with the Senate. Lodge intended to test Wilson's resolve.

As chair of the Foreign Relations Committee, Lodge did everything in his power to delay consideration of the treaty by the full Senate. He packed his committee with six "irreconcilables" and kept the agreement bottled up for weeks, first by reading the entire agreement, roughly one thousand standard pages, before a largely empty committee room, and then by holding extended hearings. His object was twofold. First, he hoped that in time popular support for the treaty would dissipate. Second, his delaying tactics gave opponents of the treaty time to get their message across.

During this period Elihu Root, Charles Evans Hughes, Lodge himself, and other important Republican leaders focused their attacks on Article X of the League Covenant, which Wilson viewed as the heart of the league. In a celebrated speech Lodge warned that this article would give "other powers" the right "to call out American troops and American ships to go to any part of the world," that America would be "bound by a moral obligation into all the quarrels of Europe." Lodge did not publicly oppose league membership per se. But he did insist that Congress ought to have the power to decide "whether we should carry out the guarantees of Article 10 or not, . . ." He also wanted it understood that Congress's refusal to implement Article 10 would not constitute a treaty violation.[5]

By mid-August most important Republican leaders in the country were on record in favor of a compromise in which the treaty would be ratified with reservations and America would join the league. The pro-Republican and proleague *New York Tribune* predicted a "practically unanimous vote" for a treaty with reservations.[6] But President Wilson was in no mood for compromise. Instead he lobbied hard for ratification without reservations. And when his efforts fell short, he decided to take his case to the people. If the Senate wanted war, he told Robert Lansing, he would give them "a belly full."[7]

Though in poor health, Wilson left Washington on September 3, 1919, on an eight-thousand-mile "swing around the circle" that took him all the way to the West Coast. Over the next twenty-two days he gave more than thirty speeches. While reaching out for public support, Wilson made his position unmistakably clear. He was especially sensitive to talk of adding a reservation to the American commitment under Article X of the League Covenant. Article X, he insisted, could not be weakened, for it was "the only instrument that will cut to the very heart of the old [balance of power] system." He told a crowd in Cheyenne, Wyoming, that "if any such reservation is adopted I shall be obliged, as chief executive, to regard it as a rejection of the treaty." And in his last speech at Pueblo, Colorado, he said that reservations would mean "asking special privileges for the United States. We cannot ask that." Then, in words that may well have brought a smile to Senator Lodge's lips, he said, "We go in on equal terms or we don't go in at all."[8]

On September 25, following the Pueblo speech, Wilson suffered a physical breakdown and was rushed back to Washington. A week later he was felled by a paralytic stroke that left him incapacitated until mid-November.

## THE LODGE RESERVATIONS

On September 10, 1919, while Wilson was in the midst of his speaking tour, the Republican majority on the Foreign Relations Committee reported the treaty to the full Senate, recommending that it be ratified along with 45 amendments and four reservations. The amendments were soundly defeated on the Senate floor, no doubt because the bipartisan majority realized that an amended treaty would have to be renegotiated and that the public would view this as a thinly disguised attempt to scuttle the league. Senator Lodge then proposed fourteen reservations to the treaty (one for each of Wilson's points). Under the terms of Lodge's proposal, there would be no need to renegotiate the treaty which would go into effect after three of the four other major signatories to the treaty accepted the American reservations.

Most of the Lodge reservations were pointless tautologies. Number 3 for example, stipulated that the United States could not accept a mandate "except by action of Congress." Of the fourteen, only two had real substance.

The first gave Congress the power to withdraw from the league by the passage of a concurrent resolution, and the second stipulated that the United States would not be obliged "to preserve the territorial integrity or political independence of any other country or to interfere in controversies between nations . . . under the provisions of Article X" of the League Covenant or to employ American forces under any other article of the treaty unless Congress first approved the action.[9]

By November, the president had recovered to the point that he was able to resume some of his duties. But the left side of his face and body remained partially paralyzed; his powers of concentration were impaired; and often for no apparent reason he broke into tears. One thing, however, had not changed. He continued to insist on an unmodified treaty.

With the agreement about to come before the Senate once again, Senator Gilbert Hitchcock, the Democratic leader in the upper house, urged Wilson to accept the Lodge reservations. Mrs. Wilson, too, urged her husband to be flexible. But the president was adamant. "Let Lodge compromise," he said.[10] Wilson was convinced that if the Versailles pact was defeated, public outrage would force the Senate to reconsider and approve the treaty unchanged. Rather than challenge Wilson's leadership, Hitchcock endorsed this strategy. Thus, when the treaty with the Lodge reservations came to a vote on November 19, it was soundly defeated by a vote of 39–55. Forty-two Democrats joined thirteen Republican "irreconcilables" in opposition. Lodge and most of the Republicans, on the other hand, voted in the affirmative. The treaty then came to a vote shorn of the Lodge reservations only to be defeated again, this time by a vote of 38–53.

The treaty's demise elicited predictable reactions. Senator William E. Borah, a leading "irreconcilable," described the outcome as "the second winning of the independence of America" and "the greatest victory since Appomattox." Supporters of the league, on the other hand, were devastated. The *New York World* said, "We have lost courage, confidence and resource; we have made the Declaration of Independence parochial instead of universal, and we have withdrawn selfishly and afraid from complications that can never be settled without our help." When it came to assessing blame, the *Philadelphia Inquirer* had it about right. The paper blamed Wilson, who "has been egotistical and has ignored the Senate." On the other hand, the editorial continued, "the opposition to the treaty" had "been malicious and with mighty little honesty in it."[11]

## EPITAPH

Wilson was right about one thing, the informed public did rise up and demand that the Senate reconsider the treaty. Pressure on the Senate and Wilson came from many quarters, including Europe, where the powers were stunned at the prospect of the United States abandoning the peace structure so recently created. With the Senate heading for another vote on the treaty in March 1920, the French ambassador, Jules Jusserand, urged the president to accept the Lodge reservations. The British joined in the appeal. American participation in the league, no matter what the terms, was absolutely vital.

Still the president remained unmoved, his instructions to Senate Democrats unmistakably clear. But Wilson's control over his party was weakening. This time twenty-one Democrats broke with the president to vote for the treaty with the Lodge reservations. As a result the pact came within six votes of the two-thirds majority required for passage. Some have made the point that had only a few more Democrats broken with Wilson the treaty would have been approved. But it is important to note that even if those six votes had been found, Wilson would never have ratified it with the Lodge reservations.

In the last analysis it was Wilson who killed the treaty. But why? What was it about those reservations that was so unacceptable? His biographer, Professor Arthur Link, believes that in the end Wilson might have compromised had "disease" not "dethroned his reason."[12] While there may be something to this assessment, it should be recalled that Wilson refused to consider a compromise with Lodge and the reservationists before his breakdown. It was his decision not to compromise that sent him on the disastrous speaking tour in the first place.

Was it, then, the president's hatred for Lodge that prompted him to react so? This feeling, too, may have been a consideration. In the midst of the struggle Wilson told one Senate Democrat that he would "never consent to adopt any policy with which that impossible man is so prominently identified."[13] Still, it is difficult to believe that illness, even when complemented by personal animus, could have led Wilson to kill his own brainchild unless the Lodge reservations themselves in some way challenged his basic beliefs.

We know that others did not view the Lodge reservations as serious infringements on America's ability to function as a member of the league. David Hunter Miller, a member of the American delegation at Paris and the author of a history of the conference, has described the Lodge reservations as "of a wholly minor character." They would, he tells us, have "interfered with the League's workings not at all."[14] Even that archenemy of the treaty, Senator William E. Borah, thought the reservations of no consequence.

Borah was more right than wrong. Even Wilson would probably have agreed that twelve of Lodge's reservations were mere irritations. On the other hand, the president believed that reservations 1 and 2 seriously weakened the American commitment to the league and raised a congressional challenge to the powers of the executive that he could not ignore. Wilson saw the first reservation, which gave Congress the power to withdraw from the league by concurrent resolution, as infringing on the president's power to conduct foreign policy. He was even more disturbed by reservation 2, which stipulated that the United States would take no action under Article X of the covenant, the collective security provision, without congressional approval.

Wilson believed that the United States ought to assume the mantle of world leadership willingly and aggressively. The United States could not be forced to act against its own interests. It had a veto power in the League Council. And in any event Congress and not the president had the power to declare war and through its budgetary function to control the activities of the armed forces. There was, therefore, no need for these two reservations. But the message they sent to the world community was that the United States could not be depended upon and that it was not genuinely committed to the preservation of the peace so recently won. For Wilson, as the historian Daniel Smith has observed, the "difference between entering the League of Nations with or without the Lodge Reservations was the very significant difference between a limited and grudging participation in world affairs, and Wilson's concept of an America willingly assuming the full burdens of a great power and becoming actively involved in making the League a success."[15]

Even after the final defeat of the Treaty of Versailles in the Senate that March, Wilson persisted in thinking that finally he would win out over his enemies by transforming the 1920 presidential election into a "great and solemn referendum" on American participation in the League of Nations. Though still partially paralyzed from his recent stroke and in frail health, he even considered running. His physician, his wife, and Democratic party leaders, however, persuaded him to abandon that idea. Instead the Democrats chose Governor James M. Cox of Ohio to carry their banner against another Ohioan, Senator Warren G. Harding. "Mr. President," Cox told the ailing Wilson during an emotional visit to the White House, "we're going to be a million percent with you and your administration, and that means the League of Nations."[16]

During the election campaign Cox and his running mate, Franklin D. Roosevelt, defended Wilson's record, focused on the importance of continuing the economic and social reform movement of the preceding two decades, and emphasized the importance of joining the league. But the public was unresponsive to their appeal. It was Harding who correctly sensed what the people wanted. He promised "not heroics, but healing; not nostrums, but normalcy; not revolution but restoration; not surgery; but serenity." And although for the most part Harding avoided taking hard and fast positions, he made himself unmistakably clear on the League of Nations when he said that as to "this particular League proposed by Wilson, I do not want to clarify the obligations. I want to turn my back on them. It is not interpretation but rejection that I am seeking."[17]

Harding went on to an overwhelming victory in the election, garnering 60 percent of the vote to the Democrats' 34 percent. "It wasn't a landslide," said Wilson's secretary, Joe Tumulty. "It was an earthquake."[18] But was it a referendum? The obvious answer is of course it was—not only on the foreign policy issue but on much more as well. After more than twenty years of social, political, and economic reform efforts, capped off by the great crusade to "make the world safe for democracy" complete with plans for the creation of an international community of nations, the people were weary. Under the circumstances, it is not surprising that Harding's appeal was as great as it was.

As president, Harding gave no thought to joining the League or to developing some theoretically more acceptable form of international organization—an idea he had hinted at during the campaign. He could not, however, roll back the clock and return to some bygone time when America played less than a leading role in world affairs. The United States had emerged from the war as the world's strongest power with global interests. Having rejected Wilson's vision of the future, the Republicans would have to make their own way through new and previously uncharted waters.

## ENDNOTES

1. Woodrow Wilson, quoted in Arthur Link, *Wilson the Diplomatist* (Baltimore: Johns Hopkins University Press, 1957), p. 130.
2. *Literary Digest*, August 9, 1919, p. 8.
3. *Nation*, September 27, 1919, p. 421.
4. William Randolph Hearst, quoted in Edward W. Chester, *The Scope and Variety of U.S. Diplomatic History* (Englewood Cliffs, N.J.: Prentice-Hall, 1990), II, 285–86.
5. Henry Cabot Lodge, quoted in *Literary Digest*, August 9, 1919, pp. 8–10.
6. *New York Tribune*, quoted in *ibid.*, August 30, 1919, pp. 11–13.
7. Wilson, quoted in Daniel Smith, *The Great Departure: The United States and World War I, 1914–1920* (New York: John Wiley and Sons, 1965), p. 189.
8. Wilson, quoted in Link, *Wilson the Diplomatist*, pp. 140–50.
9. For the debate on Article X, see John Chalmers Vinson, *Referendum for Isolation: Defeat of Article Ten of the League of Nations Covenant* (Athens, Ga.: University of Georgia Press, 1961), pp. 110–20.
10. Wilson, quoted in John Milton Cooper, Jr., *Pivotal Decades: The United States, 1900–1920* (New York: W. W. Norton, 1990), p. 352.
11. Wiliam E. Borah, *New York World*, and *Philadelphia Inquirer*, all quoted in *Literary Digest*, November 29, 1919, pp. 11–13.
12. Link, *Wilson the Diplomatist*, p. 154.
13. Wilson, quoted in Armin Rappaport, *A History of American Diplomacy*, (New York: Macmillan, 1975), p. 278.
14. David Hunter Miller, quoted in *What Really Happened at Versailles*, ed. Edward M. House and Charles Seymour, (New York: Charles Scribner's Sons, 1921), p. 424.
15. Smith, *Great Departure*, pp. 195–96.
16. James M. Cox, quoted in Cooper, *Pivotal Decades*, p. 367.
17. Warren G. Harding, quoted in *ibid.*, p. 369.
18. Joe Tumulty, quoted in *ibid.*, p. 372.

ALL DEBITS ON THE WESTERN FRONT.

The failure of the United States and the European powers to resolve the war debts–reparations tangle contributed in no small way to the financial crisis of the early 1930s.

# 20

# *BETWEEN THE WARS:*
## *Republican Foreign Policy, 1921–1933*

It has often been suggested that following the Senate's rejection of the Treaty of Versailles the United States entered a period of isolationism from which it did not emerge until World War II. While it is true that during the interwar years Americans were unwilling to assume binding international political commitments and proved reluctant to use force to achieve foreign policy ends, the country was far from isolated.

During the 1920s, Washington participated in three major disarmament conferences, signed the Kellogg-Briand agreement for the outlawry of war, and had representatives working in collaboration with a variety of League of Nations agencies. Convinced that a thriving world economy was the best guarantee of peace, Republican policy makers worked to create a stable and prosperous Europe, took the lead in creating a new political and economic order in the Far East, and reduced the American military presence in Latin America to improve America's image while advancing its interests in that economically and strategically important part of the world.

On the economic front, Americans dug for manganese and manufactured cars and trucks in the Soviet Union, competed for control of the communications industry in China, and fought for access to the oil resources of Mesopotamia. During this same exciting decade America's first multinational corporations grew up. Firestone, Ford, General Motors, and many others expanded overseas to take advantage of new opportunities. At the same time, foreign markets became more important than ever as America churned out $66 billion in exports. In brief, American business, aided by a succession of Republican administrations, sought and achieved a dominant role in the global economy.

## HARDING, HOOVER, AND HUGHES

The administration that oversaw the beginning of these dramatic developments was headed by President Warren Gamaliel Harding, a man not generally credited with an overabundance of either brains or ability. Harding rose from the obscurity of life as a small-town Ohio newspaper editor to the power of the presidency by adhering to the Republican party line, being in the right place at the right time, and looking "presidential." Ordinary and fallible beyond the norm, Harding would never have attained the presidency but for the fact that the 1920 Republican convention deadlocked. The party managers settled on the Ohio senator as a compromise candidate because he was manageable. Moreover, his silver hair and tall, broad-shouldered appearance were major attributes in a country already growing image conscious.

In contrast to Woodrow Wilson, who once scoffed at his "bungalow mind," Harding had no intellectual pretensions. As an orator he was a living, breathing disaster. Not only was his syntax poor (his trouble with suffixes gave us "normalcy"); he was prone to mistakes. "Keep Warren at home," warned one Republican stalwart. "Don't let him make any speeches. If he goes out on tour somebody's sure to ask him questions and Warren's just the sort of damned fool who will try to answer them." The great satirist, H. L. Mencken, once remarked that Harding "writes the worst English that I have ever encountered. It reminds me of a string of wet sponges; it reminds me of tattered washing on the line; it reminds me of stale bean soup, of college yells, of dogs barking idiotically through endless nights. It is so bad that a sort of grandeur creeps through it."[1]

As president, Harding was not so awful as all that. It is true that he made some remarkably bad appointments and that his administration was plagued by scandal and corruption. But there was a positive side to the Harding record as well. He intervened to help bring an end to the infamous twelve-hour day in the steel industry, advocated welfare reform, and had a far better record in the field of civil liberties than did Wilson. He even pardoned the Socialist leader, Eugene Debs, who had been imprisoned during the war for violating the Sedition Act, and invited him to the White House. Harding also made sound appointments in areas having to do with foreign relations. He made Charles Evans Hughes his secretary of state and chose Herbert Hoover to be commerce secretary.

Hoover's was one of those "poor boy makes good" stories that has universal appeal. Orphaned at the age of nine, the young Quaker boy left

President Warren G. Harding lays a wreath on the coffin of the unknown soldier who lies
in state in the Capitol rotunda.

Iowa for Oregon, where he lived with relatives. He attended Stanford
University, graduating with a degree in geology. Driven by the desire to
succeed, he worked for many years as a mining engineer in Latin America,
China, Australia, and Russia. By the time he was forty he was a millionaire
with an international reputation as a brilliant administrator. Hoover's postwar
achievements as head of the European relief program added luster to an
already impressive reputation.

Charles Evans Hughes, a former reform governor of New York,
associate justice of the Supreme court, and in 1916 the Republican candidate
for the Presidency, possessed a narrowly focused but brilliant legal mind.
Hughes understood that the structure of peace created at the Congress of
Vienna in 1815 had finally and irrevocably been destroyed by the war.
Moreover, he believed that as the world's single greatest power with far-
flung and expanding interests, the United States had a responsibility both
to itself and to the rest of the world to help restore prosperity and order
abroad.

Hughes and Hoover, who between them dominated American foreign policy in the Harding administration, believed that economic power

could be used to advance America's international ambitions. They sought to guide private foreign investment, determining where and for what purpose money would be loaned. Hoover wanted direct control over America's foreign lending so that Washington might discourage armaments and encourage foreign economic growth, thus swelling the ranks of potential consumers for American products. Hughes's purposes were similar, though he was less inclined to seek direct control over the activities of the banking community. As he explained to Hoover, "I am disposed to discountenance loans to unrecognized governments [Russia and Mexico] or loans sought by foreign governments for military purposes or for objects that appear to run counter to clearly defined policies of this government."[2]

In March 1922, after the powerful investment banker, J. P. Morgan, informed Hughes that the rest of the banking community was willing to cooperate, the State Department made it official. America's bankers were "asked to ascertain the opinion of the government in writing" before making any new foreign loans. The State Department believed that it should have the opportunity "of saying to the underwriters concerned . . . that there is or is not objection to any particular issue."[3]

The State Department's control over foreign lending was far from complete. Though Hughes could and did influence decisions taken by private bankers, that influence often waned when bankers saw opportunities for high profits. Nevertheless, the bankers did cooperate with policies designed to encourage postwar European economic recovery and political stability, to require the funding of war debts, and to force concessions from Mexico relating to control of that country's petroleum resources.

## EUROPE IN CRISIS

During the period immediately following the armistice, Western Europe experienced an extended economic boom. Wages and profits soared, while unemployment remained low. Toward the end of 1920, however, a recession set in. In France, industrial production dropped to 53 percent of its prewar level, and unemployment became a serious problem. At the same time, because Paris had financed 175 billion francs' worth of postwar reconstruction by issuing paper money and borrowing extensively, the country was hit by a serious inflation. The price index jumped from a 1918 figure of 514, already more than five times the prewar level, to 836 by 1925.

Britain was in even worse shape. The Japanese had taken advantage of the wartime situation to drive Britain from many Far Eastern markets. The United States had done the same throughout Latin America and Europe. American manufacturers were even competing successfully for an increased share of the British market. As a result of this extreme competition and a hard money policy that made British products expensive abroad, Britain's exports stood at just 50 percent of the 1913 level, while a whopping 17.7 percent of the work force was unemployed.

Europe after Versailles, 1919

NORWAY
FINLAND
Helsinki
Petrograd
SWEDEN
Tallinn
ESTONIA
DENMARK
LATVIA
Riga
NORTH SEA
BALTIC SEA
LITHUANIA
GER.
Kaunas
U.S.S.R.
NETH.
Berlin
Danzig Free State
BELG.
GERMANY
Warsaw
LUX.
POLAND
Paris
SAAR
Prague
ALSACE-LORRAINE
Munich
CZECHOSLOVAKIA
FRANCE
SWITZ.
Vienna
AUSTRIA
Budapest
HUNGARY
ROMANIA
Fiume
Belgrade
ITALY
YUGOSLAVIA
BULGARIA
Rome
ALBANIA
MEDITERRANEAN SEA
GREECE
TURKEY

New independent nations        Plebiscite area

Allied occupation zone

Germany suffered from even more serious problems. At the end of the war the country's public debt was twenty times what it had been in 1913. There was five times as much paper currency in circulation. The country had lost 13 percent of its European land area, 72 percent of its iron ore, 36 percent of its coal reserves and was saddled with a $33 billion reparations bill.

It was the reparations bill that turned a serious problem into a catastrophe. To fulfill its reparations obligation for 1922, the Weimar Republic needed to pay $375 million in cash, 26 percent of the proceeds from Germany's exports, and certain reparations in kind to the Allies. Lacking foreign currency reserves, the Weimar government tried to purchase what it needed in the international money market. But the attempt resulted in the collapse of the Mark, which fell from 14.6 Marks to the dollar in May 1921, to 10,000:1 by the end of December 1922. During that same period the German price index rose from 36.7 to 1,475. (The 1913 price index is 100.) At that point the government, having lost control of the situation, began printing money wildly in a futile attempt to stay solvent and provide the banks with the currency they needed to extend credit. By October 1923, the printing presses were turning out 400,000,000,000,000,000 Marks each day. The economy was in total disarray.

Internationally minded American businessmen such as the banker, Frank A. Vanderlip, and James Simpson, a partner in Marshall Field and Company, were convinced that if Washington did not take steps to encourage European recovery the United States, too, would suffer serious economic problems. Simpson, for example, warned that Europe was in a state of "financial and economic chaos" and that "unless something is done promptly to avert the disaster, . . . it will spread from one country to another until we are all involved in the maelstrom." Another Republican businessman noted, "Our interests are indissolubly united with the interests of Europe and until we have reorganized a sound, a normal condition of affairs in Europe . . . we shall not have normal, healthy times at home."[4]

Herbert Hoover, who agreed, believed that the "export market becomes of particular importance to us . . . in maintaining a stable and even operation of our domestic industries. It has an importance in that regard far beyond the percentage of our exports to our total production." Foreign trade was, he believed, a vital "part of our domestic progress, both socially and economically." It was really very simple, Hoover thought. Orderly, prosperous societies make good customers; chaotic conditions inhibit trade. Secretary Hughes, carrying Hoover's logic one step further, observed that "there can be no economic recuperation in Europe unless Germany recuperates" and that there would "be no permanent peace unless economic satisfactions are enjoyed." It was, therefore, in America's interest to encourage Germany's economic recovery.[5]

Considering their awareness of the connection among European recovery, international peace, and American prosperity, it is ironic that prospects for Europe's recovery were dimmed by the Republican's own protectionist tariff policy. Many Republican internationalists opposed protectionism on the ground that it would lead to shrinking markets abroad and discourage Europe's recovery. They were correct. Europe needed capital. And one of the few places it could be earned was in the rich American market. But it was the Republican party's high-tariff traditionalists and those manufacturing interests that were largely dependent on the American market who won the day in Congress. Emergency tariff legislation was enacted in 1921 to be replaced in the following year by the high Fordney-McCumber tariff. At the very moment when Europe needed dollars to pull itself out of the doldrums, Congress closed a significant portion of the American market to European goods.

The war debts owed to the United States by the Allies further complicated matters. Beginning in 1917 Washington loaned approximately $10.3 billion to the Allies, first for the conduct of the war and later for humanitarian purposes. After the war the Allies hoped that the Wilson administration would forgive a debt incurred in fighting a common enemy. The British, who had themselves loaned substantial sums to their allies, proposed a general cancellation of all inter-Allied debts. But the Wilson and Harding administrations both refused to consider this action. Instead Washington took the curious position that it would be a very good thing if the Allies canceled Germany's reparations debt, since that step would strengthen the German economy and contribute to a general European recovery. They refused to apply the same logic, however, to the war debts.

Republican internationalists realized that by insisting on repayment of the war debts Washington placed extra stress on Europe's war-weakened economies and that this pressure ran contrary to hopes for a speedy European recovery. Earlier, while serving as a member of the World War Foreign Debt Commission, Hoover, for example, supported a complete write-off. Others including Treasury Secretary Andrew W. Mellon, favored partial cancellation.

But the war debts question was a highly charged political issue. If the Allies did not pay, the American taxpayer would be left to foot the bill. It is not surprising then, that as the public's disillusionment with the wartime experience grew, so did its insistence that the war debts be funded. President Calvin Coolidge is supposed to have said, "They hired the money didn't they? Now let them pay it back." Whether he did or not is open to question. But the thought was certainly a popular one, especially in the early years of the decade when, caught in a depression, the public demanded tax relief and a balanced budget.

Policy makers in the Harding administration denied, at least publicly, that their tariff and war debt policies were in any way connected to Europe's continuing state of economic and political instability. The Europeans, they insisted, had it in their power to solve their own problems. In fact, however, the Republicans were caught in the toils of a hopelessly inconsistent policy. They wanted an economically strong and politically stable Europe. But they could not bring themselves to make the sacrifices necessary to attain it. The problem, as President Harding explained, was "how to fully assert a helpful influence abroad without sacrificing anything of importance to our own people."[6] Neither he nor his two Republican successors ever found the answer to this irritating conundrum.

## CRISIS INTERVENTION: THE DAWES PLAN

The Allied demand for war reparations from Germany proved another major stumbling block to European recovery. In late 1921, by which time inflation had gone completely out of control in Germany, Berlin notified the Reparations Commission that it could not meet its 1922 obligation. The commission agreed to a yearlong moratorium on payments and summoned a panel of international experts to propose a solution to Germany's problem.

The committee of experts, however, did not have an opportunity to make its report. Events got in the way.

In January 1923, French and Belgian troops invaded the Ruhr Valley, Germany's industrial heartland. Their object was to collect reparations in kind. In Berlin, Chancellor Wilhelm Cuno reacted angrily. He urged the workers in the Ruhr to go on strike, gave them government support when they did, and announced that there was no longer the slightest possibility that Germany would pay reparations. In London, ex-Prime Minister David Lloyd George expressed amazement at the French action claiming that "even logically it was indefensible" while the *London Outlook*, denounced France's Premier Raymond Poincaré as "one of the most colossal idiots, or the greatest of knaves, who ever strutted upon the stage of high human destinies."[7]

The reaction to the Ruhr invasion was more or less the same in the United States, where it produced some furious outcries. Senator William E. Borah denounced it as "utterly brutal and insane." And Mississippi's Senator John Sharp Williams, noted for his strong anti-German feelings, said, "France has hurt her own cause and that of her Allies and associates in the World War."[8]

Secretary of State Hughes believed from the beginning that French policy was misguided. He understood that the French viewed reparations as one method of keeping Germany weak and nonthreatening but believed that French security was best guaranteed by encouraging German economic growth. A prosperous Germany seemed to Hughes to be France's best guarantee against an uncertain future.

The crisis continued for months, until at length the exhausted Germans, their economy in ruins, ordered the workers back to their jobs and called on the United States to arrange a settlement. At that point Secretary Hughes informed the French government in no uncertain terms that "to overcome German resistance to payment of just obligations is one thing; to push matters to a point of disintegration where hope of adequate reparations payments will be destroyed is quite another, and in the long run will prove a futile reliance for French security." Because the present situation was causing "great anxiety," he considered it vital that the powers immediately adopt "an adequate financial plan based upon the capacity of Germany to pay."[9] Toward that end he now called for the creation of a new panel of experts who would be empowered to settle the reparations question.

Paris had no choice but to agree. The Ruhr invasion had been a costly fiasco. France was suffering from financial problems almost as severe as those besetting Germany. Only a major foreign loan could save the franc, and that loan would have to be funded in the United States. But no loan was to be had unless Paris accepted Hughes's recommendation.

In deference to the American public's strong opposition to any direct involvement in European political affairs, policy makers in Washington worked through private individuals in their efforts to sort out the reparations problem. Charles Gates Dawes, the Chicago banker, and Owen D. Young of the General Electric Company, headed a delegation that left for Paris in early 1924. The Dawes group was to meet with other European experts and propose a settlement to the Franco-German dispute. Before they left, the American "experts" were, of course, completely briefed by the State Department.

The problem confronting Dawes and Young was to find a compromise solution to the reparations question that all sides could live with politically. This was a weighty responsibility for a set of "private citizens," since it was clear that failure would plunge Western Europe further into chaos. Yet chances for success were good because, by 1924, the British were being cooperative and France was in no position to assert itself.

The Dawes Plan called for a $200 million loan to Germany, $110 million of which was to be subscribed by American investors. The purpose of the loan was to stabilize the German Mark, which had become worthless during the runaway inflation of 1923. The plan also scaled down the amount of reparations Germany was to pay by about 20 percent, stretched the payments out over sixty-four years, and established a graduated scale of payments for the first five years beginning with $250 million in 1924–25 and rising to $625 million in 1928–29. An American, S. Parker Gilbert, became agent general of reparations. Gilbert had the authority to determine the exact amount of each yearly payment depending on Germany's "capacity to pay."

The Dawes Plan also contained certain political conditions insisted upon by the American bankers, whose responsibility it was to arrange the all-important German loan. Before any money would be forthcoming, the parties had to guarantee "the political independence, the territorial integrity, and the sovereignty of Germany." France was also required to end the military occupation of the Ruhr within two years and to agree that if the Germans should at some future time renege on reparations, it would not take military action. What the bankers demanded, Thomas Lamont, a Morgan Company partner explained, was "a tranquilized and hard working Germany, Allies working in harmony, no more Ruhr invasion, no more sanctions, Germany paying reparations at last upon a scale steady and fairly adequate."[10]

The French were unhappy about the concessions they were forced to make. But they were desperate for a $100 million loan to shore up the franc and had no place else to turn. Hughes, who thought the Dawes Plan essential to European recovery and who saw this as a vital interest of the United States, made it clear that there would be no loan unless France was prepared to cooperate. Dependent as they were on the American banking community, the French had no choice but to give in.

Five years later a second group of experts headed by Owen Young met to reassess the reparations question. The Young Plan called for further reductions. The final reparations bill set by Young and his colleagues was $8 billion to be paid over fifty-eight years at an interest rate of 5.5 percent. Thus, within a very few years and largely as a result of the joint efforts of powerful American bankers, the State Department, and the cooperative

British, Allied reparations claims were scaled down by 70 percent, to a figure that Woodrow Wilson would probably have accepted in 1919.

## THE SPIRIT OF LOCARNO

Following the implementation of the Dawes Plan, American bankers, still working in collaboration with Washington, let it be known that future loans to European nations would not be forthcoming unless the Europeans made political commitments guaranteeing order and stability on the continent. Encouraged not only by their need for American dollars but also by the French who were assaying every possible means of enhancing their security, Britain, France, Italy, Belgium, and Germany sent delegates to an international conference in Locarno, Switzerland where they negotiated several important treaties. The Locarno Agreements legitimized the postwar French-German and Belgian-German borders and established arbitration as the preferred method of settling disputes among Germany, France, Belgium, Czechoslovakia, and Poland. By ratifying the Locarno Agreements, Berlin surrendered all claim to the provinces of Alsace and Lorraine and reaffirmed its commitment to a demilitarized Rhineland. In guaranteeing the German border, the French affirmed that if the Germans reneged on their reparations commitment, they would not again occupy the Ruhr.

American policy makers saw the Dawes Plan and the Locarno Agreements as necessary preconditions to the stable, prosperous, new order they envisioned for Europe. So did the American investing public. From the end of World War I to the implementation of the Dawes Plan and the signing of the Locarno Agreements, only modest amounts of American capital had flowed to Europe. But after Locarno, the floodgates opened. What happened next might be likened to a scene from the first day of the Oklahoma land rush, only in this instance it was American investors who rushed to acquire high-yield European securities. During those brief halcyon days, American investors sent more than $12 billion abroad. Germany alone absorbed $2.6 billion.

This astonishing flow of investment from the United States to Europe offered the Republicans a temporary solution to their dilemma. The Germans used some of these investment dollars to make reparations payments. The Allies then used the reparations money to make payments to their war debts. The flow of investment capital also allowed Europe to finance its unfavorable trade balance with the United States.

For that brief moment the United States had it all, an apparently stable and increasingly prosperous Europe that provided an expanding market, war debts payments, a high tariff to protect the home market, and a favorable balance of trade. But it was a fool's paradise, for it was the flow of American capital abroad that made it all possible. And when in 1930 the depression brought a halt to American foreign investment, the entire structure came tumbling down.

If the Republicans had, early in the decade, adopted a low-tariff policy, opened the American market more widely to foreign goods, and agreed to the cancellation of all war debts and reparations, the international economy would have been in a stronger position to absorb the shock of the depression. As the historian Joan Hoff Wilson has observed, these measures would not have prevented the catastrophe. They would "in all probability," however, "have made it less severe."[11]

## COLLAPSE IN EUROPE

The Great Depression had a disastrous effect upon both America and Europe. In 1930, with prosperity a thing of the past and unemployment at 9 percent and rising, Congress did exactly the wrong thing—enacting the Smoot-Hawley tariff. With its 59 percent *ad valorem* (according to the invoiced value) rate on imports, the new tariff was bound to have a deleterious effect on world trade. The danger was so obvious that one thousand economists signed an open letter to President Herbert Hoover, urging him to veto the measure. Whenever so many economists can agree on anything, it is probably worth paying attention. Certainly Hoover, who succeeded Calvin Coolidge in 1929, would have been well advised to pay heed. But Hoover was under intense pressure from economic nationalists, who thought it vital to defend the home market during the depression. He signed the tariff measure, and the country took the consequences.

The Smoot-Hawley tariff, which many countries viewed as a declaration of economic warfare, had the predictable effect. In short order thirty-one countries retaliated by raising their tariffs. It was the beginning of a fierce trade war that did not so much end as it flowed into the military conflict that broke out later in the decade. As a result, American foreign trade dwindled. Imports, which had peaked at $4.4 billion in 1929, dropped to $1.3 billion in 1932. Exports dropped from $5.2 billion to a low of $1.6 billion in the trough of the depression.

Before the end of 1930, American foreign investment had all but ceased, and Europe was caught up in an economic crisis. British unemployment jumped to 16 percent. The Germans were even worse off, with 22 percent of the labor force unemployed. Two years later, on the eve of elections that brought Adolf Hilter to power, German unemployment reached a catastrophic 38.5 percent. Price levels dropped too, by 30 percent in Germany, 25 percent in Britain, and 32 percent in France.

Bank reserves also dwindled, as people used their savings to meet personal obligations. This decrease in reserves, plus the lack of new infusions of capital from America, led to increasing financial difficulties for businesses, individuals, and nations as well. Before the end of 1930, Austria's central bank, the Creditanstalt, and the powerful Danatbank in Germany, were both near bankruptcy.

In an effort to avert total disaster, the Weimar government undertook negotiations with the Austrians looking toward the establishment of an Austro-German Customs Union. The French, who viewed the possible unification of Germany and Austria as threatening to their security, attempted to discourage the consummation of this union by putting intense financial pressure on both countries. As a result, in the spring of 1931 the Creditanstalt collapsed, while the economic situation throughout Germany grew desperate. Barring some action from outside, Berlin let it be known that Germany would soon be compelled to cut off reparations payments.

It had been clear for some time that the United States could relieve some of the pressure on the global financial structure by agreeing to the mutual cancellation of war debt and reparations claims. But President Hoover had been reluctant to take that step both because he was not certain that the economic situation in Europe made payment impossible and because he feared the domestic political fallout if he agreed to cancel the war debts. By May 1931, however, he believed that if he did not take some action the entire Central European banking system would collapse. And if the Germans went under, he was convinced it would set off a global crisis that would bring many of the largest financial institutions in the United States to the brink of ruin.

Even so, he was not prepared to propose a general cancellation of debts. Instead, he decided on a year's moratorium on debt and reparations payments to relieve some of the immediate pressure and give all sides an opportunity to think the problem through once again. Hoover announced his moratorium proposal on June 20 and ran head on into objections from the French, who were not yet prepared to abandon their reparations claims. The collapse of the Danatbank on July 1 may have convinced them, however, for five days afterward they, too, agreed to the moratorium.

Like so many things the Republicans tried in these extraordinary times, the moratorium was a case of too-little, too-late. Hoover's purpose had been to prevent a financial panic in Germany that would seriously undermine the American banking system. But a banking panic swept Germany even before the moratorium went into effect. As increasing numbers of German banks closed their doors, many American banks, holders of huge quantities of now-worthless German securities, followed suit.

In June 1932, at a conference in Lausanne, Switzerland, the European powers made one last attempt to resolve the interrelated war debt and reparations questions short of outright repudiation. They proposed reducing Germany's remaining reparations debt by 90 percent if the United States would do the same for the war debts. But the president, with one eye on the upcoming national elections, refused.

In December all of the nations owing war debts to the United States save France made their scheduled payments, albeit in their native currencies. But these were the last payments. By 1933, all of America's debtors save Finland had repudiated their war debts. At the same time signs ominous for the future were emanating from Germany. In March 1933, by dint of a hysterical anticommunist propaganda campaign accompanied by extreme

Adolf Hitler reviews his SA troops at a Nazi Party rally in Nuremberg. The rise of Nazism marked the beginning of an ominous new stage in the history of the West.

forms of terrorism and violence, the Nazis coerced the Reichstag (Parliament) into passing an enabling act that placed absolute power in the hands of Chancellor Adolf Hilter. A new and frightening era in world history was about to begin.

## THE ASIAN PUZZLE: COOPERATION OR CONFLICT?

In December 1920, Idaho's Senator William E. Borah introduced a Senate resolution calling on the administration to invite Japan and Britain to a naval disarmament conference. Borah and other peace advocates believed that reducing armaments would necessarily lessen international tension and create a more stable world.

Although initially skeptical, by the time Congress passed the Borah Resolution in August 1921, Secretary of State Charles Evans Hughes wanted a conference. At the time the United States, Britain, and Japan were involved in a costly naval armaments race. But Hughes believed that, with demands for a tax cut on the increase and the country in the grip of an economic recession, Congress was likely to cut the naval building program. It seemed reasonable, therefore, to seek an agreement that limited naval construction while guaranteeing the United States parity with other naval powers.

A naval limitations agreement appealed to the secretary for other reasons as well. Hughes believed that Europe's economic difficulties stemmed in part from nonproductive spending on armaments. Secretary of Commerce Herbert Hoover even claimed that the money Europe had spent on naval armaments since the war "would have contributed materially to the entire economic rehabilitation of the world."[12] A disarmament agreement, then, promised to reduce international tensions, end the naval armaments race, allow the administration to cut taxes, and free European capital for use in more productive areas.

Hughes also hoped to use the projected conference to establish a new political arrangement in the Far East. The war had radically changed the situation there. Germany was no longer a factor in the region; nor for the moment was Russia. Moreover, French and British influence had been sharply curtailed. Japan's power, on the other hand, had reached new heights. Tokyo's grip on southern Manchuria and eastern Inner Mongolia was stronger than ever. Japan occupied China's Shandong Peninsula, Kiaochow Bay, and Germany's former colonies in the western Pacific. Moreover, Japanese troops remained in Asiatic Russia.

Hughes was prepared to accept a continued Japanese presence in Manchuria and eastern Inner Mongolia but wanted Tokyo to remove its forces from Siberia and return the Shandong Peninsula and Kiaochow Bay to China. He also wanted all of the interested powers, including Japan, to adhere to the open door principle in China and give the Chinese the opportunity, free from foreign interference, to organize a viable central government. Finally, Hughes sought the abolition of the Anglo-Japanese Alliance that since 1902 had enhanced Japanese power throughout the Far East. The secretary was convinced that an end to the old alliance system and a multi-national commitment to the open door would mark the beginning of a new, more stable era in the Far East and smooth the way toward successful disarmament negotiations.

Britain's prime minister, David Lloyd George, was just as interested in a naval limitations agreement as was Hughes. He, too, recognized the importance of establishing a new status quo in the Far East. The Foreign Office and the Admiralty were by no means keen on the idea of abandoning the Japanese alliance. But with the Germans out of the picture and the Russians preoccupied, the prime minister saw no reason to hold out on the point.

Tokyo had the least reason to attend a conference such as the one Hughes envisioned. But the business, financial, and civilian political elites in Japan favored an accommodationist foreign policy because they believed that the country could not continue to pursue its imperialist drive in China without courting a war with the United States. Therefore, Prime Minister Hara Kei charted a new course, emphasizing peaceful expansion through trade, the economic penetration of previously undeveloped markets, and cooperation with the Western powers, especially the United States. Toward this end Hara was ready to accept a modified form of the open door policy that left Japan economically preeminent in southern Manchuria and eastern Inner Mongolia. He was also prepared to withdraw from the Shandong Peninsula and Siberia and under the proper conditions to abandon the Anglo-Japanese Alliance.

## THE WASHINGTON CONFERENCE

On August 11, 1921, President Warren G. Harding invited all the great powers, Germany and Russia excepted, to a conference on naval disarmament and Far Eastern affairs to be held in Washington. In nominating his delegates to the conference, Harding was careful to avoid the mistake Wilson had made before the Paris conference. Secretary Hughes was joined by Henry Cabot Lodge, who was still the chair of the Foreign Relations Committee; the Senate's leading Democrat, Oscar Underwood; and the elder statesman of the Republican party, Elihu Root.

On November 12, at the opening session of the conference, Hughes astounded his listeners with a daring proposal that called for limits on future naval construction as well as the scrapping of ships already afloat or in the building stage. This proposal, which the conference adopted as a basis for negotiations, called for the United States to scrap 845,000 tons of shipping. The British would have to give up 583,000 tons, and the Japanese 480,000 tons.

Hughes's dramatic opening captured the imagination of many in the United States, who thought disarmament the best method of securing lasting peace. Oswald Garrison Villard, writing in the *Nation*, could not say enough on the secretary's behalf. "Not in modern times has there been so clear cut, so astounding, and so brilliant a feat in statecraft as marked Mr. Hughes's opening of the conference. . . . Some of the foreign correspondents and delegates are still wandering about, as I write, in a perfect daze, unable to take it all in."[13]

The Five-Power Treaty signed at Washington by the United States, Britain, Japan, France, and Italy, committed the signatories to honor a ten-year "holiday" during which no new capital ships would be built. (A capital ship was defined as one of more than ten thousand tons displacement or having guns larger than eight-inch caliber.) The treaty also established a fixed ratio of capital ship tonnage for each nation. For every five tons of capital shipping that Britain and the United States were allowed, Japan could have three tons, while France and Italy settled for 1.67 tons each.

Although Hughes won plaudits for his efforts, the Five-Power Treaty was anything but a major disarmament achievement. The French blocked all efforts to limit land armaments and chemical weapons. And none of the nations involved was prepared to limit construction of aircraft or smaller naval vessels. Even the limits placed on capital ship construction were less impressive than they appeared. As one shrewd observer noted: "Battleships may still be the pride of the Navy but experts agree that the next war will be decided by death rained on men from the air or directed against them from beneath the waters."[14] By limiting capital ship construction the powers had in effect achieved a saving that could be put to use on more deadly weapons.

Japanese critics of the agreement complained that Tokyo had been treated unfairly, that the 5:5:3 ratio read, in effect, "Cadillac-Cadillac-Ford."

In fact, however, since the treaty also imposed a freeze on the construction or improvement of naval bases in the Pacific (Hawaii, Singapore, and the Japanese home islands excepted), the treaty gave the Japanese naval predominance in the western Pacific.

Two other agreements signed at Washington addressed Far Eastern issues. The Four-Power Treaty, described by one reporter as "the winding sheet for the corpse of the Anglo-Japanese alliance," was precisely what Hughes wanted, a meaningless consultative agreement. The Nine-Power Treaty, drafted by Hughes's mentor, former Secretary of State Elihu Root, committed the signatories to the open door in China. The signers also agreed to afford China the opportunity to organize a stable government without foreign interference. The very significant fourth clause of the treaty further committed the signatories to seek no "special rights or privileges in China that would abridge those of citizens of other states" and to take no action "inimical to the security of such States."[15]

Convincing the Japanese to sign the Nine-Power Treaty was no mean feat. They had no intention of abandoning their special position in southern Manchuria and eastern Inner Mongolia and would have much preferred a clear statement recognizing their interests in that part of the world. The Japanese delegates only signed this agreement, the most important of the conference, after being assured by Root himself that the treaty committed the signatories only with regard to future behavior and had no bearing on Japan's position in China at the time. Root even indicated that the fourth clause of the agreement—the "security clause"—though vaguely stated, affirmed Japan's special position in Manchuria and Inner Mongolia.

In other agreements signed at Washington, Japan agreed to return Kiaochow and Shandong to the Chinese and confirmed American cable rights on the island of Yap. Although the issue was not raised at Washington, within a year the Japanese also began to withdraw their forces from Siberia.

Hughes was delighted with what had been accomplished at Washington. The powers had agreed to cooperate in the creation of a liberal international order in the Far East. It seemed the beginning of a new era in which the open door would at last replace the old spheres of influence system in China. As a result, Hughes hoped, the danger of international conflict would be sharply reduced and opportunities for trade and investment increased.

## THE CHALLENGE OF CHINESE NATIONALISM

It was a sign of their myopia that the diplomats who assembled in Washington in 1921 were unable to perceive the great weakness of the Far Eastern system they created. It failed to take into account changes inside China. It assumed that China would remain inert, a market to be exploited, a playing field for great power politics. But Chinese nationalism was a major force, the Chinese Revolution already something to be contended with.

The Chinese delegates came to Washington hoping for an end to foreign domination and to the indignities heaped on China through the hated system of "unfair" treaties that had evolved over the past century. But Britain, Japan, and the United States all had significant investments in China, and each considered the China market economically important. Until the Chinese could organize a government that was capable of protecting these interests, there was no chance that they would abandon extraterritoriality, withdraw troops stationed in China, return to China control over its own tariffs, or make concessions on many lesser points.

Secretary Hughes actually warned the Chinese delegates that if they demanded too much they would end up with nothing. He told them that he was prepared to help China, but on his terms, not theirs. If the Chinese had been invited to sit at the table where the game of diplomacy was played, the secretary made it clear that they were there at the sufferance of others.

China's failure to win significant concessions in Washington fueled the flames of Chinese nationalism and antiforeignism. It also led Sun Yat-sen, the ailing head of the Guomindong (Kuomintang) in Guangzho (Canton), one of two rival governments at the time, to turn toward Moscow for support. At the suggestion of his heir apparent, Chiang Kai-shek, he asked the Soviets to help reorganize the Guomindong along Communist party lines. He also authorized Moscow to enter Outer Mongolia and ceded to the Soviets a role in managing the Chinese Eastern Railroad, which bisected Manchuria.

Though these developments could not have pleased Washington, they had no long-term significance. The Soviet connection was a marriage of convenience and was quickly ended. But the nationalist fervor that swept China in the 1920s was something else again, for it set in motion forces that in a very few years would leave the new Far Eastern order established at Washington in ruins.

In 1925, America's approach to Far Eastern affairs changed abruptly with the coming of Frank B. Kellogg to the State Department. Charles Evans Hughes had cultivated good relations with the Japanese. He recognized the special position they enjoyed in Manchuria and eastern Inner Mongolia and believed that Tokyo was within its rights in defending its interests against the growing extremism of Chinese nationalism. Kellogg, on the other hand, sympathized with China's nationalist aspirations and was deeply suspicious of Japanese purposes in China.

His pro-Chinese sentiments notwithstanding, Kellogg might never have altered America's Far Eastern policy had it not been for the rising tide of antiforeignism in China that produced numerous widespread demonstrations. The sheer fury of these demonstrations led Kellogg to the conclusion that the United States would have to surrender some of the extraordinary privileges it then enjoyed in China. He thought it absurd to believe that the powers could indefinitely suppress a nation of 400 million people.

Early in January 1927, Kellogg announced that he was prepared to negotiate a new treaty with China dealing with the subjects of extraterritoriality and the tariff. But the secretary could find no Chinese government worthy of diplomatic recognition. At the time there were two rival factions in China, one located in Beijing (Peking) and supported by various warlords, and the Guomindong, which after Sun's death was led by Chiang Kai-shek. Kellogg offered to negotiate with a delegation made up of representatives from both parties. But since the proposal clearly had no appeal to either side, negotiations had to wait until China had something approximating a government.

Over the next two years Chiang Kai-shek made the Guomindong a legitimate candidate for recognition by winning military victories against warlord armies and occupying Nanjing (Nanking) and Shanghai. He also purged the communists from Guomindong ranks, sent his Soviet advisers home, and forged an alliance with China's conservative classes. Finally, he married the Wellesley-educated Soong Mei-ling. Madam Chiang exerted a strong pro-American influence on her husband, causing him to adopt an increasingly friendly attitude toward the United States. Where once Washington had denounced Chiang as "the Red General," he thus succeeded in transforming himself into a "moderate," someone the West could do business with. Secretary Kellogg then presented Chiang with what he most wanted, diplomatic recognition and international respectability. Britain quickly followed suit.

## THE MANCHURIAN INCIDENT

During the early years of the 1920s, Japan's leaders had little reason to question their decision to cooperate with the Western powers. Charles Evans Hughes took a pro-Japanese position regarding developments in China. And throughout the decade the United States remained Japan's best foreign market, absorbing 40 percent of its exports.

But in the middle of the decade, Japanese-American relations began to deteriorate. In 1924, Hughes's strong objections notwithstanding, Congress enacted new immigration legislation that excluded Orientals from coming to the United States. The effect of this blatant assertion of race inequality was to weaken the hand of Japan's pro-Western civilian leaders while strengthening the militarists and chauvinists who argued that the Western powers would never accept Japan as an equal and advocated greater aggressiveness in China as the best means of securing Japan's interests there.

Relations grew worse after Kellogg took over the State Department. His pro-Chinese attitudes were disturbing to the Japanese, and his decision to recognize Chiang's government was a serious blow. Chiang, after all, represented a burgeoning Chinese nationalism that threatened Japan's vital interests in Manchuria.

The Japanese had been active developing southern Manchuria for a quarter-century by 1928. Their holdings in the region were more than extensive. They dug coal, manufactured steel, grew soybeans, and controlled banks and railroads. They had a permanent bureaucracy in place to manage their various interests and a well-trained army there to defend them. No Japanese government would willingly have surrendered these interests, which constituted the diadem of the Japanese empire.

And yet that was precisely the nature of the threat posed by the advance of Chinese nationalism. Encouraged by the Guomindong, local Chinese inhabitants held anti-Japanese demonstrations that frequently turned ugly, boycotted Japanese goods, and regularly harassed Japanese nationals living in Manchuria. By the early 1930s elements within the Japanese military had grown weary of their government's refusal to use force in response to the Chinese nationalist challenge. They were equally displeased with the government's domestic policies, which they blamed for leading the nation into the trough of the depression. To many in the military, especially younger officers who frequently came from poor peasant backgrounds, it seemed clear that Japan's domestic and foreign problems stemmed from the same cause. A government controlled by giant corporate interests would do nothing to resolve Japan's domestic economic problems because it could only do so at the expense of the rich. Nor would it defend Japan's honor in Manchuria because military action would disrupt the Manchurian economy, reducing profits. Reformers at home, the younger officers, a powerful force in the Japanese military, called their countrymen to duty and honor.

In the summer of 1931 the Japanese army, acting independently of the government in Tokyo but with the knowledge of the Army General Staff, made plans to secure Manchuria and in the process punish the "Chinese brigands" for their many provocations. On the night of September 18–19, following an alleged sabotage attack on a section of track on the Japanese-owned South Manchurian Railroad, the army swung into action, determined to seize all of Manchuria.

In Tokyo, Prime Minister Reijiro Wakatsuki and his foreign minister, Kujūrō Shidehara, reacted with shock and chagrin but were in no position to repudiate the army's action. Manchuria was just as important to the government as it was to the army. To have withdrawn the troops, even if that had been possible, would have been read as a sign of weakness and encouraged the Chinese to press harder. Moreover, the civilian government had no power to control the army since Japan's curious constitutional structure made the army chief of staff responsible only to the emperor.

European reaction to the Manchurian crisis ranged from outright support for the Japanese to a cautious attitude of watchful waiting. The British, for example, took the position that the Chinese had it coming. Thus the *London Daily Telegraph* reminded its readers that "the right of a government to protect its interests against barbarism and anarchy is a well recognized one." The *Times* of London agreed, suggesting that since the Chinese seemed unable to protect the lives and property of foreigners, somebody had to do it. And that somebody was Japan.[16]

At the time of the Manchurian crisis, Herbert Hoover was in the third year of this presidency and Henry L. Stimson, a protégé of Elihu Root, was the secretary of state. Stimson, who was quite disturbed by Far Eastern developments, decided for the moment to do nothing. He knew the Japanese army had acted independently and hoped that the civilian government in Tokyo would regain control of the situation. "My problem," he wrote, "is to let the Japanese know we are watching them and at the same time to do it in a way that will help Shidehara, who is on the right side." But Stimson hoped in vain. In December the Wakatsuki government gave way to a new regime controlled by the military, and the Japanese renewed their offensive in Manchuria. The secretary was in despair, for in his judgment the situation was "in the hands of virtually mad dogs."[17]

Stimson believed that with Tokyo walking all over the Washington agreements, the United States had to "take a firm ground and aggressive stand toward Japan." But President Hoover refused to go too far, fearing that if Tokyo called an American bluff he would be humiliated. The United States, he insisted, should confine itself to some sort of moral statement.

That was where matters stood in January 1932, when the Japanese completed the conquest of Manchuria. At that point, Stimson later wrote, he thought the time had come to do something. Of course, given the president's pacifist bent, there were not many options. Nevertheless, on Sunday, January 3, Stimson penned a note to be delivered to the Japanese and Chinese governments. This note, which came to be known as the Stimson Doctrine, was a reiteration of the nonrecognition formula first employed by the Wilson administration in 1915 during the crisis over the Twenty-One Demands.

> The United States, Stimson wrote, would refuse to recognize any situation de facto . . . or any treaty or agreement entered into between those governments, . . . which may impair the treaty rights of the United States or its citizens in China, including those which relate to the sovereignty, the independence, or the territorial and administrative integrity of the Republic of China, commonly known as the open-door policy.

Nor would the United States recognize any changes in the Far Eastern situation achieved through the use of force.[18]

The Stimson Doctrine was an ill-advised expression of the secretary's frustration. For one thing, he acted without consulting Britain and France, the other powers with significant Far Eastern interests. Had he done so he would have learned that neither country was willing to support him. In fact, two days after Stimson made his announcement London undermined any effect his note might have had by issuing a terse statement indicating that it was confident Japan was acting in defense of the open door in Manchuria. Worse, the Japanese paid no heed, continuing with plans for the transformation of Manchuria into the new puppet state of Manchukuo with Henry Pu Yi, the heir apparent to the Manchu dynasty, as head of state.

Japan had violated the Nine-Power and Four-Power treaties and gotten away with it. In the Far East, as in Europe, the Republican peace structure lay in ruins. But Stimson did not think that would be the end of it by any means. He saw an issue "shaping up . . . between two great theories of civilization" and thought it "almost impossible that there should not be an armed clash between" the two sometime soon.[19]

## RETREAT FROM THE ROOSEVELT COROLLARY

Theodore Roosevelt laid the foundation for American dominance in the Caribbean and Central America by proclaiming the Roosevelt Corollary to the Monroe Doctrine. In the years that followed, Washington intervened militarily in the region many times either to protect American lives and property or to forestall possible foreign intervention. During these same years, emboldened by the promise of military protection for their interests, American corporations, including such giants as United Fruit and General Electric, invested heavily in the region.

The Harding administration had no intention of abandoning the economic empire that American corporations had developed in Central America and the Caribbean. At the same time, World War I appeared to have eliminated the need for frequent interventions by ending foreign threats to American hegemony there. Moreover, policy makers realized that past interventions had created an unfavorable climate of opinion throughout Latin America, where it was generally assumed that Washington was using the Monroe Doctrine for its own imperialistic purposes.

Convinced that interventionism was bad not only for America's reputation but for business as well, Hughes hoped to improve Washington's negative image among Latin Americans by reducing America's military presence in the Caribbean region and avoiding future interventions if possible. He got off to a fast start with the 1921 ratification of the Treaty of Bogotá which granted Colombia $25 million in exchange for its recognition of the Republic of Panama. Though the treaty contained no overt apology for the Roosevelt administration's involvement in the Panamanian revolution, the payment came as close as a proud nation could to an admission of guilt. Hughes also set in motion a plan to withdraw American forces from the Dominican Republic. After elections were held there in 1924, the protectorate was abandoned. Only the customs receivership remained where once the entire country had been governed by the United States Navy. Hughes also intended to withdraw from Haiti. But he had to abandon the idea when it became clear that if the United States did pull out, the country would quickly dissolve into anarchy.

Though Hughes hoped to avoid brandishing the "Big Stick" in Latin America, he did not hesitate to do so when circumstances seemed to require it. Thus in 1923, when civil war broke out in Honduras, the administration dispatched a detachment of marines to protect American lives and property there and end the violence. Still, it was intervention with a difference, for in this case the State Department dispatched a Latin American expert, Sumner Welles, to mediate among the conflicting factions. As soon as peace had been restored and a neutral figure elevated to the Honduran presidency, the marines withdrew.

In 1924 Hughes had reason to be pleased. His policy to that point had been a moderate success. But the two greatest tests of America's new Latin American policy lay ahead in Mexico and Nicaragua.

## RESOLVING THE DISPUTE WITH MEXICO

The issues raised by the Mexican Revolution continued to trouble Mexican-American relations in the interwar years. Claims for damages sustained by American nationals in Mexico during the course of the revolutionary turmoil went unpaid. More important, under Article 27 of the Mexican Constitution of 1917, the government of Alvaro Obregón sought to nationalize the land, oil, and mineral resources sold to foreigners during the regime of Porfirio Díaz (1876–1911). Considering the large American landholdings in Mexico and the fact that American oil companies controlled 60 percent of Mexico's known oil reserves, the Mexican challenge was taken seriously in Washington.

Secretary Hughes responded to this threat of nationalization by withholding recognition and refusing to approve loans to the Obregón government. The Mexican president thus found himself in a difficult situation. Mexico's only hope of fulfilling the promise of its revolution lay in regaining control of its natural resources. On the other hand, Obregón could not afford to do without American recognition, since it meant international legitimacy and, just as important, opened the way for the negotiation of desperately needed development loans. And Hughes was adamant on the subject of loans. When Blair and Company asked about making a $12 million loan to Mexico in early 1923, he hit the ceiling, refusing even to discuss the matter. In his view, he noted angrily, citizens had a duty to support their government and not enter into business dealings with governments that Washington refused to recognize. A few months later, when the banker, Mortimer Shiff, approached Hughes about extending a loan to Mexico, he got the same answer. Mexico was to be starved for funds until it came to terms.

Obregón promised that American holdings in Mexico would not be disturbed. But the State Department wanted a binding guarantee. Since he could not agree to a treaty of that nature without admitting publicly that he had mortgaged the social purposes of the revolution to American corporations, Obregón did the next best thing. He had the Mexican Supreme Court hand down a decision which held that so long as foreign companies had taken some "positive act" to develop their claims prior to 1917, the date the Constitution went into effect, their holdings would be secure.[20]

The Mexican doctrine of "positive acts" was only the first in a series of concessions that Hughes demanded. At the Bucareli conference (named after the street in Mexico City where the conference was held) a settlement was finally worked out. The Mexicans agreed to pay for expropriated properties and as yet undeveloped oil rights. A mixed claims commission made up of representatives from both countries was established to hear complaints from Americans who believed they had not been provided with fair compensation. And perhaps most important, Obregón reiterated his earlier commitment to the positive acts doctrine. Satisfied with the Bucareli Agreement, the United States then recognized the Obregón government on August 31, 1923.

That should have been the end of Washington's differences with Mexico. But in 1924, Plutarco Calles, who succeeded Obregón as president, tried to expand Mexico's right to nationalize foreign holdings. He approached this delicate problem by having the Mexican Congress enact legislation limiting the possession of oil properties acquired by foreigners before 1917 to fifty years. Surely, Calles thought, fifty years would be enough time for the American companies to exploit their claims. At the same time it would enable him to reassert Mexico's right of expropriation.

But Calles misunderstood the problem. In the first place, oil company executives argued, if the Mexicans were allowed to limit their claims to fifty years, what was to stop them from reducing the term to five or ten years at some future time? Moreover, the oilmen feared the effect of the Mexican precedent elsewhere. If Mexico could nationalize its oil, was the same true for other countries where Americans had oil properties?

Calles's attack on American oil interests in Mexico infuriated conservatives, who equated nationalization with Bolshevism. By the end of 1926 certain elements of the conservative press were uttering dark warnings about the Bolshevik menace to Latin America. The *Philadelphia Public Ledger* claimed that "Central and South American countries are being flooded with Bolshevist propaganda in a manner that would point to Mexico City as the Soviet base in the Western Hemisphere." At the same time the *New York Commercial Bulletin*, a business journal, charged that "the present government of Mexico is directed from and dominated by Soviet Russia" and that the ongoing revolution in nearby Nicaragua was "inspired from Russia and directed from Mexico." The *New York Herald Tribune*, also evidently concerned by the Bolshevik threat, remarked menacingly that the Panama Canal and America's rights to a canal across Nicaragua "are national assets of vast importance, which the Bolshevization of Nicaragua would endanger. We cannot lightly tolerate intrigues against them, countenanced or participated in by any government."[21]

The administration, evidently seeking to prepare the ground for some sort of action against Mexico as the source of unrest in Central America, encouraged the hysteria. First, President Coolidge sent a message to Congress claiming to have "conclusive evidence" of large scale arms shipments from Mexico to rebel forces in Nicaragua. He warned that if the revolution there continued "American business interests in Nicaragua will be very seriously affected if not destroyed" and said that national interests in the region, especially the Panama Canal and the Nicaraguan Canal route which had been acquired by treaty in 1914, "place us in a position of peculiar responsibility." In a direct reference to Mexico he said that the United States could not "view with indifference" continued instability in Nicaragua or any other Central American state, "especially if such a state of affairs is contributed to or brought about by outside influences or by any foreign power." He also announced his intention of taking action "to insure the adequate protection of all American interests in Nicaragua, whether they be endangered by internal strife or by outside interference in the affairs of that republic."[22]

Two days after the president's dramatic announcement, Secretary of State Kellogg attempted to fuel the hysteria by sending a memorandum to Congress on "Bolshevist Aims and Policies in Mexico and Latin America." In it he charged that the Bolsheviks had "set up as one of their fundamental tasks the destruction of what they term American imperialism as a necessary prerequisite to the successful development of the international revolutionary movement in the New World."[23]

Administration efforts notwithstanding, it turned out to be the wrong moment for military intervention in Latin America. Even members of the President's own party attacked him. Senator William King of Utah denounced the administration's policies in Mexico and Central America as "a series of colossal blunders." And Senator William E. Borah, the powerful Chairman of the Senate Foreign Relations Committee, called for peace and the abandonment of the use of force. If the United States would "try friendly relations; seek to establish amity; seek to get in touch with the masses, with the people themselves," then, he insisted, it could "establish a policy in Central America which will protect our interest and respect our rights"[24] The overwhelming majority of the nation's newspapers as well as many influential peace groups stood with King and Borah against the administration. War was out of fashion anyway in 1926. But a war in defense of "Big Oil" in the wake of the Teapot Dome scandal was out of the question.

At the urging of Thomas Lamont, President Coolidge recalled the ambassador to Mexico, James R. Sheffield, replacing him with Dwight Morrow, one of Lamont's partners at J. P. Morgan and Company. A master of public relations, Morrow purchased a home in Cuernavaca, commissioned Diego Rivera to paint murals in the town celebrating the Mexican Revolution, and brought his famous son-in-law, Charles Lindbergh to Mexico on a goodwill mission. An equally effective diplomat, Morrow quickly won the trust and friendship of President Calles. Morrow's work paid off in 1928, when Mexico agreed to return to the doctrine of positive acts established five years before.

The arrangement worked out between Morrow and Calles left American oil company executives embittered. Still living in the age of Theodore Roosevelt, they seem to have expected nothing less than military action in support of their most extreme claims. But those days were over. And without any further support from the State Department, they were required to take what they could get.

Calvin Coolidge and Frank B. Kellogg were roundly criticized for their policies toward both Nicaragua and Mexico in 1926 and 1927.

BABES IN THE NICARAGUAN WOOD.

## THE NICARAGUAN CIVIL WAR

In August 1925, following national elections in Nicaragua, the marine contingent that had for so long been stationed there was withdrawn. Within a year, however, forty-five hundred marines returned to play a new role. A bloody civil war had broken out between the pro-American government of Adolfo Díaz and Juan B. Sacasa's Liberal party, which was supported by Mexico. The marines had gone there not simply to protect American lives and property but to help Díaz win a military victory. In 1927, however, the administration reacted to the storm of criticism its Mexican policy produced by pursuing a new conciliatory course in Nicaragua as well. President Coolidge sent Henry L. Stimson as his personal representative to work out a compromise between Nicaragua's warring factions.

Stimson got off to a fast start. The Truce of Tipitapa left the pro-American president, Adolfo Díaz, at the head of an interim coalition government with new elections (to be supervised by the marines) scheduled for 1928. This early success notwithstanding, Stimson was convinced that the coming elections would solve nothing and that the party that won power would seek to secure it by force, leaving the "outs" with no alternative but to resort to force at some later time. That was how politics worked in Nicaragua. And that, Stimson was certain, was why the country was in a constant state of turmoil.

Stimson believed that the way to achieve political stability in Nicaragua was to educate the Nicaraguans to the virtues of free, democratic elections. In his judgment, this was the only way to avoid the depressing cycle of coup and countercoup that served as a form of politics in that unhappy country.

Acting on Stimson's advice, the administration kept the marines in Nicaragua to maintain order while the State Department attempted to demonstrate to the people there the virtues of democratic politics. The marines were also responsible for training a nonpartisan constabulary. The Guardia Nacional, like the American military, was to be above politics and committed to the preservation of stability and order no matter who held power.

Washington's best efforts notwithstanding, Nicaragua's elites remained unconvinced of the merits of a democratic political system. During the years of the American occupation both major parties held power at one time or another. And each used every means at its disposal to secure itself in power. The country's indigenous political culture was too deeply rooted to be changed.

Nor were the marines able to preserve order. General Augusto Sandino, one of the leaders of Nicaragua's Liberal party, refused to accept the terms of the Truce of Tipitapa. Instead, he and a few hundred followers rode north to the mountains that straddle the Nicaraguan-Honduran border, from where they conducted a hit-and-run guerrilla war against the Yankee imperialists. The marine force, which at one time ran to fifty-eight hundred supported by a half-dozen biplanes, chased Sandino and his followers through the jungles and hills of Nicaragua for five years but never caught up with them. To the Americans, Sandino was a bandit who butchered innocent Americans. But to many Latin Americans, he was a heroic symbol of resistance to American imperialism.

By 1931, the Hoover administration was so fed up with this ill-conceived involvement in Nicaragua that it began preparing to withdraw the marines. The war they were fighting made Americans anathema throughout Nicaragua, and the costs of the adventure, as well as lengthening casualty lists, were increasingly unpopular at home. Moreover, it was embarrassing to the State Department to have marines chasing about in the jungles of Nicaragua where they often killed noncombatants while it was denouncing the Japanese for doing the same thing, albeit on a larger scale, in Manchuria.

Augusto Sandino (center) led a body of irregulars against the American presence in
Nicaragua. American officials viewed him as nothing more than a murdering bandit, but
to millions of Latin Americans he was a valiant opponent of Yankee imperialism.

The marine withdrawal, which was completed in 1933, was certainly for the
best since by that time the United States was so hated throughout Nicaragua
that American lives and property were safer there without them.

From the beginning, Augusto Sandino had promised that as soon as
the Americans left he would open negotiations with the government in
Managua. True to his word, he did just that, opening talks with President
Sacasa in 1934. Sandino had just left one of these negotiating sessions when
he was waylaid, dragged from his car, and murdered on the orders of
Anastasio Somoza, head of the Guardia Nacional.

Hughes and Stimson had envisioned a constabulary that would be
above politics. But given Nicaragua's political culture, it was inevitable that
it should develop into an essentially political organization. And it did,
becoming the instrument Somoza and his sons used to seize and hold power
in Nicaragua from 1936 until the 1978 Sandinista Revolution. Thus, curiously,
the United States did achieve one of its goals—forty years of stability in
Nicaragua. But at a terrible cost to the Nicaraguan people.

# ENDNOTES

1. Boise Penrose, quoted in William E. Leuchtenburg, *The Perils of Prosperity, 1914–1932* (Chicago: University of Chicago Press, 1958), p. 88; H. L. Mencken, quoted in Robert K. Murray, *The Harding Era: Warren G. Harding and His Administration* (Minneapolis: University of Minnesota Press, 1969), p. 122.

2. Charles Evans Hughes, quoted in Herbert Feis, *The Diplomacy of the Dollar* (New York: W. W. Norton, 1966), p. 9. See also Warren Cohen, *Empire without Tears: America's Foreign Relations, 1921–1933* (New York: Alfred A. Knopf, 1987), pp. 18–44.

3. State Department circular, quoted in Feis, *Diplomacy of the Dollar*, pp. 9–11.

4. James Simpson, quoted in *Nation*, December 14, 1921, p. 692; George Wickersham, quoted in Melvyn P. Leffler, *The Elusive Quest: America's Pursuit of European Stability and French Security, 1919–1933* (Chapel Hill, N.C.: University of North Carolina Press, 1979), p. 41.

5. Herbert Hoover, quoted in William Appleman Williams, *The Tragedy of American Diplomacy* 2d ed. (New York: Dell, 1972), p. 137; Hughes, quoted in Leffler, *Elusive Quest*, p. 82.

6. Warren G. Harding, quoted in *Leffler, Elusive Quest*, p. 68.

7. David Lloyd George and *Outlook*, both quoted in *Literary Digest*, January 27, 1923, p. 19.

8. William E. Borah and John Sharp Williams, both quoted in *ibid.*, p. 11. See also Cohen, *Empire without Tears*, p. 92.

9. Hughes to the chargé in France, October 23, 1923, *Foreign Relations of the United States, 1923* (Washington, D.C.: 1938), II, 83.

10. Thomas Lamont, quoted in Stephen A. Schuker, *The End of French Predominance in Europe* (Chapel Hill, N.C.: University of North Carolina Press, 1976), p. 316.

11. Joan Hoff Wilson, *American Business and Foreign Policy 1920–1933*, (Lexington, Ky.: University of Kentucky Press, 1971), p. 122.

12. Herbert Hoover, quoted in Wilson, *American Business and Foreign Policy*, p. 40.

13. Oswald Garrison Villard, quoted in *Nation*, November 23, 1921, p. 589.

14. Quoted in *Nation*, November 30, 1921, p. 609.

15. Nathanael Pfeffer quoted in *Nation*, December 21, 1921, p. 724; Nine-Power Treaty, quoted in Akira Iriye, *After Imperialism: The Search for a New Order in the Far East, 1921–1931* (New York: Atheneum, 1973), pp. 18–19. See also Arnold A. Offner, *The Origins of the Second World War: American Foreign Policy and World Politics, 1917–1941* (New York: Praeger, 1975), pp. 81–85.

16. *London Daily Telegraph* and *London Times*, quoted in Armin Rappaport, *Henry L. Stimson and Japan, 1931–1933* (Chicago: University of Chicago Press, 1963), p. 18.

17. Henry L. Stimson, quoted in Richard N. Current, "The Stimson Doctrine and the Hoover Doctrine," *American Historical Review*, 19, no. 3 (April 1954), p. 515; Stimson, quoted in Henry L. Stimson and McGeorge Bundy, *On Active Service in Peace and War* (New York: Harper and Brothers, 1947), p. 232.

18. Stimson and Bundy, *On Active Service*, pp. 235–36.

19. Stimson, quoted in Current, "Stimson Doctrine," p. 516.

20. Mexican Supreme Court, quoted in Howard F. Cline, *The United States and Mexico* (New York: Atheneum, 1963), pp. 206–7.

21. *Philadelphia Public Ledger, New York Commercial Bulletin*, and *New York Herald Tribune*, all quoted in *Literary Digest*, December 4, 1926, p. 14.

22. Calvin Coolidge, speech to Congress, January 10, 1927, *Foreign Relations of the United States, 1927* (Washington, D.C., 1942), III, pp. 294–98.

23. Frank B. Kellogg, quoted in Bryce Wood, *The Making of the Good Neighbor Policy* (New York: Columbia University Press, 1961), p. 20.

24. William King, quoted in *Literary Digest*, January 8, 1927, p. 13; William E. Borah, quoted in *Literary Digest*, January 29, 1927, p. 6.

# 21

# NEW DEAL DIPLOMACY, 1933–1939

GOOD NEIGHBORS?

Jan 6, 1940

With war on the horizon, a great many Americans wondered just where the neighbors to the south would stand when the fighting actually began.

When Franklin Delano Roosevelt won the Democratic party's nomination for the presidency in 1932, his running mate, Texas's John Nance Garner quipped, "All you have to do is stay alive until election day."[1] He was right. There was never any doubt that the charming, charismatic Roosevelt would win. The depression had destroyed Herbert Hoover's credibility. There had been too much talk about prosperity being just around the corner and too little concern for the needs of common people in distress.

The new president was a "gold-plated" member of the "eastern establishment." Reared in a loving environment, the only son of Sara Delano and James Roosevelt, FDR had it all. After attending the exclusive Groton school, he went to Harvard, where, true to his social class, he earned mediocre grades. Roosevelt then took a law degree at Columbia University and in 1910 jumped into politics. A Democrat, he rose quickly from the New York State Senate to the periphery of power as an assistant secretary of the navy in the Wilson administration. In 1920 Roosevelt, by this time a rising young star in the Democratic party, ran for vice-president on the ticket with Ohio's Governor James M. Cox.

Not long after Roosevelt's election defeat, personal disaster struck. He contracted polio; his legs were permanently paralyzed. But encouraged by his wife Eleanor and his friend and political adviser Louis Howe, he fought back. In 1928 he was elected governor of New York. Four years and a few months later he stood on the steps of the Capitol building, his legs held rigid in steel braces, to take the oath of office as president of the United States.

## LATIN AMERICA'S NEW DEAL

Roosevelt inherited a relationship with the Latin American republics that was much improved over the bleak days of the mid-1920s. Herbert Hoover withdrew the marines from Nicaragua and resisted the temptation to intervene elsewhere, even when chaotic conditions threatened American interests, as they did in Haiti, Panama, and most seriously Cuba, where Americans had more than $1 billion invested. He also made it clear to those Americans with Latin American investments that the marines were no longer at their beck and call. Those who chose to invest abroad would have to understand that they were subject to the laws of the country in which they

The marines, who chased Augusto Sandino through the mountainous country of northern Nicaragua for years, captured his flag but never came close to taking the man.

invested. If their holdings were threatened, they could count on help only after they had exhausted all legal remedies available to them in the country in question and only if Washington believed they had been treated unfairly.

If it can be said that Herbert Hoover adopted the attitude of a "good neighbor," it was Franklin Roosevelt who transformed that attitude into a policy. Well before he moved into the White House, FDR was on record calling for a new approach to Latin American relations. In an article published in *Foreign Affairs* in 1928, he denounced the Nicaraguan invasion and called for an end to unilateral "intervention by us in the internal affairs of other nations." Five years later, in his first inaugural address, he reiterated that point saying, "I would dedicate this nation to the policy of the good neighbor—the neighbor who resolutely respects himself and because he does so respects the rights of others—the neighbor who respects his obligations and respects the sanctity of his agreements in and with a world of neighbors."[2]

Before Roosevelt had an opportunity to put his neighborly rhetoric into practice, he was confronted with a crisis in Cuba that raised serious questions throughout Latin America about his true intentions. At the time Cuba was governed by Gerardo Machado, a dictator who practiced a form of state terrorism that involved the late night knock on the door, mysterious disappearances, the imprisonment and torture of political enemies, and the unofficially sanctioned operations of death squads. Machado's well-organized opponents also practiced terrorism, assassinating government officials and planting bombs in government buildings.

By the time Roosevelt took the oath of office Cuba was in a state of near-anarchy. As Secretary of State Cordell Hull recalled:

> Popular resentment against the brutal dictatorship of General Machado . . . was growing acute. It was becoming evident that either Machado would resign or a revolution would force him out. Bomb explosions and shootings were occurring in Havana, sugar mills and cane fields were being burned, schools were closing, and guerrilla bands . . . were operating in the hills. Political exiles streamed to the United States. Added to the political unrest was economic distress, partly caused by high United States tariffs. It was a hair-trigger situation.[3]

The president quickly decided that Machado would have to go, for if the Cuban crisis persisted he believed he would be forced to use troops to end the chaos. American investments in Cuba had to be protected.

FDR sent his friend and former school chum, Undersecretary of State Sumner Welles, as ambassador to Cuba to see what could be done. By the time Welles arrived in Havana, the Cuban economy, which depended on the sale of sugar in the American market, was in a shambles. Not only had the world price of sugar tumbled, the Smoot-Hawley tariff had reduced Cuba's share of the American market by 50 percent. Welles was prepared to offer the Cubans a reciprocity agreement that promised them a larger share of the American sugar market. This agreement, he believed, would restore the Cuban economy and reduce political activism on the island. It would have the additional benefit of providing the United States with a stranglehold on the Cuban market. In return, Welles wanted the opposing sides in Cuba to allow him to mediate a settlement. He intended to use that power to remove Machado and establish a new government more acceptable to the United States.

When attempts at a mediated settlement failed, Welles set out to drive Machado from power. The Cuban dictator struggled to save himself. But the pressure Welles exerted, especially the influence he wielded with the officer corps of the Cuban army, finally left him no choice but to go into exile.

After Machado's departure, a new government headed by Cárlos Manuel de Céspedes took power in Havana. In Washington, Welles was applauded for a job well done. But both Welles and his superiors were under the misapprehension that a change of government and the promise of a reciprocity agreement would lead to a more stable Cuba. They failed to perceive that the cruel mixture of Machado's repression, the economic crisis brought on by the depression and American tariff policy had laid the foundation for a social revolution. The Céspedes regime promised nothing new or better for the Cuban people. Nothing had really changed but the names on the doors of government offices. The Cuban economy remained a ruin, and poverty was endemic.

Within a month Céspedes was gone, driven from power by the rank-and-file of the Cuban army. Led by Sergeant Fulgencio Batista and aided by student radicals from Havana University, the soldiers mutinied against their officers and established a new government headed by a social democrat and former biology professor, Ramón Grau San Martín. Batista became the new head of Cuba's army and the most powerful man on the island.

The stunned Welles denounced the "theories" of the new Cuban Junta as "frankly communistic."[4] Nothing could have been further from the truth. If anything Grau was a Cuban version of FDR himself. Indeed, many of the reforms he attempted during his four months in power were only somewhat more liberal than those Roosevelt himself sponsored during the Second New Deal.

In spite of the reformist nature of the new Cuban government, Welles called on Washington to send troops. FDR wanted no part of that. But he did exert pressure on Grau's government, first by refusing to extend diplomatic recognition and second by dispatching some thirty warships, including the thirty-two-thousand-ton battleship *Mississippi* to Cuban waters.

Meanwhile Welles made the facts of life clear to Batista. Cuba's economic recovery depended on gaining an expanded share of the American sugar market. But the United States would never agree to make that concession so long as Grau remained in power. Economic problems and the potential for political chaos would therefore continue until a government acceptable to the United States was in place.

Batista was a pragmatist. He knew that Grau could not last without Washington's recognition. And the former sergeant was determined to survive even if the nascent social revolution he had helped create did not. And so he came to an understanding with Carlos Mendieta, an opposition leader in good standing with Washington. Like Machado before him, Grau was forced into exile, and Batista elevated Mendieta to the presidency. But it was Batista who ruled in Cuba.

Within five days the Mendieta government won American recognition and a great deal more. In 1934, Washington abrogated the Platt Amendment, surrendering the right to intervene in Cuba. In the same year Washington signed a reciprocal trade treaty with Havana that gave Cuban sugar special advantages in the American market. Thanks to these and other concessions, Fulgencio Batista, "the New Machado," remained the power in Cuba until 1959.

## MONTEVIDEO AND BUENOS AIRES

The embarrassing Cuban involvement only made it seem that much more important to the president to transform the "good neighborly" rhetoric of his first inaugural into believable policy. At the seventh inter-American conference held in Montevideo, Uruguay, Secretary Hull took the first step when he told the assembled delegates that "no government need fear any intervention on the part of the United States under the Roosevelt Administration." Hull also did what Charles Evans Hughes had refused to do at the 1928 Havana conference, committing the United States to the principle that no "state has the right to intervene in the internal or external affairs of another." The secretary held back on only a single point, insisting that the United States, like all other nations, retained the right to intervene to protect the lives and property of its citizens.[5]

In 1936 Roosevelt himself traveled to Buenos Aires on board the cruiser *Indianapolis* for the opening of the eighth inter-American conference. It was a grand gesture and clearly appreciated by all Latin America. The president of Argentina, most members of the government and legislature, and thousands of onlookers gathered at the harbor to greet him. Hull thought, "Probably no distinguished visitor to Argentina ever received so great a welcome."[6]

Until that time the Roosevelt administration had insisted that in spite of commitments made at Montevideo, there were certain extreme circumstances in which international law justified military intervention. But at Buenos Aires, Hull abandoned even this claim. The United States at last joined with other western hemispheric nations in its complete commitment to the principle of nonintervention.

By 1936, Roosevelt had also taken a number of other steps to allay Latin American suspicions. Having already abrogated the Platt Amendment, he withdrew the last contingent of troops from Haiti, closed down the customs receivership in the Dominican Republic, and renounced the right

Washington had previously claimed to intervene in Panama for the protection of the canal.

At the same time the administration extended its definition of the good neighbor to include the principle of noninterference in the internal political affairs of Latin American nations. Washington moved in this direction because its recent Cuban involvement had done it no good in the eyes of most Latin Americans and because the personal relationship that existed between the American ambassador in Nicaragua, Arthur Bliss Lane, and Anastasio Somoza, led many to conclude that the Roosevelt administration had been involved in the plot to assassinate Augusto Sandino. Hull, who was especially sensitive with regard to Nicaragua, specifically warned Lane's replacement in Managua that he was to avoid any semblance of interference, "even though such interference is requested or suggested by the Nicaraguans."[7]

## THE LATIN AMERICAN CHALLENGE

Roosevelt and Hull had by 1936 done a great deal to improve United States–Latin American relations. Still, many Latin Americans did not believe that Washington had gone far enough. They would not be satisfied until the great corporations—the banks, the mining enterprises, and the oil companies—that tied them to the American economy had been driven from their privileged positions in Latin American life. Considering the fact that the good neighbor policy seemed to deny Washington many of the weapons it had previously used to advance American economic interests in the hemisphere, it is not surprising that in the later years of the 1930s some Latin Americans tested the president's commitment.

On March 13, 1937, the Bolivian government announced that it was expropriating the holdings of the Standard Oil Company of New Jersey and that it was not prepared to offer compensation. The State Department did not dispute Bolivia's right of expropriation. But it did insist that the company, which claimed its holdings were worth $17 million, had a right to just compensation. La Paz, however, proved unmovable on the subject.

Bolivia's obstinacy frustrated Hull, who insisted that neighborliness had to be reciprocal and that all sides had to live by agreed-on and reasonable rules of conduct if the policy was to remain unchanged. Still, for three years he confined himself to peaceful efforts aimed at bringing about a settlement. Resorting to tactics the Republicans had used during the 1920s, he discouraged loans to Bolivia and refused to provide other forms of assistance La Paz needed. He also discouraged other American states from developing Bolivian oil. The pressure hurt the Bolivians. But the expropriation was so popular, and the Bolivian political situation so unstable, that the government did not feel secure enough to risk offering compensation to Standard Oil.

In July 1941, following the discovery of a German-supported plot to overthrow the Bolivian government, Washington abandoned the stick in favor of the carrot. The administration offered military assistance and dangled the possibility of a large development loan before La Paz. The Second World War, which brought with it the possibility of significant economic aid, proved more than the Bolivians could resist. And so in January 1942, a deal was struck. The Standard Oil Company would receive $1.5 million in Bolivian government bonds for its former holdings. The Bolivians won a $25 million economic development loan. And Washington ended a dispute that interfered with its push for hemispheric solidarity.

A more serious test of the good neighbor policy came on March 18, 1938, when President Lázaro Cárdenas of Mexico expropriated the holdings of the Dutch, British, and American oil companies there. Cárdenas, who at one time or another fought with Emiliano Zapata, Alvaro Obregón, Francisco Villa, and finally Venustiano Carranza and Plutarco Calles, revitalized Mexico's faltering revolutionary purposes in the 1930s. He expropriated foreign landholdings, encouraged agricultural collectives, built modern schools to reduce the power of a reactionary church, encouraged the development of workers'cooperatives, and was the patron of the powerful petroleum workers union.

In late 1936 the petroleum workers demanded a 27 percent wage hike from the foreign-owned oil companies operating in Mexico. The companies refused, and the issue landed in the courts. Early in 1938, after the Mexican Supreme Court held in favor of the workers, the companies agreed to a wage increase totaling 24 million pesos. President Cárdenas, whose control over the workers was undisputed, promised the oilmen that the offer would be accepted by the union. For a moment it appeared that the issue had been resolved. But the companies then demanded that Cárdenas put his commitment in writing. They wanted a notarized agreement. The president refused. He had given his word, and it had been judged insufficient. Meanwhile, Mexico's Federal Board of Arbitration and Conciliation gave the oil companies until March 15, 1938, to comply with the court decision on wages. When the companies refused to budge, Cárdenas nationalized their holdings.

The oilmen appealed to the State Department for support, claiming that the value of their subsoil rights (oil still in the ground) and the investments they had made in Mexico amounted to $260 million. But the State Department was in no mood to ride to the rescue. In early notes to the Mexican minister of foreign affairs, Secretary Hull made it clear that he did not support the companies' claim to compensation for subsoil rights (about $200 million of the total claim). He also admitted that Mexico City had every right to expropriate foreign holdings, asking only that the companies be paid just compensation. At the same time, Hull urged the companies to undertake direct negotiations with Cárdenas.

For more than two years the expropriation issue remained unresolved. The oil companies used boycotts, blacklists, in short every resource at their disposal to keep Mexican oil off the international market and force Cárdenas to settle on their terms. But to no avail. Meanwhile, the administration confined itself to diplomacy and the policy of the good neighbor. It urged the oilmen to exhaust their legal options in Mexican courts and tried to persuade Cárdenas to accept arbitration.

In 1941, with Axis political activity in Mexico on the increase and Mexico's foreign trade with the Axis powers also growing, the State Department decided the time had come not only to end the dispute over oil but to place Mexican-American relations on a generally sound footing. Mexico was important politically and could not be allowed to slip away. The War and Navy departments were especially anxious to improve relations with Mexico because of its proximity to the Panama Canal and the military's need for transit, naval, and air base rights. Moreover, Mexico supplied a variety of raw materials that would be important to the United States when war came.

In August 1941, Washington endorsed a Mexican proposal for a joint commission made up of one Mexican and one American representative to establish the value of the expropriated property. If the oil companies agreed to this method of assessing their claims, the Mexican government was prepared to settle the dispute. But in spite of the extraordinary dangers and the imminence of war, the oilmen refused to go along.

In November 1941, only a few weeks before the Pearl Harbor attack, Mexico and the United States entered into a series of agreements that vastly improved their relationship. Mexico agreed to pay the claims of American landholders who had suffered expropriation. The two nations entered into a reciprocal trade agreement and a currency stabilization agreement that fixed the value of the peso to the dollar. The United States also agreed to continue to purchase large quantities of Mexican silver at the world market price and to arrange substantial loans for Mexico through the Export-Import Bank, which had been incorporated by Congress in 1933 for the purpose of extending credits to foreign countries to facilitate trade and the payment of outstanding debts.

Hull hailed the agreement as the beginning of a new era in Mexican-American relations. But the dispute over Mexico's expropriation of oil properties remained unresolved until after war actually broke out. "The advent of Pearl Harbor," Hull recalled, "placed the dispute on its right footing as simply one of the elements in a perilous world situation, and eventually the companies agreed to a settlement."[8] In the end the oilmen received $29 million in Mexican bonds for their holdings.

## DEFENDING THE HEMISPHERE

There can be no doubt that Washington's concern over the growing influence of the Axis powers in Latin America was a major consideration in the evolution of the good neighbor policy during the later 1930s. Many Latin American countries, Argentina and Mexico for example, had large German populations. Moreover, the Germans had been particularly active promoting their trade with Latin America. In 1935 alone German trade in the region increased by 47 percent and continued to grow in the following year. Unable to sell in the heavily protected American market, Latin Americans turned to Germany because no better markets were open to them.

Concerned by the growth of German trade as well as by evidence of Axis political activity in the region, Washington fought back by living up to its hard-won reputation as a good neighbor, opening its market more widely through reciprocal trade agreements, and providing economic and military aid as well as development loans through a much expanded Export-Import Bank. The package that the United States offered was a powerful inducement, which FDR used to encourage the much-sought-after hemispheric solidarity prior to Pearl Harbor.

Not long after the Munich conference in 1938, President Roosevelt proposed the creation of a defensive alliance for the nations of the Western Hemisphere. In December of that year, at the eighth Pan-American conference held in Lima, Argentina blocked the American plan. But the conference did lay the foundation for future action by agreeing on consultations in the event of outside aggression.

In late September 1939, after war had broken out in Europe, the foreign ministers of all the western hemispheric nations met in Panama at Washington's request. There they agreed on a general declaration of neutrality and on the establishment of "a Hemispheric Security Zone" of from three hundred to one thousand miles around both continents. The delegates also undertook new measures of economic cooperation designed to solve some of the problems created by the European war.

After the German victories of 1940, the foreign ministers met once again, this time to decide what to do if Germany should try to take over the Dutch and French colonies in the hemisphere. The Act of Havana reiterated the old "no transfer doctrine," (first clearly articulated in 1802 when it appeared that Spain would attempt to transfer the Louisiana Territory to France) by stipulating that, if such an attempt seemed likely, the nations of the hemisphere either jointly or unilaterally would take and hold these colonies until they could "either . . . restore the possessions to their original sovereigns when security conditions permit, or recognize their independence if they are deemed capable of self-government."[9] The foreign ministers also joined in a Declaration of Reciprocal Assistance and Cooperation, which established the basis for mutual security in the event of outside aggression.

Once the outlines of a hemispheric defense program were in place, the War Department entered into conversations with military leaders in various Latin American countries. Washington wanted bases, control of key transit routes, and access to important raw materials produced in Latin America. Although most Latin American governments refused to allow American military forces on their soil, they were willing to offer other forms of cooperation, since they found the offers of the United States too tempting to resist. The good neighbor policy, when supplemented by an increasingly profitable trade as well as cash inducements, created at least an approximation of the hemispheric solidarity Washington required.

## THE LONDON ECONOMIC CONFERENCE

Early in his administration, Roosevelt agreed to send a delegation to an international economic conference scheduled for London in June 1933. At the time America's foreign trade was down by a catastrophic 75 percent from its 1929 high. The same was true for almost all trading nations. Many international financial experts believed that this decline in world trade, which was prolonging the global economic crisis, was the result of several interrelated considerations. Some nations had departed from the gold standard, devaluing their currencies to make their exports more attractive in foreign markets. Some erected high tariff walls to protect their markets from foreign competition. Some, including the United States, did both. By 1933 currency manipulation and protectionism had become widespread. The international economic situation was further complicated by the failure of interested nations to resolve the war debt and reparations questions and by the drying up of American investment abroad, which foreign debtors had used to adjust their international trade balances.

The London conference had been called because it was widely believed that these problems could only be resolved by a general international agreement. It was also thought that if tariff walls could be lowered, price levels, which had declined by more than 30 percent in all industrial nations, would rise and the world could at last begin to dig its way out of the depression.

The head of the American delegation to the London conference was Secretary of State, Cordell Hull. A former congressman and senator from Tennessee, and a devout free trader, Hull wanted the conferees to focus their efforts on reducing tariff barriers. But Italy, France, and other nations with currencies tied to the gold standard believed that currency stabilization should come first. Stabilization, said Premier Édouard Daladier of France, was "the indispensable condition of a useful economic conference."[10]

Only a month earlier Roosevelt himself had called for currency stabilization. But in the midst of the conference he changed his mind. The president's sudden turnabout is perhaps best explained this way. Early in the New Deal, domestic policy makers concluded that by abandoning the gold standard and devaluing the dollar they could boost price levels and simultaneously make American products cheaper in the world marketplace, thus encouraging exports. Since the administration hoped to manipulate the dollar in this way, it had no interest in an international agreement that would fix its value in relation to other currencies.

Having decided that he did not want stabilization after all, Roosevelt sent assistant secretary of state Raymond Moley, a former professor of economics and an important member of the president's inner circle (dubbed the "brains trust" in the press), to London to ride herd on the delegation. Moley, who immediately stole the spotlight from Hull, became the de facto head of the delegation and in that capacity signed a largely meaningless accord by which the signatories agreed to do their best to stabilize their currencies. Even this nonbinding promise was evidently too much for Roosevelt, who promptly repudiated the surprised Moley.

Two days later, while on a cruise aboard the USS *Indianapolis*, Roosevelt lobbed a "bombshell" message across the Atlantic that broke up the conference. The president attacked the very concept of currency stabilization, stating that the United States would not enter into a stabilization agreement and that he was determined to have "the kind of dollar which a generation hence will have the same purchasing and debt paying power as the dollar we hope to obtain in the near future."[11]

The economist, John Maynard Keynes, pronounced FDR "magnificently right" for rejecting stabilization at a time when price levels were so low.[12] More recently some historians have defended the president by arguing that he did not intend to undermine the conference, only to encourage it to go on to other more important issues. But the fact remains that whether consciously or not, he killed the last attempt by the industrialized nations prior to World War II to work out their economic problems in concert.

## RECOGNIZING THE SOVIETS

Roosevelt decided even before taking the oath of office that the time had come to extend diplomatic recognition to the Soviet Union. By 1925 most of Europe had recognized Moscow. And by the early 1930s a number of important business leaders, including Reeve Schley of the Chase Manhattan Bank, the financier W. W. Atterbury, Thomas Mooney of General Motors, and Thomas Watson of IBM were urging Washington to follow suit. There were, of course, those who for ideological reasons opposed recognition. To these Roy Howard of the Scripps-Howard newspaper chain remarked, "I think the menace of Bolshevism in the United States is about as great as the menace of sunstroke in Greenland or chilblains in the Sahara."[13] For Howard as for many American businessmen the "red scare" was over. America needed trade.

Roosevelt was no doubt impressed by the fact that recognition had such widespread business support. But the idea did not appeal to him because he viewed the Soviet Union as an economic cornucopia. He was thinking more in geopolitical terms. By 1932 the Japanese had overrun Manchuria, transforming it into the puppet state of Manchukuo. Though unprepared to make binding commitments, Roosevelt hoped that the appearance of Soviet-American harmony might be enough to slow the pace of Japanese expansionism. Cordell Hull later recalled that he and the president agreed that, with the Japanese moving in the Far East and the Nazis in power in

Germany, the world was becoming an increasingly dangerous place and that the Soviet Union could be "a great help in stabilizing the situation."[14]

Moscow welcomed the opportunity to establish relations with the United States and dispatched Foreign Minister Maxim Litvinov to Washington to make the formal arrangements. Following the negotiations, which went smoothly, Litvinov was given a gala send-off at the Waldorf Astoria Hotel in New York. There, financiers and industrialists—representatives of much of the accumulated wealth of this country—listened as IBM's Thomas Watson asked all Americans to "refrain from making any criticism of the present form of Government adopted by Russia."[15]

All was euphoria in 1933. If the business community saw economic opportunities opening in the Soviet Union, liberals were pleased for political reasons. The *Nation* congratulated Roosevelt upon his "realism, courage and good sense." The *New Republic* called recognition "extremely good news" and observed that as a result "Germany and Japan are today far more completely isolated in a hostile world than before; and in both cases, such isolation is a development on the side of peace."[16]

In spite of the fine beginning, Soviet-American relations quickly soured. Moscow was concerned primarily for its security. The Japanese threatened Soviet Asia, while Adolf Hitler posed an increasing threat in the west. The Soviets hoped to coax Washington into cooperating in the face of these dangers. But Roosevelt, who was well aware of the public's strong noninterventionist sentiments, would go no further, even refusing to enter into a nonaggression pact. Nor did Moscow reap significant economic benefits from the new relationship. Soviet-American trade failed to develop as hoped, and American investors proved reluctant to invest in the Soviet Union.

If Moscow was disappointed by the results of recognition, so was Washington. In spite of agreements arrived at in 1933, the prerevolutionary Russian debt owed to American creditors remained unfunded. Moreover, in 1935 Moscow repudiated its promise not to support interference in the internal affairs of the United States by becoming the official sponsor of the seventh annual congress of the Comintern created by Lenin in 1919 to advance the cause of international Communism. Nor did closer contact with the Soviets improve American policy makers' opinion of them. William C. Bullitt, whose last diplomatic assignment had been as Woodrow Wilson's emissary to Lenin, served as Roosevelt's first ambassador to Moscow. He arrived in the Soviet capital a starry-eyed romantic, a latter-day John Reed, moved by a naive enthusiasm for the social revolution he imagined was taking place. But state terrorism, the discovery that the embassy had been penetrated by Soviet spies, and the failure of the Kremlin to live up to its commitments led him to conclude that the revolution had failed. By 1935 he was arguing that Soviet policy was influenced by only two considerations, power and ideology. Convinced of Stalin's global revolutionary purposes, he came to view the Soviet government as a dangerous, expansionist force.

Bullitt's views were characteristic of those commonly held in American policy-making circles. Still, few argued that recognition had been a mistake.

The Soviet Union, no matter what its form of government, was a powerful nation. It was therefore important to have established relations.

## THE NEW NEUTRALITY

Roosevelt understood that the desire to steer clear of European political entanglements and war, sometimes described as isolationism, was a powerful force in the America of the 1930s. But at least during his first term in office this caused him no sleepless nights. His fundamental concern was the domestic economic crisis. Moreover, like the people he represented he, too, was chary about foreign entanglements.

The public's desire to avoid a repetition of "the mistake" of 1917 grew in the first instance out of the results of the war itself. The failure of "the Great Crusade" to "make the world safe for democracy" strengthened America's traditional commitment to nonentanglement in European political affairs. That feeling was reinforced during the interwar years as many wartime assumptions came into question. In 1917, for example, it had been an article of faith that the kaiser was responsible for the war, which most Americans viewed as a contest between good and evil. As early as 1928, however, the historian Sidney B. Fay demonstrated that Germany was not the only culpable power, that all of the major European states bore a degree of responsibility.[17]

Once it was accepted that the Great War had been merely another chapter in the ongoing history of balance-of-power politics, many Americans began to wonder about the "true reasons" for American intervention. A number of revisionist authors such as C. Hartley Grattan and Charles Tansill soon popularized the notion that American involvement in the war had been the result of a sophisticated Allied propaganda campaign, the pro-Allied inclinations of the policy makers, and the machinations of greedy bankers and arms makers anxious to profit from the war trade. Oswald Garrison Villard, the editor of the *Nation*, spoke for many when he wrote that "a tremendously important" cause of American involvement in the war "was the tying up of our great industrial plants and munitions factories to the allied military machine, with a resultant rain of gold from the Allies."[18]

In the spring of 1934 the publicity lavished on the wartime activities of arms makers and international bankers prompted the Senate to create a special subcommittee to investigate the munitions industry. Senator Gerald P. Nye, a populist Republican from North Dakota, headed an investigation that captured headlines and popularized the view that, as Nye himself put it, "the profits of preparation for war and the profits of war itself constitute the most serious challenge to the peace of the world. . . . The removal of the element of profit from war would materially remove the danger of more war."[19] Those who accepted the senator's reasoning believed that America could stay out of future conflicts by enacting legislation that would take the profit out of war and prohibit policy makers from adopting policies similar to those that had landed America in World War I.

Secretary of State Cordell Hull later charged that the Nye committee had "aroused an isolationist sentiment that tied the President's hands at a time when they should have been free to influence the course of events in Europe and Asia." But Nye didn't create the desire to stay out of war. He reflected and reinforced that sentiment, nothing more.[20]

War clouds began to gather over Africa late in 1934. The first sign of trouble came in December, when border guards clashed along the frontier dividing the Italian colony of Eritrea from Ethiopia. For the next several months the crisis simmered as Italy's Fascist dictator, Benito Mussolini, moved infantry units, tanks, and planes into his African colony.

During the 1935 session of Congress, with the Italo-Ethiopian crisis deepening, Senator Nye, Texas's Maury Maverick, and other congressional isolationists introduced a plethora of bills intended to keep America out of war. But Democrats in Congress loyal to the president pigeonholed these proposals.

In July advocates of what came to be called the "new neutrality" warned that they were prepared to keep Congress in session all summer if necessary to win passage of a neutrality law. The pressure on the president was intense. One New York Democratic leader urged him to accept the inevitable, warning that "Thousands and thousands of women's votes have been lost by this stalling." And Senator Key Pittman of Nevada, chair of the Senate Foreign Relations Committee, told a White House aide that if the president insisted on going up against the isolationists. "He will be licked as sure as hell."[21]

Roosevelt was not prepared to make a fight of it. He gave ground quickly, and Congress enacted the first in a series of neutrality laws intended to keep the United States out of the next war. The key provision of the 1935 law mirrored the belief that arms makers should not be allowed to profit from other people's wars. In the event of a conflict, a mandatory embargo on the sale of arms to all belligerents would come into force once the president declared American neutrality.

## NEUTRALITY ON TRIAL

In October 1935, not long after the first Neutrality Act went into effect, Italian forces crossed into Ethiopia. Once before, in 1895, the Italians had invaded that unhappy land only to suffer a humiliating defeat. But this time native spears were no match for modern weapons and the poison gas the Fascists used to achieve their conquest.

There was no lack of moral outrage in the United States as a result of the Italian attack. Thus, the *Nation* expressed shock and indignation "at Mussolini's brazen invasion of Ethiopia." But, the editorial continued,

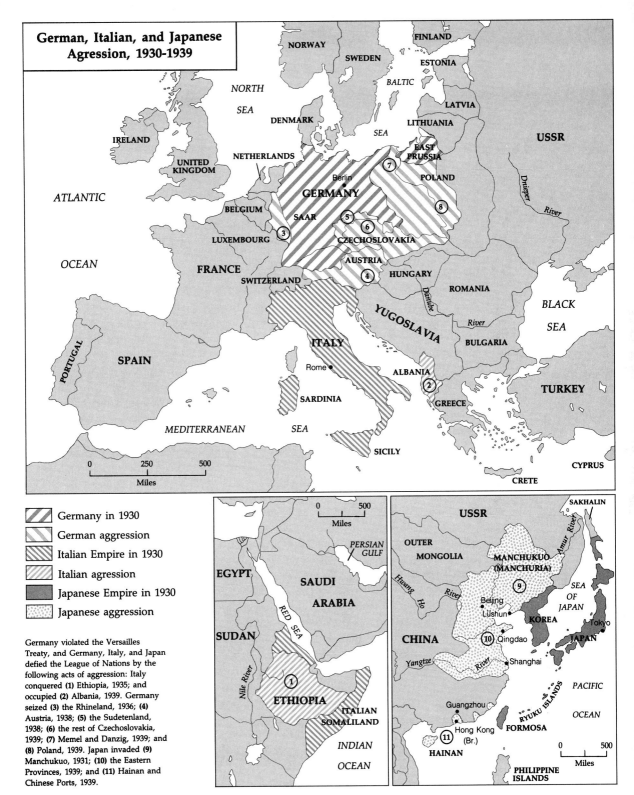

# German, Italian, and Japanese Agression, 1930-1939

Germany in 1930

German aggression

Italian Empire in 1930

Italian agression

Japanese Empire in 1930

Japanese aggression

Germany violated the Versailles Treaty, and Germany, Italy, and Japan defied the League of Nations by the following acts of aggression: Italy conquered **(1)** Ethiopia, 1935; and occupied **(2)** Albania, 1939. Germany seized **(3)** the Rhineland, 1936; **(4)** Austria, 1938; **(5)** the Sudetenland, 1938; **(6)** the rest of Czechoslovakia, 1939; **(7)** Memel and Danzig, 1939; and **(8)** Poland, 1939. Japan invaded **(9)** Manchukuo, 1931; **(10)** the Eastern Provinces, 1939; and **(11)** Hainan and Chinese Ports, 1939.

the experience of one war fought for what we believed to be the highest of idealistic principles has convinced us, . . . that the harm resulting from Il Duce's mad adventure will be slight compared with the havoc that would be wrought by another world conflict. Whatever may happen, we are determined that American youth shall not again be sacrificed to the greed of munitions makers and war profiteers.[22]

Roosevelt, who believed that the implementation of the Neutrality Act might aid Ethiopia, at least in small ways, did not wait for a declaration of war, announcing American neutrality as soon as Italian forces attacked. "They are dropping bombs on Ethiopia—and that is war," an angry president told his most intimate personal adviser, Harry Hopkins. "Why wait for Mussolini to say so?"[23] The president made his own feelings clear by warning Americans that they would travel on belligerent passenger liners at their own risk. Considering the distinct shortage of Ethiopian submarines and the large number of Italian liners and cruise ships plying the Atlantic and Caribbean, it is clear that the president was encouraging travelers to boycott Italian ships.

Roosevelt also tried to discourage trade with Italy by warning that the government would keep tabs on exporters who took advantage of Ethiopia's agony to line their pockets. When the League of Nations slapped an embargo on the sale of certain war-related materials to Italy, including cooper and steel, he even considered stretching the meaning of the Neutrality Act to include the embargoed commodities. He backed off, however, on advice from the State Department.

Roosevelt's personal views notwithstanding, he was bound by the law and the power of anti-interventionist sentiment. Thus when the British asked if the United States would join in an embargo on the sale of petroleum to Italy, a sanction that might have had an impact on Rome, Washington refused. "We have gone as far as we can," a gloomy Cordell Hull told the British ambassador.[24] Hull did announce a "moral embargo" on the sale of all types of petroleum, as well as scrap iron and steel, to the belligerents. But the oil companies and purveyors of scrap metals were not feeling cooperative. Thus the sale of scrap metal to Italy increased substantially, while petroleum sales shot up 600 percent in a few months.

If the Roosevelt administration did nothing substantive to punish Italian aggression, action by the League of Nations also proved to be ineffective. When the crisis first broke, London led the league in applying a partial embargo on the sale of war-related goods to Italy and moved fleet units into the Mediterranean in a gesture of displeasure with Rome. But neither London nor Paris ever seriously considered measures that might truly have hurt Italy. An oil embargo was never really in the cards. Nor did they think in terms of a naval blockade of Italian ports. The British did not even stop Italian ships from using the Suez Canal to supply Italian forces in Africa.

The plain fact is that the British and French governments were primarily interested in appeasing Mussolini, hoping in this way to discourage an Italo-German alliance. Ethiopian sovereignty was a matter of indifference to them. They proved this late in 1935 when, in order to keep Il Duce's good graces, the British foreign secretary, Sir Samuel Hoare, and Premier Pierre Laval of France plotted to offer the Italians control over roughly two-thirds of Ethiopia to keep on Il Duce's good side. The Hoare-Laval plan, a mortal wound to the principle of collective security, was leaked to the press in December. The storm of protest that followed forced Hoare from office and led to the collapse of the Laval government. The demise of the secret plan was all well and good except it did nothing for Ethiopia. In May 1936, the Italians took Addis Ababa, Marshal Pietro Badoglio became viceroy of Italy's newest African colony, and subsequently the league as well as the United States abandoned sanctions against Rome.

## APPEASEMENT IN THE RHINELAND AND SPAIN

During his first two years as German chancellor Adolf Hitler had gone from one triumph to another. In 1935 the Ethiopian war provided new opportunities that he was quick to exploit. He violated commitments made under the Versailles settlement and the 1921 German-American peace treaty by ordering rearmament, conscription, and the creation of an army of 500,000. He also revealed the existence of a large German air force. Britain and France, seeking guarantees in the face of what appeared to be a growing German threat, called on Hitler to reaffirm Berlin's commitment to the Locarno Agreements, which guaranteed Europe's postwar boundaries. In a speech before the Reichstag, Hitler refused, informing the democracies that he no longer considered the Locarno Agreements valid. Even as he spoke German troops were entering the Rhineland in violation of the Versailles and Locarno Agreements.

Remilitarizing the Rhineland was a major gamble. Germany was unprepared for war, and had the French been willing to fight, Hitler would have found himself in serious trouble. But Paris vacillated, looking to Britain for support. Unhappily, when Premier Pierre Flandin raised the issue with Downing Street, Foreign Secretary Anthony Eden was no help, telling Flandin that Hitler's Rhineland venture was "a matter of judgment for the French government."[25] The British lion was clearly unprepared to come roaring to the rescue.

The same state of mind prevailed in the houses of Parliament. Harold Nicolson, who had been with David Lloyd George at Paris in 1919, was one of the few who saw the real danger. He confided in his diary, "General mood of the house is one of fear. Anything to keep out of war." Again he noted, "The country will not stand for anything that makes for war." It was, Nicolson remarked, "all very tragic and sad."[26]

In remilitarizing the Rhineland, Hitler had accomplished far more than simply moving into what some in England described as "his own back garden." A system of prepared defenses, the Siegfried Line, gave Germany a shield against any future French invasion, freeing Hitler to pursue his expansionist ambitions in Southern and Eastern Europe. It also struck a decisive blow at France's security system, so carefully crafted in the interwar years. Its allies on the Reich's eastern flank could count on little help from Paris once the Wehrmacht was firmly entrenched west of the Rhine. Hitler had won a major gamble, while Britain and France lost their best opportunity to stop him short of all-out war.

In July 1936, Europe was thrown into further turmoil when the Spanish army in Morocco, commanded by General Francisco Franco, revolted against the liberal republican government in Spain. Franco began his rebellion with powerful allies. His army had been receiving arms and ammunition from Italy for two years prior to the revolt. And Hitler's Luftwaffe ferried Franco's forces by air across the Mediterranean. Without this initial aid as well as continued support from his Fascist and Nazi friends, Franco could never have overthrown the Spanish Republic.

In Paris, Leon Blum's socialist government was at first inclined to provide Madrid with the weapons it not only needed but as a legitimate government had every right to purchase. But probably because he feared the power of French rightists, Blum soon abandoned the idea. In London, the situation was rather different. Stanley Baldwin's government had no love for the Spanish left and no wish to alienate Franco who it was assumed would win the war. Baldwin also wanted to avoid alienating Italy. He was, therefore, delighted to join the French in establishing the nonintervention committee, a group of twenty-seven nations pledged not to intervene in the war or to provide aid to either side.

Three members of the committee, Germany, Italy, and the Soviet Union, failed to abide by the terms of the agreement. The Germans and Italians provided Franco with infantry units, tanks, and aircraft. The Soviets provided some direct aid to the Madrid government, while the Comintern aided in a general mobilization of volunteers from Europe and America who fought on the government's side. London and Paris were aware that members of the Nonintervention Committee were violating the agreement but were unwilling to do anything about it. Appeasement was the policy and nonintervention a convenient masquerade.

The Spanish Civil War aroused deep passions and stimulated a furious public debate in the United States. Conservatives viewed the Madrid government as "communistic," while its anticlerical policies aroused the ire of the American Catholic hierarchy and many lay Catholic groups. For these people, Franco appeared to be an anticommunist crusader and defender of the mother church. On the other hand, many socialists, liberals, and intellectuals viewed Franco as another Hitler. For them the war was an ideological struggle between social democracy and fascism, an allegory for the world in which they lived.

As in the case of Ethiopia, Roosevelt sympathized with the Madrid government. But as was also true in the case of Ethiopia, the president was

"WHAT'S NEXT, ADOLF?"

Without help from Germany and Italy, General Francisco Franco could never have overthrown the Spanish Republic and established his Falangist dictatorship.

unprepared to take on the isolationists. On the contrary, he outdid many of them in supporting noninvolvement.

Since existing neutrality legislation did not apply to civil wars, Roosevelt might have allowed Madrid to purchase weaponry in the United States. Instead, however, Secretary Hull declared a moral embargo (his second in two years) on the sale of weapons to either side in Spain. And in January 1937, when Congress reconvened, administration supporters rushed to enact supplementary legislation to apply the provisions of the Neutrality Act to the Spanish situation. In Spain, Ambassador Claude Bower's emotions ran the gamut from anger, to bitterness, to sheer frustration. "My own impression," he wrote, "is that with every surrender beginning long ago with China, followed by Abyssinia and then Spain, the Fascist powers, with vanity inflamed, will turn without delay to some other country—such as Czechoslovakia—and that with every surrender the prospects of a European war grow darker."[27]

During 1937, while Britain, France and the United States stuck to their noninterventionist policy, Italian troops and German equipment poured into Spain until the outcome of the war became a forgone conclusion. In the spring of 1938, with his army bolstered by 100,000 Italian troops, Franco launched a massive offensive. It took a year, but in early 1939 Barcelona and then Madrid fell. Thousands of Spaniards fled the country to escape persecution as Franco established yet another fascist state in Europe.

American policy during the Spanish Civil War was so thoroughly reprehensible that in 1941, two years after the Spanish Republic had been overthrown, even the president admitted that it had been a mistake. Why, then, had it been the policy? Secretary Hull explained in his *Memoirs* that he believed since the Italians, Germans, and Soviets were all involved, the Spanish situation might erupt into a full-scale war and that under the circumstances it made sense to cooperate with Britain and France in attempting to quarantine the fighting. He also pointed out that Roosevelt's policy was popular, a fact that cannot be denied since only one member of Congress, a Farmer-Laborite, had the gumption to oppose enactment of the January, 1937 neutrality act.

While Hull's explanation has a certain plausibility, it ignores domestic political considerations that were also important to Roosevelt. Public opinion polls taken at the time indicated that a large bloc of Catholic voters supported General Franco. Moreover, the powerful Catholic hierarchy and the Catholic press were universally pro-Franco. Roosevelt was loath to alienate his Catholic supporters, especially since they far outnumbered those on the left who were deeply committed to the Republican cause. The point was brought home in 1938 when the president gave momentary consideration to lifting the arms embargo. He was then warned by several congressional Democrats that raising the embargo would cost the party the Catholic vote in the coming congressional elections. After that Roosevelt dropped the idea. "This is the cat that was actually in the bag," wrote the interior secretary, Harold Ickes, "and it is the mangiest, scabbiest cat ever."[28]

Roosevelt began his second term in 1937 committed to the established policy of noninvolvement and neutrality. But increasingly, as time passed, he showed signs of moving in more assertive directions. His change in approach was due in part to the fact that he had not yet given any thought to breaking the long-standing tradition that presidents should serve no more than two terms. He therefore enjoyed a greater degree of independence than before. But to give the president his due, the world situation had also grown more threatening. It was increasingly difficult to believe that a policy of noninvolvement would work or was even in the national interest given the growing Nazi threat, Italy's conquest of Ethiopia, one war in Spain and another that broke out between China and Japan in July 1937.

On October 5, 1937, Roosevelt gave vent to his feelings in a speech in Chicago, the center of isolationist sentiment in the United States. He spoke of a "reign of terror and international lawlessness" that threatened to destroy "the very foundations of civilization." It was impossible, he insisted, to "escape" the dangers of the current world situation "through mere isolation or neutrality." Peace-loving nations ought therefore to respond to war as any community would to the spread of a communicable disease by joining "in a quarantine of the patients in order to protect the health of the community."[29]

The Quarantine Speech suggested that FDR was contemplating a major shift in American foreign policy. Naturally, then, when a group of reporters met with the president a few days after the speech, they were anxious to learn more. But Roosevelt was evasive. When asked if he intended to apply sanctions against aggressor nations, he said, "Look, . . . 'sanctions' is a terrible word to use. They are out of the window." Nor would he clarify just what "quarantine" meant.[30]

It may be, as some have argued, that Roosevelt intended the speech as a "trial balloon" and that he was intimidated by the outcry of the isolationist press. It may also be true, however, that he was simply letting off a little steam. Whatever the case, one thing is certain: the Quarantine Speech changed nothing. If FDR had any clear idea of what America's role was to be as the world headed for the abyss, he was not saying.

## MUNICH

Before the end of 1937 Hitler had decided to bring all Germans living under foreign flags into an expanded Reich. This meant annexing Austria, Czechoslovakia's Sudetenland, and the Polish city of Danzig as well as the corridor of land connecting Poland proper to that city. He then planned to expand eastward into Poland and the Ukraine, a move that was certain to mean war with the Soviet Union.

In March 1938, Hitler achieved the first of his objectives when the Austrian government surrendered to his bullying and agreed to annexation. Hardly had the land of his birth been incorporated into the Reich before Hitler focused on his next target, Czechoslovakia's Sudetenland, where 3 million Germans lived. The leader of the Nazi party in the Sudetenland, Konrad Henlein, working closely with Hitler, began the campaign against Prague by demanding local autonomy. The Czechs made a number of concessions to the Sudeten Germans but refused to go that far. At the same time, President Eduard Beneš appealed to his ally, France, for help. The French government sensed that Hitler would not stop until he had taken the Sudetenland. But unwilling to act alone, Paris looked to the British for support.

Unhappily for the Czechs, the French, and the entire world, Neville Chamberlain, who replaced Stanley Baldwin in May 1937, was stubbornly committed to a policy of appeasement. He not only refused to support the Czechs, he convinced Paris to join him in forcing Prague to give in to the demands of the Sudeten Germans.

Early in September 1938, with no hope of support from London or

The German police march into Imst, Austria, after the *Anschluss.* Contrary to their later claims, most Austrians were pleased with this development.

Paris, Prague agreed to grant the Sudeten Germans autonomy. But this concession only produced new demands from Henlein, who now insisted on outright annexation to Germany. Hitler thundered, the Czechs announced partial mobilization, and Chamberlain flew to Berchtesgaden for a meeting with the Führer. At Berchtesgaden, Hitler demanded the transfer of the Sudetenland and warned that the alternative was war.

Convinced that he was acting in the interest of peace, Chamberlain flew to Prague, where he made it abundantly clear that Czechoslovakia would receive no help from France or England in the event it resisted Germany's demands. President Beneš then agreed to surrender the Sudetenland and its 800,000 Czechs to the Reich. On September 22, the flying prime minister was off once again, this time to Godesberg, where he informed Hitler that Beneš had accepted his terms.

During the Czech crisis, Roosevelt continued to live a double life. Officially, he confined himself to a polite, general appeal for peace that netted him a curt rebuff from the democracies and a lesson in the art of the harangue by the Führer. Privately Roosevelt expressed doubts that Chamberlain's diplomacy would succeed. He thought the Berchtesgaden meeting could at best "result in a temporary postponement of what looks to me like an inevitable conflict within the next five years." He also told Harold Ickes that Chamberlain wanted "peace at any price" and predicted that the British and French would abandon the Czechs and would later try to "wash the blood from their Judas Iscariot hands."[31]

On learning that the British and French had, in fact, conspired with Hitler to force the Czechs to cede the Sudetenland, Roosevelt told Sir Ronald Lindsay, the British ambassador, that he thought they had sanctioned "the most terrible remorseless sacrifice that had ever been demanded of a state."

But Roosevelt was not prepared to express his feelings publicly because, as he also explained to Lindsay, the American people remained committed to noninvolvement and he did not wish to "encourage the Czechs to vain resistance."[32]

The crisis in Central Europe should have ended with Prague's agreement to cede the Sudetenland. But when Chamberlain arrived in Godesberg bearing news of the Czech surrender, Hitler had yet another demand. The territorial transfer would have to be completed in two days time, and the Czechs were not to remove a single material object. Industrial equipment, military fortifications, everything was to be left in place; otherwise, he said, there would be war. Hitler's Godesberg demand went too far for the Czechs, who mobilized their army of 1.5 million. France called up 600,000 reservists, and war talk swept across Europe.

At this point Roosevelt became a more active player in the diplomatic game. The key decision had already been made. One way or another Czechoslovakia would lose the Sudetenland. Now the problem was to preserve the peace. The West needed time to prepare for what the president viewed as an inevitable war.

On September 26, Roosevelt issued an appeal to the powers calling for a peaceful settlement. He cabled Hitler urging him to be patient and asked Mussolini to organize one final conference. When Roosevelt learned that Chamberlain had accepted Hitler's invitation to a meeting in Munich, he sent a two-word cable to Number 10 Downing Street. It read "Good man." The reference was not to the fact that Chamberlain had sacrificed the Czechs but that he agreed to make one more journey in the interest of preserving peace if only for a time.

During the last week of September 1938, Hitler, Chamberlain, Premier Daladier of France, and Mussolini met in Munich. There the Western democracies agreed that the Sudetenland should be in German hands before October 7. In return Hitler agreed to guarantee the independence of a truncated Czechoslovakia and to seek no further territory in Europe, a promise he broke less than six months later. The Czechs, who had not even been invited to the conference, were then confronted with a four-power *démarche* (diplomatic representation) they could not resist.

## THE MARCH TOWARD WAR

Following the Munich crisis, the president moved an important step down the road to a more assertive foreign policy. He decided not only to encourage arms sales to Britain and France but also to seek the revocation of the arms embargo clause of the latest neutrality law, the Peace Act of 1937. In March 1939, after Hitler tore up the Munich agreement and absorbed the remainder of Czechoslovakia, administration supporters in Congress tried to free the president from the bondage of the arms embargo. But they ran into a stone wall. "The President has no more intention of taking us into war than he

Britain's Prime Minister Neville Chamberlain and Adolf Hitler met in Munich in September 1938 to decide the fate of Czechoslovakia.

had 6 years ago of taking us into debt," remarked one Republican isolationist. "But we have learned that despite good intentions, if you spend enough you get into debt, and if you threaten enough you get into war."[33]

In July 1939, with Congress about to adjourn, Roosevelt held an unusual evening meeting at the White House hoping to convince key legislators to support repeal of the arms embargo. During the meeting Secretary Hull described some of the many war warnings coming over his desk from America's foreign embassies. But Idaho's Senator William E. Borah, still a power in Congress, insisted that his sources of information were superior to the State Department's and that there would be no war. Borah appears to have been more persuasive than Hull, for at the end of the meeting Vice-President John Nance Garner, having taken a head count, told the president, "Well, Captain, we may as well face the facts. You haven't got the votes, and that's all there is to it."[34]

After Hitler seized the remainder of Czechoslovakia and began the propaganda campaign that preceded his attack on Poland, a general European war became all but certain. In London, Prime Minister Chamberlain, at last aware that appeasement would not bring peace, launched a major rearmament program and extended military guarantees to Poland as well as Greece, Rumania, and Turkey. France followed suit.

With the United States still out of the picture, it was obvious that the Soviets held the balance of power in Europe. Aware of their role, Chamberlain undertook negotiations with the Soviets, hoping to conclude a defensive

Here Foreign Minister V. M. Molotov of the Soviet Union (center) is about to sign the Soviet-German Nonaggression Pact that cleared the way for the German attack on Poland. A smiling Josef Stalin (fourth from the left) looks on.

alliance. The Soviets were amenable, proposing a mutual security pact that would guarantee the integrity of all countries from the Baltic to the Black Sea. But at the last moment the British rejected this proposal. The Tory government in London simply could not bring itself to form an alliance with the Soviets.

This was the last rebuff that the Soviet dictator, Josef Stalin, intended to take at the hands of the West. He had been excluded from the Munich conference and viewed the agreement arrived at there as an attempt by Britain and France to direct Nazi aggression southward and eastward in his direction. But appeasement was a game that two could play. After the Western democracies scuttled the negotiations for a mutual security pact, he signed a nonaggression pact with Hitler, hoping to remain neutral while Germany and the Western democracies fought it out. A secret protocol to the agreement, which was initialed on August 23, a week before the German invasion of Poland, divided much of Eastern Europe into two spheres of influence. Germany was to have control over Lithuania and western Poland. The Soviets were given a free hand in Finland, Estonia, Latvia, eastern Poland, and Bessarabia.

The Soviet-German Nonaggression Pact, which stunned the West, gave rise to the hope in Berlin that England and France would abandon Poland as they had Czechoslovakia and that this latest crisis might end in another Munich. But it didn't work that way. Hitler sent his Panzer divisions

"I MADE THAT MISTAKE."

Like the kaiser before him, Adolf Hitler believed that he could attack Poland without precipitating a war in the West.

crashing into Poland on September 1, 1939. Two days later Britain and France declared war on Germany. The Führer took the blow quietly. His translator would later recall: "For a while Hitler sat in his chair deep in thought, and stared rather worriedly into space. Then he broke his silence to say, 'What are we going to do now?'"[35] What he was about to do was fight the most costly war in history.

## ENDNOTES

1. John Nance Garner, quoted in Arthur Schlesinger, Jr., *The Crisis of the Older Order* (Boston: Houghton Mifflin, 1957), p. 416.

2. Franklin D. Roosevelt, "Our Foreign Policy: A Democratic View," *Foreign Affairs*, July 1928, pp. 573–86; Roosevelt, quoted in Irwin F. Gellman, *Good Neighbor Diplomacy: United States*

*Policies in Latin America, 1933–1945* (Baltimore: Johns Hopkins University Press, 1979), p. 11.

3. Cordell Hull, *Memoirs* (New York: Macmillan, 1948), I, 312.

4. Sumner Welles to the secretary of state, September 5, 1933, *Foreign Relations of the United States, 1933* (Washington, D.C., 1952), V, 382.

5. Cordell Hull, *Memoirs*, I, pp. 333–35.

6. Ibid., p. 497.

7. Hull, quoted in Bryce Wood, *The Making of the Good Neighbor Policy* (New York: Columbia University Press, 1961), p. 145.

8. Hull, *Memoirs*, pp. 1140–42. See also Wood, *Making of the Good Neighbor Policy*, pp. 203–59; and Howard F. Cline, *The United States and Mexico* (New York: Atheneum, 1963), pp. 215–70.

9. The Act of Havana, quoted in John A. Logan, *No Transfer, an American Security Principle* (New Haven, Conn.: Yale University Press, 1961), p. 338.

10. Edouard Daladier, quoted in William E. Leuchtenburg, *Franklin D. Roosevelt and the New Deal* (New York: Harper and Row, 1963), p. 200.

11. Roosevelt, quoted in James MacGregor Burns, *Roosevelt: The Lion and the Fox* (New York: Harcourt, Brace and World, 1956), p. 178.

12. John Maynard Keynes, quoted in Arthur Schlesinger, Jr., *The Coming of the New Deal* (Boston: Houghton Mifflin, 1959), p. 223.

13. Roy Howard, quoted in Leuchtenburg, *Roosevelt and the New Deal*, pp. 205–06.

14. Hull, *Memoirs* I, p. 297.

15. Thomas Watson, quoted in Leuchtenburg, *Roosevelt and the New Deal*, p. 207.

16. *Nation* and *New Republic*, both quoted in Edward Bennett, *Recognition of Russia: An American Foreign Policy Dilemma* (Waltham, Mass., Blaisdell, 1969), p. 132.

17. Sidney B. Fay, *The Origins of the World War* (New York: Macmillan, 1928).

18. Oswald Garrison Villard, quoted in *Nation*, May 1, 1937, p. 492.

19. Gerald P. Nye, quoted in Wayne Cole, *Gerald P. Nye and American Foreign Relations* (Minneapolis: University of Minnesota Press, 1962), p. 76.

20. Hull, *Memoirs*, I, 404.

21. Fred Sisson and Key Pittman, both quoted in Leuchtenburg, *Roosevelt and the New Deal*, p. 219.

22. Villard, quoted in *Nation*, October 16, 1935, p. 425.

23. Roosevelt, quoted in Robert E. Sherwood, *Roosevelt and Hopkins* (New York: Harper and Brothers, 1948), p. 79.

24. Hull, *Memoirs*, I, 442.

25. Pierre Flandin quoting Anthony Eden, in Telford Taylor, *Munich: The Price of Peace* (New York: Random House, 1979), p. 131.

26. Harold Nicolson, *Diaries and Letters*, ed. Nigel Nicolson (London: Collins, 1966), I, 248.

27. Claude Bowers, quoted in F. J. Taylor, *The United States and the Spanish Civil War, 1936–1939* (New York: Bookman Associates, 1956), 152–55.

28. Harold L. Ickes, *The Secret Diary of Harold L. Ickes* (New York: Simon and Schuster, 1953–55), II, 390.

29. Roosevelt, speech of October 5, 1937, quoted in Department of State, *Peace and War: United States Foreign Policy, 1931–1941* (Washington, 1943), pp. 383–87.

30. Roosevelt, quoted in Leuchtenburg, *Roosevelt and the New Deal*, p. 227.

31. Ickes, quoted in Wayne S. Cole, *Roosevelt and the Isolationists, 1932–1945* (Lincoln, Nebr.: University of Nebraska Press, 1983), p. 284.

32. Ronald Lindsay quoting Roosevelt, in Taylor, *Munich*, pp. 846–47.

33. J. M. Vorys, quoted in Leuchtenburg, *Roosevelt and the New Deal*, p. 292.

34. Garner, quoted in Robert A. Divine, *The Reluctant Belligerent: American Entry into World War II*, 2d ed., (New York: John Wiley and Sons, 1979), p. 66.

35. Paul Schmidt, quoted in David Thompson, *Europe since Napoleon* (New York: Alfred A. Knopf, 1957), pp. 715–16.

Adolf Hitler, the conquerer of France, has his picture taken in Paris with the
Eiffel Tower in the background.

# 22

# THE ROAD
# TO WAR,
# 1939–1941

On September 5, 1939, four days after Hitler moved against Poland, President
Franklin Roosevelt declared American neutrality. Recalling Woodrow Wilson's 1914 neutrality declaration, he declined, however, to ask the people to
be neutral in thought. "Even a neutral cannot be asked to close his mind or
his conscience," he said. Nor should Americans deceive themselves into
believing that a mere declaration of neutrality would protect the United
States from involvement. When war breaks out anywhere, he warned, the
"peace of all countries everywhere is in danger."[1]

Roosevelt honestly seems to have wanted to remain at peace. At the
same time, however, he was determined to use "methods short of war" to
aid the democracies. He therefore called a special session of Congress to
convene on September 21 for the purpose of repealing the arms embargo
provision of the Peace Act of 1937.

Isolationist leaders believed they now faced a moment of truth for,
as Senator Gerald P. Nye warned, "If we repeal the act, we will not be able
to avoid subsequent steps which will lead us into war."[2] But President
Roosevelt was a formidable opponent. He eliminated partisan considerations
from the debate by enlisting the support of such Republican luminaries as
former Secretary of State Henry L. Stimson and Alf Landon, the 1936
Republican nominee for president. He further undermined the credibility

of the opposition by pointing out that their views were music to the ears of policy makers in Rome and Berlin.

That was dirty politics as far as isolationist members of Congress were concerned. "I hate Hitlerism and Naziism and Communism as completely as any person living," wrote the discomfited Arthur Vandenberg, Republican senator from Michigan. "But I decline to embrace the opportunist idea—so convenient and so popular at the moment—that *we* can stop these things in *Europe* without entering the conflict with everything at our command, including men and money. There is no middle ground. We are either *all the way in* or *all the way out*."[3]

If Vandenberg's position was valid, it was also politically untenable. The great majority of the American people, like FDR himself, wanted to stay out of the war and to help the democracies at the same time. The isolationists found it impossible to be naysayers without also identifying themselves with the aggressor nations. Not surprisingly then, on November 4, 1939, Congress repealed the arms embargo. Although the revised neutrality law still forbade arms suppliers from extending credit to prospective purchasers, the way was now open for the democracies to purchase weaponry on a "cash and carry" basis.

While the battle over neutrality was being fought in Congress, the war in Europe developed in curious ways. Warsaw surrendered to the Germans on September 27. But in the West little or nothing happened. The French, with one hundred ready divisions, waited on the defensive when they might have advanced all the way to the Rhine. The Royal Air Force confined itself to dropping leaflets over German cities. It was the time of "the phony war," a six-month period of inactivity in the West that ended in the spring of 1940, when the Germans launched a devastating offensive.

Hitler made his first move on April 10, 1940, when on a single day German forces occupied Denmark and Norway. These quick German thrusts had a profound political effect in England, where, after losing a vote of confidence in the House of Commons on that same day, Neville Chamberlain resigned and was replaced by Winston Churchill. Later Churchill wrote that on the day he took power he "was conscious of a profound sense of relief. . . . I felt as if I were walking with destiny and that all my past life had been a preparation for this hour and this trial. I was sure I should not fail. Therefore, though impatient for the morning, I slept soundly."[4]

If Churchill did in fact sleep soundly that night, one can only wonder at the man's constitution. For on that day—May 10— the Germans launched their *Blitzkrieg* (lightning war) against the Low Countries. Holland surrendered in five days; Belgium succumbed on May 28.

## SIGNS AND PORTENTS

The fall of the Low Countries came as a terrific shock in the United States. Now, for the first time, Americans felt exposed and vulnerable. Even some of the president's heretofore most strident critics began to alter certain long-held notions. Thus the *Christian Science Monitor* reported "many signs" that "sentiment is crystallizing for the United States to take a strong stand for aid in every way to the Allies."[5]

William Allen White, the Republican editor of the *Emporia Gazette* in Kansas, and formerly a strong advocate of neutrality legislation, was among those who concluded that the United States should now do something to help the Allies. Encouraged by Roosevelt, White organized the Committee to Defend America by Aiding the Allies. "Our idea," White explained, "is to fill the radio and the newspapers and the Congressional mail with the voice of prominent citizens urging America to become the nonbelligerent ally of France and England. I am afraid it is too late and I stand aghast at what will happen if the English either scuttle their ships or turn them over to Germany."[6]

The White committee confined itself to advocating military aid. But an offshoot of that organization, the New York–based Century Group, published a full page advertisement in the *New York Times* calling for immediate intervention. With the Allied armies already in disarray, the advertisement boldly proclaimed: "The frontier of our national interest is now on the Somme. Therefore, all disposable air, naval, military and material resources of the United States should be made available at once to help maintain our common front."[7]

Following the example of the White committee, the isolationists also organized in the battle for control of public opinion. With initial funding provided by General Robert E. Wood of Sears Roebuck and Company, R. Douglas Stuart, Jr., a Yale Law School student, organized a grass-roots organization committed to keeping America out of the European war. The organization, America First, attracted some strange bedfellows. The best known "America Firster" was, without question, Charles A. Lindbergh, the first man to fly solo across the Atlantic. Lindbergh was joined by an odd assortment that included Republican conservatives, idealistic college students, pacifists, members of the American Communist party, a smattering of Irish and German Americans, and followers of "the Radio Priest," Father Charles Coughlin, many of whom were crazed, right-wing, antisemitic fanatics. The public debate continued unabated through 1941. Only the Japanese attack on Pearl Harbor ended the dispute.

## AFTER THE FALL OF FRANCE

Following the fall of the Low Countries, the main German thrust was directed at a soft spot in the Allied front between the Maginot Line, a sophisticated system of defenses that reached from the Alps to the Belgian border near Sedan, and the southern fringe of Belgium's defensive system. German tanks raced through country the French thought too thickly wooded and hilly for mechanized warfare, driving straight to the English Channel. The British Expeditionary Force, along with a large number of French and Belgian

They called it "the miracle of Dunkirk." But not all Allied troops were lucky enough to escape. These dispirited British and French soldiers are being herded off to a German prisoner-of-war camp.

troops who were caught in a pocket to the northwest of the advancing Germans, had no choice but to retreat to Dunkirk, where the Royal Navy, aided by hundreds of merchant ships and pleasure craft, evacuated some 338,000 Allied troops. The press called it "the miracle of Dunkirk." But England could afford few such miracles. The evacuees left behind all of their heavy equipment and a large portion of their small arms.

To escape the oncoming Germans, the French government declared Paris an open city, withdrew to the south, and replaced General Gustave Gamelin, the author of France's catastrophe, with General Maxime Weygand. But Weygand proved no more effective. By June 7 the war was in effect over. Unable to organize a coherent defense, Weygand told Premier Paul Reynaud that "the final break in our defense line may take place at any moment." Once that happened, he continued, it would be "only a question

In the dark days of 1940, Britain, standing alone, came under attack from the Nazi *Blitz*.
Here, with the city wrapped in smoke and flames, St. Paul's Cathedral stands out, a
symbol of Britain's determination to resist.

of time" before total disintegration took place. "The battle of France is lost."[8]
A few days later Reynaud resigned in favor of the aged General Philippe
Pétain, the hero of Verdun during the First World War.

Pétain immediately asked for an armistice, which was signed on the
afternoon of June 21 in the same railroad car in which Marshal Ferdinand
Foch had taken the German surrender at the end of the first war. This, the
greatest moment in Hitler's life, was without doubt also the greatest humiliation in modern French history. The terms of the settlement were just as
humiliating as the signing ceremony. Northern and Western France including
Paris were occupied by German forces. Pétain moved his capital to Vichy in
the south. From there he governed a truncated demilitarized France until
the day of liberation came in 1944.

Even after France collapsed, Roosevelt was a long way from advocating intervention. He did, however, react in a variety of ways. First, he
broadened his administration by bringing two Republican interventionists
into his cabinet. Henry L. Stimson took over the War Department, while
Frank Knox became secretary of the navy. Next, he asked Congress for a
vastly increased military budget including funds to build fifty thousand
aircraft a year. Congress was in no mood to quibble. Roosevelt got more
than he asked for and soon found that it was not enough. He also sent some

$37 million in "surplus" equipment to Britain, allowed Royal Air Force pilots to train in Florida, and authorized American shipyards to repair and refit British ships fighting the battle of the Atlantic against German submarines.

FDR might have done more. But it was at this time, just after France surrendered, that he decided to seek a third presidential term. This decision caused him to be even more cautious than he otherwise might have been about becoming identified with unpopular policies. Thus, although the world situation made military conscription an obvious necessity, he refused to get out in front on that explosive issue. Others were called upon to fight that battle, while he stood in the wings.

On another important subject Roosevelt was even less forthcoming. Not a week after moving in at 10 Downing Street, Churchill asked Roosevelt to transfer as many as fifty destroyers to the Royal Navy for use in the battle of the Atlantic. At the time Roosevelt was not certain how the public would react to such a move or if the Republicans would make it an issue in the coming November election. Nor was he confident that it would be a sound military decision. Roosevelt therefore refused, telling the prime minister that Congress would never approve the transfer and that he had no authority to act on his own. Roosevelt's explanation may have reflected his view at the time. But it is interesting to note that when other obstacles had been cleared away, he discovered he had the authority after all.

By mid-August 1940, when Roosevelt decided to transfer the destroyers, he had been assured through the good offices of William Allen White that Wendell Willkie, the Republican presidential candidate, would not make this an issue during the political campaign. The British helped him over another obstacle by indicating a willingness to offer something in exchange for the ships. FDR himself then had the idea that they should be traded for leases on western hemispheric naval bases. That gave him the opportunity to defend the transfer before the public as enhancing America's national security. Finally, Roosevelt received an important intelligence estimate from William Donovan, soon to be the head of the Office of Strategic Services. Following a fact-finding mission to London, Donovan indicated that he believed the British could hold on against the Germans. The ships, therefore, would not fall into the hands of the Axis powers.

Critics denounced the "destroyers for bases deal" on a number of counts. To many it seemed a clear-cut violation of the Constitution. Thus Professor Edward S. Corwin, an eminent constitutional authority, denounced it as "an endorsement of unrestrained autocracy in the field of our foreign relations." Senator Nye, more concerned by the apparent danger that yet another president was balancing on the brink of war than by constitutional considerations, charged that "it was a belligerent act, making us a party to the war." And the *New York Daily News* agreed, remarking: "The United States has one foot in the war and the other on a banana peel." The public does not appear to have been impressed by these or similar warnings, however. Opinion polls taken at the time showed conclusively that the president stood on firm political ground in trading the warships for bases in the Caribbean.[9]

## THE ARSENAL OF DEMOCRACY

Not long after FDR was returned for another four years in the White House, Churchill appealed for more aid, at the same time indicating that Britain's ability to pay for this support was fast evaporating. Interventionists inside the administration, especially Secretary of War Stimson, urged the president to take the nation to war before Britain collapsed. But Roosevelt, cautious as ever, was not ready for that. He was ready, however, to sponsor a major program of military aid for Britain. In a speech delivered on December 29, 1940, he warned:

> If Great Britain goes down, the Axis powers will control the continents of Europe, Asia, Africa, Australasia, and the high seas—and they will be in a position to bring enormous military and naval resources against this hemisphere. It is no exaggeration to say that all of us in the Americas would be living at the point of a gun—a gun loaded with explosive bullets, economic as well as military. . . .
> We must be the great arsenal of democracy. For us this is an emergency as serious as war itself. We must apply ourselves to our task with the same resolution, the same sense of urgency, the same spirit of patriotism and sacrifice, as we would show were we at war.[10]

Not long after this speech, the lend-lease bill, authorizing the president "to sell, transfer title to, exchange, lease, lend or otherwise dispose of" military equipment to "the government of any country whose defense the President deems vital to the defense of the United States," was promptly introduced into both houses of Congress.[11] Isolationists were quick to charge that lend-lease would make the United States a nonbelligerent ally of Britain and was bound to lead to war. But the opposition notwithstanding, lend-lease became law on March 11, 1941.

Secretary of War Stimson viewed the Lend-Lease Act as an enormous accomplishment. It solved the problem of financing the British war effort, gave the administration total control over military procurement, and sent a clear message to the Axis, for it was unquestionably "a declaration of economic war."[12]

In spite of the fact that lend-lease was clearly unneutral, opinion polls showed that the public approved of it. Either the people were unconvinced by the argument that it brought the nation a large step closer to war, or they were having difficulty maintaining a commitment to neutrality in the face of Axis aggression.

An agreement to provide England with war material was one thing. Actually moving the goods was quite another. The 1939 Neutrality Act stipulated that American ships could not carry war material to belligerents.

Sidestepping the law, however, proved no problem. Washington simply encouraged the reflaging of American merchant vessels, which in increasing numbers came under Panamanian registry. The administration also sponsored an expanded ship-building program and seized Axis merchant ships interned in American ports for use in the lend-lease trade.

Germany's submarines posed a more formidable barrier to the fulfillment of the American commitment. Beginning in early 1941 Admiral Erich Raeder's wolfpack tactics began paying off in a big way. In April alone, U-boats sank 653,960 tons of British shipping. The German submarine campaign led Admiral Harold Stark, chief of naval operations, to urge the president to begin convoying ships carrying lend-lease goods. The collapse of the British empire, he argued, would pose a major threat to the security of the Western Hemisphere.

But Roosevelt refused to sanction convoys. He hadn't the naval resources to keep the Pacific Fleet up to strength as a check against the Japanese and provide naval escorts in the Atlantic, too. Moreover, he doubted that the public would approve such a direct involvement in the fighting. Roosevelt did, however, authorize the navy to begin offensive operations against German submarines that ventured into the western Atlantic. He also extended the Hemispheric Security Zone halfway across the Atlantic and ordered the navy to patrol this area, trailing British-protected convoys and reporting the position of German submarines, ships, or planes in the vicinity to British naval and air units. He also took over the defense of Greenland to forestall the Germans from establishing bases there.

In the spring of 1941, while Roosevelt continued his cautious ways, in Europe the Wehrmacht won another series of striking victories. In April, Axis armies swept through Yugoslavia in a matter of days. Greece, where fifty-six thousand British troops had been stationed, fell before the end of the month. In May, a daring airborne attack on the British-held island of Crete resulted in another dramatic German victory. Meanwhile, on the other side of the Mediterranean, General Erwin Rommel's Deutches Afrika Korps completed a five-hundred-mile dash that came to a halt before British positions at el-Alamein. Rommel might have made it all the way to Suez, gateway to Britain's eastern empire, had he not run short of fuel, equipment, and replacements.

The grim news from Europe worsened in June when Hitler launched Operation Barbarossa, the invasion of the Soviet Union. The Wehrmacht struck with four hundred divisions, dwarfing Napoleon's attempt to conquer Russia of a century before. In the first weeks of the fighting German forces drove deep into Soviet territory, leading military analysts in the West to predict another great victory for the world's best army. The Soviets, it was thought, would not last three months.

Isolationists in America were overjoyed at the news, believing it inconceivable that the United States would ever ally itself with the Soviets. "The entry of Communist Russia into the war certainly should settle once and for all the intervention issue here at home," wrote America First's

On June 22, 1941, Germany attacked the Soviet Union. Four million German troops, including the two shown above, fought their way deep into the Soviet heartland.

General Robert Wood. "The war party can hardly ask the people of America to take up arms behind the Red Flag of Russia."[13]

But Roosevelt saw the situation quite differently. He thought the invasion of the Soviet Union was Hitler's "first big political miscalculation," one that could mean "the liberation of Europe from Nazi domination."[14] At the very least, it took the pressure off England and gave Roosevelt the time he needed to prepare for war. Almost immediately the State Department negotiated a lend-lease agreement with the Soviets. In August the president made it public and waited for the outcry he more than half expected. But none came. Most Americans evidently felt rather like Winston Churchill who, in spite of his impeccable anticommunist credentials, remarked, "If Hitler invaded Hell I would make at least a favorable reference to the Devil in the House of Commons."

## AN UNDECLARED NAVAL WAR

Early in August, Roosevelt boarded the presidential yacht *Potomac* supposedly to do a little fishing. Instead, the *Potomac* kept a secret rendezvous with the USS *Augusta,* which, with the president aboard, sailed for the fog-enshrouded

Franklin Roosevelt (seated right) and Winston Churchill (seated center) meet for the first time at the Atlantic conference off Newfoundland in August 1941. Though Churchill was unable to win any specific commitments from Roosevelt, he returned to London confident that before very long the United States would become involved in the struggle against the Axis.

waters off the coast of Newfoundland and a meeting with Prime Minister Churchill, who had made the crossing on board HMS *Prince of Wales*.

The Atlantic conference of August 1941 marked the beginning of a warm personal relationship between Roosevelt and Churchill. But in spite of the cordiality that marked this their first meeting, the prime minister failed to win any specific commitments from the president. American and British naval officers agreed that the United States Navy should soon begin protecting convoys from U-boat attacks in the western Atlantic. But Roosevelt refused to set a date for the beginning of convoy operations. Churchill urged a joint *démarche* to check further Japanese expansion in the Far East. But again Roosevelt demurred, fearing this might provoke a war in the Pacific he hoped to avoid.

The two leaders did agree on a general statement, which they dubbed the Atlantic Charter. A wonderfully mushy declaration that could mean any number of things or nothing, the charter endorsed the principles of national self-determination, disarmament, and freedom of the seas. Following "the final destruction of the Nazi tyranny," the charter called for the creation of a new world order based on liberal economic principles and "a peace which will afford to all nations the means of dwelling in safety within their own boundaries, and which will afford assurance that all the men in all the lands may live out their lives in freedom from fear and want."[15]

In spite of his failure to extract any specific commitments from Roosevelt, Churchill sailed for England confident that the United States would soon enter the war. He told the cabinet: "The President had said that he would wage war but not declare it," that "he would be more and more provocative," and that "he would look for an 'incident' which would justify him in opening hostilities."[16] It is difficult to say whether Roosevelt actually said these things or simply left Churchill believing that he had. In any event, incidents did occur and Roosevelt did take advantage of them.

On September 4, a German submarine attacked the American destroyer *Greer* while on patrol southeast of Iceland. Although the U-boat commander no doubt felt justified since the *Greer* was tracking him and radioing his position to nearby British aircraft, the president used the incident to serve his own purposes. In a national radio broadcast he described the attack as more evidence of Hitler's desire to create "a permanent world system based on force, on terror, and on murder." American ships, he announced, would no longer wait to be attacked but would undertake an "active defense." He also announced that effective immediately American naval vessels would protect convoys inside America's "defensive waters." German and Italian warships entering these waters, he warned, would do so "at their own peril."[17] A few days later the first convoy protected by American naval vessels left on the journey across the Atlantic.

Other incidents occurred. The destroyer *Kearny* was torpedoed while on convoy duty. The destroyer *Reuben James* was sunk with the loss of 115 lives. And with each new submarine attack, Roosevelt responded by escalating the crisis. By November 1941, the 1939 Neutrality Act had been reduced to a nullity, American merchant ships had been armed for war, and the United States was in a full-scale if undeclared naval war in the Atlantic. Interventionists in the cabinet—Secretary of War Stimson was perhaps the most strident—urged FDR to ask for a declaration of war. But Roosevelt remained cautious to the end, preferring to leave that decision to his enemies.

## THE FAR EASTERN CRISIS

Following their annexation of Manchuria in 1932, the Japanese announced that in the future they would act as the protector of foreign rights and interests in China proper. Tokyo also warned the United States and other interested powers against encouraging the Chinese to resist this new order of things and asked that they recognize Japanese preeminence in the region.

Roosevelt had no intention of accepting what amounted to a Japanese Monroe Doctrine for Asia. But neither did he develop a coherent response to Japan's growing aggressiveness during his first term in office. He recognized the Soviet Union, hoping that a rapprochement with Moscow would serve as a check on Japanese expansion. But he then allowed Soviet-American relations to sour. And even though he sympathized with China's efforts at nation building, he did not implement an actively pro-Chinese Asian policy. It was a dead period in the history of America's approach to the Far East.

By 1936 the Japanese government was firmly under the control of the military. From that point on Tokyo abandoned all talk of maintaining the open door in China or living up to other commitments made at Washington in 1922. Instead Japan sought preeminence in China and began to caste covetous eyes in the direction of Southeast Asia and the East Indies, areas controlled by the European colonial powers. As a check on Soviet ambitions in Asia, Tokyo also entered into the Anti-Comintern Pact of 1936 with Germany.

In spite of the increasingly extreme tendency of Japanese foreign policy, as late as 1937 a hot debate continued to rage inside Japan's ruling circles over whether to attempt the actual conquest of China. A number of military officers, especially among those serving in Manchuria and China proper, wanted to forcibly integrate China into the Japanese empire. Others, however, favored a more conservative policy. Fearing that renewed military action would lead the country into an endless quagmire, this more cautious group hoped to secure what Japan had already attained, control over Manchuria and a special position in northern China, through negotiations with Chiang Kai-shek's Nanjing regime.

Tokyo had not yet decided which course to follow when fate took a hand. On July 7, 1937, at the Marco Polo Bridge near Beijing, a small-scale shooting incident between Chinese and Japanese troops escalated into a full-scale undeclared war that curiously enough continued to be known as "the China incident."

For a brief moment in the autumn of 1937, it seemed that the United States might bestir itself on China's behalf. Aware that the arms embargo and other aspects of the neutrality law would work to China's disadvantage in its conflict with Japan, Roosevelt refused to declare the law in effect, using as an excuse the fact that war had not officially been declared. Isolationists complained. But most Americans, sympathetic to the Chinese, were satisfied that the president had done the right thing. Then, on October 5, 1937, Roosevelt delivered the Quarantine Speech, which in the context of the time could only be viewed as a sharp rebuke to the Japanese. Not long after this the League of Nations condemned Japan for its aggression and called for an international conference in Brussels to deal with the situation. When Secretary of State Cordell Hull announced that the United States would attend the Brussels conference, the stage seemed set for some potentially significant international action.

While Roosevelt and the League of Nations were busy organizing world opinion against Japan, the government of Prince Fumimaro Konoye, having stumbled into war in China without a clearly defined purpose, sought to extricate itself from its predicament. Tokyo asked Germany, which was

This traumatized child appears to be the only soul left alive after a Japanese bombing raid on the railroad station in Shanghai.

then on good terms with China, to mediate. But buoyed by Roosevelt's Quarantine Speech and the false hope that the Brussels conference might produce increased foreign support, the Chinese refused to negotiate.

Chiang's unwillingness to talk left Prince Konoe with no attractive options. Japan could not unilaterally withdraw from China proper without encouraging the Chinese, who might then threaten its interests in northern China and Manchuria. The lesser evil seemed to be to pursue the war in China and hope for the quick victory that hard-line military men promised. And so Japan plunged deeper into the morass.

In that last year before war broke out in Europe, nothing went well for Tokyo. Hitler signed a Nonaggression Pact with Josef Stalin, leaving the Soviets free to focus on their Far Eastern problem. Japanese forces were badly mauled in a brief but fierce border war with the Soviets. And the quick victory in China failed to materialize. Finally, the United States refused to be intimidated, protesting Japanese aggression in China with increasing vehemence.

## JAPAN LOOKS SOUTH

The outbreak of war in Europe stimulated considerable debate inside Japan's ruling circles. Some, especially in the military, saw the European crisis as a superb opportunity to end the China incident on favorable terms and pursue a more aggressive course in Southeast Asia. But more cautious observers noted that American pressure was growing. Washington's decision to abrogate the Treaty of Commerce and Navigation of 1911 put the Roosevelt administration in a position to embargo all trade with Japan. Should that happen, how would Japan survive, dependent as it was on the United States for petroleum, scrap metal, and a variety of other vital raw materials?

Unwilling to run any serious risks during the first several months of the European war, Tokyo at first behaved cautiously. But German victories in the spring of 1940 opened new vistas for Japanese policy makers. The oil and resource-rich Dutch East Indies, French Indochina, and the British colonies of Burma and Malaya now lay before them like fruit ripe for the picking. Ambassador Joseph Grew, a seasoned observer of the Japanese, had not seen anything like it before. The German victories in Europe, he reported, had "gone to their heads like strong wine."[18]

In July 1940, the government of Mitsumasa Yonai fell. The new government headed once again by Fumimaro Konoye, with the flamboyant Yosuke Matsuoka as foreign minister and General Hideki Tojo as war minister, was committed to the creation of "a new order in Great East Asia." Japan, China, and Korea were to form the nucleus of a vast empire that would include the area "east of India and north of Australia and New Zealand."[19] Once in possession of these areas, the Konoye government believed Japan would be economically independent and able to resist pressures from the democracies.

Matsuoka and others who advocated this strategy did not believe it would lead to war, since the Dutch and French had already been defeated and England had troubles of its own. To discourage Washington from interfering, Matsuoka proposed negotiating a nonaggression pact with Moscow and establishing a much closer relationship with the Axis powers in Europe. An alliance, Matsuoka insisted, "would force the United States to act more prudently in carrying out her plans against Japan."[20]

The Roosevelt administration was at least as anxious to avoid war as was Matsuoka. But American policy makers were disinclined to enter into any arrangement that compromised their long-standing commitment to the open door or allowed Japan to advance into Southeast Asia. Only tactical questions divided American leaders. Japan was dependent on the United States and the Dutch East Indies for petroleum products. Hard-liners in the administration believed that a complete embargo on the sale of key raw materials, but especially oil, would force the Japanese to give in without a fight. Secretary of State Hull and the president, on the other hand, feared that a complete embargo would lead the Japanese to seize the oil and other resources of the Dutch East Indies and Southeast Asia. If that happened, all agreed America would have to fight.

Given these views, it is not surprising that Roosevelt and Hull opted for a policy of limited economic sanctions intended to make the cost of aggression increasingly unacceptable to Tokyo. At length, they hoped, the Japanese would realize they were playing a losing game.

In July 1940, the administration made its first move—placing an embargo on the sale of aviation-grade gasoline, lubricating oil, and certain grades of scrap metal to Japan. These sanctions were intended to create discomfort and stimulate an awareness in Tokyo's ruling circles of America's vast economic power, not to provoke a war.

These limited sanctions had no effect on Japanese planners. On September 23, 1940, Japanese forces moved into northern Indochina, where they established military and air bases. A few days later Matsuoka signed the Tripartite Pact with Germany and Italy, a defensive alliance, one clause of which was aimed directly at Washington.

Matsuoka believed the Tripartite Pact would chasten the United States and allow Japan to pursue its "southern strategy" unhindered. But it had the precisely opposite effect. Roosevelt increased the pressure on the economic front by forbidding the export of all types of scrap metal to Japan and arranged a $100 million loan to China. He also promised Generalissimo Chiang Kai-shek fifty fighter aircraft and began allowing fighter pilots in the U.S. Army Air Force to resign their commissions and join General Claire Chennault, who was then organizing the "Flying Tigers," a fighter group, flying for the Chinese. At the same time the British reopened the Burma road, closed earlier at Tokyo's insistence, allowing supplies to once again flow to Chiang Kai-shek from the south.

Some in the administration argued for a total trade embargo, cutting Japan off from its principal supplier of oil. If the United States indicated by "bold action" that it would not tolerate Japan's move south, Secretary Stimson argued, Tokyo would "yield to that policy even though it conflicts with her own Asiatic policy and conceived interests." But again FDR refused to go that far. When asked why, he explained that an embargo on oil might force Japan to seize the Dutch East Indies, and that would mean war. "At this writing," he wrote, "we all regard such action on our part as an encouragement to the spread of war in the Far East." He told Interior Secretary Harold Ickes that it was "terribly important for the control of the Atlantic for us to help keep the peace in the Pacific. I simply have not got enough Navy to go around."[21]

In March 1941, Secretary Hull and the Japanese ambassador in Washington, Admiral Kichisaburo Nomura, began a lengthy negotiation aimed at forestalling the war that neither side wanted. Admiral Nomura, who had earlier served in the United States and had as foreign minister in 1939 tried in vain to improve Japanese-American relations, was well thought of in Washington. But even the well-intentioned Nomura had no success in breaking the deadlock. The talks, which took place in Secretary of State Hull's Washington hotel suite, dragged on for months before ending inconclusively. There was simply no give on either side. Tokyo insisted that the United States recognize Japan's dominant position in China as well as its claim to Southeast Asia. Hull, on the other hand, continued to insist on the withdrawal of Japanese forces from all of China proper and a return to the principles of the open door—in other words, the status quo as defined in 1922.

## THE END OF DIPLOMACY—THE FREEZE

From Tokyo's perspective, Hitler's June 1941 attack on the Soviet Union was a disastrous setback. Now Churchill and Stalin were allies, and the United States would no doubt join the coalition when it entered the war. Japan's three principal rivals in the Far East were drawing closer together. In light of these developments, Prime Minister Konoye wanted to reconsider the entire thrust of Japanese foreign policy and establish improved relations with the United States. But the military refused to go along, continuing to insist on a southward move. Convinced that Britain and America were too preoccupied with their European problems to accept a war in Asia, the Japanese forced the Vichy French authorities to allow them to advance into southern Indochina. From bases there Japanese air and naval forces were in easy striking distance of the Dutch East Indies, the Philippines, Burma, Malaya, and even India.

The move south was a crucial misjudgment on the part of the Japanese military. They simply refused to believe that Washington would risk war over southern Indochina. They were, of course, wrong. The threat that Japan now posed to Britain's Asian empire and the rest of Southeast Asia could not be ignored. Even Admiral Stark and the army chief of staff, General George C. Marshall, both of whom had previously urged caution, hoping to buy time in which to build their forces, now believed the Japanese had gone too far. Secretary Hull took the occasion to break off his long and fruitless negotiations with Ambassador Nomura. And on July 25, the president signed an executive order freezing all Japanese assets in the United States.

The practical effect of the freezing order was to give the president the power to cut off as much or as little of the trade between Japan and America as he wished. At the stroke of a pen he could have cut the flow of oil to Japan to zero. But that was not his intention. Roosevelt wanted to use his new weapon flexibly, to discipline the Japanese while still avoiding war. Thus, before boarding the *Augusta* for the Atlantic conference, he left orders to free sufficient Japanese funds to allow a continued but reduced flow of petroleum products to Japan.

But things did not work that way. Assistant Secretary of State Dean Acheson, who headed the State Department's Foreign Funds Control Commission, established an unofficial but nevertheless total embargo on petroleum sales to Japan. It was several weeks before Roosevelt and Hull learned of Acheson's action. By that time they could not allow oil to flow again even in reduced quantities without sending the wrong message to Tokyo. And so the freeze on all oil sales to Japan remained official policy.

The Japanese were shocked by the oil embargo, which seemed to leave them only two choices. They could advance southward and seize the oil-rich Dutch East Indies even at the risk of war, or they could surrender. But surrender meant giving up their dreams of a Southeast Asian empire and getting out of China and probably Manchuria, too. The military refused to accept that. The problem was that a war against the United States, Britain, China, and perhaps the Soviet Union as well, was an uninviting alternative. Still, there was a growing feeling in military circles that fighting and losing a war was more acceptable than surrender.

The war minister, General Hideki Tojo, made just that point to Prime Minister Konoye when he remarked that "sometimes a man has to jump with his eyes closed, from the veranda of Kiyomizu Temple." Konoye may be forgiven if he did not agree. With the military driving the country toward a war that Japan would certainly lose, he resigned. Tojo became prime minister in a new government and decided from that moment that "diplomacy must keep pace with military preparations."[22] If a settlement with Washington could not be arranged by December 1, 1941, it would be war.

Foreign Minister Shigenori Togo, the lone moderate in the Tojo cabinet, urged his colleagues to be cautious. The United States wanted to concentrate its efforts on the Axis powers in Europe and would not fight in the Pacific unless attacked. Under the circumstances, there was no danger in awaiting the outcome of the war in Europe before deciding on war or peace with America.

But military leaders argued that the freeze made such a policy impossible. Japan had but an eighteen-month supply of petroleum in storage. Every day that passed thousands of tons of the precious stuff disappeared, and the country became more vulnerable. Moreover, the United States would only grow stronger as time passed. The Japanese navy believed it could hold its own against the United States and its allies for from eighteen to twenty-four months. During that time, the military men argued, Japan could strengthen itself by exploiting the resources of Southeast Asia and the Indies, using that strength to fight a longer war if necessary. Military planners also pointed out that a war with the Anglo-Saxon powers would provide a significant bonus, for it would then be possible to end the flow of supplies to China up the Burma road. Clearly, Foreign Minister Togo's was a voice crying in the wilderness. Short of a diplomatic miracle, war had become inevitable.

## THE LAST CHANCE FOR PEACE

Between September and December 1941, Tokyo made its last attempt to stave off war. Japan's first proposal, dubbed Plan A by the Tojo government, showed some flexibility on basic questions. Tokyo offered to withdraw from the Tripartite Pact and to neutralize Southeast Asia so long as it continued to have access to the resources of the region. The United States for its part would be required to restore trade and restart the flow of oil to Japan. Washington would also be required to offer its good offices for a settlement to the war in China that would leave Japan dominant there.

Washington's refusal to consider Plan A moved Ambassador Nomura to urge his government to delay any military action until the European situation had been clarified. "Even though I will be harshly criticized for it," he wrote, "I would like to caution patience for one or two months in order to get a clear view of the world situation." But Foreign Minister Togo, himself anxious to avoid war, told Nomura that delay was out of the question. With plans for the Pearl Harbor attack already maturing, there could be no delays. "The deadline for the solution of these negotiations is set . . . and there will be no change."[23]

On November 20, Nomura and a newly arrived special emissary, Saburo Kurusu, submitted Plan B, Japan's last offer. This modus vivendi proposal stood in marked contrast to Plan A and perhaps deserved more serious consideration than Secretary Hull accorded it. In this final bid for peace Japan agreed to withdraw from southern Indochina immediately and from all of Indochina after the China incident had been settled. In return, Tokyo asked only for the restoration of trade with the United States and access to the resources of Southeast Asia and the East Indies.

In all likelihood the Tojo government offered these concessions because its geopolitical situation did not look as promising in late November as it had two months before. The German offensive against the Soviet Union was stalled. Britain remained undefeated, and the United States was on the brink of intervening. The Japanese had never wanted a war. Now, close to taking the last irretrievable step, it is not surprising that Tokyo should have at last shown some real, if belated, flexibility.

In spite of its attractive features, Hull rejected Japan's modus vivendi proposal. He may have been responding, at least in part, to the same geopolitical factors that influenced Tokyo. It is more likely, however, that for Hull, China remained the sticking point. Like Plan A, Tokyo's latest proposal would have required the administration to give Japan a free hand in China, and Japan's presence in China had been the issue from the beginning. As the Far Eastern crisis matured, the United States responded by creating a coalition with Chiang as a major partner in a strategy that isolated Japan. As the historian Akira Iriye has pointed out, the abandonment of China would have left the coalition in ruins, the United States without an Asian strategy, and Japan free to do her worst in China.[24]

## PEARL HARBOR

At 8:00 A.M. on the morning of December 7, 1941, the war that neither side wanted came with dramatic suddenness when planes from six Japanese aircraft carriers launched a devastating attack against the Pacific Fleet at Pearl Harbor. In a matter of two hours, eight battleships, three cruisers, and a number of destroyers and smaller vessels had been sunk or damaged. One hundred eighty planes had been destroyed on the ground, and 128 others were damaged. All told, nearly thirty-six hundred Americans were killed or wounded.

The Japanese attack on the American Pacific Fleet at Pearl Harbor was a stunning blow to America's national pride.

Ever since then the public and historians alike have asked how the base could have been taken so completely by surprise. The success of the surprise attack has been especially puzzling since prior to the outbreak of war in the Pacific policy makers and military leaders in Washington had access to much of Japan's most secret naval and diplomatic correspondence. MAGIC, a sophisticated decrypting device stolen from the Germans by Polish intelligence and provided to the United States courtesy of the British, allowed Naval Intelligence to crack some of Japan's naval and diplomatic codes. Throughout the prewar period American policy makers and military leaders had an enormous amount of information about Japanese military planning that should have prepared them for the attack.

In the years immediately following the war a number of revisionist scholars pointed an accusing finger at President Roosevelt, claiming that he "planted the fleet" at Pearl Harbor in a deliberate attempt to provoke the Japanese into an attack and involve the United States in a war that the people would otherwise have refused to support. Some of these revisionists even argued that with all of the information MAGIC was providing it is inconceivable that high-level policy makers did not know when and where an attack would come. They allege that Roosevelt, Hull, and other high-level officials conspired to withhold information from Admiral Husband E. Kimmel and General Joseph C. Short, the commanders in Hawaii, because they wanted the fleet to be attacked.

While there is a certain plausibility to this argument—presidents before and since have tried to maneuver an adversary into firing the first shot—the weight of the evidence does not support the revisionist view. It is true that Washington had a great deal of information indicating that an attack was coming somewhere and soon. It is also true that the Pearl Harbor command did not have the mass of information at its disposal that MAGIC was providing Washington. But Admiral Kimmel and General Short were provided with a large portion of the data. Moreover, prior to December 7, they received clear warning that an attack was coming. On November 24 a dispatch from Admiral Stark warned that Japan might mount "a surprise aggressive movement in any direction." On November 27 the Navy Department sent a "war warning" to all Pacific commanders. An "aggressive move by Japan," the dispatch read, "is expected within the next few days."[25] General Short received a similar message on the following day. A week after this message the command at Pearl Harbor was informed that Japanese diplomats were destroying all of their sensitive papers, another sure sign that war was imminent.

It is also worth noting that Admiral Kimmel and General Short were not caught napping, at least in the conventional sense. They were convinced from the information received that the Japanese were going to move. They simply did not believe that the attack would come in their direction. It was inconceivable to them that the Japanese could, undetected, move a carrier task force five thousand miles across the Pacific. It was almost equally inconceivable that the Japanese would strike at Pearl Harbor—the most heavily defended United States holding in the Pacific. Convinced that Tokyo would move against Southeast Asia and the Dutch East Indies, they prepared against the possibility of sabotage attacks, which they believed might be undertaken by disloyal Japanese Americans on the island. In the final analysis, the Pearl Harbor command was taken by surprise because they simply did not believe that the Japanese would mount an attack on the fleet. This disbelief, and not some sort of elaborate conspiracy emanating from Washington, was the basic cause of the disaster.

Finally, even assuming the president was attempting to manipulate Japan into firing the first shot, he had no motive for keeping information indicating that Pearl Harbor was going to be the point of attack from Kimmel and Short. He did not need a debacle to involve the United States in the war. All that was required was an attack. The Pearl Harbor command could have been prepared with more than two hundred P-40s hiding in the sun waiting for the first wave of Japanese attackers while bombers flew northward in search of the Japanese carriers. Antiaircraft crews might have been at their guns. And the ships sunk at their moorings might have put to sea, moving out of range of the Japanese planes before the attack came. Instead of a disaster, Pearl Harbor could have been a great victory for American arms. What better way to start a war?

By late November policy makers in Washington and America's Pacific commanders knew that the Japanese were preparing to attack soon. Naval intelligence officers even tentatively placed the first day of a possible attack as the weekend of November 30. When nothing happened, they then suggested December 7 as the logical day for a Japanese move. The real problem was not when but where the attack would come. In this area MAGIC was of little use. The messages being decrypted indicated that attacks might come in a number of places, including Burma, Malaya, the Dutch East Indies, the Philippines, Singapore, and even Siberia.

Some of MAGIC's intercepts did suggest that the Japanese had an inordinate interest in the mooring arrangements for the Pacific Fleet at Pearl Harbor, and critics have suggested that this interest was or should have been the tip-off regarding Japanese intentions. After the fact, it was easy to read great significance into such MAGIC intercepts. But it was quite another thing to read special significance into such messages beforehand when they were buried in hundreds of messages indicating impending attacks in several different directions.

American intelligence experts had too much conflicting information to point with certainty to the likely target. As one shrewd student of Pearl Harbor has noted, "We failed to anticipate Pearl Harbor not for want of the relevant materials but because of a plethora of irrelevant ones.[26] Under the circumstances, Washington did the only appropriate thing—putting all Pacific commands on alert.

## WAR AT LAST

Down to the day of the attack, American policy makers refused to take Japan seriously. America's war production was up, and Britain and the Soviet Union remained in the war. Under the circumstances, Japan seemed a second-rate power, no real threat. Secretary of the Interior Harold Ickes, reflecting a view held by hard-liners throughout the administration, wrote that he enjoyed seeing Japan on "the anxious seat" and predicted that the United States and its allies "could probably crush her within a few months." Stanley K. Hornbeck, a Far Eastern expert in the State Department, simply refused to believe that Japan would be foolish enough to fight. No sane nation would go to war, he argued, "out of desperation."[27]

The news from Pearl Harbor had a sobering effect on everyone in the administration, including the hard-liners. Secretary of the Treasury Henry Morgenthau told key aides that what happened in Hawaii was "unexplainable" and "much worse than anyone realizes." He described Secretary of the Navy Knox as feeling "something terrible," while Secretary of War Stimson, who earlier thought the Japanese were "rattled and scared," spent much of December 7 "mumbling that all the planes were in one place. . . . They have the whole fleet in one place . . . the whole fleet in this little Pearl Harbor base. They will never be able to explain it."[28]

High-level policy makers were impressed by Japan's daring in striking at the most heavily defended point in the Pacific and stunned at the cost. At the same time, after months of tension Pearl Harbor, came as something of a release. Secretary Stimson recalled, "When the news first came that Japan

In a shocking violation of human rights the U.S. government rounded up Americans of Japanese descent living on the West Coast and placed them in internment camps for the duration of the war.

had attacked us, my first feeling was of relief that the indecision was over and that a crisis had come in a way which would unite all our people." At a cabinet meeting held while the smoke still rose from the ruins that had once been the Pacific Fleet, Harry Hopkins, Roosevelt's most intimate adviser, noted that this mood was shared by the cabinet as a whole. "The conference met in not too tense an atmosphere because I think that all of us believed that . . . the enemy was Hitler and that he could never be defeated without force of arms; that sooner or later we were bound to be in the war and that Japan had given us an opportunity."[29]

But would the United States be able to go to war against Germany? It was Japan, after all that had attacked. Secretary Stimson argued that Hitler had no doubt encouraged the Japanese to strike and that the president ought to ask Congress for a declaration of war against both Axis powers. But the president, ever cautious and evidently unconvinced that Congress or the people would support a war against Hitler on the basis of what happened at Pearl Harbor, refused. On December 8 he asked for a declaration of war against Japan, and Congress quickly complied. What Roosevelt would have done had Hitler not come to his aid at this point is difficult to tell. In any event, the president never had to face that problem, for on December 11 Germany declared war on the United States. Italy followed suit. At the president's request, Congress then enacted a resolution recognizing the existence of a state of war with Germany and Italy.

Faraway in London, Winston Churchill exulted. With the United States at last in the war, he had no further doubts as to the final outcome.

On December 8, 1941, a grim-faced President Franklin Roosevelt signed the declaration of war against Japan.

## ENDNOTES

1. Neutrality declaration, in *Public Papers and Addresses of Franklin Delano Roosevelt,* ed. Samuel Rosenman (New York: Random House, 1941), VIII, 460–64.

2. Gerald P. Nye, quoted in Wayne S. Cole, *Roosevelt and the Isolationists, 1932–1945* (Lincoln, Nebr.: University of Nebraska Press, 1983), pp. 328–29.

3. Arthur Vandenberg, quoted in ibid.

4. Winston Churchill, *The Second World War: The Gathering Storm* (Boston: Houghton Mifflin, 1948–52), I, 667.

5. *Christian Science Monitor,* quoted in William L. Langer and S. Everett Gleason, *The Challenge to Isolation* (New York: Harper and Row, 1964), p. 486.

6. William Allen White, quoted in ibid., p. 487.

7. Century Group advertisement, quoted in ibid., p. 507.

8. Maxime Weygand, quoted in M. K. Dziewanowski, *War at Any Price: World War II in Europe* (Englewood Cliffs, N.J.: Prentice-Hall, 1987), p. 108.

9. Edwin S. Corwin, Nye, and *New York Daily News,* all quoted in William L. Langer and S. Everett Gleason, *The Challenge to Isolation: The World Crisis of 1937–1940 and American Foreign Policy* (New York: Harper and Row, 1964), p. 772.

10. Franklin D. Roosevelt, quoted in Department of State, *Peace and War: United States Foreign Policy, 1931–1941* (Washington, D.C., 1943), pp. 483–85.

11. Lend Lease Act, *Documents on American Foreign Relations, 1940–1941* (Boston: World Peace Foundation, 1941), pp. 712–15.

12. Henry L. Stimson, quoted in Henry L. Stimson and McGeorge Bundy, *On Active Service in Peace and War* (New York: Harper and Brothers, 1947), p. 360.

13. Robert Wood, quoted in Cole, *Roosevelt and the Isolationists,* pp. 434–35.

14. Roosevelt, quoted in Waldo Heinrichs, *Threshold of War: FDR and American Entry in World War II* (New York: Oxford University Press, 1988), p. 102.

15. Atlantic Charter, quoted in ibid., p. 152.

16. Churchill, quoted in Robert A. Divine, *The Reluctant Belligerent: American Entry into World War II*, 2d ed. (New York: John Wiley and Sons, 1979), p. 141.

17. Roosevelt, quoted in *Documents on American Foreign Relations, 1941–42* (Boston: World Peace Foundation, 1942), pp. 16–22.

18. Joseph C. Grew, *My Ten Years in Japan* (New York: Simon and Schuster, 1944), p. 325.

19. Fumimaro Konoye Policy Statement, quoted in Akira Iriye, *The Origins of the Second World War in Asia and the Pacific* (New York: Longman, 1987), p. 107.

20. Yosuke Matsuoka, quoted in John Toland, *The Rising Sun* (Garden City, N.Y.: Doubleday, 1970), II, 80.

21. Harold Ickes quoting Roosevelt, in Cole, *Roosevelt and the Isolationists*, p. 355.

22. Hideki Tojo, quoted in Toland, *Rising Sun*, II, 142.

23. Kichisaburo Nomura and Shigenori Togo, both quoted in Herbert Feis, *The Road to Pearl Harbor* (New York: Atheneum, 1962), pp. 305–6.

24. Iriye, *Origins of the Second World War.*

25. Dispatch, quoted in Gordon W. Prang, *At Dawn We Slept: The Untold Story of Pearl Harbor* (New York: Penguin Books, 1981), p. 406.

26. Roberta Wohlstetter, *Pearl Harbor: Warning and Decision* (Stanford, Calif.: Stanford University Press, 1962), p. 387.

27. Harold L. Ickes, *The Secret Diary of Harold L. Ickes* (New York: Simon and Schuster, 1953–55), III, p. 592; Stanley K. Hornbeck, quoted in Charles E. Neu, *The Troubled Encounter: The United States and Japan* (New York: John Wiley and Sons, 1975), pp. 193–94.

28. Henry Morganthau and Stimson, quoted in Prang, *At Dawn We Slept*, pp. 559–60. See also Neu, *Troubled Encounter*, pp. 194–95.

29. Stimson, quoted in Stimson and Bundy, *On Active Service*, p. 393; Harry Hopkins, quoted in Robert E. Sherwood, *Roosevelt and Hopkins* (New York: Harper and Brothers, 1948), p. 431.

The Burma road was the only land route by which lend-lease supplies could be transported to China in 1941. Even this tortuous route was closed to the Allies when Japan drove the British from Burma in 1942.

# 23

# THE WAR IN ASIA, 1941–1945

China's leaders hoped for big things after the Japanese attack on Pearl Harbor. Where previously they counted American support in the millions, now they expected billions. But American aid failed to materialize in the quantities they expected. Chiang Kai-shek's government was low on Washington's priority list, behind Britain, the Soviet Union, and America's own needs. Moreover, the rapid advance of Japanese forces throughout Southeast Asia left China isolated. Even the Burma road was cut. The only method of delivering lend-lease material was by air over the Himalayas. But the flight was dangerous, and the twin engine C-47s that flew "the hump" had a limited cargo capacity.

Chongqing (Chungking), China's wartime capital, complained constantly about the inadequacy of American aid. But this counted for little in Washington. America's policy, Secretary of War Henry L. Stimson explained, was designed to provide just enough to keep China in the war "and so to strengthen her that she might exact a constantly growing price from the Japanese invader."[1] Money, which was often easier for the administration to come by than military equipment, was another matter. Therefore, in 1942, when Chiang threatened to negotiate a separate peace with Tokyo, the administration came up with a $500 million loan to keep China in the war.

Washington wanted Chiang to use the money to strengthen himself

**455**

internally by checking inflation and supporting the national currency (the yüan), which was rapidly losing its value. Predictably, however, the money disappeared into the dark and mysterious recesses of the Chinese government. Inflation worsened, and the yüan became nearly worthless.

The level of corruption in Asia has often astonished Americans. But the level of corruption in Chiang's China may even have astonished Asians. It was the life-blood of the regime. Chiang, who mouthed platitudes about democracy and freedom but who ruled like a traditional despot, had long since spent most of his political capital. In lieu of popular support, he used financial resources to purchase the loyalty of bureaucrats, generals, and the more or less autonomous warlords who made up the Guomindong coalition. Though Chiang managed somehow to maintain his position at the top of this unstable pyramid, his regime was never secure. The threat of a coup d'état was ever present.

General Joseph ("Vinegar Joe") Stilwell was sent to China in 1942 to head the American military effort in the China-Burma-India (CBI) theater and to serve as Chiang's chief of staff. In retrospect it seems clear that conflict between these two very stubborn and determined men was inevitable. The conflict was not so much a clash of personalities (though that was an important consideration) as a reflection of crossed-purposes. Stilwell hoped to lead Chinese forces into combat. But Chiang, who wanted to husband his resources for the war after the war with Mao Zedong's (Mao Tse-tung) communists, had no desire to tangle with the Japanese. As Ambassador Clarence Gauss explained, he (Chiang) intended to let the Anglo-American allies defeat Japan while "the Chinese . . . concentrate their planning upon China's post-war political and economic problems."[2]

Early in their relationship Chiang did turn over a few of his treasured divisions to Stilwell. But after the Allies were defeated in the 1942 Burma campaign that saw Japanese forces march almost to the Indian border, he was virtually unmovable on the subject. Nor would Chiang approve Stilwell's plan to train and equip thirty new Chinese divisions. At first glance Chiang's obstinacy makes no sense, since these troops would have been under his command. Stilwell criticized "the little dummy" for failing to "realize that his only hope is the 30-division plan, and the creation of a separate, efficient, well-equipped and well-trained force."[3] But it was Stilwell who didn't understand. Chiang's insecurity ran so deep that he feared an American-trained force would vastly enhance Washington's influence in China. The regime was weak enough without introducing a disruptive foreign element into Chinese affairs.

Under the circumstances, it is not surprising that relations between Chiang and the plain-spoken Stilwell quickly hit rock bottom. Chiang wanted the general replaced by someone less anxious to fight the Japanese and more sympathetic to his regime. On the other hand, the frustrated Stilwell soon became convinced that nothing could be accomplished in China until Chiang had been replaced. He took to referring to Chiang as "peanut" in his diary and wrote that "something [must] be done to clean up this stinking gang and put some real people at the head of things." Later he lamented, "Here I am in this pile of shit, after forty-three years in the army."[4]

Reports coming out of the Chongqing embassy and from a number of younger foreign service officers on Stilwell's staff warned Washington against tying the United States too closely to Chiang. John Carter Vincent, the genteel southerner who served as counselor at the embassy, described the government as little more than a collection of corrupt cliques whose members sought power for the sole purpose of lining their own pockets. Vincent reminded his superiors that China was in the midst of a social revolution and that Mao Zedong's communists had an excellent chance of driving the Nationalists from power. Continued support for the Chongqing government, therefore, might well earn the United States the hatred of those who sought and might well achieve Chiang's downfall. Like Stilwell, Vincent believed that the only hope of saving the situation was to replace the current Chongqing power structure with new men committed to reform.

Vincent was an optimist. Writing in 1944, John Patton Davies, a China expert attached to Stilwell's staff, thought that civil war in China was inevitable and that Chiang would no doubt lose.

> If the Generalissimo neither precipitates a civil war nor reaches an understanding with the Communists, he is still confronted with defeat. Chiang's feudal China can not long co-exist alongside a modern dynamic popular government in North China.
> The Communists are in China to stay. And China's destiny is not Chiang's but theirs.[5]

Because civil war and Chiang's defeat appeared likely, John Service, another of the young "China hands" serving Stilwell, urged a mission at Mao's capital in Yan'an (Yenan). At the time American policy makers knew next to nothing about the Chinese communist movement. It seemed particularly important to learn the degree to which it was connected to Moscow.

## FDR AND CHINA

Chiang's inadequacies notwithstanding, during the first two years of the war President Franklin Roosevelt insisted that China was to be elevated to the status of a great power, one of "the four policemen" who would maintain order and stability in the postwar world. If Roosevelt was engaging in wishful thinking—and there is every reason to believe that he was—he at least had good reason. The president knew that Japan's defeat would produce a vast power vacuum throughout East Asia. Since nation states, like nature, abhor vacuums, Roosevelt could see but two possibilities. Either Soviet influence would expand throughout the region, or China would fill the void. Of the two possibilities FDR naturally preferred the latter.

Roosevelt had another reason for clinging to and cultivating Chiang. American military strategists continued to hope that Chiang would finally agree to establish a real fighting front in Burma and southern China and allow the construction of more air bases in China from which American bombers might attack the Japanese home islands.

Since there was not much else Roosevelt could do, he addressed Chiang's repeated complaints and threats of a separate peace with Japan by arranging small increases in military aid and a succession of loans and by flattering the Generalissimo's ego. Thus at their first and only meeting, in Cairo in November 1943, the president assured Chiang that he would be placed on a footing equal to the other members of the alliance, which would from then on be known not as the Big Three (Britain, the Soviet Union, and the United States) but the Big Four, and that all territory taken from China by Japan since 1895 would be restored.

Not long after their Cairo meeting, Chiang sent another in what had become a long string of demands to the White House. He wanted his lend-lease aid doubled as well as a $1 billion loan. Secretary of the Treasury Henry Morgenthau, infuriated by Chiang's corrupt mismanagement of the 1942 loan, urged the president to refuse this latest request. Morgenthau confided to his diary that no further aid should go to Chiang, who was a "crook," and that as far as he was concerned the Nationalist leader could "go jump in the Yangtze."[6]

Roosevelt not only turned Chiang down, but rebuked him for mismanaging the earlier loan and warned that no more aid would be forthcoming unless he freed Chinese forces for service with General Stilwell. After two years of coddling Chiang, Roosevelt was clearly hardening.

A Chinese sentry stands guard over a number of P-40 Warhawks sent to China under the lend-lease program.

An agreement made at the Tehran conference, which took place in late November 1943, only days after Roosevelt met with Chiang in Cairo, partially accounts for Roosevelt's shift. He was under considerable pressure from his military advisers (probably because of China's woefully inadequate military performance) to secure Soviet involvement in the Far Eastern war. Stalin made that commitment when he and Roosevelt met in the Iranian capital, thus reducing America's need for the Chinese. Then, too, by early 1944 the navy's island-hopping campaign and the development of a new long-range bomber, the B-29 Superfortress, had nearly put the U.S. Army Air Force within range of the Japanese home islands from bases in the Pacific. Chinese air bases were therefore of decreasing military importance to the United States.

But perhaps most important, Roosevelt's changed attitude toward Chiang was a reflection of his growing conviction that the Nationalist leader's hold on power was slipping and that something had to be done to stabilize China's internal political situation. Roosevelt believed that unless Chiang and Mao Zedong organized a coalition government, China would be racked by civil war, postwar Asia would be destabilized, and Manchuria would be opened to Soviet penetration.

Shortly after threatening a cutoff in aid, Roosevelt asked Chiang to allow a team of American observers to go to Yan'an, ostensibly for the purpose of forestalling a possible communist attack on Guomindong forces. In fact, however, the president had more important things on his mind. Few in the United States had any knowledge of China's communists save that they claimed to want China to enjoy the benefits of democracy and were willing to fight the Japanese. But talk is cheap, and there remained the very fundamental question of Yan'an's connection to Moscow. Roosevelt needed to find out more.

Chiang was, as usual, unwilling to cooperate. But Roosevelt would not be put off. In June 1944, he sent Vice-President Henry Wallace to Chongqing on a special mission. Under pressure from the vice-president, Chiang agreed that an observer group could go into Yan'an and set up shop in Mao's northern capital.

During Wallace's visit, Chiang made it clear that Stilwell would have to go. And Wallace was inclined to agree. After all, he reasoned, Chiang was the head of a sovereign state. And if Stilwell could not get along with him, then the president should find someone who could. At the same time Wallace was so unimpressed with Chiang that he recommended replacing him, too. He thought "our attitude should be flexible enough to permit utilization of any other leader or group that might come forward offering greater promise." Wallace thought Chiang was "at best . . . a short-term investment" who had neither the "intelligence nor the political strength to run post-war China." New leaders, he thought, would be "brought forward by evolution or revolution, and it now seems more likely the latter."[7]

The members of the observer group, the Dixie Mission, who settled in Yan'an, confirmed through firsthand exposure what America's China experts had suspected for some time. First, the communists' policy was heavily influenced by their view that the United States had a major role to play in China's future. Mao believed that if his movement could attain American aid equivalent to that being provided for Chiang, he could win control of the country, perhaps without a fight. On the other hand, the continuation of an exclusive American commitment to Chiang would make the task of overthrowing the Nationalist government far more difficult and ensure the inevitability of a civil contest.

Obviously, the United States was in a position to do China's communists a great deal of good or harm. They feared Washington as a potential enemy but sought a good relationship. And they thought the basis for future friendship existed because the president's desire for a strong, stable China correlated with their own ambitions and because it was obvious that China under Chiang would be neither strong nor stable.

But what about the ideological dimension of the issue? Were China's communists devoted Marxists committed to social revolution and the destruction of capitalism? If they succeeded in driving Chiang from power, would they become Moscow's surrogates? The general consensus among the Americans in Yan'an, as expressed by John Davies, was that:

> Yenan is no Marxist New Jerusalem. The saints and prophets of Chinese Communism, living in the austere comfort of caves scooped out of loess cliffs, lust after the strange gods of class compromise and party coalition, rather shamefacedly worshipping the Golden Calf of foreign investments, and yearn to be considered respectable by worldly standards.[8]

Given these judgments, it is not surprising that the dispatches coming out of Yan'an should have been filled with optimism for the prospects of improved relations with China's communist leaders and warnings not to tie America's future too closely to the fortunes of Chiang Kai-shek.

## THE HURLEY MISSION

While the members of the Dixie Mission worked to unravel the mysteries of the Chinese communist movement, back in Washington Roosevelt wrestled with the question of how to respond to Chiang's demand that Stilwell be replaced. Giving into Chiang seemed a poor tactic since Roosevelt was determined to keep the pressure on Chongqing. And so he took another tack, sending one of his favorite agents, the Oklahoma oilman, Patrick Hurley, to China. Hurley was to act as a buffer between Chiang and Stilwell while promoting the hoped-for coalition between Chiang and Mao.

Hurley, six feet two inches tall in his stocking feet, with a flowing silver mane and handlebar mustache to match, was a striking figure of a man. He was also appallingly eccentric. He could belt out a Choctaw war whoop and had been known to dive into a snake dance under the most unusual circumstances. An egotist who talked incessantly, he hadn't the vaguest idea of how to listen. A less-than-enthusiastic constituent back home in Oklahoma once remarked of Hurley that he was "the only man I ever saw who can strut sitting down." Mao Zedong, who quickly took the measure of the man, dubbed him Chu Teh, "the clown." In Chongqing the Nationalists knew him as "the big wind."[9]

Hurley began his mission on a promising note, journeying first to Moscow, where he secured a commitment from Josef Stalin to steer clear of Chinese affairs. The Soviet dictator, who described Mao and his followers as "margarine" communists, promised that the Soviet Union would offer no aid or encouragement to Yan'an and would keep clear of internal Chinese political affairs. Hurley thus isolated the diplomatic battlefield. It was a sound tactic for a man who hoped to maximize his political clout before going to work on Chiang and Mao. With the Soviets out of the picture, neither side had any place to turn but toward Washington.

Hurley arrived in Chongqing at a critical point in the kaleidoscopically changing Chinese situation. In the summer of 1944 the Japanese began a major offensive in southeastern China. General Stilwell reacted by urging Washington to demand that he be placed in command of all Chinese military forces. Encouraged by General George C. Marshall and Secretary of War Henry L. Stimson, Roosevelt agreed that the time had come to send a strong note to Chiang.

The Generalissimo was put in a truly awkward position by Roosevelt's request. The divisions he controlled represented the key to his remaining power. Yet under the circumstances he found it impossible to issue a flat refusal. Instead he temporized, agreeing in principle to Stilwell's elevation but delaying the appointment.

In September, with the Japanese still on the offensive and Chiang still stalling, Stilwell informed the War Department that, unless he took command of Chinese forces soon, there was going to be a catastrophe. General Marshall, Stilwell's most staunch supporter in Washington and no admirer of Chiang, then sent the Chinese leader a caustic message in which he warned of an impending "military disaster" and demanded that all Chinese forces be turned over to Stilwell immediately. If Chiang refused, Marshall continued, aid to China would be cut off.

Though apparently cornered, Chiang sensed that Patrick Hurley could save him. Instead of surrendering to Marshall's ultimatum, he told Hurley that he would no longer even consider turning the military command over to Stilwell. Instead he demanded that General Stilwell be immediately replaced.

Hurley had been in China only a short while. Nevertheless he intervened decisively on Chiang's behalf. According to Hurley, Chiang had already agreed to begin major military operations against the Japanese. He believed that other agreements were certain to follow once Stilwell, who seemed to be the crux of America's problem in China, was out of the way. The envoy insisted that the president would have to choose between an irascible general and Chiang. "My opinion," he wrote, "is that if you sustain Stilwell in this controversy you will lose Chiang Kai-shek and possibly you will lose China with him."[10]

Given the popularity that Chiang and Madam Chiang had attained in the United States, and the enormous sympathy that the American people felt for China as the victim of Japanese aggression, there was no good time for a break with Chongqing. But as the historian Michael Schaller points out, Roosevelt no doubt viewed the period just prior to the 1944 presidential election as the worst possible moment.[11] It is not surprising, then, that he decided in favor of political expediency, removing Stilwell and sending in his place General Albert Wedemeyer, a staff officer with strong anti-Communist credentials.

Roosevelt's decision to remove Stilwell was more than a simple matter of presidential politics, however. He had for some time been concerned by the growing friction between Chiang and the general. As early as June, 1943, he told Harry Hopkins that Stilwell "obviously hated the Chinese" and that fact was "undoubtedly known to the Generalissimo."[12] He also knew that Chiang had no use for the general. Patrick Hurley's letter advising the president to replace Stilwell, then, did not come out of the blue. On the contrary—it was the final filip in a situation that had been growing worse for some time.

Roosevelt followed up on Stilwell's removal by appointing Hurley to be his ambassador to China. The ebullient Oklahoman took his new assignment seriously, flying to Yan'an where he quickly won Mao's endorsement of a five-point program calling for a joint military effort against Japan, a coalition government, and the creation of a democratic system of government. Mao and Zhou Enlai (Chou En-lai) were delighted with the American

Ambassador Patrick Hurley (fourth from left) meets with Mao Zedong (second from left) and Zhou Enlai (extreme right) in Yan'an.

proposal. Unlike Hurley, they knew that Chiang could not survive in a democratic environment, that he had no popular support. Colonel David Barrett, a member of the Dixie Mission who was there when Hurley unveiled his proposals, recalled being "astounded, because up to then Hurley had always struck me as a pretty shrewd negotiator, and Mao and Chou seemed flabbergasted by his proposals, too. They were beside themselves with joy that Hurley had made what seemed to me to go far beyond any reasonable offer."[13]

Back in Chongqing, Hurley presented his five-point plan to T. V. Soong, Chiang's brother-in-law and his foreign minister, who wanted no part of the agreement. "The Communists have sold you a bill of goods," Soong said. "Never will the National Government grant the Communist request." (One wonders what the foreign minister would have said had he known the plan was Hurley's brainchild.) Instead, Soong and Chiang proposed a three-point plan that had the virtue from Chongqing's point of view of placing the Chinese communist movement entirely under Chiang's control.

Mao's angry rejection of Chiang's obviously unacceptable counter-proposal put an end to Hurley's first attempt at finding a resolution to the differences dividing the Guomindong and the Chinese communists. Undiscouraged, Hurley continued his efforts to bring the two sides together. But even a competent ambassador would have found it impossible to bridge the gap between Chiang and Mao. And ebullience was no substitute for competence. Meanwhile America's China policy remained in limbo, a prisoner of circumstances beyond Washington's control to the end of the war.

## ENDNOTES

1. Henry L. Stimson, quoted in Henry L. Stimson and McGeorge Bundy, *On Active Service in Peace and War* (New York: Harper and Brothers, 1947), p. 528.
2. Clarence Gauss, quoted in Herbert Feis, *The China Tangle: The American Effort in China from Pearl Harbor to the Marshall Mission* (New York: Atheneum, 1965), pp. 76–77.
3. Joseph Stilwell, quoted in Michael Schaller, *The U.S. Crusade in China, 1938–1945* (New York: Columbia University Press, 1979), p. 126.
4. Stilwell, quoted in ibid., p. 111.
5. John Patton Davies, quoted in E. J. Kahn, Jr., *The China Hands: America's Foreign Service Officers and What Befell Them* (New York: Penguin Books, 1972), p. 137.
6. Henry Morganthau, quoted in Schaller, *U.S. Crusade in China*, p. 154.
7. Henry Wallace, quoted in Kahn, *China Hands*, p. 111.
8. Davies memorandum, "How Red Are the Chinese Communists?" November 7, 1944, *Foreign Relations of the United States, 1944* (Washington, D.C., 1967), VI, p. 669. See also Feis, *China Tangle*, p. 263.
9. Kahn, *China Hands*, pp. 122–24.
10. Patrick Hurley, quoted in Feis, *China Tangle*, pp. 198–99.
11. Schaller, *U.S. Crusade in China*, pp. 174–75.
12. Harry Hopkins, quoted in Robert E. Sherwood, *Roosevelt and Hopkins* (New York: Harper and Brothers, 1948), p. 739.
13. David Barrett, quoted in Kahn, *China Hands*, pp. 138–39.

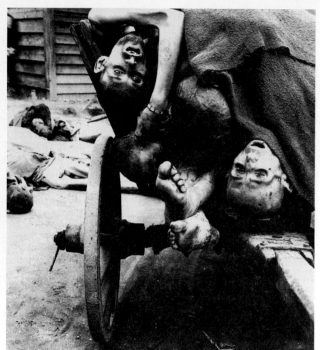

The bodies of some of the 6 million who were enslaved, starved, and then murdered in Nazi concentration camps are here stacked like so much cordwood.

# 24

# *COALITION DIPLOMACY, 1941–1945*

America's plunge into World War II led to the creation of the most powerful military coalition in history. It has been called "the strange alliance," and by any stretch of the imagination it was. The Allies had little in common save a mutual enemy. Adolf Hitler brought them together, and expediency kept them together. It is not surprising, then, that the Grand Alliance was under constant stress, the result of dark suspicions and conflicting ambitions. Josef Stalin made no secret of his intention to maintain control of the Baltic states, a substantial portion of eastern Poland, and that part of Finland acquired during the just-concluded Soviet-Finnish war. Another of Stalin's ambitions, which became clear in the later stages of the war, was to establish a Soviet sphere of influence in Eastern Europe. Winston Churchill, on the other hand, sought to preserve the British empire and restrain postwar Soviet expansion through the creation of a new balance of power. In contrast, Franklin Roosevelt, who championed the principle of national self-determination, hoped to eliminate traditional European imperialism and establish a new liberal political and economic world order.

The conflicting war aims of the Allies notwithstanding, Roosevelt was convinced that postwar cooperation was crucial if there was to be a lasting peace. Though Roosevelt and Churchill often disagreed, the president was reasonably confident that Anglo-American harmony was assured. His main concern was to secure Soviet support.

To many, especially among those who had observed the Soviet state at close quarters, Soviet cooperation seemed problematic. Convinced that Stalin was driven by ideological convictions, they believed that his true purpose was the triumph of international communism. Thus George F. Kennan, the American charge d'affaires in Moscow during the war, later wrote that in 1943 Stalin was "already resolved to exploit a German defeat . . . for the purpose of expelling the British and Americans from Europe and assuring the early communization of the continent."[1] Kennan and like-minded observers faulted Roosevelt for failing to perceive that the Soviets were not prepared to be reasonable.

Roosevelt was not unaware of this point of view. But he chose to be guided by another set of assumptions. There were those inside the Washington establishment, including Vice-President Henry Wallace and Roosevelt's most intimate adviser, Harry Hopkins, who believed Stalin was a more or less traditional Russian statesman who was not moved fundamentally by ideological zeal. Shortly before his death in 1945, Hopkins wrote: "The great enigma about the Soviet Union in the years to come is the policy which the new leaders of Russia will have toward the promotion of world-wide Communism. There is every indication that the Soviet Government today is becoming more and more nationalistic." The fact that the Soviets were even then establishing a sphere of influence in Eastern Europe did not trouble Hopkins. "They are going to see to it that their borders are protected from unfriendly states and I, for one, do not blame them for that."[2]

Hopkins and others of this persuasion believed that though the Soviets often behaved churlishly, it was nevertheless possible to arrive at an accommodation with them. Trust could be built, but only slowly. The Soviet Union's bleak relations with the West, especially the interventions in the Russian Civil War, would not quickly be forgotten.

During the war, Roosevelt adopted a policy of "openhandedness" toward the Soviets, hoping to build the atmosphere of trust and mutual understanding that seemed essential to future cooperation. The president had good reasons for pursuing this course. It was apparent that the distribution of power in the postwar world would be far different from the situation before 1939. German and Japanese power would be destroyed, and France would be of little consequence. British power, too, would be sharply reduced. On the other hand, the Soviet Union was bound to emerge from the war as the second most powerful nation on earth. If Stalin remained a dissatisfied outsider, he could do limitless harm. It therefore seemed essential to cultivate improved relations.

Still, Roosevelt's policy of openhandedness went only so far. For example, he was entirely willing to share information relating to the atomic bomb project (code-named the Manhattan Engineer District) with London. Agreements signed in 1943 and 1944 in fact amounted to an Anglo-American atomic alliance. On the other hand, Washington did everything in its power to keep information regarding the bomb from reaching the Soviets. Security on the project was extraordinarily tight. Scientists who had liberal or left-wing connections (with the single exception of the indispensable Dr. J. Robert Oppenheimer, who headed the scientific team at Los Alamos) were kept off the project. As one security officer explained, his job "was primarily concerned with the formation of judgments as to who were or were not Communists." Later, General Leslie R. Groves, who ran the Manhattan Project, testified:

> There was never from about two weeks from the time I took charge of this project any illusion on my part but that Russia was our enemy and the project was conducted on that basis. I didn't go along with the attitude of the country as a whole that Russia was a gallant ally. . . . Of course, that was so reported to the President.[3]

The army also organized a team of scientists and intelligence officers to gather information on Axis nuclear research. Code-named Alsos, the team traveled with Allied forces, often moving into formerly Axis-held areas before they had been completely secured. The Alsos team's fundamental purpose was to deny the advancing Red Army access to German nuclear data and personnel. So anxious were team members to capture German scientists that they were nicknamed "the body snatchers." They seized all uranium stocks from Strassfurt just ahead of the Soviets and kidnapped scientists and snatched uranium stocks from around Hechingen, inside the already-approved Soviet occupation zone. When Alsos couldn't acquire nuclear materials and data ahead of the Soviets, it sought to destroy it. It was on Alsos's recommendation that the U.S. Army Air Corps bombed nuclear facilities at Orienienburg before the Soviets could move into the area. As General Groves explained, "Our principal concern . . . was to keep information and atomic scientists from falling into the hands of the Russians."[4]

Clearly there were two sides to Roosevelt's Soviet policy. He wanted a friendly relationship. But if Moscow proved intractable, he would rely on an Anglo-American nuclear monopoly to bolster the West's position in dealing with the Kremlin. There might be four policemen in the postwar world, but as the historian Martin Sherwin has noted, only two would have the bomb.[5]

## A SECOND FRONT IN EUROPE

Roosevelt's hopes for postwar cooperation among the Allies rested on the premise that he could win Stalin's confidence. But it soon became clear that good intentions notwithstanding, there were going to be problems. In 1942 the hard-pressed Soviets called on Britain and America to establish a second front in Europe. At that time Soviet soldiers and fliers were bearing the brunt of the fighting. And they were taking horrific losses doing it. Stalin knew it. So did Churchill and Roosevelt. But no second front materialized to divert Hitler's armies from the eastern front in 1942 or 1943.

Although British and American military leaders agreed upon a "Europe first" strategy, they disagreed over the timing of a cross-channel invasion of France. American strategists, who feared that the Soviet army of eight million would collapse if relief did not come quickly, were anxious to strike at the heart of the beast. The British saw things differently. Their World War I experience and their more recent encounter with the Wehrmacht made them reluctant to attempt a frontal assault on Hitler's "Fortress Europe." They preferred a strategy of nibbling away at the peripheries of German power first. Moreover, from London's standpoint it was vital to secure the Mediterranean, Britain's lifeline to its empire, before challenging the Wehrmacht head on. In 1942, the threat to that lifeline seemed quite real. If General Erwin Rommel took Suez, and Spain's Francisco Franco jumped into the war and seized Gibraltar, the Mediterranean would become an Axis lake; Britain would be cut off from the east and done perhaps irreparable harm.

In May 1942, with British and American strategists still squabbling, the Soviet foreign minister, V. M. Molotov, journeyed to London seeking a second front and recognition of the Soviet Union's 1941 boundaries. But he got next to nothing from Foreign Secretary Anthony Eden. The Soviet diplomat was more successful in Washington. Aware that Stalin suspected his Western partners of being only too happy to see Soviets and Germans killing each other in record numbers, Roosevelt promised Molotov a second front in Europe before the end of 1942.

The president's promise had long-run negative effects, for it soon became apparent that he could not keep it. Fearing a debacle, Churchill absolutely refused to participate in a cross-channel invasion in 1942. Instead, he urged the president to consider securing North Africa. At length Roosevelt gave in. He had to admit that Churchill was correct about chances for a successful invasion of France in 1942. The North African operation, code-named Torch, would not relieve the pressure on the Soviets. But it appeared to be better than nothing.

Generals George C. Marshall and Dwight D. Eisenhower were distressed by the president's commitment to Operation Torch. They feared that the British would convert the president to a "peripheral" strategy, which they considered a waste of scarce resources that also risked a Soviet collapse. Their greatest concern, however, was that Torch would divert resources from the planned 1943 invasion of Europe. And that is precisely what happened. Because the North African operation used up more men and material than had been expected, Roosevelt and Churchill settled on two more Mediterranean operations for 1943, the Sicilian and Italian campaigns, and postponed the cross-channel invasion of France for another year.

Roosevelt realized that this further postponement of a second front

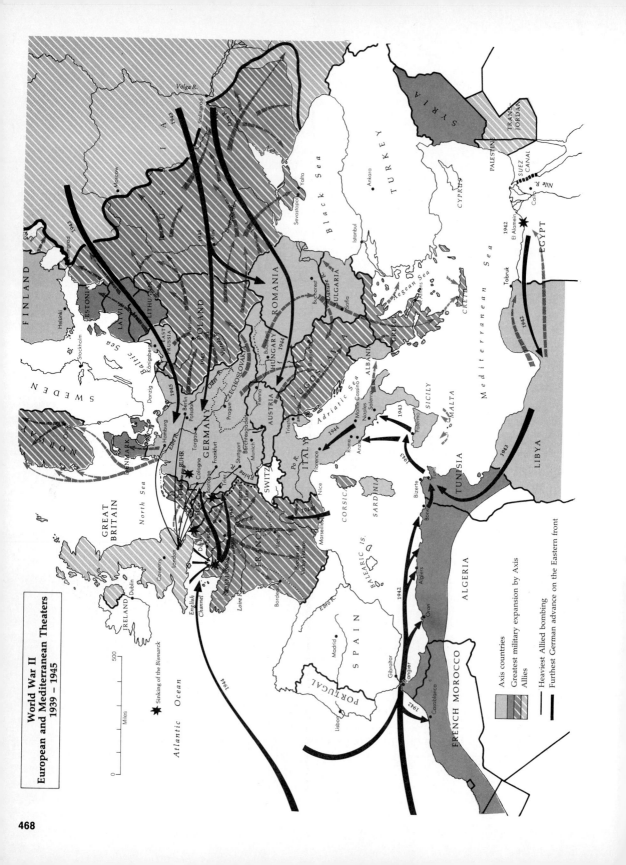

## World War II
### European and Mediterranean Theaters
### 1939 – 1945

**FINLAND**

**SWEDEN**

**NORWAY**

**RUSSIA**

Volga R.

Moscow

Stalingrad 1943

Helsinki

Stockholm

ESTONIA

LATVIA

LITHUANIA

Leningrad 1941

Königsberg

Danzig

EAST PRUSSIA

**POLAND**

Dnieper R.

Don R.

Warsaw

**Black Sea**

Yalta

Sevastopol

**TURKEY**

Ankara

Istanbul

**SYRIA**

**TRANS-JORDAN**

PALESTINE

SUEZ CANAL

Nile R.

Cairo

**EGYPT**

El Alamein 1942

**CYPRUS**

*Aegean Sea*

Athens

CRETE

RHODES

1942

Tobruk

**LIBYA**

1943

**Mediterranean Sea**

**GREAT BRITAIN**

*North Sea*

Coventry

London

*English Channel*

Dunkirk

**IRELAND**

Dublin

**Atlantic Ocean**

DENMARK

Hamburg

Elbe R.

Berlin

Potsdam

Torgau

Cologne

RUHR

Frankfurt

Trier

**GERMANY**

Prague

CZECHOSLOVAKIA

Dresden

Oder R.

Munich

Berchtesgaden

Stuttgart

Magino t Line

Rhine R.

**SWITZ.**

Vienna

**AUSTRIA**

**HUNGARY**

Budapest

Danube R.

1944

**ROMANIA**

Bucharest

**BULGARIA**

Sofia

Belgrade

**YUGOSLAVIA**

**ALBANIA**

*Adriatic Sea*

Trieste

Venice

Po R.

Florence

**ITALY**

Rome

Anzio

Monte Cassino

Naples

Salerno

1943

**SICILY**

Palermo

**MALTA**

**SARDINIA**

**CORSICA**

Nice

Marseilles

**FRANCE**

Bordeaux

Vichy France

Loire R.

NORMANDY

1944

1944

1944

**SPAIN**

Madrid

Lisbon

**PORTUGAL**

BALEARIC IS.

Ebro R.

Gibraltar

Tangier

Oran

Algiers

1942

Casablanca

1942

**FRENCH MOROCCO**

**ALGERIA**

**TUNISIA**

Bizerte

Bône

1943

Tripoli

Sinking of the Bismarck

500

Miles

0

**468**

### Legend

Axis countries

Greatest military expansion by Axis

Allies

Heaviest Allied bombing

Furthest German advance on the Eastern front

in Europe would irritate Stalin, who of course feared treachery. Therefore, on the last day of the Casablanca conference with Churchill, in January 1943, Roosevelt announced that the Allies would settle for nothing less than the unconditional surrender of the Axis powers. It was a promise to the Soviets that there would be no separate peace and that England and America were in the war to the finish.

Though the unconditional surrender doctrine pleased Stalin, he continued to berate his allies for their laggardly ways, warning Roosevelt two months after Casablanca that any further delay in opening a second front would be "fraught" with "grave danger."[6] The president didn't have to be overly perceptive to understand the Soviet leader's meaning. At the end of January 1943, the Red Army raised the siege of Stalingrad and captured an entire German army. After this Soviet victory, Soviet and German forces on the eastern front fought on relatively equal terms. The opportunity for a separate peace was there if Stalin wanted to pursue it.

From Stalin's point of view the second front in France, which the

The invasion of Europe in June 1944 was the largest amphibious military operation ever undertaken. Here General Dwight Eisenhower, commander of all Allied forces in Europe, meets with some of the assault troops prior to the invasion.

Western Allies opened in 1944, was better than no second front at all. But it came two years late. Mounting a cross-channel invasion in early 1943 would have meant a great deal to the Soviet dictator. By the following year, however, the military situation had changed, and the suspicious Stalin was no doubt prone to dwell on the three years that the Red army had faced the Wehrmacht alone. It is debatable whether Stalin was capable of feeling gratitude. But in any event, by 1944 the time for gratitude had passed.

## THE ITALIAN PRECEDENT

Allied forces landed in Sicily on July 10, 1943, and secured the island in a month's time. Two weeks after the initial landing a group of Italian Fascists, led by Marshal Pietro Badoglio, overthrew Benito Mussolini in a coup d'état. Badoglio and his followers, seeing the hopelessness of Italy's situation, wanted to negotiate with the Allies while they still had some leverage.

General Eisenhower, who commanded all Allied forces in Western Europe, did not relish the idea of dealing with Fascists. He had done it once before when problems associated with the North African invasion led him to make a deal with the Vichyite admiral, Jean Darlan. At that time the public outcry had been intense. "What the hell are we fighting for?" cried the popular radio commentator Edward R. Murrow.[7] Others wondered angrily whether the allies would someday make a deal with Mussolini. And now here was Eisenhower perilously close to doing exactly that.

But Eisenhower had a problem. Because the Allies were gearing up for the 1944 invasion of France, the force he was about to put ashore in Italy was vastly inferior to the German and Italian armies it would face. Under the circumstances, he felt he had no choice but to recommend to Roosevelt and Churchill that they negotiate terms with Badoglio and neutralize the Italian army. Reluctantly, Roosevelt and Churchill agreed.

Under the terms of the agreement, the Badloglio regime would administer Italy, with overall control vested in an Allied Advisory Council made up of British and American representatives. The Soviets were not allowed to participate.

At first, Moscow protested Anglo-American policy in Italy. It was a clear violation of the unconditional surrender doctrine. Moreover, there were some 300,000 Italian troops fighting in support of the Germans on the Eastern Front. Under the circumstances Stalin had every right to play a role in Italy's political reorganization. It wasn't long, however, before he abandoned all complaints. The Soviet dictator recognized a precedent when he saw one. The Western Allies controlled developments in Italy because their military forces were on the scene and because as a Mediterranean country it was important to Britain's future security. Stalin saw an exact analogy between this situation and the one developing in Eastern Europe. Later he told the Yugoslav communist Milovan Djilas: "This war is not as in the past; whoever occupies a territory also imposes on it his own social system. Everyone imposes his own system as far as his army can reach. It cannot be otherwise."[8]

The Red Army's advance into Eastern Europe caused grave concern in Washington and London. Stalin seemed determined to create a sphere of interest there. Yet his policies ran contrary to Churchill's hopes for restricting Soviet expansionism as well as Roosevelt's commitment to the principle of national self-determination.

Nevertheless, though fragmentary, there is evidence to suggest that before the end of 1943 Roosevelt had begun to reconcile himself to the creation of a Soviet sphere in Eastern Europe. In the autumn of that year he noted to Churchill that the West had "set the precedent for all such future activities in the war" by its actions in Italy.[9] And in face-to-face conversations with Stalin at the Tehran conference in November, he partially satisfied the Soviet leader's Eastern European ambitions, telling him that he would support the Soviet claim to the Baltic states and the Polish territory it had seized in 1939.

Churchill, who made the same commitment to Stalin at Tehran, later sought an agreement with the Soviet dictator regarding the Balkans. In October 1944, he journeyed to Moscow for an extraordinary meeting. After a series of negotiating sessions between Foreign Secretary Anthony Eden and Molotov, the principals sat down across the table from one another in the Kremlin. According to Churchill's dramatic description of their meeting, he handed Stalin a slip of paper on which was written his proposal for the division of influence in the Balkans. The Soviets would enjoy 90 percent of the "say" in Rumania, while the Western Allies exercised similar predominance in Greece. Influence would be divided evenly in Yugoslavia, while the Soviets would have the lion's share—75 percent—in Bulgaria and Hungary. Stalin listened to the translation and agreed, marking the paper with a tick of his blue pencil. It was all done in a matter of moments.

Later Churchill complained that he had not intended this agreement to decide the future of South Central Europe and the Balkans. He thought of it only as an agreement designed to keep the Allies from getting "at cross-purposes" as the war wound down. But this argument bears little scrutiny. Certainly London had no intention of allowing Greece the luxury of political self-determination. How can it be that Churchill expected the Soviets to be less aggressive in pursuit of their interests in Eastern Europe?

## THE POLISH QUESTION

After the German attack on the Soviet Union in June 1941, Churchill arranged a reconciliation between Moscow and the Polish government in exile, which had set up shop in London. The two governments exchanged ambassadors, but the relationship was troubled from the start. There was first of all the nagging question of Poland's eastern boundary. The 1921 Treaty of Riga concluded a Soviet-Polish conflict in which, at the Soviet

Union's expense, the Poles extended their boundary 150 miles east of the Curzon Line, the boundary established at the Paris peace conference. As a result, during the interwar years 5 million Belorussians and Ukrainians found themselves living under Polish rule. In 1939, Stalin took back this territory, establishing a boundary that roughly approximated the Curzon Line. The Polish government in exile, however, refused to accept this change, insisting on the prewar boundary.

The Big Three decided the issue among themselves at the Tehran conference. Churchill and Roosevelt believed that Stalin had a good case and were in any event unwilling to risk rupturing the alliance for the sake of the Poles. They agreed that the 1939 boundary would stand and that after the war Poland might be compensated by acquiring territory to the west at Germany's expense. The Western Allies then had to convince the Poles to accept this compromise. But that turned out to be impossible. Even after Churchill publicly endorsed the Soviet position early in 1944, the Poles refused to concede the point.

Another issue that troubled Soviet-Polish relations erupted in April 1943, when the Germans announced the discovery of a mass grave in the Katyn forest near Smolensk that contained the remains of four thousand Polish army officers who they claimed (correctly) had been massacred by the Soviets. When the Polish government in exile demanded a Red Cross investigation, Moscow denounced the "slander" and broke relations. A few months later Stalin announced that he would tolerate no government in postwar Poland that was not "friendly" to the Soviet Union. He then established the Polish Committee of National Liberation, a communist group headquartered in Lublin, a city already liberated by the Red Army. In July 1944, the Lublin committee began administering portions of occupied Poland.

In October 1944, Churchill made a desperate stab at staving off Soviet recognition of the Lublin regime. He took Stanislaw Mikolajczyk, the head of the Polish government in exile, to Moscow for direct talks with Stalin. Churchill hoped to strike a compromise in which the London Poles would accept the boundary arrangements tentatively worked out at Tehran in return for Stalin's agreement to restore relations. But even under intense pressure the Pole stood firm. Churchill was furious, warning Mikolajczyk: "We are not going to wreck the peace of Europe because of quarrels between Poles. In your obstinacy you do not see what is at stake. . . . You are absolutely incapable of facing facts. Never in my life have I seen such people."[10]

Late in 1944, Stalin ignored a last-minute appeal from Roosevelt and recognized the Polish provisional government in Lublin. Now that unfortunate country had two governments. But only one was supported by the might of the Red Army.

As President Roosevelt prepared for the conference at Yalta to be held in February 1945, he was advised by State Department officials that the time had come to get tough with the Soviets both as to the Polish boundary and to Poland's future government. But FDR saw things differently. His military advisers insisted on the importance of bringing the Soviets into the

Winston Churchill (left), Franklin Roosevelt, and Josef Stalin met for the last time in February 1945, at the Crimean resort town of Yalta. The president, though smiling broadly, looks weary and frail.

Asian war. Tens of thousands of American lives were at stake. Moreover, like Churchill, he was unwilling to jeopardize possibilities for future Soviet-American cooperation in the postwar world over an issue of such relative insignificance as Poland's boundary or even its form of government. The president was prepared to make representations on behalf of Poland. But he was not willing to push matters to extremes.

At Yalta, Roosevelt and Churchill appeared to make some headway with regard to Poland's future. After heated debate, Stalin agreed to expand the Lublin regime (which had by this time moved to Warsaw) by including a small number of noncommunist Poles. He also agreed that Poland should hold elections in which all "antifascist parties" could participate. The Declaration of Liberated Europe, also signed at Yalta, called for the establishment of Eastern European provisional governments that were "broadly representative of all democratic elements in the population and pledged to the earliest possible establishment through free elections of governments responsive to the will of the people."[11]

These fine-sounding words obscured the fact that the Yalta agreements on Poland only papered over wide differences among the Allies. To suggest that elections would be held as soon as possible guaranteed nothing, since the Soviets could define the appropriate circumstances. Moreover, Roosevelt himself had agreed that Stalin had every right to expect that a new Polish government should be "friendly" toward the Soviet Union. Since the vast majority of Poles despised the Soviets, truly free elections would undoubtedly have produced a government unfriendly to Moscow. It might not then be "possible" to hold such elections for a very long time. Even if elections were held, the Soviet leader had his own definition of who the "fascists" were that might be excluded from the political process and what constituted a democratic election. In the Soviet Union, it began with a slate of candidates offered by the Communist party.

Admiral William D. Leahy remarked to the president that the agreement on Poland was "so elastic that the Russians can stretch it all the way from Yalta to Washington without ever technically breaking it." The president's revealing reply was: "I know, Bill—I know it. But it's the best I can do for Poland at this time."[12] Roosevelt was right. He had no leverage. The Red Army controlled Eastern Europe, the Germans had not yet surrendered, Roosevelt needed Soviet aid for the war in Asia, and he had to keep in mind the importance of postwar cooperation among "the four policemen." If the price he had to pay was a Soviet sphere of influence in Eastern Europe, he felt a growing compulsion to accept that despite growing increasingly uneasy about Soviet intentions.

## THE GERMAN QUESTION

Strange though it may seem, even in the late summer of 1944, with Allied armies converging on Germany, the United States had yet to develop a clear policy regarding the Reich's future. In August, Secretary of the Treasury Henry Morgenthau stepped into that void with a plan calling for the partition and deindustrialization of Germany. Mines would be flooded, factories dismantled, and machine tools as well as other capital equipment shipped to the victims of Nazi aggression as reparations. The smaller German states created by partition would have pastoral and agricultural economies and would never again be in a position to threaten the peace of the world.

The idea of partitioning Germany had earlier been discussed at the Tehran conference, where it won the endorsement of the Big Three. Winston Churchill had even gotten down to specifics, suggesting the creation of a north German and a south German state with the Saar and Ruhr to be placed under international control. It is not surprising, then, that he and Franklin Roosevelt both initially endorsed Morgenthau's ideas. The president was convinced that after World War I the Allies had let the Germans off too easily. This time, he said, "we have got to be tough with Germany and I mean the German people, not just the Nazis." It had to be "driven home to them that the whole nation has been engaged in a lawless conspiracy against the decencies of modern civilization."[13]

Secretary of State Cordell Hull and Secretary of War Henry L. Stimson, resentful of Morgenthau's interference, tried to convince the president that the partition of Germany would sow the seeds of future wars by encouraging German irredentism (the desire to restore the country to its prewar status even at the risk of war). They also pointed out that such a policy was contrary to America's own economic interests. Europe could not prosper unless Germany did. And a prosperous Europe was essential as a market for American agricultural and industrial products. Recalling the economic circumstances that surrounded Hitler's rise to power, they also suggested that the best security against future aggression in Europe was a prosperous Germany. Charles E. Bohlen, a leading State Department expert on Soviet affairs, added a final fillip to the argument against partition when he noted with a certain amount of concern that a divided Germany would leave the Soviet Union "the only important military and political force on the continent of Europe."[14]

With opposition to the Morgenthau plan growing inside the government as well as in the press, the president quickly backtracked. Admitting that he had endorsed the idea without giving it much thought, Roosevelt said, "No one wants to make Germany a wholly agricultural nation again."[15]

By the time the Big Three met at Yalta, the Morgenthau plan was dead. It is not surprising, then, that when Stalin pressed for Germany's dismemberment Churchill objected and the president turned the proposal aside in favor of creating a commission to study the question. The Western Allies, in fact, had no coherent policy for postwar Germany, but they were reasonably certain that partition and deindustrialization were bad ideas.

The changed attitude of Roosevelt and Churchill toward Germany's dismemberment inevitably affected their position on reparations. The post–World War I experience made Western policy makers skeptical about the wisdom of insisting on reparations to begin with. As the idea that Germany should be rehabilitated took root, reparations payments that would act as a drag on the country's postwar revival became increasingly unappealing. Josef Stalin suggested that the Germans should pay $20 billion in reparations, half to the Soviet Union. Churchill and Roosevelt agreed to use the $20 billion figure "as the basis" for future discussions. But again nothing was decided.

Although the Allies found no satisfactory solution to either the German or Polish questions at Yalta, the conference did produce a wide-ranging understanding on Far Eastern issues. Pressed by his military chiefs, Roosevelt secured Stalin's promise that the Red Army would march against Japanese forces on the Asian mainland within three months of the end of the war in Europe. The Soviet leader also made an important political concession, agreeing to turn his back on the Chinese communists and negotiate "a pact of friendship and alliance" with the Chinese Nationalists. In return Roosevelt and Churchill agreed that Stalin could have the Kuril Island chain that stretches south from the Kamchatka Peninsula toward Japan, and the southern half of Sakhalin Island, which Tokyo had taken from Russia as part of the settlement following the Russo-Japanese War of 1904–05. Contingent on the approval of the Guomindong the Soviets were also to have the use of the internationalized port of Lüda (Dairen) and a lease on Lüshan (Port Arthur). The Chinese Eastern and South Manchurian railroads were to be placed under the control of a Soviet-Chinese company that would protect Soviet interests in the region. At the same time the Soviets recognized Chinese sovereignty over Manchuria. The agreement also called for the maintenance of the status quo in Outer Mongolia, an area the Soviets had transformed into a people's republic in the 1920s.

Here Adolf Hitler surveys bomb damage during the last days of the Third Reich.

Stalin's commitment to the Declaration on Liberated Europe, his endorsement of the Atlantic Charter, his formal agreement to enter the Pacific war within three months of victory in Europe, and the generally harmonious atmosphere that prevailed during the conference led some on the American delegation at Yalta to describe the gathering as the beginning of a new more positive era in East-West relations. Harry Hopkins said: "We believed in our hearts that this was the dawn of a new age we had all been praying for."[16] But Yalta was hardly that. On the contrary, it exposed growing differences between the Allies over Poland and Germany, issues of enormous consequence. None of the Big Three wanted to press these questions to the point of a break. There was still a war to be won. But the differences, which were quite real, grew more pronounced as the European aspect of the war wound down.

In the waning days of the war in Europe, the optimism generated at the Crimean conference began to fade. Western observers were prohibited from entering Eastern European nations liberated by the Red Army. But the stories of mass arrests and political intimidation that leaked to the West made Stalin's intentions increasingly obvious. Another setback to Roosevelt's hopes for postwar cooperation came when Stalin abruptly announced that he would not send Foreign Minister V. M. Molotov to San Francisco for the conference to organize the United Nations. Then, only weeks before the president's sudden death, the Soviet leader accused the Western Allies of planning to make a separate peace with the Germans. He charged that in return for the promise of easier terms, the Germans had agreed to allow Anglo-American forces to move east unhindered. Roosevelt, of course, denied the allegation. "Frankly," he told Stalin, "I cannot avoid a feeling of bitter resentment toward your informer . . . for such vile misrepresentations of my actions or those of my trusted subordinates."[17]

There is no way of knowing how Roosevelt would have handled the problems of the postwar era. He died suddenly on April 12, 1945, before the German surrender and before the first successful test of the atomic bomb. It is clear, however, that his hopes for postwar cooperation were slipping and that he believed chances for a Soviet-American confrontation were on the increase.

## A NEW HAND AT THE HELM

Vice-President Harry Truman was stunned at the news of Roosevelt's death. "I'm not big enough," he told a Senate friend.[18] Back home in Independence, they knew the feeling. It was like having a load of hay dropped on you. "President Truman" sounded all wrong to the man who was happiest with three aces in his hand, a bottle of bourbon nearby, and political friends to jaw with. Still, if deep inside Truman felt insecure, he knew he could not show it. Roosevelt had left a pair of very large shoes to fill. He would have to appear confident and act decisively.

But what a job it was. The war in Europe was winding down, leaving the continent in a state of political confusion and economic chaos. The war in the Pacific continued to rage. There was the new collective security organization to be organized. And on the day he was sworn in Truman learned for the first time of the Manhattan Project, a development that Secretary of War Stimson described as "a first step in a new control by man over the forces of nature too revolutionary and dangerous to fit into the old concepts."[19] Finally, there were the Soviets, whose behavior in Eastern Europe raised serious doubts about the future of the wartime coalition.

Truman was certain about one thing: he wanted no deviation from the policies of his illustrious predecessor. The problem was that, aside from a general commitment to maintaining a spirit of cooperation among the Allies, it was impossible to get a clear fix on what they had been. For years Roosevelt had conducted his own diplomacy, relying on face-to-face meetings with world leaders and on personal representatives like Harry Hopkins. He had removed the State Department from the policy making loop, thus denying Truman a clear record for study. Moreover, some of his most important commitments—for example his agreement with Stalin that the Polish government must be "friendly" to the Soviet Union—were nowhere written down.

The new president's difficulties were especially acute because on the fundamental issue—how to handle the Soviets—there were wide differences of opinion among those in government. Secretary of the Navy James Forrestal believed the Soviets were determined "to make their system global" and advised Truman that it would be wise to "have a showdown with them now" rather than wait. On the other extreme, Harry Hopkins and former Vice-President Henry Wallace spoke for those who had not yet given up on the possibility of postwar cooperation with Moscow. Hopkins warned against those like Forrestal "who have already made up their minds that there is no possibility of working with the Russians. . . . From my point of view that is an untenable position and can but lead to disaster." Hopkins believed that Stalin's purposes were highly nationalistic, that his ambitions were limited to the creation of a sphere of influence along Soviet borders, and that Washington had little room to criticize considering America's insistence on a sphere of influence in the Caribbean and Central America. Secretary of War Stimson made the same point when he observed that "some Americans are anxious to hang on to exaggerated views of the Monroe Doctrine and at the same time bite into every question that comes up in Central Europe."[20]

The president was most influenced by the views of Admiral William D. Leahy, who had served in the White House throughout the war, and W. Averell Harriman, the ambassador to the Soviet Union who returned to Washington after Roosevelt's death and quickly established himself as a key insider in the new administration. Originally, Roosevelt selected Harriman, one of the richest and most powerful men in America, to go to Moscow because he had done business in the Soviet Union in the 1920s and was sympathetic toward the Soviets. But three years of butting heads with Soviet bureaucrats and observing the Stalinist regime at close quarters had soured him. Harriman did not believe that Stalin was driven by ideological conviction. He saw the Soviet ruler as a latter-day czar, an expansionist who would stop only when he was stopped. "Russian plans for establishing satellite states are a threat to the world and to us," he said. Once Stalin "had control of bordering areas," he would attempt to penetrate the next adjacent countries." Logically, then, the "issue ought to be fought out in so far as we could with the Soviet Union in the present bordering areas."[21]

Harriman's message was clear. The Soviets understood only the language of strength. But if confronted by strong counterpressure, they could be restrained. And the place to make the stand was in Eastern Europe, particularly in Poland where, Harriman insisted, the Soviets were violating their agreement to hold free elections.

Here was a message that appealed to the forthright and plainspoken Truman. Yet if he took quickly to the idea of adopting a stronger line toward the Soviets, he refused to go too far in that direction. Thus he rejected Churchill's proposal that American forces race for Prague to improve the West's bargaining position in Central Europe at the end of the war. Nor would he renege on the Far Eastern commitments FDR had made to Stalin at Yalta. Truman wanted to be assertive with the Soviets, but not so assertive that the alliance would collapse.

Truman had the opportunity to try out his new approach on April

22, 1945, when Foreign Minister Molotov arrived in Washington. Prior to their meeting on the next day Truman told his cabinet that as far as Eastern Europe was concerned, he did not "expect to get 100 percent of what we wanted." But he thought that "on important matters . . . we should be able to get 85 percent."[22]

One such important matter was the Polish question, and the president intended to settle that during his first meeting with the Soviet foreign minister. Molotov attempted to defend the Soviet position on Poland. But he had not gotten far before Truman first cut him off and then read him off. Molotov was furious. "I have never been talked to like that in my life," he complained. But Truman was unrelenting. "Carry out your agreements and you won't get talked to like that," he said.[23]

The scene was vintage Truman. But even in the president's mind it raised some questions. In a conversation with Joseph E. Davies, a former ambassador to the Soviet Union and one of those who feared that the president's tough line would prove counterproductive, Truman remarked proudly, "I gave it to him straight—a one two to the jaw, I let him have it straight." But then, revealing his own uneasiness, he asked Davies, "Did I do right?" Davies let Truman know that he hadn't "done right." But the president remained intent on pressuring the Soviets, still hoping to force them to loosen their grip on Eastern Europe.[24]

It was clear that the Soviet Union, devastated by the war, would need capital to rebuild its shattered economy. Harriman, who had previously discussed a possible reconstruction loan with Molotov, thought a trade might be in order: the United States would provide a large loan, and, in return, the Soviets would make concessions to Washington's point of view in Eastern Europe.

Following the German surrender, Truman, who found Harriman's idea attractive, initiated a policy that was intended to put a slow economic squeeze on the Soviets, thus making them even more needful of a loan. He adopted a hard line in opposition to German reparations payments to the Soviet Union and also ordered Leo Crowley, head of the Foreign Economic Administration, which administered the lend-lease program, to slowly reduce the aid being sent to the Soviet Union, thus further increasing Moscow's economic difficulties. The idea was to increase the pressure slowly so that it would not appear that Washington was, in fact, attempting to use its economic weapon. But Crowley mishandled the assignment, stopping all aid instantaneously. He even ordered ships at sea carrying lend-lease aid to return to the United States.

The Soviets and the British, who were also cut off, complained about what Stalin called this "brutal" treatment.[25] Truman then relented, authorizing the shipment of goods already in the pipeline. He also tried to extricate himself from this embarrassing situation by claiming that he was bound by legislation to end aid when the fighting had stopped. But the Soviets understood the cutoff as a threat and reacted predictably by standing pat in Eastern Europe.

Not long afterward the first tangible indication that Soviet-American relations were heading for the rocks took place at the San Francisco conference, which convened in late April for the purpose of organizing the United Nations. Sparks first flew when the Soviets objected to naming the American secretary of state, Edward Stettinius, permanent chair. Moscow's insistence that the communist-dominated Warsaw government be recognized as the only legitimate representative of Poland further annoyed Washington. When the American delegates violated an earlier agreement by proposing that profascist Argentina be admitted as a member of the organization, it was the Soviets' turn to be angry. They deadlocked the conference by insisting (in violation of another agreement made at Yalta) that members of the UN Security Council should be enabled to use their veto power not simply to block action on substantive questions but to prevent any issue from appearing before the council.

Within a month Truman had presided over a serious slide in Soviet-American relations. That was not the plan. Something had to be done. And so the president and his advisers conceived the idea of sending the ailing Harry Hopkins to Moscow. Roosevelt's most intimate adviser, Hopkins had, during several wartime meetings, established a solid relationship with Stalin. In his *Memoirs* Truman recalled that he instructed Hopkins to tell Stalin that he would carry out the agreements entered into at Yalta and that the Soviets must do the same. He also told Hopkins "he could use diplomatic language or he could use a baseball bat if he thought that this was the proper approach to Mr. Stalin."[26]

Hopkins, who left his bat at home, told Stalin that recent Soviet behavior, especially in Poland, had eroded popular sympathy for the Soviet Union in the United States. Unless Moscow was prepared to alter course, it would be increasingly difficult for the president to carry out Roosevelt's policies.

But Stalin refused to budge on the Polish question. Instead, he reminded Hopkins that over the past twenty-five years Poland had twice served "as the corridor" for German invasions. It was "therefore in Russia's vital interest that Poland should be both strong and friendly." The Soviet leader added that if the recent suspension of lend-lease aid had been "designed as pressure . . . in order to soften" him up, "it was a fundamental mistake." He said that if he were "approached frankly on a friendly basis, much could be done." On the other hand, "reprisals in any form would bring about the exact opposite effect."[27]

Unshakable on the Polish question, Stalin did, however, make other gestures of goodwill. He told Hopkins that Soviet forces would be deployed on the Manchurian border and ready to join in the Far Eastern war by August 8. He also promised to cooperate with Generalissimo Chiang Kai-shek, thus alleviating the fear that he might offer his support to the Chinese communists. Finally, he ended the stalemate in San Francisco by accepting the American position on voting procedures in the UN Security Council and agreed to a Big Three meeting at Potsdam, presumably for the purpose of resolving remaining issues and restoring friendly relations among the Allies.

## POTSDAM

The meeting of the Big Three at Potsdam just outside Berlin in mid-July 1945 represented the last real hope for postwar cooperation among the wartime allies. At Yalta, Churchill, Roosevelt, and Stalin had sidestepped the major issues that threatened Allied unity. But now, with the war in Europe over, the fate of the Continent had to be decided. The Allies had little difficulty settling lesser issues, including the "de-Nazification" and disarmament of Germany, the creation of an Allied Control Council to decide questions relating to the whole of Germany, and the cession of German territory east of the Oder and Neisse rivers to Poland. But they found no solutions for the basic questions that had gone unanswered at Yalta. Until his defeat in Britain's general elections, which came partway through the conference (he was replaced at that point by the new Labor prime minister, Clement Attlee), Churchill pounded away at the whole question of Eastern Europe with particular emphasis on the future of Poland. But Stalin was unmovable, pointing out that the British were unwilling to allow true national self-determination in Greece.

The Western Allies proved just as determined to resist Stalin's demands for the partition of Germany. Stalin gave in on this point, agreeing to the ultimate reunification of Germany. But reunification was in any event a moot question since the Soviet dictator had it in his power to keep Germany east of the Elbe River under his control for as long as he deemed it expedient. De facto partition of the Reich was an accomplished fact no matter what London and Washington wanted.

The last major question dividing the Allies was the reparations question. And again East and West could find no basis for agreement. The Soviets revived their earlier proposal that the Germans pay $20 billion in indemnities, half of this to them. But Washington and London, having already decided that Germany should be restored as a nation of some (though as yet indeterminate) consequence in Central Europe, rejected this proposal. The Western Allies saw reparations as a drain on a German economy that needed to be strengthened. As President Truman later explained, it was clear that to some extent Germany would have to be restored after the war. He was not going to agree to reparations that would drain the Reich's already devastated economy, leaving the American taxpayer to foot the bill.

In the face of this complete deadlock, the Allies agreed to accept only what they could not prevent. The occupying power in each zone was authorized to take appropriate reparations from that zone. Beyond that, the Western Allies, who controlled the industrial part of Germany, agreed to turn over to the Soviets 10 percent "of such industrial capital equipment as is unnecessary for the German peace economy."[28] The Soviets could also have an additional 15 percent of western Germany's industrial production in exchange for food and raw materials of an equivalent value.

Centrifugal forces were now tugging hard at the Grand Alliance. Major issues remained unresolved, and each of the two superpowers that had emerged from the war was looking to its own interests. The result, already apparent in outline, was the emergence of political bipolarity. The cold war had not yet begun. But the alliance was clearly coming to pieces as American and Soviet leaders pursued conflicting ambitions.

## ENDING THE PACIFIC WAR

The first successful test of an atomic bomb took place on July 16, 1945, the day before serious talks began at the Potsdam conference. This news changed a great many things for Truman, among them his attitude toward Soviet intervention in the Asian war. Suddenly possessed of virtually limitless power,

This poster by James Montgomery Flagg plays upon the strongly felt desire of most Americans for revenge against Japan following the attack on Pearl Harbor and atrocities committed by Japanese forces in the Philippines.

he and his recently appointed Secretary of State, South Carolina's James F. Byrnes, now believed that their problem was to find some method of discouraging Soviet intervention. After conferring with Truman on the outcome of the atomic test, Prime Minister Winston Churchill cabled London, "It is quite clear that the United States do not at the present time desire Russian participation in the war against Japan."[29]

Truman and Byrnes quickly contrived a strategy to delay a Soviet declaration of war against Japan. Moscow and Chongqing were then negotiating the precise terms of the territorial and economic concessions the Soviet Union was to receive in Manchuria at war's end. Byrnes cabled Chiang Kai-shek urging him to prolong the talks. The secretary hoped that while the negotiations continued a nuclear attack on Japan would bring the war to an abrupt conclusion before the Soviets could intervene and claim the concessions offered them at Yalta.

Truman was walking a thin line. He hoped to limit Soviet expansion in Asia. At the same time he had not yet entirely given up hope for a cooperative relationship with Moscow in the postwar era. He therefore felt obliged to tell Stalin something (but not too much) about the powerful new weapon American and émigré scientists, who had come to the United States fleeing Nazism and Fascism, had developed. It would certainly do Soviet-American relations no good if the Soviet leader first read about the atomic bomb in the newspapers.

Doing his level best to underplay the significance of what he was about to say, Truman ambled up to Stalin after one of their negotiating sessions at Potsdam and offhandedly mentioned that the United States had "perfected a very powerful explosive which we are going to use against the Japanese and [which] we think ... will end the war."[30] Stalin asked no questions, only indicating that he hoped the weapon would be effective. The Soviet leader's lack of interest was as much a disguise as Truman's casual air. He understood precisely what the president was not exactly trying to tell him. That evening Stalin informed Marshal G. K. Zhukov that the Americans had successfully tested an atomic bomb and that Soviet scientists would have to accelerate their own research efforts.

On July 26, toward the end of the conference, Truman, Prime Minister Clement Attlee, and Chiang Kai-shek issued the Potsdam Declaration, a demand that the Japanese surrender unconditionally or face "utter devastation." When Tokyo failed to respond appropriately, Truman ordered the immediate use of nuclear weapons against Japanese targets.[31]

Eleven days later, on the morning of August 6, the *Enola Gay,* a B-29 bomber piloted by Colonel Paul Tibbets and carrying a nine-thousand-pound atomic bomb, rumbled down the runway on the island of Tinian in the Marianas. Engines screaming, the plane lurched heavily into the air and began a slow ascent. On reaching a cruising altitude of thirty thousand feet, the plane leveled off and headed for Hiroshima. At a little past eight in the morning the plane approached its target. At 8:14 A.M. the bomb bay doors

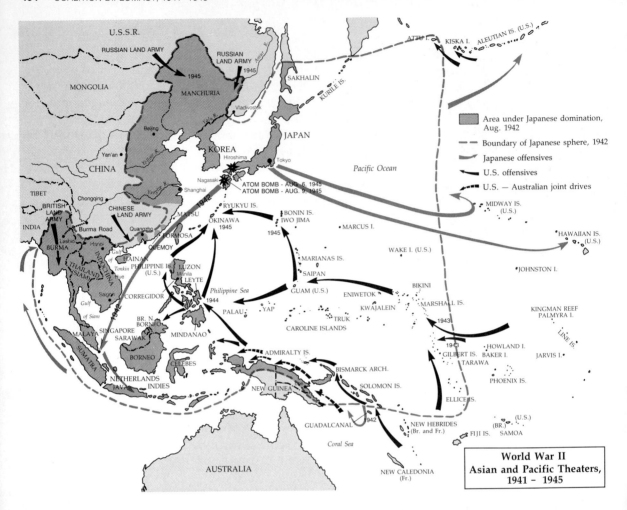

World War II
Asian and Pacific Theaters,
1941 – 1945

opened, and a minute later Tom Ferebee, the bombardier shouted, "Bomb away" and watched as the bomb began its descent.

In a few seconds the center of Hiroshima was transformed into a charred waste, four miles square. More than 130,000 persons, including a dozen American navy fliers imprisoned in the city jail, were killed promptly; another 70,000 were to die by 1950, making the total fatalities for that city 200,000. Three days later, Nagasaki was the target of a second nuclear attack. Seventy thousand persons were killed, including some Dutch prisoners of war; by 1950, 140,000 had died as a result of the second bombing.

One day after the Nagasaki bombing, Tokyo offered to surrender on the basis of the terms outlined in the Potsdam Declaration and "with the understanding that the said declaration does not comprise any demand which prejudices the prerogatives of His Majesty as Sovereign Ruler."[32]

Washington might have rejected this offer of conditional surrender. But Stalin had declared war on Japan on August 8, thus legitimizing his

On August 9, 1945, the city of Nagasaki, Japan, was destroyed by a single atomic bomb. One hundred forty thousand people died.

claim to the economic and territorial concessions he had won at Yalta. With Soviet forces racing across Manchuria while American forces were no closer to Japan and the Asian mainland than Okinawa, it would have been insane to prolong the war. In his carefully drafted reply to Japan's offer of surrender, Secretary Byrnes therefore affirmed the "authority of the Emperor and Japanese Government to rule the state" subject only to "the Supreme Commander of the Allied Powers."[33] Although President Truman announced to the public that Japan had surrendered unconditionally, that was clearly not the case.

## THE BOMB AND HISTORY

The horrifying results of the attacks on Hiroshima and Nagasaki have been at the center of a debate that has raged ever since. Exactly why did President Truman decide to use the atomic bomb? Were the nuclear attacks on Japan really necessary? The president himself never wavered in his explanation. He viewed the bomb, he said, as "just another piece of artillery" and used it to end the war quickly and thus save American lives that otherwise would have been lost in an invasion of the Japanese home islands. In his memoirs, Secretary of War Stimson, who oversaw the Manhattan Project from beginning to end, expressed the same view:

My chief purpose was to end the war in victory with the least possible cost in the lives of the men in the armies which I had helped to raise. In the light of the alternatives which, on fair estimate, were open to us I believe that no man, in our position and subject to our responsibilities, holding in his hands a weapon of such possibilities for accomplishing this purpose and saving those lives, could have failed to use it and afterwards looked his countrymen in the face.[34]

Stimson admitted that at the time the decision to use the atomic bomb was taken, a peace movement was gaining momentum inside Japan's ruling circles. But he argued that it was the nuclear attacks that gave Japan's peace advocates the strength required to overcome the military fanatics, who otherwise would have insisted on fighting to the last, at a terrible cost to both sides.

This explanation of the decision to use nuclear weapons against Japan has for years enjoyed wide currency. Yet it is vulnerable at key points. For example, the contention that by using the bomb the United States avoided the enormous casualties that American forces would have suffered in an invasion presupposes the need for an invasion. Yet there is considerable evidence to suggest that the invasion, which was scheduled for November 1, 1945, would not have been necessary. For example, the 1946 report of the government's Strategic Bombing Survey suggests that Japan was in such a bad way by the summer of 1945 that it would probably have surrendered prior to an invasion whether or not the atomic bomb was used. Colonel R. C. Kramer, the chief of the Economic and Scientific Section at General

The ruins of a Roman Catholic cathedral in this picture only serve to accentuate how complete the destruction of Nagasaki actually was.

Douglas MacArthur's occupation headquarters in Tokyo, made the same point. According to Kramer, American officers then in Japan were "amazed by the fact that resistance continued as long as it did." Bomb or no bomb, Kramer asserted, Japan could not have held out for long.[35]

Even more surprising, a number of high-ranking military officers did not believe an invasion would be necessary. General Dwight D. Eisenhower, informed of the bomb in July 1945 while at Potsdam, argued fervently against using the weapon. Like high-level members of the government, Eisenhower knew that Tokyo had recently asked Moscow to mediate a peace settlement. With Japan on the verge of surrender and in his judgment looking for a way out of the war with "a minimum loss of face," Ike argued that the administration should avoid "shocking world opinion by the use of a weapon whose employment was . . . no longer mandatory to save American lives."[36] High-ranking naval officers felt similarly. Fleet Admiral Ernest J. King was convinced that a naval blockade would have starved Japan into submission without an invasion and without the use of the bomb. Admiral William D. Leahy, in total agreement with King, added:

> My own feeling was that in being the first to use it we had adopted an ethical standard common to the barbarians of the Dark Ages. I was not taught to make war in that fashion, and wars cannot be won by destroying women and children.[37]

Did the nuclear attacks give the peace faction in Tokyo the strength it needed to overcome the militarists and end the war short of an invasion, as Stimson contends? Kazuo Kawai, who was the editor of the *Nippon Times* at the time and well connected in the Japanese government, long ago pointed out that Hiroshima and Nagasaki changed nothing in Tokyo. Those militarists who had opposed surrender before the bombs continued their opposition afterward, while those in the government, including Emperor Hirohito, who were working for a surrender, also continued to do so. According to Kawai, the attacks on Hiroshima and Nagasaki sped the peace process, which was already well under way, by no more than a few days. Kawai and Colonel Kramer agree on that basic point. Bomb or no bomb, Japan would have surrendered without an invasion.

The official explanation for the use of nuclear weapons against Japan, resting as it does on such questionable foundations, has led some to argue that the president used the bomb not to end the war against Japan, which had in effect already been won, but to strengthen his hand for the difficult negotiations with Moscow over Eastern Europe that lay ahead. These scholars have alleged that the administration used the bomb against Japan to demonstrate to Stalin that it not only had this power but the will to use it.

Today most historians reject this extreme view. In recent years it has become fashionable to explain Truman's actions in simpler terms. He used the bomb because it existed. President Roosevelt made the key decision when he signed the executive order creating the Manhattan Project. It was implicit

Americans celebrated the end of World War II each in his or her own way. This young lady was walking down the street minding her own business when the navy made perhaps its last conquest.

in that decision that if a bomb was perfected during the war it would be used.

Military men understood how the momentum of war worked. In the winter of 1945, Samuel Goudsmit, the civilian who headed the Alsos team, remarked to an army major, "Isn't it wonderful that the Germans have no atom bomb? Now we won't have to use ours." But the soldier, who knew better, replied, "Of course you understand, Sam, that if we have such a weapon we are going to use it."[38] The decision was, as Truman always maintained, a routine matter to which he gave no prolonged consideration.

Although today most historians tend to agree that Truman's decision to use the atomic bomb against Japan was fairly routine, this is not to say that the president and his advisers did not have the Soviets on their minds at the time of Hiroshima. As we have already seen, it is beyond question that Truman hoped the bomb would end the war before the Soviets could intervene and claim the concessions offered at Yalta. Nor can there be any doubt that he believed the existence of an American atomic monopoly would prove advantageous in future negotiations with Moscow.

In his influential book, *The Tragedy of American Diplomacy* (1972), the late Professor William Appleman Williams put Truman's decision in the proper perspective when he argued that the president used the bomb against Japan to end the war in the Pacific quickly "and thereby stop the Russians in Asia, and give them sober pause in eastern Europe."[39] Another student of the Truman administration, Professor Barton J. Bernstein, makes an equally subtle and important point. He argues that Truman did not use the bomb to improve his chances of imposing a postwar settlement on the Soviets. He assumed the bomb would be used to end the war. The diplomatic advantages that he thought would accrue to the government as a result of having a nuclear monopoly were by-products of the fact that the United States controlled such power, not the reason for using it.[40]

# ENDNOTES

1. George F. Kennan, quoted in John Snell, *Illusion and Necessity: The Diplomacy of Global War* (Boston: Houghton Mifflin, 1963), p. 139.

2. Harry Hopkins, quoted in Robert E. Sherwood, *Roosevelt and Hopkins* (New York: Harper and Brothers, 1948), pp. 922–23.

3. Leslie R. Groves, quoted in Martin F. Sherwin, *A World Destroyed: Hiroshima and the Grand Alliance* (New York: Random House, 1975), p. 62.

4. Groves, quoted in Gerard Clarfield and William Wiecek, *Nuclear America: Military and Civilian Nuclear Power in the United States, 1940–1980* (New York: Harper and Row, 1984), pp. 39–40.

5. Sherwin, *World Destroyed,* pp. 90–115.

6. Josef Stalin, quoted in Snell, *Illusion and Necessity,* p. 117.

7. Edward R. Murrow, quoted in Stephen E. Ambrose, *Rise to Globalism: American Foreign Policy since 1938,* 5th ed. (New York: Penguin Books, 1988), p. 24.

8. Stalin, quoted in Milovan Djilas, *Conversations with Stalin* (New York: Harcourt, Brace and World, 1962), p. 114.

9. Franklin D. Roosevelt, quoted in John L. Gaddis, *The United States and the Origins of the Cold War, 1941–1947* (New York: Columbia University Press, 1972), p. 90.

10. Winston Churchill, quoted in Edward W. Rozek, *Allied Wartime Diplomacy: A Pattern in Poland* (New York: Wiley, 1958), pp. 278–83.

11. Declaration of Liberated Europe, quoted in Diane Shaver Clemens, *Yalta* (New York: Oxford University Press, 1970), pp. 303–4.

12. William D. Leahy and Roosevelt, both quoted in William D. Leahy, *I Was There* (New York: Whittlesey House, 1950), pp. 315–16.

13. Roosevelt, quoted in John L. Gaddis, *The United States and the Origins of the Cold War, 1941–1947* (New York: Oxford University Press, 1972), p. 214.

14. Charles A. Bohlen, quoted in Snell, *Illusion and Necessity,* p. 185.

15. Roosevelt, quoted in Henry L. Stimson and McGeorge Bundy, *On Active Service in Peace and War* (New York: Harper and Brothers, 1947), p. 581.

16. Hopkins, quoted in Sherwood, *Roosevelt and Hopkins,* p. 870.

17. Roosevelt, quoted in Daniel Yergin, *Shattered Peace: The Origins of the Cold War and the National Security State* (Boston: Houghton Mifflin, 1977), p. 67.

18. Harry Truman, quoted in Robert J. Donovan, *Conflict and Crisis: The Presidency of Harry S. Truman, 1945–1948* (New York: W. W. Norton, 1977), p. 15.

19. Stimson, quoted in Stimson and Bundy, *On Active Service,* p. 644.

20. Hopkins, quoted in Sherwood, *Roosevelt and Hopkins,* pp. 922–23; James Forrestal and Stimson, both quoted in Yergin, *Shattered Peace,* pp. 80–81.

21. W. Averell Harriman, paraphrased in minutes of a State Department staff meeting, April 20, 1945, *Foreign Relations of the United States, 1945* (Washington, D.C., 1967), V, 841–843.

22. Truman, quoted in Ambrose, *Rise to Globalism,* p. 61.

23. Truman and V. M. Molotov, both quoted in ibid. See also Gaddis, *United States and the Origins of the Cold War,* p. 204.

24. Truman, quoted in Yergin, *Shattered Peace,* pp. 100–101.

25. Stalin, quoted in ibid., p. 94.

26. Truman, quoted in ibid., p. 102.

27. Hopkins quoting Stalin in Sherwood, *Roosevelt and Hopkins,* pp. 887–916.

28. Potsdam agreement on reparations, quoted in Herbert Feis, *Between War and Peace; The Potsdam Conference* (Princeton, N.J.: Princeton University Press, 1960), pp. 344–45.

29. Churchill, quoted in Kenneth M. Glazier, Jr., "The Decision to Use Atomic Weapons against Hiroshima and Nagasaki," *Public Policy,* (Summer 1970), XVII, 472.

30. Truman, quoted in Walter Smith Schoenberger, *Decision of Destiny* (Athens, Ohio: Ohio University Press, 1969), p. 262.

31. Potsdam proclamation, quoted in Robert J. C. Butow, *Japan's Decision to Surrender* (Stanford, Calif.: Stanford University Press, 1954), pp. 243–44.

32. Japanese surrender offer, quoted in ibid., p. 245.

33. James F. Byrnes, *Speaking Frankly* (New York, Harper and Brothers, 1947), pp. 209-10.

34. Stimson, quoted in Stimson and Bundy, *On Active Service,* pp. 631–32.

35. R. C. Kramer quoted by Edwin A. Locke, Jr., to Truman, October 19, 1945, Truman Papers, President's Secretaries files, Harry S Truman Library, Independence, Mo.

36. Dwight D. Eisenhower, *The White House Years: Mandate for Change, 1953–1956* (New York: Doubleday, 1963), pp. 312–13.

37. Leahy, *I Was There,* p. 441.

38. Samuel Goudsmit, quoted in Clarfield and Wiecek, *Nuclear America,* pp. 68–69.

39. William Appleman Williams, *The Tragedy of American Diplomacy* 2d ed. (New York: Dell, 1972), p. 253.

40. Barton J. Bernstein, "The Atomic Bomb and American Foreign Policy: An Historiographical Essay," *Peace and Change,* (Spring 1974), III 1–16.

Secretary of Commerce Henry Wallace objected to the hard-line approach toward the Soviets taken by the Truman administration in 1946. He believed that more understanding toward Moscow could save the relationship and said so publicly. Finally the president enforced conformity in the government by dismissing Wallace.

# 25

# THE WINDS OF CHANGE, 1945–1949

The deadlocked Potsdam conference did not mark the end of the Truman administration's efforts to force a Soviet withdrawal from Eastern Europe. Secretary of State James F. Byrnes remained convinced as he left in September, 1945, for a meeting of the Council of Foreign Ministers in London that finally the American nuclear monopoly would make the Soviets more "manageable" on that question. Byrnes's attitude worried Secretary of War Harry L. Stimson, who feared that the South Carolinian's tendency to wear the bomb "a little too ostentatiously on his hip" would make the Soviets more rather than less difficult to deal with. Stimson was correct. In London, Byrnes learned just how ineffective the bomb was as an instrument of diplomacy.

During the conference itself the secretary made no mention of the American nuclear monopoly, relying on its mere existence to influence the course of the talks. It was the Soviet foreign minister, V. M. Molotov, who raised the issue, but only to warn that the Soviet Union would not be intimidated. After three weeks of butting heads with Molotov and getting nowhere, Byrnes realized it was true. He returned to Washington convinced that far from softening the Soviet position on Eastern Europe, the bomb was having the reverse effect. The Soviets, he remarked, were "stubborn, obstinate, and they don't scare."[1]

The London experience convinced Byrnes that there was practically no give in the Soviet position regarding Eastern Europe. At the Moscow meeting of the Council of Foreign Ministers held in December, he therefore modified the American position. After Josef Stalin promised that the Soviet-installed regimes in Rumania and Bulgaria would be modestly broadened to include some noncommunist elements, Byrnes agreed to recognize and negotiate peace treaties with these governments.

Stalin responded with cooperative gestures of his own. He accepted mere token representation in Japan, where American occupation authorities were in complete control; agreed to a continued American military presence in China, where fifty thousand marines were supporting Chiang Kai-shek's efforts to extend his control over the country; reaffirmed his support for Chiang's government; and agreed to the reunification of Korea, which had been divided into American and Soviet zones of occupation at the end of the war.

As far as Byrnes was concerned, the capstone to the conference came when the Soviet leader endorsed the creation of a United Nations Atomic Energy Commission. After the London conference, Byrnes belatedly realized that the world was on the brink of a runaway nuclear arms race that could destroy all hope of a lasting peace. Like most observers, he believed that international control of nuclear energy was the only solution to the problem—hence his interest in the creation of a UN commission. But since the Soviets had not yet solved the mystery of the atom, Byrnes did not expect them to go along. It seemed a very positive sign, then, when Stalin agreed to cooperate in the search for a solution. "Much to everyone's surprise," the scientist-bureaucrat James Conant remarked, "the Russians did not argue or talk back."[2]

Byrnes was pleased with what he had accomplished in Moscow. He had conceded to the Soviets something he was in any event in no position to deny them—preeminence in Rumania and Bulgaria. And Stalin had been conciliatory in return. Byrnes thought the conference had gone a long way toward restoring harmony between East and West, which was, after all, vitally important for the peace of the world.

That was definitely not the view of the White House, where the president and his advisers had absolutely no inclination to give ground on the Eastern European question. In a Navy Day speech given in October, Harry Truman had stated categorically that he would never agree to recognize any government that was not created by the freely expressed will of its people. Now he told Byrnes flatly that he would neither recognize nor sign peace treaties with Rumania and Bulgaria until those communist-dominated regimes had been "radically changed." Furthermore, he said: "I do not think we should play compromise any longer." The Soviets, he added, understood only one language: "How many divisions have you." That being the case, he intended to confront Moscow "with an iron fist and strong language." He was "tired of babying the Soviets."[3]

Truman's new "get tough" policy was the result of twin considerations.

First, and most obviously, the pressure he had exerted on the Soviets to surrender their position in Eastern Europe had failed. Second, Moscow's Eastern European policy had undermined popular admiration for the once "glorious Russian ally." Republicans and Democrats, too, were demanding that the administration stand firm. Thus Representative Joseph W. Martin of Massachusetts denounced "any betrayal of the small nations of the world in the making of the peace." And Senator Arthur Vandenberg of Michigan insisted that the United States demand that the Soviet Union fulfill promises made at Yalta. If the Soviets refused, he said, the United States should "go to the forum of the United Nations and demand judgment from the organized conscience of the world." The Michigan senator called for the abandonment "of the miserable fiction, often encouraged by our own fellow travelers, that we somehow jeopardize the peace if our candor is as firm as Russia's always is, and if we assume a moral leadership which we have too frequently allowed to lapse."[4]

Truman, cognizant of the fact that the political coalition that had kept the Democrats in power since 1933 was made up in part of working-class voters of Eastern European origins, could not afford to allow the Republicans to steal this issue. Nor could he afford to be labeled an appeaser. Munich and the rape of Czechoslovakia had left an ineradicable mark in the collective memories of Western Europeans and Americans. Truman could not allow himself to be tarred with that brush.

## IRAN AND TURKEY: EARLY SIGNS OF ESTRANGEMENT

An early manifestation of the administration's hardening attitude toward the Soviets came in the winter of 1946. During World War II, oil-rich Iran was a nation of considerable importance to the Grand Alliance. Iranian oil fed the Allied war machine. And a railroad running from the Persian Gulf to the Soviet Union served as a conduit for lend-lease goods. In 1941, Soviet and British forces invaded the country, dividing it between them. The Soviets occupied the north, while British and American forces took over in the south. The Allies deposed Reza Shah Pahlavi, who was sympathetic to the Axis, and set his twenty-two-year-old son Muhammad Reza Pahlavi on the throne. They then signed a treaty with Tehran agreeing to remove their occupation forces within six months of the end of the war.

During the war, Iran came under pressure from American as well as Soviet sources. American oil companies, anxious to penetrate what until then had been a British preserve, were angling for oil leases. The Soviets, too, were after oil.

Tehran responded to these pressures by refusing to do business with either side. In 1944 the Fourteenth Majlis (Parliament) enacted legislation barring the government from agreeing to any new oil concessions and prohibiting the election of the Fifteenth Majlis so long as foreign troops remained on Iranian soil. Since the legislature would have to approve new oil leases, it became impossible for either the Americans or the Soviets to win concessions until all foreign troops left Iran.

At the end of the war, Washington and London withdrew their forces from Iran. But the Soviets, remained, as Moscow continued to press the Iranians for oil concessions. The Kremlin added to the pressure by giving aid and encouragement to separatist rebels in Iran's northern province of Azerbaijan.

On January 19, 1946, with the deadline for Soviet troop withdrawal less than two months away, Iran took the issue to the United Nations. But the Iranians harbored no illusions about how useful international opinion alone would be in convincing Moscow to withdraw. Their real hope lay in a combination of outside pressure and direct negotiations. Things worked out as Tehran hoped. With the spotlight of world opinion turned his way, Stalin invited Ahmed Qavam es-Saltanah, the Iranian prime minister, to Moscow for talks.

In Washington these developments were viewed with alarm. American policy makers believed that any compromise between Iran and the Soviets would result in an expanded Soviet presence in Iran. And if Iran was transformed into a Soviet satellite, the entire Middle East and Southwest Asia would be threatened. "There is a very dangerous situation developing in Iran," the president told W. Averell Harriman. "The Russians are refusing to take their troops out . . . and this may lead to war."[5]

In March 1946, Washington sent a strongly worded protest to the Soviet Foreign Ministry, objecting to the continued presence of Soviet forces in Iran. Washington also urged the Iranians to make no compromises but instead to bring the issue once again before the UN Security Council. The American initiative had little effect on the major players. Far from being intimidated, the Soviets added to their garrison in northern Iran. As for Qavam, he was no doubt pleased to have Washington's moral support. But he had a powerful neighbor with troops occupying Iranian soil to deal with. Compromise seemed far wiser than confrontation.

Qavam was a clever man. Though it was not to be the main arena of his diplomacy, he did return the issue to the UN Security Council to please Washington and once again expose the Soviets to outside pressure. At the same time, however, he sought to reassure Moscow by ordering a crackdown on those extreme right-wing elements inside Iran that were unrelentingly hostile to Iran's Tudeh (Communist) party.

Embarrassed by the attacks emanating from the UN Security Council and reassured by Qavam's domestic strategy, the Soviets abandoned the Azerbaijan separatists. In return, Qavam agreed to the creation of a joint Soviet-Iranian Oil Company that would work fields in northern Iran. Once the oil agreement with Moscow had been arranged, Qavam pointed out that it could not be ratified because a new Majlis had not been elected and no election could be held until Soviet forces had been withdrawn.

The Soviets then withdrew from Iran, trusting Qavam to steer the agreement through the Majlis. But things did not work out that way. In

1947 the Fifteenth Majlis, influenced by the American ambassador in Tehran, George Allen, rejected the agreement creating the Soviet-Iranian Oil Company.

President Truman later claimed that it was he who forced the Soviets to withdraw from Iran by issuing an ultimatum. But a more convincing explanation focuses on Qavam's stratagems. Still, even though the American role in the Iranian affair was largely peripheral, it is interesting to note that Washington first discouraged Tehran from negotiating with Moscow and then used its influence to defeat the oil agreement in the Majlis. The old allies were now clearly estranged. Toughness was coming into its own as a hallmark of America's Soviet policy.

Later in 1946 the Truman administration acted boldly when it appeared that the Soviets might be making a move to expand into the eastern Mediterranean. During World War II, Turkey had remained neutral but had tilted in favor of the Axis, allowing German U-boats through the straits into the Black Sea, where they preyed upon Soviet shipping. At Yalta and again at Potsdam the Western Allies agreed to support a Soviet demand for revision of the Montreux Convention of 1936 that granted Turkey complete control over the straits. With the approval of the Western Allies, Moscow would demand joint control.

By early 1946 Washington had, of course, changed its mind about who should control the straits. With Soviet expansionism considered a serious threat, the last thing the administration wanted was a Soviet presence in the eastern Mediterranean.

In August 1946, Moscow sent a strong note to Ankara demanding a revision of the Montreux Convention. This Soviet pressure on the Turks was viewed in Washington as further proof of Moscow's expansionist design. At a meeting in the White House, Truman and his national security advisers decided to make a stand. "We might as well find out whether the Russians are bent on world conquest now as in five or ten years," the president said.[6] The navy sent a carrier task force into the eastern Mediterranean for "maneuvers," and the State Department fired off a strong note to Moscow.

The Soviets did not follow up on that first note to the Turks, and the crisis soon dissipated. Just why the Soviets backed off is a question still debated by historians. But in Washington the episode suggested nothing more clearly than that being "tough" was exactly the right policy.

## THE TRUMAN DOCTRINE

In February 1946, with Soviet-American relations already strained, Josef Stalin made a rare public appearance at the Bolshoi theater, where he spoke on the eve of the 1946 Soviet elections. For the most part he discussed plans for rebuilding the Soviet economy. But in that part of his speech dedicated to ideological concerns, Stalin emphasized the incompatibility of capitalism and communism. During the next several days Molotov, Laurentia Beria,

WHAT WE'RE DRIVING AT

COMMUNIST INFILTRATION AND DICTATORSHIP THREATS

U.S. AID

TURKEY

NON-COMMUNIST SMALL NATIONS

GREECE

S.J.Ray

NO. 16   MARCH 13, 1947

The Truman Doctrine speech made it clear that the administration was aiming at nothing less than the total containment of communism.

Lazor Kaganovich, and other Soviet leaders followed with speeches of their own, each warning of increasing problems abroad and the danger of "capitalist encirclement." *Newsweek* found in these speeches "a depressing common denominator: The same men had been saying the same thing ten years ago." Their remarks "raised the dark prospect that war has taught them very little about the world they have to live in."[7]

The State Department reacted to Stalin's speech by asking George F. Kennan, the chargé d'affaires in Moscow and a respected Sovietologist, to offer an analysis of what to expect from the Soviets. Kennan's response, an eight-thousand-word telegram, set the department and the entire bureaucracy on its ear. "At bottom of Kremlin's neurotic view of world affairs is traditional and instinctive Russian sense of insecurity," Kennan wrote.

We have here a political force committed fanatically to the belief that with

US there can be no permanent *modus vivendi,* that it is desirable and necessary that the internal harmony of our society be disrupted, our traditional way of life destroyed, the international authority of our state be broken if Soviet power is to be secure.

Still, Kennan continued, this did not mean inevitable war. While clearly bent on expanding their power as far as possible the Soviets were cautious and would usually "withdraw . . . when strong resistance is encountered." In the long run, Kennan argued, the contradictions inside Soviet society would force internal change, making Moscow more susceptible to reason. A patient, long-term policy aimed at checking Soviet expansionism, he believed, would bear fruit without a war.[8]

Eloquent and with a flare for the melodramatic, Kennan had articulated what by February 1946, was becoming conventional wisdom while at the same time offering an attractively packaged response. The "long telegram" attracted widespread approval throughout the government and led to Kennan's swift rise in the bureaucracy. In 1947 he became the head of the State Department's Policy Planning Staff.

Not long after Kennan sent his long telegram, Winston Churchill delivered his famous Iron Curtain Speech on the campus of Westminster College in Fulton, Missouri. With President Truman sitting on the platform behind him, Churchill said:

> From Stettin in the Baltic to Trieste in the Adriatic, an iron curtain has descended across the Continent. Behind that line lie all the capitals of the ancient states of central and eastern Europe. Warsaw, Berlin, Prague, Vienna, Budapest, Belgrade, Bucharest, and Sofia, all these famous cities and the populations around them lie in the Soviet sphere and all are subject in one form or another, not only to Soviet influence but to a very high and increasing measure of control from Moscow.

These evidences of Soviet expansionism notwithstanding, Churchill did not believe that the Soviets wanted war. "What they desire," he said, "is the fruits of war and the indefinite expansion of their power and doctrines."[9]

In the face of this threat Churchill urged Western unity. If the democracies stood together "in strict adherence to the principles of the United Nations Charter, their influence for furthering these principles will be immense and no one is likely to molest them." And so Churchill proposed an alliance between the "English-speaking commonwealth" and "the United States with all that such co-operation implies in the air, on the sea and in science and industry."[10]

The Kennan analysis and Churchill's Iron Curtain Speech had two points in common. First, they both assumed that Soviet foreign policy was driven by a grand expansionist design. Second, they both insisted that the Kremlin did not want war. Therefore, a strong but measured response to Moscow's probing could keep this aggressive force in check without war. These important judgments became the basis of a new approach to the

The refugee problem in Europe at war's end was quite literally overwhelming.

Kremlin taking shape in Washington. The policy, which Kennan further elaborated in a famous article published anonymously in the summer of 1947 in *Foreign Affairs,* came to be known as "containment," the economic aspect of which took shape in 1947.

In the early postwar years few American policy makers were concerned about the danger of Soviet military adventurism. The United States still held the nuclear monopoly, and in any event Moscow was preoccupied consolidating its position in Eastern Europe and rebuilding a shattered economy. The war had cost the Soviets 20 million dead and almost their entire economic infrastructure. Hardly a town or city west of the Urals remained intact. When Trygve Lie, the secretary general of the United Nations, visited the Soviet Union after the war, he found only "the chaos of charred and twisted villages and cities," not a country preparing for war. Even in 1948 Kennan explained, "we do not think the Russians, since the termination of the war, have had any serious intentions of resorting to arms."[11]

If the Soviets were not prepared for war, they were not without means of advancing their interests. It was an article of faith in Washington that they would use political, diplomatic, and subversive methods to destabilize governments and expand their power. The area of greatest concern to Washington was Western Europe, which was at the time in near chaos.

Western Europe was desolate in the immediate postwar years. Its reconstruction seemed essential to an administration determined to check communist expansion.

Industrial production was down, millions were unemployed, and millions more, so-called displaced persons, roamed the Continent. In July, 1945, Secretary of War Stimson warned the president that if "famine, disease, and distress" continued, "individual liberty and free political action" could not survive in Europe.[12] Stimson was only one of a bevy of American policy makers who viewed Europe's economic revival as a vital national security consideration. The misery and chaos that existed there, they believed, lent strength to local communist parties throughout Europe. They were especially concerned about Italy and France, where the communists won considerable support in the 1946 elections.

The Truman administration saw a direct analogy between the situation that had confronted the nation after World War I and existing conditions in Europe. The war-weary peoples of the continent needed to be put back on their feet again. Once that had been achieved, their confidence would return, the threat of a communist takeover would dissipate, and valuable markets would be restored in the bargain. But unlike the generation of the 1920s, this group of Washington policy makers was convinced that it could not rely on unplanned private investment to produce the recovery. They viewed a coordinated, large-scale program of foreign aid as essential.

There was a political problem, however. After four years of war, the American public wanted military demobilization, reduced government spending, and lower taxes. President Harry Truman however, had not been able to give the people what they wanted. Because of America's new position in the world, he retained a military establishment of 1.6 million, larger than any in America's peacetime history. The costs of this enlarged military establishment as well as a major international relief effort left him no choice but to oppose excessive tax cuts. At least in part because of his stand on taxes, his approval rating in the polls dropped to a dismal 32 percent. Foreign aid had no political constituency. Assuming that he wanted to be elected in 1948, Truman was in no position to recommend a large aid package.

The Republican victory in the 1946 congressional elections only made matters worse. The GOP climbed back into control of both houses of Congress by calling for a 20 percent tax cut and draconian reductions in government spending. In early 1947, then, congressional support for large-scale spending on a major foreign aid program seemed politically out of reach.

It was at this time and in this context that the Greek Civil War, which pitted the communist-led EAM (National Liberation Front) against a British-backed conservative royalist government, attracted concern inside the Truman administration. "If Greece falls to Communism," one State Department official warned, "the whole Near East and part of North Africa as well is certain to pass under Soviet influence."[13] It was this sort of thinking combined with an awareness that economic problems would soon force the British to end their commitment to the Greek government that prompted the administration to begin planning a foreign aid program for Athens.

On February 21, 1947, the British ambassador informed the State Department that England would discontinue its support for Greece as of March 31. The news came as no surprise. Within a week a State Department study group headed by Undersecretary Dean Acheson produced a plan for aid to Greece and Turkey, a program that would substitute American for British influence in the eastern Mediterranean. The administration's problem then became selling the idea to a hostile Congress.

At a White House briefing session held for congressional leaders, Acheson pulled out all the stops in appealing for support. He warned that if Greece fell to the communists, the Middle East and parts of North Africa would go next. And if that should come to pass, Italy and France might well collapse, making America's position in Germany untenable. With dominoes falling all about them, the members of Congress quickly climbed aboard the administration bandwagon. Michigan's Arthur Vandenberg, however, cautioned President Truman that if he wanted to sell the foreign aid idea to the whole Congress he would have to be no less effective than Acheson. He would have to "scare hell" out of Congress and the people.[14]

On March 12, 1947, the president went before a joint session of Congress and did as Vandenberg advised. In a speech that one observer described as "tantamount to a declaration of ideological or religious war," Truman characterized both Greece and Turkey as nations struggling for freedom against the encompassing tentacles of international communism. Arguing that the United States must aid Greece and Turkey or risk losing all the oil-rich Middle East to communism, he warned that failure to act "in this fateful hour" would have "far-reaching" effects on "the West as well as . . . the East." Truman made a sweeping commitment when he said, "I believe that it must be the policy of the United States to support free peoples who are resisting attempted subjugation by armed minorities or by outside pressures."[15]

The Truman speech, which the press quickly elevated to the level of a "doctrine," was denounced in the Soviet newspaper, *Izvestia,* as "a smoke-screen" for American expansion. In the United States opinion was more or less divided. *Time* noted that Truman's speech "sounded almost like a declaration of war" and that most Americans were not ready for that. The magazine itself, while hardly ecstatic, nevertheless thought Truman was right. "Communist imperialism must be contained. U.S. influence must expand to contain it; otherwise the U.S. might be engulfed." Others were not so certain. Senator Robert Taft, "Mr. Republican," shrewdly observed that the foreign aid program was tantamount to an acceptance of "the policy of dividing the world into zones of political influence." Both Joseph P. Kennedy, the former Ambassador to Great Britain, and Bernard Baruch, financier and adviser to presidents from Wilson to Truman, also expressed concern. Such a sweeping commitment, they feared, would lead to unchecked spending, major economic dislocations and, finally, "the destruction of the very democratic system which the policy sought to protect."[16]

Perhaps the most trenchant critic of the Truman speech was George Kennan, who objected to the "sweeping nature of the commitments which the speech implied." It "placed our aid to Greece in the framework of a universal policy rather than that of a specific decision addressed to a specific set of circumstances." Kennan thought it doubtful that it would always be in America's interest "or within our means to extend assistance to countries (provided only that they face) the threat of 'subjugation' by armed minorities or outside pressures."[17]

Kennan was of course correct, as Americans would learn to their regret in years to come. But Truman no doubt understood this, too. He had a political problem: how to convince a reluctant Congress to support foreign aid. His answer was to confront them with a dilemma. As Georgia's Carl Vinson told Navy Secretary James Forrestal, "They [the Congress] don't like Russia, they don't like the Communists, but still they don't want to do anything to stop it. But they are all put on the spot now, and they all have to come clean."[18] And come clean they did, enacting a bill that provided $400 million in aid for Greece and Turkey.

## THE MARSHALL PLAN

The Truman Doctrine speech was only a warm-up for the major foreign aid proposal to come. Just back from Europe, where he witnessed at firsthand the extent of the crisis, Secretary of State George C. Marshall, who had only recently replaced Byrnes, gave a radio address urging a major program of economic aid for the Continent. "Disintegrating forces are becoming evident," he said. "The patient is sinking while the doctors deliberate."[19]

The recovery program recommended by George Kennan's Policy

Planning Staff (it became the Marshall Plan) focused on the importance of Germany to all of Western Europe. Without Germany's coal and steel production, as well as its industrial know-how, American planners believed that Western Europe would find recovery next to impossible. At the same time, because the planners were anxious to restore Germany economically without reviving "the German threat," the plan they developed was designed to encourage economic integration. "Without the Germans," Kennan noted, "no real European federation is thinkable. And without federation the other countries of Europe can have no protection against a new attempt at foreign domination."[20]

During the Marshall Plan's period of gestation, Kennan made this important point. Though the United States had no interest in contributing to the Soviet Union's recovery, neither did it want to appear responsible for dividing Europe into separate camps by deliberately excluding Moscow and the Eastern European satellites from the recovery program. Kennan, then, had two objectives. First, he wanted a program that would restore Germany's economic strength but not its military potential. Second, the program had to be designed so as to lead the Soviets to exclude themselves.

On June 5, 1947, in a speech delivered at Harvard University's commencement ceremony, Secretary Marshall focused on the importance of Europe's recovery "as a whole." He described American thinking in brief outline, urged the European powers to join in the effort, and noted that while the United States was willing to make recommendations, the Europeans should lead in producing a plan "agreed to by a number, if not all, European nations."[21] London and Paris, alerted to the significance of the speech beforehand, responded immediately with a call for a general European conference to meet in Paris on June 16, 1947.

There was much speculation prior to the conference as to whether the Soviets would send representatives. But when the conference convened, Molotov was on hand at the head of a large delegation. Though the Soviets appeared to be serious about seeking foreign aid, they were prepared to do so only under certain conditions. Molotov wanted separate recovery programs to be administered by individual nations. But the other conferees, led by Britain and France, insisted on taking the multilateral approach advocated by the United States.

The joint planning that Washington and the Western Europeans envisaged required the exchange of vital economic information, the integration of all European economies for purposes of trade, and the opening of Eastern Europe to Western capital penetration. When it became apparent that the Soviets could not participate in the aid program without opening their hard-won Eastern European sphere to Western penetration, Molotov warned that the plan would split "Europe into two groups of States" and left, taking the satellites with him.[22]

The sixteen nations remaining at the Paris conference developed a plan for the economic revival of Western Europe that called for a $28 billion commitment from the United States. In Washington that figure was slashed to \$17 billion, to be stretched over four years. In late December 1947, this version of what was officially designated the European Recovery Program but was even then known as the Marshall Plan was sent to Congress.

The Marshall Plan appealed to a wide variety of constituencies. Those worried about communist expansion found in it a peaceful method of responding to that threat. Others, more concerned with the future of America's export trade, supported the plan, too. At the time the United States was exporting roughly \$16 billion in goods to Europe annually and importing only \$8 billion in return. At that rate the Europeans would soon be out of dollars and unable to purchase American products. The result, of course, would be a serious domestic economic problem for the United States.

If certain powerful constituencies rallied in support of the Marshall Plan, there was significant opposition to the program as well. Senator Robert Taft and former President Herbert Hoover called for a scaling back of the recovery program. Taft warned that the Marshall Plan would produce domestic scarcities and that a program of this magnitude would discourage the Europeans from doing as much as they could on their own and would probably lead them further down the road to socialism.

The opposition, while probably not powerful enough to have killed the Marshall Plan, did manage to stall its progress in Congress and might have affected reductions and other changes in the administration proposal had it not been for developments elsewhere. In February 1948, a political crisis in Czechoslovakia gave the administration the leverage required to push its program through Congress.

## THE CZECH COUP: 1948

The 1946 elections in Czechoslovakia, in which the communists emerged with 38 percent of the popular vote, produced a coalition government made up of communist and noncommunist ministers. The aged and infirm Eduard Beneš was president, and the foreign minister was Jan Masaryk, the son of the nation's founding father. For the next two years the government in prague operated in a sort of political limbo. It enjoyed a substantial amount of local autonomy but only because it rigidly adhered to pro-Soviet foreign and economic policies.

Not long after the 1946 elections, Washington promised desperately needed economic aid to Czechoslovakia if Beneš would throw the communists out of the government. But Beneš, fearing a Soviet reaction, refused. In early 1948 a number of noncommunist ministers re-ignited the idea and made a deal with Beneš. The plan was to create a political crisis that would require Beneš to reorganize the government. He would do so but without the communists.

Early in February 1948, a dozen noncommunist cabinet ministers resigned en masse, creating the necessary crisis. But when the moment came to act, Beneš lost his nerve. In the chaotic days that followed Klement

Gottwald, the leader of the Czech Communist party, used his control of the Interior Ministry and the police to intimidate the opposition. With Red Army forces close to Czech borders and a Soviet trade delegation actually in Prague at the time, rumors of an imminent Soviet intervention flew through the city. A thoroughly intimidated Beneš surrendered to Gottwald's demand and agreed to a communist-controlled government for Czechoslovakia. In the period that followed, Gottwald, supported from Moscow, began a brutal purge of noncommunist Czech leaders and transformed his country into a Soviet satellite.

Washington had little time to absorb the shock of the coup in Czechoslovakia before receiving another jolt. General Lucius Clay, the military governor in the American zone of occupation in Germany had long argued that the Soviets would be in no position to go to war for at least a decade. But in recent days, he explained, he "felt a subtle change in the Soviet attitude . . . which now gives me a feeling that it may come with dramatic suddenness."[23] Clay's warning was followed by the news that Jan Masaryk, who had agreed to stay on as Czechoslovakia's foreign minister in the Gottwald government, either jumped or was thrown to his death from a window of the Foreign Ministry.

When Washington learned that on top of everything else the Soviets were pressing the Finns for a military alliance, the bureaucracy went into what might be described as a minipanic. The Central Intelligence Agency (CIA), created by the National Security Act of 1947, did an intelligence estimate and came to the not wholly reassuring conclusion that war was not likely for at least sixty days. Secretary Marshall held a press conference at which he denounced "the reign of terror" in Czechoslovakia and warned that the "situation is very serious." Truman followed up on the next day with a news conference of his own at which he announced that his faith in peace "had been shaken."[24]

Though rattled, administration leaders nevertheless took quick advantage of the political opportunities created by the European crisis. On March 17 the president went before Congress and in the gravest tones warned that the Soviets had "destroyed the independence and democratic character of a whole series of nations in East and Central Europe. It is this ruthless course of action and the clear design to extend it to the remaining free nations of Europe that have brought about the critical situation in Europe today."[25] Time was short, Truman warned. He urged Congress to pass the European Recovery Program and reestablish the military draft, and to do so quickly. The president got all that he asked for and more, as Congress also authorized a major increase in the size of the air force.

## THE RISE OF THE NEW GERMANY

Since a revived Germany was an essential ingredient in Washington's plans for Western European recovery, the administration next took steps to create a new Germany out of the three Western zones of occupation. The French

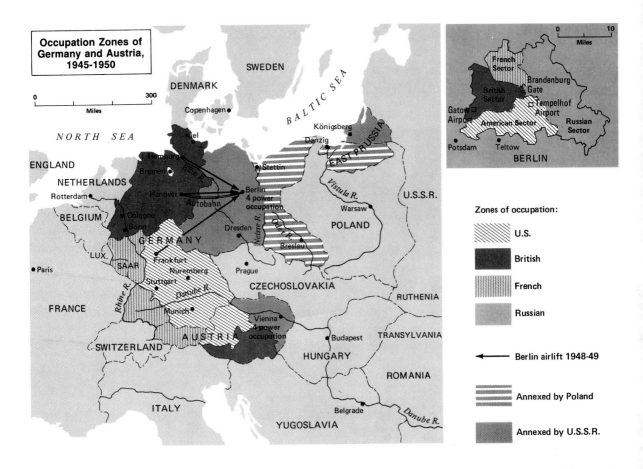

Occupation Zones of Germany and Austria, 1945-1950

posed the most serious threat to plans for West German recovery. Just as in the period following World War I, they saw their security threatened by a revived Germany. But pressure from Washington brought Paris into line. Within two weeks of the Czech coup, France joined Britain and America in an agreement calling for the economic integration of the three western zones of occupation and West Germany's participation in the European Recovery Program. Three months later the Western Allies announced plans for the creation of an independent West Germany with an economy integrated into Western Europe's and established the Deutchmark as the official currency of the three western zones of occupation. At the same time, no doubt to reduce French fears, Washington announced that American forces would remain in Europe for the indefinite future.

Washington viewed the initiatives it took during the first half of 1948 as purely reactive. But Moscow saw the Marshall Plan and the West's German initiative as ominous threats to its security. Stalin had no solution to the troublesome German question beyond continued military occupation. But he knew very well that he did not want an economically strong Germany with substantial military potential. And so in March and April 1948, he responded to Western moves by instituting a partial blockade of rail and road traffic from the west into Berlin, which lay 110 miles inside the Soviet occupation zone. This partial blockade was a warning of stronger action to come if the West persisted in encouraging the rise of the German phoenix.

In June, following the Western Allies' announcement of final plans for a new West German government, the Soviets declared that since the West had taken unilateral action to divide Germany they claimed complete control over Berlin, which had by a wartime agreement been divided into four zones of occupation. In an attempt to drive the Western Allies out of Berlin, the Soviets cut all land routes into the city from the west and stopped electrical service to those parts of the city under Western control.

American policy makers viewed the Berlin crisis as a test of wills. The United States could not allow itself to be driven from its position in Berlin without losing its claim to leadership in the West. General Clay warned: "If we mean that we are to hold Europe against Communism, we must not budge, . . . If America does not know this, does not believe the issue is cast now, then it never will and Communism will run rampant." Clay urged his superiors to shoot their way into Berlin.[26]

The president had no intention of leaving Berlin. "We are going to stay, period," he remarked.[27] But neither the president nor General Omar Bradley, chair of the Joint Chiefs, wanted to fight if the city could be saved in some other way. The shooting might escalate into a global war for which the United States was not prepared.

In fact, General Clay himself had earlier pointed the way toward an alternative method of keeping Berlin supplied. When the Soviets first implemented their partial blockade, he used transport planes to fly in necessary supplies. Truman and Bradley adopted the same strategy on a much larger scale, organizing the Berlin airlift. The Western Allies also implemented a counterblockade, refusing to provide eastern Germany with vital industrial goods. As tension mounted during the summer of 1948, the air force also deployed B-29 bombers at bases in England. From there these planes, which were known to be capable of carrying nuclear weapons, could reach targets in the Soviet Union.

The airlift was an astonishing success. The Soviets had hoped that winter weather conditions would restrict access to Tempelhoff Airport in Berlin. But pilots and crews flew round the clock and in all kinds of weather. By the spring of 1949 they were delivering eight thousand tons of supplies each day, as much as had been transported by land prior to the blockade.

By January 1949, Stalin realized that the blockade had failed. Moreover, the counterblockade was having a serious effect on the economy of the Soviet occupation zone. He was looking for a graceful way out when he informed the Western Allies that he would lift the blockade if they would agree to delay the establishment of a West German state at least until after one more foreign ministers' conference. Several more months of sparring followed. Finally, however, Stalin lifted the blockade, the Western powers

The Berlin airlift, which delivered thousands of tons of supplies to besieged West Berlin, captured the imagination of Berliners of all ages. Here, four German children use model cargo planes to play "airlift" amid the ruins of Berlin.

ended their counterblockade, and a foreign ministers' conference was scheduled for Paris on May 23.

By the time the Paris foreign ministers' conference convened, significant personnel changes had taken place on both the American and Soviet sides of the negotiating table. Andrei Vishinsky had replaced Molotov as foreign minister. George Marshall was gone, too, replaced by the urbane, sophisticated Dean Acheson. The new secretary, a brilliant attorney with an incisive, rapierlike wit, had served in the State Department since 1941. As undersecretary he played a leading role in the development of America's postwar foreign policy and was without question the quintessential cold warrior. The conservative Republican senator, Arthur Vandenberg, who went to Paris as a member of the delegation, described the secretary as "so totally anti-Soviet" that he doubted "whether there [was] any chance at all" that the conference could succeed. That was fine with Vandenberg, who had long since decided that negotiation was simply a modern-day synonym for appeasement.[28]

The Paris talks went more or less as expected. Vishinsky proposed what amounted to a return to the four-power arrangement for the governance of occupied Germany. Such an approach, of course, would have undermined the Marshall Plan and so was immediately rejected by Acheson, Britain's Ernest Bevin, and France's Robert Schuman. Aware that he was holding all the cards, Acheson gave nothing away. The conference deadlocked when Vishinsky rejected a Western proposal for a unified Germany under terms and conditions already agreed upon by Washington, London, and Paris. From Washington's point of view, German unification continued to be a desirable objective. But Acheson would only agree to it "under conditions which help and do not retard the unification of a free Europe." Thus by mutual consent Germany, like the rest of Europe, was divided into separate camps.[29]

## THE NORTH ATLANTIC TREATY ORGANIZATION

The North Atlantic Treaty Organization (NATO) was in the first instance the brainchild of French and British diplomatists. From their viewpoint, the permanent presence of the United States in Europe was an important guarantee, a psychological anchor in an unsettled, insecure environment. But in the early years of the postwar era the Western Europeans had no reason to believe that the Americans would stay indefinitely. The popular clamor to "bring the boys home" that rang across the United States in 1946 was heard very clearly in Europe's foreign ministries, where it was feared that, as in the 1920s, the United States would once again withdraw behind the Atlantic.

Western European policy makers made much of the fact that Moscow had twenty-five ready divisions in Central Europe alone and warned that if the Soviets decided to take Western Europe they could reach the English Channel in a few weeks. Recent scholarship suggests that the Western Europeans may not have been so concerned about the threat of a Soviet invasion as they said at the time. They knew, however, how concerned Washington was and exploited that fear to bring the United States into a permanent relationship with Europe. That relationship, they hoped, would mean advantageous economic ties and the creation of a stable balance of power as a guarantee against both a revanchist Germany and any future Soviet threat.

In 1947 these considerations prompted London, Paris, and the Benelux (Belgium, the Netherlands, and Luxembourg) countries to begin negotiating a mutual security treaty. The talks went on for several months, until the Czech coup provided the catalyst for final agreement. At the same moment that Congress was approving the Marshall Plan, the Western Europeans signed the Brussels Pact. Wasting no time, Georges Bidault, the French foreign minister, then appealed to the Truman administration to enter negotiations looking toward the creation of a more formidable alliance.

Negotiations between the United States, Canada, and the five members of the Brussels Pact began in the spring of 1948 and continued against the backdrop of the Berlin blockade until October, when a final agreement was reached. At that point the powers already involved invited Norway, Denmark, Iceland, Italy, and Portugal to enter the alliance, and a second round of negotiations got under way.

At length, on April 4, 1949, the twelve original members initialed the NATO agreement. That night at a dinner in Washington attended by the representatives of the NATO powers, President Truman remarked on the extraordinary nature of what the diplomats had achieved. NATO was the first peacetime military alliance the United States had ever negotiated and the first true alliance of any sort since the Franco-American Alliance of 1778. As the president noted, the agreement marked the passing of one era and the beginning of another, for with NATO Washington asserted its claim to leadership over the nations of Western Europe.

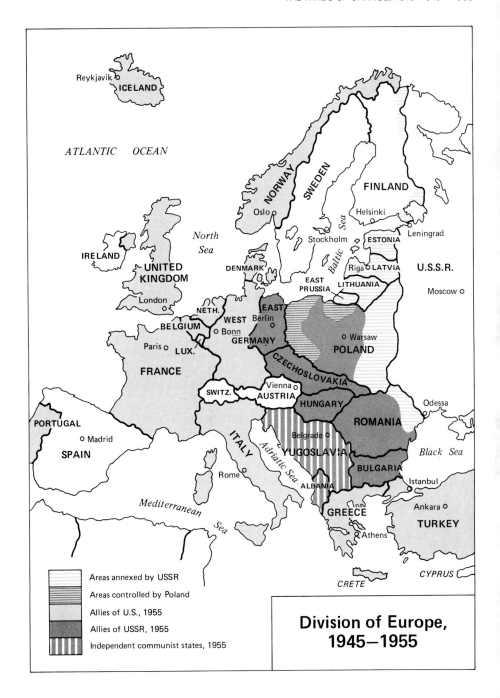

Areas annexed by USSR

Areas controlled by Poland

Allies of U.S., 1955

Allies of USSR, 1955

Independent communist states, 1955

## Division of Europe, 1945–1955

President Harry Truman, surrounded by the NATO ambassadors, signs the NATO Treaty. It was the first peacetime alliance in American history.

If one asked what substantive changes were brought about by the creation of NATO, the answer, at least in 1949, was few if any. The West's conventional military posture remained unchanged. Nor were there as yet any plans afoot to rearm Germany or dispatch large numbers of American troops to Europe. These decisions all lay in the future. But at a psychological level, NATO meant a great deal. The Western Europeans had found it difficult, almost impossible, to believe that the United States was on the Continent to stay. The Truman Doctrine, Marshall aid, the Berlin airlift— these were all good omens. But the Europeans wanted a guarantee that this time, unlike the period after World War I, the United States would not withdraw. NATO was that guarantee.

## NSC 68

From the time that he took over the State Department in early 1949, Dean Acheson was troubled by the fact that American foreign and military policies were so far out of sync. The United States was playing a dominant role in world affairs. But the armed forces languished with budgets that seemed hopelessly inadequate. Still, the situation did not appear to be terribly serious until August, when the Soviets exploded an atomic bomb, ending America's nuclear monopoly. After that Acheson concluded that it was imperative to build America's military strength in both conventional and nuclear forces while at the same time rearming the NATO Allies.

Aware that there was strong domestic opposition to increased government spending, Acheson prepared the ground carefully. He first convinced the budget-conscious Truman that, in light of the Soviet atomic bomb and the likelihood that Moscow would go forward with the development of fusion weapons, the administration should reconsider its entire defense posture. It seemed clear, Acheson later wrote, that "changes in power relationships were imminent."[30]

After winning presidential approval for a study, Acheson turned the job over to his Policy Planning Staff, where Paul Nitze, a former investment banker, had replaced Kennan as director. Since Nitze and Acheson shared the same world view and were both advocates of a massive peacetime military establishment, the outcome of the study was a forgone conclusion. Though no one was saying so publicly, it was more or less assumed even before Nitze's study group set to work that the defense budget would have to increase from $13.5 billion to about $50 billion. This was an extraordinary idea, since at the time the entire federal budget stood at about $37.5 billion.

While Nitze's group worked on its report, the State Department was the scene of a major internal debate over rearmament. It seemed logical to Acheson that any attempt to predict America's defense needs should be based on an analysis of Soviet purposes and capabilities. But George Kennan and Charles Bohlen, the department's leading Soviet experts, opposed the attempt to reduce the department's understanding of Moscow's ambitions to a position paper. They feared that in the process complicated problems would be oversimplified, subtlety and nuance abandoned in favor of clarity. The process, both diplomats insisted, would very probably lead to incorrect conclusions and misguided policy. Moreover, even assuming that a position paper did somehow accurately gauge current Soviet policy and purposes, documents of this sort had a tendency to be transformed into immutable wisdom, robbing policy makers of the flexibility they required to react to changed circumstances.

Kennan and Bohlen also clashed with Acheson over the nature of the Soviet threat. They insisted that the Soviet leaders were primarily concerned with preserving what had already been achieved. Communist expansion, then, was at best a secondary consideration. That being the case, the Soviets posed no serious military threat since war in the nuclear age would mean the destruction of the Bolshevik Revolution. The Soviet threat, the two diplomats insisted, was political, economic, and diplomatic. A major military buildup, therefore, was not only needless but dangerous in that it increased international tensions and the possibility of war.

Acheson had no patience with such arguments. He was committed to rearmament and to the view that the department ought to produce "communicable" ideas to the president. Kennan and Bohlen, he thought, especially Kennan, produced mere poetry; he needed more than "educated hunches" on which to base policy.[31]

In the spring of 1950 Nitze's study group presented their conclusions to the National Security Council (an advisory body to the President created under the 1947 National Security Act) in the form of a long paper designated

NSC 68. It was an extraordinary piece of work, presenting an overdrawn, not to say outlandish evaluation of Soviet intentions and capabilities. The authors contended that "the Soviet Union, unlike previous aspirants to hegemony, is animated by a new fanatic faith, antithetical to our own, and seeks to impose its absolute authority over the rest of the world." As the leader of a "world-wide revolutionary movement" and "the inheritor of Russian imperialism," the Soviet Union would not, indeed could not rest until the United States had been destroyed. This threat to the continued existence of the American republic, the paper made plain, was both immediate and extreme.[32] Though the authors of NSC 68 sounded overwrought, almost hysterical, when describing the Soviet menace, they reverted to standard, bureaucratic lingo in explaining how the United States might respond. In the style characteristic of national security managers then and now, they laid out four options. Two of these, however, were never seriously considered. There was no support for a do-nothing response to the Soviet threat. Nor was there any enthusiasm for the "Fortress America" concept advanced by Republican conservatives including Senator Taft and former President Herbert Hoover.

The first option to receive any consideration at all by members of the National Security Council was the proposal to fight a "preventive war" against the Soviet Union. Air Force General Nathan Twining, who became chairman of the Joint Chiefs of Staff under Dwight Eisenhower, later recalled that "pre-emptive action" was vigorously advocated by "some very dedicated Americans." Taking their cue from the document itself, they argued that since Moscow was bent upon America's destruction, sooner or later the United States would be forced to fight. It was only reasonable, then, for the United States to launch nuclear strikes against the Soviets before they developed "nation-killing capabilities."[33]

A majority on the council rejected the preventive war option. Some took the moral position that the United States could not sully its reputation by striking first. More to the point, however, many on the council "believed that the Red Army could quickly seize . . . Western Europe even if we used our small existing stock of nuclear weapons in a direct attack upon the U.S.S.R."[34] The United States would then be faced with the prospect of fighting a costly conventional war to liberate Western Europe and defeat the Soviets and their Eastern European allies. For this reason, preventive war was not considered a viable option. As Acheson later observed, it would only have complicated matters immeasurably.

In due course the council recommended that the president adopt a fourth option, the one Acheson and Nitze advocated from the beginning. This proposal called for the expansion of American conventional and nuclear forces for the purpose of deterring war and meeting the Soviet challenge in any form it might appear. The price of deterrence would be high. But Acheson believed that any other course would prove more costly.

In April 1950, the president gave conditional approval to NSC 68, thus committing himself in principle to an arms race in conventional as well as nuclear weaponry. But Truman, who had consistently insisted on a balanced federal budget, refused to approve the specific programs recommended in the document until he had seen cost estimates.

Winning even conditional presidential approval was an important step forward on the road to rearmament. But for the supporters of NSC 68, many obstacles still loomed. It would be difficult to persuade Congress and the public to foot the bill for rearmament. Nor could one predict how the president would respond once he saw the rearmament program's price tag.

During the spring of 1950 elements of the federal bureaucracy outside the national security establishment were given access to NSC 68. The director of the Bureau of the Budget was particularly critical of the plan, claiming it would have a disastrous impact on efforts to balance the budget. He argued so persuasively that even some of the Joint Chiefs of Staff began to waver. For a time NSC 68 was sitting dead in the water while the Budget Bureau took potshots at it and the Joint Chiefs waffled. Advocates of rearmament were stymied. Their program, one later recalled, was "being nibbled away by the ducks."[35]

The Korean War changed everything. Literally overnight, opposition to rearmament withered. As President Truman explained, the North Korean attack "made danger clear to everyone." Years later Secretary Acheson was still almost gleeful as he recalled how doubtful it was "whether anything like what happened in the next few years could have been done had not the Russians been stupid enough to have instigated the attack on South Korea."[36]

NSC 68 stands as a landmark in the history of the cold war. From 1947 until 1950 Washington had used economic and political means to strengthen nations outside the Soviet sphere of influence and in that way contain Soviet power. Few gave serious thought to the possibility that the Soviet Union might use force to achieve its foreign ambitions. But five events—the Berlin blockade, the Czech coup, the successful test of a Soviet atomic bomb, the Chinese Revolution, and the North Korean attack on South Korea (which most believed had been instigated by Stalin)—reshaped official opinion in the United States. And so, clearly overextended and sporting a militaristic foreign policy that proved a major drag on the nation's domestic economic well-being, America moved resolutely forward into the second half of the twentieth century.

## ENDNOTES

1. James F. Byrnes, quoted in Gregg Herken, *The Winning Weapon: The Atomic Bomb in the Cold War, 1945–1950* (New York: Random House, 1982), p. 43.

2. James Conant, quoted in ibid., pp. 82–83.

3. Harry Truman, quoted in Daniel Yergin, *Shattered Peace: The Origins of the Cold War and the National Security State* (Boston: Houghton Mifflin, 1977), p. 161.

4. Joseph W. Martin and Arthur Vandenberg, both quoted in *Newsweek*, March 11, 1946, p. 25.

5. W. Averell Harriman quoting Truman, in Yergin, *Shattered Peace*, p. 188.

6. Truman, quoted in ibid., p. 235.

7. *Newsweek,* February 18, 1946, p. 47.

8. George F. Kennan to secretary of state, February 22, 1946, *Foreign Relations of the United States, 1946* (Washington, D.C., 1969), VI, 696–723.

9. Winston Churchill *Vital Speeches,* Speech of Feb. 12 (March 15, 1946), 329–32.

10. Ibid.

11. Trygve Lie, quoted in Thomas G. Paterson, *On Every Front: The Making of the Cold War* (New York: W. W. Norton, 1979), p. 8; Kennan, quoted in John L. Gaddis, *Strategies of Containment* (New York: Oxford University Press, 1982), p. 62.

12. Henry L. Stimson and McGeorge Bundy, *On Active Service in Peace and War* (New York, Harper and Brothers, 1947), p. 594.

13. Quoted in Yergin, *Shattered Peace,* p. 280.

14. Vandenberg, quoted in Richard M. Freeland, *The Truman Doctrine and the Origins of McCarthyism* (New York: Alfred A. Knopf, 1972), pp. 89–93.

15. Truman special message to Congress, March 12, 1947, *Public Papers of the Presidents: Harry S. Truman, 1947* (Washington, D.C., 1963), pp. 178–79.

16. Robert Taft, Joseph Kennedy, and Bernard Baruch, all quoted in *Time,* March 24, 1947, pp. 18–21.

17. George F. Kennan, *Memoirs, 1925–1950* (New York: Bantam Books, 1969), pp. 337–39.

18. Carl Vinson, quoted in Robert J. Donovan, *Conflict and Crisis: The Presidency of Harry S. Truman, 1945–1948* (New York, Norton, 1977), p. 286.

19. George Marshall, quoted in Walter LaFeber, *America, Russia, and the Cold War, 1945–1984,* 5th ed. (New York: Alfred A. Knopf, 1985), p. 58.

20. Kennan, quoted in Gaddis, *Strategies of Containment,* p. 38.

21. Marshall, speech of June 5, 1947, *State Department Bulletin,* June 15, 1947, pp. 1159–60.

22. V. M. Molotov, quoted in Stephen E. Ambrose, *Rise to Globalism: American Foreign Policy since 1938,* 5th ed. (New York: Penguin Books, 1988), p. 90.

23. Lucius Clay to Stephen J. Chamberlain, March 5, 1948, *The Papers of General Lucius D. Clay: Germany, 1945–1949,* ed. Gene E. Smith (Bloomington, Ind.: Indiana University Press, 1974), II, 569.

24. Marshall and Truman, both quoted in Freeland, *Truman Doctrine,* pp. 269–74.

25. Truman special message to Congress, March 17, 1948, *Public Papers of the Presidents: Harry S. Truman, 1948* (Washington, D.C.; 1964), pp. 182–86.

26. Teleconference between Clay and Omar Bradley, April 10, 1948, *Clay Papers,* II, 623.

27. Truman, quoted in Yergin, *Shattered Peace,* p. 377.

28. Vandenberg, *The Private Papers of Senator Vandenberg,* ed. Arthur H. Vandenberg, Jr. (Boston: Houghton Mifflin, 1952), p. 485.

29. Dean G. Acheson, quoted in Robert J. Donovan, *Tumultuous Years: The Presidency of Harry S. Truman, 1949–1953* (New York, W. W. Norton, 1982), p. 42.

30. Dean G. Acheson, *Present at the Creation: My Years in the State Department* (New York: W. W. Norton, 1969), p. 345.

31. Acheson, quoted in ibid., p. 347.

32. NSC 68, quoted in Yergin, *Shattered Peace,* pp. 401–3. See also Gaddis, *Strategies of Containment,* pp. 89–126.

33. Nathan Twining, *Neither Liberty Nor Safety* (New York: Holt, Rinehart and Winston, 1966), pp. 48–50.

34. Ibid.

35. Quoted in the Princeton Seminars, July 9, 1953, Harry S. Truman Library, Independence, Mo.

36. Acheson, *Present at the Creation,* p. 374.

This ten-year-old Chinese soldier was conscripted by the Chinese Nationalists for their war against the communists.

# 26

# *THE COLD WAR IN ASIA, 1945–1950*

The period immediately following the end of World War II was a time of extraordinary volatility in China. Japanese power disappeared along with the Japanese themselves, millions of whom were repatriated to the home islands. Then in the summer of 1946 the Soviets, who entered Manchuria during the last stages of the war and stayed to strip the region of much of its industrial equipment and rolling stock, withdrew. The Chinese communists expanded into Manchuria, an area of vital concern to the Chinese Nationalists. Chiang Kai-shek, meanwhile, aided by fifty thousand American marines, established a strong presence in North China, an area controlled by the communists. With the Nationalists and communists both on the move and the foreign presence diminished, the stage was set for the long-anticipated Chinese civil war.

During World War II, Mao Zedong tried to cultivate American friendship, hoping for the lend-lease aid that could spell victory over Chiang, perhaps without a civil war. But Washington's policy was to provide aid only to the Nationalists. Vastly underestimating the power of the communist movement in China as well as Mao's resolve, Ambassador Patrick Hurley, the author of this approach, assumed that, with the Soviets sitting on the sidelines and Chiang's armies well armed and equipped, the communist leader would have no choice save to accept minority status in a coalition government.

A number of foreign service officers stationed in China, including John Patton Davies and John Stewart Service, warned the State Department that a policy of unilateral aid to Chiang would only stiffen his resolve to crush the communists militarily, making it more rather than less likely that China would be caught up in civil war. These China experts were correct. By September 1945, tension between the rival Chinese factions was intense; civil war seemed imminent.

At this point Hurley returned to the United States, ostensibly to brief administration leaders on developments in China. His real purpose, however, was to resign before his failed China policy came to pieces. Hurley told Truman that a coalition government was a distinct prospect but that he was exhausted and unable to carry on with his work. He offered to resign urging the president to find a younger, fresher man to take his place. But Truman, who apparently believed Hurley was merely seeking a reaffirmation of his support, refused to accept his resignation.

Hurley then confronted the president with a fait accompli. In a letter of resignation that hit the newspapers before it was received at the White House, he charged that the State Department's China experts were working hand in glove with the Chinese communists to undermine his efforts at creating a coalition government in China. The letter went on to allege that "a considerable section of our State Department is endeavoring to support Communism generally as well as specifically in China."[1]

Since Hurley had seen the president only the day before and given no indication of what was coming, Truman was naturally furious. But he handled the situation skillfully, prevailing on General George C. Marshall, who only a few months before had resigned as the army chief of staff, to accept an appointment as his envoy to China. Marshall's job would be the same as Hurley's—to mediate between the rival factions and forestall a civil war by encouraging the creation of a coalition government. The president had enormous admiration for and confidence in Marshall—one of the most respected Americans of the age and the architect of victory in World War II. Truman believed that Marshall's appointment was certain to put a stop to talk of communists running the State Department's China policy.

General Marshall's mission to China began on a positive note. A military truce was followed by a conference in Chongqing that went exceedingly well. There, aided by Marshall, the communists and Nationalists hammered out a series of agreements that laid the foundation for the coalition government the United States sought.

The truce between the two factions soon broke down, however, and the fighting began once again. Marshall worked feverishly for a cease-fire. But in May he cabled the president that the situation was at "an impasse." The outlook, he thought, was "not promising and the alterative to a compromise arrangement is, in my opinion, utter chaos in North China, to which the fighting will inevitably spread."[2]

General George C. Marshall (extreme left) failed completely in efforts to convince Chiang Kai-Shek (third from left) that he could not win a military victory over the communists.

In June, Marshall managed to arrange a second truce. But Chiang, who by this time believed that no matter what he did the United States would not withdraw its support, was completely uncompromising. Marshall tried to convince the Nationalist leader that he could not win a military victory over the communists. But the Generalissimo would not listen, preferring instead to resume the war.

By October 1946, Marshall was satisfied that there remained no chance that China's warring factions would accept a mediated settlement or agree to a coalition government. The last of the fifty thousand American marines to enter China after the war were withdrawn before the end of November. A month later Marshall himself was on his way home to begin his new assignment as secretary of state in the Truman cabinet. The long-shot attempt to create a coalition government in China had failed. The Chinese themselves would decide their future on the battlefield.

## THE COMMUNIST VICTORY IN CHINA

Marshall's return to the United States marked a significant turning point in America's China policy. The administration was now prepared to abandon Chiang Kai-shek. This willingness to break the long-standing relationship was based on three considerations. First, Marshall was convinced that Chiang's incorrigibly corrupt government had no chance of winning back the popular support it had long since squandered. Chiang seemed destined to lose to the communists, and American policy makers did not want to be caught in the impending debacle. Second, the Soviets had surprised the administration by withdrawing from Manchuria. It seemed unlikely, therefore, that Moscow would attempt to take advantage of the civil conflict to move back into China's frontier province. Third, Marshall and the Joint Chiefs of Staff had concluded that even without China the United States could defend its Asian interests from bases in the western Pacific, Japan, and other offshore islands.

Though prepared to sever their ties with the Nationalist Chinese, Truman and Marshall were not free agents. Chiang still had powerful friends in the United States. A substantial portion of the daily press, as well as Henry Luce's *Time-Life* media empire, continued to back the Chinese leader. The China lobby, a powerful group of foreign agents and rabid Asia Firsters lavishly funded by the Nationalist regime, worked tirelessly to popularize Chiang's cause. And in Congress there was the China bloc, a small but vocal group of representatives and senators that included, among others Styles Bridges of New Hampshire, William Knowland of California, Walter Judd of Minnesota, Pat McCarran of Nevada, and the junior senator from Wisconsin, Joseph R. McCarthy.

Pressure from these sources made it impossible for the administration to abandon Chiang. And so between 1946 and 1949 the Nationalists received another $2 billion in aid (much of which corrupt Chinese officials seem to have invested in the United States). Moreover, an American military advisory group remained in China almost to the very end.

But nothing the Americans did had the least effect on the outcome of the civil war. Though well equipped with American weapons, the Nationalists, who outnumbered the communists 3:1, suffered one defeat after another. "No battle has been lost since my arrival due to lack of ammunition or equipment," Major General David Barr reported. "Their military debacles in my opinion can be attributed to the world's worst leadership and many other morale destroying factors that lead to a complete loss of will to fight."[3] By 1949 it was clear that Chiang, who fled to the island of Taiwan, had lost the battle for China.

The communist victory in China confronted the Truman administration with separate but related questions. First, should the United States extend diplomatic recognition to the Beijing government? And what should Washington do regarding the future of Taiwan, where Chiang still claimed to head the only legitimate Chinese government?

The State Department's earliest position regarding the Beijing government was based on the assumption that it was possible to keep China outside the Soviet orbit. Toward that end Washington adopted a wait-and-see attitude on the question of diplomatic recognition, avoided all further interference in the ongoing civil war in China (meaning no more aid for Chiang), raised no insuperable barriers to Beijing's membership in the United Nations, and allowed occupied Japan to trade with China.

Unhappily, this early policy, which had considerable merit, was soon overtaken by events. Inevitably, Americans in China became targets of opportunity for angry, xenophobic Chinese. Thus Mao's troops violated the diplomatic immunity of American officials in China, overrunning the American embassy compound in Nanjing and harassing American diplomats and consular officials in all of China's major cities. The most celebrated incident of this sort took place in Mukden, Manchuria, where the American consul, Angus Ward, and four other consular officials were kept under house arrest for a full year before being expelled from the country.

Repeated anti-American incidents in China gave conservative critics the opportunity they needed to lambast the administration. Many, including of course Senator McCarthy, charged that Nationalist China had been the victim of communist traitors operating in the State Department. Dean Acheson himself, one of the principal architects of America's anticommunist foreign policy, was the victim of frequent, vitriolic attacks. Thus Kenneth Wherry of Nebraska charged: "It is known—somehow it is common knowledge—that Acheson has been an appeaser of Russia." Senator Robert Taft, meanwhile, charged that the communists in the Acheson State Department were "the greatest Kremlin asset in our history." Months of such sustained political turmoil made it impossible for Washington to open the dialogue with Beijing that might have led to recognition.[4]

This is not to say that the administration would have extended recognition to the People's Republic but for its domestic critics. The president himself was so angered by Chinese behavior that he considered adopting extreme retaliatory measures. During the Angus Ward affair he talked of blockading China's seaports and supporting anticommunist Chinese Muslims, who some believed might form the nucleus of a Chinese counterrevolution. Truman even went to the extreme —(unusual for him) of requiring Acheson to review and defend his moderate China policy.

In February 1950, with Sino-American relations already seriously deranged, Mao and Josef Stalin signed a thirty-year treaty of friendship. This development triggered a hardening of the administration's attitude. O. Edmund Clubb, an experienced China hand, saw the Sino-Soviet agreement as proof that the Chinese Communist party had "oriented its own program to Moscow's and attached China to the Soviet chariot, for better or worse." There was, he thought, "no reasoning" with that "[m]adness born of xenophobia." The same John Patton Davies, who with a certain amount of equanimity informed Washington in 1944 that China's future belonged to Mao and not Chiang, now urged support for the remaining noncommunist elements inside China and a policy of encouraging "revolution from the ground up against the unified strength of the whole Communist apparatus."[5] And Assistant Secretary of State Dean Rusk urged a major overhaul of America's Far Eastern policy. He called for the defense of Taiwan, a major aid program for Southeast Asia, and a peace treaty with Japan on terms that would ensure a close and lasting relationship between Washington and Tokyo.

By March 1950, a reconsideration of the State Department's early moderate policy toward the People's Republic was clearly under way. Toughness was becoming the order of the day, and if a policy of nonrecognition had not yet been decided upon, recognition was becoming increasingly

UNION OF SOVIET SOCIALIST REPUBLICS

*BERING SEA*

*SEA OF OKHOTSK*

Irkutsk     *Lake Baikal*

(U.S.S.R.)
(U.S.)     ATTU
KISKA

SAKHALIN I.
(U.S.S.R.)

MONGOLIA
Ulan Bator

KURILE IS.
(U.S.S.R.)

MANCHURIA

Vladivostok

Beijing
Pyongyang
NORTH KOREA

*SEA OF JAPAN*

CHINA

Seoul     SOUTH KOREA

JAPAN

*PACIFIC*

Shanghai

BONIN IS.

TIBET

TACHEN IS.

RYUKYU IS. (Jap.)

IWO JIMA

NEPAL

MATSU I.

QUEMOY I.

OKINAWA

MARCUS I.

E. PAKISTAN
Calcutta

BURMA

Hanoi

Hong Kong (Br.)

TAIWAN (FORMOSA)
PESCADORES IS.

*OCEAN*

WAKE I. (U.S.)

INDIA

LAOS
Vientiane
NORTH VIETNAM

*SOUTH CHINA*

*PHILIPPINE*

MARIANAS IS.

Rangoon

THAILAND
Bangkok

CAMBODIA

SOUTH VIETNAM
Saigon

*SEA*

Manila

*SEA*

GUAM (U.S.)

M I C R O

MARSHALL IS.
(U.S. trust)

*BAY OF BENGAL*

PHILIPPINES
(also member of SEATO)

N E S

CEYLON

BRUNEI (Br.)

CAROLINE ISLANDS
(U.S. trust)

I A

GILBERT IS.
(Br.)

MALAYSIA
Kuala Lumpur
SARAWAK

M E L A N E S I A

SUMATRA
Singapore
KALIMANTAN

SULAWESI

IRIAN
(To U.S. 1962,
Indonesia 1963)

NEW GUINEA
(Aust.)

ELLICE IS.
(Br.)

I N D O N E S I A

Djakarta     JAVA

SOLOMON IS.
(Br.)

PAPUA
(Aust.)

TIMOR
(Port.)

*INDIAN*

*CORAL SEA*

NEW HEBRIDES IS.
(Br. and Fr.)

FIJI IS.
(Br.)

*OCEAN*

NEW CALEDONIA
(Fr.)

# The Alliance System in the Far East, 1945-1966

A U S T R A L I A

Brisbane

*TASMAN SEA*

Perth

Sidney
Canberra

Melbourne

NEW ZEALAND
Wellington

TASMANIA

Members of SEATO

Nations having bilateral treaties with the U.S.

Communist bloc

unlikely. Before the year was out, Mao's decision to intervene in the Korean War settled the issue for the next quarter-century.

## CHIANG AND THE FUTURE OF TAIWAN

After Chiang's flight to Taiwan, the question of the island's future also became a major issue in Washington. The China lobby, the China bloc, as well as many others believed the United States should do everything possible to save the Nationalist regime. The most prominent spokesperson for this point of view was General Douglas MacArthur, the supreme commander of Allied powers in Japan, who described Taiwan as a stationary aircraft carrier and submarine tender from which an adversary could strike devastating blows at the American position in the western Pacific. The general insisted that because of its strategic location, Taiwan should at all costs be kept in friendly hands.

The Joint Chiefs of Staff, too, hoped to keep Taiwan from falling to a potential adversary. They did not covet bases on the island themselves, however. Nor were they willing to commit troops to the island's defense. Because their forces were stretched to the limit, they argued instead that the administration should use diplomatic and economic means to strengthen the Nationalist regime and in that way save the island from falling under Beijing's control.

Dean Acheson was baffled by talk of Taiwan's importance. Had the island been a peninsula, he observed, no one would have worried about its strategic importance. Would not military bases on the China coast only a few miles away be just as threatening to American interests? More to the point, the secretary was convinced that the Joint Chiefs' prescription for keeping Taiwan out of communist hands would not work. He had no reason to believe that Chiang, who had failed to create a viable government in China, would succeed on Taiwan. Nor had he any desire to tie American prestige yet again to the Nationalist cause. Acheson thought it far more sensible to persist in the administration's policy of noninvolvement in China's civil war.

Supported by a 1949 National Intelligence Estimate, which predicted that Taiwan would fall before the end of 1950, Acheson challenged the Joint Chiefs to put up or shut up. He insisted that if the island was of such enormous strategic importance the Joint Chiefs should be prepared to defend it. Their refusal to make that commitment gave him the bureaucratic victory. On December 29, 1949, the president approved NSC 48/2, which stipulated that there would be no new aid for Chiang.

The substance of the administration's Taiwan policy was quickly leaked to the press by the Defense Department and General MacArthur's headquarters in Tokyo. As soon as it became known that Chiang was to be abandoned, members of the China bloc, Senator Robert Taft, and former President Herbert Hoover all howled in anger at this "Far Eastern Munich." The administration, of course, fought back. On January 5, the president stated bluntly that he would "not pursue a course which will lead to involvement in the Civil conflict in China." Nor would America "provide military aid or advice to Chinese forces on Formosa."[6] One week later Secretary Acheson followed up on the president's statement. In a speech before the National Press Club in Washington, he reiterated the president's position and described the line that the United States was prepared to defend against communist encroachment in the Pacific as extending from the Aleutians through Japan, the Ryukyus, and the Philippines. Taiwan and South Korea, another position the Joint Chiefs were unprepared at the time to defend, were pointedly excluded. In spite of the uproarious opposition, America's China policy appeared set. Chiang and the Nationalists would sink or swim—probably sink—on their own.

Though in January the Truman administration's Taiwan policy seemed written in stone, it changed immediately after North Korean forces invaded South Korea in late June 1950. Within two days of the invasion the administration not only committed itself to the defense of Korea but sent the U.S. Seventh Fleet into the Taiwan straits to protect the sagging Nationalist regime. A month later, in another startling move, the administration renewed its aid programs for Chiang Kai-shek.

Obviously, what had been acceptable to Washington prior to the outbreak of hostilities in Korea was not so any longer. In Acheson's judgment, more was at stake than part of the Korean peninsula and Taiwan. It seemed clear to the secretary that if South Korea and Taiwan both fell under the control of the Kremlin's surrogates, the United States would find it difficult to keep an independent Japan from steering a neutralist course or worse, drifting into the Soviet orbit. Taiwan, then, was to be preserved not for its strategic importance but because its loss would prove a serious blow to American hopes regarding Japan's future and the Asian balance of power.

## OCCUPIED JAPAN

At the end of World War II, though not without serious misgivings, President Truman appointed General Douglas MacArthur the supreme commander of Allied powers (SCAP) in Japan. The plainspoken Truman and the aristocratic, egoistic general had no liking for one another. The general conceived of himself as more important than the president and often behaved as he felt. Truman, never a man to mince words, once described his Asian proconsul as "Mr. Prima Donna, Brass hat, Five Star MacArthur. He's worse than the Cabots and the Lodge's—they at least talked with one another before they told God what to do. Mac tells God right off. It is a very great pity we have stuffed shirts like that in key positions."[7] Truman even opined that in 1942, during the siege of Bataan, Roosevelt had made the wrong decision. He should have left MacArthur to rot in a Japanese prison and brought General Jonathan Wainwright out.

Had there been a feasible option, Truman would have selected someone other than MacArthur to head up the Japanese occupation. But the liberator of the Philippines and the conqueror of Japan could not be denied. The next best thing, Truman may have mused, was to keep him ten thousand miles from Washington.

MacArthur was instructed to implement a wide variety of reforms. Japan was to be disarmed, its military forces demobilized. He was also to establish a new democratic political order that guaranteed basic freedoms to all Japanese, including women. He was to restructure the economy by destroying the *zaibatsu* (huge family-owned economic conglomerates that dominated the Japanese economy) and encourage the development of a competitive free enterprise system. At the same time he was to reduce or eliminate those industries that contributed to Japan's war-making capabilities. The new Japan was to be left with an industrial base sufficient to provide an acceptable standard of living for its people but not sufficient ever again to dominate the economy or threaten the security of the rest of Asia.

General MacArthur's staff pursued the administration's reformist purposes with mixed feelings and results. The Japanese government, which functioned as an administrative arm of SCAP, adopted a liberal democratic constitution that included a provision forbidding the creation of a national army and denied the state the right to make war. SCAP also implemented a major land reform program, breaking up large estates and redistributing the land among formerly landless peasants. The police and school systems were reformed, and for a brief time labor unions flourished.

At the same time SCAP officials connived with Japanese officials to thwart the reparations and anti-*zaibatsu* programs. And although Washington called for a thorough purge from political and economic life of all those thought to have been involved in leading Japan on an imperialist course before the war (about 2.5 million people), SCAP derailed this experiment in social engineering by the simple expedient of leaving the implementation of the purge in the hands of the conservatives who controlled the Japanese government.

In 1947 the Truman administration began gradually to abandon its reformist goals in favor of restoring Japan's economic strength. In May 1949, this became established policy. NSC 13/3 stated categorically: "economic recovery should be made the primary objective of United States policy in Japan for the coming period." SCAP was instructed "not to press upon the Japanese Government any further reform legislation."[8]

The anti-*zaibatsu* and purge policies as well as the reparations program, none of which had ever been enthusiastically pursued, were scuttled. Instead of shipping factories to the victims of Japanese aggression, SCAP now began to stimulate Japan's textile, iron and steel, and other basic industries. Trade unionism, which had been encouraged in the early years of the occupation, was now crushed in the interest of political stability, economic efficiency, and growth.

There were two major reasons for this dramatic turnabout. First, two years into the occupation Japan's economy remained in the doldrums.

Occupation costs ran into the hundreds of millions of dollars, all of which came directly from the American taxpayer. Obviously something had to be done to turn this situation around. Second, and far more important, were geopolitical considerations. By 1947 the cold war was the central fact of international life. As the Soviet-American crisis intensified, American policy makers looked to Germany as a key to checking Soviet expansionism in Europe. After the failure of the Marshall mission to China, they decided that Japan should play a similar role in Asia. As Secretary of the Navy James Forrestal explained, success in the competition with the Soviet Union meant that "Japan, Germany, and other affiliates of the Axis" would have to be put "back to work."[9]

Before Japan could play its new role, it was essential that its economic vitality be restored. But reviving the economy was a tricky business. Japan was a trading nation dependent on outside sources for food and many of the basic raw materials its industry required. It was also dependent on Asian markets to absorb its surplus production. Prior to World War II, China, Manchuria, Korea, and Southeast Asia had been areas of vital economic importance to Japan. Therefore, the CIA believed that Japan's revival appeared to depend in part on a French success in Indochina where they were attempting to put down an uprising by the communist leader Ho Chi Minh. Moreover, because Japan's traditional trading partner was China, it was thought that a modus vivendi with Beijing would have to be arranged. Once political stability had been restored and relations regularized, trade and economic growth would follow.

The Sino-Soviet accord of 1950 convinced Washington that it was no longer desirable to seek a modus vivendi between Japan and China. On the contrary, Washington now feared that such a relationship would encourage the Japanese to drift into the Soviet orbit.

SCAP responded to this changed situation first by slapping an embargo on all trade between Japan and China. Then State Department planners set out to create a modern-day version (minus China and Manchuria) of Japan's old Co-Prosperity Sphere, an integrated regional economy that would include Japan, South Korea, Southeast Asia, and India. Japan was to be the "workshop of Asia," providing manufactured goods for the region in exchange for food and raw materials.

Because the other participants in this envisioned regional economic arrangement were too poor to provide adequate markets for Japan's export needs, policy makers also planned to initiate aid programs to encourage economic growth throughout the region. In this way the State Department hoped to encourage an increase in food and raw material production as well as growing markets for Japanese manufactures. According to NSC 61:

> Continuing, or even maintaining Japan's economic recovery depends on keeping Communism out of Southeast Asia, promoting economic recovery there and in further developing these countries, together with Indonesia, the Philippines, Southern Korea and India as the principal trading areas for Japan. In this way Japan's revived economy, with its more than adequate

plants, know-how and labor, which now lacks sufficient markets, could be employed with maximum effectiveness in achieving U.S. objectives.[10]

## A PEACE TREATY FOR JAPAN

In 1947 General MacArthur called for an international conference to negotiate a peace treaty that would restore sovereignty to Japan and end the occupation. But the great man had, characteristically, not bothered to clear his proposal either with the State Department or the Joint Chiefs of Staff before making his views public. Both bureaucracies strongly opposed the general's proposal.

The Joint Chiefs were unwilling to accept any treaty that did not guarantee the United States extensive base rights in postoccupation Japan. MacArthur's proposal did not include the appropriate provisions. The State Department was equally opposed to a Japanese peace treaty in 1947. In the first place, America's eleven World War II Far Eastern allies were not yet ready to accept Japan back into the family of nations. Nor was Japan prepared to play the new role in postwar Asia only recently assigned to it. If the former enemy was to become the key to the containment of Soviet expansionism in the Far East, it would first have to be restored economically, stabilized politically, and conditioned to accept American leadership. Then at the very beginning of this process, the State Department joined the Joint Chiefs in burying the MacArthur proposal.

Two years later the State Department revived the idea of a Japanese peace treaty. By this time Secretary Acheson and his Far Eastern advisers were convinced that they had set Japan on the right road and that the occupation had become a "wasting asset," which, if continued, would alienate the Japanese. Consequently, State Department planners drafted a treaty calling for a neutralized and demilitarized Japan. The treaty gained wide acceptance among America's old Pacific allies but ran into serious difficulties in the Pentagon. American military planners insisted that the United States retain numerous bases in Japan. Moreover, they opposed the idea of a disarmed Japan, arguing that at the very least Japan should have a self-defense force capable of defending the home islands against attack. Nor were they impressed by the view that the occupation could not be continued indefinitely without provoking an anti-American backlash.

The vehement opposition of the Department of Defense might have been overcome had the president been willing to make a decision in the matter. But the year was 1949, and the administration was already under withering attack for its failures in China. Under the circumstances, Truman, who generally came down on Acheson's side when the State and Defense departments tangled, refused to second-guess the military. And so the stalemate over the future of Japan continued into mid-1950, when events surrounding the Korean War led the feuding bureaucracies to compromise their differences. The Pentagon got most of what it wanted, and plans went forward for the peace treaty with Japan that was signed at San Francisco in September 1951.

## AMERICA IN SOUTHEAST ASIA

During much of World War II, Franklin Roosevelt had opposed the reestablishment of French colonial rule in Indochina. He was contemptuous of the French, and he despised the arrogant Charles de Gaulle, leader of the "Free French." In 1944 he told Cordell Hull that "France has had the country [Indochina]—thirty million inhabitants—for nearly one hundred years, and the people are worse off than they were at the beginning." It was time, he believed, to let the Indochinese peoples rule themselves.[11]

Toward the end of the war, Roosevelt reversed himself. Pressure exerted by the British, who at the time had every intention of hanging on to as much of their overseas empire as possible, led him to abandon his earlier views. It was simply inexpedient to apply one standard to the French and another to the British. The Truman administration went even further. Not only did Secretary of State James F. Byrnes assure Paris that the United States would not object if France sought to reestablish control over Indochina, he agreed to transport French troops there.

In 1946, after fruitless negotiations with Ho Chi Minh, president of the recently proclaimed Democratic Republic of Vietnam, the French decided to reassert their control over Indochina by force. In November of that year a French cruiser shelled the city of Haiphong, center of Ho's power, killing upward of six thousand people. The French war for Indochina had begun.

American policy toward the war was no doubt influenced by the administration's interest in maintaining a close relationship with France, an important European ally. But it is also true that ideological considerations influenced American policy from the start. American intelligence operatives could find no connection between Ho and Moscow. There were no Soviet military or political advisers attached to Ho's movement. Nor were the Vietnamese receiving any Soviet aid. Moreover, Ho made a number of gestures intended to convince the United States that he owed nothing to Moscow and was inclined to lean toward the West. He even encouraged Washington to believe that an independent Vietnam would welcome American investment and look with favor on the establishment of an American naval base on its territory. But nothing he could say or do changed the fundamental fact that he was a communist. Consequently, Washington assumed that his talk of a pro-Western policy was a sham and that his insurgency was Moscow controlled.

Between 1947 and 1949, Washington adopted a low-key policy of benevolent neutrality toward the French in their struggle for control of Indochina. The administration did not want the insurgents to win in Vietnam. But neither did it wish to become identified with the attempt to reestablish colonial rule there. Convinced that the French could never maintain control over a country caught up in the postwar wave of Asian nationalism, Washington urged Paris to abandon its colonial effort and instead work to establish a viable noncommunist government for Vietnam as an alternative to Ho Chi Minh's revolutionary movement.

Though far less concerned about the threat posed by international communism than the United States, Paris did create a government for Vietnam headed by Bao Dai, formerly the emperor of Annam. But this puppet government had no real power or popular support. The embattled French created it in hopes of undercutting Ho Chi Minh's popularity by offering the appearance of sovereignty while withholding its substance. These efforts notwithstanding, by late 1949 Ho's Viet Minh forces controlled 90 percent of the land area of the country and claimed the loyalty of 80 percent of the people of Vietnam. The French, who were confined to the cities and controlled only certain tenuous lines of communication, seemed on the verge of defeat.

By this time Washington had come to view the possible loss of Vietnam and Southeast Asia to communism as completely unacceptable. According to a 1949 State Department report, the area was "a vital segment on the line of containment, stretching from Japan southward around to the Indian peninsula. The security of the three major non-communist base areas in this quarter of the world—Japan, India and Australia—depends in a large measure on the denial of Southeast Asia to the Kremlin." "If Southeast Asia is held," the report continued, "the links will exist for the development of an interdependent and integrated counter-force to Stalinism in this quarter of the world."[12]

In another analysis done in the same year, the Joint Chiefs warned that a French defeat would have catastrophic global implications. The loss of China had been a severe blow. But "if Southeast Asia is also swept by communism we shall have suffered a major political rout the repercussions of which will be felt throughout the rest of the world, especially in the Middle East and in a then critically exposed Australia."[13]

Washington was obviously already in a state of panic when, in January 1950, Moscow and Beijing recognized Ho Chi Minh's government. That decision set off warning bells all over official Washington. State Department experts quickly declared that the war in Indochina was just one element in a larger Soviet plan to gain control of all Southeast Asia. Both the State Department and the CIA agreed that if the Chinese should come to the aid of Ho Chi Minh the French would be defeated and Indochina lost to Soviet communism.

Because the domino theory was already accepted doctrine, it necessarily followed that the other countries of Southeast Asia would also fall. The last domino would, of course, be Japan, which, without access to the markets and resources of the region, would have little choice but to drift into the Soviet orbit. According to NSC 48/2:

If Japan, the principal component of a Far Eastern war making complex, were added to the Stalinist bloc, the Soviet Asian base could become a source of strength capable of shifting the balance of world power to the disadvantage of the United States. Should India and Pakistan fall to Communism, the United States and its friends might find themselves denied any foothold on the Asian mainland.[14]

Given the extraordinary importance analysts in the State and Defense departments placed on "denying Southeast Asia to the Kremlin," Washington was loath to ignore French pleas for help. Acheson and Truman realized that the government of Vietnam, created by the French and headed by the Emperor Bao Dai, was a mere facade, a disguise for continued French colonial rule. But they nevertheless reacted to the Sino-Soviet recognition of Ho by extending recognition to Bao Dai's regime and establishing a small military aid program for the French. Simultaneously, they placed themselves in the curious position of arguing that the French were the true defenders of Vietnamese independence while Ho was the agent of a foreign imperialism

American military aid was vital to the French in their war against the Viet Minh for control of Indochina.

and, as Acheson put it, "the mortal enemy of native independence in Indochina."[15] Strange though it may seem, this assessment was not entirely an act of dissimulation on the secretary's part. The fact that Ho was a nationalist was in Acheson's judgment irrelevant since he was convinced that once Ho had achieved his nationalist aims he would quickly subordinate Vietnam "to Commie purposes" and "Kremlin control."

The outbreak of the Korean War took the administration another important step down the road toward intervention in Southeast Asia. On the same evening that the president and his national security bureaucracy decided to send the Seventh Fleet into the Taiwan straits, they also moved to provide vastly increased quantities of military aid to the French in Vietnam. Only the fact that the American military was already stretched to the limit deterred them from giving serious consideration to active intervention.

The American decision to step up its support for the French war in Vietnam put the United States squarely on the side of European imperialism in Asia and dealt a damaging blow to America's reputation among nationalists throughout the underdeveloped world. Even those Asians friendly to the United States were appalled. Thus the Philippines' Carlos Romulo, who was at the time the president of the United Nations General Assembly, urged Truman and Acheson to reconsider this policy. But neither Romulo nor Jawaharlal Nehru, the Indian prime minister, who also tried to educate official Washington on the differences between Soviet imperialism and local Asian forms of communism, had the slightest impact on official thinking. The idea that the Soviets were using local communist movements to create a Soviet-dominated empire in Asia was utterly compelling. President Truman was so convinced of it that he could only explain Nehru, the leader of a neutralist bloc, as either a dupe of the Soviets or worse, a closet communist. Thus he told Chester Bowles, who was about to leave for India as the American ambassador: "The first thing you've got to do is find out whether Nehru is a Communist. He sat right in that chair [the President pointed to a chair in the corner of his office] and he talked just like a Communist."[16]

The Cambridge-educated Indian prime minister found it difficult to believe that anyone could consider him a communist. In a humorous aside he once quipped to Bowles, "I have more Communists in prison than any man in the world, except Stalin." Nehru believed that Washington's policy, which was based on the assumption of "a monolithic bloc from central Germany to the China Sea and the Pacific," was essentially "bankrupt." The primary worldwide political force, he insisted, was not communism "but an intense nationalism."[17]

The administration's decision to throw its lot in with France was clearly a high-stakes gamble. And it was a gamble they lost. The French were, of course, delighted to accept aid, but they rejected Washington's advice. French strategists ignored the military advisory group sent by Washington to aid in military planning. Nor would Paris make any concessions to Bao Dai, whose regime remained a government in name only.

In spite of French obstructionism, Acheson never pushed Paris too

far. He feared that if he did, one or another of the revolving-door governments that ruled France in these years would simply decide to leave Vietnam.
That would have left the United States in an impossible position, for as the
secretary explained, "another Korea was out of the question; we could not
put ground forces into Indochina."[18]

In August 1950, George Kennan, then clearly an outsider at the
State Department, warned Acheson that "we are getting ourselves into the
position of guaranteeing the French in an undertaking which neither they
nor we, nor both of us together, can win."[19] He urged the abandonment of
the involvement there, even at the risk of seeing the country come under
Ho Chi Minh's control. But Acheson was not buying. He still had his eye on
all those dominoes, with Japan as the ultimate prize.

By 1953 the struggle in Vietnam had been transformed from a local
insurgency into an international conflict. Washington was not only funding
nearly 40 percent of the French war effort but had agreed to provide air
and naval support in the event that the Chinese, who were providing the
Viet Minh with "volunteer" workers and thousands of tons of supplies each
month, should decide to intervene with troops. The Viet Minh had evolved
from a guerrilla force into a well-armed and disciplined army, and the
outlook for French success ranged from grim to dismal. Carlos Romulo tried
to convince Acheson that Ho Chi Minh was an Asian Tito and left to his
own devices would chart a course independent of Moscow. But Truman and
Acheson had chosen another path and gone far toward sowing the whirlwind.

## ENDNOTES

1. Patrick Hurley, quoted in Robert J. Donovan, *Conflict and Crisis: The Presidency of Harry S. Truman, 1945–1948* (New York: W. W. Norton, 1977), I, 149–52.

2. George C. Marshall to Truman, May 6, 1946, *Foreign Relations of the United States, 1946* (Washington, D.C., 1972), IX, 818.

3. David Barr, quoted in E. J. Kahn, Jr., *The China Hands: America's Foreign Service Officers and What Befell Them* (New York: Penguin Books, 1972), p. 198n.

4. Kenneth Wherry, and Taft, both quoted in Foster Rhea Dulles, *American Foreign Policy toward Communist China, 1949–1969* (New York: Thomas Y. Crowell, 1972), pp. 74–77.

5. O. Edmund Clubb, John Patton Davies, and Dean Rusk, all quoted in Michael Schaller, *The American Occupation of Japan: The Origins of the Cold War in Asia* (New York: Oxford University Press, 1985), pp. 253–54.

6. Harry Truman, quoted in presidential press conference, January 5, 1950, *Public Papers of the Presidents: Harry S. Truman, 1950* (Washington, D.C., 1965), pp. 11–17.

7. Truman, quoted in Donovan, *Conflict and Crisis*, p. 141.

8. NSC 13/3, May 6, 1949, *Foreign Relations of the United States, 1949* (Washington, D.C.: 1976), VII:2, pp. 733–34.

9. James Forrestal, quoted in Schaller, *American Occupation of Japan*, p. 78.

10. NSC 61, January 27, 1950, *Documents of the National Security Council* (University Publications of America microfilm), reel 2.

11. Cordell Hull, *Memoirs* (New York: Macmillan, 1948), II, 1597.

12. NSC 51, July 1, 1949, *Documents of the National Security Council*, reel 2.

13. NSC 48/1, December 23, 1949, ibid.
14. NSC 48/2, December 30, 1949, ibid.
15. Dean Acheson, quoted in George C. Herring, *America's Longest War: The United States in Vietnam, 1950–1975* (New York: Alfred A. Knopf, 1979), p. 11.
16. Chester Bowles, oral history interview, Columbia University, New York.
17. Ibid.
18. Acheson, memorandum, June 17, 1952, quoted in Herring, *America's Longest War,* p. 20.
19. George F. Kennan, quoted in Dean Acheson's Official Conversations, August 21, 1950, Acheson Papers, Harry S. Truman Library, Independence, Mo.

# 27

# *THE KOREAN WAR, 1945–1953*

In October 1950, President Harry Truman met General Douglas MacArthur at Wake Island for a conference following the Inchon landings.

At the Yalta conference in February 1945, the Big Three tentatively agreed to administer liberated Korea as a four-power trusteeship. Roosevelt had at least two reasons for sponsoring this arrangement. First, though he understood that after forty years of Japanese occupation the Korean people yearned for independence, he questioned their political maturity. More important, he feared that if Korea was granted its independence, as Josef Stalin proposed, China and the Soviet Union would soon be at odds over the country's future and that finally Moscow would gain control of not only Korea but Manchuria as well.

Originally, American policy makers hoped to occupy the entire Korean peninsula before the end of the war. But on August 14, 1945, when Tokyo surrendered, the closest American forces were six hundred miles away on Okinawa. The Soviets, on the other hand, had troops in Manchuria and could easily have occupied all of Korea before the first American soldier set foot on the Asian mainland. State Department planners therefore had to scramble to stake a claim to even part of the peninsula.

The American proposal, which Moscow quickly accepted, called for a temporary division of Korea into two zones of occupation, with the Soviets taking the Japanese surrender down to the 38th parallel while American forces occupied Korea south of that line. The four-power trusteeship was to be organized later.

The American occupation force that arrived in South Korea in September 1945 was commanded by General John Hodge, a combat officer with no experience in military government. Following instructions from General Douglas MacArthur's headquarters in Tokyo, Hodge at first relied on the established Japanese bureaucracy to run South Korea's civil affairs. It wasn't long, however, before press reports revealed this fact while noting that in the North the Soviets allowed the Koreans to govern themselves. That was enough for President Harry Truman, who blamed MacArthur for the foul up and ordered an immediate change. Hodge then had to find capable Koreans to administer civil affairs in the American zone.

At the time the most representative political organization in Korea was the Korean People's Republic (KPR), a nationalist, center-left coalition. Fundamentally anti-Japanese, it advocated land reform, the nationalization of Japanese holdings, the legalization of labor unions, political freedom, and, above all, national independence. Prior to the arrival of the Americans, the KPR, which claimed governmental status, removed many Japanese bureaucrats and Korean collaborators from office, replacing them with local governments that functioned through people's committees.

Very early in his tenure and without justification, Hodge concluded that the KPR was a communist-front organization. He refused to recognize it and quickly moved to oust the people's committees. In their place he created the Korean Advisory Council. Nine of the eleven members appointed by Hodge to this new governing body were also members of the Korean Democratic party, a small right-wing group made up largely of political conservatives, landlords, and capitalists, many of whom were former Japanese collaborators. Professor Bruce Cumings, a leading expert on the history of postwar Korea, has described the KDP as a coalition of "discredited Plutocrats."[1]

To strengthen the power of the KDP-controlled Advisory Council, Hodge organized a constabulary (army) that was officered in the main by former Japanese collaborators. He also armed and equipped a national police force of eighteen thousand. Minus their Japanese officers, these were by and large the same men who had tyrannized Korea during the Japanese occupation. Finally, Hodge convinced Washington to allow certain important right-wing politicians then living in exile to return to Korea. These included Kim Koo, who headed the Korean provisional government in Chongqing, and, more important, the best-known Korean nationalist leader of his age, Syngman Rhee, who had spent years living in the United States.

Washington's unwillingness to sanction Korean independence, combined with Hodge's suppression of the KPR and support for rightist policies, looked to many Koreans like an effort to reestablish the old repressive colonial system under a new flag. The fact that the American command relied so heavily on former Japanese collaborators certainly did not help matters, especially since in northern Korea the Soviets, working with the KPR's people's committees, had not even bothered to create a military government.

In 1946, Korean frustration with American policy boiled over into a general strike that was accompanied by widespread rioting. In the counter-action undertaken by the constabulary and police, thousands were killed and injured. American forces helped break the strike and destroy the All Korean Council of Labor, South Korea's most powerful union, "We set up concentration camps outside of town and held strikers there when the jails got too full," recalled one American. "It was war. We recognized it as war. And that is the way we fought it."[2]

As in any war, prisoners were taken. By March 1947, the rumor that South Korea's jails held thousands of political prisoners aroused the interest of both the American Civil Liberties Union and the press. The occupation authorities vehemently denied the charge, contending that four thousand of those described as political prisoners had in fact been convicted of crimes. But when they were asked to explain the nature of these crimes, it turned out that these people had been convicted of creating disorder by passing out handbills or holding political meetings. The authorities then admitted that another 3,773 persons then being held for trial were also accused of political crimes of this sort.

Following a visit to South Korea, Roger Baldwin of the American Civil Liberties Union charged that Washington had established an anticommunist police state there. And in a report to the Foreign Policy Association, George M. McCune of the University of California argued that South Koreans were being driven toward communism by the repressive, anti-democratic behavior of the occupation authorities. McCune did not believe everything he read about the level of political freedom enjoyed by North Koreans. Still, he thought it was undeniably true that under the Soviets, North Koreans were being encouraged to participate actively in their own government. And that could not be said for life in the American zone.

## KOREA DIVIDED

General MacArthur, who realized that Washington was wearing out its welcome in Korea, warned that anti-Americanism was burgeoning there and that "The word pro-American is being" equated with the phrases "national traitor" and "Japanese collaborator."[3] MacArthur believed that if the country was not soon reunited and granted its independence, the Korean people would turn toward communism. Any attempt to create a trusteeship, he was certain, would precipitate a revolution. He therefore urged Washington to support Korean unification and independence. Failing that, he recommended a mutual withdrawal of Soviet and American forces, leaving the Koreans to settle their differences.

Secretary of State James F. Byrnes refused to consider granting

Korea its independence, since he was certain that this would mean Russian control. Instead, at the Moscow meeting of the Council of Foreign Ministers in December 1945, he and V. M. Molotov agreed to create a five-year trusteeship over Korea. During this period a Soviet-American Joint Committee would consult with legitimate political groups in Korea and then organize a representative provisional government for the entire country. Once this government was in place and functioning, all occupying forces would be withdrawn.

Predictably, the joint Soviet-American committee created under the Moscow agreement deadlocked over which Korean groups were to be consulted prior to organizing the government. The stalemate continued into the summer of 1947, at which point the Truman administration reviewed its options. It could, as MacArthur suggested, withdraw American forces from the peninsula. That would satisfy the Pentagon, which wanted the forty-five thousand troops it had stationed there removed as soon as possible. But if the American forces left, State Department officials were convinced the North Koreans would overrun the peninsula, transforming all of Korea into a Soviet satellite.

Because the administration viewed a simple troop withdrawal as unacceptable, the question became how to liquidate the American presence in southern Korea without abandoning it to communist domination. American planners decided that the only solution was to create a separate state in the South and hope that international recognition, when complemented by economic aid, would serve to sustain a government there.

Washington sent General Albert Wedemeyer, an officer with impeccable anticommunist credentials and considerable Far Eastern experience, to Korea for a firsthand look at the situation there. Wedemeyer's report was by no means encouraging. He pointed out that the terrorist tactics employed by the Korean rightists and their "youth groups" had intimidated moderates and noncommunist leftists, discouraging them from participating in public affairs. He also noted that the activities of the South Korean police, "80 percent of whom are holdovers from the period of Japanese occupation," were doing vast damage since "they are hated by all save the extreme rightists who support them." Nor was Wedemeyer optimistic about possibilities for the creation of a South Korean government. "So long as there is no reform of the present police system and police brutality and partisanship continue, there seems to be little hope that a government can be established fully representative of the freely expressed will of the people in South Korea."[4]

Wedemeyer's report notwithstanding, the State Department pressed ahead with plans to create a separate state in the South. Late in 1947, after the Soviets rejected a call for nationwide elections, a compliant but unenthusiastic UN General Assembly passed the resolution Washington wanted, calling for elections in the South to be held in May 1948.

As soon as it became clear that Washington intended to divide the country permanently, a wave of violence gripped South Korea. Railway lines were cut, telephone and telegraph communications were interrupted, and a call went out for a general strike, the withdrawal of American troops, the creation of a people's republic, land redistribution, and the nationalization of industry. On February 8, the *New York Times* reported widespread rioting in which twenty-seven persons were killed and ten persons injured. Two days later the *Times* reported that one thousand demonstrators had been arrested and forty-seven more persons killed.

As election day approached, the Korean Advisory Council, which was to all intents and purposes an arm of the Korean right, used the police to intimidate the opposition. The United Nations Temporary Commission on Korea, a watchdog committee, demanded the release of all political prisoners and warned General Hodge that it might refuse to certify the elections as valid if he did not stop the intimidation. But the committee's efforts were in vain. The *Times* reported that prior to the elections nearly four hundred persons had been killed, thousands more had been injured, and scores of homes burned. Many election officials and opposition candidates were missing and presumed dead.

On May 10, 1948, the Korean elections at last took place. But the United Nations' presence (a tiny thirty-five person team) did not mean that the voting was an honest expression of the will of the South Korean people. The Korean left boycotted the elections, claiming correctly that they were rigged. Even on election day, while the American military government looked on, the police and the youth gangs practiced extreme forms of political intimidation. Street violence was rampant. On that day alone forty-five persons were killed. The outcome of the election was never in doubt. Syngman Rhee's right-wing party won control of the National Assembly, and Rhee assumed the presidency.

Following the South Korean elections, the Soviets performed their own travesty on the democratic process in the North, creating a government headed by the young Moscow-trained Kim il Sung, a Korean who had fought with the Red Army during the war. But if two Koreas had emerged on the map, the fundamental issue in Korean politics was and would remain the reunification of the country. Kim il Sung was committed to it. So, too, was Syngman Rhee. Neither man gave the slightest consideration to forming a coalition government, and each was willing, even anxious, to use military means to achieve his ends. It is not surprising, then, that in 1949 and 1950 there were frequent clashes between North and South Korean army units along the 38th parallel or that the possibility of war seemed ever present. One State Department official described the 38th parallel as "a real front line" with "very real battles involving perhaps one or two thousand men."[5]

For two years, beginning in 1947, the Defense Department fought a running battle with the State Department to remove American forces from Korea. By June 30, 1949, with the exception of a military assistance group of five hundred, the troop withdrawal had been completed. Withdrawal did not mean, however, that the United States had abandoned Seoul. Washington had been midwife to the birth of the new nation. America's prestige and credibility were tied to South Korea's survival.

Keeping the young country afloat was not easy. Syngman Rhee's government was corrupt, administratively inept, and fiscally irresponsible. The Americans who administered the economic aid program in Korea had both to cajole and to threaten in order to force fiscal and economic responsibility on an uncooperative Rhee. The military side of the equation was equally complex. Because of the threat of a North Korean invasion, Seoul had to be able to defend itself. Yet at the same time, given Rhee's undisguised determination to unify the country by force, the United States was reluctant to provide him with an offensive military capability. As William Sebald, MacArthur's political adviser explained, "It was feared that, properly armed for offense, Rhee promptly would punch northward across the 38th parallel."[6]

The administration attempted to resolve its dilemma by providing South Korea with defensive weapons only. But was it possible to create a military force with only defensive capabilities? General William Roberts, head of the Military Advisory Group that trained the South Korean army, certainly thought so. He repeatedly assured Washington that the South Koreans could repel any attack launched from the North. On his departure from Korea in April 1950, General Roberts even pronounced South Korea's the "best damn army outside the United States." Two months later he would have reason to regret those words.

## WAR COMES TO KOREA

On June 25, 1950, after a long period of tension punctuated by frequent fire fights along the 38th parallel, North Korean forces invaded the South. At the time most policy makers in Washington (and elsewhere for that matter) assumed that the Soviets had ordered the Korean attack. More recently, however, that view has begun to give way to one that emphasizes local, indigenous causes of the war.

The Soviets never established the kind of control over North Korea that became the rule throughout Eastern Europe. There is no doubt that Kim il Sung was installed as the head of the North Korean state at Soviet insistence. But Kim was not a puppet. By the same token he could not expect to survive by relying on Moscow's support alone. At least in the early days he had to prove himself in the rough and tumble of competitive politics.

In 1950 Kim's leadership was being challenged by Pak Hŏn-yŏng, head of the Democratic Front for the Unification of the Fatherland. Both men, like most Koreans, were passionately committed to national reunification. And Pak, claiming that the military buildup the United States was funding in the South would soon give Seoul a military edge, was advocating an early invasion. What better way for Kim to consolidate his position and deflate Pak's appeal than to do just that?

Kim was considering invasion as early as February 1950. At that time, while visiting Stalin in Moscow, he raised the issue with the Soviet

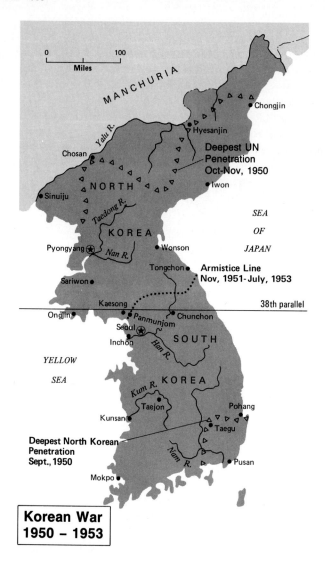

**Korean War
1950 – 1953**

dictator. Stalin appears to have approved Kim's planned attack while at the same time making it clear that if he ran into difficulties with the United States he was on his own.

Once he had Stalin's qualified approval, Kim simply waited for the proper moment to strike. And for a number of reasons June 1950, appeared to be the right time. First, he had recently received an arms shipment from the Soviets that gave him at least a temporary advantage over Republic of Korea (ROK) forces. Second, he thought he had little to fear from Washington since in a widely reported speech given before the National Press Club in January, Dean Acheson had quite clearly excluded Korea from America's defense line in the Pacific. Finally, and perhaps most significant, Kim had reason to believe that his soldiers would be welcomed as liberators in the South since by that time Syngman Rhee had spent virtually all of his political capital.

Once Rhee attained the presidency of South Korea, he went about consolidating his power in the tradition of all despots—by throwing out the constitution and attempting to crush his opponents. In a single eight-month period he arrested more than eighty thousand persons, charging them with political crimes. He discharged about one-third of his army's officers—those whose personal loyalty he doubted—and he imprisoned a number of his opponents in the National Assembly. At the same time his fiscal policies, especially his addiction to printing press money, led to a runaway inflation that ate the heart out of the South Korean economy. He was, all things considered, doing a fairly good imitation of Chiang Kai-shek in China.

Rhee's fall from grace became clear in the May 30, 1950, parliamentary elections. His party won only 47 of the 210 seats in the assembly, and he was able to continue in the presidency only by organizing the shakiest of political coalitions. No wonder, then, that Kim believed national unification would be welcomed by most South Koreans, even if it did come at the wrong end of a Soviet built tank.

## THE AMERICAN RESPONSE

If in retrospect it seems clear that the North Koreans were primarily responsible for the attack on South Korea, it did not seem so to American policy makers, who never doubted that the invasion was part of Moscow's scheme for world conquest. It also appeared to mark a new stage in the evolution of the cold war. To this point the Soviets had tried to advance their interests through psychological warfare, mass propaganda campaigns, and subversion. Now Washington believed Moscow was willing to use force to achieve its ends. A new and more threatening period in the cold war had apparently begun.

Confident that the South Koreans could hold against a purely North Korean invasion, the administration at first reacted cautiously. General MacArthur was ordered to resupply the ROK forces, while air and naval units provided protection for American dependents then evacuating the war zone. The United States also introduced a resolution in the United Nations Security Council condemning North Korea as an aggressor and demanding that North Korean forces withdraw behind the 38th parallel. The Soviets were at this time boycotting the United Nations because of the Security Council's earlier refusal to seat the Beijing government in place of the Nationalist Chinese. The American resolution therefore passed easily by a vote of 9–0.

By June 26, reports from Ambassador John Muccio in Seoul made it clear that the situation in Korea was deteriorating. ROK forces were in retreat; Seoul was about to fall; and the Rhee government was preparing to flee southward. At this point, and without any hesitation, the administration took decisive steps. Naval and air forces were authorized to aid ROK units by attacking North Korean forces anywhere below the 38th parallel.

On June 27 the United Nations Security Council approved another American-sponsored resolution, this one calling on member nations to aid in the military defense of South Korea. On June 28, North Korean forces occupied Seoul, and General MacArthur warned that, if the United States did not commit troops to the fighting, the peninsula would probably be lost. President Truman reacted promptly, approving the immediate dispatch of a regimental combat team. Other forces soon followed. In a matter of a few days America's military power and national prestige were thus committed to the battle for Korea.

Sixteen nations ultimately contributed to the United Nations force that fought in Korea, but most made only token contributions. Ninety-five percent of the effort was shared between American and South Korean forces. General MacArthur served as the UN commander, and all key policy decisions were made in Washington.

Once it became evident that the United States would have to intervene militarily to save South Korea, no one in authority in Washington gave serious consideration to any other course of action. There were a number of reasons for this lack of questioning—one based on "the lessons of history," others more cold war oriented.

Convinced that the Korean attack was part of Moscow's global strategy, this generation of American statesmen, so deeply imprinted with recollections of Munich, felt it had no choice but to intervene. As soon as the fighting began, John Foster Dulles, the Republican party's principal foreign policy spokesperson, urged the administration to save South Korea or face a graver challenge somewhere else. "To sit by while Korea is overrun by unprovoked armed attack," he warned, "would start a disastrous chain of events leading most probably to world war."[7] President Truman, who agreed with Dulles, described Korea as the Greece of the Far East:

> If we are tough enough now, if we stand up to them like we did in Greece three years ago they won't take any next steps. But if we just stand by, they'll move into Iran and they'll take over the whole Middle East. There's no telling what they'll do if we don't put up a fight now.[8]

Dean Acheson's State Department, also influenced by the Munich analogy, believed that if the Soviets succeeded in Korea, Beijing would increase the pressure on Indochina. A Soviet controlled Korea would also give Moscow extra leverage over the Japanese, who, when they regained their sovereignty, would have to decide on their future role in a divided world. Finally, policy makers believed that if the communists won in Korea, American prestige would suffer a crushing blow not only in Asia but among the European Allies and especially in Germany, where questions already abounded about America's reliability as an ally.

If the State Department saw dangers arising from a do-nothing policy in the face of Soviet-inspired aggression, it also saw advantages to an intervention. State Department analysts did not believe that the Soviets, who had tested their first nuclear device only months before, were ready for war with the United States. Therefore, Washington could be reasonably confident that an American intervention in Korea would not prompt the Soviets to jump in, touching off World War III.

And what would the political effect be if Moscow remained aloof while the United States intervened to chastise a Soviet satellite and save South Korea? The answer seemed obvious. By this single act the administration could raise doubts throughout Asia regarding Soviet power, reduce the growing influence of the Chinese, secure Japan for the West, and send a message of strength and determination to America's European friends.

It would be going too far to suggest that American policy makers were pleased by the coming of war in Korea. But they certainly believed that Moscow had blundered and that the United States could profit from that blunder, putting the Soviets and their satellite, China, on the defensive throughout Asia.

During June and the early part of July the North Koreans drove UN forces before them until General MacArthur's command was confined to a small perimeter at the tip of the peninsula near the port city of Pusan. Then, however, the UN lines held. Reinforcements poured in, and General MacArthur laid plans for a counteroffensive.

At that point American policy makers began considering how far to proceed northward once the anticipated counteroffensive began. The president ordered the National Security Council to study the implications of ground action above the 38th parallel. He was weighing the advantages to be gained from an attempt to unite Korea by force against the danger that the effort might provoke a wider war with China and or the Soviet Union.

The president was not the only one thinking about the next stage in the war. Inside the State Department George Kennan and John Allison, director of the Office of Northeast Asian Affairs, were at odds over what to do. Allison insisted that the only proper course was to unify the peninsula by force and sponsor free democratic elections for all of Korea. Anything less, he insisted, would be appeasement. Kennan, on the other hand, argued that the Soviets would not permit a United Nations army to approach the very "gates of Vladivostok." By repelling the aggressors and stopping at the 38th parallel, Kennan believed, the United States could vindicate its leadership, check aggression, and still claim a victory in the cold war.

As the date for General MacArthur's planned counteroffensive approached, the tide of opinion in Washington ran heavily in favor of the Allison view. Still, the threat of Soviet or Chinese intervention deterred the administration from making the crucial decision then and there. Even the usually decisive Dean Acheson was ambivalent. He thought it would be nearly impossible to stop military operations at some artificially imposed line

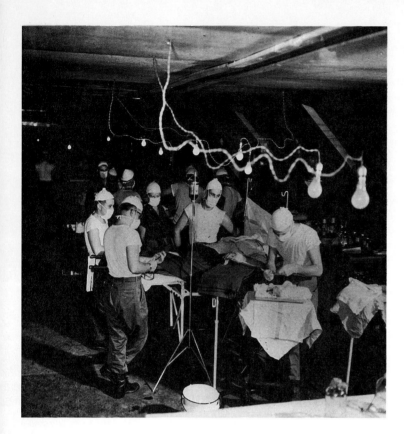

Here a mobile army surgical hospital (a MASH unit) performs an emergency operation on a wounded GI.

on a map. On the other hand, he feared that not doing so might provoke a Chinese or Soviet intervention.

MacArthur's brilliantly conceived and executed counteroffensive began on September 13. Two days later an amphibious landing at Inchon, about 20 miles from Seoul and 175 miles north of Pusan, took the North Koreans completely by surprise. The lightly defended city quickly fell, and the American Tenth Corps began a drive southward toward Seoul. Meanwhile the Eighth Army, commanded by General Walton Walker, broke out at Pusan and drove north to link up with the Tenth Corps. The North Koreans, caught in the jaws of a huge vice, broke and fled. Of the original invasion force of 110,000 no more than 30,000 managed to make it back above the 38th parallel.

General MacArthur was widely praised for his success at Inchon. Admiral William ("Bull") Halsey actually told him that it was "the most masterly and audacious strategic stroke in all history." Such praise, which came from many sources, fed an ego that needed little nourishment and may have contributed to the disaster that soon befell MacArthur's command. Be that as it may, there is no question that the general's early success whetted

The navy, fearing a disaster because of tidal conditions, argued strongly against an amphibious landing at Inchon. But General Douglas MacArthur (center) insisted. Here the general observes as the troops go ashore.

his and the administration's appetite. With total victory now seemingly within reach, talk of stopping at the 38th parallel ceased. After Inchon, as the president's special assistant W. Averell Harriman later noted, given "the possibility of destroying the North Korean army, it was not possible to stop."[9]

A great political and military victory beckoned, and no one, least of all the grandiloquent General MacArthur, was prepared to ignore the opportunity. Still, the nagging fear that the Soviets or the Chinese might intervene would not go away. Thus the Joint Chiefs instructed MacArthur to employ only ROK forces above a line stretching from Wŏnsan to Pyongyang. And under no circumstances was he to violate the Manchurian or Soviet border.

MacArthur had been a willful man before Inchon. Afterward he was driven by a sense of infallibility and personal destiny. Thus he immediately violated his instructions by ordering not only South Korean units but all of his forces across the Wŏnsan-Pyongyang line. They headed for the Yalu River that marked the Manchurian border. In Washington there was concern. The Joint Chiefs asked for an explanation. But when the general claimed military necessity nobody was willing to second-guess him.

## CHINA ACROSS THE YALU

On the same day that MacArthur received his marching orders Zhou Enlai, the Chinese foreign minister, informed the Indian government that Beijing would not stand idly by if United Nations forces crossed into North Korea. Over the next several days Washington was deluged with warnings from K. M. Panikkar, the Indian ambassador in Beijing, from Prime Minister Nehru, and from British and European sources, all indicating that China was not bluffing. On September 29, Zhou issued a public statement warning that "the Chinese people absolutely will not tolerate seeing their neighbors being savagely invaded by the imperialists." A few days later he dragged Ambassador Panikkar out of bed and over to the Foreign Ministry at 1:00 A.M. and told him point blank that "if U.N. armed forces crossed [the] thirty eighth parallel China would send troops across [the] frontier to defend North Korea."[10]

Despite repeated and emphatic warnings, Washington refused to pay heed. In part, policy makers simply did not want to believe that the enormous victory seemingly within reach could be denied to them. Moreover, many of the Chinese warnings had come through Indian intermediaries deemed untrustworthy by administration leaders. President Truman, for example, thought that Prime Minister Nehru was at least a communist sympathizer and that Panikkar "had in the past played the game of the Chinese Communists fairly regularly."[11]

Washington's refusal to take Beijing's warnings seriously was based on other considerations as well. Acheson did not believe that it was in China's interest to intervene. Mao's government was none too stable. Why, then, would he want a war with the United States and its allies, especially when by making war against a United Nations force he would alienate the world community and end any chance of replacing the Nationalists at the United Nations? Washington had gone out of its way to assure Beijing that it had no intention of threatening China. Surely the Chinese would accept that.

Acheson and other policy makers saw themselves as on the defensive in the cold war and viewed their policies as obviously and incontrovertibly benign. They were incapable of viewing the world situation through Chinese eyes. And the Chinese saw things very differently. During the recently concluded civil war the United States had provided the Nationalists with billions of dollars in aid. More recently they had intervened to deny Beijing both Taiwan and its legitimate place in the United Nations. Now a military force that flew a UN flag but was in fact largely American and under Defense Department orders was heading for the Manchurian border. What were the Chinese, a people who had been victimized for more than a century by foreign imperialists, to think?

On October 26 advance units of the Eighth Army reached the Yalu River that divided Korea from Manchuria. But on that same day ROK units further south were savaged by the first Chinese "volunteers" to enter the

Korean War. These engagements were serious enough to force the Eighth Army to halt its advance and regroup.

This first sign of a Chinese presence in Korea caused concern in Washington but did not produce any new orders for MacArthur. The fighting continued into early November, when, without consulting Washington, the general suddenly ordered the bombing of the bridges connecting Manchuria and Korea. On learning that American planes were about to hit targets on the Manchurian border, the Joint Chiefs issued an immediate stop order, demanding to know why MacArthur had authorized an action that was so obviously provocative. MacArthur's virtually hysterical response made Washington even more nervous. Chinese forces were coming across those bridges "en masse," he said. They had to be destroyed. He demanded that the issue be brought to the president for a decision "as I believe your instructions may well result in a calamity of major proportion for which I cannot accept the responsibility."[12] MacArthur had always been good at making a point. The president really had no choice but to authorize the bombing of the Yalu bridges.

On November 7, after more than two weeks of fierce fighting, the Chinese suddenly and mysteriously broke off the action, leaving the Eighth Army to lick its wounds. Beijing probably intended this early contact as a warning that it would not let the United Nations force march to the Yalu unopposed. Policy makers in Washington should have paid heed. It was their last chance to avoid a much larger, more costly war for Korea.

But no one in Washington was confident enough or strong enough to seize the initiative from General MacArthur and halt the "home by Christmas" offensive he planned for late November. As Acheson recalled, the Joint Chiefs were thousands of miles from the action. MacArthur was on the scene and presumably had better intelligence than did they. Moreover, the general was an extremely determined man. The only way to stop him, Acheson observed, would have been to remove him. And especially after his dramatic success at Inchon that was out of the question.

If policy makers in Washington were nervous, the British, with Hong Kong and large investments in China proper to protect, were deeply concerned. Though they had contributed troops to the UN force, they had always disagreed with American policy toward Beijing. Now Foreign Secretary Ernest Bevin proposed establishing a demilitarized zone south of the Yalu to reassure the Chinese. Acheson liked the idea and suggested private contacts with Beijing to see if such a zone would satisfy them.

But MacArthur denounced the British proposal as appeasement. When the Joint Chiefs suggested going over to the defensive until Chinese intentions became clear, the general bridled, insisting that he was on the brink of complete victory and that such a move would have disastrous psychological effects on his army.

It was a curious performance. First MacArthur created panic in Washington by warning that the Chinese were flooding North Korea with troops and that his command was at risk. Then, ignoring the warnings he

For these marines, General Douglas MacArthur's "home by Christmas" offensive ended at Koto-ri, Korea in December 1950. A wounded chaplain reads a service for them.

had issued only days before, he denigrated the Chinese threat and successfully fought off attempts to delay his planned offensive.

MacArthur's "home by Christmas" offensive began on November 24 and immediately ran into big trouble in the form of 300,000 Chinese troops who had infiltrated mountainous North Korea over the preceding weeks. On November 28, MacArthur confirmed the worst. His forces were in retreat and unable to stem the advance of Chinese and North Korean units. He needed reinforcements urgently. His prognosis: "We face an entirely new war."[13] During the next several days the general's cables became increasingly grim. His entire command, it appeared, faced destruction.

The Chinese intervention did, as General MacArthur noted, change the entire situation. Secretary Acheson, who believed that the Soviets were behind this latest move, thought that the danger of a general war was now "very close." He wanted badly to find a way to disengage from Korea and would happily have accepted a settlement on the basis of the prewar status quo. Generals Omar Bradley and J. Lawton Collins, the army chief of staff, agreed that disengagement would be wise. Their resources were stretched thin. They had no reinforcements to provide. Besides, no one in Washington wanted to be locked in a war with China.

## GROPING TOWARD A POLICY

Early in December 1950, General Collins flew to Korea to assess the situation firsthand. He returned on December 8 with the only good news the Truman administration had received in many days. Earlier, basing their judgments on MacArthur's cables, they had concluded that the United Nations force might be expelled from Korea at any time. But the field commanders, Generals Walker and Edward M. Almond, agreed that though evacuation might become necessary, even without reinforcements they could regroup and hold in Korea for some time to come.

Basing their thinking on this new intelligence, officials in the State and Defense departments together with the Joint Chiefs, decided on a new strategy. The UN command would establish a defense line, perhaps across Korea's narrow waist, and inflict maximum casualties on the enemy in hopes that Beijing would accept a cease-fire and the restoration of a boundary at the 38th parallel.

General MacArthur, who opposed this new approach, urged the administration to accept an offer of troops made earlier by Chiang Kai-shek and commit itself to a full-scale war with China. But diplomatic and military leaders in Washington would have none of it. They were convinced that a war for Asia would shatter the Western alliance, leave Western Europe open to Soviet aggression, and cost the United States its majority in the United Nations.

Furiously, MacArthur retorted that his army could not hold indefinitely against the hordes the Chinese could throw at it. "As I have before pointed out," he wrote, "under the extraordinary limitations imposed upon the command in Korea its military position is untenable, but it can hold for any length of time up to its complete destruction if overriding political considerations so dictate."[14]

It was at this time that Acheson first began to question whether the general's "colorful rhetoric" could be trusted. The members of the Joint Chiefs were also beginning to have their doubts. In January, Generals Collins and Hoyt Vandenberg, the air force chief of staff, journeyed to Korea to find out for themselves. They arrived to find the Eighth Army, now under the command of General Matthew Ridgway (General Walker had been killed when his jeep overturned) in good condition and preparing for a limited offensive. From that point on MacArthur's credibility plummeted in Washington.

Ridgway's offensive, which began on January 26, went so well that by April the Eighth Army had retaken Seoul and was approaching the 38th parallel. From that point on no one doubted that the United Nations forces in Korea could hold indefinitely. American policy was to punish the enemy as severely as possible to gain a cease-fire and reestablish something like the prewar status quo without offering any political concessions in return. United Nations ground forces would be allowed to operate north of the 38th parallel but only within clearly defined limits. It was no longer the policy of the United States to seek the unification of Korea by force.

If the United States had decided to settle for a standoff, the Chinese were still thinking in terms of victory. In December 1950, Zhou Enlai rejected a cease-fire proposal put forward by thirteen nonaligned nations. Stating that the 38th parallel had been "obliterated forever," he claimed that China would accept no cease-fire before all major Far Eastern political issues had been resolved. He demanded that all foreign troops be withdrawn from Korea, called for a settlement of Korean affairs "by the Korean people

Here North Korean and American negotiators attempt to agree on a truce line.

themselves," required the withdrawal of "American aggression forces" from Taiwan, and insisted that his government should replace the Nationalists in the United Nations.[15]

Not long afterward, in May 1951, the Chinese launched their most ambitious offensive of the war. But their human wave tactics failed decisively. The massed firepower of Ridgway's command, now well entrenched near the 38th parallel, took an awful toll. The reports of Chinese casualties coming in from the field were in fact so high that Ridgway himself at first refused to credit their validity.

Following the failure of its massive spring offensive, Beijing agreed to peace talks, which began on July 10, 1951, at the village of Kaesŏng. The Chinese and North Koreans proposed a military truce during the negotiations. But General Ridgway demurred because during a truce the Chinese would be able to strengthen their positions and add to their forces unhindered by his naval and air power. And so, while the talks went on, the war did, too.

It took two long years before the fighting was finally brought to a conclusion by what is best described as "a lasting truce." The dividing line between North and South Korea approximated the existing battle line, which ran close to the 38th parallel.

After the fighting ended, India's Prime Minister Nehru pointed out to Chester Bowles, the American ambassador to India, that the United States could have established that boundary in September 1950, before twenty-six thousand Americans were killed in action. "And yet," Bowles recalled Nehru saying, "presumably responsible American leaders had called him a Communist or 'fellow traveller' because he had warned them accurately of the consequences of their efforts to move to the Yalu."[16]

## THE GENERAL AND THE PRESIDENT

During his years as the supreme commander of Allied powers in Japan, General MacArthur behaved as though his authority was at least coequal to that of the president. When officials from the State or Defense departments visited Tokyo, it was as though they had come to negotiate with a "foreign potentate." Often, if they were not important enough, they would merit only brief audiences with the great man. As Secretary Acheson later remarked, "MacArthur was practically a chief of state at this time. He was the Mikado of Japan and Korea."

MacArthur's difficulties with the Truman administration stemmed from more than his own unfortunate personality disfunction. As the patron saint of all "Asia Firsters," he was out of sympathy with the entire thrust of administration foreign policy. A succession of secretaries of state, Acheson preeminently, were "Atlanticists," committed to a "Europe First" strategy and preoccupied with the danger posed by Soviet imperialism. MacArthur, on the other hand, was the latest in a line of soldiers and statesmen going at least as far back as William H. Seward who believed that America's destiny lay across the Pacific. The Far East's "billions of inhabitants," he insisted "will determine the course of history for the next ten thousand years."[17]

Serious differences between MacArthur and the Truman administration first surfaced in 1949 when the general lent his support to those Republican conservatives who were then attacking Washington's Taiwan policy. The problem became more acute early in the Korean War, when he paid a personal visit to Taiwan for two days of talks with Chiang Kai-shek.

The general had a plausible reason for going to Taiwan. By this time the United States was committed to aid Chiang. But press photographs of the general kissing Madam Chiang's hand, Nationalist press releases indicating that Chiang and MacArthur had agreed on the importance of close cooperation in the struggle against Asian communism, and unconfirmed rumors that MacArthur intended to station fighter aircraft on Taiwan, put the president in an awkward position. Britain and America's other NATO and United Nations allies believed that cooperation with Chiang could only provoke Beijing and might well lead to a wider war in Asia, something they devoutly hoped to avoid. Officials in the State and Defense departments shared these concerns.

The President sent W. Averell Harriman to Tokyo to confer with MacArthur and explain the reasoning behind his unwillingness to tie the United States too closely to Chiang. The aristocratic Harriman told MacArthur that by involving the Nationalists in the Korean War the United States risked losing the support of a majority in the United Nations, fragmenting NATO, and striking a spark that could ignite much of Asia.

Though the general gave the proper assurances, Harriman left Tokyo uneasy, explaining to the president that he "did not feel we came to a full agreement on the way we believed things should be handled on Formosa and with the Generalissimo."[18]

Not long afterward the text of a letter from General MacArthur to the annual convention of the Veterans of Foreign Wars appeared in newspapers from coast to coast. In it he again took exception to the administration's Taiwan policy. This time a furious president ordered MacArthur to withdraw the letter, and he did. At their Wake Island meeting in October 1950, the general even apologized for any embarrassment his letter had caused. His apology, however, could not undo the impact of the widely published letter.

After the Chinese intervened in Korea, the always-tense relationship between the president and the general went to pieces. Failing in his effort to convince Washington to expand the war, MacArthur again went public with his criticism of administration policy. In a prepared statement released on February 13, 1951 he declared that the "concept advanced by some that we should establish a line across Korea and enter into positional warfare" was "wholly unrealistic."[19]

A few weeks later MacArthur actually intervened to thwart an administration effort to end the war. In March 1951, with the Eighth Army advancing on the 38th parallel, the president was preparing to make a statement that he hoped might open the door to peace talks. But before he could act, MacArthur, who knew what was coming, made a statement of his own designed to eliminate any possibility of a settlement. Claiming that China's "military weakness" had at last been "revealed," he implied that the war would soon be expanded to include China proper unless the Chinese and North Koreans were prepared to accept a settlement on the basis of "the political objectives of the United Nations in Korea."[20]

MacArthur's statement not only preempted the president; it was a clear violation of a standing order that statements of this sort were to be cleared by the White House before being made public. President Truman, who was furious, considered removing MacArthur from his command then and there, but was dissuaded from doing so largely for political reasons. It made little difference, however, for the end was near.

In March 1951, the Republican Speaker of the House of Representatives, Joseph W. Martin, who was himself an advocate of "unleashing" Chiang Kai-shek's forces on the Chinese mainland, wrote MacArthur asking his opinion whether such a move would be wise. In his letter Martin specifically asked MacArthur to indicate whether he wanted his views to be kept confidential or not. In a March 20 reply MacArthur told Martin that he believed Chiang's forces ought to be used against the mainland. Then, attacking the entire thrust of administration foreign policy, he added:

> It seems strangely difficult for some to realize that here in Asia is where the Communist conspirators have elected to make their play for global conquest,

and that we have joined the issue thus raised on the battlefield; that here
we fight Europe's war with arms while the diplomats there still fight it with
words; that if we lose the war to Communism in Asia the fall of Europe is
inevitable, win it and Europe most probably would avoid war and yet preserve
freedom. As you point out, we must win. There is no substitute for victory.[21]

On April 5, Martin rose in the House of Representatives and delivered a
speech attacking the administration's conduct of the war. Because MacArthur
had not indicated that his views should be kept confidential, he read the
MacArthur letter in the context of that speech.

The general's letter to Martin proved to be the last straw for the
president, who, not long after this, dismissed him from his commands. The
nation was stunned by the news. Senator McCarthy told reporters, "The son-
of-a-bitch [Truman] ought to be impeached." Another Republican conservative, William Jenner of Indiana, claimed that MacArthur's dismissal proved
that the country "was in the hands of a secret inner coterie which is directed
by the Soviet Union. Our only choice," he said, "is to impeach President
Truman."[22]

For a time it almost appeared that Jenner and McCarthy might have
their way. The public outrage was general and palpable. On April 17, when
MacArthur flew into San Francisco, more than a million people were on
hand to greet him. They filled the airport, lined the miles of highway leading
into the city, and crowded Union Square outside the St. Francis Hotel to
greet him.

Two days later in a nationally televised speech delivered before a
cheering throng in the House chamber in Washington, MacArthur again
stated his case for victory in Asia. In an elegant, understated performance,
he captivated the heart and soul of a nation yearning for victory. After thirty
minutes of brilliant oratory the general concluded by recalling the lyric of
an old song, "Old soldiers never die, they just fade away." Looking out at
his audience he said, "and like the old soldier of that ballad, I now close my
military career and just fade away—an old soldier who tried to do his duty
as God gave him the light to see that duty. Good-bye."[23]

It was a bravura performance. Even congressional Democrats wondered whether the president could survive the withering fire being directed
his way. The public had taken the general to their hearts. Only a few days
after his dramatic appearance before Congress he was given a parade in
New York City that attracted 7.5 million people. Certainly there was no
ignoring a Republican demand for the creation of a joint committee to hold
hearings on the circumstances of MacArthur's dismissal.

The hearings, which began on May 3, disappointed those anxious to
pillory the president. MacArthur was dignified and articulate during his
three days of testimony. But his credibility was undermined when first
Secretary of Defense George C. Marshall, a soldier of some note himself,
and then each member of the Joint Chiefs of Staff testified in support of
administration policy. The chair of the Joint Chiefs, General Bradley, was
particularly effective in supporting administration actions. When he re-

marked that a war against China would involve the United States "in the wrong war, at the wrong place, at the wrong time, and with the wrong enemy," senators and representatives of both parties realized that no matter how articulate he was, General MacArthur hadn't a leg to stand on.[24] It was, as he himself had said not long before, his time to fade away.

# ENDNOTES

1. Bruce Cumings, "American Policy and Korean Liberation," in *Without Parallel: The American Korean Relationship since 1945,* 2 ed. Frank Baldwin (New York: Random House, 1973), pp. 57–58.

2. Quoted in ibid., p. 83.

3. Douglas MacArthur to the Joint Chiefs of Staff, December 16, 1945, *Foreign Relations of the United States,* 1945, (Washington, D.C., 1969), VI, 1145.

4. Albert Wedemeyer, report, Sept., 1947, *Foreign Relations of the Untied States, 1947* (Washington, D.C., 1972), VI, 796–803.

5. Quoted in Robert R. Simmons, "The Korean Civil War," in *Without Parallel,* pp. 151–52.

6. William Sebald, quoted in ibid., p. 150.

7. John Foster Dulles, quoted in John L. Gaddis, *Strategies of Containment* (New York: Oxford University Press, 1982), p. 109.

8. Harry Truman, quoted in George Elsey, diary, June 26, 1950, George Elsey Papers, Harry S. Truman Library, Independence, Mo.

9. William Halsey, quoted in Burton I. Kaufman, *The Korean War: Challenges in Crisis, Credibility, and Command* (New York: Alfred A. Knopf, 1986), p. 82; W. Averell Harriman, quoted in the Princeton Seminars, February 14, 1954, Truman Library.

10. Dean Acheson, recounting the message from K. M. Pannikar, in Richard H. Rovere and Arthur Schlesinger, Jr., *The MacArthur Controversy and American Foreign Policy* (New York: Farrar, Straus, Giroux, 1965), p. 148.

11. Harry S. Truman, *Years of Trial and Hope* (New York: Doubleday, 1956), p. 148.

12. MacArthur, quoted in James Schnabel and Robert J. Watson, *The History of the Joint Chiefs of Staff* (Wilmington, Del.: Glazier, 1979), III, 293.

13. MacArthur, quoted in Rovere and Schlesinger, *MacArthur Controversy,* p. 146. See also Schnabel and Watson, *History of the Joint Chiefs of Staff,* III, 335–37.

14. MacArthur, quoted in Schnabel and Watson, *History of the Joint Chiefs of Staff,* III, 412.

15. Zhou Enlai, quoted in *State Department Bulletin,* January 22, 1951, pp. 165–66.

16. Jawaharlal Nehru, quoted in Chester Bowles, *Promises to Keep: My Years in Public Life* (New York: Harper and Row, 1971), p. 492.

17. MacArthur, quoted in John Spanier, *The Truman-MacArthur Controversy and the Korean War* (New York: W. W. Norton, 1965), p. 67.

18. Harriman, quoted in Donovan, *Tumultuous Years: The Presidency of Harry S. Truman, 1949–1953* (New York: W. W. Norton, 1969), p. 261.

19. MacArthur, quoted in Schnabel and Watson, *History of the Joint Chiefs of Staff,* III, 524.

20. MacArthur, quoted in ibid., p. 527.

21. MacArthur to Joseph W. Martin, March 20, 1951, quoted in Rovere and Schlesinger, *MacArthur Controversy,* pp. 171–72.

22. Joseph McCarthy and William Jenner, both quoted in Donovan, *Tumultuous Years,* p. 359.

23. MacArthur, quoted in Kaufman, *Korean War,* p. 166.

24. Omar Bradley, quoted in Spanier, *Truman-MacArthur Controversy,* p. 247.

# 28

# EISENHOWER AND DULLES, 1953–1957

As the arms race heated up in the 1950s, interservice rivalry, which centered on control of sophisticated weapons programs and resulted in appalling waste and duplication, became a major political issue.

Two decades of Democratic party dominance ended on January 20, 1953, when former General of the Army Dwight David Eisenhower took the oath of office as the president of the United States. Born in Denison, Texas, and raised in Kansas, Eisenhower entered West Point in 1911. A tolerably good student and a fine athlete, he graduated in 1915 at a time when Europe was caught up in the fury of World War I. When America intervened, Eisenhower, like most young officers, hoped for a European assignment. But instead he sat out the war at a training camp near Gettysburg.

Promotions were hard to come by in the interwar period, and, though he was a talented officer, Eisenhower rose only slowly through the ranks. In 1940, on the eve of America's involvement in World War II, he was still only a lieutenant colonel with little chance of ever wearing a star on his shoulder.

The war changed all that. Experienced officers were scarce. And Eisenhower's impressive performance during the army's 1941 field maneuvers caught the attention of the Army Chief of Staff General George C. Marshall, who brought Eisenhower to Washington. Eisenhower's talent for military planning, his extraordinary organizational skills, and his personal charm contributed to his meteoric rise. Before the end of 1941 he had been named the army's chief of operations. In 1942 Marshall chose him to command all American forces in the European theater. And in 1943 Eisenhower became the supreme commander of Allied forces in Europe.

Working with men as diverse and egotistical as General George Patton and Britain's Field Marshall Bernard Montgomery, not to mention Winston Churchill, Franklin Roosevelt, and General Charles de Gaulle, was an enormous challenge. But Eisenhower, a naturally gifted diplomat, did a superb job. Even Montgomery, who was often at odds with him, admitted that Ike had "the power of drawing the hearts of men towards him as a magnet attracts the bits of metal. He merely has to smile at you, and you trust him at once." As one reporter later explained, Ike had the "absolutely unique ability to convince people that he has no talent for duplicity."[1]

Eisenhower seems to have been thinking of a run for the presidency as early as 1943. General Patton, among the first to suspect that Ike had political ambitions, thought he wanted "to be President so badly you can taste it."[2] But catching the presidential virus and going after the presidency itself were two entirely different things. Eisenhower stayed out of the political wars until 1950. But when he resigned the presidency of Columbia University to become the first NATO commander, he had more on his mind than getting back into military harness. The NATO command gave him enormous visibility both at home and in Europe. In 1952 he allowed his name to be entered in the New Hampshire primary. A few months later he resigned the NATO command and began his successful campaign for the Republican nomination. In November he went on to an easy victory over the eloquent but politically outclassed Democratic candidate, Adlai E. Stevenson of Illinois.

Most observers assumed that Eisenhower would select John Foster Dulles to be his secretary of state. The dour international lawyer certainly had the background for the job. His grandfather, John W. Foster, had been secretary of state in the Benjamin Harrison administration. And his uncle, Robert Lansing, held the same position in Wilson's cabinet. Dulles himself had been the architect of the Japanese peace treaty and, following the death of Senator Arthur Vandenberg, had emerged as the premier foreign policy spokesperson for the Republican party.

Numerous photographs attest to the fact that Dulles, a large and ungainly man, could when the moment was right break into a wide, appealing grin. But when the muscles of his face were in repose, his mouth formed a censorious semicircle that bespoke both self-righteousness and a general disapproval of the world around him. Some church deacons have been noted for this. And the analogy is not entirely inappropriate, for Dulles was a Christian moralist in politics. The quintessential cold warrior, he was convinced that the United States and its allies were engaged in a no-holds-barred struggle against the political embodiment of evil.

Dulles believed that the containment policy was not only futile but immoral. The 1952 Republican party's platform plank on foreign policy, his handiwork, called not for containment but for the liberation of Europe's captive peoples. "We shall again make liberation into a beam of light . . . that will penetrate dark places. It will mark the end of the negative, futile, and immoral policy of 'Containment' which abandons countless human beings to a despotism and godless terrorism."[3]

Though Dulles was the obvious choice for the State Department job—one observer noted wryly that "Foster has been studying to be Secretary of State since he was seven"—Eisenhower, who had himself been schooled in the intricacies of European affairs first during the war and later as NATO commander, was not overawed. Dulles troubled him. There was something about the man, about the quality of his thinking, that raised doubts in the new president's mind. Too often, Eisenhower thought, Dulles was swept away by his own extreme and unrealistic rhetoric. At length, but only after becoming convinced that Dulles would not be a loose cannon on the deck, Eisenhower offered him the State Department job.

Until his death from cancer in 1959, it was generally assumed that Dulles was the principal architect of American foreign policy. In fact, however, the secretary, who never forgot that his uncle, Robert Lansing, had been sacked by Woodrow Wilson, was always the loyal subordinate. As Eisenhower's secretary, Ann Whitman, once explained, "Dulles and the President consulted on every decision and then Dulles went back to the State Department and carried them out." Dulles was not without influence, to be sure. But he was the junior partner in a firm run from the Oval Office.[4]

It suited the president to have the outside world believe that Dulles made foreign policy. In public Eisenhower played the calm, utterly confident father figure. But behind the scenes he was a far different person. Given to fits of anger, even rage, and extremely sensitive, he wanted to appear above the political fray while subordinates deflected criticism. Richard Nixon once remarked that Eisenhower always needed someone around to do the dirty work. During the war it was General Walter Bedell Smith. Later Nixon himself and to an extent Dulles played that role. Much later the press dubbed Ronald Reagan "the Teflon president." It was too early for Teflon in 1953, but Eisenhower understood the principle.

## "CLEANING UP" AT STATE

Eisenhower and Dulles more or less assumed that with the Republicans in power Senator Joseph R. McCarthy and his followers, whose anticommunist witch-hunts had transformed the previous four years into a nightmare for the Truman administration, would exercise a certain amount of restraint. They were mistaken. In 1953 the Wisconsin senator became chair of the Senate Permanent Investigations subcommittee and used his position to step up his attacks against the State Department.

Instead of coming to the defense of the Department, Dulles and Eisenhower, no doubt to satisfy the demands of the extreme right wing of the Republican party and preserve party unity, gave the senator the ritual sacrifices he coveted. Dulles fired John Patton Davies, who as a member of General Joseph Stilwell's staff in China had made the mistake of expressing his belief that Mao Zedong would best Chiang Kai-shek in the struggle for control of China. He also forced George Kennan into retirement. When the government's Loyalty Review Board recommended that John Carter Vincent, a high-ranking China expert in the department, should be terminated, Dulles, who found no evidence of disloyalty in Vincent's service record, nevertheless gave the genteel southerner the Hobson's choice of being fired and losing his pension or accepting forced retirement.

Dulles also approved the appointment of Scott McLeod, a former FBI agent and right-wing extremist, to be the deputy for personnel security in the State Department. Though he uncovered not a single case of disloyalty, McLeod's zealotry led to the forced retirement or termination of hundreds of employees.

Eisenhower was no more willing than Dulles to take on the extremists. He despised McCarthy but did nothing to check his growing power. On the contrary, he actually cooperated with the witch-hunters who ended the public career of J. Robert Oppenheimer, the father of the atomic bomb. Even when McCarthy attacked the army, Ike did nothing more than fume. It was a group of senators, sensing that the Army-McCarthy hearings had turned the public against the Wisconsin senator, who led the movement for censure.

## KOREAN DISENGAGEMENT

During most of the 1952 presidential campaign Eisenhower was relatively silent on the subject of the Korean War save to make it clear that while he had no magic formula for ending the conflict, he would accept nothing less than an honorable settlement. Late in October, Emmet John Hughes, one of his speech writers, suggested that Ike include in one of his campaign speeches a promise that if elected he would go to Korea. Eisenhower, who liked the idea, made the promise several times during the remaining days of the campaign.

As president-elect, Eisenhower did go to Korea. He visited the battlefront, called on Syngman Rhee, and conferred with General Mark Clark, who had replaced Matthew Ridgway as UN commander. During their talks Clark laid out a plan for winning the war by widening it to include China. But Eisenhower explained that he intended to end the war, not win it. He instructed Clark to exert maximum pressure on the enemy while taking no unnecessary casualties. Meanwhile he would find other means of forcing the enemy to settle.

At the time the cease-fire talks in Korea had been deadlocked for more than a year. The issue blocking progress was the Truman administration's insistence upon a novel form of prisoner repatriation. An international conference held in Geneva in 1949 established the principle of prompt and compulsory repatriation of prisoners at the end of future wars. In spite of commitments made at Geneva, Washington argued that since nearly half of the approximately 140,000 POWs in its hands did not want to repatriated to

China and North Korea, they should have freedom of choice regarding their future.

The administration claimed that its insistence on the voluntary repatriation of POWs was based on humanitarian considerations. Many Chinese prisoners, especially former Nationalist troops, wanted to be repatriated to Taiwan, claiming they would be killed if they fell into Beijing's hands. Several thousand South Koreans, impressed into service by the North Koreans during the invasion, claimed they faced an equally bleak future if they were returned to the North.

But Washington also had cynical reasons for abandoning the Geneva standard. It would be a major propaganda coup if thousands of POWs refused to return to communism. Moreover, administration leaders calculated that if Chinese and North Korean troops learned they could find sanctuary behind UN lines, enemy forces might be faced with mass defections.

Eisenhower refused to reconsider the Truman administration's stand on voluntary repatriation. At the same time he was convinced that the United States "could not stand forever on a static front and continue to accept casualties without any visible result."[5] The enemy had to be made aware that Washington's patience was wearing thin. Therefore, in his first state of the union message he announced that the Seventh Fleet would no longer prevent Nationalist Chinese forces from raiding the China coast. Since the Seventh Fleet had in fact been aiding Nationalist raiders for some time, nothing substantive had changed. It was the message that mattered. By publicly "unleashing" Chiang, Eisenhower hoped to let Beijing know that he might

The Korean truce negotiations were delayed for many months because first the Truman and then the Eisenhower administration insisted that Chinese and Korean prisoners like those shown here should have the right to choose whether to return to communism.

be preparing to widen the war. He reinforced that point by sending a private message to Beijing via Indian Prime Minister Jawaharlal Nehru, threatening to expand the war if an acceptable truce was not soon arranged. Simultaneously, he deployed nuclear weapons on Okinawa, within striking distance of mainland China.

Not long after Eisenhower made these threatening gestures, Beijing gave in on the issue of the voluntary repatriation of POWs, thus opening the way toward a final settlement. Eisenhower and Dulles believed that their new tough line and the implied threat of nuclear attack on the Chinese mainland turned the tide at the talks. It is just as likely, however, that changes then taking place inside the Soviet Union had as much or more to do with China's sudden change of heart. Josef Stalin died of a brain hemorrhage on March 5, 1953. Not long afterward Moscow's new collective leadership made a number of moves intended to reduce international tensions. It may well be that as part of this "peace offensive" the new Soviet leaders pressed the Chinese and North Koreans (who depended on the Soviets for military aid) to get the peace talks off dead center.

Procedural questions caused further delays in the cease-fire negotiations. But finally, on July 27, 1953, an armistice was signed. Korea's "lasting truce" had begun. The fighting ended roughly where it had started, with South Korea in possession of about one thousand square miles of new territory. As to the war itself, it has never officially ended. Talks between the two sides have continued intermittently ever since. Today, Panmunjom, the site of the talks, has even become something of a tourist attraction.

## MASSIVE RETALIATION

By 1953, as a result of the Korean War and the implementation of NSC 68, defense spending stood at a record $50.4 billion, four times the 1950 level. Although economic growth led to an increase in government revenues, these did not keep pace with the Defense Department's seemingly insatiable appetites. A budget deficit of more than $4 billion appeared in the 1951–52 fiscal year, rising to $9.5 billion for 1952–53. Simultaneously, unmistakable signs of inflation appeared in the statistics regularly churned out by the government's economy watchers.

During the 1952 campaign Eisenhower attacked the Truman administration for running a deficit and promised that he would win total victory in the struggle against communism while at the same time reducing defense spending, the cause of the deficit. This goal was not mere rhetoric. Eisenhower believed that a weak economy was just as dangerous to the nation's security as the Soviet threat. "Our military strength and our economic strength are truly one," he said. And neither could "sensibly be purchased at the price of destroying the other."[6]

But was it possible for the United States to fulfill its global commitments while at the same time reducing defense expenditures? What sort of military strategy would accomplish both goals? As a former NATO commander, Eisenhower thought a conventional defense of Western Europe was impossible. Nor was he satisfied that the Truman administration had been wise in making a large-scale conventional commitment to Korea. The Soviets, he thought, could easily precipitate similar crises elsewhere. But the United States could not respond as it had in Korea without risking economic and military exhaustion.

Once Eisenhower arrived at these conclusions, he saw no need to retain all of the 3.4 million men and women then serving in the armed forces. He instructed the Joint Chiefs to develop a new low-cost strategy based on reduced force requirements. The Joint Chiefs abandoned the idea that future wars could be fought without recourse to nuclear weapons. By assuming that nuclear striking power could substitute for military personnel, they were able to recommend a 600,000-person force reduction, which meant, of course, substantially lower funding for defense.

The press dubbed the administration's strategy the "new look." Paris designers had just decreed their own "new look," requiring hemlines on women's clothing to drop. Now defense expenditures and hemlines would come down simultaneously.

In January 1954, Secretary Dulles focused national and international attention on the new look when he announced that in responding to aggression the United States would not rely heavily on conventional forces for defense but would "depend primarily upon a great capacity to retaliate, instantly, by means and at places of our own choosing."[7] It seemed clear from what the secretary said that there were to be no more Koreas—no more peripheral wars—and that in the event of such a challenge the United States was prepared to respond with massive nuclear firepower directed at the source of the problem.

Writing just a few days after Dulles gave this celebrated speech, James Reston interpreted the new strategy of "massive retaliation" to mean that "in the event of another proxy or brushfire war in Korea, Indochina, Iran or anywhere else, the United States might retaliate instantly with atomic weapons against the USSR or Red China." Dulles denied that the administration would respond in this way to any and all provocations. He was even willing to admit that the United States would not be able to react at all on occasion and that, given the nation's limited resources, certain foreign policy setbacks might have to be accepted. While admitting this much, however, neither Dulles nor Eisenhower was prepared to state precisely what set of circumstances might call forth nuclear lightning. It was vital to the success of the strategy, Dulles explained, that no one know "in advance precisely what would be the scope of military action if new aggression occurred. . . . That is a matter as to which the aggressor had best remain ignorant."[8] By keeping this nuclear sword of Damocles forever suspended, Dulles and Eisenhower hoped to maximize its deterrent effect.

Massive retaliation was the subject of intense controversy from the start. The physicist J. Robert Oppenheimer pointed out that the Soviets would soon rival the United States as a nuclear power and that under the circumstances, initiating a nuclear war would be suicidal. "We may anticipate a state of affairs in which the two Great Powers will each be in a position to put an end to the civilization and life of the other, though not without risking its own," Oppenheimer said. "We may be likened to two scorpions in a bottle, each capable of killing the other, but only at the risk of his own life." William Kaufmann of the Rand Corporation, another critic, pointed out that if "the Communists should challenge our sincerity, . . . we would either have to put up or shut up. If we put up, we would plunge into all the immeasurable horrors of atomic war. If we shut up, we should suffer serious loss of prestige and damage our capacity to establish deterrents against further Communist expansion."[9]

Both Robert Bowie and Gerard Smith, his successor as head of the State Department's Planning Council, tried to convince Dulles that growing Soviet nuclear capabilities made a heavy reliance on nuclear striking power noncredible. They advocated a "flexible" military strategy that included conventional as well as nuclear capabilities. Dulles saw the point but feared the effect a change would have on the NATO Allies. Eventually, however, he agreed that a change was necessary and ordered defense planners to come up with an alternative.

But that was easier said than done. Eisenhower and Dulles were grappling with a dilemma for which there was no completely satisfactory answer. The nation had assumed global commitments that it did not have the resources to honor. The nuclear option left gaps, to be sure. But the conventional military option also appeared to Eisenhower to be an "unrealistic solution." Little wonder, then, that planners found no resolution to their dilemma or that, despite its shortcomings, massive retaliation remained official policy throughout Eisenhower's eight years in office.

## EISENHOWER, DULLES, AND THE SOVIETS

Premier Josef Stalin's sudden death left a power vacuum at the head of the Soviet state that was filled for a time by a collective leadership with Georgi Malenkov, Stalin's chosen heir, serving as premier and first Secretary of the Communist party. Almost immediately Malenkov signaled his interest in improved relations with the West. In a speech given at Stalin's funeral he called for "peaceful co-existence and competition" between capitalist and communist systems, and in subsequent statements he warned of the dangers of nuclear war. Eisenhower reacted quickly to this apparent change in Soviet policy by calling for an end to the arms race and for "total war, not upon any human enemy but upon the brute forces of poverty and need."[10]

These initiatives by Malenkov and Eisenhower were received enthusiastically in Western Europe. Winston Churchill, once again Britain's prime minister, urged a summit conference. He hoped that in this era of improved

John Foster Dulles (extreme left), Winston Churchill, Dwight Eisenhower, and Foreign Secretary Anthony Eden met in the Bahamas early in Ike's administration.

relations the Big Four might at last settle some of the unfinished business left over from the war, especially the German question.

The weak French government of Joseph Laniel was even more anxious for direct talks. Laniel was under intense pressure from Washington to approve a treaty creating a Western European army that would integrate the forces of the continental NATO Allies into a single fighting force. The European Defense Community (EDC) was exceedingly unpopular in France, where it was generally assumed that without British and American participation the Germans would dominate the organization. Laniel was, therefore, interested in pursuing any opening that promised détente with the Soviets and reduced the need for the EDC.

John Foster Dulles, alone among major policy makers, opposed working for improved relations with Moscow. He believed that Malenkov's speech signaled serious troubles inside the "Soviet empire" and that the West should increase, not reduce, the pressure on the communist system. The Soviet leaders, Dulles insisted, were fanatics, ideologues committed to the strategy and tactics of Karl Marx and V. I. Lenin. If they now called for peaceful co-existence, he believed it was only because they needed time to sort out their affairs at home before resuming the international struggle. Dulles believed that a state of controlled crisis was the best of all possible worlds for the Western Allies, since it encouraged unity. This strategy seemed especially important in 1953, for he was then devoting much of his energy to maneuvering the reluctant French into joining the EDC.

Dulles won the battle against a summit in part because Churchill, a formidable opponent, was suddenly incapacitated by a stroke. From his sickbed the old lion grumbled: "This fellow preaches like a Methodist minister and his bloody text is always the same; that nothing but evil can come out of a meeting with Malenkov. Dulles is a terrible handicap."[11]

Still, the secretary continued to have his troubles with the French, who refused to make a decision regarding the EDC. Finally, in a fit of pique he warned that if Paris didn't join the EDC, Washington might be forced into an "agonizing reappraisal" of its entire commitment toward Europe.[12] This bold threat to return to isolationism netted the secretary little save the hostility of the French, who called Dulles's bluff by rejecting the EDC treaty. Needless to say, the United States did not withdraw from Europe.

The decade of the 1950s was a busy and productive time in the history of Soviet foreign policy. Led by Nikita Khrushchev, who replaced Malenkov as party secretary in 1955, the Soviets healed the breach with Yugoslavia that developed after Marshal Josip Tito broke with Stalin in 1948. They also established diplomatic relations with West Germany and strengthened that connection by inviting the German chancellor, Konrad Adenauer, to visit Moscow. They even cooperated with the Western powers in arranging a peace treaty with Austria that ended ten years of military occupation. To many observers outside the United States, the Soviets seemed to be earnest in their quest for détente. It was the United States that appeared to prefer continuing crisis.

During this same period, the Soviets consolidated their claim to superpower status by moving rapidly ahead in the development of nuclear weaponry and delivery systems. In 1953 they exploded their first thermonuclear weapon. In 1954 they unveiled the Bison, a bomber that appeared to have intercontinental range. In 1957 came Sputnik, the world's first earth satellite. Then in 1958 Moscow exploded a fifty-eight megaton monster, larger than any weapon ever exploded either before or since. Soviet nuclear strength was clearly becoming a major factor in the equation of international politics.

With the world becoming an increasingly dangerous place and Soviet foreign policy moving in new, more creative directions, it became clear to Eisenhower that a summit conference was desirable "in order to see whether in this time of stress and strain we cannot devise measures that will keep from us the terrible scourge [of war]."[13] And so, over Dulles's strenuous objections, the president agreed to meet the Soviet leaders at Geneva.

The Geneva summit, which opened on July 18, 1955, was a cordial gathering, devoid of the rancor, suspicion, and backbiting that had characterized East-West relations for so long. Still, nothing positive came of it. Neither side was willing to consider the reunification of Germany except on its own terms. And no progress was made toward nuclear disarmament. Nevertheless, whatever the conference lacked in substantive achievement, it made up for in atmospherics. The press wrote of "the spirit of Geneva," and for most people it was enough to know that the two sides were at least talking once again.

## THE SUEZ CRISIS

In 1952 the wave of nationalism then sweeping the underdeveloped world produced a revolution in Egypt that left power in the hands of the man who came to symbolize Arab nationalism, Gamal Abdel Nasser. Nasser's objective was to purge the Arab world of the last vestiges of colonialism and bring Arab peoples together into a single federation dominated by Egypt.

In the years following his rise to power, Nasser's pan-Arab activities created increasing concern in Israel as well as Western capitals. The French, who were embroiled in a war in North Africa, where the Algerians were fighting for independence, believed that Nasser was the source of the revolutionary ferment they faced and wanted him crushed. The Israelis saw him as a direct threat to their security. And the British feared him as a threat to their vital interests throughout the Middle East.

Nor did the Eisenhower administration have any use for Nasser, who adopted a policy of nonalignment in the cold war. Convinced that neutralism was simply a way station on the road to communist domination, Ike and Dulles both believed it was a "short-sighted" and "immoral" policy.

In 1955, after an Israeli raid in the Gaza Strip revealed the extraordinary weakness of the Egyptian army, Nasser tried to negotiate arms deals with Washington, Paris, and London. But none of the Western powers would sell him weapons. And so, having been rebuffed by the West, he turned to Moscow. Nikita Khrushchev and Premier Nicolai Bulganin, who had been hoping for entré into the Middle East, saw this request as an opportunity not to be missed. Nasser not only consummated an arms deal with the Soviets; he also negotiated a mutual security treaty with Syria, Saudi Arabia, and Yemen, broke relations with Taiwan, and recognized the People's Republic of China.

These developments led Dulles and Eisenhower to the mistaken conclusion that Egypt and Syria had joined Moscow in an alliance directly threatening to Western control of Middle East oil. Still, administration leaders did not feel they could deal cavalierly with Nasser, who was the recognized leader of a nationalist movement sweeping the region. His "removal" would have provoked an anti-Western reaction of enormous magnitude.

With that in mind, policy makers in Washington and London sought to co-opt Nasser by offering him a package of aid and loans to be used for the construction of the Aswan high dam. This project, the centerpiece of Nasser's plan for the economic modernization of Egypt, would dwarf the pyramids. Once in operation it was supposed to produce huge quantities of electrical energy for industry, vastly expand the amount of arable land available for cultivation, and in some places allow two crops to be grown each year instead of one.

In July 1956, after months of inconclusive negotiations during which he attempted to play Moscow and Washington off against one another, Nasser called his ambassador to Washington, Ahmed Hussein, home for

consultations. In the ambassador's absence Dulles learned that while negotiating with the West for funds to build the Aswan dam, Nasser was
simultaneously working out another big arms deal with Moscow and Prague.
That fact alone did not sit well with the secretary. But when Ambassador
Hussein returned to Washington and informed him that if the United States
was not prepared to make a multi-year commitment to finance most of the
Aswan dam project, the Soviets would, Dulles decided Nasser had gone too
far. He informed Hussein that the United States would not submit to
blackmail and withdrew the offer to fund the project.

Dulles had never been comfortable dealing with Nasser, a man he
viewed as a dangerous pro-Soviet radical. He was even less inclined to do
business with him after learning of the new arms deal. Moreover, the Aswan
project was extremely unpopular in Congress, where pro-Israeli senators
and representatives opposed it and cotton state representatives wanted to
know why the administration was going to fund a project that would result
in an increase in the size of the Egyptian cotton crop.

Dulles also thought that by withdrawing his offer to help finance the
Aswan project he would expose the Soviets, who, he was convinced, did not
have the resources to expend on a project of this magnitude. He even
calculated that since the dam was a central feature of Nasser's domestic
economic program, the longer it remained unbuilt, the weaker Nasser would
become politically. In time, assuming the Aswan project came to nothing, he
might even be deposed. And Dulles thought the Middle East would be a far
better place without Gamal Abdel Nasser muddying the waters.

Dulles both miscalculated the strength of the hand he was playing
and underestimated Nasser's creativity. Interpreting the American decision
as an attempt to undermine his government, the Egyptian leader told an
enthusiastic crowd at a gathering outside Cairo that the Soviets had offered
to help build the great dam but that he was determined to remain independent
of both superpowers. Instead, he announced that Egypt would nationalize
the Suez Canal and pay for the dam's construction with the user's fees it
collected. The canal, which at the time was owned and operated by the Suez
Canal Company, served as the conduit for more than 100 million tons of
cargo annually, much of it oil for Western Europe. Aware of its strategic
significance, Nasser took pains to assure the world community that he would
adhere to the 1888 international convention guaranteeing all nations the
free and unhindered use of the waterway.

Nasser was within his rights in nationalizing the canal so long as he
compensated its stockholders. But that was beside the point as far as London
was concerned. Prime Minister Anthony Eden, who succeeded the aged
Churchill, was determined to use Egypt's nationalization of the canal as a
pretext for overthrowing Nasser, whose actions threatened both Europe's
access to Middle East oil and Britain's standing as a great power.

In the immediate aftermath of the seizure, Eden cabled Eisenhower:
"My colleagues and I are convinced that we must be ready, in the last resort,
to use force to bring Nasser to his senses. For our part we are prepared to

do so. I have this morning instructed our Chiefs of Staff to prepare a military plan accordingly."[14] Appalled, Eisenhower and Dulles made three separate but unsuccessful attempts between August and October 1956 to find a diplomatic solution to the crisis.

Britain, France, and Israel, meanwhile, hatched a plot that was to begin with an Israeli invasion of Egypt. Once the fighting was under way, the British and French, posing as innocent but interested bystanders, would demand that both sides respect the neutrality of the Suez Canal. The Egyptians, having claimed sovereignty over the waterway, were certain to refuse. British and French forces would then attack Egypt from the air, land troops, secure the canal, and oust Nasser.

During that fateful autumn, the three allies did their best to keep Eisenhower, who firmly opposed the use of force against Nasser, ignorant of their precise plans. Even so, Washington policy makers learned enough to give them a good case of the jitters. Dulles warned London not once but many times against attempting to remove Nasser. So did the president. "I must tell you frankly," Ike cabled Eden, "that American public opinion flatly rejects the thought of using force."[15]

The president also sent Robert Murphy, a longtime career diplomat, to London to restrain his allies. Murphy, who ran into a stone wall, later recalled that the British made it abundantly clear that they viewed the seizure of Suez as "a test that could only be met by the use of force." According to Murphy, the French were even more determined. Christian Pineau, the French foreign minister, was not only contemptuous of "what he called American naivete" but behaved "as though he had received a blank check from" Washington.[16]

Murphy's remark about Pineau points up one of the more curious aspects of this unfortunate business. The allies had ample evidence, or so it would seem, that Eisenhower opposed any attempt to unseat Nasser by force. Yet Murphy describes Pineau as confident that the administration would not interfere. Shimon Peres, who as an official of Israel's ministry of defense conferred with French officials prior to the Egyptian invasion, makes the same point, stating categorically that the French "do not think the United States will interfere." An Israeli source too, suggests that Tel Aviv was being encouraged to attack Nasser. Thus, following Egypt's 1955 arms deal with the Soviets, Israeli Prime Minister Moshe Sharett confided to his diary that he had received a "hint from a CIA source which reached Jerusalem through a highly secret channel, intimating that if Israel hit Egypt upon the arrival of the Soviet weapons, America would not protest."[17]

Was Washington playing a double game? Were the French and Israelis actually receiving secret encouragement from Washington? Sharett's diary entry notwithstanding, the answer is most certainly no. Eisenhower feared that a Middle East war would open the door to Soviet penetration and possibly a superpower confrontation. The risk was definitely not worth the gamble.

By late October 1956, it was no longer possible for Britain, France, and Israel to disguise their purposes. The American ambassador in Tel Aviv reported "an enormous mobilization in Israel." The roads, he said, were clogged with tank columns.[18] At the same time intelligence flights over Malta, then a British crown colony, revealed a huge Anglo-French military buildup there. In light of these developments, Dulles called Abba Eban, the Israeli ambassador, to the State Department and demanded to know what was going on. But Eban, who had been deliberately kept in the dark by Tel Aviv, knew nothing.

## THE HUNGARIAN UPRISING

At this juncture, with Dulles and Eisenhower wringing their hands over what America's closest allies might be planning, a crisis boiled up in Eastern Europe. For one brief moment it appeared that the "liberation" of at least some of Eastern Europe's "captive peoples" might be at hand.

In February 1956, at the Twentieth Communist Party Congress, Nikita Khrushchev stunned the communist world with a speech denouncing the crimes of Stalin. Khrushchev's speech and his attempts to liberalize the Soviet system had a profound effect on Eastern Europeans, who had long chafed under Soviet domination. In Poland, the de-Stalinization program moved forward cautiously and stopped short of provoking Soviet counter-measures.

In Hungary, where a thousand-year-old cultural tradition had not been erased by a decade of Stalinist repression, students and workers rioted against their government. At first the Soviets sought compromise, agreeing to place Imre Nagy, a reformist leader, in power. At that the Hungarian rebels escalated their demands, calling for the removal of all Soviet troops and the creation of an opposition political party. Khrushchev replied by offering to negotiate for the removal of Red Army forces from Hungary and the creation of a new relationship between Moscow and the Eastern Europeans based on the principle of "noninterference in each other's internal affairs." Unhappily, extremists in the Nagy government, thinking they had Moscow on the run, raised the ante once again, this time calling for Hungary's withdrawal from the Warsaw Pact, the Eastern European military alliance created at Moscow's insistence in 1955. That was going too far for the Kremlin. On November 4, the Red Army entered Budapest and stamped out the rebellion. Nagy was taken prisoner and later executed.

## WITHDRAWAL AT SUEZ

Ordinarily the West would have been in an excellent position to take full advantage of this manifestation of Soviet brutality. But Moscow's action came six days after the Israelis invaded Egypt and after the British and French

When the Suez crisis broke in 1956, John Foster Dulles and Dwight Eisenhower went on the radio to explain their position to the American people.

began air operations against Egyptian targets. The West was, all things considered, in no position to claim moral superiority over the Soviets.

On learning of the Israeli strike, Eisenhower flew into a towering rage. He told Dulles, "all right, Foster, you tell 'em that, goddam it, we're going to apply sanctions, we're going to the United Nations, we're going to do everything that there is so we can stop this thing." He then called Ambassador Eban to the White House, where, as the Israeli envoy later explained, "We had to deal with Eisenhower in his full righteous fury."[19]

The Israeli attack on Egypt was hardly twenty-four hours old when Ambassador Henry Cabot Lodge, Jr., introduced a resolution before the United Nations Security Council calling for a cease-fire and the withdrawal of Israeli forces from the Sinai Peninsula. After the British and French vetoed this resolution, Lodge took it to the General Assembly, where it passed overwhelmingly.

The Egyptians reacted to the American sponsored UN resolution quickly, agreeing to a cease-fire on November 3. The Israelis, who had by this time taken control of the Straits of Tiran as well as the Sinai, and who could not afford to irritate Washington further, followed suit on the following day, thus eliminating the supposed reason for an Anglo-French invasion. Yet even after Egypt and Israel had agreed to a cease-fire, on November 5 a paratroop drop put Anglo-French forces on Egyptian soil. Transports steaming toward Port Said landed a larger force on the following day.

Washington was, of course, appalled. The whole purpose of American policy in the eastern Mediterranean had been to keep the Soviets from insinuating themselves into the affairs of the oil-rich, strategically vital Middle East. And now the British and French had provided Bulganin and Khrushchev with the opportunity to do exactly that while posing as the champions of Arab nationalism. And the Soviets were quick to seize the opportunity. In notes to London, Paris, and Tel Aviv, Khrushchev threatened to intervene, while Premier Bulganin announced that the Red Army was prepared "to crush the aggressors and restore peace in the East." Enjoying every moment of Washington's embarrassment, Bulganin even suggested a joint Soviet-American intervention to drive the invaders out.[20]

Eisenhower was not seriously concerned about the threat of Soviet intervention. He thought Khrushchev's rocket rattling so much propaganda. The Soviets were not about to commit nuclear suicide over the fate of the Suez Canal or Nasser. Nor did he think Moscow was in a position to intervene with conventional forces. "Look at the map," he told members of his staff. "Geography makes effective Soviet intervention in Egypt difficult, if not impossible."[21]

It was the political ramifications of the crisis that troubled Eisenhower. To bring the intervention to a swift conclusion and limit the damage, he subjected Britain and France to intense diplomatic pressure. He put the economic squeeze on them as well. Arab oil had already become unavailable because the Egyptians sank ships to block the Suez Canal and the Syrians blew up portions of the pipeline to the Mediterranean. Eisenhower added to Anglo-French distress by sharply reducing the flow of oil from Western Hemispheric sources. At the same time the Treasury Department put intense pressure on the French franc and British pound. Starved for petroleum and with the rest of the world firmly arrayed against them, London and Paris had little choice but to withdraw. Before the end of December their forces had left Egyptian soil. Ike had made his point, but at great cost to the NATO alliance, which was shaken to its very foundations.

## THE EISENHOWER DOCTRINE

The Suez crisis, which finally eclipsed British and French power in the Middle East, led Eisenhower and Dulles to conclude that a power vacuum had been created there. Concerned lest Nasser or the Soviets move to fill it, Dulles suggested that the president ask congress to enact a resolution granting him the authority to use military force if necessary to stop communist aggression there.

Congress did not surrender its prerogatives easily. However, after two months of intense debate it passed a resolution in March 1957 that was promptly dubbed the Eisenhower Doctrine. The resolution authorized the president to provide economic and military aid to Middle Eastern nations desiring such help and if necessary "to use armed force to assist any such nation or group of nations requesting assistance against armed aggression from any country controlled by international communism."[22] This last not-too-oblique reference was, of course, to Nasser's Egypt.

The international response to the Eisenhower Doctrine was about what might be expected. The Soviets called it an unjustified intrusion into the internal affairs of Arab countries. The radical Arab states—Egypt and Syria,—denounced it as an imperialist plot. Iraq, which was ruled before the Baathist revolution by young King Faisal, endorsed the doctrine. Other states like Saudi Arabia and Jordan, weak countries that survived at the sufferance of more powerful neighbors, said as little as possible.

The president of Lebanon, Camille Chamoun, was the only Arab leader to respond enthusiastically to the Eisenhower Doctrine. He had good reason. At the end of World War II Lebanon was divided more or less evenly between Christians and Muslims. But in 1948, following the creation of the state of Israel, war broke out between neighboring Arab nations and the new Jewish country. During this conflict, which ended in a tense truce in 1949, thousands of Arabs fled or were driven from Israeli-held territory in Palestine to Lebanon. In the years that followed more Arab refugees found their way to Lebanon, so that by 1957 the little country had become considerably more Muslim than Christian. President Chamoun, who was a Christian, was feeling more than a little insecure, especially because Arab nationalists were working to agitate the country's Muslim population against his government and because the Syrians were providing antigovernment groups in Lebanon with arms. Given these circumstances, Chamoun's enthusiasm for the promise of American support in the event that his government came under attack is completely understandable.

According to the Lebanese constitution, Chamoun, who was scheduled to conclude his eight-year-term in office in September 1958, was ineligible to succeed himself. A wise man might have decided, given Lebanon's unstable political situation, to play by the rules. But in May 1958, Chamoun pressed the Lebanese Parliament for a constitutional amendment that would allow him to retain power. As a result, civil strife broke out, pitting Christians against Muslims.

Chamoun ordered General Fuad Chehab, commander of Lebanon's army of seven thousand, to crush the Muslims. But since his army was, like the country itself, divided between Christians and Muslims, Chehab wisely decided to do nothing. He feared that if he took action the army would simply dissolve, with the soldiery joining the different factions.

Chamoun then appealed to the United Nations, claiming that the Muslim insurrectionists were being supported by Nasserite infiltrators from Syria and Egypt. Secretary General Dag Hammarskjöld sent a UN observer group to Lebanon. But the UN team came up with little evidence of foreign interference there.

Finally, Chamoun invoked the Eisenhower Doctrine, calling on Washington to send troops. But Eisenhower, who doubted that outsiders had much to do with events in Lebanon, refused to come riding to the rescue. He did, however, send the Sixth Fleet steaming into the eastern Mediterranean and had arms shipments hurried to the Lebanese army. At the same time, in the unlikely event that there actually were some Nasserite agents skulking about in Lebanon, Dulles warned in an extraordinary assertion of rights that the Eisenhower Doctrine gave the United States "a mandate to do something if we think that our peace and vital interests are endangered from any quarter."[23]

It appeared for a time that the Lebanese crisis would pass without an American intervention, for in July 1958 Chamoun, who feared for his life, announced that he would leave office when his term expired in September. At that point, however, with Lebanon's Muslims and Christians still battling one another, Nasserite officers in Iraq staged a coup, slaughtered the prime minister and King Faisal, and dragged their bodies through the streets of Baghdad. A thoroughly hysterical Chamoun, who evidently envisioned himself suffering a similar fate, again asked for an American landing, warning that otherwise his government would surely fall. King Hussein of Jordan, equally fearful of a Nasserite coup, also appealed for help.

This time Eisenhower paid attention. At a White House meeting with Dulles and career diplomat Robert Murphy, Ike explained that a feeling seemed to be developing in the Middle East "that Americans were capable only of words." He feared that unless he actually did something the Iraqi coup might stimulate a general outbreak that could engulf Jordan, Lebanon, and oil-rich, strategically vital, Saudi Arabia. According to Murphy, Eisenhower "wanted to demonstrate in a timely and practical way that the United States was capable of supporting its friends."[24] Within days, sixty-eight ships of the Sixth Fleet were anchored off Beirut; fourteen thousand soldiers and marines equipped with tanks, artillery, and even nuclear cannon had been put ashore; and navy jets were screaming across Lebanese skies. Meanwhile the British airlifted three thousand troops to bolster Hussein's regime in Amman.

Eisenhower sent Robert Murphy to Lebanon to find out what was really going on there. It took Murphy no time at all to realize "that much of the conflict concerned personalities and rivalries of a domestic nature, with no relation to international issues."[25] The Muslim rebels wanted Chamoun out and did not believe he would surrender the presidency willingly. Murphy suggested—and Chamoun, who quite justifiably feared assassination, agreed—that the Lebanese Parliament should elect a new president immediately. The legislators met and selected General Chehab. It was a brilliant choice. A Maronite Christian, he was acceptable to one important element of the population. And as the nonpolitical, neutralist army commander who had refused to act against the Muslim rebels, he was acceptable to the other. Peace was quickly restored, and the American forces reembarked and sailed away.

## WAR IN INDOCHINA

By early 1953, the war in French Indochina had evolved into a major conflict. Ho Chi Minh's Viet Minh, with large quantities of military aid from China (some of it captured American equipment), had grown into a well-trained and disciplined, battle-hardened army. The French had committed a half-

Viet Minh guerrillas captured by the French did not have a long life expectancy.

million men to the struggle, but they controlled only the cities of Hanoi, Haiphong, and Saigon, their environs, and a small area close to the Cambodian border. The remaining 90 percent of the country was under Viet Minh control.

The war-weary French were clearly nearing the end of their resources. Though not yet prepared to accept a humiliating defeat, they were ready to explore possibilities for a negotiated settlement. Paris therefore accepted an invitation extended by Britain and the Soviet Union to attend a conference in Geneva in April 1954 for the purpose of discussing a variety of Asian problems, among them the war in Indochina.

With the Geneva conference only weeks away, General Henri Navarre, the French commander in Vietnam, committed upward of sixteen thousand troops to a heavily fortified position in northwestern Vietnam near a village called Dienbienphu. Navarre hoped to lure the Viet Minh into a set-piece battle in which he could bring his superior firepower to bear on large formations of enemy troops.

The site for the fortress, a low-lying area surrounded by high hills, was badly chosen. General Vo Nguyen Giap, the Vietnamese commander, took quick advantage of this French blunder. Viet Minh forces seized the surrounding hills, used artillery they placed there to knock out the French airstrip, and laid siege to the outpost. Dienbienphu, which from that point on could be supplied only by parachute drop, was hopelessly isolated.

The siege of Dienbienphu caused panic in Paris and Washington alike, for it was understood that the surrender of an entire French army could force the government in Paris to withdraw from Indochina. On March 23, General Paul Ely, chief of staff of the French army, made a hurried trip to Washington seeking additional military aircraft for his Indochina command. But during his visit, Admiral Arthur Radford, chair of the Joint Chiefs, suggested something more dramatic. Operation Vulture was to be a mass raid by American B-29s and carrier-based aircraft against the Viet Minh positions ringing Dienbienphu. Radford, who believed the entire Viet Minh army could be destroyed in a single strike, suggested that the aircraft might even use tactical nuclear weapons in the attack.

Ely returned to Paris believing that Radford was speaking for the president. In fact, however, Radford stood alone, even among military leaders. To a man, the Joint Chiefs of Staff opposed Vulture. Army Chief of Staff Matthew Ridgway derided the fatuous view that the war in Indochina could be won from the air and warned that a land war there would be extremely costly in men and material. "One cannot go over Niagara Falls in a barrel only slightly," said one high-ranking analyst who agreed with Ridgway.[26]

Though the administration had no enthusiasm for Radford's scheme, it was prepared to intervene if it became necessary to stave off a French withdrawal from Indochina. Dulles was thinking in terms of "united action"

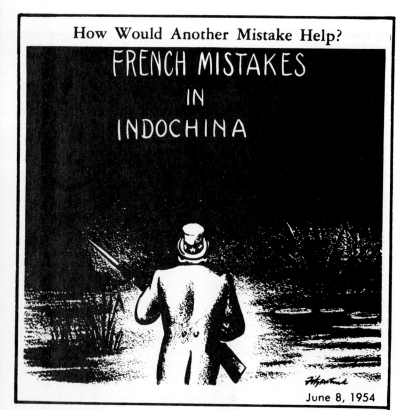

How Would Another Mistake Help?

FRENCH MISTAKES IN INDOCHINA

June 8, 1954

Many Americans opposed the idea, then being considered by the Eisenhower administration, that America should replace France in Indochina.

by a coalition of states including the United States, Britain, Australia, New Zealand, the Philippines, and France along with its puppet states of Vietnam, Laos, and Cambodia.

The immediate problem, as Dulles and Eisenhower saw it, was that Dienbienphu might surrender and the French decide to abandon Vietnam before arrangements could be made for the creation of this coalition. And so, early in April the administration sought congressional support for the use of American air and naval forces in Indochina if it appeared that Paris might otherwise withdraw.

Congress proved a difficult nut to crack. The congressional leaders who met with Dulles and Admiral Radford refused to support any sort of military action until the administration had allies who were also committed to intervention. Moreover, they insisted that if there was to be another coalition war, as in Korea, this time the allies would be expected to bear an appropriate share of the burden. Nor would Congress agree to a war in support of French colonialism. Before a single combat soldier embarked for Indochina, congressional leaders insisted, the French would have to agree on true independence for Vietnam, Laos, and Cambodia.

The administration moved quickly to seek Allied support for the internationalization of the Indochina war. On April 5, Dulles flew to London for conferences with Churchill and Anthony Eden. But the British would not be moved. As co-hosts of the upcoming Geneva conference, they much preferred to work out a diplomatic solution to the war. Bitterly disappointed, Dulles flew on to Paris, where he found even less enthusiasm for the administration's scheme. Foreign Minister Georges Bidault was not interested in becoming a junior partner in a war in which the United States would inevitably make the important political and military decisions. He, too, preferred to take his chances at the negotiating table.

## THE GENEVA ACCORDS

Unable to organize the support Congress required, Eisenhower and Dulles abandoned the idea of intervention. Instead, American delegates were on hand when the Geneva conference convened in late April 1954. But Dulles, who led the delegation, was not happy about it. According to Townsend Hoopes he behaved "with the pinched distaste of a puritan in a house of ill repute, 'quite bruskly' refusing to shake hands with Chou En-lai and instructing the American delegation to ignore at all times the presence and existence of the Chinese delegation." His extraordinary behavior prompted Churchill to remark that "Foster is the only case of a bull I know who carries his china closet with him."[27]

On May 8, 1954, one day after the fortress at Dienbienphu surrendered to the Viet Minh, the Geneva conference at last addressed the problem of Indochina. The negotiations moved slowly, for, in spite of their weak bargaining position, the French explored every possible avenue in hopes of avoiding complete humiliation. Then, on June 12, the French government fell. On taking office the new premier, Pierre Mendés-France, pledged that he would either have a settlement by July 21 or resign. He was almost as good as his word. On the early morning of July 22 the last details of a settlement fell into place.

The Geneva Accords of July 1954 temporarily divided Vietnam along the 17th parallel, with a demilitarized zone established on either side of the line. French forces and their Vietnamese allies were to retire south of the cease-fire line, and Viet Minh forces would move north. But the agreement made it clear that the 17th parallel was not a "political or territorial boundary." It was a convenience, a means of separating the warring armies. Vietnam was to be unified by elections to be held no later than July 1956. A committee made up of neutrals (Canadians, Poles, and Indians) was to work with the "competent authorities" in the North and South to prepare for the elections.[28]

The United States refused to commit itself in writing to the Geneva Accords. The head of the American delegation, General Walter Bedell Smith, did, however, promise that Washington would "refrain from the threat or the use of force to disturb them."[29]

Bedell Smith's statement notwithstanding, Dulles immediately set out to undermine the Geneva Accords. It is clear that the conferees intended to unify Vietnam through supervised national elections. But it was equally clear to Eisenhower and Dulles that Ho Chi Minh would win those elections. It therefore became American policy to transform the temporary dividing line along the 17th parallel into a permanent division between two sovereign states, North and South Vietnam.

At a press conference held on July 23, Dulles explained that the United States was not pleased with the Geneva Accords. But, he said, there was little the United States could do about the loss of northern Vietnam to communism. This acquiescence did not mean, however, that Washington was prepared to see the southern part of the country go the same way. On the contrary, he explained, the United States would do everything in its power to help the vehemently anticommunist president of the French-sponsored government of Vietnam, Ngo Dinh Diem, build a viable noncommunist government south of the 17th parallel.

To strengthen his nation-building effort in South Vietnam, Dulles championed the creation of a Southeast Asian security agreement. The South East Asia Treaty Organization (SEATO) treaty, signed in Manila in 1954, bore no resemblance to NATO. Three of the major nations of the region—Indonesia, India, and Burma—refused to have anything to do with it, while Laos, Cambodia, and Diem's government of Vietnam were prohibited from joining under terms agreed upon at Geneva. Moreover, the agreement (which was signed by the United States, Britain, France, New Zealand, Australia, Thailand, the Philippines and Pakistan) had no teeth in it. A purely consultative arrangement, the SEATO pact stated that any threat to Laos, Cambodia, or South Vietnam would be considered as threatening the "peace and security of the signatories." But it required nothing more than that they "consult" together in the event that some "common danger" should emerge.[30]

Though no more than a paper agreement, the SEATO treaty served administration purposes reasonably well since it established a basis for future American intervention in Vietnam. At the same time it put China, the Soviet Union, and the Viet Minh on notice that the United States considered the area among its vital interests.

## IKE'S SECRET WARS

Once it became evident that the nuclear stalemate could not be broken, that war was not a feasible method of resolving the differences that divided East from West, the major battleground of the cold war shifted to the developing world. In the mid-1950s, Moscow began to court these nations with aid programs not unlike those pioneered by the United States. The Soviets built steel making facilities in India and penetrated the Middle East, courting revolutionary regimes in Nasser's Egypt and Iraq through arms sales and technical assistance programs.

At first Dulles showed little concern over these new Soviet initiatives. But administration leaders did become concerned when the Soviets proved, as in Egypt, that they would fulfill their commitments. Washington was distressed, too, at the number of leaders in underdeveloped countries who rejected the capitalist approach to economic development in favor of state planning and who looked to Moscow as a model. Those nations, such as Jawaharlal Nehru's India, that chose the course of neutralism rather than joining the Western camp were another source of irritation to Washington, where neutralism was viewed as a way station on the road to communism.

In attempting to prevent Third World countries from "falling to communism," the Eisenhower administration had frequent recourse to covert actions engineered by the Central Intelligence Agency. At the time the agency was headed by Allen Dulles, the brother of the secretary of state and a former officer in the wartime Office of Strategic Services. When the CIA was first organized under the National Security Act of 1947, its main function was intelligence gathering and analysis. But within a year President Harry Truman was using the CIA for a variety of covert activities ranging from propaganda broadcasts behind the Iron Curtain to political and economic warfare and even small-scale paramilitary activities. Still, it wasn't until the Dulles years that the CIA, for better and worse, came into its own.

The Eisenhower administration first had recourse to covert action in Iran, where Premier Mohammad Mossadegh, a progressive nationalist, was in a life-and-death struggle with the Anglo-Iranian Oil Company (AIOC), a British firm. For years the AIOC had operated in Iran under a contract that at best provided the Iranians with 10 percent of the profits from the oil produced in that otherwise destitute country. Mossadegh wanted to renegotiate the agreement between his government and the AIOC to guarantee

Iran half the profits, an arrangement similar to that worked out not long before between American oil companies and Venezuela.

In 1951, after three years of fruitless bargaining, the Iranian Parliament, the Majlis, nationalized Iran's oil resources, promising to use 25 percent of the revenues it received to pay the AIOC for its assets. This decision was based on political as well as economic considerations. Powerful British economic interests had for years exerted influence over Iran's national life. As Mossadegh explained, the "Iranian people finally became convinced that so long as this company continued to operate within Iran, its systematic interference in Iranian internal life would continue." They therefore saw no option other than to exercise their sovereign rights by nationalizing their oil and terminating the activities of the former company in Iran."[31]

London reacted to Mossadegh's nationalization order by freezing all Iranian assets under its control. Meanwhile the AIOC entered into an agreement with the other major oil producers to boycott Iranian oil. Smaller independent oil producers were warned off by threats of legal action should they attempt to make any deals with Iran.

Britain's object—the destabilization of Mossadegh's government—drew criticism from the Truman administration, which feared that the British "might drive Iran to a Communist coup d'etat, or Iran might drive Britain out." Secretary of State Dean Acheson viewed "either development" as a "major disaster" for the West. The British, less concerned by the communist threat, saw things differently. "I did not accept the argument that the only alternative to Mossadegh was communist rule," wrote Anthony Eden. "I thought that if Mossadegh fell, his place might well be taken by a more reasonable government."[32]

By 1952, Iran's oil production had fallen from 241 million to 10.6 million barrels annually. The economic hardships created by the Western oil boycott created internal divisions inside Iran. Mossadegh, once the leader of a powerful coalition, was losing control of the situation as an opposition movement spearheaded by members of the armed forces began to coalesce around the weak and until then relatively powerless figurehead Shah, Muhammad Reza Pahlavi.

Not two weeks after coming to power, the Eisenhower administration entered into discussions with London looking toward Mossadegh's overthrow. The final decision was taken on June 22, 1953, at a high-level meeting in Secretary Dulles's State Department office. Satisfied that Mossadegh was leading Iran into the Soviet orbit, Dulles authorized Kermit Roosevelt, a Middle East expert with the CIA who also happened to be the Rough Rider's grandson, to plot the overthrow of the regime. In the summer of 1953 Roosevelt left for Iran with a million dollars in his pocket and a gleam in his eye.

In mid-August 1953, a crowd of toughs bought and paid for by Roosevelt, took to the streets of Tehran and toppled the already faltering Mossadegh. In the aftermath of the coup the new Iranian government, now headed by Fazollah Zahedi, a retired general in the pay of the CIA, negotiated an oil agreement that was enormously beneficial to American companies. From then until the shah nationalized Iran's oil sixteen years later, American firms controlled 40 percent of Iran's oil production. The AIOC (renamed British Petroleum) took an equal share. The other 20 percent was divided among Dutch and French companies.

In the years following the anti-Mossadegh coup it was the shah, backed by the United States, who held power in Iran. And he used it to create a ruthless absolutist state. Between 1954 and 1966 the United States provided him with $1.3 billion in aid, much of it to train the army and SAVAK, the infamous Iranian secret police force that he used to crush dissent.

CIA involvement in the coup that set the shah on the road to absolutism would not be forgotten by Iranians. This fact goes a long way toward explaining the deep and abiding hostility toward the United States that helped sustain the extremist postshah regime in power for so long.

## THE ARBENZ AFFAIR

Southwest Asia was only one of a number of global trouble spots that attracted the attentions of the CIA. Eisenhower and Dulles were also disturbed by developments in Guatemala, where the United Fruit Company and other foreign corporations had major interests. Guatemala had been in the midst of what might be described as a moderate revolution since 1944, when a brutal dictator, General Jorge Ubico, was overthrown by a group of reform-minded military officers. In the next few years President Juan Arevalo implemented a number of welfare state reforms, including minimum wage and social security laws.

In 1951 President Jacobo Arbenz Guzman, one of the officers involved in the 1944 coup, sought to carry the reform program further. Because a mere 2 percent of the population controlled 70 percent of the country's arable land, Arbenz focused his attentions on land reform. As a beginning, he expropriated 234,000 acres of uncultivated land belonging to the United Fruit Company and offered in payment $600,000 in twenty-five year 6-percent bonds. United Fruit, contending that the land in question was worth nearly $16 million (although it was listed on the tax rolls at $600,000) complained to the State Department and began a public relations campaign charging that Arbenz was a communist.

Though he was a leftist, Arbenz was not associated with the Guatemalan Communist party. He received no aid from Moscow and had no connection with other communist nations. He did use local communists, however, both in his government and as advisers on important social issues. That connection plus the fact that he had expropriated American-owned assets was enough for Dulles and Eisenhower, who quickly concluded that he must go.

Late in 1953 the CIA began planning a Guatemalan coup and found its candidate for president in Colonel Carlos Castillo Armas, a right-wing military officer. Early in 1954 the CIA established a base camp for Armas and his 150 followers in Honduras and began preparing for an invasion. On learning of the planned coup, Arbenz, blocked from purchasing arms in the West, bought weapons from Soviet-bloc suppliers and prepared to resist.

Armas and his "army" crossed the border into Guatemala on June 18, 1954. At the same time American pilots flying World War II–vintage aircraft bombed and strafed Guatemala City. On June 27, after the Guatemalan army deserted him, Arbenz fled the country, and Armas took power as Guatemala's new president. One of the more tawdry aspects of this tawdry affair took place immediately after the coup when Secretary Dulles actually took to the airwaves to congratulate "the people of Guatamala" for having eliminated a communist threat to the hemisphere without outside interference.[33]

Once installed in office, Armas returned the expropriated land to United Fruit and reversed most of the domestic reforms implemented after 1944. The Armas coup could not, however, turn back the clock. The reform movement set in motion by presidents Arévalo and Arbenz continued to have adherents inside Guatemala who resisted Armas's dictatorship. Unable to rule with the consent of the governed, he ruled by terror until his assassination in 1957. In 1963 a right-wing military junta seized outright control of Guatemala and retained power by brute force for the next two decades. Its troops, trained and equipped by the United States, held the country in a reign of terror. The Guatemalan military did not take political prisoners; it simply assassinated those suspected of harboring dangerous thoughts.

Nobody really knows how many have died at the hands of the Guatemalan military. But one generally accepted estimate places the figure at more than 100,000.

## ENDNOTES

1. Sir Bernard Montgomery and anonymous, both quoted in Robert A. Divine, *Eisenhower and the Cold War* (New York: Oxford University Press, 1981), pp. 3–7.

2. George Patton, quoted in ibid.

3. 1952 Republican party platform, quoted in Louis L. Gerson, *John Foster Dulles* (New York: Cooper Square, 1967), pp. 87–88. See also Townsend Hoopes, *The Devil and John Foster Dulles* (Boston: Little, Brown, 1973), pp. 135–41.

4. Ann Whitman, quoted in Divine, *Eisenhower and the Cold War,* p. 23.

5. Dwight David Eisenhower, *Mandate for Change, 1953–1956* (Garden City, N.Y.: Doubleday, 1963), p. 24.

6. Eisenhower, quoted in Richard A. Aliano, *American Defense Policy from Eisenhower to Kennedy* (Athens, Ohio: Ohio University Press, 1975), pp. 30–31.

7. John Foster Dulles, quoted in *State Department Bulletin,* June 25, 1954, p. 108.

8. James Reston and Dulles, quoted in Gerard Clarfield and William Wiecek, *Nuclear America: Military and Civilian Nuclear Power in the United States, 1940–1980* (New York: Harper and Row, 1984), p. 155.

9. J. Robert Oppenheimer, quoted in ibid., p. 156; William Kaufmann, quoted in Michael Mandelbaum, *The Nuclear Question: The United States and Nuclear Weapons, 1946–1976* (New York: Oxford University Press, 1979), p. 57.

10. Eisenhower, "The Chance for Peace," Speech of April 16, 1953, *Public Papers of the Presidents: Dwight David Eisenhower, 1953* (Washington, D.C., 1960), pp. 179–88.

11. Winston Churchill, quoted in Delman Morin, *Dwight David Eisenhower: A Gauge of Greatness* (New York: Simon and Schuster, 1969), p. 175.

12. Dulles, quoted in Hoopes, *Devil and John Foster Dulles*, p. 189.

13. Eisenhower, *Mandate for Change*, p. 509.

14. Anthony Eden, quoted in Robert Murphy, *Diplomat among Warriors* (Garden City, N.Y.: Doubleday, 1964), p. 378.

15. Eisenhower, quoted in Hoopes, *Devil and John Foster Dulles*, p. 360.

16. Murphy, *Diplomat among Warriors*, p. 382.

17. Shimon Peres and Moshe Sharett, quoted in Philip J. Briggs, "Congress and the Middle East: The Eisenhower Doctrine, 1957," in *Dwight David Eisenhower: Soldier, Statesman, President*, ed. Joann P. Kreig (New York: Greenwood Press, 1987), pp. 251, 254.

18. U.S. ambassador to Israel, quoted in ibid., p. 254.

19. Eisenhower, quoted in Hoopes, *Devil and John Foster Dulles*, p. 374; Abba Eban, quoted in Briggs, "Congress and the Middle East," p. 254.

20. Nicoli Bulganin, quoted in Divine, *Eisenhower and the Cold War*, pp. 86–87.

21. Eisenhower, quoted in Murphy, *Diplomat among Warriors*, pp. 390–91.

22. Eisenhower Doctrine, quoted in Hoopes, *Devil and John Foster Dulles*, pp. 406–8. See also Gerson, *John Foster Dulles*, pp. 298–99.

23. Dulles, quoted in Richard J. Barnet, *Intervention and Revolution: America's Confrontation with Insurgent Movements around the World* (New York: Meridian Books, 1968), p. 143.

24. Murphy, *Diplomat among Warriors*, p. 398.

25. Ibid., p. 404.

26. Defense Department analyst, quoted in George C. Herring, *America's Longest War: The United States and Vietnam, 1950–1975* (New York: Alfred A. Knopf, 1979), p. 31.

27. Hoopes, *Devil and John Foster Dulles*, p. 222, including quotation from Churchill.

28. Geneva Accords, quoted in George Donelson Moss, *Vietnam: An American Ordeal* (Englewood Cliffs, N.J.: Prentice-Hall, 1990), p. 60.

29. Ibid.

30. South East Asia Treaty Organization treaty, September 8, 1954, *Documents of American History*, ed. Henry Steele Commager and Milton Cantor, 10th ed. (Englewood Cliffs, N.J.: Prentice-Hall, 1988), II, 598–600.

31. Mohammad Mossadegh to Eisenhower, January 9, 1953, *The United States and Iran: A Documentary History*, ed. Yonah Alexander and Allan Nanes (Frederick, Md.: Aletheia Books, 1980), p. 231.

32. Dean G. Acheson, *Present at the Creation: My Years in the State Department* (New York: W. W. Norton, 1969), p. 506; Anthony Eden, *Full Circle: The Memoirs of Anthony Eden* (Boston: Houghton, Mifflin), p. 222.

33. Dulles, quoted in Walter LaFeber, *Inevitable Revolutions: The United States in Central America* (New York: Norton, 1984), p. 125. See also Barnet, *Intervention and Revolution*, pp. 229–236.

Following the launching of Sputnick, Nikita Khrushchev attempted to use the leverage it created to advance Soviet interests. Americans called it "Sputnik diplomacy."

# 29

# IKE'S TIME OF TROUBLES, 1957–1961

In November 1956 Dwight Eisenhower was overwhelmingly re-elected to a second term as president. Ironically, it was at this time, while he was at the height of his popularity, that things began to go wrong for him. On the domestic front he would have to deal with a major economic recession as well as the beginnings of the civil rights revolution. In foreign affairs there would be the "missile gap" controversy as well as crises in Europe, the Caribbean, Asia, and Africa.

One of the most serious problems Eisenhower faced in his second term boiled up in October 1957, when Radio Moscow announced that Soviet scientists had successfully placed in orbit Sputnik, the world's first artificial earth satellite. Two more satellites soon followed, one of which weighed 2,925 pounds. Not only had the Soviet Union preceded the United States into space; it had in the process demonstrated that it possessed a launch vehicle of enormous power with a guidance system that was probably capable of delivering a nuclear warhead to a target thousands of miles away.

Hysteria swept the United States. In a vehement denunciation of the president's defense policy, John F. Kennedy, Lyndon Johnson, and other Congressional Democrats charged that he had placed fiscal considerations ahead of national security and warned that the Soviets would soon have a missile force capable of raining death on the United States. The news commentator, Eric Sevareid, agreed, warning his millions of viewers that it wouldn't be long before the Soviet Union could "stand astride the world, its military master."[1]

In a television address to the nation Eisenhower conceded that the Soviets enjoyed a temporary lead in missile development but maintained that "the overall military strength of the free world is distinctly greater than that of the Communist countries." Moreover, while some might talk of a "missile gap," he assured his viewers that there was no "deterrent gap." He also pointed out that missile research had not been neglected in the United States, that the Atlas, a first-generation intercontinental ballistic (ICBM), was ready for testing, and that the more sophisticated Titan was not far behind.[2]

The president called for calm and moderation. But not even Eisenhower, among the most trusted of presidents, could quiet the hysteria produced by Sputnik. In spite of the fact that even as late as the summer of 1960 the American intelligence community had not uncovered a single operational Soviet ICBM, Eisenhower had no choice but to authorize a major escalation in the nuclear arms race. By the end of his administration Ike had approved the deployment of 255 Atlas and Titan ICBMs, 450 silo-based and 90 mobile Minuteman missiles, and 19 Polaris-type submarines, each carrying 16 missiles. In all he approved a strategic missile force that approached the 1,100 mark before intelligence sources could uncover even one operational Soviet ICBM.

## A SECOND BERLIN CRISIS

A decade after the first Berlin crisis Nikita Khrushchev took a very big chance. Gambling that the West believed his claim that Soviet factories were producing ICBMs on an assembly line basis, he tried to use the leverage Sputnik provided to force a solution to the Berlin and German questions on his terms.

In a speech given on November 10, 1958, and in subsequent notes to the Western Allies, Khrushchev announced that the time had come to end the four-power occupation of Berlin. Arguing that when they rearmed West Germany the NATO Allies had in effect nullified the 1945 Potsdam agreements establishing the quadripartite occupation of the old German capital, Khrushchev called for a reunified but neutralized Germany with Berlin to become a "free city." The Soviet leader also announced that if the Western Allies refused to come to an agreement within six months, he would recognize the East Germans as the legitimate authority throughout all of Berlin. Had Khrushchev done this, and had the East Germans attempted to exert authority over the Western-occupation zones, the stage would have been set for a major confrontation and possibly nuclear war.

Khrushchev's extraordinary gamble was based on a number of important considerations. First, Moscow was troubled by the growing military strength of West Germany, a member of NATO since 1955. Just as disturbing

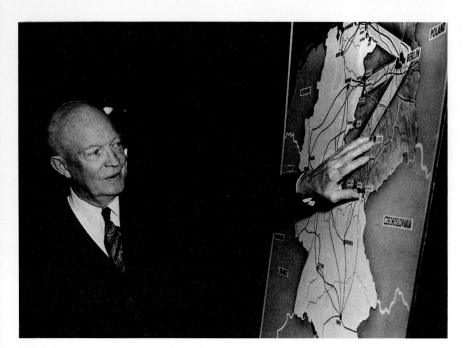

Dwight Eisenhower was the first president to use the new medium of television effectively. Here he is shown explaining the Berlin situation to a national television audience.

was the American decision to station nuclear weapons on German soil. Though the weapons remained under American control, having German hands anywhere in the vicinity of such weapons inevitably raised serious concern in Moscow. Finally, thirteen years after World War II the Western Alliance was showing signs of fragmentation, especially with regard to France, where President Charles de Gaulle sensed the end of the bipolar world. Sputnik appeared to have strengthened the Kremlin's bargaining position in international affairs. Why not, then, exert pressure along the fault lines of the NATO alliance and see what developed?

Western unity was sorely tried by Khrushchev's initiative. Harold Macmillan, who succeeded Anthony Eden as Britain's prime minister, wanted a summit. Macmillan believed that a resolution to the Berlin and German questions could only come at the highest level and that unless agreement could be reached, Khrushchev would, as he had threatened, plunge the world into a crisis. The West Germans, on the other hand, fearing that the United States and Britain would give ground on the Berlin question, wanted no compromise and therefore no summit. The Germans need not have worried. Eisenhower had no intention of being summoned to a summit meeting by the Soviets. To pacify London, he did, however, agree to a foreign ministers' conference, which opened at Geneva in May 1959.

To nobody's surprise, the Geneva foreign ministers' conference was a nonstarter. The West's nonnegotiable position was that German unification would be acceptable only if it came about as a result of free, democratic elections and if the new Germany was allowed to join NATO. Nor would

Dwight Eisenhower and Nikita Khrushchev (second from right) pose for a photograph during the Soviet leader's visit to the United States in 1959.

there be any concessions relating to Berlin, where the Western Allies insisted on their rights as occupiers. The Soviet position, equally clear, called for the neutralization of a reunified Germany with Berlin to become a "free city."

Khrushchev's six-month deadline passed uneventfully during the Geneva conference, dissipating much of the tension that had gripped Europe and America through the first half of 1959. What remained of the crisis atmosphere completely evaporated in August when the Soviet premier announced that he was contemplating a goodwill visit to the United States. Conservatives were appalled at the prospect of a Soviet premier touring America. Even Harry Truman objected. But Eisenhower, who hoped to reduce Soviet-American tensions, quickly extended an invitation.

Khrushchev arrived in September 1959, for a two-week whirlwind journey across the United States. It was, according to one White House insider, "a transcontinental display of political showmanship." He sparred with and generally got the best of Henry Cabot Lodge, Jr., who escorted him on his trip, inquired of the two-time Democratic candidate for president, Adlai Stevenson, whether he might not "be investigated by the Bureau of Un-American Affairs" for talking with him, and, when he was barred from Disneyland because of inadequate security, asked puckishly, "Do you have rocket-launching pads there?"[3]

All in all, Khrushchev was quite impressive. One observer remarked, "He's a little like a candidate in the late stages of the campaign. He has heard all the questions many times, and his answers are sharp as hell."[4] When he left the United States following three days of private talks with Eisenhower at the president's retreat, Camp David, Maryland, the entire political atmosphere seemed to have changed for the better. The cold war remained a fundamental fact of international life. But détente was an idea whose time appeared to have come.

## PARIS AND THE U-2

There was really no reason to hold a great power summit meeting in 1960. Sputnik had killed any possibility that the United States might consider nuclear disarmament. And the German question remained impossible to resolve. But Khrushchev's visit had been an enormous public relations success, and all sides were anxious to build on the spirit of goodwill it had engendered. Unhappily, a CIA reconnaissance flight that went awry over the Soviet Union just prior to the conference ended any hope of improved relations between Washington and Moscow for the remainder of Eisenhower's administration.

The CIA and the air force had been using U-2 spy planes to fly reconnaissance missions over the Soviet Union since 1956. This remarkable aircraft could fly at eighty thousand feet and still photograph the terrain below in sharp detail. The Soviets were aware of these flights but could do little about them. Nothing in the Soviet air force could fly high enough to attack the astonishing U-2. And that was a fact both Washington and Moscow, each for its own reasons, preferred to keep confidential.

On May 1, 1960, just two weeks before the summit meeting was scheduled to begin, the Soviets, using a recently developed surface-to-air missile (SAM), bagged their first U-2 twelve hundred miles inside Soviet territory over the industrial city of Sverdlovsk. The damaged plane fell to earth with its cameras intact. The pilot, Francis Gary Powers, parachuted to safety carrying with him, among other personal effects, an unused poison needle issued by the CIA for just such emergencies.

Unaware that the Soviets had Powers as well as the photographs he had taken, Washington began to grind out lies to explain the missing plane. First, the National Aeronautics and Space Administration (NASA) informed the press that it had lost a weather research plane over Turkey. But two days later, when Khrushchev announced in a speech before the Supreme Soviet that an American plane had been shot down over Soviet territory, it was clear that something more would have to be said. And so the State Department dug the administration in more deeply. A government spokesperson admitted the possibility that the plane's pilot might have lost consciousness for lack of oxygen and that the plane, while flying on automatic pilot, could have crossed into Soviet air space. At the same time, however, he told reporters, "There was absolutely no-No-no deliberate attempt to violate Soviet air space, and there never has been." This lie blew up in Washington's face the next day when the Soviets informed the American embassy, "We've got the pilot."[5]

Khrushchev, anxious to save the upcoming summit conference, tried to leave the president out of the picture by blaming the incident on the Pentagon. The State Department, also hoping to keep Ike out of what was becoming a messy situation, then finally admitted that U-2 reconnaissance flights over Soviet territory had been going on for some time. But, it claimed, "There was no authorization for any such flights" from the White House.[6]

This latest lie left Eisenhower in a dreadful bind. He could have saved the upcoming summit meeting by claiming ignorance of the U-2 flights. But that would have been tantamount to admitting that he did not know about or authorize actions that had grave national security implications. Under the circumstances he did what any smart politician would have done. On May 11, he took full responsibility for the U-2 flights.

The president's announcement that he was personally responsible for ordering the violation of Soviet air space had the predictable result. It destroyed the Paris summit. Khrushchev came, but only to excoriate Eisenhower as "a thief caught red handed in his theft."[7] He refused to hold talks and withdrew an invitation previously extended for the president to visit the Soviet Union later in the year.

Khrushchev really had no choice. He was at the time engaged in an ongoing struggle with conservative critics inside the Soviet hierarchy who deplored his efforts on behalf of domestic reform, his commitment to co-existence, and his willingness to negotiate with the West. The crash of Gary Powers's U-2 was a serious embarrassment to him, for it clearly strengthened the hand of those who opposed his liberal policies. Washington's mismanagement of the affair, culminating in Eisenhower's decision to accept full responsibility for the flights, created an impossible situation for Khrushchev. The collapse of the summit was a sad ending to the tentative beginning he and Eisenhower had made toward détente.

## FIDEL

In March 1952, Fulgencio Batista, who allowed the Cuban presidency to slip out of his control when his handpicked candidate lost the 1944 election, overthrew Prío Socarras, the constitutionally elected president of Cuba, in an almost bloodless coup. For the next six years he ruled Cuba with an iron hand. A ruthless dictator, Batista was nevertheless acceptable to the Eisenhower administration because he provided political stability, encouraged economic development and tourism, and offered protection to foreign investors.

The old *caudillo* appeared to be presiding over the prosperous, orderly protectorate that Theodore Roosevelt and the imperialists of his generation once envisioned. But behind the glitter and swank of Havana's nightclubs, gambling casinos, and beach resorts, Cuban nationalism was developing into a force to be reckoned with. American investors controlled much of the island's economic life, and a reciprocal trade agreement with the United States ensured the fact that Cuba would remain an economic colony, exchanging sugar and tobacco for a myriad of American manufactured goods. At the same time land reform remained the unfulfilled promise of the Cuban revolution of 1933 and the Constitution of 1940. Cuba's quasi-colonial status, the popular longing for economic reform, and a desire for true political independence contributed to a rising resentment against the

United States and its agent, Batista, that culminated in Fidel Castro's seizure of power in 1959.

Castro, the son of a wealthy landowner and a young lawyer in a country overrun with lawyers, was driven by his own quest for personal power as well as the desire to achieve a true revolution for Cuba. A political activist from his student days in the mid-1940s, he spent the years just prior to Batista's 1952 coup working to advance the cause of reform in Cuba. The renewal of the Batista dictatorship, however, convinced him that social and economic change could be achieved only by violence.

In 1953 Castro led a small band of rebels in his first attempt to overthrow Batista. The attack on the Moncada barracks was easily crushed. Those rebels who weren't killed in battle or "shot while trying to escape," were given long prison terms. Castro, one of the lucky ones, was sentenced to fifteen years imprisonment on the Isle of Pines. But Fidel served less than two years in prison. He was turned loose in 1955 when Batista, confident of his hold on power, declared a general amnesty.

Following his release from prison, Castro went into exile in Mexico where, together with the Argentinean radical Ernesto ("Ché") Guevara and a few others, he planned a second more elaborate effort at overthrowing Batista. During his exile, while on a fund-raising tour in the United States, Castro told an audience of Cuban exiles, "In 1956 we will be free, or we will be martyrs."[8] Many of those who went with the "maximum leader" on the subsequent filibustering expedition achieved their martyrdom just days after landing on Cuban shores. Only Fidel and a small remnant of his force evaded Batista's soldiers and made it to the Sierra Maestra mountains of Oriente Province. From there for the next two years they carried on an increasingly successful guerrilla war against the government while at the same time building political support among the Cuban people.

Events in Cuba placed the Eisenhower administration in an awkward position. Castro had a superb press in the United States, where he was viewed as a cross between Robin Hood and Tom Paine, fighting for freedom, democracy, and social justice. In contrast, Batista was seen for what he was, a brutal dictator who was responsible for the murder or disappearance of perhaps as many as twenty-thousand persons during his six-year rule. The fact that Batista's army had been trained and equipped by the United States and that he received military aid from Washington was an added embarrassment to the government.

Still, it was not until 1958, by which time Batista's grip on power was slipping, that the Eisenhower administration decided to distance itself from the Cuban dictator. In March of that year the State Department signaled its changed attitude by instructing the American ambassador in Havana to adopt a policy of strict neutrality regarding the turmoil in Cuba. Washington also imposed an embargo on the sale of arms to the regime. Batista should have been the handwriting on the wall and left quietly. That, at least, is what Eisenhower hoped. But Lord Acton was right about power; it corrupts. And so Batista hung on.

Fearing that the Cuban revolutionary movement was heavily influenced by communists, the administration was not prepared to accept Castro as Cuba's new leader. Eisenhower hoped instead to replace Batista with someone else. This mythical person, whom no one in the administration had as yet identified, was to be a "moderate" who would win the support of the Cuban people through democratic political reforms while at the same time protecting American economic interests. It was, of course, a forlorn hope, since American economic domination of the island blocked the path to meaningful economic and social reform. But if Eisenhower understood the inconsistency, he never acknowledged it.

In December 1958, Washington urged Batista to resign in favor of someone with a greater chance of remaining in power. Though he was promised asylum in Florida, the Cuban dictator continued to deceive himself about his changes for survival. In any event by that time it was far too late to implement such schemes. On New Year's Eve, Batista fled to the Dominican Republic, and the regime crumbled. Castro's victorious army entered Havana on New Year's Day, 1959.

## THE CASTRO REVOLUTION

Scholars have long debated exactly when Fidel Castro became a convert to communism. Some believe that the decision came even before his ill-fated assault on the Moncada barracks. Others think it came as late as 1958, while he was still operating out of the Sierra Maestra mountains. In any event, it is certain that by the time Castro seized power he was committed to transforming Cuba into a communist state. It is also clear, however, that to cultivate support in the United States and reduce the danger that Washington might act against him, he kept his ideological commitment a profound secret.

During the long struggle with Batista, Castro was careful to keep the small Cuban Communist party at arm's length. He had no contact with the Soviets and stated categorically that he had "no plans for the expropriation or nationalization of foreign investments." On a visit to the United States in April 1959, Castro again announced that he would not allow the communists to play a role in his government, that he had no intention of nationalizing anything, and that he was committed to the restoration of democracy and the Cuban Constitution of 1940. Aware that his beard made a bad impression on the American middle classes, he explained it as a symbol. When the revolution was completed, he told reporters, "We will cut our beards off."[9]

Castro's visit to the United States was a public relations triumph. But it did not result in any substantive improvement in his relations with Washington. During his stay the Cuban leader was careful to appear friendly. But he sensed no reciprocal indications of friendliness. President Eisenhower made his feelings plain by taking a long vacation while Castro was in Washington. Those American officials he did see, especially Vice-President

Richard Nixon, appeared interested only in his suspected communist connections.

Following his visit to the United States, Castro was forced to face the hard fact that, his recent statements notwithstanding, to address problems of social and economic injustice he would have to undertake reform programs that were certain to alienate Cuba's privileged middle and upper classes as well as the foreign interests (mostly American) that controlled a large part of the Cuban economy. As a first step, his government enacted agrarian land reform legislation that was designed to break up Cuba's large landed estates. Under the new law most landholdings were limited to 1,000 acres. Sugar plantations, the exception, were limited to 3,333 acres. All land over these limits was expropriated by the state and transformed into cooperative farms or 67-acre plots for peasant farmers.

The government offered compensation for expropriated land in the form of twenty-year bonds paying 4.5 percent interest. But the law stipulated that funds realized from these bonds could not be converted into dollars and had to be reinvested in Cuba. American sugar producers complained bitterly that the new policy amounted to confiscation. But when the State Department lodged a vigorous protest demanding compensation, Havana rejected the protest.

Castro's dispute with the Eisenhower administration over his land reform program seems to have marked a turning point in the history of his relations with Washington. Some time later he told Herbert Matthews, a reporter who interviewed him on many occasions, that the vehement American objections "made me realize there was no chance to reach an accommodation with the United States."[10] From this point onward Castro operated on the assumption that Washington was his enemy and that his survival would depend on his ability to maintain the credibility of his revolution with the Cuban people.

By the end of 1959 Castro had expropriated American holdings valued at more than $1 billion. The Eisenhower administration, meanwhile, began to consider methods of fomenting a counterrevolution in Cuba. The American ambassador in Havana was called home "for consultations," and the CIA was let loose to perform a variety of dirty tricks that included everything from burning sugarcane fields to sabotaging industrial equipment. On March 17, 1960, the agency was further instructed to begin organizing anti-Castro Cuban exiles for possible guerrilla war. Ultimately the president approved a budget of $13 million for this purpose.

It was at this point that Castro first looked toward Moscow for support. The Soviets had until then steered clear of the developing situation in the Caribbean, believing the region to be within the American sphere of influence. But the adventurous Khrushchev now saw an opportunity to embarrass Eisenhower in his own backyard. And he took it. First Deputy Premier Anastas Mikoyan, who visited Havana in February 1960, arranged a $100 million credit for Cuba and offered technical assistance for the modernization of Cuban industry. He also signed a multi-year sugar purchase agreement.

Mikoyan drove a hard bargain. The price that Moscow paid for Cuba's sugar was lower than the subsidized price Havana had been receiving from the United States. Moreover, because the Soviets had no foreign exchange to spare, payment for Cuban sugar was to be in bartered goods. This arrangement meant that Cuba, too, would remain short of foreign exchange and tied closely to the Soviet economy. Still, Castro had no choice but to accept Soviet terms. There was no place else to turn. It is not surprising, then, that by the end of 1961 four-fifths of Cuba's trade was with East bloc countries.

As the Soviet-Cuban relationship developed, Cuban-American relations quickly deteriorated. When Castro seized three American and British oil refineries, the president reacted by suspending the Cuban sugar quota for the rest of the year, an act that cost Cuba about $140 million in foreign exchange. Castro retaliated by nationalizing the remaining American sugar mills on the island. Then, in an effort to cripple the Cuban economy and encourage counterrevolution, Eisenhower placed an embargo on all trade with Cuba. When, early in January 1961, Castro insisted that the American embassy staff, which numbered in the hundreds (many of whom were CIA agents), be reduced to eleven persons, Eisenhower broke relations. The time had come, the president thought, for a showdown. When Ike left office plans were nearly complete for a force of anti-Castro Cubans, armed and equipped by the United States, to land on an isolated strip of beach called the Bay of Pigs.

## THE COVERT WARS CONTINUE

The Cuban operation, which took place early in the Kennedy administration, was the best known of those covert actions planned and or carried out by the CIA during Eisenhower's second term. But two others, one in Indonesia and a second in the Congo, are also worthy of note.

In 1957 the United States offered its support to a revolutionary movement aimed at overthrowing the apparently left-leaning Indonesian government of Achmed Sukarno. While the CIA provided small arms and air support for the rebels, the official State Department position, announced by Secretary of State John Foster Dulles himself, was that the Indonesian rebellion was a purely "internal affair" and that Washington would remain neutral.[11] It must have been an awfully embarrassing moment for the secretary when one of the Americans flying for the rebels, Allan Pope, was shot down and captured alive with documents linking him to the CIA and authorizing him to fly his missions from Clark Field, an American air base in the Philippines.

Sukarno's charge that the rebels would long since have given up save for the aid they were receiving from the United States may have been the cause, or it may simply have been the realization that the CIA was backing the losing side; in any event, shortly after Pope's capture, Washington began providing Sukarno with aid. After that the uprising against Jakarta quickly died away.

In 1960 the CIA became involved in another, far more complex situation in the Republic of the Congo (the name was changed to Zaire in 1971). Only weeks after the Congo gained its independence from Belgium, a four-way struggle developed between President Joseph Kasavubu; the premier and defense minister, Patrice Lumumba; the army commander Sese Seko Mobutu, and Moise Tshombe, whose power base lay in mineral-rich Katanga Province. Tribal rivalries, money, and power—these were the forces driving each of the four.

The Congo Republic was only weeks old when signs of internal crisis appeared. First the Congolese army mutinied, attacking a number of whites still living and working in the former Belgian colony. Then, Tshombe, working closely with Belgian businessmen as well as the Belgian government, declared rich Katanga Province independent. Tshombe had earlier tried to separate his province from the rest of the Congo. Now, with the army in rebellion, he saw his chance and took it. The Belgians, too, saw an opportunity. Early in July, Brussels reinforced the contingent of troops that had remained in Katanga after independence. The announced purpose of this expanded Belgian presence was to protect the lives of Belgian citizens in the area. But Brussels's real object was to support Tshombe, the defender of Belgium's special interests.

Lumumba, by far the most popular of the four rivals for power in the Congo, called on the United Nations for help. The Security Council told the Belgians to leave and sent a peacekeeping force to the Congo to restore order. But the UN force refused to help end the rebellion in Katanga, which it considered a purely internal affair.

At this point Lumumba made a serious mistake, turning to the Soviet Union for aid. Roger Hilsman, who served as an assistant secretary of state in the Kennedy administration, once described Lumumba as a man who, though he "played with Marxist verbiage," was first and foremost a Congolese nationalist. Hilsman was no doubt correct. But Lumumba's appeal to the Soviets, combined with his socialist rhetoric, led hypersensitive American observers to conclude that his real objective was to transform the Congo into a Soviet satellite. When in September 1960, Soviet military equipment along with Czech and Soviet advisers turned up in the Congo, the CIA station chief there became convinced that something had to be done about Lumumba. He cabled Washington: "Embassy and [CIA] station believe Congo experiencing classic Communist takeover [of] government."[12]

That seems to have settled the issue for President Eisenhower, who, at a meeting of the National Security Council, ordered Lumumba's removal. Some of those sitting around the table had no doubt about what the president meant. One NSC staffer later testified that Ike's words "came across to me as an order for the assassination of Lumumba. . . . I remember my sense of that moment quite clearly because the president's statement came as a great shock to me." Undersecretary of State C. Douglas Dillon, who attended the same NSC meeting does not believe that the assassination order was quite so "clear cut." But he does admit that the President could have said, "We will have to do whatever is necessary to get rid of him."[13] One thing *is* certain, The CIA took Eisenhower's remark to mean that Lumumba should die.

Before the CIA could "hit" Premier Lumumba, President Kasavubu dismissed him from office and placed him under house arrest. Joseph Ileo replaced him as premier and, with CIA support, Sese Seko Mobutu, head of the army, emerged as Kasavubu's ally and the Congo's new strong man. But this was not the last of Lumumba or the crisis that, like the Cuban crisis, remained to be played out during the Kennedy administration.

## CRISIS IN SOUTHEAST ASIA

In 1954, when John Foster Dulles first considered a serious nation-building project in South Vietnam, he was aware that he faced formidable obstacles. After years of warfare, the economic infrastructure of the region was in a shambles. Moreover, he had only the government of Vietnam (GVN) to work with. A creature of the French, the GVN had little credibility among the Vietnamese people. Dulles tried to console himself with the thought that because French colonialism was no longer a factor in Vietnamese affairs chances for creating a viable government in the South were better than they otherwise might have been. But even he was skeptical. At the beginning of the experiment he told General J. Lawton Collins, "Frankly, Collins, I think our chances of saving the situation there are not more than one in ten."[14]

Dulles understood one point very clearly. The fundamental problem confronting the United States and the GVN was political. Success or failure would depend on the acumen of Ngo Dinh Diem, who became prime minister of South Vietnam at Washington's insistence in the summer of 1953.

In some respects Diem appeared to be an excellent choice to create a viable state. He came from a powerful Vietnamese family. Moveover, he had not collaborated with the Japanese during World War II and had been a vehement critic of French colonialism in the postwar era. Most important from Washington's point of view, Diem was passionately anticommunist.

If in some ways Diem seemed well chosen for the task at hand, he nevertheless suffered from a number of inadequacies. First, he was a devout Catholic in a country where Catholics were a distinct minority. Even more important, though he often spoke eloquently of the revolution he intended to bring about, Diem was in fact a cross between a Trappist monk and an Oriental mandarin, an absolutist who expected to rule in the traditional way. An introvert cut off from his people and hopelessly inflexible, he lacked the personal and political skills required to succeed in a country already caught up on a tidal wave of revolutionary change.

In 1955, after holding fraudulent elections in which he claimed to have received 98.2 percent of the vote for prime minister (according to the tally he received 200,000 more votes in Saigon than the city had registered voters), Diem announced that there would be no nationwide national elections as called for under the Geneva Accords. In what was a clear violation of its own commitment, the Eisenhower administration sanctioned Diem's decision, since it was clear that if elections were held Ho Chi Minh would win control of the country.

Between 1955 and 1961 the United States sent more than $1 billion in foreign aid to Diem. Most of it went to train and equip the 150,000-person Army of Vietnam (ARVN) and a civil guard. Nonmilitary aid was used to balance South Vietnam's burgeoning trade deficit and to fund reconstruction projects, school construction, and the training of government functionaries.

The aid programs contributed to the impression during the later 1950s that Washington was succeeding in its effort in South Vietnam. The people in the cities were well dressed and appeared prosperous. But the prosperity did not reach beyond the cities. The villages, where 90 percent of the people lived, did not share in the largess. Moreover, those who material existence had been improved as a result of American aid were dependent on the continued flow of dollars to maintain that new higher living standard. Virtually none of the money pouring into Vietnam was invested in the country's economic infrastructure. During this period the South Vietnamese economy grew hardly at all.

The Eisenhower administration based its hopes for South Vietnam on the ability of the Diem regime to implement a wide variety of economic and political reforms designed to create popular support for the government. But Diem was not interested in reform. Instead, he tried to rule by force. He muzzled the press and quickly transformed the Vietnamese legislature into his creature. Those who would not conform were killed or imprisoned. Early in January 1956, Diem promulgated Presidential Ordinance Number 6, which stated that "all persons considered dangerous to national defense or collective security . . . may be sent to concentration camps by decision of the President of the Republic."[15] Within two years Diem had placed at least forty thousand persons in concentration camps.

By 1957 Diem's repressive measures had reduced the number of former Viet Minh political cadres remaining in South Vietnam by about 75 percent, to a total of some twenty-five hundred. Although discouraged from doing so by the communist leadership in North Vietnam, which was unprepared for another war, these southern cadres together with old Viet Minh military personnel organized to fight back. In so doing they quickly learned that Diem's repressive measures had alienated a large proportion of the peasantry and that he had, in effect, laid the foundation for a revolution in the South.

The Viet Minh was not the only group that by 1957 was in open rebellion against Diem. Others included the noncommunist National Salvation Movement and the Dai Viet. Communist and noncommunist opponents of the regime had one thing in common. They had no future in a country controlled by Diem. The coalition these groups formed came to be known as the National Liberation Front (NLF).

By late 1958 South Vietnam was in the throes of a full-scale guerrilla war. And by that time Ho Chi Minh was prepared to assume the leadership in this struggle. In the autumn of 1959, following the monsoon rains, the first trickle of North Vietnamese fighters began infiltrating South Vietnam, swelling the ranks of the southern rebels, whom Diem and later the Americans called the Viet Cong. Though at the time some observers believed the NLF and the Viet Cong were independent of Hanoi, it is now clear that they were at least from this time forward agencies of the North in a struggle to achieve the national unification that should have come after Geneva.

Diem responded to the stepped-up guerrilla campaign with greater repression in the cities and increased military action to eliminate the NLF and the Viet Cong from the villages. The government's actions, including the ill-conceived "agroville" program, which alienated Vietnam's peasants by removing them from the land of their ancestors, only made matters worse. By the end of 1960, Diem's government was in deep trouble. It had lost the political battle in the countryside, where the NLF had gained wide support. Moreover, its control of Vietnam's cities was clearly slipping. A crisis was developing in South Vietnam. Nation building was not working.

A *Reader's Digest* article published in 1956 described Diem as "the Biggest Little Man in Asia."[16] The little man was now in big trouble. It would be up to the incoming Kennedy administration to make some vital decisions.

## ENDNOTES

1. Eric Sevareid, quoted in Richard A. Aliano, *American Defense Policy from Eisenhower to Kennedy* (Athens, Ohio: Ohio University Press, 1975), pp. 49–50.

2. Dwight Eisenhower, television address, November 7, 1957, *Public Papers of the Presidents: Dwight David Eisenhower, 1957* (Washington, D.C., 1958), pp. 789–90.

3. Nikita Khrushchev, quoted in Emmet John Hughes, *Ordeal of Power: A Political Memoir of the Eisenhower Years* (New York: Atheneum, 1963), pp. 290–92.

4. Unnamed U.S. senator, quoted in ibid.

5. Soviet Foreign Ministry spokesperson, quoted in C. Bernard Noble, *Christian Herter* (New York: Cooper Square, 1970), pp. 77–102.

6. State Department statement, quoted in ibid., p. 82.

7. Khrushchev, quoted in Hughes, *Ordeal of Power*, p. 305.

8. Fidel Castro, quoted in Tad Szulc, *Fidel: A Critical Portrait* (New York: William Morrow, 1986), p. 345.

9. Castro, quoted in ibid., pp. 488–90; Castro, quoted in Peter G. Bourne, *Fidel* (New York: Dodd, Mead, 1986), p. 180.

10. Castro, quoted in Szulc, *Fidel*, pp. 488–90.

11. John Foster Dulles, quoted in Richard J. Barnet, *Intervention and Revolution: America's Confrontation with Insurgent Movements around the World* (New York: Meridian Books, 1968), pp. 236–37.

12. Lawrence Devlin, quoted in Jonathan Kwitny, *Endless Enemies: The Making of an Unfriendly World* (New York: Penguin Books, 1986), p. 59.

13. Robert Johnson and C. Douglas Dillon, quoted in ibid., p. 62.

14. John Foster Dulles, quoted in Barnet, *Intervention and Revolution,* p. 196.

15. Ngo Dinh Diem, Presidential Ordinance Number 6, quoted in ibid., p. 202.

16. O. K. Armstrong, "The Biggest Little Man in Asia," *Reader's Digest,* February 1956, pp. 144–53.

The danger that a superpower confrontation over Berlin might result in all-out nuclear war was clear to all.

# 30

# A NEW GENERATION, 1961–1963

At age forty-three, John Fitzgerald Kennedy, the youngest man ever to be elected president, was a tonic for Americans. The country was more prosperous than at any time in its history. Yet if the people commanded wealth, they seemed to lack purpose. Sensing that, Kennedy tried to galvanize the national spirit. Youthful, charismatic, and intellectually quick if not deep, he promised to "get the country moving again." At home that meant attending to problems of poverty and racism while generating new growth for an economy that had, like the country, grown sluggish. In the foreign field it meant seizing the initiative in the cold war. In his brilliantly conceived inaugural address, Kennedy said:

> Let the word go forth from this time and place, to friend and foe alike, that the torch has been passed to a new generation of Americans—born in this century, tempered by war, disciplined by a hard and bitter peace. . . .
> Let every nation know, whether it wishes us well or ill, that we shall pay any price, bear any burden, meet any hardship, support any friend, oppose any foe to assure the survival and the success of liberty.[1]

Though in some ways more enlightened than his predecessors,—he understood, for example, that revolutionary movements in developing nations had their own indigenous causes and that neutralism was not necessarily

595

a way station on the road to communism—Kennedy remained a captive of cold war assumptions. He believed that a Soviet-led communist conspiracy was bent on world domination. He was also satisfied that in the struggle between good and evil, evil seemed to be winning. Thus, sounding for all the world like the ghost of Joe McCarthy, Kennedy once warned that the Soviet Union and China were on the verge of conquering the entire Eurasian landmass. Only the United States stood between them and the onset of a new dark age. "We are the captains at the gate," he warned. "If we fail, all fail."[2]

If Kennedy's foreign policy views were rooted in the anticommunism of the past, it was anticommunism with a difference. The president was convinced that the Third World was the field on which the struggle with the Soviets would be played out and that the battle would be fought on many planes and in a variety of ways. Because he believed that communism thrived on ignorance and poverty, Kennedy created the Peace Corps. The young, enthusiastic, and idealistic volunteers who joined in this aspect of the Kennedy crusade were to bring technological advancement, economic and educational opportunity, and a message of friendship and peace to the "have not" nations of the world. Because there were places where idealistic young volunteers could not go, Kennedy also created the Green Berets or Special Forces to conduct counterinsurgency warfare against militant revolutionaries. Economic aid programs had an important place in Kennedy's scheme of things as well. The Alliance for Progress, a grandiose but ill-fated plan to create an international partnership for the purpose of stimulating economic growth throughout Latin America, is a prime example of how Kennedy hoped American economic power would be put to use in the anticommunist struggle.

Kennedy wanted his administration to be made up of "the best and the brightest" of the generation, a "ministry of all the talents." That befitted a president who viewed himself as besieged by a powerful and relentless foe. Nor did it matter which political party his advisers came from. He wanted the best, he told Clark Clifford, the head of his transition team. And so Douglas Dillon, who had made a sizable contribution to the 1960 Nixon campaign, took over the Treasury Department. Another at least nominal Republican, Robert McNamara, the president of the Ford Motor Company, moved into the Pentagon. And a political outsider, McGeorge Bundy, former dean of the faculty of arts and sciences at Harvard University, became Kennedy's special assistant for national security affairs.

Kennedy's most controversial cabinet appointee was his brother Robert, who took over as attorney general. The press was all over the young president for that decision. But John Kennedy greeted the criticism with winning humor. When one reporter observed that "Bobby" had no courtroom experience, the president quipped, "I can't see that it's wrong to give him a little legal experience before he goes out to practice law."[3]

Kennedy's choice of Dean Rusk to run the State Department was not in keeping with his other top-level appointments. The soft-spoken, former undersecretary and assistant secretary of state who later headed the Rockefeller Foundation was the exception in an inner circle dominated by assertive, confident, some would say arrogant men. But it was precisely because Rusk was less an advocate than an adviser that the president selected him for the job. Kennedy intended to make his own foreign policy. For that reason he wanted a capable but low-profile figure at State. The loyal Rusk was ideal for the role.

## THE BAY OF PIGS FIASCO

The final break in relations between Castro's Cuba and the United States came in January 1961, just days before Kennedy took the oath of office. But planning for Castro's demise had begun a full year before. The man behind the project was the deputy director of the CIA, Richard Bissell. Ivy League–educated with a Ph.D. in economics from Yale, Bissell was energetic, intelligent, and persuasive. He was also obsessive on the subject of ousting Castro.

During the latter part of the Eisenhower administration, Bissell masterminded the first in a series of assassination plots against Castro. Reasoning that the Mafia, which had lost its gambling and prostitution interests in Cuba as a result of the revolution, had an incentive to eliminate the Cuban leader, he authorized a "hit." Acting for the CIA, a former FBI agent, Robert Mahew, offered the mobster Johnny Roselli, $150,000 to murder Castro. Roselli sent Mahew to Mafia chieftains Salvatore Giancana and Santos Trafficante, formerly a major crime figure in Havana. But not even the Mafia could get to Castro. Later, the Cuban dictator told Senator George McGovern that he had survived twenty CIA-supported attempts on his life. But Castro exaggerated. A special Senate subcommittee investigating America's covert activities in 1975 documented only eight.

Bissell's other scheme for eliminating Castro, a plan approved by Eisenhower, was modeled on the CIA's Guatemalan experience. The agency would establish a government in exile made up of Cuban expatriates. At the same time the Cuban people would be subjected to a propaganda barrage designed to undermine their support for Castro. Finally, a small paramilitary force, trained and equipped by the CIA, would make a landing on Cuban soil. When it had secured a beachhead, the government in exile would come ashore and proclaim a counterrevolution that the CIA believed, would spark a popular uprising against Castro. The success of this uprising was considered central to the project. In January 1961, plans for the invasion were nearing completion. Some fourteen hundred Cuban exiles who had been trained on an isolated coffee plantation in Guatemala were waiting expectantly for orders to move out.

Many inside the administration expressed serious doubts either about the workability of the scheme or the effect it would have on world opinion. Undersecretary of State Chester Bowles, White House aide Arthur Schlesinger, Jr., Senator J. William Fulbright, and Dean Acheson all raised objections.

For Acheson it was a matter of simple mathematics. One did not need the services of a high-priced accounting firm, he warned the president, "to discover that fifteen hundred Cubans weren't as good as [Castro's army of] twenty-five thousand Cubans." But Kennedy, who admitted to having doubts about the operation, was as obsessive on the subject of Fidel Castro as Bissell himself. He therefore preferred to listen to those such as CIA Director Allen Dulles, who assured him "that the prospects for this plan are even better than our prospects were in Guatemala."[4]

On April 14, 1961, the Cuban brigade put to sea from a Nicaraguan port bound for an obscure piece of Cuban beach known as the Bay of Pigs. On the following day, two days before the landing, CIA-trained Cuban exiles flying World War II–vintage B-26 bombers that sported Cuban markings, bombed military airstrips in Cuba in an attempt to destroy Castro's tiny air force on the ground. The air attack failed. Worse, as a result of these attacks the public learned even before the Cuban brigade hit the beaches that the administration was directly involved in the attempt to overthrow Castro.

The CIA's plan had been to claim that defecting Cuban Air Force pilots attacked their own airfields before seeking asylum elsewhere. To support this story, one of the CIA planes flew to Florida, where the pilot told his story, asked for asylum, and was whisked away by the Immigration Service before he could be identified. Unhappily, an alert newsman noticed that the plane he flew had a metal nose, while Castro's B-26s had plexiglass noses. The CIA's cover was blown, and American involvement in the operation was clear. Fearing a domestic as well as an international backlash, President Kennedy then refused to provide air support for the invaders. They would have to make do with the planes already provided by the CIA.

Fidel Castro was well prepared to meet the invaders. His intelligence service, operating in Miami's "Little Havana," had tracked the developing CIA operation from its beginnings. The April 15 bombing attack made it clear that a landing was imminent. When Brigade 2506 hit the beach the Cuban army of 20,000 and a force of 200,000 militia were prepared for combat.

Castro's tiny air force controlled the sky over the beach and sank or drove away the eight ships carrying supplies, ammunition, and reinforcements. Within twenty-four hours the invaders were surrounded by a force of 20,000 armed with tanks and artillery. Defeat came quickly. On April 19, 1,180 members of the invasion force surrendered. More than 100 had been killed or wounded, and a few disappeared into the countryside.

Some critics argued that the debacle at the Bay of Pigs could have been avoided had Kennedy allowed the air force to provide air cover for the invaders. But the real flaw in the operation had to do with certain political judgments made by the CIA. Bissell and his colleagues predicted that the Cuban people would rise in support of the counterrevolution. Although there was a growing opposition to Castro, at the time of the invasion he had no fear of the people. On the contrary, he was confident enough of his support to put weapons in the hands of 200,000 militia. Put simply, the CIA

The Bay of Pigs fiasco was a humiliation for John Kennedy. In fact Fidel Castro did trade his prisoners, but not for dozers. He asked for and received medical supplies and other such essentials in exchange.

and the president made a very bad guess on a fundamental point—and paid for it.

## CRISIS IN THE CONGO

The continuing crisis in the Congo occupied John Kennedy's attention from the moment he first sat down behind the desk in the Oval Office. At the time President Joseph Kasavubu, the head of the central government, was holding Patrice Lumumba prisoner; Moise Tshombe continued to hold Katanga Province against the central government; Antoine Gizenga, a friend and supporter of Lumumba, headed another government in Stanleyville that had been recognized by the Soviet Union as well as a number of Afro-Asian nations; and a United Nations peacekeeping force was in the Congo, sent there in 1960 to protect the lives and property of Belgians and other Westerners.

Kasavubu tried to untangle at least part of this political mess by cutting a deal with Lumumba, offering him a subordinate role in his government. But Lumumba, who was after all the legitimate premier and the most popular political figure in the Congo, rejected the offer. Kasavubu then decided to be rid of his rival. He and Sese Seko Mobutu had Lumumba flown to Katanga Province and into the hands of his most bitter enemy, Moise Tshombe, who had him murdered. Lumumba's assassination solved little as far as Kasavubu, Mobutu, or the United States (which recall had earlier authorized his murder) were concerned. They still had Tshombe and Gizenga to deal with.

Washington's strategy, developed by Undersecretary of State George Ball, was to end the Katanga secession and eliminate Gizenga as a power in the Congo while strengthening the central government of Kasavubu and Mobutu. Ball based his policy on the assumption that the Congo was a region of vast strategic importance, the "keystone of central Africa." He was convinced that if the Katanga secession succeeded, other areas would break away, creating chaos throughout the continent and opening the door to communist infiltration. Ball even seems to have believed that in the event the central government failed to restore its control over Katanga, Gizenga, as the Soviet's "chosen agent," would make a "bid to take over the central government in the name of Congolese unity." If that happened, Ball believed Moscow would have established "a base in the heart of Africa," leaving the United States no choice but "to drive them out."[5] As Ball saw things, then, it was essential to restore stability in the Congo to avoid a dangerous confrontation with Moscow.

In the summer of 1961 President Kasavubu, in cooperation with the Kennedy administration, the United Nations, and a number of Afro-Asian states, called the Congolese Parliament into session for the purpose of electing a new premier to replace Lumumba. When Parliament met, it became apparent that Gizenga, who controlled a plurality of the members, might be elected. Kasavubu tried to forestall this possibility by nominating a candidate of "national reconciliation," Cyrille Adoula, who had long been on the CIA's payroll.

Adoula's election victory was evidently very much in doubt down to the moment of the balloting. Rumor has it that even as the voting was proceeding CIA operatives were circulating among the members of Parliament distributing bribes. This claim may in fact be true, since one declassified CIA memorandum relating to the Adoula's election contains this remark: "The U.N. and the United States in closely coordinated activities played essential roles in this significant success over Gizenga."[6]

The disappointed Gizenga,, perhaps recalling Lumumba's fate, agreed to serve as vice-premier in the new Congolese government. But not long after this he denounced the United States as the latest in a series of Western nations to despoil the Congo and created a new anti-Western political organization. Colonel Mobutu responded by accusing Gizenga of antigovernment activities and placing him under house arrest. Convinced that Gizenga hadn't much of a future, and perhaps hoping to avoid the chaos that might follow yet another political murder, UN soldiers spirited Gizenga out of Mobutu's clutches and placed him under guard on an island in the Congo River, where he was physically safe and politically irrelevant.

Gizenga's elimination left only Moise Tshombe, leader of the Katanga secessionists, to be dealt with. Tshombe, described by George Ball as "cynical," "ambitious," and "a bold and skillful operator," had a large following in the United States, especially among political conservatives, who viewed him as the valiant defender of free enterprise struggling against the radicals (Kasavubu and Mobutu) who controlled the central government.[7] The Committee for Aid to the Katanga Freedom Fighters, organized in 1961, kept up a drumbeat of criticism, claiming that Kennedy policy was leading to a communist-dominated Congo. Major political figures of both parties, including Richard Nixon and Senator Richard Russell of Georgia, joined in the criticism.

Administration leaders were unwilling to move against Tshombe directly. A troop commitment would have infuriated domestic conservatives. Moreover, policy makers did not believe they could send troops into the Congo without running the risk that the Soviets would do the same. What Washington could and did do was to convince the United Nations to use the peacekeeping force already in the Congo to achieve its ends. The UN force, which was financed and given substantial logistical support by Washington, then went after Tshombe, something it had refused to do when Lumumba made the same request earlier. In 1963, Tshombe was defeated and rich Katanga Province was returned to the Congo.

The end of Gizenga's power and the Katanga secessionist movement did not bring peace to the Congo. The worst of the bloodletting was in fact ahead. For five years, between 1964 and 1969, the Simbas, followers of Lumumba and Gizenga, ran amok, systematically burning, killing, and pillaging across a huge area of the Congo. In a terrorist campaign reminiscent in some ways of that later undertaken in Cambodia by the Khmer Rouge, they murdered anyone with even a smattering of Western education or culture. No one knows how many thousands died.

## NEUTRALIZING LAOS

During the early weeks of his administration, while George Ball was unraveling the mysteries of Congo politics, President Kennedy spent much of his time puzzling over the Laotian situation, where a civil war was under way between the central government in Vientiane and the communist Pathet Lao, who were being aided by Moscow and North Vietnam. The Laotian crisis was the result of earlier meddling in the affairs of that tiny country by John Foster Dulles. The Geneva Accords of 1954 called for a neutral Laos. In keeping with the terms of the convention, Prince Souvanna Phouma, the head of the government in Vientiane at the time, negotiated an agreement with his half-brother Souphanouvong, head of the communist Pathet Lao. Under the terms of this agreement, Laos was to be governed by a coalition government.

Dulles, who viewed any coalition with communists as unacceptable, had the CIA replace Souphanouvong, who was imprisoned, with Phoui Sananikone. But Phoui's performance evidently failed to satisfy Washington, since in less than eighteen months the CIA created a Laotian Committee for the Defense of the National Interest and brought in a right-wing military officer, one Phoumi Nosovan, to run it. Phoumi then replaced Phoui, which as George Ball later quipped, "could have been either a significant event or a typographical error."[8]

The next development in what George Ball thought was beginning to resemble the story line from a Kung Fu movie was Souphanouvong's escape from jail. Fleeing to the north, he resumed control of the Pathet Lao, and the civil war began once again. Encouraged by Washington, Phoumi, the recipient of substantial military aid, then marched on Vientiane, forcing Prince Souvanna to flee north, where he joined his half-brother in the war against Phoumi. Thus, as the journalist Bernard Fall remarked, Washington succeeded in throwing "into Communism's arms a great many people who essentially were *not* Communists . . . but who, by deliberate action on our side, were left with no alternative."[9]

Not only did the heavy-handed activities of Phoumi and the CIA drive the Laotian neutralists to form a coalition with the Pathet Lao, American involvement prompted Moscow and Hanoi to provide aid to the other side. By the beginning of 1961, in spite of $300 million in American aid (most of which went into the pockets of corrupt political and military leaders) the Pathet Lao clearly had the initiative in the struggle for control of the country.

John Kennedy had at least three reasons for believing that keeping Laos out of communist hands was a vital interest of his administration. First, he accepted as valid a CIA analysis which argued that other Southeast Asian governments "tended to regard the Laotian crisis as a symbolic test of strength between the two major powers of the West and the Communist bloc."[10] A defeat in Laos, therefore, could lead to the collapse of American influence throughout the region. Kennedy was also concerned by the political fallout that would result from "losing" Laos. The Republicans would make mincemeat out of him. Finally, Laos was important militarily because the North Vietnamese used the Ho Chi Minh trail, much of which ran through that country, to funnel men and supplies to Viet Cong fighters then trying to overthrow the South Vietnamese government of Ngo Dinh Diem.

All of these considerations notwithstanding, Kennedy was by no means anxious to intervene militarily in Laos. In the first place, Phoumi's Royal Laotian Army was a joke. John Kenneth Galbraith, Kennedy's ambassador to India, warned that as a "military ally the entire Laos nation is clearly inferior to a battalion of conscientious objectors from World War I."[11]

Moreover after the Bay of Pigs debacle he was chary about risking another setback.

The Joint Chiefs of Staff seemed ready, even anxious, to intervene. But when asked how they would introduce and supply an army in landlocked Laos, they were short on answers. At the same time, they made it abundantly clear that if Kennedy was considering intervention they would support no halfway measures. They even insisted on the right to use nuclear weapons and to attack China proper if Beijing sent troops into the fray.

These depressing considerations convinced Kennedy that the wisest course was to seek a neutralized Laos. The problem was in getting the Soviets, who were supplying the Pathet Lao, to accept that outcome. Kennedy first made a series of military moves intended to let Moscow know that he would if necessary intervene in Laos. At the same time, Secretary of State Rusk issued a statement indicating that President Truman's 1947 commitment to defend freedom had "no geographical barriers." He also wrenched troop commitments from the Philippines, Thailand, and Pakistan and extracted from the reluctant members of SEATO a resolution supporting any action in Laos that Washington might take.[12]

On May 3, by which time it appeared that the United States might very well intervene, Prince Norodom Sihanouk of Cambodia arranged a cease-fire among the rival Laotian factions. Then all sides accepted a British invitation to a conference at Geneva, which in July 1962 produced an agreement for the creation of a coalition government headed by Prince Souvanna Phouma.

The creation of a neutralist government in Vientiane by no means ended the American involvement in Laos. On the contrary, while the diplomats worked in Geneva to create a new Laotian government, General Edward Lansdale was busy organizing a counterinsurgency force under CIA control in Laos. Before Lansdale and the CIA were through they had created a "clandestine army" of thirty thousand that had as its objective the closing of the Ho Chi Minh trail. Some of the bloodiest fighting of the Vietnam war took place in "neutral" Laos. Before the struggle was over, nearly a quarter of a million Meo people had lost their lives.

## KENNEDY, KHRUSHCHEV, AND BERLIN

Even before Kennedy took the oath of office, a storm was brewing up in East-West relations. And once again the focal point of the crisis was Berlin, that "splinter" stuck in that heart of Europe, that "bone" in Nikita Khrushchev's throat. On January 6, 1961, in a speech before the Moscow Communist party, Khrushchev reiterated his commitment to peaceful co-existence with the West but made it clear that he was through waiting; the Berlin question would soon have to be resolved. In a note to the West German government, he stated that the Soviet Union could no longer tolerate the existing situation and indicated that he wanted to negotiate a German settlement in which

When John Kennedy and Nikita Khrushchev met in Vienna they smiled for the cameras. But their meetings were tense, and the threat of war over Berlin hung in the air.

Berlin would become a free city. If the West refused to negotiate, he threatened to sign a separate treaty with East Germany ending all occupation rights. Khrushchev also warned that if, following a settlement between Moscow and the East Germans, the Western nations tried to force their way into Berlin, the Red Army would come to East Germany's aid.

Khrushchev once described Berlin as "the testicles of the West. Every time I give them a yank, they holler."[13] But in 1961 the Soviet leader probably had more on his mind than simply producing Western discomfort. A neutralized Germany would strengthen his hand domestically in the battle against the Stalinists and establish the groundwork for the cuts in military spending that were essential if anything was to be done to improve the Soviet Union's domestic economic situation.

The Berlin pot, then, was already simmering when Kennedy and Khrushchev met in Vienna in June 1961. There Khrushchev stated his position bluntly. Europe had gone too long without a final peace treaty. If the Western powers were not prepared to negotiate an agreement along lines he had described, he would sign a separate treaty with Walter Ulbricht's East German government that would have the effect of nullifying all Western rights in Berlin. And if the NATO powers violated East German territory in the attempt to assert their claim to occupy West Berlin, the Soviet Union would defend its ally. It would mean war.

Kennedy, equally blunt, made it clear that he was not prepared to play the Neville Chamberlain of the 1960s. The United States and its allies were in Berlin by right of conquest, and they intended to stay. To give in, he pointed out, would surely lead to the fragmentation of the Western alliance and America's isolation. Just as Moscow would not agree to be separated from its Eastern European allies, so the United States would not consider such a step on its part.

On the second day of the conference, just before the two leaders parted, Khrushchev said, "I want peace . . . but if you want war, that is your problem." He also threatened once again to sign a separate treaty with East Germany if a general agreement was not arrived at prior to December. That decision, he said, was "irrevocable." Kennedy replied that "it is you and not I who wants to force a change." He warned Khrushchev that if he did in fact provoke a crisis, "it will be a cold winter."[14]

Kennedy was shaken by Khrushchev's seeming willingness to risk nuclear war over Berlin. One reporter along on the plane as the president and his entourage flew from Vienna to London described the entire party as "a chastened group." They had, he wrote, "come face-to-face with the enemy, a cunning, shrewd, clever, earthy, incisive . . . enemy . . . unlike anything anybody's ever seen." Kennedy, he thought, "looked kind of tired and a bit used up when he went into London."[15]

Kennedy was grimly determined to hang on to Berlin. At the same time, and more keenly than ever, he felt trapped in a paradox brought on by the nuclear revolution. Moscow seemed to be driving toward a war that would be suicidal. And yet Kennedy believed he would have to risk "holocaust" to avoid "humiliation" and the potential collapse of NATO. Khrushchev was tough. He would try to take advantage of any indication that the United States was not prepared to fight. As Kennedy later remarked, the unhappy reality was that "if Khrushchev wants to rub my nose in the dirt, . . . it's all over." Yet how was he to convince the Soviet leader that he meant what he said? The president later answered that question for himself. "That son-of-a-bitch won't pay any attention to words. . . . He has to see you move."[16]

Kennedy reacted to Khrushchev's challenge by emphasizing the seriousness of the crisis and advocating extraordinary military preparations while at the same time holding out the possibility of a negotiated settlement. He told White House aide Kenneth O'Donnell: "Before I back Khrushchev against the wall, the freedom of all Western Europe will have to be at stake."[17]

On July 25, in a major television address, Kennedy said, "West Berlin has now become the great testing place of Western courage and will, a focal point where our solemn commitments . . . and Soviet ambition now meet in basic confrontation." He asked that Congress approve an extra $3.25 billion for defense, authorize him to call up the army reserves as well as certain National Guard units, and establish fallout shelters to protect the civilian population in the event of nuclear war. In the same speech he announced his willingness to meet the Soviets to settle differences over Berlin peacefully.[18]

As East-West tensions mounted, the flow of refugees crossing from East Germany into West Berlin grew to a flood. In July alone some thirty thousand persons used that route to the West. On a single day, August 12, four thousand took flight. This literal hemorrhage of people led the Soviets to approve an East German request to close the border. Early on the morning of August 13, barbed wire barricades went up. Four days later the East

The Berlin crisis set off a fallout shelter craze. Here mom, dad, and daughter wait in the Kidde Kokoon for the all-clear to sound on the radio.

German authorities began construction of a concrete wall that would separate East and West Berlin.

The United States and Western Europe reacted to the construction of the Berlin wall with public outrage and diplomatic protest, but nothing more. President Kennedy was in fact relieved. "Why should Khrushchev put up a wall if he really intended to seize West Berlin?" he asked. "This is his way out of his predicament. . . . A wall is a hell of a lot better than a war."[19]

Critics charged the administration with weakness for not immediately knocking down the wall. But administration leaders judged correctly that had they done so Khrushchev would have had no choice but to fight. Besides, the wall challenged none of the West's basic interests. Allied rights in West Berlin remained intact, and access to the city was not impeded.

To reassure the West Germans that the United States would honor its commitments, Kennedy sent Vice-President Lyndon Johnson to Berlin, where he gave a stirring speech pledging "our lives, our fortunes, our sacred honor" to the defense of West Berlin. Kennedy also ordered an armored column to drive the Autobahn from West Germany to Berlin as an assertion of the West's right of access. Finally, he called the hero of the Berlin airlift, General Lucius Clay, out of retirement and sent him to Berlin for a prolonged stay.

By authorizing the wall's construction, Khrushchev admitted he could not force the West to accept his terms for a German settlement. At the same time he did achieve certain minimum objectives. He ended the flow of refugees to the West, stabilized the weak East German regime, reduced Berlin's effectiveness as a center of Western espionage activities, and reasserted his control over Eastern Europe. He also laid the foundation for an end to the diplomatic crisis. Two months after construction of the wall began, the Soviet foreign minister, Andrei Gromyko, informed the State Department that Moscow would drop its December deadline for a German settlement providing Washington was ready to negotiate. And so the crisis ended in prolonged, unproductive talks.

## THE NUCLEAR CONUNDRUM

At the very beginning of his administration Kennedy undertook to resolve a problem that had troubled him since the mid-1950s—the need to find an alternative to Eisenhower's policy of massive retaliation. The president did not believe that the Soviets wanted a nuclear war any more than he did. He was convinced, therefore, that they would never attack the United States directly but would instead nibble away at Western strength using "Sputnik diplomacy, limited brushfire wars, indirect nonovert aggression, intimidation, subversion, [and] internal revolution" to advance their interests. Yet so long as the United States failed to develop effective conventional means of meeting limited challenges, there could be no appropriate response, for while "each Soviet move" would "weaken the West," none would "seem sufficiently significant by itself to justify our initiating a nuclear war which might destroy us." Massive retaliation, Kennedy declared in one speech given while he was still in the Senate, had not worked in the past and would not work in the future. "We have been driving ourselves into a corner," he exclaimed, "where the only choice is all or nothing at all, world devastation or submission."[20]

The 1961 Berlin crisis highlighted another aspect of the awesome problem of national security in the nuclear age that proved deeply troubling to Kennedy. Though neither side wanted to fight a nuclear war, there was always the possibility that they might stumble into a confrontation. In the event that a crisis should "go critical," the massive retaliation doctrine committed the United States to an all-out first-use strategy that gave the Soviets an incentive to use their nuclear weapons early in a crisis, too. It was as though Moscow and Washington had entered into a mutual suicide pact. J. Robert Oppenheimer was right. The superpowers were like two scorpions in a bottle.

Just how bad the situation actually was became clear when the Kennedy team gained access to the Pentagon's planning documents. In the event of a war with the East bloc, the Joint Strategic Capabilities Plan, which had been approved by President Dwight Eisenhower, called for an all-out nuclear attack on the Soviet Union, China, and Eastern Europe. Daniel Ellsberg, who reviewed the plan in 1961, noted that if it had been implemented "we would have hit every city in the Soviet Union and China in addition to all military targets." The Joint Chiefs estimated prompt fatalities from the initial strikes at 360–425 million people.[21] This figure did not include persons who would die later as a result of overexposure to radiation. In Hiroshima and Nagasaki, the only examples available, prompt fatalities accounted for less than 50 percent of the total number of deaths from nuclear attack.

Kennedy did not want to play Robert Oppenheimer's game of "two scorpions in a bottle." He hoped to get out of the bottle by developing a new, more flexible military strategy. He wanted conventional forces capable of meeting Soviet challenges in the Third World and for the defense of Europe so that in the event of war he could possibly avoid an all-out nuclear exchange. He also wanted a nuclear strategy that provided him with options short of that exchange.

The man Kennedy chose to develop the new strategy that came to be known as "flexible response" was Secretary of Defense Robert McNamara, the forty-four year-old former president of the Ford Motor Company. Demanding and "utterly merciless in criticism of error or in achieving a goal," McNamara seemed the archetypal corporate manager. He was born "fully programmed when somebody flipped a switch at the Harvard Business School," remarked one particularly bitter Pentagon colonel.[22] No secretary of defense, either before or since, has so shaken the American military establishment. Yet even this extraordinary man found it impossible to arrive at a solution to the problem Kennedy had set before him.

## A CONVENTIONAL DEFENSE FOR EUROPE?

Until 1961 it had been taken for granted that the Warsaw Pact countries enjoyed such conventional military superiority that a nonnuclear defense of the West was impossible. But in the McNamara years, Defense Department analysts arrived at an entirely different conclusion. White House aide Theodore Sorensen later wrote that the administration:

> refused to concede that the Warsaw Pact nations ... were automatically more powerful in conventional strength than the members of NATO, who had a hundred million more people, twice as large an economy, one-half million more men in uniform, and the capability of placing in time more combat forces on the ground in Central Europe and more tactical bombers in the air.[23]

If McNamara and Kennedy thought a conventional defense of Europe was feasible, Western European leaders were cool to the idea. In their view NATO existed not to fight a war but to deter one by making it clear to Moscow that an invasion would be quite literally suicidal. A serious conventional buildup, they feared, would lower the threshold for a major European war by indicating to the Soviets that the West was prepared to fight with conventional arms only.

To an administration bent on finding some method of surviving the next war, this Western European view seemed utterly insane. As McNamara insisted, "One cannot make a credible deterrent out of an incredible action."[24] Nevertheless, Western Europe's leaders preferred to stick with the nuclear deterrent rather than increase the possibility of another war that would probably turn nuclear anyway by admitting that they would even consider fighting a nonnuclear contest.

Ironically, the Kennedy administration's desire to develop a conventional capability for the defense of Europe shook the NATO Allies' confidence in America's commitment to Europe. Thus French President Charles de Gaulle concluded that Washington's vulnerability to a Soviet nuclear strike made it unlikely that the United States would in fact come to the aid of its allies in the event they were attacked.

De Gaulle contended that no one, not even an American president, could know what he would do until the time came for decision. But in his judgment, America would use nuclear weapons "only when its own territory was actually threatened." De Gaulle had a point. Why, after all, was the administration so anxious to find a conventional method of defending Europe? Clearly it was because Moscow's nuclear retaliatory capability made massive retaliation an extraordinarily unappealing option. European security, de Gaulle insisted, could only be ensured by European countries, "not without the United States but not exclusively through the United States" either.[25]

McNamara won the battle inside NATO but lost the war. The NATO allies finally agreed to substantial increases in conventional military strength. But that paper commitment never came to fruition. To this day NATO continues to depend on its nuclear striking power to deter an attack.


## THE NO CITIES DOCTRINE: ESCALATING THE ARMS RACE

Kennedy commented repeatedly during his less than three years in office on the dangers posed by nuclear weapons. Yet, paradoxically, his actions seemed to belie his words. Aware that the missile gap was a fiction, he nevertheless authorized a major increase in the size of America's strategic nuclear arsenal, thus escalating the arms race. Just how to explain this apparent contradiction has been a matter of some interest to scholars.

The economist Seymour Melman contends that Kennedy's commitment to expanded conventional as well as nuclear forces was driven by economic considerations and that "having just concluded that an infusion of capital funds was needed in order to raise American economic activity to a higher level, the White House decided that an outlay of capital for missiles, as well as other military forces was necessary."[26] Kennedy may indeed have viewed increased military spending as a stimulant for a sluggish economy. But his commitment to increased missile forces was strategy driven. Ironically, it was his desire for options short of "massive retaliation" that led the administration to authorize increases in the size of the nuclear arsenal.

In 1962 the Defense Department developed a strategy that, providing both sides played by the same rules, could limit the destruction from a nuclear exchange. In the event of a Soviet attack (first strike), this new approach was designed to provide the president with a range of options that together constituted a primitive ladder of escalation. In the initial stages of a war, while attempting to end the fighting through diplomacy, the president would respond to a Soviet strike by attacking not densely populated cities but missile-launching sites, air bases, and submarine pens inside the Soviet Union. If the war continued, he might next order attacks on air defense systems that were some distance from Soviet cities but along routes to be used by American bombers. If it still proved needful, he could then order attacks on air defenses near cities and go on to strike Soviet command and control facilities. Finally, if all else failed, he could use a large reserve force of strategic missiles in a full-scale attack on East bloc and Chinese cities.

The new strategy also called for certain defensive or "damage-limiting" features, including an elaborate civil defense program and a missile defense system to destroy in flight at least some of the attacking Soviet missiles. Because the new strategy focused first on military targets rather than large population centers, it was soon dubbed the "no cities doctrine."

To implement the new strategy, it was obvious that the United States would require a far larger inventory of strategic nuclear weapons than was needed to carry out the spasmodic attack called for under massive retaliation. For this reason a Defense Department study group recommended a Minuteman missile force of 2,000 missiles; 150 new RS-70 bombers, each armed with 18 cruise missiles; 370 Skybolt air-to-ground missiles to be launched from B-52 bombers; and as many as 47 missile-firing submarines, each armed with 16 missiles.

In June 1962, McNamara used a commencement address at the University of Michigan as the occasion for the public unveiling of the no cities doctrine. Reaction to his Ann Arbor speech came swiftly and was almost universally negative. In Western Europe the speech fed already established fears that Washington was having second thoughts about protecting the NATO Allies against a Soviet attack and thus further undermined America's claim to leadership of a united alliance.

The Soviets were critical for other reasons. *Pravda* denounced the doctrine as "monstrous" and pointed out that Washington appeared to have abandoned a deterrent strategy in favor of finding some method of making nuclear war feasible. At the same time, the Red Army's Marshal V. D. Sokolovskii made the cogent observation that there was no way to distinguish between McNamara's new doctrine and a plan to initiate a nuclear war by developing a first-strike capability. "A strategy which contemplates attaining victory through the destruction of the armed forces" of an adversary, he wrote, "cannot stem from the idea of a 'retaliatory' blow: it stems from preventive action and the achievement of surprise."[27]

The new strategy fared no better at home. Critics pointed out that the nuclear deterrent worked primarily because all sides accepted the premise that nuclear war would be suicidal. But the no cities doctrine signaled a shift away from deterrence. It seemed evident that Pentagon planners were thinking not in terms of deterring but of fighting and winning a nuclear war. Other critics, suspicious of administration purposes, agreed with Marshal

Sokolovskii. The new strategy made no sense unless the United States was planning a preemptive war. How else could one explain targeting Soviet air bases and missile installations? If the Soviets struck first, these facilities would be empty. The new strategy made sense only if the Pentagon was planning to attack such targets preemptively.

The criticism took McNamara by surprise. He had from the beginning been habituated to thinking in terms of deterrence and the importance of developing a retaliatory (second-strike) damage-limiting strategy. It had never entered his mind that the "no cities doctrine" could be viewed as a plan for striking the initial blow. One aide remarked in McNamara's defense that he "wasn't thinking for himself. He was listening to his Whiz Kids and accepting too much of what they said at face value." Even this loyalist was forced to admit, however, that "he should have known there could be no such thing as primary retaliation against military targets after an enemy attack. If you're going to shoot at missiles, you're talking about first strike."[28]

In January 1963, McNamara publicly abandoned the no cities doctrine in favor of another proposed answer to the nuclear puzzle. He now admitted that there could be no complete security against the danger of nuclear war and that a deterrent strategy which incorporated certain damage-limiting capabilities was the safest approach to avoiding such a catastrophe. Toward this end, he explained, the United States would maintain " a clear and convincing capability to inflict unacceptable damage on an attacker, even were that attacker to strike first."[29] This approach, which postulated the total devastation of both parties in a nuclear exchange, came to be known as mutually assured destruction.

MAD, a wonderfully descriptive acronym, was not a strategy at all but a recognition that there was in fact no way out of America's nuclear dilemma. Deterrence was fallible and might one day fail. But under the circumstances it appeared to be the only available option.

Although the no cities doctrine remained policy for only a brief time, the process of expanding the nuclear arsenal that began during its period of gestation could not be stopped. The ambitions of the military services, especially the air force, and the reluctance of the administration to provoke an open quarrel with the Joint Chiefs and Congress over questions of national security, assured the continued growth of the strategic missile force. Ironically, then, it was the administration's attempt to develop options short of an all-out nuclear war that triggered the expansion of an already more-than-adequate American missile force and further fueled the nuclear arms race.

## THE MISSILE CRISIS

Kennedy and McNamara were right to be concerned about the possibility that the nuclear deterrent might one day fail, bringing the world to the brink of nuclear holocaust. In fact, that day very nearly came in October 1962, as a result of a Soviet attempt to place nuclear-armed missiles in Cuba.

In the summer of 1962 Soviet ships carrying a wide variety of weapons began arriving in Cuban ports. Before the summer was over some twenty-two thousand Soviet military personnel had also arrived, ostensibly for training purposes. The appearance of surface-to-air (SAM) missiles together with other rumblings from intelligence sources inside Cuba led John McCone, who replaced Allen Dulles as head of the CIA, to suspect that the Soviets were placing offensive missiles on the island. But McCone's evidence was sketchy. Secretaries Rusk and McNamara, who studied the McCone allegations, agreed that the Soviets were helping Castro build a defensive capability. But they refused to credit his allegations about offensive weapons without supporting evidence. They were not alone. Most intelligence experts also thought McCone was mistaken.

Khrushchev himself had stated categorically that he had no intention of using Cuba as a military base. On September 6, 1962, he even assured the president that "nothing will be undertaken before the American Congressional elections that could complicate the international situation or aggravate the tension in the relations between our two countries."[30] Lacking evidence to the contrary, policy makers took Khrushchev at his word, especially since to that point Moscow had never deployed nuclear weapons outside Soviet borders.

If the administration doubted that the Soviets would risk placing missiles in Cuba, the Republicans thought otherwise and made Cuba the central issue in the 1962 congressional election campaign. New York's Senator Kenneth Keating, Homer Capehart of Indiana, and other Republican stalwarts blasted the administration for allowing the Soviets to provide the Cubans with weaponry. Keating was quite specific about what he believed was happening in Cuba. In a speech on the Senate floor he charged point blank and with what turned out to be embarrassing accuracy that intermediate-range missiles capable of hitting targets almost anywhere in the continental United States were being installed in Cuba.

Kennedy responded to these charges by challenging Keating to reveal his sources (the senator refused) and stating categorically what the American intelligence community had no evidence of Soviet missiles in Cuba. But he also repeatedly warned the Soviets that if missile bases were found, "the gravest issues would arise."[31]

One month after Kennedy made that last statement, on October 14, 1962, a U-2 spy plane photographed unmistakable signs of offensive missile installations under construction in Cuba. His promises notwithstanding, Khrushchev was attempting to place an initial force of seventy-two medium- and intermediate-range nuclear armed missiles in western Cuba. From this base, just as Kenneth Keating charged, these missiles could attack targets everywhere in the United States save the extreme Northwest.

Both policy makers at the time and scholars since have speculated on Khrushchev's motives for taking such an extraordinary gamble. The Soviet leader himself explained that: "At the request of the Cuban government we shipped arms there. . . . Our purpose was only the defense of

MRBM LAUNCH SITE 1
SAN CRISTOBAL, CUBA
23 OCTOBER 1962

MISSILE ERECTOR

CABLE

MISSILE SHELTER TENT

FUEL TANK TRAILERS

TRACKED PRIME MOVERS

OXIDIZER TANK TRAILERS

American reconnaissance planes uncovered indisputable evidence of missile construction in western Cuba in October 1962. The result was the most dangerous Soviet-American confrontation ever to take place.

Cuba." The arms, he wrote on another occasion, were intended "to prevent an attack on Cuba—to prevent rash acts."[32] At a 1989 gathering of surviving Soviet and American officials from the days of the missile crisis, the Soviet representatives continued to maintain that the defense of Cuba was their one and only consideration. Even so, it is difficult to dismiss the possibility that Moscow was also influenced by strategic considerations.

By 1962 the Soviets, who had never placed any emphasis on the development of a bomber force, had clearly fallen behind in the strategic missile race. America's vast superiority in bombers and missiles, combined with an administration program calling for even more nuclear weapons, may well have appeared to Soviet strategists as an attempt to develop the capability to launch a preemptive first-strike against the Soviet Union. If so, and considering the difficulties the Soviets were encountering in developing a reliable ICBM, placing available medium- and intermediate-range missiles in Cuba may have been seen as a vital stopgap measure, a method of strengthening the Soviet deterrent while work continued on long-range missiles.

On being informed that Soviet missiles were being deployed in Cuba, the president, aware that he had a multi-dimensional crisis on his hands, organized an ad hoc committee made up of top ranking policy makers, military officers, White House officials, and former Secretary of State Dean

Acheson to advise him on what course of action he should take. This group quickly became known among its members as the Executive Committee or the ExCom.

Members of the ExCom identified three possible methods of handling the situation. The administration could do nothing, allowing the Soviets to establish their Cuban missile base. It might try quiet diplomacy in hopes of convincing the Soviets to withdraw the missiles. Finally, it could opt to force Moscow to withdraw the missiles.

Early in the ExCom debate, Secretary of Defense McNamara did in fact argue that the missiles posed no threat to America's deterrent force and were not worth bothering about. "A missile is a missile," he has been quoted as saying. "It makes no great difference whether you are killed by a missile fired from the Soviet Union or from Cuba."[33] McNamara even suggested that since these missiles would to an extent close the actual missile gap, which was very much in America's favor, they created a more stable balance of terror and reduced the danger of nuclear war.

McNamara was quickly shouted down by others on the committee, who believed that the strategic issues was less important than political considerations. In the broader international context, a Soviet success in planting missiles almost literally under Kennedy's nose would be viewed worldwide as another cold war victory for Moscow. Moreover, domestic political considerations had to be taken into account. The Republicans had for weeks been warning that the Soviets were placing missiles in Cuba. And the administration had, with increasing vehemence, warned of grave consequences should the charges be true. If the news of a Soviet missile field in Cuba leaked prior to the congressional elections, as it almost certainly would, the president's credibility would be blasted and the administration could look forward to a disaster at the polls—unless it reacted forcefully.

Quiet diplomacy had no more support on the ExCom than McNamara's proposed do-nothing approach. Kennedy had staked his political reputation as well as the hopes of his party in the approaching congressional elections on Khrushchev's promise not to deploy offensive weapons in Cuba. Moreover, the president had repeatedly stated that any attempt to deploy missiles there would lead to grave consequences. In his judgment the time for diplomacy was past, especially since once the missile sites had been finished and the missiles were deployed (a matter of perhaps two weeks) the Soviets were certain to reject any call for their removal.

## AIR STRIKE OR BLOCKADE?

A consensus quickly developed among the members of the ExCom. The Soviets would have to be forced to remove their missiles from Cuba before they became operational and could threaten the United States. From that point on the debate focused on the level of force to be employed.

The more hawkish among the president's advisers advocated air strikes to knock out the missile installations. Others, including McNamara, Bobby Kennedy, and Theodore Sorensen, feared that such an attack would kill a large number of Cubans and Soviets, giving Khrushchev little choice but to retaliate and thus touching off a general war.

This second group urged the president to demand that the Soviets withdraw the missiles and back up that demand with a naval blockade of Cuba for the purpose of turning away Soviet ships carrying missile components. The blockade was a forceful response. It was, in fact, an act of war. Yet because no Soviet ships were within three days' sail of Cuba, it had the virtue of giving the Soviets time to think things through before they plunged into a shooting war. But the blockade had its weaknesses, too. Foremost among these was the fact that it did not address the problem of the missile installations then under construction in Cuba. Clearly the administration could not allow these weapons to become operational.

For days the debate seesawed back and forth. Finally, when it became clear that no complete consensus among his advisers was possible, the president made his decision. At 7:00 P.M., on Monday, October 22, he informed the public in a dramatic television address that the Soviets were attempting to establish a missile base in Cuba. He demanded the withdrawal of the missiles and established a naval blockade five hundred miles from Cuba (out of range of Cuban MIGs) to turn back Soviet ships carrying missiles or their components. Kennedy also announced that the firing of a single missile from Cuba against the United States or any other western hemispheric nation would require "a full retaliatory response against the Soviet Union."[34]

Even as Kennedy spoke, preparations were under way for an invasion of Cuba should Khrushchev refuse to remove the missiles. Hundreds of military aircraft were moved to airfields on the Gulf Coast. An invasion force of more than 180 ships, including transports carrying 100,000 soldiers and marines, was sent into the Caribbean. Polaris missile–firing submarines moved into position within striking distance of the Soviet Union. The bombers of the Strategic Air Command and the land-based strategic missile force were placed in a high state of readiness.

The president's speech seems to have taken the Soviets by surprise. Khrushchev responded with bluster, calling the blockade "piracy" and warning that Soviet ships would not stop at the blockade line and that if they were attacked Soviet submarines operating in the Caribbean would attack American warships. But rhetoric aside, Khrushchev behaved warily. When Kennedy first announced the blockade, twenty-five Soviet ships were detected heading for Cuba. Two days later twelve of these, no doubt those carrying missile components, put about and headed for home. The rest, most of them tankers, continued on course.

Kennedy, too, behaved cautiously. Over the protests of the navy brass he ordered the blockading squadron to let the first two ships, a tanker and an East German cruise ship, pass through the blockade line without being boarded and searched. In fact, in subsequent days only one ship, the

*Maracola,* a Panamanian freighter under charter to the Soviets, was stopped and searched. At the same time, because he judged that the missiles in Cuba would be deployed and ready for firing before the end of the following week, Kennedy scheduled air strikes and an invasion for Tuesday, October 30. It was up to Khrushchev to give ground or accept the consequences.

The tension in Washington was intense when, on October 26, Aleksander F. Fomin, the head of Soviet intelligence in the United States and a personal friend of Khrushchev's, asked John Scali of ABC News to meet him for lunch. An obviously flustered Fomin asked Scali if the State Department would be interested in a trade. Moscow would agree to dismantle and remove its Cuban missiles if Washington would pledge not to invade the island. Scali returned this reply (given to him by Secretary Rusk) that evening. "I have reason to believe that the USG sees real possibilities and supposes that the representatives of the two governments in New York [the United Nations] could work this matter out with [Secretary General] U Thant and with each other. My impression is, however, that time is very urgent." Scali was also told to inform Fomin verbally that if no settlement was arrived at within forty-eight hours, things were going to happen.[35]

A few hours later the State Department teletype clattered out a personal message from Khrushchev to the president proposing the same arrangement Fomin had earlier outlined. The letter, meandering and at times philosophical, was pure Khrushchev:

> If you have not lost your self-control and sensibly conceive what this might lead to, then, Mr. President, we and you ought not to pull on the end of the rope in which you have tied the knot of war, because the more the two of us pull, the tighter that knot will be tied. And the moment may come when that knot will be tied so tight that even he who tied it will not have the strength to untie it, and then it will be necessary to cut that knot, and what that will mean is not for me to explain to you, because you yourself understand perfectly well of what terrible forces our countries dispose.[36]

On Friday peace seemed at hand. But on Saturday morning, before the administration had framed its reply to Khrushchev, the crisis once again intensified. First, Washington received news that a U-2 reconnaissance plane had been shot down over Cuba. Major Rudolph Anderson, Jr., the pilot who first photographed the missile sites, had been killed. Then Radio Moscow transmitted a second letter to Washington. Completely different in tone, this message raised the stakes by demanding that the administration agree not to invade Cuba *and* to dismantle and remove its Jupiter-C missile installations in Turkey.

The two events, coming hard on one another, led Assistant Secretary of Defense Paul Nitze, CIA Director McCone, and the Joint Chiefs of Staff to press for an immediate invasion. Though under extraordinary pressure, the president refused to alter the already-established invasion schedule. On the other hand, he also refused to give in on the second of the two Soviet demands. To have withdrawn the Jupiters from Turkey under threat from

Moscow would have dealt a major blow to NATO by confirming what President Charles de Gaulle had alleged all along, that in the last analysis the United States could not be trusted to defend an ally when its own security was threatened.

The irony was that the Jupiters were obsolete. McNamara described them as "junk." According to one State Department official, "no one could even be sure they were operable. In a purely military sense, we did not even need them; Polaris submarines stationed in or near Turkish waters would be far more effective."[37]

Robert Kennedy finally came up with a brilliant solution to his brother's problem, suggesting that he ignore the second letter with its demand for the removal of Turkey's Jupiter missiles and respond to Khrushchev's personal letter as though it were the only proposal on the table. That approach at least had the virtue of leaving the final decision as to war or peace in Soviet hands.

The president's brother had something else in mind as well. On Saturday evening, after Washington's response to the Khrushchev letter had been forwarded to Moscow, he went to see the Soviet ambassador, Anatoly Dobrynin. He told Dobrynin that an invasion was imminent and that the United States could not withdraw the Jupiter missiles under existing conditions. He added, however, that "within a short time after the crisis was over, those missiles would be gone."[38] In other words the Soviets could look forward to the removal of the Jupiters, but on Washington's terms not theirs, and certainly not under existing circumstances.

At just a few minutes before nine o'clock on Sunday morning, Radio Moscow beamed another long letter from Khrushchev to Kennedy agreeing that in return to a promise not to invade Cuba he would dismantle the missiles and have them returned to the Soviet Union. With less than two days to spare before the scheduled invasion, the Soviets gave in.

Washington and Moscow had gone to the brink of war and, through a combination of statesmanship and plain good luck, managed to survive. But it was a near thing. Looking back on the moment when the crisis was finally resolved, one ExCom member remarked, "I shall never forget the relief we all felt that morning."[39]

## IN SEARCH OF DÉTENTE

The Cuban missile crisis had a chastening effect on John Kennedy and Nikita Khrushchev. Both leaders now recognized the importance of reducing political tensions and finding a way of reining in the nuclear arms race.

On the same day that he agreed to remove the missiles from Cuba, Khrushchev called on Kennedy to open discussions "on the prohibition of atomic and thermonuclear weapons, on general disarmament and other problems relating to the relaxation of international tension." Kennedy quickly agreed, remarking that "perhaps now, as we step back from danger, we can make some real progress in this vital field."[40]

A United Nations disarmament conference that convened in November 1962, provided the forum for the test-ban negotiations between Washington and Moscow. The talks soon bogged down, however, over the issue of verification. Relying on a recent American Defense Department study, the Soviets, who assumed the CIA would use the inspection process for espionage purposes, claimed that well-placed seismic instruments could detect any clandestine tests that either side might undertake. On-site inspections were, therefore, unnecessary. The Joint Chiefs of Staff and the Atomic Energy Commission (AEC) thought differently. Rejecting the conclusions of the Defense Department study, Glenn Seaborg, head of the AEC, argued that it was doubtful seismic instruments could detect low-level nuclear explosions and that much valuable research could secretly be done unless a comprehensive test-ban agreement included ample provision for on-site inspections.

The opposition of the Joint Chiefs and the AEC killed any prospect for Senate passage of a comprehensive test-ban treaty. Once that became evident, Kennedy and Khrushchev decided to settle for what they could get, a partial test-ban agreement. The treaty, which prohibited nuclear tests in the atmosphere, space, or under water but allowed both sides to continue testing underground, was hardly a major disarmament agreement. Nor did the president describe it as one. In a major television address he called it "a step toward reason" and "an opening wedge" in what was to be an ongoing campaign for the limitation of nuclear weapons. "Let us, if we can, get back from the shadows of war and seek out the way of peace. And if that journey is one thousand miles, or even more, let history record that we, in this land, at this time, took the first step."[41]

Kennedy's hopes notwithstanding, the Partial Test-Ban Treaty led nowhere. Whatever plans he may have had for future negotiations died with him in Dallas. Not long after this, Nikita Khrushchev was stripped of his power by colleagues less interested in controlling the arms race than in achieving nuclear parity with the United States. And so for the next several years the nuclear arms race sped out of control.

## THE GROWING COMMITMENT TO VIETNAM

John Kennedy had been thinking more or less seriously about the political situation in Vietnam since the early 1950s, when he first became a prominent supporter of Ngo Dinh Diem. He endorsed the Eisenhower administration's policy of "nation building" and in 1956 applauded Diem's refusal to hold national elections. At that time Kennedy argued that the "fundamental tenets of this nation's foreign policy depend in considerable measure upon a strong and free Vietnamese nation." South Vietnam, he argued, "represents the cornerstone of the Free World in Southeast Asia, the keystone in the arch, the finger in the dike."[42]

As president, though his rhetoric was less florid, he remained committed to the basic assumption that had guided America's Vietnam policy since Dean Acheson's time: that a communist victory there would lead to losses elsewhere in Asia and ultimately to a shift in the global balance of power. But if Kennedy's commitment was genuine, he was nevertheless cautious. In spite of a deteriorating political and military situation in South Vietnam, he proved reluctant to follow the advice of his more hawkish advisers.

In late 1961, after Diem issued an urgent appeal for increased aid, Kennedy sent General Maxwell Taylor and Walt W. Rostow, a professor of economics turned White House aide and counterinsurgency expert, to Vietnam on a fact-finding mission. On returning from Saigon, Taylor and Rostow issued a report that recommended not only more aid but the deployment of a minimum of eight thousand troops to be used in non-combat situations in South Vietnam as "a visible symbol of the seriousness of American intentions," a warning to the Viet Cong and North Vietnamese that they could not win the war.[43]

Debate over the Taylor-Rostow report revealed a significant division of opinion inside the administration between those who believed the United States should under no circumstances allow South Vietnam to collapse and a few advisers, especially Undersecretary of State George Ball, who argued against involvement. Ball warned that a social revolution was under way in Vietnam, that the Viet Cong were extremely tough, and that the United States ran the risk of following in France's footsteps. He told the president that if he decided to make even a small commitment, in "five years we'll have three hundred thousand men in the paddies, and jungles and never find them again. That was the French experience. Vietnam is the worst possible terrain both from a physical and political point of view." Ball would have said more, but the president cut him off. "George," he said, "you're just crazier than hell. That just isn't going to happen."[44]

The president, who no doubt shared some of Ball's misgivings, had other concerns that made it seem imperative to shore up the crumbling Diem regime. During his first year in office he had suffered humiliation at the Bay of Pigs, had agreed to a neutralized Laos, had not come off well during a face-to-face confrontation with Khrushchev in Vienna, and had let the Berlin wall stand. Considering all these events, he may have believed that anything less than a strong stand in Vietnam would be viewed as an indication of weakness both abroad and domestically.

At the same time he told the White House aide and historian Arthur Schlesinger, Jr., that he opposed the idea of sending ground forces to Vietnam. "The troops will march in; the bands will play; the crowds will cheer; and in four days everyone will have forgotten. Then we will be told we have to send in more troops. It's like taking a drink. The effect wears off, and you have to take another." The war in Vietnam, the president insisted, was Diem's to win or lose.[45]

After listening carefully to the arguments of all sides, Kennedy decided against sending ground troops. But he did send more economic aid while increasing the number of American military advisers in South Vietnam. Kennedy may have thought that in this way he had squared the circle. But in the months that followed the American military commitment in Vietnam grew by small increments to almost seventeen thousand persons. Whether he understood it or not he had made a major decision. America's credibility as a great power was now at stake.

## A COUP IN SAIGON

Better armed and equipped than ever before, transported on helicopters flown by Americans, and protected from the air by American-crewed helicopter gunships, ARVN went on the offensive in 1962 and, in spite of a corrupt and incompetent officer corps, had some initial success. But it was not long before the Viet Cong developed tactics to cope with ARVN's newfound mobility and acquired the automatic weapons needed to deal with the helicopters. By early 1963 the Viet Cong again held the initiative, a fact it demonstrated in a battle near Ap Bac, where, though outnumbered 10:1, they mauled an entire South Vietnamese division and downed five helicopters. The legendary American military adviser, Colonel John Paul Vann, ascribed this South Vietnamese defeat, like most of the rest, to ARVN's utterly worthless officer corps. It was a "miserable damn performance, just like it always is."[46]

Throughout 1961 and 1962 Kennedy was confused by conflicting reports coming out of Vietnam. Young reporters such as Neil Sheehan (whose 1988 biography of Colonel Vann won a Pulitzer price) and David Halberstam of the *New York Times* were reporting on a debacle in the making. On the other hand, the official reports from Saigon were consistently optimistic.

Kennedy sent his old friend Senator Mike Mansfield to Saigon to get the real story. Mansfield, who like Kennedy had once been a Diem enthusiast, reported that American policy had failed and that the moment had come for Washington to reconsider its commitment. America's investment in Vietnam, he told Kennedy, had been a waste since "substantially the same difficulties remain, if indeed, they have not been compounded." Mansfield also warned Kennedy that it would be foolhardy to send American troops to Vietnam; the war was for the South Vietnamese to win or lose. "To ignore that reality will not only be immensely costly in terms of American lives and resources, but it may also draw us inexorably into some variation of the unenviable position in Vietnam that was formerly occupied by the French."[47]

If Mansfield's report shook Kennedy's confidence, his doubts about Diem's viability as well as the soundness of his own policy grew more pronounced in mid-1963 after South Vietnamese troops fired on a group of Buddhist monks during a religious celebration at Hue, the ancient capital. Vietnam's Buddhist community responded by organizing hunger strikes and protest meetings at Hue and Saigon. When a Buddhist monk, Quang Duc, poured gasoline over his body, sat down in the lotus position in the middle of a busy Saigon intersection, and immolated himself, it was the signal for a general uprising in which a large cross-section of the city's population participated. The crisis continued through the summer. Before it was over six more monks followed Quang Duc in acts of self-immolation.

Washington put intense pressure on Diem to stop the persecutions. But Diem, influenced by his brother, Ngo Dinh Nhu, paid no heed. Only days after Washington made its demands, Vietnamese Special Forces attacked Buddhist pagodas nationwide, imprisoning more than fourteen hundred monks. The government also declared martial law, and government troops cracked down hard on rioting students, shooting into crowds and killing women and children.

At the same time Washington received intelligence reports indicating that Nhu was in contact with the North Vietnamese and seemed to be trying to work out a settlement that would involve an American withdrawal and the creation of a coalition government. George Ball thought it likely that Nhu and Madam Nhu, a powerful force in her own right in Saigon, were "deliberately trying to destroy the Saigon government to advance their own personal power." He wondered how United States policy could succeed when Diem was so completely under Nhu's "poisonous influence."[48] Others in the administration were probably thinking along similar lines.

Almost immediately following the attack on the pagodas, the president approved a cable instructing Ambassador Henry Cabot Lodge, Jr., to assure a group of senior Vietnamese officers who were then conspiring to overthrow Diem that the United States would support them. The August conspiracy collapsed. But when another plot materialized, Lodge again assured the conspirators of Washington's backing. On November 1, 1963, the coup, so long in the making, began with an attack on the presidential palace. Diem and Nhu were taken prisoner on the following day and murdered.

John Kennedy met his own death at the hands of the assassin, Lee Harvey Oswald, not three weeks later in Dallas, Texas. Considering the subsequent disastrous course that American policy makers followed in Vietnam, many have wondered whether he would have traveled the same path as Lyndon Johnson.

There can be no doubt that Kennedy was distressed over the deepening involvement of the United States in Vietnam. Moreover, it is unquestionably true that he hoped to find a way out of what he recognized as a dangerous situation. He told Senator Mansfield that he wanted all American troops out of Vietnam after the 1964 elections. And in the spring of 1963 he told Assistant Secretary of State Roger Hilsman that it would be "great" if the South Vietnamese could win the war against the Viet Cong.

"But if they don't," he said, "we're going to Geneva and do what we did with Laos."[49]

That remark was typical of Kennedy, who, despite his well-cultivated reputation for toughness, usually seemed to be looking for an appropriate compromise between extremes. A neutralized Vietnam would have allowed the United States to withdraw its troops and might not be construed as a cold war defeat for the administration. But Vietnam was not Laos. There was a genuine social revolution going on there that left no room for the sort of compromise that neutralization implied.

And so the question becomes what would Kennedy have done if he had been forced to choose between intervention and acquiescing in a Viet Cong victory? Obviously that is a question that cannot be answered with certainty. Yet two factors do encourage speculation. First, by increasing the number of advisers in South Vietnam from a mere 400 to 16,700, Kennedy substantially increased the American commitment to the war. Moreover, as the historian George C. Herring has observed, by sanctioning the coup that overthrew Diem and supporting the council of generals that replaced him, he deepened Washington's responsibility for South Vietnam's survival.[50]

If Kennedy felt that he could not abandon a faltering Diem regime in 1961 when the United States had only a few advisers and a comparatively small investment in the country, is it possible that he would have pulled out in 1964 or 1965 when so much more had been invested? The question, of course, can never be answered with certitude. But if one were called upon to speculate, the answer would probably be no.

## ENDNOTES

1. John F. Kennedy, inaugural address, January 20, 1961, *The Inaugural Addresses of the American Presidents*, ed. Davis N. Lott (New York: Holt, Rinehart and Winston, 1961), pp. 269–71.

2. Kennedy, quoted in Richard A. Aliano, *American Defense Policy from Eisenhower to Kennedy* (Athens, Ohio: Ohio University Press, 1975), pp. 235.

3. Kennedy, quoted in Paul Boller, *Presidential Anecdotes* (New York: Oxford University Press, 1981), p. 302.

4. Dean Acheson, quoted in Herbert S. Parmet, *JFK: The Presidency of John F. Kennedy* (New York: Dial, 1982), p. 163; Allen Dulles, quoted in Trumbull Higgins, *The Perfect Failure* (New York: W.W. Norton, 1987), pp. 104–5. Dulles in fact deceived Kennedy about his actual feelings. He believed he was in a "now or never" situation with the young president. Anxious to depose Castro, he neglected to tell Kennedy that he hadn't in fact been optimistic prior to the Guatamalan invasion.

5. George Ball, *The Past Has Another Pattern* (New York: W. W. Norton, 1982), pp. 226–32.

6. CIA memorandum, quoted in Jonathan Kwitny, *Endless Enemies: The Making of an Unfriendly World* (New York: Penguin Books, 1986) pp. 77–78.

7. Ball, *Past Has Another Pattern*, pp. 226–27.

8. Ibid., pp. 362–63.

9. Bernard B. Fall, *Anatomy of a Crisis* (Garden City, N.Y.: Doubleday, 1969), p. 199.

10. CIA estimate, quoted in Parmet, *JFK*, p. 133.

11. John Kenneth Galbraith, quoted in George C. Herring, *America's Longest War: The United States and Vietnam, 1950–1975* (New York: Alfred A. Knopf, 1979), p. 77.

12. Dean Rusk, quoted in Warren I. Cohen, *Dean Rusk* (Totowa, N.J.: Cooper Square, 1980), pp. 128–29.

13. Nikita Khrushchev, quoted in ibid., p. 137.

14. Khrushchev and Kennedy, both quoted in Arthur Schlesinger, Jr., *A Thousand Days: John F. Kennedy in the White House* (Boston: Houghton Mifflin, 1965), p. 374.

15. Peter Lisagor, quoted in Parmet, *JFK*, p. 190.

16. Kennedy, quoted in Schlesinger, *Thousand Days*, p. 391.

17. Kennedy, quoted in David Burner, *John F. Kennedy and a New Generation* (Boston: Little, Brown, 1988), p. 77.

18. Kennedy, television address, July 25, 1961, *Public Papers of the Presidents: John F. Kennedy, 1961* (Washington, D.C., 1962), pp. 533–40.

19. Kennedy, quoted in Burner, *John F. Kennedy*, p. 77.

20. Kennedy, quoted in William W. Kaufmann, *The McNamara Strategy* (New York: Harper and Row, 1964), p. 40.

21. Daniel Ellsberg, quoted in Desmond Ball, *Politics and Force Levels: The Strategic Missile Program of the Kennedy Administration* (Berkeley, Calif.: University of California Press, 1980), p. 190.

22. Pentagon colonel, quoted in Henry Trewhitt, *McNamara* (New York: Harper and Row, 1971), p. 18.

23. Theodore Sorensen, *Kennedy* (New York: Harper and Row, 1965), p. 627.

24. Robert S. McNamara, quoted in Alain Enthoven and Wayne K. Smith, *How Much Is Enough?* (New York: Harper and Row, 1971), p. 124.

25. Schlesinger paraphrasing Charles DeGaulle, *Thousand Days*, p. 353.

26. Seymour Melman, *Pentagon Capitalism: The Political Economy of War* (New York: McGraw-Hill, 1970), p. 108.

27. *Pravda* and V. D. Sokolovskii, both quoted in Lawrence Freedman, *The Evolution of Nuclear Strategy* (New York: St. Martin's Press, 1981), p. 239.

28. McNamara aide, quoted in Trewhitt, *McNamara*, p. 115.

29. McNamara, quoted in Gerard Clarfield and William Wiecek, *Nuclear America: Military and Civilian Nuclear Power in the United States, 1940–1980* (New York: Harper and Row, 1984), p. 259.

30. Khrushckev, quoted in Graham T. Allison, *Essence of Decision: Explaining the Cuban Missile Crisis* (Boston: Little, Brown, 1971), p. 40.

31. Kennedy, quoted in ibid., p. 189.

32. Khrushchev, quoted in ibid., p. 47.

33. McNamara, quoted in Roger Hilsman, *To Move a Nation* (Garden City, N.Y.: Doubleday, 1967), p. 195.

34. Kennedy, television address, October 22, 1962, *Public Papers of the Presidents: John F. Kennedy, 1962* (Washington, D.C., 1963), pp. 806–9.

35. John Scali, quoted in Allison, *Essence of Decision*, p. 220.

36. Khrushchev, quoted in ibid., pp. 221–24.

37. Ball, *Past Has Another Pattern*, pp. 305–7.

38. Robert F. Kennedy, *Thirteen Days: A Memoir of the Cuban Missile Crisis* (New York: W. W. Norton, 1969), pp. 86–87.

39. Ball, *Past Has Another Pattern*, p. 307.

40. Kennedy, quoted in Glenn Seaborg, *Kennedy, Khrushchev, and the Test Ban* (Berkeley, Calif.: University of California Press, 1981), p. 176.

41. Kennedy, quoted in ibid., p. 257.

42. Kennedy, quoted in Herring, *America's Longest War*, p. 43.

43. Maxwell Taylor and Walt W. Rostow, report, quoted in ibid., p. 81.

44. Kennedy, quoted in Ball, *Past Has Another Pattern*, p. 366.

45. Kennedy, quoted in Schlesinger, *Thousand Days*, p. 547.

46. John Paul Vann, quoted in Neil Sheehan, *A Bright and Shining Lie: John Paul Vann and America in Vietnam* (New York: Random House, 1988), p. 277.

47. Mike Mansfield, quoted in Stanley Karnow, *Vietnam: A History* (New York: Viking, 1983), p. 268.

48. Ball, *Past Has Another Pattern*, pp. 370–74.

49. Kennedy, quoted in Burner, *John F. Kennedy*, p. 104.

50. Herring, *America's Longest War*, pp. 73–107.

A grim-faced Lyndon Johnson takes the oath of office. Jacqueline Kennedy, the widow of the slain president, stands at his side.

# 31

# "THAT BITCH OF A WAR," 1963–1969

On November 22, 1963, with Jacqueline Kennedy standing by his side in the cabin of *Air Force One*, a grim-faced Lyndon Johnson took the oath of office as president of the United States. Not long afterward the plane rose from the runway at Dallas and headed northeast, toward Washington and Lyndon Johnson's date with destiny.

The big, raw-boned Texan has been described as crude, vulgar, egocentric, manipulative, ruthless, and a bully. He certainly was—and a slave driver to boot. "I don't have ulcers," he once bragged. "I give 'em." On another occasion he remarked, "There are no favorites in my office. . . . I treat them all with the same general inconsideration." At the same time LBJ drove himself relentlessly. Few people recall ever seeing him walk. They called what he did "the Johnson trot." The Senate had never seen such an energetic majority leader. When one senator complained, "What's the hurry? After all, Rome wasn't built in a day," a colleague replied, "No, but Lyndon Johnson wasn't foreman on that job." On another occasion, after becoming president, Johnson called Bill Moyers, his press secretary, to say that he was going to Honolulu. Moyers said, "Fine, Mr. President; I'll come over and talk to you about it. Where are you?" Johnson replied, "Over Los Angeles."[1]

Johnson's ego was legendary in Washington. Once, or so the story goes, Chancellor Ludwig Erhard of West Germany remarked that he had heard Johnson was born in a log cabin. "No, Mr. Chancellor," Johnson supposedly replied, "I was born in a manger."[2]

Though Lyndon Johnson did not enjoy the most enviable of reputations, he was a man with a vision, anxious to fulfill the promise of Franklin Roosevelt's New Deal by ending poverty and discrimination in America. He called his vision "the Great Society." "I do not want to be the President who built empires, or sought grandeur, or extended dominions," he once remarked. "I want to be the President who educated young children . . . who helped to feed the hungry . . . who helped the poor to find their own way and who protected the right of every citizen to vote in every election."[3]

Like so many other presidents, before and since, Johnson lacked foreign policy experience. He was not so woefully unprepared as some, however. First, as the majority leader in the Senate and later as vice-president, he gained more than a nodding acquaintanceship with the issues that formed the focus of American foreign policy during the cold war. He had been present at meetings of the National Security Council and had often served as President John Kennedy's roving ambassador. Indeed, Kennedy seems to have taken a certain perverse delight in sending LBJ to foreign hotspots. In May 1961, he sent the vice-president to Berlin as a symbol of the administration's determination not to be driven out. Earlier Johnson had been hustled off to Saigon. While there, in typical Texas style, he anointed Ngo Dinh Diem "the Winston Churchill of Asia." Later, the reporter, Stanley Karnow, asked him if he really meant that. "Shit," Johnson said, "Diem's the only boy we got out there."[4]

## VIETNAM'S CONTINUING CRISIS

From the moment he took office, Johnson was forced to grapple with the deteriorating situation in Southeast Asia. Following the assassination of Ngo Dinh Diem, the political situation in South Vietnam became if anything more chaotic. Returning from a trip to Saigon in December 1963, Secretary of Defense Robert McNamara reported that the military junta that had replaced Diem was "indecisive and drifting," that the generals were "so preoccupied with essentially political affairs" that neither the army nor the government "were being properly directed."[5]

In January 1964, the junta was overthrown in a coup led by General Nguyen Khanh. Nobody in Washington grieved. But nobody cheered either, for it seemed clear, as George Ball noted, that Khanh's was another of those "Saigon coups that hatched out obscure military leaders with the political life span of June bugs who fluttered briefly in the limelight only to disappear."[6] Intelligence estimates done at this time indicated that unless something changed soon South Vietnam would certainly collapse.

The prospect of South Vietnam's imminent demise prompted the Joint Chiefs of Staff to recommend the immediate Americanization of the war. But Johnson refused to consider what then appeared to be a rash

# The Vietnam War

CHINA

● Nanning

**Gulf of Tonkin Incident 1964**

20th parallel

*Gulf of Tonkin*

HAINAN

NORTH VIETNAM

● Deinbienphu

Hanoi ✷ ● Haiphong

Paksong ●

● Luang Prabang

PLAIN OF JARS

Vientiane ✪

LAOS

● Vinh

**Demilitarized zone (DMZ) 1954**

Dong Hoi

17th parallel

Udon Thani △

Phanom △

KORAT PLATEAU

**Quang Tri Province ✷ 1966-67 1971**

△ Hue

SOUTH CHINA

THAILAND

△ Takhli △ Ratchasima

Uban △ Ratchathani

✷ Danang

△ Chulai

✷ **Dak To 1967**

SEA

△ Dan Muang

✪ Bangkok

Battambang

**Ia Drang Valley 1965** ✷

△ Pleiku

Ankhe △ Quinhon

SOUTH VIETNAM

CAMBODIA

"Fishhook"

Nhatrang △

△ Sattahip

✪ **Zone C 1967** ✷

Phnom Penh

**ARVN thrust Feb., 1971**

△ Camranh Bay

Phanrang

Kompong Som ●

"Parrot's Beak"

△ Bienhoa

△ ✪ Saigon

Tan Son Nhut

*Gulf of Thailand*

Cantho △

Mekong Delta

Ho Chi Minh Trail

✷ Major battles

△ U.S. bases

✕ Areas of guerilla activity

Communist countries

Allied with U.S.

Neutral countries

measure. He was convinced, at least early on, that the appearance of large numbers of white-skinned soldiers in Vietnam would turn most of the people there against the Saigon regime. Moreover, he believed that a major war in Asia would have a disastrous effect on his hopes for the Great Society program at home.

Still, Johnson felt trapped. "I knew from the start," he later recalled, "that I was bound to be crucified either way I moved. If I left the woman I really loved—the Great Society—in order to get involved with that bitch of a war . . . then I would lose everything at home." On the other hand, recalling how the Republicans had used the "loss" of China to paralyze the Truman administration, he was certain that the loss of Vietnam would "shatter my presidency, kill my administration and damage our democracy."[7] Unprepared either to fight or to withdraw, the president increased the amount of aid going to South Vietnam and added seven thousand advisers to those already stationed there, hoping in this way to stave off disaster.

But there were no positive developments in South Vietnam during 1964. No effective government emerged there; the military continued its internecine strife, and the Viet Cong's threat to the regime grew increasingly serious. The "best thing that can be said about Khanh's government," Ambassador Henry Cabot Lodge Jr., cabled in August, "is that it has lasted six months and has about a 50–50 chance of lasting out the year."[8]

Ten years of nation building had failed. From this experience policy makers might have concluded that the time had come to withdraw from South Vietnam. But domestic political considerations precluded any such move. Lyndon Johnson intended to win the 1964 presidential election. He was not, therefore, about to hand his Republican opponent, the conservative Arizona Senator Barry Goldwater, an issue such as the "loss" of Vietnam on the eve of the election.

Cold war imperatives also impelled the administration to find methods of "saving" South Vietnam. Echoing thoughts first articulated more than a decade and a half earlier, Secretary of State Dean Rusk argued that Vietnam was "a region of great strategic importance, not only to all the people who live in the great arc from Karachi to Tokyo but to the free world as a whole." The loss of Southeast Asia, he warned, would lead to a basic shift in the global balance of power.[9]

It is now clear that Rusk was terribly wrong. But his argument, which had underlain America's Vietnam policy since the days of Harry Truman and Dean Acheson, remained compelling. Until policy makers were able to free themselves from those assumptions—to break the cold war paradigm— events would carry them along like so much debris caught in a spring flood.

As Johnson and his top aides looked desperately about for some means of preventing a Viet Cong victory, they lost sight of the fact that the essential failure had taken place in South Vietnam, where neither Diem nor his successors had created a stable government. Instead, they focused on the role played by the North Vietnamese who were infiltrating men and supplies into the South. Whereas it should have been clear that a viable government in South Vietnam would have been able to deal with the guerrillas, official Washington turned logic on its head. By the middle of 1964 conventional wisdom in policy making circles held that forcing the North Vietnamese to end their intervention was an essential precondition to the creation of a stable government in the South.

To blame the North Vietnamese because the corrupt military cliques that controlled the South failed to organize a stable and responsible government was, of course, absurd. But that argument did allow policy makers to believe that South Vietnam might yet be saved. Unhappily, it also led them to the conclusion that North Vietnam was the cause of all South Vietnam's problems. By the summer of 1964 official Washington had redefined its principal Southeast Asian problem. South Vietnam was not a victim of its own incompetent, corrupt leadership but of outside aggression.

The Johnson administration was itching for a chance to fire a warning shot in Hanoi's direction when, on the morning of August 1, 1964, the opportunity presented itself. While on an espionage mission off North Vietnam, the USS *Maddox* was attacked by three North Vietnamese torpedo boats. On the previous night South Vietnamese rangers had raided Hon Me island, near where the *Maddox* was cruising. The North Vietnamese evidently believed the American ship was part of that operation. In a brief action the North Vietnamese boats launched a number of torpedoes at the *Maddox*, which fired back. Crusader jets from the aircraft carrier *Ticonderoga* eventually drove the attacking boats off.

The president might have avoided further trouble by withdrawing the *Maddox* from North Vietnamese waters. Instead, however, he approved the navy's plan to send another destroyer, the *Turner Joy*, to join it. Together the two ships steamed nervously along North Vietnam's coast, while in Washington Pentagon planners selected targets for air strikes in the event they were molested.

On the dark, storm-tossed night of August 4, the *Maddox* and the *Turner Joy* reported being attacked by North Vietnamese torpedo boats. In Washington, the president quickly authorized air strikes against torpedo boat bases and oil storage facilities in North Vietnam. Before the orders could be delivered, however, messages from Captain John Herrick, the commander of the *Maddox*, indicated that there had probably been no attack after all. Radar and sonar contacts were unreliable in rough seas. Jumpy sonar men might have mistaken the sounds of their own ships or the storm-tossed sea for torpedoes. There had been no actual sightings of enemy boats. And in spite of the fact that numerous torpedoes were thought to have been launched at the American ships, neither one sustained any damage. All things considered, Captain Herrick was inclined to think that bad weather and nervous crews had combined to make something out of nothing.

A pugnacious administration, anxious to hit North Vietnam, disregarded Captain Herrick's message and went ahead with the planned air strikes. A compliant Congress then passed the Tonkin Gulf Resolution, granting the president the authority to take all "necessary measures to repel any armed attacks against the forces of the United States and to prevent further aggression."[10]

From a purely political point of view Johnson's management of the Tonkin Gulf affair was a tour de force. Barry Goldwater, the Republican presidential candidate in 1964, never had much of a chance of winning the November election. But he did try to make an issue of the president's handling of the deteriorating Southeast Asian situation. Johnson's brilliantly conceived reaction to North Vietnam's "challenge" sent exactly the right message to the voting public. At the same time, the air strikes satisfied the administration's foreign policy purposes by letting Hanoi know that the United States did not intend to lose South Vietnam.

Lyndon Johnson won an overwhelming victory in 1964 in part, at least, because he succeeded in labeling Senator Goldwater as "trigger happy." The people voted for the presidential candidate they believed was most inclined to keep them out of war. Ironically, even as the votes were being tabulated, policy makers in Washington were laying plans for a bombing campaign that proved to be a major step toward involvement in the ground war in Vietnam.

## ARMS CONTROL: THE ORIGINS OF SALT

In the same year that Lyndon Johnson defeated Barry Goldwater, the Politburo of the Soviet Union unceremoniously deposed Nikita Khrushchev. A new team of Soviet leaders, Alexsei Kosygin and Leonid Brezhnev, abandoned Khrushchev's aggressive diplomacy in favor of a more low-key approach to the United States. In part this shift occurred because they had their hands full with the burgeoning Sino-Soviet conflict. But it was also a fact that in the aftermath of the Cuban missile crisis the Soviet leadership wanted no further difficulties with Washington at least until it had achieved something approaching nuclear parity.

It would be an exaggeration to suggest that the years of the Johnson administration represented a period of détente in Soviet-American relations. On the other hand, it was a time of relative calm. Ironically, it was also a period during which both countries made decisions that sent the nuclear arms race spiraling out of control.

By 1964 Robert McNamara had concluded that mutually assured destruction, a deterrent strategy that depended on the existence of a stable nuclear balance between the superpowers, provided the greatest possible security against the threat of all-out nuclear war. (A stable nuclear balance is thought to exist when each side is confident that its nuclear forces can survive an initial attack and respond effectively. In theory it is the existence of this "second-strike" capability that deters either side from attacking first.) Unhappily, as the secretary soon learned, advances in technology can undermine the stability that is the key to a credible deterrent strategy.

The first hint that the Soviets might be attempting to discredit Washington's nuclear retaliatory capability came when America's Discoverer satellites photographed a number of mysterious black buildings rising on the outskirts of Moscow. Soon, the Defense Intelligence Agency was able to state with certainty that these buildings housed the Galosh antiballistic missile (ABM) system. Had the Soviets developed a technology capable of defending against a retaliatory missile attack? If so, America's missiles would be useless, and Moscow might be tempted to launch a first strike.

The discovery that the Soviets were deploying the Galosh system set off a furious debate in the United States. The army, which had long been at work developing its own ABM system, wanted to deploy the Nike X. But McNamara refused. The system could not always distinguish decoys from real targets; its complex radars were unreliable; and it would be monstrously expensive. More to the point, McNamara opposed the deployment of any weapon system that threatened nuclear stability. As the secretary saw it, the Soviets had created instability by deploying Galosh. By mimicking the Soviets, the United States would only add to the instability.

McNamara also knew that the Nike X, even if it was technically perfect, could not protect the country. The Soviets would always be in a position to overwhelm it by simply increasing their offensive capability. He was convinced that if the United States countered Galosh with the Nike X, both sides would be forced to add to their offensive forces. That step, in turn, would require increased defensive measures. In the end the offensive and defensive aspects of the arms race would spiral out of control. Each side would have more weapons and be less secure than ever.

Instead of compounding the instability produced by the appearance of Galosh, McNamara believed the United States ought to add to its offensive forces, thus neutralizing the Soviet ABM system and restoring a stable nuclear balance. A cost-effective technology for such a coup was at hand in the form of the multiple, independently targetable, reentry vehicle (MIRV). In this system the last stage of an offensive missile becomes a "space bus" carrying many separate warheads, each of which can be directed toward a different target. McNamara proposed neutralizing the Soviet ABM threat (and demonstrating how easy and it would be for the Soviets to do the same to an American system) by modifying the Minuteman missile to deliver three warheads and equipping missile-firing submarines with the MIRVed Poseidon missile. Each boat would then be capable of launching not 16 but up to 160 warheads at different targets.

McNamara was able to fight off pressure for the deployment of the army's ABM system until 1967, when, for domestic political reasons, Congress appropriated an initial $167.9 million for that purpose. He then concluded that the only way to head off a massive escalation of the arms race was to convince the Soviets to agree to a joint ban on the deployment of ABM systems. Unhappily, talks in Moscow between Ambassador Llewellyn Thompson and Premier Alexsei Kosygin went nowhere. In June, McNamara himself made a direct appeal to Kosygin. The Soviet leader listened attentively and was impressed by McNamara's obvious sincerity but not by his argument. Kosygin had not yet fathomed how a purely defensive system could threaten the nuclear balance. He may not even have understood the importance of such a balance in the nuclear age.

In January 1968, with political pressure for an American ABM system growing and Moscow unwilling to negotiate, President Johnson asked Congress for another $1.2 billion for the NIKE X, now renamed Sentinel. Ironically, by this time the ostensible reason for deploying the system had all but disappeared. The Soviets had not expanded Galosh, that imagined

At the 1967 Glassboro summit, Secretary of War Robert S. McNamara (far left) attempted to convince Premier Alexei Kosygin (third from left) to abandon plans for a Soviet ABM system. President Lyndon Johnson is seated at the far right.

threat to the credibility of the American deterrent. On the contrary, the system was so ineffective they had virtually abandoned it.

There were other ironies as well. First, the decision to deploy Sentinel was taken for purely political reasons—to satisfy the Joint Chiefs and their supporters in Congress. There was no dissent among weapons experts on the basic question. No matter how effective the system, it could not protect the United States from missile attack because the other side would always be able to overwhelm it by adding to its offensive capabilities.

Of the many curious twists to this story, perhaps the most unfortunate is that in authorizing the MIRVing of American missiles, Secretary McNamara himself inadvertently contributed to the massive destabilization of the nuclear balance. The secretary was so fixated on the dangers posed by an ABM deployment that he failed to see that MIRV, too, was one of those technologies that undermine stability. It was an astonishing oversight. In making this decision, as one strategist has since observed, he went a long way toward restoring the "first strike capability, which he was [committed] to avoiding."[11]

As Herbert York, the former head of the Livermore arms laboratory, has pointed out, MIRV permanently destabilized the arms race by "making it easily possible for *each* side to have many more warheads than the *other* side has missiles." If each side increased the number of warheads in its arsenal while improving the accuracy and reliability of its missiles, it would "eventually be able to wipe out better than ninety-five percent of the other side's silo-based missile force in a surprise attack." During a period of crisis, York concluded, having MIRVed missiles substantially increased the danger of all-out nuclear war. "Each side, believing the other could make a preemptive attack, would certainly be stimulated to consider doing so first." "Use them or lose them," York was saying, might well become the motto of both superpowers.[12]

It was the missile gap all over again. The United States responded to an imagined threat from Galosh by MIRVing its offensive missile forces and beginning the deployment of an ABM system. The threat of a Soviet ABM system then disappeared. But MIRV and an American ABM were harsh realities. The arms race had reached a new level of intensity.

In the spring of 1968, not long after President Johnson decided to seek further funding for Sentinel, the Soviets finally signaled an interest in arms control talks. "It's too bad we waited so long," one Soviet arms controller later lamented. "If only we had gone ahead with talks when McNamara was pressing for them. Don't think we weren't studying the problem. It was just too soon. We didn't think we were ready."[13] Unhappily, by the time the Soviets were ready, technology was again in the saddle and running out of control.

The Strategic Arms Limitation Talks (SALT) might have opened in the summer of 1968. But with President Johnson poised to announce that the two countries would soon meet, the Soviets invaded Czechoslovakia to put down a reform movement there. After that it was politically impossible for the administration to proceed. SALT would have to wait for the new year and a new administration in Washington. In any event, however, the great preoccupation of Soviet-American relations for the next two decades—arms control—was at last about to be addressed.

## ESCALATING THE VIETNAM WAR

In August 1964, when the president authorized those first limited air strikes against North Vietnam, one of his objectives was to discourage Hanoi from continuing its support for the Viet Cong. At the time the CIA warned that such an approach would have exactly the opposite effect. The agency was correct. By the time the presidential election rolled around in November, the Saigon regime was crumbling and the Viet Cong had become stronger and bolder than ever.

In response to this deteriorating situation, a consensus was building inside Washington's policy-making elite in favor of a large-scale bombing campaign against North Vietnam. Though it was doubtful that air attacks could interdict the flow of men and supplies moving from North to South, many in the administration believed that the bombing would have a positive effect on Saigon. Thus Assistant Secretary of State William Bundy argued that by bombing North Vietnam, Washington would create "at least a faint hope" of strengthening the Saigon government. And General Maxwell Taylor, who had taken over as ambassador in Saigon, thought the alternative to bombing was "to accept defeat in the fairly near future."[14]

The lone dissenter inside the administration was George Ball, who later commented on how those in positions of power in Washington turned "logic upside down" to argue that the virtual collapse of the Saigon regime and the growing power of the Viet Cong proved not that the United States should leave Vietnam "but rather that we must promptly begin bombing to stiffen the resolve of the corrupt South Vietnamese government." It was, he thought, "classical bureaucratic casuistry."[15]

The bombing campaign against the North began in February 1965. During the next few months events were in the saddle, and policy makers struggled merely to hang on. In March, General William C. Westmoreland, the commander of American forces in Vietnam, asked for two battalions of marines to guard the air base at Danang. Ambassador Taylor objected but was overruled. A short while later, Westmoreland asked for two combat divisions to undertake offensive operations. Johnson again approved his request but lied to the public about the significance of this. Not until June 1965 did the public and Congress learn that American troops had for two months been active participants in the war.

In July 1965, after a spring offensive by the Viet Cong left ARVN a virtual ruin, Westmoreland, backed to the hilt by McNamara, requested a total of 179,000 troops for Vietnam and told the president, "We are in for a long pull. . . . I see no likelihood of achieving a quick, favorable end to the war."[16] Johnson was thus forced to make a choice, total commitment to a ground war in Asia, with all of its attendant risks, or defeat. George Ball, the only naysayer in the administration, urged him to withdraw. But Ball's was a lonely voice in 1965. The assertive McNamara, who bolstered his arguments with reams of data and computer printouts and who was ably seconded by Secretary Rusk and Special Assistant to the President for National Security McGeorge Bundy, won an easy victory—easy because at bottom the president could not accept defeat.

Although Johnson committed American ground forces to the war, he denied the military complete freedom of action. For example, he prohibited bombing attacks around Hanoi and Haiphong where large numbers of noncombatants were likely to be killed. Nor would he allow air strikes near the Chinese border with North Vietnam. Recalling Korea, he explained that he did not want to wake up one morning and find 2 million Chinese coming down the Ho Chi Minh trail. Nor would he give the military as much latitude in ground operations as the Joint Chiefs wanted.

Originally the Joint Chiefs called for an invasion of North Vietnam to a point above the demilitarized zone. To stop the flow of men and supplies south, they also envisioned expanding the war into Laos and Cambodia. But Johnson, who feared that an expanded war might grow to include China and possibly the Soviets, insisted that ground operations be limited to South Vietnam.

Westmoreland and the Joint Chiefs reluctantly accepted these limits but continued to pressure the president to extend their field of operations. In 1967, when it became clear that the war probably could not be won so long as ground operations were restricted to South Vietnam, they even considered threatening mass resignation as a method of forcing Johnson's hand.

Nothing worked out quite as administration leaders hoped. The

Lyndon Johnson visited the troops in Vietnam in 1966.

intervention, which was in part designed to bolster the sagging government in Saigon, in fact stripped it of most of its remaining credibility. The overwhelming American presence in South Vietnam convinced most Vietnamese that the Saigon government was a mere dependency of Washington. Nor did the increased American presence serve to stabilize South Vietnam's political situation. The power struggle went on just as before. The constant political turmoil angered more than a few Americans in Vietnam. "We're fighting to save these people," one volunteer complained, "and they're fighting each other."[17]

The massive American intervention also had a devastating effect on the South Vietnamese economy. The influx of American goods destroyed local industries, while the increased demand for services of all sorts—ranging from cooks to prostitutes and shoeshine boys—made the people of Vietnam dependent on a continued American presence. At the same time inflation, which ran at close to 100 percent annually in 1966 and 1967, ripped and tore at the fabric of society.

Nor did the war itself go as the military had hoped. General

Westmoreland intended to destroy the enemy main force in a war of attrition, using firepower to keep casualties low. He called it "search and destroy." But this approach could only work if air and ground action stopped the flow of men and material coming into South Vietnam from the North. And that proved to be impossible. With 200,000 young men coming of draft age each year in the North, Hanoi had no trouble escalating its efforts to match those of the United States. During the mid-1960s, an average of 5,000 men a month infiltrated South Vietnam.

During 1966, their hopes of a quick victory dashed, some in the administration began thinking in terms of a negotiated settlement to the war. In fact, however, there was no basis for a compromise. Johnson was unwilling to sacrifice the vision of an independent noncommunist South Vietnam. Not even some sort of coalition would do, since it was clear that the Saigon government had little political support. Nor were the battle-hardened leaders in Hanoi interested in a compromise settlement. They had been fighting the war for independence and unification since 1946 and had by no means run out of patience.

Toward the end of 1966 the Joint Chiefs of Staff began pressing the president to approve a massive increase in the number of troops committed to the war, the mobilization of the reserves (an act that would have placed the country on a war footing), and an expansion of the bombing campaign to allow attacks on Hanoi, Haiphong, and targets near North Vietnam's border with China. But others in the administration, even Robert McNamara, were having second thoughts. Just back from a depressing visit to Saigon, McNamara argued that no amount of bombing could slow the flow of men and supplies from the North. On the other hand the bombing was doing the United States a lot of harm. "The picture of the world's greatest superpower killing or seriously injuring 1,000 non-combatants a week, while trying to pound a tiny, backward nation into submission on an issue whose merits are hotly disputed, is not a pretty one," he told the president.[18]

Satisfied that the United States could not win on the battlefield, McNamara advocated deescalation. He urged the president to stop the bombing, hoping that this gesture might bring the other side to the bargaining table.

Johnson not only rejected McNamara's advice; he got rid of McNamara, appointing him president of the World Bank. The new Secretary of Defense was Clark Clifford, a friend and longtime Washington insider who supported the war.

Johnson's angry rejection of McNamara's proposals did not mean that he supported the Joint Chiefs' call for a further escalation of the war. "If we add divisions, can't the enemy add divisions?" he asked. "If so, where does it all end?"[19] Johnson resolved his dilemma in 1967 by authorizing an expanded air war and a small increase in the number of troops in West-moreland's command. He did so aware that these gestures would make no real difference. Their sole purpose was political—to pacify the Joint Chiefs

Death often came swiftly and without warning in Vietnam.

and their congressional allies. With victory unattainable and defeat unacceptable, the war had turned into a quagmire.

## TROUBLE IN THE DOMINICAN SHOWCASE

In April 1965, while the administration concentrated on its troubles in Southeast Asia, new problems developed closer to home in the Dominican Republic. From 1930 until his assassination in 1961, Rafael Trujillo ruled there with an iron hand. When he was murdered by some of his own military officers, the deed was done with the knowledge and tacit approval of the CIA. Trujillo had become more than an embarrassment to the United States. His ruthless dictatorship was thought to be a breeding ground for a leftist uprising. Fidel Castro had already failed in one attempt to overthrow Trujillo. Unless the dictator was replaced by a more liberal regime, Washington feared that the Dominican Republic might become the Caribbean's next Cuba.

In December 1962, in the first free elections held in the Dominican Republic in forty years, Juan Bosch was elected president. Described by Ambassador John Bartlow Martin as "a divider, a splitter, a schemer, a destroyer," and by Undersecretary of State George Ball as "a muddle-headed, anti-American pedant committed to unattainable social reforms," Bosch was nobody's favorite in Washington.[20] But he was a Social Democrat committed to constitutional government. As such the Kennedy administration reluctantly embraced him and spent the next several months attempting to transform the island republic into a showcase for reform.

The administration wanted Bosch to use the economic aid it was providing to implement moderate reforms while concentrating on establishing a stable political order in the Dominican Republic. It did not want him tampering with American economic interests there. But Bosch had other ideas. In attempting to assert his independence from Washington he proclaimed " a revolutionary democracy," negotiated a large loan from European sources, and implemented a number of economic reforms that alienated both American business interests and the United States government.[21]

Once it became clear that Bosch had fallen out of favor with the United States, the Dominican army deposed him. The new president, General Donald Reid Cabral, had plenty of support from Washington, but little at home. Unable to resolve his country's growing economic problems—unemployment stood at 40 percent—he sealed his fate by adopting an austerity program mandated by Washington that called for a substantial cut in the military budget. These cuts cost him the support of the army, which was all that he had going for him at the time, and opened the way for another coup.

A group of younger, reform-minded army officers forced Reid Cabral from power in April, 1965. They chose as his successor José Rafael Molina Urena, who had once been part of the Bosch government. But Urena's elevation prompted Colonel Elí Wessín y Wessín, one of the officers who had overthrown Bosch in 1963, to organize a countercoup.

In the tug of war between Wessín and Urena, the new American ambassador, W. Tapley Bennett, clearly favored the conservative Wessín. When it appeared that Urena was likely to prevail, Bennett warned the White House that his faction was dominated by communists and urged an immediate military intervention which, he insisted, was necessary "to prevent another Cuba."[22] Bennett also circulated false atrocity stories which no doubt contributed to President Johnson's decision to intervene. According to one such tale, some fifteen hundred persons had been murdered and decapitated by rampaging leftist rebels. The embassy even provided reporters with a list of fifty-three Dominican communists who, it charged, dominated the group supporting Urena. This list was appallingly inaccurate. Many of those named were not on the island at the time; still others were in prison. More to the point, not one had anything to do with Urena. While Bennett worked on the President from long distance, closer to home FBI Director J. Edgar Hoover fed the president similar "information" about the communists who were supposedly behind the Dominican coup.

Fearing another Cuba, Johnson sent twenty-five thousand troops to the island. In spite of the fact that there was hardly a leftist to be found in rebel ranks and reporters like Tad Szulc of the *New York Times* debunked much of what the embassy claimed, President Johnson argued then and later that "the danger of a communist takeover in the Dominican Republic was a real and present one" and that the communists "controlled much of the

Street fighting in the Dominican Republic in 1965.

military strength in the rebel movement." In spite of an embarrassing lack of evidence, the ever-loyal secretary of state, Dean Rusk, backed the president to the hilt. The "danger of a Communist takeover," he insisted "was established beyond question." Rusk also claimed that "what began in the Dominican Republic as a democratic revolution was taken over by Communist conspirators who had been trained for, and had carefully planned, that operation."[23]

The American intervention spelled exile not only for Urena but for Colonel Wessín y Wessín as well. Washington quickly decided that what the Dominican Republic needed most was a fresh start in the direction of constitutional government. It seemed reasonable, then, that the man who had fomented two military coups in as many years would have to go. When Wessín resisted, he was given no choice. "Never would I have imagined," he later said, "that an army officer of my rank would have been taken to the airport in full uniform and forced out of the country with a bayonet at his back."[24] And one has to admit it was an astonishing come-down for a man who, not long before, had been pictured on *Time's* cover as the savior of his country.

Once order had been restored, the Marines were withdrawn from the Dominican Republic and replaced by an Organization of American States peace-keeping force that remained for some months while policy makers in Washington decided what came next. The provisional government of General Antonio Imbert had no future. It was too repressive and too closely identified with the Johnson administration to provide the stable order Washington required. And so new presidential elections were held June 1, 1966. The winner was Joaquin Belaguer, a former president from the days of Trujillo, who had the unqualified support of the Army and financial backing from the American embassy. In this way stability, order, and constitutional government were restored to the Dominican Republic. The Johnson administration had made its point. Clearly, reform and sovereignty both had limits.

## WAR IN THE MIDDLE EAST

Overwhelmed with a myriad of other problems, the Johnson administration paid scant attention to developments in the Middle East, where for eleven years following the Suez crisis, Israel and its Arab neighbors shared an uneasy peace. That all changed in mid-May 1967 when Israeli-Egyptian relations took a turn for the worse and war became not simply possible but highly likely.

Egypt's Gamal Abdel Nasser had for years advocated the destruction of the state of Israel and the establishment in its place of an Arab Palestine. But Nasser had not matched his rhetoric with deeds. By the mid-1960s his rivals for leadership in the Arab world were demanding more than words. Nasser had to do something. And so in mid-May 1967, he began the remilitarization of the Sinai Peninsula, ordered the withdrawal of a United Nations peacekeeping force that had been in the Sinai for some years, and, in spite of a long-standing warning from Tel Aviv that it would mean war, blockaded the Straits of Tiran, cutting Israeli shipping off from the Red Sea and the Indian Ocean. Quite suddenly, while in the midst of its Vietnam agony, the Johnson administration found itself confronted with a probable war in the Middle East and the possibility of a great power confrontation should the Soviets become involved on behalf of their surrogates, Egypt and Syria.

Prior to the outbreak of the 1967 Arab-Israeli war, President Lyndon Johnson (seated on couch) tried to convince Israeli ambassador Abba Eban (facing him) not to fight.

The president urged the Israelis to act with restraint. He suggested that they take the Israeli-Egyptian dispute to the United Nations and promised that if the UN failed to act he would organize a multi-national naval force to keep the Straits of Tiran open. Pulling out all the stops, he also warned Israeli Foreign Minister Abba Eban that if Israel took preemptive action it would be acting alone and without American support. But not even Johnson's famed persuasive powers could alter Israel's course. After Eban left the Oval Office, Johnson told his advisers, "I've failed. They'll go."[25]

Early on the morning of June 5, the Israeli air force struck devastating blows, virtually destroying the Egyptian and Syrian air forces on the ground. In the six days of fighting that followed, Israeli tanks and infantry routed the combined forces of Egypt, Syria, Jordan, and Iraq. The cease-fire that followed the Six Days' War, as it came to be known, left Israel in control of the entire Sinai Peninsula including the Gaza Strip, the West Bank of the Jordan including the cities of Hebron, Nablus, and the Holy City of Jerusalem, and the Golan Heights on the Syrian-Israeli border.

Policy makers in Washington looked for and thought they found a silver lining in these astonishing developments. Tel Aviv, they hoped, could be induced to return the occupied territories in exchange for an Arab agreement to recognize Israel and live in peace.

Five months of painstaking diplomacy produced unanimous UN Security Council support for Resolution 242, a proposed "package settlement" for the Middle East's problems. The resolution called for the recognition of freedom of the seas and the right of innocent passage, a reference to Israel's right to use the Gulf of Aqaba and the Straits of Tiran. But in other ways it was vague. It called for a "just" solution to the Palestinian refugee problem (which became more serious after 1967 as Palestinian Arabs fled or were driven from the newly occupied territories) but made no specific recommendations. The resolution was even less clear in calling for the "withdrawal of Israeli armed forces from territories occupied in the recent conflict" and the "termination of all claims of belligerency and respect for and acknowledgement of the sovereignty, territorial integrity, and political independence of every state in the area and their right to live in peace within secure and recognized boundaries free from threats or acts of force."[26] These carefully chosen words failed to demand either that Tel Aviv withdraw from *all* the territory it had acquired or that the Arab states make a final and definitive peace with Israel.

The vague phraseology used in Resolution 242 was necessary if Moscow and Washington were to cooperate in pushing it through the Security Council. But deliberate vagueness meant that basic issues remained to be resolved in subsequent negotiations. Consequently the resolution called for the appointment of a United Nations representative who was to work with the Arab states and Israel to arrange the details of a settlement. That unenviable task went to the Swedish diplomat, Gunnar Jarring.

To the end of his administration Lyndon Johnson remained committed to Resolution 242. But in the face of an Israeli policy that aimed at

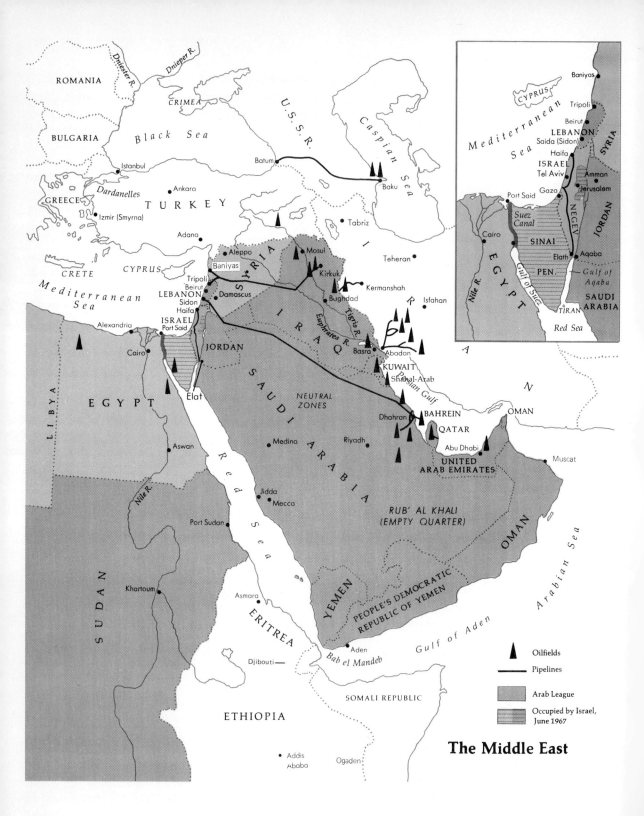

ROMANIA

Dniester R.
Dnieper R.

BULGARIA

CRIMEA

Black Sea

U.S.S.R.

Caspian Sea

Istanbul

Batum

Baku

GREECE

Dardanelles

Ankara

TURKEY

Izmir (Smyrna)

Tabriz

Teheran

Adana

CYPRUS

Aleppo

Mosul

SYRIA

Kirkuk

Kermanshah

CRETE

Mediterranean Sea

Tripoli
Beirut

Baniyas

Damascus

Isfahan

LEBANON

Sidon

Haifa

Bughdad

ISRAEL

Euphrates R.

Tigris R.

Port Said

JORDAN

IRAQ

Basra

Alexandria

Abadan

Cairo

KUWAIT

Shatal-Arab

LIBYA

Elat

SAUDI ARABIA

NEUTRAL ZONES

Persian Gulf

EGYPT

Dhahran

BAHREIN

OMAN

QATAR

Aswan

Medina

Riyadh

Abu Dhabi

Muscat

UNITED ARAB EMIRATES

Red Sea

Jidda
Mecca

RUB' AL KHALI (EMPTY QUARTER)

OMAN

Nile R.

Port Sudan

Arabian Sea

SUDAN

Khartoum

Asmara

YEMEN

PEOPLE'S DEMOCRATIC REPUBLIC OF YEMEN

ERITREA

Aden

Gulf of Aden

Djibouti

Bab el Mandeb

ETHIOPIA

SOMALI REPUBLIC

Addis Ababa

Ogaden

**The Middle East**

Oilfields

Pipelines

Arab League

Occupied by Israel, June 1967

*Inset map:*

CYPRUS

Mediterranean Sea

Baniyas

Tripoli

Beirut

LEBANON

Saida (Sidon)

SYRIA

Haifa

ISRAEL

Tel Aviv

Amman

Gaza

Jerusalem

Port Said

NEGEV

JORDAN

Suez Canal

Cairo

SINAI

Elath

Aqaba

EGYPT

PEN.

Gulf of Aqaba

Gulf of Suez

SAUDI ARABIA

TIRAN

Nile R.

Red Sea

integrating the occupied territories into a greater Israel, Arab unwillingness to make peace with Israel, and the growing power of the Palestine Liberation Organization (PLO), there was no hope of achieving a Middle East settlement.

## DOVES AND HAWKS

The war in Vietnam created deep divisions in American society. In 1965, not long after President Johnson committed the first ground troops to the fighting, "teach-ins" designed to inform students and raise questions about American policy spread from one university campus to another. The early teach-ins focused on the validity of the domino theory, the morality of undermining the Geneva Accords of 1954, and the worthiness of the government in Saigon that Americans were fighting to sustain.

Soon the antiwar movement spread to the society as a whole, attracting the support of such diverse people as actress Jane Fonda, the famed pediatrician Benjamin Spock, and several regiments of folk singers including (to name but a few) Joan Baez, Pete Seeger, and Peter, Paul, and Mary. Leading senators including J. William Fulbright, George McGovern, and Mike Mansfield also joined in the movement against the war.

Early in 1966, Fulbright, who was the chair of the Senate Foreign Relations Committee (and the man who in 1964 steered the Tonkin Gulf resolution through the Senate) held nationally televised hearings on the war. Leading military figures, including retired Generals Matthew Ridgway and James Gavin, criticized administration policy at the hearings. But it was the testimony of George Kennan, a principal architect of the containment policy, that perhaps hurt the administration's case most. Kennan testified that he had never envisioned the use of force as part of the policy he helped create, especially with regard to places of no consequence to American security, such as Vietnam.

Antiwar protesters soon took their cause off the campuses and into the streets. Draft card burnings became common. Storefront draft counseling centers sprang up, where young men could go for advice on how to avoid military service. Some fled to Canada or the Scandinavian countries. Others remained, preferring jail to service in a war they considered immoral. Still others were able to avoid the draft with the help of antiwar physicians who diagnosed them for problems that made them unfit for service. A desperate few even avoided induction into the armed forces by self-inflicted wounds.

Civil rights leaders, unhappy because blacks were doing a dispro-portionate share of the fighting and dying (while many middle-class white youths sat out the war with college deferments) and because the Great Society programs were being gutted to finance the war, joined in the struggle. In March 1967, the Reverend Martin Luther King, Jr., charged that the "pursuit of this widened war has narrowed domestic welfare programs, making the poor, white and negro, bear the heaviest burdens both at the front and at home."[27] A month later King led an army of protesters in an antiwar march through downtown New York City.

King's was only one of a series of mass protests that rocked the administration. On October 21, 1967, 100,000 protesters gathered in Washington. On another occasion some 35,000 tried to close down the Pentagon. And often young protesters could be found outside the White House chanting, "Hey, hey, LBJ, How many kids have you killed today?" The opposition became so widespread that before he left office Johnson was forced to limit his public appearances to "safe" forums, which for the most part were military bases.

At the same time that antiwar protests were on the increase, a significant portion of the media, including even the normally conservative *Time* magazine, grew critical of the war. Opposition developed inside the Democratic party as well. Senator Eugene McCarthy of Minnesota announced at the end of 1967 that he would enter the presidential primaries, which began in March in New Hampshire. It seemed clear, too, that Robert Kennedy was standing in the wings, waiting for the proper moment to throw his hat into the ring.

## THE TET OFFENSIVE

Johnson responded to the tide of criticism both from the antiwar movement and from those who insisted that he ought to become more aggressive in Vietnam with repeated assurances that the war was being won. General Westmoreland, too, assured the public that America was winning in Vietnam. Late in 1967, in an appearance before the National Press Club, Westmoreland claimed that his command had "reached an important point when the end begins to come into view." Later, he told a reporter that he hoped the other side would attempt a large-scale operation because, as he put it, "we are looking for a fight."[28]

On January 30, 1968, the general got the fight he said he was spoiling for. In the early hours of that morning Viet Cong sappers blew a hole in the outer wall of the heavily fortified American embassy compound in Saigon, rushed through the courtyard, and attempted to break into the embassy itself. Unable to blow open the embassy door, the attackers took up positions in the courtyard and fought it out with American forces and were all either killed or seriously wounded.

The attack on the embassy was but one element in a large-scale offensive begun by the Viet Cong that day. All told, Viet Cong troops launched coordinated attacks on thirty-six provincial capitals, sixty-four district capitals, and five cities. Caught off guard by the offensive, which began during a truce called for the celebration of Tet, Vietnam's lunar new year, American and South Vietnamese forces rallied quickly and in the days that followed delivered a crushing tactical defeat to the Viet Cong.

General Westmoreland pronounced the outcome of this battle a

The city of Saigon is enveloped in smoke during the surprise Tet offensive of 1968.

victory for the United States. And in one sense he was correct. Hanoi had miscalculated, believing that the Tet offensive would incite a general uprising of the South Vietnamese people against the Americans and the Saigon regime. Instead, American and ARVN units delivered a counterblow that crippled the Viet Cong in the South.

But if Westmoreland viewed the outcome of the Tet offensive as a major victory, it meant something entirely different to large numbers of Americans. For more than two years the Saigon command had issued nothing but optimistic reports indicating that, as the president put it, there was "light at the end of the tunnel." Tet made a mockery of those claims, convincing most even moderately alert observers that three years of fighting had produced no improvement in the situation. Even some former supporters of the war had a change of heart after Tet. The news commentator Walter Cronkite, whose bluff, straightforward manner made him the most trusted man in America, returned from Saigon at the end of February in a downcast mood. It seemed "more certain than ever," he told his huge television audience, "that the bloody experience of Vietnam is to end in a stalemate."[29]

## THE ROAD TO THE PARIS PEACE TALKS

President Johnson appeared to react to the Tet offensive with grim determination. America, he insisted, would not cut and run. General Earle Wheeler, the chair of the Joint Chiefs of Staff, interpreted the president's demeanor to mean that finally he might be maneuvered into calling up the reserves and expanding the war. Wheeler briefed General Westmoreland on the opportunity at hand, and the field commander responded by urging the president to send another 206,000 troops, more than the president could provide without putting the country on a war footing. Sounding just a little like General Douglas MacArthur after the Chinese intervened in Korea, Westmoreland tried to force the president's hand by warning that his army was in jeopardy. "A setback is fully possible if I am not reinforced," he warned. "I desperately need reinforcements. Time is of the essence." General Wheeler's own briefing for the president and high-level policy makers was even more depressing. Clark Clifford, who had replaced Robert McNamara at the Defense Department, later described it as "somber" and "really shocking."[30]

The president was thus confronted with a set of unpalatable alternatives. He could refuse Westmoreland's request and risk military setbacks or at the very least the indefinite prolongation of the war. On the other hand, he could provide the troops, call up the reserves, further gut his Great Society programs, and probably be forced to raise taxes, all in an election year. Unwilling to make a snap decision, he asked Clifford to advise him.

Johnson had appointed Clifford to the Defense Department job because of his hawkish views on the war. But even Clifford was now developing doubts about continuing the struggle. After a full-scale reevaluation of policy, the Defense secretary became convinced that the United States should leave Vietnam.

Clifford's budding dovishness was encouraged by a number of civilians in the Pentagon. But the decisive factor in his transformation was the fact that the military could not explain how the 206,000 additional men it wanted would change anything. Once he was satisfied that the military had no answer to America's dilemma, Clifford set out to convince the president that the time had come to disengage from Vietnam. This was no easy task, since Johnson viewed the Defense secretary's changed views as evidence of disloyalty. He did, however, allow Clifford to seek the advice of a group of elder statesmen that Johnson had used on certain earlier occasions. Dubbed "the Wise Men" by the press, this group included Dean Acheson, Generals Omar Bradley and Matthew Ridgway, Douglas Dillon, George Ball, McGeorge Bundy, Johnson's close friend Abe Fortas, and a number of others.

At a similar meeting held only five months earlier "the Wise Men" had endorsed the president's Vietnam policy. But that was before the Tet offensive. This time, after a depressing briefing by State Department and Pentagon officials, the consensus of the group was that the United States should disengage. Acheson, normally the most hawkish of advisers, told the president bluntly that given the domestic turmoil and the limited resources available, the United States could not achieve its goal in Vietnam. He urged Johnson to find some way out of the war before mid-summer, warning that otherwise domestic problems would probably reach critical proportions.

This latest blow, coming on the heels of Senator Eugene McCarthy's strong showing in the New Hampshire presidential primary election, was too much for Lyndon Johnson. Less than a week after "the Wise Men" rendered their verdict, the president delivered a major television address in which he announced that he was restricting the bombing of North Vietnam to areas just above the demilitarized zone. He also offered to deescalate the ground campaign if Hanoi would reciprocate, and he appointed W. Averell Harriman to be his personal peace negotiator. Then, in an astonishing finale, Johnson informed the country that he would not be a candidate for reelection.

President Johnson's dramatic speech served to disguise the fact that at the policy level nothing had changed. His new tactics—the limit on bombing, the offer to deescalate, the appointment of a peace negotiator—were primarily designed to reduce the influence of the antiwar movement so that he could pursue the same objective he had sought all along—the preservation of South Vietnam's independence.

Peace talks between Washington and Hanoi opened in Paris on May 13, 1968. But neither side was truly interested in serious negotiations. The North Vietnamese were anxious to see the bombing stopped entirely but unwilling to make any concessions that might further weaken their already battered position in South Vietnam. Nor would they agree to negotiate with the Saigon government. The United States, meanwhile, was unwilling to further deescalate the war unless it could claim some quid pro quo from the North Vietnamese and Viet Cong, and it would not negotiate unless Saigon was represented in Paris.

In October 1968, probably to help the Democratic party's presidential candidate, Hubert Humphrey, who was running behind Richard Nixon in the polls, the president at last agreed to the complete bombing halt the North Vietnamese had demanded as a precondition to serious talks. In return, Hanoi stopped rocket and mortar attacks on South Vietnamese cities, cut its infiltration of men and material into the South, and agreed that the Saigon government should have a seat at the Paris peace talks.

Even so, serious negotiations never actually began. The Saigon government feared the talks would lead to a "sell-out" by the Johnson administration. President Nguyen Van Thieu was encouraged in these views by Republican leaders in the United States who mistakenly believed that the administration would do anything to end the war before the presidential election. Thieu himself no doubt also calculated that South Vietnam's future would be more secure in Republican hands than if he allowed the Johnson administration to control the negotiations. And so he balked, blocking progress in Paris until Johnson was replaced by Richard Nixon.

Thieu's obstructionism, especially the long quarrel at Paris over the shape of the conference table, infuriated many in the United States. Americans were dying while the South Vietnamese stalled. It is doubtful, however, whether much would have come of these talks even if they had begun without delay. Time was short. And more to the point, neither Washington nor Hanoi was as yet willing to make major concessions. President Johnson had assured Thieu that he would not compromise on the basic issues. That had been his position from the beginning, and there is no reason to believe that he had changed his mind at this point in time. Nor had North Vietnam's leaders abandoned their ambitions. There was still no basis for a settlement. Nor would there be for years to come.

## ENDNOTES

1. Lyndon Johnson, quoted in Paul Boller, *Presidential Anecdotes* (New York: Oxford University Press, 1981), p. 308.
2. Johnson, quoted in ibid., p. 311.
3. Johnson, quoted in ibid., p. 313.
4. Johnson, quoted in Stanley Karnow, *Vietnam: A History* (New York: Viking, 1983), p. 214.
5. Robert S. McNamara, quoted in ibid., p. 325.
6. George Ball, *The Past Has Another Pattern* (New York: W. W. Norton, 1982), p. 377.
7. Johnson, quoted in Doris Kearns, *Lyndon Johnson and the American Dream* (New York: Harper and Row, 1976), p. 252.
8. Henry Cabot Lodge, Jr., quoted in *The Pentagon Papers*, Senator Gravel ed. (Boston: Beacon Press, 1971), III, 82.
9. Dean Rusk, quoted in Warren I. Cohen, *Dean Rusk* (Totowa N.J.: Cooper Square, 1980), p. 235.
10. Gulf of Tonkin Resolution, quoted in George Donelson Moss, *Vietnam: An American Ordeal* (Englewood Cliffs, N.J.: Prentice-Hall, 1990), p. 147.
11. McNamara aide, quoted in Henry Trewhitt, *McNamara* (New York: Harper and Row, 1971), pp. 127–28.
12. Herbert York, *Race to Oblivion* (New York: Simon and Schuster, 1970), pp. 178–80.
13. Soviet strategist, quoted in John Newhouse, *Cold Dawn: The Story of SALT* (New York: Holt, Rinehart and Winston, 1973), p. 102.
14. William Bundy and Maxwell Taylor, both quoted in George C. Herring, *America's Longest War: The United States and Vietnam, 1950–1975* (New York: Alfred A. Knopf, 1979), pp. 127–28.
15. Ball, *Past Has Another Pattern*, p. 383.
16. William Westmoreland, quoted in Karnow, *Vietnam*, p. 422.
17. Unnamed U.S. official, quoted in ibid., p. 446.
18. McNamara, quoted in Herring, *America's Longest War*, p. 176.
19. Johnson, quoted in ibid., pp. 177–78.
20. John Bartlow Martin, *Overtaken by Events: The Dominican Crisis from the Fall of Trujillo to Civil War* (New York: Doubleday, 1966), p. 329; Ball, *Past Has Another Pattern*, p. 327.
21. Juan Bosch, quoted in Martin, *Overtaken by Events*, p. 325.
22. W. Tapley Bennett, quoted in ibid., pp. 656–57.
23. Lyndon Baines Johnson, *The Vantage Point: Perspectives of the Presidency, 1963–1969* (New York: Holt, Rinehart and Winston, 1971), pp. 200–201; Dean Rusk, quoted in Cohen, *Dean Rusk*, p. 266.
24. Elí Wessin y Wessin, quoted in Hal Draper, "The Dominican Crisis," *Commentary*, December 1965, p. 39.
25. Johnson, quoted in William B. Quandt, *Decade of Decisions* (Berkeley, Calif.: University of California Press, 1976), p. 54.
26. U.N. Resolution 242, quoted in Congressional Research Service, Library of Congress, "The

Search for Peace in the Middle East, 1967–1979: Report for the House Committee on Foreign Affairs," Committee Print CP-957 (Washington, D.C., 1979), p. 227.

27. Martin Luther King, quoted in Alexander Kendrick, *The Wound Within: America in the Vietnam Years, 1945–1974* (Boston: Little, Brown, 1974), pp. 234–35.

28. Westmoreland, quoted in Karnow, *Vietnam*, p. 514.

29. Walter Cronkite, quoted in ibid., p. 547.

30. Clark Clifford, quoted in ibid., p. 547. See also Moss, *Vietnam*, pp. 256–60.

This antiwar demonstration was led by Coretta Scott King (center) and Dr. Benjamin Spock (just behind her) and took place outside the gates of the White House.

# 32

# "PEACE WITH HONOR," 1969–1973

On January 20, 1969, Richard M. Nixon took the oath of office as the thirty-seventh president of the United States. Few, even inside the White House inner circle, ever came to understand this curious, insecure loner. The White House chief of staff, H. R. ("Bob") Haldeman, called him "inexplicable, strange, hard to understand." Another aide thought Winston Churchill's description of the Soviet Union—"a mystery wrapped in an enigma, enclosed in a paradox"—might with equal accuracy be applied to his boss.[1]

A political gutter-fighter, Nixon made his way in the southern California of the 1940s by practicing his own brand of McCarthyism. After an impressive start, his political career almost came to an abrupt end during the 1952 presidential campaign when, while he was running for the vice-presidency on the Republican ticket, it was discovered that he had a secret slush fund made up of contributions from wealthy friends. Eisenhower, who never liked Nixon, momentarily considered dropping him from the ticket. Only Nixon's famous "Checkers Speech," dubbed by Darryl F. Zanuck, the Hollywood film mogul, the "most tremendous performance I've ever seen," saved him from political oblivion then and there.[2]

Following Nixon's defeat in the 1960 presidential election, the press wrote the first of what became a series of political obituaries for this tenacious, unlikable man. After a second loss, this time in the 1960 California gubernatorial election, Nixon wrote one for himself. In a rambling and emotional concession speech given before a group of gaping reporters at his Los Angeles hotel, Nixon blamed the press for his defeat. In a statement still recalled with a certain amount of amazement by those who witnessed it, he concluded: "As I leave you I want you to know—just think how much you're going to be missing. You won't have Nixon to kick around anymore, because, gentlemen, this is my last press conference."[3]

Of course it was not Richard Nixon's last press conference. During the next six years he worked assiduously for the Republican party and for another chance to win the presidency. In 1968 all the hard work and tenacity paid off.

Of all the presidents who had come before, Nixon most admired Woodrow Wilson, so much so that he had the desk Wilson was thought to have used during his years in the White House moved into the Oval Office. Though he lacked Wilson's intellectual power, there were similarities between the two men. Both were humorless, self-absorbed, intolerant of criticism, and extremely thin skinned. On a more positive note each man came to the White House anxious to leave a mark. But unlike Wilson, who hoped to focus on domestic reform, Nixon intended to go down in history as the president who revolutionized American foreign policy and ended the cold war.

Nixon chose William Rogers to be his secretary of state. A successful corporation lawyer and an old acquaintance from their days together in the Eisenhower administration, Rogers was neither a forceful person nor an effective bureaucratic infighter. And that is precisely why Nixon selected him. Determined to run foreign policy from the White House, he excluded the unassertive Rogers and the State Department from the policy-making process.

Nixon was to be the grand strategist of his administration. But he had neither the time nor the inclination to deal with the details. What he needed, and what he found in Henry Kissinger, a former Harvard political science professor with a thick German accent and a knack for public relations, was an extremely talented second. As national security adviser, Kissinger became, next to Nixon himself, the most powerful person in the foreign policy establishment.

Kissinger was an unlikely candidate for service in the Nixon White House. He had played an advisory role in the two preceding Democratic administrations and had most recently worked for Nelson Rockefeller, Nixon's nemesis in the Republican party. Moreover, prior to his appointment, Kissinger made no secret of the fact that he had a low opinion of Nixon. Still, it is not difficult to understand why Henry Kissinger accepted the president's offer. Nixon gave him more raw power than most secretaries of state have enjoyed.

Kissinger never learned to like or even respect Nixon. Nor did the president ever feel comfortable with his national security adviser. At the same time Kissinger never lost sight of the fact that the president was the

Richard Nixon and Henry Kissinger confer over Woodrow Wilson's old desk in the Oval Office.

source of his power. Until mid-1973, by which time the Watergate fiasco had eroded the president's power and undermined his ability to concentrate, there was never any question about who made American foreign policy. Kissinger remained the loyal subordinate.

## THE VIETNAM MEAT GRINDER

Nixon viewed the Vietnam War as an annoyance, a distraction from the more important business of restructuring American foreign policy. His basic objective during his first months in office was to end the war quickly. Otherwise, he feared, domestic discord would paralyze the administration and prevent him from getting on with the real work at hand. "I'm not going to end up like LBJ," the president told Bob Haldeman, "holed up in the White House afraid to show my face on the street. I'm going to end that war. Fast."[4]

At the same time Nixon was unwilling to leave Vietnam on anything less than "honorable" terms. In a practical sense this meant that, like LBJ before him, he insisted on preserving an independent, noncommunist South Vietnam. Johnson had not been able to achieve a settlement on those terms. It was hubris that led Nixon to believe he could succeed where his predecessor had failed.

Although Nixon alluded to a "secret plan" for ending the war during the election campaign, he had no new ideas about how to achieve what he loosely described as "peace with honor." In spite of the fact that the State and Defense departments as well as the CIA agreed that bombing could "not significantly raise the cost of the war to North Vietnam," he intended to bludgeon Hanoi into surrendering by escalating and expanding the air war. A "fourth rate power like North Vietnam," Henry Kissinger observed, "must have a breaking point." The essence of Nixon's strategy was to find that point.[5]

By escalating the bombing campaign and authorizing the secret and illegal bombing of Cambodia, Nixon hoped to signal the North Vietnamese that they were now dealing with an extremist. "I want the North Vietnamese to believe I've reached the point where I might do *anything* to stop the war," he told his White House chief of staff. He wanted them to believe in "the madman theory"—that he was even desperate enough to use nuclear weapons. If he could do that, he predicted, "Ho Chi Minh himself will be in Paris in two days begging for peace."[6]

Nixon's brutal tactics failed. Repeated secret meetings in Paris between Kissinger and the North Vietnamese negotiator, Le Duc Tho, produced no movement on the diplomatic front. Hanoi continued to call for the withdrawal of all American forces from Vietnam, President Nguyen Van Thieu's removal as the head of government in Saigon, and the establishment of a coalition South Vietnamese government made up of representatives from the Saigon government, the People's Revolutionary Government (the PRG was a South Vietnamese government in exile), and a group of neutralists.

During the initial nine months of his administration, Nixon had not been troubled to any significant degree by the antiwar movement—for two reasons. First, as a new president publicly committed to ending the war, he enjoyed a "honeymoon" period during which the great majority of Americans were willing to allow him time to put his "secret plan" into operation. He also managed to keep the antiwar movement off balance by committing himself to the phased withdrawal of American forces from Southeast Asia. In May 1969, he announced that twenty-five thousand troops would be withdrawn immediately, with further withdrawals to be announced periodically. In August another thirty-five thousand troops left Vietnam.

These early troop withdrawals were relatively insignificant, since a half-million American service men and women remained in Vietnam at the time. But they did serve to convince the general public that Nixon was acting to end the involvement there. And that was enough to give him several more months during which he remained relatively free from domestic criticism.

All of his stratagems notwithstanding, in the autumn of 1969 the antiwar movement again emerged as a political force to be reckoned with. And when it did, it proved to be more powerful than before. On October 15, and again on November 15, 1969, large-scale demonstrations against the war were held all across America. The most impressive of these took place in Washington, where 250,000 protesters, led by Coretta Scott King, the widow of the slain civil rights leader, marched against the war. And if some of the speakers at these gatherings were seasoned antiwar activists, others were clearly new to the movement. A crowd on Long Island, for example, even heard W. Averell Harriman, until recently the head of the American delegation to the Paris peace talks, call for an end to the war.

By the autumn of 1969 Richard Nixon had nearly run out of options. He was no closer to a peace settlement than before. And the antiwar movement was clearly gaining momentum. Still unwilling to accept anything less than "peace with honor," he decided on a desperate gamble. Sir Robert Thompson, the British counterinsurgency expert, believed that if properly armed and equipped ARVN could be made strong enough to stand against the North Vietnamese and Viet Cong without American help. Secretary of Defense Melvin Laird, who had been advocating withdrawal all along, made the same argument, dubbing the transfer of responsibility for the conduct of the ground war to Saigon "Vietnamization." Now, though skeptical about Saigon's ability to survive on its own, Nixon adopted Vietnamization as policy.

Nixon, a shrewd political tactician, saw in Vietnamization a method of muzzling his critics while actually extending the period of time that he could keep American ground forces in Vietnam. In a nationally televised address delivered on November 3, 1969, he explained that he intended to train and equip ARVN to assume responsibilities currently being handled by American ground forces and promised the gradual withdrawal of all remaining American forces from Vietnam. But Nixon also explained that Vietnamization would take time and appealed to the "great silent majority' to grant him that time. Then, in an attack on the patriotism of the antiwar protesters, he said, "Let us be united for peace. Let us be united against defeat. Because let us understand: North Vietnam cannot defeat or humiliate the United States. Only Americans can do that."[7]

Nixon's speech was a political tour de force, a bravura performance that once again temporarily hamstrung the antiwar movement. The White House was overwhelmed with telephone calls, telegrams, and letters from citizens rallying to the president's support. Congress, where antiwar sentiment had been on the rise, now gave the president broadly based bipartisan support. "We've got those liberal bastards on the run now," Nixon crowed, "and we're going to keep them on the run."[8]

This speech, in which Nixon appealed for support from the middle class, America's great "silent majority," gave him a major victory over his domestic foes; there is no doubt about that. But the commitment to Vietnamization placed him in the untenable position of having to withdraw American forces while at the same time attempting to force Hanoi to accept the continued existence of an independent South Vietnam. He could not have it both ways. Since the North Vietnamese were convinced that once the Americans left they could achieve total victory, Vietnamization reduced to the vanishing point any incentive they had to negotiate.

Aware of his problem, Nixon knew that somehow he had to demonstrate to Hanoi that his commitment to South Vietnam was unchanged and that his ability to inflict punishment remained very great. In the spring of 1970 he believed an opportunity to do that was at hand in Cambodia.

## THE CAMBODIAN INCURSION

The Joint Chiefs had long been frustrated by the Johnson administration's unwillingness to widen the war by invading neutral Cambodia, where the North Vietnamese and Viet Cong had established staging areas for incursions into South Vietnam. President Nixon modified that policy in 1969 when he authorized the secret bombing of those sanctuaries. But not even Nixon would authorize the invasion of an officially neutral country over the objections of its government. And Prince Norodom Sihanouk, Cambodia's head of state, did emphatically object.

Early in 1970, the political situation in Cambodia changed, when Sihanouk was overthrown in a coup headed by the pro-American General Lon Nol. The new Cambodian government authorized the South Vietnamese to undertake limited military action against the North Vietnamese and Viet Cong operating in Cambodia and offered the same opportunity to the United States.

The president, encouraged by the Joint Chiefs, saw the changed situation in Phnom Penh as creating an opportunity to destroy the enemy sanctuaries in Cambodia, strengthen Lon Nol, who was then involved in what appeared to be a losing battle with the Communist Khmer Rouge, and demonstrate to Hanoi that Vietnamization and recent troop withdrawals did not mean that he was abandoning South Vietnam. But there was a grave risk to be run in expanding the war as well. As Secretaries Laird and Rogers both pointed out, there would be a major domestic outcry.

For a time Nixon vacillated. But in the end, encouraged by the Joint Chiefs' promises of a great victory, he authorized an invasion. The operation, which began on April 29, 1970, set off a chain reaction of disasters for the nation and the Nixon administration. The invading force did destroy large quantities of war material stored in the enemy sanctuaries. But the supplies Hanoi lost were quickly replaced by the Soviets and Chinese. On the other hand, the political effect of the "incursion" was long lasting. The invading American forces drove the North Vietnamese deeper into Cambodia, where they established new bases from which they gave increased support to the Cambodian communists, the Khmer Rouge, in their war against Lon Nol. To combat this development, the United States committed itself to a large-scale program of aid to Phnom Penh. Thus, one significant result of Nixon's Cambodian adventure was a wider war in Indochina with American prestige linked to yet another crumbling government.

The Cambodian adventure also had a negative impact on the process of Vietnamization. Because of the furious domestic reaction to the invasion, Nixon felt compelled to withdraw American forces from Cambodia only weeks after they had launched the attack. But to keep Lon Nol's government afloat, South Vietnamese forces had to remain in Cambodia to deal with the North Vietnamese and the Khmer Rouge. This added burden made it impossible for Saigon to fulfill its expanding responsibilities under the Vietnamization program.

At home the Cambodian invasion set off a domestic uprising that rocked the Nixon administration to its foundations. All told, somewhere between four and five hundred colleges and universities experienced antiwar demonstrations and student strikes. Kent State University in Ohio became the scene of a great tragedy and the focus of national attention after national guardsmen fired into a group of students killing four and wounding several others. Only days later, at Jackson State University in Mississippi, two more student demonstrators were gunned down by police.

Angry protesters, more than 100,000 strong, converged on Washington. Unlike earlier demonstrations, the mood of the crowd was so ugly that the police cordoned off the White House, ringing it with buses to keep protesters away. It was a modern metaphor for the old western practice of circling the wagons during an Indian attack. And that was precisely the mood in the White House. Charles Colson, a Nixon aide, later wrote, "Within the iron gates of the White House a siege mentality was setting in."[9]

Congress responded to Nixon's Cambodian adventure by rescinding the Gulf of Tonkin Resolution. This action had no practical effect. But legislation offered by Senators John Sherman Cooper of Kentucky and Idaho's Frank Church would have stopped all funds for the Cambodian operation by July 1. An even more far-reaching proposal, the work of Senators George McGovern and Mark Hatfield, called for the withdrawal of all American forces from Vietnam before 1972. Neither of these bills passed. But the fact that they were seriously considered was a clear indication of how tenuous the president's control over the war power had become.

## SERIOUS TALKS BEGIN

In spite of the fact that his policies had failed to produce the slightest movement toward peace, Nixon stayed the course during 1971, hoping, one supposes, that accumulated military pressure would have a telling effect on Hanoi. By the middle of that year, however, it was clear that dry rot was eating away at the American commitment to the war. Opinion polls showed that 71 percent of the people believed the original decision to fight in Vietnam had been a mistake. Even worse from Nixon's point of view, only 31 percent of the people believed he was managing the war properly. A large antiwar group, of course, wanted America out of Vietnam. But another group made up of conservatives and blue-collar workers did not believe the president was being tough enough.

At the same time serious problems had developed inside the military establishment. Once the president abandoned the goal of victory in favor of a staged withdrawal, morale collapsed. There were even occasional "mutinies" (one covered by CBS News) in which enlisted men refused to follow officers they judged to be incompetent. The military also confronted a serious drug problem in Vietnam. Every GI could easily acquire all the "Hanoi Gold" (a high-potency marijuana) he wanted. Harder drugs were also cheap and available. Racial tensions rose inside the military, especially after the assassination of Martin Luther King, Jr. And "fragging" incidents—attacks by enlisted men against their officers—were all too common.

The 1971 peace talks between Kissinger and Le Duc Tho produced movement but no settlement. The major sticking point was the future of South Vietnam's President Nguyen Van Thieu. As before, Le Duc Tho insisted that Thieu be removed and his government replaced by a coalition. And that was a commitment Nixon and Kissinger refused to make. Only if Thieu remained in power after American forces withdrew could the president claim he had left Vietnam under honorable circumstances.

The failure of the 1971 Paris peace talks led each side once again to seek on the battlefield what it had failed to achieve at the bargaining table. For President Nixon this decision meant continuing with Vietnamization while pursuing an aggressive air war. For North Vietnam's leaders, tempted by the fact that American ground combat strength had shrunk almost to the vanishing point, it meant a large-scale offensive.

On April 1, 1972, the North Vietnamese struck across the demilitarized zone with 120,000 men supported by tanks and artillery. The fighting was fierce, and both sides took appalling casualties. The president responded quickly to this new challenge. "Damn it," he raged, "The bastards have never been bombed like they're going to be bombed this time."[10] While American and South Vietnamese fighter-bombers pounded the North Vietnamese invaders, B-52 bombers attacked targets in the North. The giant planes also flew thousands of sorties against North Vietnamese forces in the South.

The massive bombing campaign slowed but did not stop the North Vietnamese advance. In early May, after the fall of the city of Quang Tri, General Creighton Abrams, the American commander in Vietnam, warned that "it is quite possible that the South Vietnamese have lost their will to fight, or to hang together, and that the whole thing may well be lost."[11]

The potential collapse of South Vietnam put Nixon in a difficult position. If he was to save the Saigon government, his only option was to escalate the war against North Vietnam. In practical terms that meant an expanded bombing campaign against Hanoi and Haiphong, the mining of Haiphong Harbor, which was used by Soviet and other East-bloc vessels to deliver supplies, and the bombing of the rail lines between China and North Vietnam. Kissinger along with others warned that escalating the war might undermine relations with Beijing and lead the Soviets to cancel an upcoming summit meeting which was politically important in an election year. But Nixon was in no mood to be restrained. "The summit," he said, "isn't worth a damn if the price for it is losing in Vietnam."[12] Gambling that Beijing and Moscow wanted improved relations badly enough to look the other way, he ordered the mining of Haiphong Harbor and increased bombing raids on Hanoi and Haiphong.

In Washington policy makers braced themselves for a furious reaction from the Soviets. But nothing happened. One Soviet official even told Stanley Karnow of the *Washington Post* that the summit would not be cancelled.

"Listen," this embassy official said, "we've done enough for those Vietnamese. We're not going to let them interfere with our relations with you."[13]

Nixon's gamble paid off in other ways as well. First, his hard-line approach won him increased support from those who had been critical of him for not going all out against North Vietnam. More important, the expanded American bombing campaign apparently made the difference between victory and defeat for ARVN. Aided by American air power, the South Vietnamese stopped the North Vietnamese advance.

## BACK TO THE BARGAINING TABLE

The failure of their 1972 offensive led the North Vietnamese Politburo to make a major concession at the bargaining table. They dropped their demand for the immediate creation of a coalition government in South Vietnam and agreed that President Thieu could remain as South Vietnam's head of state. This shift was the break that Nixon and Kissinger had been looking for. If President Thieu remained in place following a cease-fire and an American withdrawal, Nixon could claim, albeit with a certain amount of disingenuousness, that he had in fact achieved "peace with honor."

Kissinger and Le Duc Tho reopened their secret negotiations late in September 1972. On October 11 they had an agreement that called for a cease-fire, the repatriation of all American prisoners of war, and a complete American withdrawal from Vietnam within sixty days of the cease-fire. In keeping with an earlier concession offered by the administration, North Vietnamese forces would be allowed to remain in place in the South following the cease-fire.

Under terms of the agreement President Thieu would remain as South Vietnam's head of state. But in a major concession Kissinger agreed that the People's Revolutionary Government had legitimate political status in South Vietnam. That innocent sounding phrase meant that the PRG would de facto be recognized as sovereign in those portions of South Vietnam then under North Vietnamese or Viet Cong control.

On the most vital issue, the political future of South Vietnam, Kissinger and Le Duc Tho conspired in a charade that offered form without substance and had no chance of producing a peaceful settlement to the long struggle. The agreement called for the creation of a tripartite commission made up of representatives from the Saigon government, the PRG, and a body of neutralists. This National Council of Reconciliation and Concord was to administer new elections in South Vietnam. But no method was devised to identify who the neutralists on this council might be, and no mechanism was established that would require either Saigon or the PRG to cooperate in establishing the council. In fact, neither Kissinger nor Tho expected the Vietnam question to be settled peacefully. All sides clearly understood that the commission idea was nothing more than a convenient fiction, an elaborate pretense.

After Kissinger and Tho wrapped up their work in Paris, the national security adviser flew to Saigon, where for some curious reason he expected President Thieu to be pleased with the agreement. Kissinger did quite a selling job. But Thieu was not impressed. His American-educated aide, Hoang Duc Nha, described Kissinger's performance as "pure bullshit."[14]

Thieu, who had been excluded from the negotiations, told Kissinger that he would never agree to allow North Vietnamese forces to remain in his country after a cease-fire. Nor was he prepared to accept the People's Revolutionary Government as a legitimate political entity. He also refused to participate as a member of the tripartite National Council of Reconciliation and Concord.

Kissinger urged President Nixon to approve the October accords in spite of Thieu's opposition. But Nixon, who had earlier given tentative approval to the October deal, now supported Thieu. It may be that on reflection he came to share some of the South Vietnamese leader's concerns about the agreement. It is more likely, however, that election year politics influenced his thinking. Even without peace in Vietnam, he was heading for a landslide victory over Senator George McGovern, his Democratic opponent. But if he approved the Paris accords and Thieu complained loudly enough of a sell-out, that could cost him votes.

Nixon would probably have won the election in any event. But he had no incentive to approve a flawed peace and run the risk of being denounced by his ally before the election. General Alexander Haig, an aide to Kissinger and a rising star inside the Nixon White House, later explained to a *Washington Post* reporter that if the president had endorsed the Kissinger-Tho agreement prior to the election he would have placed himself in a "messy" situation. He chose, therefore, to "expose himself to what he regarded as the lesser hazard, . . . a charge of duplicity by North Vietnam."[15]

Just prior to the presidential election Nixon sent Henry Kissinger back to Paris to reopen negotiations with Le Duc Tho. But Tho was not in a cooperative frame of mind. The negotiations dragged on until mid-December. At that point a frustrated Kissinger broke off the talks, flew back to Washington, and urged the president to begin bombing North Vietnam once again.

Following his landslide election victory, Richard Nixon resolved not to spend another four years caught in the toils of an unwanted war in Vietnam. To make his point and bring Le Duc Tho back to the bargaining table, he unleashed a furious bombing campaign against North Vietnam. "I don't want any more of this crap about the fact that we couldn't hit this target or that one," he told the chair of the Joint Chiefs of Staff. "This is your chance to use military power to win this war and if you don't, I'll consider you responsible."[16]

The so-called Christmas bombing campaign, which saw American aircraft drop thirty-six thousand tons of bombs on North Vietnam in less than two weeks, created widespread public outrage. Congress was on its annual Christmas holiday at the time. But opposition to the bombing was so intense that the administration feared when the legislators returned they would cut off funding for the war unless the bombing was stopped. Even the air force was calling for an end to the bombing. Hanoi was not only the most heavily bombed city in the history of aerial warfare; it was the most heavily defended. In a mere twelve days the air force lost twenty-six aircraft to SAM missiles.

Kissinger and Nixon subsequently claimed that the Christmas bombing campaign forced the North Vietnamese to accept terms dictated by the United States. Nor can there be much doubt that Kissinger's promise to stop the bombing if Tho would return to Paris influenced the North Vietnamese. But Hanoi's leaders did not agree to return to Paris hat in hand to accept terms dictated from Washington. On the contrary, they appear to have agreed to renew the talks only because Washington promised that the October accords—the terms Hanoi had already agreed to—would form the basis for future discussions.

On January 8, 1973, Kissinger and Le Duc Tho met once again and in a few days produced an agreement that was essentially the same as the one worked out in October. As before, South Vietnam's President Thieu opposed the settlement. But this time President Nixon used both the carrot and the stick to force him into line. Nixon ordered the transfer of $1 billion in military equipment to the Saigon government and gave Thieu his verbal and subsequently his written commitment that if the North Vietnamese violated the pact he would order quick and decisive retaliation by American forces. But at the same time he made it abundantly clear that if Thieu refused to initial the January accords he would withdraw from Vietnam and leave Saigon to struggle on alone. Very much against his will, then, President Thieu approved the January peace accords.

In 1973, as the last American combat troops left Vietnam, President Nixon proclaimed "peace with honor." It is true that North Vietnam returned American prisoners of war and that as the last regimental flag was rolled and packed away for shipment back to the United States, an independent noncommunist government ruled (however unsteadily) in Saigon. But it is also true that the political future of South Vietnam—the issue that prompted American intervention in the first place—remained to be decided and that all the parties involved knew that the decision would come not as a result of elections but on the battlefield. The American withdrawal signaled not the end of the Vietnam War but the beginning of a final struggle that ended two years later when North Vietnamese tanks rumbled into Saigon.

In the spring of 1973, Congress acted to finally, if belatedly, end all American military involvement in Southeast Asia. In August, after a long legislative struggle, legislation was enacted requiring an end to the bombing of Cambodia and Laos as well as all other American military involvements in the Indochinese area. Then in November Congress passed the War Powers Act over a presidential veto. This legislation requires the president to inform Congress within forty-eight hours of any deployment of American troops abroad, and to withdraw those forces within sixty days unless Congress approves. The long struggle over the power to make war had taken an interesting turn. But the issue was by no means resolved. Nixon, weakened by the unpopularity of his Vietnam policy and the Watergate scandal (see Chapter 33) was unable to challenge Congress. But two of his Republican successors, Ronald Reagan and George Bush, have refused to be bound by the law, claiming that it is unconstitutional. Given the Supreme Court's natural reluctance to decide matters of this nature, the struggle between the two branches of government is likely to go on for some time to come.

## ENDNOTES

1. H. R. Haldeman, and anonymous White House aide, quoted in Paul Boller, *Presidential Anecdotes* (New York: Oxford University Press, 1981), pp. 325–27.
2. Darryl F. Zanuck, quoted in ibid.
3. Richard M. Nixon, quoted in ibid., pp. 329–30.
4. Nixon, quoted in H. R. Haldeman, *The Ends of Power* (New York: Times Books, 1978), p. 81.
5. Bureaucratic estimates, quoted in Tad Szulc, *The Illusion of Peace* (New York: Viking, 1978), pp. 25–26; Henry Kissinger, quoted in George Donelson Moss, *Vietnam: An American Ordeal* (Englewood Cliffs, N.J.: Prentice-Hall, 1990), p. 303.
6. Nixon, quoted in Stanley Karnow, *Vietnam: A History* (New York: Viking, 1983), p. 582.
7. Nixon, television address, November 3, 1969, *Public Papers of the Presidents: Richard M. Nixon, 1969* (Washington, 1971), pp. 901–9.
8. Nixon, quoted in George Herring, *America's Longest War: The United States and Vietnam, 1950–1975* (New York: Alfred A. Knopf, 1979), p. 225.
9. Charles Colson, *Born Again* (Old Tappan, N.J.: Chosen Books, 1971), pp. 37–41.
10. Nixon, quoted in Seymour M. Hersh, *The Price of Power: Kissinger in the Nixon White House* (New York: Summit Books, 1983), p. 506.
11. Nixon paraphrasing Creighton Abrams, in ibid., pp. 506, 516.
12. Nixon, quoted in Karnow, *Vietnam*, p. 644.
13. Soviet official, quoted in Hersh, *Price of Power*, p. 526.
14. Hoang Duc Nha, quoted in ibid., p. 596.
15. Alexander Haig, quoted in ibid., p. 611.
16. Richard Nixon, *RN: The Memoirs of Richard Nixon* (New York: Grosset and Dunlap, 1978), p. 734.

# 33

# *AN ERA OF NEGOTIATIONS, 1969–1977*

During the 1970 Jordanian crisis, Richard Nixon and Golda Meir cooperated to save King Hussein from the combined forces of the Palestinians and Syrians.

Richard Nixon was committed to shaping a new, innovative foreign policy for the United States. Changed circumstances, he believed, had rendered cold war policies obsolete. Western Europe and Japan could no longer be treated as subordinates. Nor could American policy be founded on the old assumption that there existed a monolithic communist bloc controlled from Moscow. Divisions in the communist world, especially between the Soviet Union and China, were all too apparent. He told C. L. Sulzberger of the *New York Times*, "The present trend was one of disintegration rather than unity and this was true all over the world, in Europe, in Asia, in the free world and in the Communist world." The cold war was over; the bipolar world created in the postwar era was gone for good.[1]

Nixon's object, like Woodrow Wilson's before him, was to establish a "structure of peace." But unlike Wilson, Nixon was no believer in international organization. The nation-state was the fundamental unit in international politics. And Nixon was convinced that peace could only be based on a balance of power. Nor did Nixon believe that it was necessary to concern himself overly much with the problems of the Third World. As he saw it, there were five great centers of power: the United States, the nations of Western Europe, Japan, the Soviet Union, and China. If these countries had a vested interest in cooperating to preserve the established order, then, he believed, the entire world would be a safer place and Third World problems could be easily managed.

In his inaugural address Nixon announced that the "era of confrontation" was over, to be replaced by an "era of negotiations."[2] In keeping with changes that had taken place in world affairs, his administration would seek improved relations with both the Soviet Union and China.

Détente with both communist superpowers was essential to the creation of Nixon's "structure of peace." By negotiating with Moscow and Beijing on a wide variety of issues, including trade, scientific and cultural exchange, technology transfers, arms control, and the like, he hoped to reduce the danger of global war. He also imagined that a network of mutually beneficial and reinforcing relationships would create an awareness on all sides that cooperation was in the general interest.

Nixon believed that the way to improve relations with each of the major communist powers was through the other, that improved relations with China would inevitably lead to closer relations with Moscow as well. The Sino-Soviet split placed the United States in a superb bargaining position with both powers. It was the split, he later wrote, that made the rapprochement between Moscow and Washington possible. "Together with continuing Soviet belligerence, it also made the rapprochement indispensable from both the Chinese and American viewpoints."[3]

## THE CHINA COURTSHIP

Nixon's grandiose ambitions for the creation of a new global balance of power notwithstanding, his first three years in office were anything but glorious. At the beginning of 1972 the Vietnam War remained the central issue in American life. And by that time it was no longer "McNamara's War" or "Johnson's War"; it was "Nixon's War," and he saw no way of ending it. Considering his many difficulties, it is remarkable that the year 1972 should have produced so many successes for him. Yet, brilliantly seconded by Henry Kissinger, he went from one dazzling foreign policy triumph to another.

One of Nixon's most visible achievements was the establishment of open if not quite formal diplomatic relations with mainland China, a country the United States had steadfastly refused to recognize. In 1969 the situation was absolutely right for this dramatic development. Nixon had made it plain in an article he published in *Foreign Affairs* before taking office that he thought the nonrecognition policy was not only absurd but counterproductive. As for the Chinese, they were more than ready to reestablish economic and political ties with Washington. They needed the trade and access to Western technology. Moreover, as Nixon clearly understood, the Sino-Soviet dispute which threatened to break into open war gave Beijing another solid reason for seeking friendly relations.[4]

In spite of these good auguries, the Sino-American courtship got off to a tentative start, probably because neither Washington nor Beijing wanted to risk a rebuff. It took ten months before there even began what Henry Kissinger described as "an intricate minuet between us and the Chinese so delicately arranged that both sides could always maintain that they were not in contact, so stylized that neither side needed to bear the onus of an initiative."[5]

On January 20, 1970, the first direct talks between American and Chinese representatives took place at the Chinese embassy in Warsaw. The meeting went smoothly. But the future of Taiwan and the question of whether Beijing or Taipei would sit in the United Nations proved to be major obstacles to diplomatic progress. Although the China lobby lacked the power it had wielded during the 1950s, conservatives still viewed America's commitment to the Nationalists as nearly sacred. And Nixon, whose conservative credentials remained impeccable, was reluctant to risk alienating the right wing of his party. Thus, on March 4, 1970, he told reporters that while he was interested in establishing relations with China, "under no circumstances will we proceed with a policy of normalizing relations . . . if the cost of that policy is to expel Taiwan from the family of nations."[6]

Nixon toyed with the idea of a "two-China policy," in which the United States would retain its relationship with the Nationalists on Taiwan and continue to support their claim to a seat on the United Nations Security Council while simultaneously establishing relations with mainland China. But Beijing's leaders, who insisted that the future of Taiwan was an internal matter to be decided by the Chinese themselves, found this proposal entirely unacceptable.

In the autumn of 1970, Beijing broke the impasse with an offer Nixon found too tempting to pass up. First, Zhou Enlai informed the president though his Rumanian contacts that he and Mao Zedong wanted improved relations providing the president "could find a solution for Taiwan." Then, having clearly defined the single obstacle to a successful negotiation, Chairman Mao gave an interview to the author, Edgar Snow, in which he said that he would welcome a visit from the president. In "discussing Nixon's possible visit to China," Snow wrote, "the Chairman casually remarked that the Presidential election would be in 1972, would it not? Therefore, he added, Mr. Nixon might send an envoy first, but was not himself likely to come to Peking before early 1972."[7]

Beijing's message came through loud and clear. If the president could find a "solution" to the Taiwan problem, he could look forward not only to the normalization of relations, a major foreign policy achievement in itself, but a trip to China that would unquestionably be given worldwide media coverage. The impact that a media blitz of this kind could have on his hopes for reelection would be incalculable.

After the Snow interview, the substance of which was immediately forwarded to the president, events moved quickly. On March 15 the administration lifted many long-standing restrictions on trade with and travel to China and followed up with a proposal to reopen talks at the ambassadorial level in Warsaw. But the Chinese were not interested in continuing the minuet. Instead they opted for something more dramatic. It so happened that in April 1971 the American and Chinese national ping-pong teams were both competing in an international tournament in Nagoya, Japan. At the conclusion of the tourney, on instructions from their government, the Chinese players invited their American counterparts to play in China. The meaning of the invitation was clear. Beijing was making a gesture designed to speed the diplomatic process along.

To make the point that this was no ordinary visit by a foreign athletic team, the American players were feted at a banquet in the Great Hall of the People. There Zhou Enlai himself explained that he considered the American team's visit as foretelling a new era in relations between Washington and Beijing. "You have opened a new page in the relations of the Chinese and American people," he said. "I am confident that this beginning again of our friendship will certainly meet with majority support of our two peoples."[8]

In Washington policy makers saw Zhou's initiative—the press dubbed it "ping-pong diplomacy"—as the breakthrough they had been looking for. At last, absolutely confident that there could be no embarrassing hitches, Washington moved quickly. Early in July, Henry Kissinger went on a secret mission to China, where he and Zhou Enlai laid the groundwork for the normalization of relations as well as a presidential visit early in 1972.

Kissinger and Zhou agreed that the future of Taiwan was an internal problem to be settled by the Chinese themselves and that at some future but unspecified time the United States would remove its military forces from the island. Because domestic political considerations made it impossible for the president to break diplomatic relations with Taiwan, Kissinger and Zhou also agreed that for the time being Washington and Beijing would establish liaison offices that would function as unofficial embassies until the Taiwan question was finally resolved.

Zhou and Kissinger agreed on other sensitive questions as well. Both sides were aware that unless the United States lobbied hard during the 1971 session, Taiwan would doubtless be expelled from the United Nations and replaced by a delegation from Beijing. Though nothing was put in writing, it was understood that Nixon would let this happen. And he did. Though Zhou made no hard-and-fast commitments, he also seems to have agreed to exert what influence he had in Hanoi to help President Nixon get "peace with honor" in Vietnam.

## JOURNEY FOR PEACE

On the morning of February 17, 1972, a crowd of eight thousand federal employees and schoolchildren (who had been bused in for the benefit of the television networks) were on hand cheering and waving American flags outside the White House to bid farewell to President and Mrs. Nixon as they boarded the president's helicopter for the first leg of a twenty-thousand-mile "journey for peace." This extravagant send-off, carefully staged by the

Here, during his stay in Beijing, President Richard Nixon (second from right) chats with Chairman Mao Zedong (center) as Zhou Enlai (far left), and Henry Kissinger (far right) look on.

White House staff, was just the beginning of one of the most impressive media events in American political history.

After a leisurely trip across the Pacific (to avoid "jet-lag") the president and his party landed at Beijing airport at 11:40 A.M. local time (10:40 P.M. Eastern Standard Time) on February 21. The Chinese having allowed the American television networks to install satellite ground stations, Nixon received prime-time live coverage as he deplaned to be greeted by Premier Zhou Enlai, other high-level dignitaries, and a military honor guard.

The president was annoyed by the fact that the Chinese had not brought out huge crowds to welcome him. But nothing else about the visit disappointed him. The Nixons were hardly settled in the Chinese government's guesthouse before he was invited for a chat with seventy-eight-year old Chairman Mao. That ninety-minute interview was followed by a brief talk with Zhou and later by an elaborate banquet that was held in the Great Hall of the People and televised live.

The foreign policy fallout from Richard Nixon's visit to China was far more important than the results of the trip itself, which was largely ceremonial and undertaken for domestic political reasons. Once the president had broken the ice, the Japanese moved quickly to reestablish relations with China. Tokyo then broke its ties with Taiwan and began the economic penetration of China. At this writing Japan is the most important foreign economic power in China in terms of both trade and investment. The United States ranks second.

Moscow, too, was influenced by the Nixon trip to China and the dramatic improvement in Sino-American relations that it signaled. The Soviets, who viewed this change as threatening to their interests, adopted a more conciliatory demeanor in dealing with the United States. The Sino-Soviet split made that move imperative.

## THE MOSCOW SUMMIT

In May 1972, only a few months after his triumphant visit to China, Richard Nixon journeyed to Moscow for the first of three superpower summit meetings he was to hold with Leonid Brezhnev. Sometime later Brezhnev quipped that Nixon went to China to attend a banquet but that when he came to Moscow it was to do business. The business Nixon came to complete in 1972 included the signing of a number of agreements on trade as well as scientific and cultural exchange. But the centerpiece of the Moscow summit was the first strategic arms limitation agreement of the nuclear age.

SALT I had been a long time in the making. On January 20, 1969—inauguration day in Washington—the Soviets announced their readiness to enter into serious negotiations for the limitation and reduction of offensive and defensive launch vehicles. Kissinger and Nixon were not, however, about to be hurried into talks. Before they did anything they were determined to make a thorough review of all major policy questions, including, of course, arms control under the administration of Lyndon Johnson.

In spite of the administration's unwillingness to move too quickly, it is clear that the president had significant incentives for wanting an arms control agreement. The United States had reached the point of diminishing returns in terms of the size of the American strategic arsenal. More weapons would not produce greater security. Moreover, the unpopularity of the Vietnam War had bred an opposition to increased defense budgets that left the Pentagon struggling to make ends meet. The situation was so grim that Assistant Secretary of Defense David Packard thought "an early freeze on offensive [strategic nuclear] weapons was imperative because the squeeze on our defense would make it nearly impossible to maintain existing strategic forces, much less increase them."[9] With the Soviets free to add to their forces, unless an arms control agreement was negotiated Washington might find itself with fewer deliverable warheads than Moscow.

The Soviets, too, had incentives to negotiate. Following the Cuban missile crisis their efforts had been focused on developing nuclear parity with the United States and a genuine second-strike capability. By the time Nixon took office, they had achieved these goals. But the Johnson administration's decision to deploy the Sentinel antiballistic missile system and Nixon's decision to rename and expand the system raised questions about the effectiveness of the Soviet deterrent. If Washington wanted a freeze on the number of launch vehicles the Soviets could deploy, Moscow was just as anxious to eliminate the threat posed by the American ABM system.

The Soviet leaders were also finding it increasingly difficult to ignore mounting economic pressures at home. For years they had diverted badly needed resources from the domestic economy to the military. By the end of the decade, as Soviet economic growth slowed, the Kremlin's leadership felt a need to redirect efforts toward strengthening the domestic side of the economy.

Finally, the Soviets wanted an arms control agreement as part of an attempt to achieve a general improvement in relations with the United States. As arms controller Paul Warnke once quipped, "The Soviet Union is the only nation in the world entirely surrounded by hostile Communist states." Moscow was having problems keeping the Eastern European satellites in line. China posed a more serious problem. As Moscow's relations with Beijing deteriorated, the Soviet leaders became increasingly interested in détente with the West. They may even have envisioned some sort of alliance with Washington to keep China in check.

Thirty months of often frustrating negotiations on the part of American and Soviet delegations, supplemented by "back-channel" talks among Henry Kissinger, Andrei Gromyko, and Leonid Brezhnev, led to the SALT I agreement. Although it is easy to overestimate its importance, SALT I was a solid achievement. It improved hot-line communications in the event of a Soviet-American confrontation, ensured against the accidental launch of nuclear weapons by either side, and authorized the use of "national technical means" (spy satellites and electronic eavesdropping devices) to gather data for verification of treaty compliance.

The ABM treaty was by far the most important of the agreements known cumulatively as SALT I. By limiting the number of ABM sites that could be established to two (the figure was later reduced to one) in each country, the agreement headed off a costly and futile competition in defensive systems that would have destabilized the nuclear balance.

For all of its virtues, it is important to note that SALT I left open some enormous loopholes that allowed the arms race in offensive strategic weaponry to escalate sharply. Most significant, while the agreement called for a five-year freeze on the deployment of new offensive launch vehicles, each side was allowed to "modernize" its existing forces. As a result, the American missile force was so rapidly MIRVed that, whereas in 1967, 1,710 warheads were aimed at Warsaw Pact and Chinese targets, eight years later, with the same number of launchers the United States deployed upward of 7,000 warheads. Similar developments took place in the Soviet Union. Additionally, as newer and more accurate guidance systems replaced older ones, each side developed what seemed to the other to be something approaching a first-strike capability. Finally, SALT I entirely ignored cruise missiles. These small, extremely accurate weapons brought a frightening new dimension to the arms race. Once developed, there would be no way for either superpower to know exactly how many its adversary possessed because there was no method of verifying the number or deployment of these easily concealed weapons.

The high-profile arms control agreements signed at the 1972 summit obscured the fact that Washington and Moscow were simultaneously pursuing détente on a number of different tracks and that other agreements of consequence signed both at the conference and shortly thereafter were designed to broaden and deepen the relationship. For example, while in Moscow the president committed the United States to cooperative ventures

At the 1972 Moscow summit, Richard Nixon and Leonid Brezhnev signed the first significant arms control agreement of the nuclear age.

with the Soviets in space exploration, environmental protection, and medical as well as scientific research. Not long afterward he agreed to the sale of $750 million in food grains to the Soviets and followed up by negotiating an agreement designed to increase trade between the two countries. At the same time the Soviets agreed to pay a lend-lease debt they had refused to honor since the end of World War II. Détente seemed to be working. Although the Soviet-American rivalry remained a basic fact of international life, relations between the two superpowers were closer than they had been at any time since the breakup of the Grand Alliance.

## CRISIS IN THE MIDDLE EAST

Richard Nixon recognized from the very beginning of his administration that continued instability in the Middle East posed a significant danger. He knew that a renewal of the war between Israel and its Arab neighbors could involve both Washington and Moscow in a superpower confrontation. Yet curiously, Nixon did not at first choose to become personally involved in the search for peace in the Middle East. It may be that he had his hands full with Vietnam, a new China policy, and détente with the Soviets. It is just as likely, however, that he was reluctant to become involved because he thought the problems of the region were intractable. Kissinger certainly believed they were. According to one NSC staffer, the national security adviser had "a real hesitancy" about involving himself in Middle East affairs. His "attitude was: So why jump in and not be successful and make a lot of enemies in the process?"[10]

Though Nixon and Kissinger hoped to steer clear of the Middle East and its problems, the escalating level of violence there and a growing Soviet presence in the region made that impossible. The cease-fire that ended the Six Days' War in 1967 left Israeli and Egyptian troops confronting each other on either side of the Suez Canal. In 1970 the fighting that had punctuated the uneasy truce intensified. Cairo sponsored Fedayeen (Palestinian guerrilla) attacks on Israeli settlements and military installations. The Israelis responded with commando raids inside Egypt and "deep penetration" air strikes that reached the outskirts of Cairo.

The likelihood that the fighting would blossom once again into full-scale war prompted Gamal Abdel Nasser to journey to Moscow seeking increased aid. The Soviets responded generously. Not long after Nasser's return from the Soviet capital the first of approximately fifteen thousand Soviet advisers arrived in Egypt. They brought with them surface-to-air missiles (SAM IIIs) to defend against Israeli air attacks, MIG fighters, tanks, and artillery. In a surprising move, the Soviets even provided pilots to fly the MIGs against Israeli intruders.

As far as Nixon was concerned, the increased Soviet involvement in Egypt transformed the basic nature of the Arab-Israeli dispute from a regional question to a superpower confrontation. Commenting on a meeting he had with Nixon, Kissinger, and Secretary of State William Rogers in the Oval Office, Israel's defense minister, Moshe Dayan, recalled that all three "were very worried by what they called the Sovietization of the Egyptian war." Dayan concluded from the level of their concern that "if the Soviet Union actively intervened, the United States would not be able to stand aside."[11]

The Nixon administration responded to this growing Soviet presence in the Middle East by agreeing to a moderate increase in the flow of arms to Israel and by brokering a cease-fire among Israel, Egypt, and Jordan. The cease-fire didn't last long, however. Within a week Israeli reconnaissance planes photographed Soviet and Egyptian crews in the act of installing SAM III missiles in the supposedly demilitarized cease-fire zone on the Egyptian side of the Suez Canal.

From the speedy way in which the Soviets and Egyptians violated the cease-fire accord, Nixon and Kissinger concluded that Moscow opposed a Washington-brokered settlement to the Arab-Israeli dispute and had chosen this method of derailing their efforts. The president was furious. Earlier he had deliberately kept a tight rein on arms sales to the Israelis, hoping that Brezhnev would take the same tack toward Egypt and Syria. Instead, the

Soviets had expanded the arms race as well as their own presence in the area and had undermined the cease-fire agreement. The president's angry reaction was to authorize the sale of eighteen new fighter-bombers to the Israelis along with air-to-ground missiles specifically designed to attack the SAM sites.

The developing superpower confrontation along the Suez Canal was exacerbated by an even more serious situation that developed in Jordan immediately after the cease-fire went into effect. There King Hussein was threatened internally by the growing power of a radical Palestinian movement and externally by Syria and Iraq, countries Washington thought of as Soviet surrogates.

The 1967 Arab-Israeli war and consequent Israeli occupation of the West Bank territory led to a vast influx of homeless, poverty-stricken Palestinians into Jordan, where they joined the ranks of refugees who had fled Israel after the 1948 Arab-Israeli war. Soon, this large Palestinian population became an organized political force in Jordan. Alongside such organizations as the Palestine Liberation Organization (PLO), there emerged guerrilla groups, including Fatah led by Yasser Arafat and the even more radical Popular Front for the Liberation of Palestine (PFLP) headed by the Christian Arab George Habash. These guerrilla organizations had as their objective the destruction of the state of Israel and the establishment in its place of an Arab Palestine. By August 1970, the Palestinians living in Jordan constituted "a state within a state." They were numerous, well armed, and disdainful of the government in Amman. A confrontation was inevitable.

It was the short-lived cease-fire among Egypt, Jordan, and Israel that triggered the crisis. Until then the Palestinians had viewed Nasser as a firm supporter of their cause. After he agreed to the cease-fire, however, Habash and others concluded that he was preparing to make peace, an act that would vastly diminish their hopes for the destruction of Israel.

The Palestinians lacked the power to create trouble in Egypt. But Jordan was another matter. It was George Habash who brought on the crisis. On September 6 and 9, 1970, Popular Front guerrillas hijacked two airliners and had them flown along with more than three hundred hostages to Dawson Field in Jordan. The stated reason for the hijackings was to induce Israel to release a large number of Palestinian guerrillas it was then holding. But Habash's real purpose was to force a showdown with King Hussein (who could hardly allow this air piracy to go unnoticed) at a time when Iraq, with twenty thousand troops in Jordan, and Syria, with an army on the Jordanian border, appeared willing to support the Palestinians.

King Hussein knew that his army could handle the Fedayeen. But he feared that if he engaged the Palestinians, Syria and Iraq would join his enemies. He therefore requested Washington's assistance. Nixon and Kissinger wanted to help Hussein not only because he was a moderate in a part of the world where moderates were few and far between but also because a Palestinian victory in Jordan would have exacerbated the Middle East crisis.

Nixon later described the Jordanian situation as "a ghastly game of dominoes, with a nuclear war waiting at the end." He explained that had the Palestinians succeeded in overthrowing Hussein,

> the Israelis would almost certainly take pre-emptive measures against a Syrian-dominated radical government in Jordan; the Egyptians were tied to Syria by military alliances; and Soviet prestige was on the line with both the Syrians and the Egyptians. Since the United States could not stand idly by and watch Israel being driven into the sea, the possibility of a direct U.S.-Soviet confrontation was uncomfortably high.[12]

Nixon's strategy during this crisis was designed to discourage the Syrians and Iraqis as well as the Soviets from intervening while avoiding intervention himself. As soon as heavy fighting broke out between the Jordanian army and the Fedayeen, the president ordered major fleet units into the eastern Mediterranean to strengthen the Sixth Fleet. At the same time he warned against foreign intervention in Jordan and announced that he was "prepared to intervene directly in the Jordanian war" if Syria and Iraq moved.[13]

The Syrians ignored Nixon's warnings, sending a column of tanks and infantry into Jordan. Nixon responded by placing the Eighty-second Airborne Division and other American units in Germany in a high state of readiness and ordering the Sixth Fleet closer to Jordan. Simultaneously, he urged the Soviets to restrain the Syrians.

The Syrian intervention stunned King Hussein, who informed Washington that under the circumstances he would welcome support from a most unlikely source, the Israelis. The next hours were filled with frantic discussions among Kissinger, Israel's Ambassador Yitzhak Rabin, and Prime Minister Golda Meir, who happened to be in the United States on a fund-raising tour. At length, after Nixon agreed to jump in if the Soviets intervened, the Israelis agreed to ride to Hussein's rescue.

At last assured of joint Israeli-American support, Hussein loosed his small air force against the Syrian tank column. On the next day, probably as a result of gestures by the United States, Jordanian air attacks, the threat of Israeli intervention, and warnings from Moscow, the Syrians turned back toward their own border. Israeli forces never crossed into Jordan. Nor did the Iraqi troops in Jordan make any move to help the Palestinians, who were left to fight it out alone with Hussein's army. Thousands were killed and injured in a combat that destroyed Palestinian power in Jordan.

## THE YOM KIPPUR WAR AND AFTER

On September 28, 1970, as the Jordanian crisis was winding down, Gamal Abdel Nasser died of a heart attack. His successor, President Anwar el-Sadat, viewed the continuing low-level warfare between Egyptian and Israeli forces along the Suez Canal as intolerable. The costs of maintaining an abnormally large military establishment placed unacceptable stress on the weak Egyptian economy. More important, Sadat was convinced that the longer the Israelis held Egyptian territory in the Sinai Peninsula, the more likely it was that they would keep it. He wanted the Sinai returned to Egypt. To achieve that he was ready to accept United Nations Security Council Resolution 242 as the basis for a settlement and to sign a peace accord with Tel Aviv, thus becoming the first Arab state to recognize the state of Israel.

Sadat tried in vain to involve the Nixon administration as a mediator between Egypt and Israel. But the president, with the 1972 election and the Jewish vote very much on his mind, refused to become involved, adopting instead a frankly pro-Israeli position that gave Tel Aviv no reason to want to negotiate.

In July 1972, Sadat made a final dramatic attempt to involve Washington in the peace process when, quite suddenly, he expelled all Soviet advisers from Egypt. Sadat had many reasons for this action. He was angered by Moscow's refusal to supply his military with high-technology weapons and by the limited quantity of weapons the Soviets were providing. But most important, he was aware that so long as the Soviets remained in Egypt, Washington would refuse to alter its pro-Israeli policy. By removing the Soviets from the political equation he hoped to entice Nixon into playing the role of honest broker in an Israeli-Egyptian negotiation.

Sadat's dramatic gesture produced the desired results. Nixon promised that after the November election he would offer to mediate between Egypt and Israel. But a series of distractions—the Vietnam negotiations, an energy crisis, and the Watergate scandal—left the Middle East off his list of priorities. That was unfortunate, since at length a frustrated Sadat decided to challenge the status quo by force. Otherwise, he feared, the Sinai would be lost forever.

On October 6, 1973, Yom Kippur, the holiest day in the Hebrew calendar, Egyptian and Syrian forces struck at Israeli positions in the Sinai and along the Golan Heights. No one should have been surprised. As early as May, State Department intelligence analysts had placed the odds at "better than even" that there would be another Middle East war before autumn.[14] And in June, Leonid Brezhnev warned Nixon that only American pressure on Israel to restore occupied Egyptian territory could prevent war. Nevertheless, the so-called Yom Kippur War caught both Washington and Tel Aviv unawares.

Henry Kissinger, who had by this time replaced William Rogers as secretary of state, hoped to use the war to bring about a final Middle East settlement. Confident of Israel's military superiority, he expected the Egyptian-Syrian offensive to bog down in a day or two and assumed that the Israeli counteroffensive would be devastating. After the Israelis had gained the upper hand, Kissinger planned to call for a cease-fire. Assuming that the Israelis would have the initiative, he was certain the Arab states and the Soviets would agree. And since the Israelis were dependent on the United States for military equipment, he was confident that he could force Tel Aviv into line as well. Once the cease-fire was in place, he would begin negotiations for a permanent Middle East peace settlement.

It soon became apparent that Kissinger had miscalculated. The Israelis were in trouble on both fronts, losing far too many aircraft to Soviet-supplied SAM missiles. To head off what appeared to be an impending Israeli disaster, President Nixon proposed a cease-fire in place on October 12. But Sadat was not interested. Egypt's Third Army had penetrated Israel's Bar Lev defense line in the Sinai and, having been resupplied by the Soviets, was preparing for a push farther east.

Nixon, furious with the Soviets for having thus fueled the conflagration, then belatedly began a large-scale airlift of military equipment to Israel. A compliant Congress also voted an extra $2.2 billion in emergency aid to Israel. On October 14, the Israeli army won the decisive battle of the war, turning back a major Egyptian thrust in the Sinai. Two days later an Israeli force crossed the Suez Canal, attacked and destroyed many of the SAM sites that protected the Egyptian army in the Sinai from air attack, and in the next few days all but encircled the overextended Egyptians.

The changed battlefield situation was only marginally satisfactory to Nixon and Kissinger. Another crushing Israeli victory over the Egyptians would do no good diplomatically, for under such circumstances the Arab states would certainly refuse to negotiate. Nor would the Israelis be easy to satisfy. It seemed imperative to stop the fighting before the Israelis destroyed the Egyptian army. Toward that end, Kissinger flew to Moscow, where he and Brezhnev quickly agreed on a cease-fire. Sadat, haunted by the prospect of the destruction of his army, also climbed on board. The Israelis were more difficult to convince. But Kissinger gave Prime Minister Meir no choice save to go along.

Even as Kissinger moved to establish a cease-fire, the international situation was complicated by the actions of the Arab oil-producing states. On October 20, King Faisal of Saudi Arabia announced that he would join other Arab oil exporters in cutting production by 10 percent and placing an embargo on the sale of oil to the United States, Portugal, and Holland, countries that in one way or another lent support to Israel in the war. The result was a severe energy crisis in the United States, Japan, and Western Europe.

The Arab oil embargo, which came at a time when the administration was already doing all it could to head off another crushing defeat for Egypt and Syria, was a model of bad timing. It had no effect on American diplomacy. At the same time it seriously undermined the already negative image of the Arab states in the United States.

## SOVIET-AMERICAN CONFRONTATION

The cease-fire in the Sinai broke down almost immediately as Israeli forces, now fully resupplied by the United States, began closing the noose on the trapped Egyptian Third Army. The Soviets protested, and Kissinger warned the Israeli ambassador in Washington against any attempt to destroy the trapped Egyptians. Kissinger's warnings notwithstanding, Israeli forces continued their advance. The Soviets, clearly agitated, reacted by mobilizing seven airborne divisions. Brezhnev asked Nixon to join him in intervening to "compel observance of the cease fire." If the United States was not prepared to cooperate, however, he threatened to go it alone. "I will say it straight, that if you find it impossible to act with us in this matter, we should be faced with the necessity urgently to consider the question of taking appropriate steps unilaterally. Israel cannot be permitted to get away with the violations."[15]

Were the Soviets really preparing to move against the Israelis? It seems unlikely, since Brezhnev understood that intervention would have led to a confrontation with the United States. Why, then, make the gesture? The most obvious answer is that Moscow hoped to deter the Israelis from finishing off the Egyptian army. A less obvious answer, but one that deserves serious consideration, is that Moscow hoped in this way to force Washington to exert greater pressure on Israel. If that was Brezhnev's purpose, he succeeded.

Kissinger and Nixon responded to the threat of Soviet intervention in two ways. First, they warned Moscow off and to make the point placed all American forces, including the Strategic Air Command, in a relatively high state of readiness. At the same time, they came down hard on the Israelis, making it clear that under no circumstances would they tolerate the destruction of the Egyptian Third Army. The Israeli defense minister at the time, Moshe Dayan, has even been quoted as saying that Kissinger threatened to send United States forces into the Sinai to resupply the Egyptians.

If that seems unlikely, it is nevertheless certain that whatever Kissinger said to the Israelis worked. Not long after this Israeli and Egyptian officers agreed to return to positions occupied at the time of the original cease-fire, to allow the trapped Egyptian army to be resupplied, and to exchange all war prisoners.

Once the fighting stopped, Kissinger, who played an increasingly important role in policy formulation as the Watergate scandal engulfed the White House, set out to end the Arab oil embargo and bring about a permanent settlement to the Arab-Israeli dispute. The secretary proceeded step by step, hoping that small agreements would produce the momentum needed for a general settlement.

After months of shuttling back and forth among Israel and the Arab capitals, Kissinger had stabilized the situation in the Sinai, reduced the danger of renewed war, and ended the oil embargo. He and the president may also have headed off a large-scale Soviet involvement in the region. These were impressive achievements. Yet at the same time the Middle East was no closer to a settlement than before. Indeed, in one sense the area's problems had become more complicated since in the aftermath of the Yom Kippur War the Palestine Liberation Organization, which remained committed to Israel's destruction, emerged more powerful than ever.

## A FORD, NOT A LINCOLN

January 20, 1973, was cold in Washington—inauguration weather. But Richard Nixon was probably oblivious to the chill. As he watched the inaugural parade from a reviewing stand in front of the White House, he must have reflected on how splendidly things had worked out. Relations with the Soviet Union were closer than at any time since World War II; he had just negotiated the first significant arms control agreement since the dawn of the nuclear age; his China policy was not only a success but had proven enormously popular; and he was on the verge of achieving a Vietnam settlement. Finally, he had just won a great election victory, garnering more than 60 percent of the popular vote while losing only Massachusetts and the District of Columbia to Senator George McGovern, his Democratic opponent.

To all outward appearances Richard Nixon's political position was unassailable. Yet in less than two years time he was forced to resign in disgrace to avoid impeachment. A deeply insecure man, Nixon had sown the seeds of his own destruction long before. As one White House aide subsequently wrote, he was "absolutely paranoid about criticism" and convinced that he was surrounded by enemies, especially members of the "eastern establishment" who, he believed, were trying to destroy him. The antiwar demonstrations and the activities of various radical groups deepened his paranoia and led him to undertake not only unsavory but illegal activities. Nixon once told Charles Colson, a White House aide: "One day we'll get them—we'll get them on the ground where we want them. And we'll stick our heels in, step on them hard and twist."[16]

The White House staff, responding to that contorted fear and hatred, drew up an "enemies list" with every intention of using agencies of the federal government to harass the president's enemies. They employed a variety of illegal means including interfering with the mails, electronic bugging, and even burglary to plug leaks inside the administration and gather political intelligence that could be used against those Nixon considered a threat.

On June 17, 1972, members of the secret "plumbers unit" used for these purposes were arrested while burglarizing the offices of the Democratic National Committee in Washington's Watergate building. Whether the president knew of the attempted burglary in advance remains unclear. But it is certain that others close to him were involved, that he learned about it immediately thereafter, and that he tried to cover up the White House involvement. The cover-up attempt failed. And in the subsequent congressional investigation so much that was tawdry, unethical, and illegal came to light that the House Judiciary Committee voted three articles of impeachment against the president. On August 9, 1974, rather than face an impeachment trial, Richard Nixon resigned. Later that day Gerald Ford took the oath of office.

The new president's self-deprecating humor (on being sworn in as vice-president he remarked that the people were getting "a Ford, not a

Lincoln"), his honesty and frankness, came as a welcome relief to a people grown cynical over the corrupt and unethical behavior of a succession of national leaders. Some, especially among the Democrats, thought little of Ford, a man who under other circumstances would never have made it to the White House. Lyndon Johnson, angered by Ford's opposition to parts of his Great Society program, once remarked that Ford, who once played football for the University of Michigan, had "played football too long without a helmet."[17] But Ford was a decent man and generally well liked by his former colleagues on Capitol Hill. And that was enough for a nation shaken to its foundations by the Vietnam War and Watergate.

Unprepared for national leadership, Gerald Ford quickly decided to leave foreign policy in the hands of Henry Kissinger, whom he retained as secretary of state. At the height of his popularity following the American withdrawal from Vietnam in 1973, a Gallup poll found Kissinger to be the most admired man in America. A British opinion survey done at the same time concluded that he was the most popular man in the entire Western world. He shared the Nobel Peace prize with Le Duc Tho and was portrayed on the cover of *Newsweek*, cartoon style, as Superman.

But by 1974 Kissinger's star was already in decline. Détente with the Soviets, once so popular, was coming under increasing scrutiny, especially in conservative Republican circles. The Vietnam settlement quickly unraveled, demonstrating that "peace with honor" had been a hollow claim. And Kissinger showed himself to be less than adept at handling foreign policy problems in the Third World. Kissinger's service as secretary of state in the Ford administration can most charitably be described as undistinguished.

## THE COLLAPSE OF SOUTH VIETNAM

The 1973 cease-fire agreement negotiated between Kissinger and Le Duc Tho changed nothing politically in Vietnam, where the civil war was only temporarily adjourned. The North Vietnamese remained committed to the unification of the country. The regime of Nguyen Van Thieu was just as determined that South Vietnam should remain independent. And both sides recognized that the National Council of Reconciliation and Concord, which was in theory to arrange elections, would never meet.

It was a forgone conclusion not only in Vietnam but in Washington, too, that the war would continue after American ground forces had been withdrawn. Nixon fully intended to continue large-scale aid to Saigon and to provide naval and air support for South Vietnamese troops in the field. He meant it when he told President Thieu that he would "respond with full force" if the North Vietnamese violated the 1973 agreement.[18] To back up that pledge he kept large air and naval forces in Southeast Asia and discharged more than nine thousand military advisers and technical experts, who then became "civilian" advisers employed by Saigon.

At the beginning of the truce period in 1973, South Vietnam was in a relatively strong military position. ARVN had been well supplied by the departing Americans, and the South Vietnamese flag flew over roughly three-quarters of the country. Buoyed by President Nixon's promise of aid, President Thieu announced the beginning of the third war for Vietnam and sent his army on expeditions to grab as much more territory as possible.

In little more than a year, however, the situation changed dramatically. Richard Nixon was out of the White House, and President Thieu could no longer count on support from American naval and air forces. Moreover, when the Americans left, they took billions of dollars out of the South Vietnamese economy. Congress did not take up the slack, allocating only $1 billion in aid for South Vietnam that year. The result of this vast cutback was an economic crisis in South Vietnam.

For years the war had been that country's major industry. Hundreds of thousands of persons—more than a million if one counted ARVN and those working for the Saigon government as well as the servants, shoeshine boys, prostitutes and bartenders who earned a living because of the American presence—had in effect been in the employ of the United States government. When the country's major employer all but disappeared, the economy went to pieces. The country experienced massive unemployment and inflation simultaneously.

Aid cutbacks had a direct effect on military operations, which had to be reduced for lack of ammunition, spare parts, and fuel. At the same time, the realization that the United States was leaving Vietnam for good proved disastrous for military morale. The desertion rate skyrocketed. Corruption, always a problem, reached unheard-of levels. Pilots demanded bribes to fly. Soldiers in the field went hungry because supply officers sold their rations on the black market. Officers appropriated payrolls intended for their men.

South Vietnam, then, was already in an advanced state of internal disintegration when in early 1975 Hanoi launched an offensive that was intended to "create conditions for a general uprising in 1976."[19] Once the offensive began, however, the North Vietnamese found they were pushing on an open door.

The collapse of South Vietnam came with dramatic suddenness. After Hanoi's forces won easy victories in the Central Highlands of South Vietnam, President Thieu ordered a general withdrawal that turned into a rout. In April, North Vietnam's Politburo, astounded at its own success, ordered General Van Tien Dung, the North Vietnamese field commander, to redirect the offensive toward Saigon before Thieu could reorganize his forces.

In spite of the critical situation, President Ford could not, as Nixon had done in 1972, use air power to halt the North Vietnamese advance. He did, however, request $722 million in emergency aid for the Thieu regime, only to be turned down by Congress. It is not at all clear what good the extra money would have done for Saigon. South Vietnamese forces had already abandoned vast quantities of military equipment in their headlong flight. Moreover, aid requests, even when funded, are not magically transformed into military equipment. Procurement and shipment would have taken months. And it was plain that South Vietnam did not have weeks.

With North Vietnamese forces closing in on Saigon, the war in Cambodia, now some five years old, came to its bloody conclusion. Early in April, Prime Minister Lon Nol resigned. A few days later those Americans who remained in Phnom Penh were evacuated. Less than a week after this, the Khmer Rouge entered the city and began the forced evacuation of its more than 1 million inhabitants. A reign of terror that by most estimates cost some 2 million lives and is directly traceable to Richard Nixon's decision to widen the Vietnam war had begun.

Not long after the Khmer Rouge took Phnom Penh, the final curtain fell on the tragic history of South Vietnam. With North Vietnamese forces advancing on Saigon, President Nguyen Van Thieu resigned, denounced the United States as "an inhumane ally" and fled to Taiwan. Curiously, given the fact that the war was clearly lost, Ambassador Graham Martin failed to initiate procedures for an orderly evacuation of the Americans remaining in Vietnam. Finally, in an utterly chaotic operation, with the North Vietnamese already on the outskirts of the city, the last thousand Americans along with several thousand Vietnamese were airlifted out of Saigon to ships waiting offshore. The operation was completed on the night of April 29—30. On the next day the victorious North Vietnamese entered Saigon, at last ending the war that began in 1946, twenty-nine years before.

## AMERICA DISCOVERS SOUTHERN AFRICA

During the post–World War II era the African continent proved almost as mysterious to American policy makers as once it had been to the European explorers and colonizers who swarmed there during the nineteenth century. In Africa colonialism and white racism were the major political issues. The cold war was irrelevant, and a Soviet presence was hard to find. Consequently, a succession of American administrations showed a profound ignorance of and lack of concern about Africa.

Like their predecessors, Kissinger and Nixon knew next to nothing about African affairs and had no interest in learning. Indifferent to the plight of native Africans living under the exploitative rule of white minority governments, the administration's policy, clearly expressed in a 1969 National Security Decision memorandum, was that there being "no hope for the blacks to gain the political rights they seek through violence," the United States should adopt a friendly policy toward the white minority regimes in South Africa, Rhodesia, and the Portuguese colonies of Mozambique and Angola.[20]

Critics called this Nixon-Kissinger policy the "tar baby option" because they were convinced that once associated with southern Africa's exploitative governments Washington's reputation would be permanently smeared and

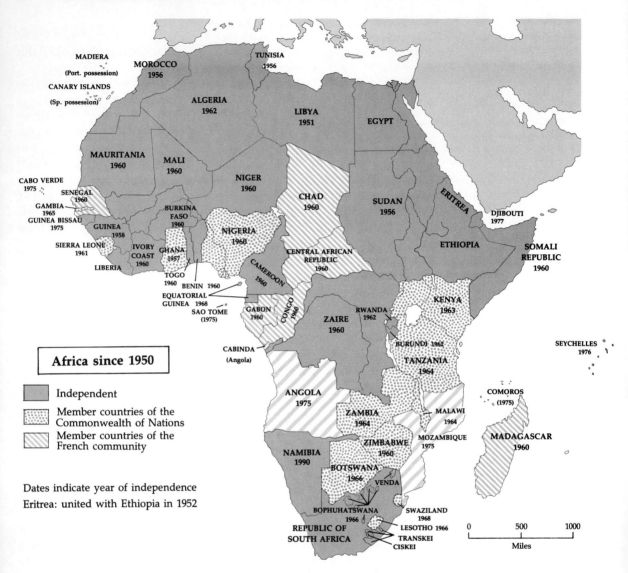

Africa since 1950

■ Independent

▦ Member countries of the Commonwealth of Nations

▨ Member countries of the French community

Dates indicate year of independence
Eritrea: united with Ethiopia in 1952

that black Africans would never forget the role Washington chose to play. But nobody listened to the critics until the mid-1970s.

In 1974 the administration was confronted with a totally unexpected development. The government of the Portuguese dictator, Marcello Caetano, was overthrown in a military coup that was prompted at least in part by the seemingly endless war of attrition the Portuguese army was fighting against Angolan nationalists. The new Portuguese government, anxious to be rid of an empire that had already cost far too much in blood and treasure, quickly set Mozambique and Angola free.

Political chaos ensued in Angola, where three factions locked horns in a struggle for power. The fast-talking Holden Roberto, the brother-in-law of Zaire's Sese Seko Mobutu and the CIA's man in Angola, headed the National Front for the Liberation of Angola (FNLA). The Popular Movement for the Liberation of Angola (MPLA) was headed by Agostinho Neto. A Portuguese-educated medical doctor and the son of a Methodist minister, Neto organized the MPLA during the 1960s to fight Portuguese repression. A third group, the National Union for the Total Independence of Angola (UNITA) was under the control of Jonas Savimbi. A charismatic revolutionary leader, Savimbi, who later became the darling of the Reagan administration, was in the mid-1970s clearly the most radical of the three.

In January 1975, it appeared that the civil strife in Angola would soon end. The three factions agreed to create an interim government and scheduled national elections for October. But Kissinger, who until that time had shown not the slightest interest in Africa, would not hear of any sort of coalition government that included representatives from the MPLA, since it had been receiving aid from Moscow. And so Roberto's FNLA, with increased funding from the CIA, abandoned the agreement, opting instead to continue the civil war.

The connection between Moscow and the MPLA convinced Kissinger that southern Africa had become a target of Soviet expansionism. Once he arrived at that conclusion, the rest followed logically. Before the end of 1975 the CIA had secretly funneled $32 million in aid to Roberto's group. Another $100 million went to Mobutu in Zaire, who sent troops and armor into Angola to aid in what was rapidly becoming a big war. The Soviets responded with a large aid program of their own to the MPLA. As the war escalated foreign troops joined the fray—Cubans for the MPLA, and white South Africans (encouraged by Kissinger) for the FNLA and UNITA. Kissinger thus managed to escalate a minor civil war, more reflective of tribal than ideological differences, into a major cold war confrontation.

In late 1975 Congress learned of the CIA's covert activities in Angola and cut off funding. Meanwhile, the public revelation that Washington had joined with the South Africans in a war against the MPLA besmirched America's reputation throughout sub-Saharan Africa and vastly elevated Neto's standing there. The limited military victory that he won over Roberto's FNLA left him in control of Angola's capital, Luanda, as well as some surrounding territory, and gave his government the international recognition and respectability it needed to survive.

Henry Kissinger could not have mishandled the Angolan civil war more completely had he set his mind to it—which he obviously did not. Even he seems to have realized as much, for in the aftermath of the Angolan debacle he executed a drastic change in African policy.

Until mid-1976 Kissinger had been content to stand by the "tar baby option" and do business with the white minority governments in the region, including Ian Smith's in Rhodesia (despite the fact that London had declared the former British colony in a state of rebellion and the United Nations had applied economic sanctions against the Smith government). In May 1976

Kissinger made his first trip to Africa the occasion for announcing a change in policy. By that time it was clear that the Smith government could not survive the pressure being brought against it by the international community and that unless the situation in Rhodesia was resolved, the guerrilla war being fought there under the leadership of Robert Mugabe and Joshua Nkomo might well spread to South Africa. In an effort to check the spread of this revolutionary ferment, Kissinger repudiated the policy that had guided American policy makers since 1969, telling an audience of black Africans: "We know from our own experience that the goal of racial justice is both compelling and achievable, . . . Our support for this principle in southern Africa is not simply a matter of foreign policy but an imperative of our moral heritage."[21] In the same speech he called for majority rule in Rhodesia, condemned South Africa's system of apartheid, and demanded that Pretoria commit itself to a clear timetable for free elections in Namibia, which it had held in violation of international law since the end of World War II. It was a strong speech and may have impressed some as a turning point in Washington's approach to southern Africa. But years of support for racist, exploitative regimes could not be erased so easily. It remained to be seen whether Kissinger's rhetoric was really the forerunner of new policies.

## THE DECLINE OF DÉTENTE

The policy of détente with the Soviet Union achieved enormous popularity after the 1972 Moscow summit. But it was not long before many Americans began to have second thoughts about a policy that was understood differently in Washington and Moscow and that had clearly been oversold by the administration.

Nixon and Kissinger envisioned the relationship they were building as the beginning of a superpower partnership for the preservation of global stability. "Our approach proceeds from the conviction that in moving forward across a wide spectrum of negotiations," Kissinger wrote, "progress in one area adds momentum to progress in other areas. By acquiring a stake in this network of relationships with the West," Kissinger hoped "the Soviet Union may become more conscious of what it would lose by a return to confrontation. Indeed it is our hope that it will develop a self-interest in fostering the entire process of relaxation of tensions."[22]

Unhappily, the Soviets' view of détente was far more limited. To them it meant improved relations with Washington and specific bilateral agreements where the interests of both countries meshed, as in the case of arms control and expanded trade relations. At the same time the Soviets felt no compunction about pursuing other policies that ran contrary to American interests. They continued, for example, to encourage wars of national liberation in the Third World, though Washington saw these struggles as politically destabilizing and threatening to Western economic interests. During the latter part of the Nixon-Ford administration, Moscow was particularly active in Africa, providing military aid not only to the MPLA in Angola but to the notorious Idi Amin in Uganda, to the "Emperor" Jean-Bédel Bokassa of the Central African Republic, and to Somalia as well as Marxist governments in Ethiopia and Mozambique.

The unwillingness of the Soviets to cooperate with Washington in the preservation of a stable world order was demonstrated in other settings as well. During the 1973 Yom Kippur War in the Middle East, for example, Moscow's major resupply operations prolonged the fighting at a time when Kissinger was seeking to arrange a cease-fire. And in November 1974, when Kissinger asked for Brezhnev's aid in restraining the North Vietnamese from overwhelming President Thieu's government, the Soviet leader refused.

Nor did the Soviets feel obliged to live up to commitments they made regarding human rights. In July 1975, representatives of the United States, the Soviet Union, and more than thirty other nations assembled in Helsinki, Finland, to sign the Helsinki Accords. One of the several agreements signed at this conference committed Moscow to relaxing its restrictions on Jewish emigration to Israel and to allowing greater freedom of expression inside the Soviet Union. Nevertheless, Soviet Jews who tried to emigrate continued to be harassed and detained against their will. And dissidents—the physicist Andrei Sakharov and the novelist Aleksandr Solzhenitsyn were only the most prominent—were often sent to labor camps, imprisoned in mental hospitals, or sent into internal or external exile.

By 1976, détente had fallen into disrepute among large portions of the American population. Liberals approved of arms control and improved cultural relations with Moscow but were appalled by the Soviet record on human rights. Conservatives argued that détente had proven to be a one-way street in which the Soviets took as much as they could get but gave nothing in return. They were especially disturbed by the deterioration in American military power, which they ascribed to the fatuous view, encouraged by talk of détente, that the Soviets had abandoned their revolutionary purposes.

The conservative view was clearly expressed in the 1976 Republican party platform. Drafted by the supporters of former Governor Ronald Reagan of California, it attacked détente in all of its various permutations, condemned the administration for agreeing in 1975 to legitimize the map of Europe established after World War II that, it averred, condemned the "captive peoples" of Eastern Europe to life in perpetuity behind the Iron Curtain, insisted on a tougher line in dealing with the Soviets, and called for substantial increases in defense spending. Seldom has the political platform of a party in power more completely repudiated the main tenets of its own administration's foreign policy.

President Ford barely survived Ronald Reagan's challenge to win his party's nomination in 1976. And he did so only by moving in a sharply conservative direction himself. One of the casualties of this change was the very word "détente," which came into such disrepute that during the election campaign the president dropped it from his vocabulary and insisted that all others in his administration do the same. The new key to Ford's policy toward the Soviets was the old standby, "peace through strength." President Ford lost the closely contested 1976 presidential election to the Democratic candidate, Jimmy Carter. But even if he had won, the odds are that he would have excluded Henry Kissinger from a reorganized cabinet. The times were changing. And in a more conservative era it is very unlikely that the man most closely associated with the idea of détente could have survived as a figure of prominence in a Republican party moving rapidly to the right.

## ENDNOTES

1. C. L. Sulzberger paraphrasing Richard M. Nixon, in Sulzberger, *The World and Richard Nixon* (New Jersey: Prentice-Hall, 1987), p. 29.
2. Nixon, inaugural address, January 20, 1969, *Public Papers of the Presidents: Richard M. Nixon, 1969* (Washington, 1971), p. 3.
3. Nixon, quoted in Sulzberger, *World and Richard Nixon*, p. 78.
4. Richard Nixon, "Asia after Vietnam," *Foreign Affairs*, October 1967, pp. 111–25.
5. Henry Kissinger, *The White House Years* (Boston: Little, Brown, 1979), p. 187.
6. Nixon, quoted in Tad Szulc, *The Illusion of Peace* (New York: Viking, 1978), pp. 350–51.
7. Edgar Snow, *The Long Revolution* (New York: Random House, 1972), pp. 172, 180–83.
8. Zhou Enlai, quoted in *Time*, April 26, 1971, p. 25.
9. Kissinger paraphrasing David Packard, *White House Years*, p. 546.
10. Anonymous Kissinger aide, quoted in Seymour M. Hersh, *The Price of Power: Kissinger in the Nixon White House* (New York Summit Books, 1983), p. 217.
11. Moshe Dayan, quoted in ibid.
12. Richard Nixon, *RN: The Memoirs of Richard Nixon* (New York: Grosset and Dunlap, 1978), p. 483.
13. *Chicago Sun Times* report of an interview with Nixon, in William Quandt, *Decade of Decisions* (Berkeley, Calif.: University of California Press, 1978), p. 114.
14. State Department intelligence estimate, quoted in ibid., p. 166.
15. Leonid Brezhnev, quoted in ibid., p. 196.
16. Charles Colson, *Born Again* (Old Tappan, N.J.: Chosen Books, 1971), p. 45.
17. Lyndon Johnson, quoted in Paul Boller, *Presidential Anecdotes* (New York: Oxford University Press, 1981), p. 335.
18. Nixon, *RN*, pp. 749–50.
19. Van Tien Dung, quoted in George C. Herring, *America's Longest War: The United States and Vietnam, 1950–1975* (New York: Alfred A. Knopf, 1979), p. 259.
20. National Security decision memorandum, January 1970, quoted in Szulc, *Illusion of Peace*, p. 221.
21. Kissinger, quoted in *State Department Bulletin*, May 31, 1976, p. 673.
22. Kissinger, quoted in Coral Bell, *The Diplomacy of Detente* (New York: St. Martins Press, 1977), p. 69.

Presidents Jimmy Carter and Leonid Brezhnev meet in Vienna to sign the SALT II Treaty.

# 34

# *THE CARTER PROMISE, 1977–1981*

Every administration since Harry Truman's, even Richard Nixon's, had been more or less fixated on the threat of Soviet expansionism. For three decades American policy makers viewed foreign affairs as a deadly contest in which any gain for the Soviets was a defeat for the United States and vice versa. In this ruthless world of power politics the end always seemed to justify the means. Thus a succession of American presidents interfered in foreign elections, overthrew governments, sanctioned political assassinations, supported right wing dictatorships, and fought two major land wars in Asia in order to prevent the expansion of communist power.

Jimmy Carter, the former governor of Georgia and lay preacher who defeated Gerald Ford in the 1976 presidential election, set out to change the tone and substance of American foreign policy. Carter was not quite the political evangelist William Jennings Bryan had been. Nor did he have the grasp of history or the intellectual power of this century's greatest political moralist, Woodrow Wilson. But he began his administration determined to redirect American foreign policy away from cold war issues and toward universal moral questions. Thus during the election campaign he called for new initiatives to end the nuclear arms race and the international traffic in arms. Above all, Carter believed that the United States ought to become the international champion of human rights.

Carter chose Cyrus Vance to be his secretary of state. A longtime Washington insider, Vance had served as chief counsel to the Defense Department and then as secretary of the army during the Kennedy-Johnson administration. Though Vance did not share Carter's moralistic approach to foreign policy, his emphasis on the importance of finding peaceful solutions to international problems and his belief that the use of force often created more problems than it solved correlated well with the president's own thinking. Moreover, he saw eye to eye with Carter on a number of basic issues including the importance of arms control and the pursuit of détente with the Soviets. Perhaps most importantly, he was determined that cold war themes should not be allowed to determine the course of American policy.

Zbigniew Brzezinski, who served as Carter's national security adviser, held views of a strikingly different nature. The author of several books on Soviet affairs, he viewed virtually all international issues through the prism of the Soviet-American conflict. Like any good Machiavellian, he also believed that the fundamental purpose of the state was to accumulate power and that toward that end blood sometimes had to be spilled. International relations, he once told the president, was "not a kindergarten."[1] Brzezinski also believed it should be Washington's purpose to exert continuous pressure on the Soviet empire for the purpose of forcing its fragmentation.

Carter believed that these two very different men would each serve an important function in the policy-making process. He looked to Brzezinski for creative new ideas. Vance, on the other hand, was to be the traditionalist who represented the State Department's point of view and implemented policy.

The president also liked the idea of having a variety of opinions

President Jimmy Carter (left), Cyrus Vance, and Zbigniew Brzezinski talk things over in the White House.

presented to him during policy debates. This had been John Kennedy's approach and it had worked for him. But Carter had a problem Kennedy never encountered, a competition between the national security adviser and the secretary of state for control of foreign policy. As a result, his administration was marred by an ongoing struggle between Brzezinski and Vance that too often left foreign policy in a muddle and the public skeptical about Carter's ability to control his administration.

## CRUSADE FOR HUMAN RIGHTS

Jimmy Carter did more than any other major political figure of his generation to focus national and international attention on the issue of human rights. He did so for both personal and political reasons. In the first place he believed it "was time for us to capture the imagination of the world again" after the twin debacles of Vietnam and Watergate. What better cause could there be than the struggle for human freedom? As James Fallows, once a Carter speech writer, remarked, this "moral theme was right in Carter's soul . . . *realpolitik* was not what he wanted to do."[2]

It is important to note that in 1976 there was also a domestic political dimension to Carter's crusade for human rights. It had universal appeal. Liberals applauded because at long last a president seemed to be prepared to stand up for basic principles even against ruthless right-wing dictators who happened to be America's allies. Many conservatives were equally enamored of the idea because they believed the Soviets and their East bloc allies were prime violators of human rights. Finally, by emphasizing the issue Carter took the moral high ground, placing himself in opposition to the often sordid and amoral policies of Nixon and Kissinger. The human rights issue was, according to Carter's pollster, Patrick Caddell, "a very strong issue across the board."[3]

During the 1976 election campaign Carter was particularly outspoken in attacking the Soviets for imprisoning dissidents and persecuting Soviet Jews anxious to emigrate to Israel. At the same time he chastised President Ford for failing to do more to protect human rights abroad. Carter continued in this vein after taking the oath of office. He deplored communist Czechoslovakia's harassment of dissidents, sent a letter of encouragement to Andrei Sakharov, a leading Soviet dissident, and, over the objections of the Kremlin, received Vladimir Bukovsky, a prominent Soviet exile, in the Oval Office.

Moscow responded angrily to Carter's criticisms. The Soviet ambassador, Anatoly Dobrynin, protested to the State Department while at the same time the Kremlin stepped up its campaign against dissidents, arresting both Yuri Orlov and Alexander Shcheransky, the latter being the best known of Russia's Jewish dissidents. President Brezhnev then warned Washington that "we will not tolerate interference in our internal affairs by anyone and under any pretext. A normal development of relations on such a basis," he said, "is, of course, unthinkable."[4] When Cyrus Vance visited Moscow in

March, 1977, the Soviet leader also made it clear that the Carter human rights campaign was damaging chances for a successful SALT II negotiation. Since nuclear arms reduction was the number one foreign policy priority in Washington, this threat was taken seriously.

By the summer of 1977 the administration's human rights campaign, insofar as it was directed against the Soviet Union, had all but petered out. The president concluded that in the real world of international politics choices have to be made, that when the vital economic and security interests of the nation are at issue it is often necessary to ignore human rights considerations.

From that point on, Carter's human rights campaign became extremely selective. Washington did bring pressure to bear on a number of states including Uruguay, Argentina, Augusto Pinochet's dictatorship in Chile, and the barbarous regime of Idi Amin in Uganda. It also cooperated in a United Nations–imposed embargo on trade with the white minority government in Rhodesia and refused to endorse internationally financed loans to a number of governments believed to be violating basic human rights. Aid programs to Nicaragua and El Salvador were also cut off.

At the same time many of America's allies, who also happened to be notorious violators of human rights, were exempted not only from sanctions but from criticism as well. Thus, though the shah of Iran's secret police, SAVAK, tortured and killed thousands, and held thousands more as political prisoners, Carter said nothing. In the Philippines, Ferdinand Marcos headed a ruthless and corrupt dictatorship that was dependent on American economic and military aid and therefore should have been susceptible to pressure. But Marcos was never bothered because the Pentagon feared he might refuse to renew the leases on the naval bases at Subic Bay and Clark Field. Nor was the repressive South Korean regime ever brought to book for its many human rights violations.

Carter's inconsistencies left him vulnerable to criticism from all points on the ideological compass. Liberals denounced him for his unwillingness to take on American allies, while conservatives cringed whenever he criticized or imposed sanctions against anticommunist dictatorships. Meanwhile, many argued with considerable justification that the entire policy had become hopelessly hypocritical. Thus the liberal historian, Arthur Schlesinger, Jr., wrote that:

> Washington was fearless in denouncing human rights abuses in countries like Cambodia, Paraguay and Uganda, where the United States had negligible strategic and economic interests; a good deal less fearless toward South Korea, Saudi Arabia, Yugoslavia and most of black Africa; increasingly circumspect about the Soviet Union; totally silent about China.[5]

Carter's human rights policies clearly left much to be desired. Still, his failings and inconsistencies notwithstanding, it is worth remembering that by focusing national and international attention on human rights, he made the issue more important than at any time in the recent past. Since his time it has remained a factor in international politics, something governments—at least those concerned with their image abroad—have to be concerned about. Carter's role as a defender of human rights, when placed in historical perspective, may yet turn out to be of some importance. The jury is still out.


## CARTER AND THE SOVIETS

In spite of Carter's frequent attacks on the Soviets for their human rights abuses, he wanted good relations with Moscow. He was especially anxious for a follow-on treaty to SALT I, since he viewed nuclear arms control as the most important international issue confronting his administration.

There was no conflict inside the government on the fundamental point. All agreed that the United States should pursue an aggressive arms control policy. There was a serious difference of opinion, however, on how to go about it. Two years earlier, in November 1974, Ford and Leonid Brezhnev initialed the Vladivostok communiqué, which laid out the framework for a second SALT treaty. But the agreement they reached was not an important achievement. The ceilings on the number of strategic missile launchers that each side could deploy—2,400 with a subceiling of 1,320 that could be MIRVed—were high enough to accommodate the ambitions of both the Soviet and American defense establishments. Moreover, the accord left unresolved a number of vital questions, among them whether Moscow's newly developed Backfire bomber and the American cruise missile were to be limited.

The question before the Carter administration was whether to pursue an agreement based on the Vladivostok communiqué and follow up with a SALT III negotiation aimed at achieving deep cuts in each side's strategic arsenal or to seek substantial cuts immediately. Secretary Vance and the head of the Arms Control and Disarmament Agency, Paul Warnke, argued for the two-stage approach. Brzezinski disagreed. Impatient with the tedious pace of the SALT talks, he was loath to begin his career as national security adviser by ratifying an agreement his longtime rival, Kissinger, had negotiated. "Why should Zbig just accept Henry Kissinger's strait jacket?" asked one aide.[6]

Secretary of Defense Harold Brown also wanted to bypass Vladivostok. Brown was concerned by the growing number of "heavy" SS-18 missiles the Soviets might deploy in the coming years. These weapons were large enough to carry up to thirty MIRVed warheads each. Brown feared that if the Soviets deployed too many of them they would have the ability to destroy America's land-based missile force in a first strike. The only way to stop this extremely destabilizing development was by an agreement limiting the number of "heavy" missiles the Soviets deployed.

Carter needed little convincing. Anxious for a major arms control achievement, he decided to scrap the Vladivostok framework in favor of something more meaningful. As it finally emerged, the administration's proposal called for the deployment of no more than two thousand strategic missile launchers on each side, with no more than twelve hundred of these to be MIRVed. More significant, it required the Soviets to limit the number of SS-18 missiles they deployed to 150 while dismantling another 150 operational launchers. While the Soviets would be required to make all of these concessions to get in under the proposed limits, the United States would have to do nothing more than abandon plans to develop the new ten-warhead MX mobile missile. The inequity of the proposal was obvious. As one American negotiator quipped, "We would be giving up future draft choices in exchange for cuts in their starting lineup."[7]

Leonid Brezhnev was infuriated by the administration's abandonment of the Vladivostok accords. It had taken two years of negotiations not only with Henry Kissinger but inside his own political and military bureaucracies to arrive at a consensus on the follow-on treaty to SALT I. He had knocked more than a few heads, especially among the military, before going to Vladivostok to sign the 1974 agreement. Now here was Jimmy Carter, who spent much of his time attacking the Soviet Union for its human rights violations, abandoning what he considered to be a binding commitment and offering instead a proposal that would require Moscow to make all the tangible sacrifices. Foreign Minister Andrei Gromyko called the Carter proposal "a cheap and shady maneuver," while Brezhnev denounced it as not only "unconstructive and one-sided" but "harmful to Soviet security."[8]

Needless to say, the 1977 Moscow arms control talks were a dismal failure. In the aftermath of that disaster, Carter contrived to make matters worse by warning the Soviets that if they did not soon come around to his way of thinking he would "be forced to consider a much more deep commitment to the development and deployment of additional weapons." To Anatoly Dobrynin, the longtime Soviet ambassador in Washington, it appeared as if the entire SALT structure was about to come tumbling down. "President Carter seemed to be saying, 'Either you accept our position or we start the arms race and the cold war again.' His statement was taken as a *diktat* or ultimatum."[9]

## SALT II

Carter's amateurish foray into the complex world of arms control left Soviet-American relations in disarray. In the aftermath of the debacle, however, American and Soviet arms controllers worked diligently to save the situation. Not quite two years later their efforts were rewarded when the SALT II Treaty came together. No one would describe this agreement as a major breakthrough. But it did demonstrate that Soviet and American negotiators could still find common ground, and it was a step in the right direction.

SALT II left a number of troubling issues unresolved, such as the number of "heavy" missiles and Backfire bombers the Soviets could deploy.

But the ceilings it established for both MIRVed and single-warhead launchers were lower than those agreed upon at Vladivostok. Moreover, the treaty also placed a freeze on "fractionization," prohibiting both sides from MIRVing their missiles to a greater extent than had already been achieved through testing. Thus, although a single giant Soviet SS-18 could conceivably deliver thirty warheads to geographically separated targets, under the terms of SALT II the missile would be allowed to carry no more than ten. Finally, the treaty allowed the United States to deploy three hundred new MX mobile missiles, thus closing the so-called window of vulnerability, which had become a political issue in Washington.

The SALT II Treaty, which was signed at an elaborate ceremony held in Vienna in June 1979, left the president with a lot of work still to be done. Two-thirds of the Senate had to be convinced to vote for the treaty, and that was not going to be easy. Opposition to any form of arms control was growing in the increasingly conservative political climate of the late 1970s. To counteract this trend, the administration mounted a major lobbying effort. "Thousands of speeches, news interviews and private briefings were held," Carter recalled.[10]

The opposition employed some big guns of its own. Paul Nitze, the principal drafter of NSC 68 and a member of the SALT I delegation, was opposed to the treaty, as were former secretary of defense James Schlesinger, Lane Kirkland of the AFL-CIO, former Deputy Secretary of Defense David Packard, and Eugene Rostow, who was destined to head the Arms Control and Disarmament Agency under Ronald Reagan. In the Senate the administration had to contend not only with the Republican opposition but with influential conservative Democrats, especially Senator Henry Jackson of Washington, who was generally considered to be the Senate's leading expert on military affairs.

Much of the testimony given before the Foreign Relations Committee by supporters and opponents of SALT II focused on technical questions. But the essence of the debate was ideological. Administration spokespersons held that the Soviet leaders accepted the view that neither side could win a nuclear war and that a strategic nuclear balance between the two superpowers was a fact of international life. Moreover, they insisted that Soviet nuclear weapons programs were, like America's, designed to enhance deterrence. As Raymond Garthoff, an experienced arms controller, put it, the Soviets developed new weapons systems "to ensure that they do not fail to maintain their side of the balance, which they see as in some jeopardy, given planned American programs."[11]

Opponents of the treaty, on the other hand, continued to embrace the precepts of NSC 68: that the Soviets were uncompromising fanatics determined to destroy Western liberalism, that they were searching for a method of fighting and winning a nuclear war, and that real safety lay in continued confrontation. As the American Security Council, a private lobbying group put it, America's security could best be protected not by arms control agreements but by a "national strategy based on over-all military and technological superiority over the Soviet Union."[12]

All the sound and fury of the opposition notwithstanding, the president was reasonably confident that SALT II would pass the Senate. To ensure that outcome he did far more than lobby undecided senators. His first move was to bring the Joint Chiefs of Staff on board and quiet the fears of many senators who might otherwise have opposed the treaty by approving the development of the $30-billion MX mobile missile system. He then brought Georgia's Senator Sam Nunn and others into the fold by promising a 5 percent annual increase after inflation in the defense budget for each of the next five years. These actions, Carter and Secretary Vance both believed, should have assured Senate approval of SALT II. And they might have, had it not been for a storm that suddenly blew up over the presence in Cuba of a Red Army brigade.

The Soviet brigade, which had been in Cuba since 1962, was of course no threat to the United States. But when the story broke in the press that the Soviets had troops in Cuba, it came as news to most Americans. Opponents of SALT II howled that the Senate should not ratify the treaty until the brigade had been removed. And as Vance sadly noted, "in the political climate of 1979, a rational separation of the Brigade issue and SALT was not possible."[13] Under the circumstances the administration was hamstrung. The SALT II Treaty suffered what to many seemed a mortal wound.

In November, after the storm over Soviet troops in Cuba had blown itself out, the Senate Foreign Relations Committee voted 9–6 in favor of the treaty, which it sent with a favorable recommendation to the Senate floor. But that was the end of the road for SALT II. Aware that it would not pass, the Senate majority leader, Robert Byrd of West Virginia, refused to bring the treaty to a vote.

## THE WAR IN AFGHANISTAN

Late in December 1979, with SALT II still bottled up in the Senate, Soviet-American relations hit a new low when Soviet troops invaded Afghanistan. Ostensibly they went in as friends to help the communist government of Prime Minister Hafizullah Amin deal with a rising tide of Islamic insurgency. The Soviets had a strange way of showing their friendship, however, as they were almost certainly responsible for Amin's murder and the creation of a new government led by Babrak Karmal.

President Carter was shocked by this blatant act of Soviet aggression. At the same time there can be no doubt that he saw certain advantages in this development. By the time the Soviets acted, Carter was in deep political trouble. His administration had failed to deal effectively with a serious energy crisis; double-digit inflation plagued the country; economic growth had been slowed by interest rates that topped 20 percent; and on top of everything else America was being humiliated by the Iranian hostage crisis. As a result, Carter's rating in the polls, never high, had fallen to a dismal 19 percent.

Moscow's Afghanistan adventure gave Carter the opportunity to get tough with the Soviets, always a popular ploy in postwar America. At the same time, as Brzezinski pointed out, he could withdraw SALT II from the Senate, blaming the difficulties it was encountering there on Soviet behavior.

On December 27, Carter delivered a blistering message to Brezhnev over the hot line, warning him that the Afghan invasion "could mark a fundamental and long-lasting turning point in our relations." When Brezhnev replied that Kabul had requested protection against a foreign threat, Carter went on national television to call him a liar. "My opinion of the Russians has changed more drastically in the last week," he told the American people, "than even the previous two-and-one-half years before that."[14] At the same time Carter requested that the Senate postpone indefinitely any consideration of SALT II, explaining (disingenuously since the treaty lacked the necessary support) that he could not possibly ratify the treaty until after the Soviets had withdrawn from Afghanistan.

Carter also applied economic sanctions against the Soviets, including an embargo on grain sales, a prohibition on the sale of high-technology items, and sharp restrictions on the right of Soviet trawlers to fish in American waters. Among the most hotly debated of the president's actions was the pressure he exerted on the U.S. Olympic Committee to withdraw from the 1980 Moscow Olympics.

The Olympic boycott, which spread to include a significant number of noncommunist countries, ruined what the Soviets had hoped would be a major public relations triumph. But it had no effect on their Afghanistan policy. The president's other sanctions proved not only futile but self-defeating. The Soviets found other sources to make up for the 14 million tons of grain they were unable to purchase from the United States. But the loss of the Soviet market precipitated a major economic crisis in the American farm community. Moscow also acquired the technology that was no longer available from the United States from Japanese and Western European suppliers. And although the UN General Assembly voted to denounce the Soviet invasion of Afghanistan, Soviet troops remained there for almost a decade.

In his January 1980 annual address to Congress, the president continued to emphasize cold war themes. Evoking fears first raised in the 1947 Truman Doctrine speech, he warned that the invasion of Afghanistan, which placed "Soviet military forces . . . within 300 miles of the Indian Ocean and close to the Straits of Hormuz—a waterway through which most of the world's oil must flow," posed a "grave threat to the movement of Middle East oil." He warned Moscow that the United States would not tolerate any attempt to interfere with that flow. "Let our position be absolutely clear," he said. "An attempt by any outside force to gain control of the Persian Gulf will be regarded as an assault on the vital interests of the United States of

America and such an assault will be repelled by any means necessary including military force."[15] Congress responded with wild applause.

The announcement of the so-called Carter Doctrine marked the completion of the president's conversion to cold warrior. It may be as Carter himself claimed that the Soviet invasion of Afghanistan led him to accept Brzezinski's view that the Soviets were aiming at control of the Persian Gulf and the Middle East's oil. But it is also true that Afghanistan provided the president with what he hoped might be a new lease on his political life. Being tough with the Soviets had been a key to political success in the United States for decades. It is not unlikely that as the 1980 elections approached Carter hoped it might work for him, too. Certainly it could not hurt.

## THE CAMP DAVID ACCORDS

Within days of taking office, Carter and Vance began orchestrating a major attempt at achieving a permanent settlement to the Arab-Israeli dispute. The president laid the foundation for new initiatives by conferring with all of the important Middle East political figures except for representatives of the Palestine Liberation Organization, with whom he refused to deal because they practiced terrorism and were committed to the destruction of Israel. He also met with the leaders of Western European nations with Middle East interests. At the same time the administration developed a peace plan based on its interpretation of United Nations Security Council Resolution 242. The American program called for:

1. Israeli forces to withdraw from territories seized after 1967.
2. Israel to be guaranteed secure and defensible borders.
3. The signing of a regional peace treaty by which all states in the region would recognize Israel.
4. The establishment of "a homeland" for the Palestinian refugees displaced since the establishment of the State of Israel.[16]

Carter's early efforts to find a solution to the problems of the Middle East netted Washington nothing. Indeed, in the summer of 1977 peace in the troubled region appeared further off than ever. The Israeli elections, which took place in June, produced a new right-wing government dominated by the blatantly expansionist Likud party and headed by Menachem Begin, a tough-minded defender of Israeli control over the Gaza Strip and the Left Bank of the Jordan River, territories occupied by the Israelis after the 1967 war. Begin both opposed the creation of a Palestinian state and expanded the policy of establishing Israeli settlements in these occupied territories.

With a general Middle East settlement apparently out of reach, Egypt's Anwar Sadat made an extraordinary, not to say courageous move designed to keep the peace process alive. In November 1977, he flew to Jerusalem, and in a dramatic appearance before the Israeli Knesset (Parliament) that was given worldwide television coverage, he appealed for peace. Sadat offered the Israelis diplomatic recognition and a guarantee of Israel's future security in exchange for an Israeli withdrawal from the occupied territories.

The Egyptian president won widespread acclaim in the West and equally widespread condemnation from the leaders of the Arab states for his offer. Unhappily, he did not win enough from Menachem Begin to justify the gamble.

It was at this point, with peace in the Middle East still seemingly out of reach, that Carter decided to become personally involved in the search for a solution. In August he invited Sadat and Begin to meet with him at Camp David, the presidential retreat in the Maryland hills. There, where the press could not intrude, he hoped to hammer out the framework for a settlement.

At the conclusion of a thirteen-day marathon negotiating session during which he shuttled back and forth between the Israeli and Egyptian delegations, Carter went before a joint session of Congress. With both Begin and Sadat seated in the House chamber, he announced the signing of a document called "Framework for Peace in the Middle East" and told an astonished Congress that the two leaders had agreed on the basis of a peace settlement to be concluded between Israel and Egypt within three months time. "Today," he said, "we are privileged to see the chance for one of the

The Camp David Accords stand out as perhaps President Jimmy Carter's major foreign policy achievement. Here Menachem Begin (seated second from left) and Anwar Sadat (to Begin's left) meet with their aides during the negotiations.

sometimes rare, bright moments in human history. . . . We have a chance for peace, because these two brave leaders found within themselves the willingness to work together."[17]

The president won widespread approval for his efforts—more perhaps than he deserved. The media and the public assumed that the Camp David Accords represented a breakthrough that would lead to peace. In fact, however, the Framework for Peace in the Middle East was too weak to bear much weight. It made no mention of the future disposition of the Israeli-occupied Golan Heights on the border with Syria or the Holy City of Jerusalem, then also occupied by the Israelis. It ignored the question of Israeli settlements in the occupied territories that had grown up under government sponsorship following the 1967 war. It also ignored the existence of the Palestine Liberation Organization, which an Arab summit in 1974 had recognized as the only legitimate representative of the Palestinians. In fact the accords did not even specifically call for a separate peace treaty between Israel and Egypt. Rather, they envisioned an Egyptian-Israeli settlement emerging as part of a regional agreement.

Considering the many inadequacies of the Camp David Accords, it is hardly surprising that Egyptian and Israeli negotiators made little progress toward a separate peace in the months that followed. In March 1979, with the negotiations going nowhere and his Middle East initiative in danger of collapsing, Carter flew to Cairo and Jerusalem for conferences with Sadat and Begin. Again acting as mediator and conciliator, he helped the two leaders arrive at a settlement. This time the wheels of diplomacy were greased with promises of substantial military aid for both countries. In addition Carter promised Begin that if Israel should be denied access to the oil then being produced from fields in the Sinai (which under terms of the agreement would be returned to Egypt), Washington would make up the shortfall.

The Egyptian-Israeli peace treaty, signed in Washington on March 26, 1979, though in itself a major achievement, marked the end of all progress toward a Middle East settlement during the Carter years. The Israelis returned the Sinai to Egypt but hung on to the Gaza Strip, the Golan Heights, and the West Bank territories. Nor was any progress made on the key issue of Palestinian autonomy. The Palestine Liberation Organization continued to be recognized by the Arab states as the only legitimate spokesperson for the Palestinian people. But neither the United States nor Israel would deal with that organization.

## MAJORITY RULE FOR AFRICA?

In the last year of the Ford administration, Henry Kissinger made a rhetorical commitment to human rights and majority rule in Africa that President Carter seemed determined to broaden and deepen. He traveled to Nigeria in 1978 to declare his commitment, telling a huge gathering at Lagos that "we share with you a commitment to an Africa that is at peace, free from colonialism, free from racism, free from military interference by outside nations, and free from the inevitable conflicts that can come when the integrity of national boundaries is not respected."[18]

Carter backed up that commitment by appointing Andrew Young, a former aide to the Reverend Martin Luther King Jr., to be his ambassador to the United Nations. Young, who was widely credited with helping Carter win the African-American vote in 1976, did not believe that cold war issues should play a role in the formulation of African policy. "The Africa policy of the Carter administration," he said, "ought not to be a reactionary policy simply to stop the Soviet Union." It ought instead to take aim against apartheid, colonialism, and white minority rule. It was the existence of these evils, he argued, that created a breeding ground for Marxist revolutions in Africa. Young's high-profile approach—his commitment to majority rule, and his willingness to meet and confer even with radical Africans such as Robert Mugabe, then a leader in the struggle for a free Zimbabwe—won him and the administration high marks among African blacks.[19]

If there was one place on the face of the earth where human rights were being abused more than anywhere else, it was probably the Union of South Africa. Carter knew it. And he knew that his African-American and liberal constituents not only knew it but were anxious to do something about it. It is not surprising, then, that only two days after taking the oath of office he launched a blistering rhetorical attack on the South African government and called for "majority rule" there. During a meeting in Vienna with South Africa's Prime Minister Balthazar J. Vorster, Vice President Walter Mondale reiterated that point, stating unequivocally that the United States would not be satisfied until South African blacks enjoyed complete political freedom. That, Mondale said, meant "one man, one vote."[20]

The Carter rhetoric had little positive effect on political developments inside South Africa. During the 1977 elections, Prime Minister Vorster's Nationalist party won a sweeping victory by campaigning against foreigners who interfered in South Africa's internal affairs. Later in the year Pretoria actually increased the level of repression there. Publications critical of the government's policies were routinely censored and sometimes closed down. *The World*, the only South African paper edited by a black, was a special target of the government. White sympathizers of the black movement were prosecuted and increasing numbers of blacks were imprisoned. One black leader, Steve Biko, achieved martyrdom when he died in prison, beaten to death by his jailers.

President Carter's response to all of this was, to say the least, disappointing to many of his constituents. Though liberals and African Americans called for economic sanctions against Pretoria, he did nothing more than lend his support to a UN Security Council decision to apply an embargo on the sale of weaponry to South Africa, an action that had no practical effect since Pretoria was always able to purchase arms from Israel and other arms suppliers.

The administration was considerably more impressive in searching for a solution to the Namibian question. The South Africans had taken Namibia (formerly German Southwest Africa) during World War I and held it after that under a League of Nations mandate. Following World War II, the United Nations attempted to transform Namibia into a UN trusteeship. But the South Africans rejected that idea, instead governing the province as though it were an integral part of the country. Finally the General Assembly of the United Nations passed Resolution 2145, vacating Pretoria's old League of Nations mandate. Still the South Africans hung on. When in 1971 the Permanent Court of International Justice declared South Africa's presence in Namibia illegal and called on her to "withdraw . . . immediately," no one was surprised that Pretoria refused.[21]

This was the situation when the Carter administration took office. From the start Andrew Young made it clear that the United States would not stand idly by while South Africa continued to ignore the will of the international community. At a conference of black African leaders held in Maputo, Mozambique, he explained that Washington viewed the end of South African control of Namibia as a forgone conclusion. He also amazed and delighted his listeners by endorsing the efforts of SWAPO (the South-West African People's Organization), which was then fighting a guerrilla war against the South Africans in Namibia.

Young and Donald F. McHenry, his second at the United Nations, organized a group of UN Security Council members that worked with Nigeria and other "front line" African states as well as with Pretoria. Months of painstaking negotiations bore fruit when Prime Minister Vorster agreed in principle to Namibian independence to be arranged under the aegis of the United Nations. There was a long way to go before this 1978 promise became a reality. But the Carter administration was responsible for moving Namibia an important step down the road to independence.

## THE COLD WAR IN AFRICA

Though Carter stood by his liberal and moral principles when dealing with Namibia, in other parts of sub-Sahara Africa his behavior was virtually indistinguishable from the ideologically based cold war positions staked out by his predecessors. This approach held even with regard to the situation in the British crown colony of Rhodesia, which was in some ways analogous to South Africa's.

In the years following World War II the British moved to divest themselves of their African holdings. One by one black majority governments emerged where once colonies had been. But the 250,000 white settlers of Rhodesia, who constituted less than 3 percent of the colony's population, refused to conform to the pattern. In 1965, led by Prime Minister Ian Smith, they declared their independence rather than accept majority rule for the country.

London reacted by declaring Rhodesia in a state of rebellion, and the United Nations Security Council established an embargo on all imports from Rhodesia. Since the Rhodesian economy was not nearly so strong as that of South Africa and a guerrilla movement led by Robert Mugabe and Joshua Nkomo threatened the regime from within, the British assumed that before long, white Rhodesians would realize they had no choice but to accept majority rule.

The United States supported the British position until 1971, when Congress passed an amendment offered by Senator Harry Byrd of Virginia, exempting Rhodesian chrome from the embargo. Since chrome was a material of considerable strategic importance and the only other source was the Soviet Union, Senator Byrd and his supporters were able to claim that they were simply attempting to protect the strategic interests of the United States. It is clear, however, that their real purpose was to lend aid and comfort to the Smith government. From that time until the end of the Ford administration, American policy remained in conflict with the purposes of both London and the United Nations.

Things seemed to change when Carter moved into the Oval Office. Two months after assuming the presidency, he engineered the repeal of the Byrd amendment. But after this initial move, when cold war considerations intruded, the president began to waver in his support for majority rule in Rhodesia. Hoping to avoid a complete surrender, Ian Smith sought to establish a new government in Rhodesia under the titular leadership of the Methodist bishop, Abel Muzorewa, a moderate black leader who had not been involved in the guerrilla war against the white regime. Rigged elections were held in 1979, and Muzorewa was elected prime minister. But under the new government whites continued to monopolize power.

The British denounced Muzorewa as a puppet and Smith's so-called internal solution as a mere charade. But Carter was attracted to the Muzorewa solution. The president was being influenced by Brzezinski, who feared that a government organized under the leadership of the likes of Mugabe and Nkomo would move quickly to the left, opening up possibilities for Soviet penetration. The national security adviser cajoled the president into allowing Ian Smith to come to the United States to make the case against Mugabe, Nkomo, and African communism in person. He even convinced Carter to invite Muzorewa to Camp David.

In the autumn of 1979, with Carter waffling, the new Conservative government in London headed by Margaret Thatcher hosted a conference intended to bring the Rhodesian question to a proper end. Three months of negotiations produced an agreement under which the British temporarily resumed control of Rhodesia, supervised free elections, and saw to the creation of a new independent nation. In 1980, Robert Mugabe became prime minister of an independent Zimbabwe. But Washington's contribution to this outcome was at best minimal.

Carter's Angolan policy again demonstrates how cold war imperatives governed his behavior toward southern Africa. Andrew Young, who wanted to extend diplomatic recognition to the MPLA, at first seemed to have the support of the president. Encouraged by Carter, the UN ambassador met with the Angolan leader, Agostinho Neto, in what he hoped would be the first in a series of talks leading to recognition. But that meeting was as close as the administration ever came to recognizing Angola.

The presence of some twenty thousand Cuban troops in Angola proved to be an overwhelming obstacle to the normalization of relations. Young argued that the Cubans were there primarily to protect the Neto government against the South Africans, who frequently raided across the border and even occupied a portion of the country. He went so far as to suggest that the Cuban presence actually contributed to stability in the region. But Young was never able to best Brzezinski in the argument over Angola. So long as the Cubans remained, normalization was impossible.

Brzezinski's cold war views prevailed not only in Angola but wherever a Soviet presence could be discerned in Africa. Even the suspicion of a Soviet involvement could arouse these concerns in the president's mind. A situation that developed in Zaire is a case in point.

In 1978 the remnants of Moise Tshombe's once-powerful forces, long exiled in northern Angola, crossed the border into Zaire and took over Kolwezi, a mining center in Shaba (once Katanga) Province. Although they had not a shred of evidence, Carter and Brzezinski immediately blamed the Soviets and the Cubans for the incursion and might well have intervened but for the fact that Congress, still gun-shy over the Vietnam intervention and appalled by recent revelations regarding CIA activities in Africa and elsewhere, refused to fund the government's plan to help Zaire's Mobutu. Though the prohibition remained in force, it did not stop Carter from supplying air and logistical support for the Belgian and French forces who did intervene.

Agostinho Neto and President Mobutu both realized that recent events in Shaba Province had nothing to do with Soviets, Cubans, or the cold war. With the aid of Donald McHenry, they signed an agreement undertaking to pacify the border, which remained quiet from then on. None of these actions, however, had the slightest effect on American policy, which continued to be founded on the assumption that the Soviets were attempting to export the cold war to Zaire.

In the late 1970s the cold war came to the Horn of Africa as well. The dispute between Ethiopia and Somalia over control of the Ogaden desert had been going on for years when the Soviets foolishly became involved, providing Mohamed Siad Barre of Somalia with military aid in exchange for the Berbera naval base. Then, in 1974 the Emperor Haile Selassie of Ethiopia was overthrown in a coup. The new Marxist government in Addis Ababa seemed a fitting ally to the men in the Kremlin, who soon found themselves providing support for both Somalia and Ethiopia.

In March 1977, the relationship between Somalia and the Soviets came to grief when Barre ignored Moscow's pleas and launched an invasion of the Ogaden that put Moscow in the absurd position of supplying both belligerents. President Barre ended his relationship with the Soviets, forcing them to leave the naval base at Berbera. The Soviets responded by airlifting arms and twenty thousand Cuban troops to aid the Ethiopians. This avalanche of support allowed the Ethiopians to drive the Somali invaders from the Ogaden in 1978.

The war at the Horn of Africa produced a major debate inside the Carter administration. Brzezinski saw the Soviet-Cuban presence there as a major strategic threat to American interests in the Middle East as well as the Indian Ocean, and he was eager to provide large-scale military aid to Somalia. Secretary Vance, on the other hand, insisted that the war was fundamentally a local dispute, that by providing Somalia with aid the United States would strengthen Moscow's influence in Addis Ababa, and that intervention would damage chances for a successful conclusion to the SALT talks between Washington and Moscow then in progress. Since Vance was able to extract from Moscow and Addis Ababa a commitment (which they kept) that they would drive the invaders out of the Ogaden but would not invade Somalia, he saw no sound reason for providing military aid to Barre, who had started the war with an act of aggression in the first place.

President Carter held out against providing Somalia with military aid until 1979, when the Iranian revolution and the Soviet invasion of Afghanistan led him to change his mind. At that point the president announced the Carter Doctrine and negotiated an aid agreement with Somalia. Inevitably, Ethiopia's dependence on Cuban troops and Moscow's military aid grew commensurately.

In 1977, Jimmy Carter had announced an African policy that was committed to social justice and basic human rights. By the end of his administration, however, Soviet adventurism in Africa had his complete attention. His preoccupation with cold war issues had become compelling.

## THE PANAMA CANAL TREATIES

Prior to 1977, with the exception of John Kennedy whose Alliance for Progress at least indicated an interest in the region, few postwar administrations paid much attention to Latin American affairs. When asked about the importance of South America, Henry Kissinger, for example, quipped that it was vital, "a dagger pointed at the heart of Antarctica." Only when the threat of a leftist revolution emerged, as for example in Guatemala or Cuba, did Washington pay much attention. And then it used its power to defend the status quo.

At the beginning of his administration, Jimmy Carter promised a new and more creative policy for Latin America. Even Vance and Brzezinski, who agreed on little else, saw eye to eye on this. The interventionist policies of their predecessors would have to be quietly abandoned.

Carter's first order of business for Latin America was achieving an agreement with the Panamanian government of General Omar Torrijos over the future of the Panama Canal. Ever since 1964, when rioting took place in the Canal Zone, a succession of administrations had been involved in delicate negotiations pointing toward a solution to this troublesome problem.

Most Latin Americans viewed the American-controlled canal as a tangible symbol of United States imperialism. And the Panamanians were determined that one way or another they would restore their sovereignty over this important strip of territory. On the other hand, most Americans opposed surrendering the canal. During the 1976 election campaign, Ronald Reagan, campaigning for the Republican ticket, made no bones about it when he said, "We bought it, we paid for it, it's ours and we're going to keep it." Candidate Carter agreed. "I would not be in favor of relinquishing actual control of the Panama Canal or its use to any other nation, including Panama," he said.[22]

But Carter could not have it both ways. If the United States could not find some compromise that would at once restore sovereignty over the Canal Zone to Panama while guaranteeing that the waterway would remain open, there was bound to be renewed anti-American rioting in Panama that might well require military intervention. There was always the possibility, too, that the canal itself, which was highly vulnerable, could be sabotaged.

Finding a solution took months of painstaking negotiations between the Torrijos government and an American delegation led by Sol Linowitz, the former head of the Xerox Corporation, and the onetime ambassador to South Vietnam, Ellsworth Bunker. At length the negotiators produced two treaties. The first provided for joint operation of the canal until the year 1999, after which it would revert to Panama. The second guaranteed to the United States the right to defend the canal, keeping it open in perpetuity. These two agreements were signed in Washington on September 7, 1977. But final ratification of the agreements would depend on winning the votes of two-thirds of the Senate, where a powerful opposition lay in wait.

During the six months following the signing of the treaties, the Panama Canal issue was among the hottest in American politics. The administration pulled out all the stops to win ratification. Carter himself proved to be a tireless promoter of the agreement, speaking in its defense and meeting with skeptical senators to win their support.

In spite of this all-out effort, however, the public remained unconvinced. In the Senate, where the decision would be made, the vote was for the longest time too close to call. At length, in the spring of 1978, the treaties passed with only two votes to spare. Carter had won a major victory, heading off a potentially serious crisis with Panama. But at home he won no plaudits for his achievement. The public remained skeptical, and Republican conservatives, led by Ronald Reagan, fed that skepticism with a drumbeat of criticism directed against the Panama Canal "giveaway."

## CENTRAL AMERICAN REVOLUTION

During much of the postwar period, Nicaragua's economy grew at a healthy rate while inflation remained low. Yet most of the Nicaraguan people failed to benefit from this growth because Anastasio Somoza, who came to power after his father's assassination in 1956, corrupted about everything there was to corrupt in his little country.

A revolutionary atmosphere was already apparent in Nicaragua when a major earthquake nearly leveled Managua in 1972. The United States and other governments provided generous amounts of aid. But Somoza stole a large portion of this money. He also monopolized Managua's rebuilding process (which was never completed) while freezing out local businesspeople and bankers who were not part of his clique. Two years later, over the strong objections of the church and what remained of the free press in Nicaragua, he corrupted the national elections and in effect made himself president for life.

By the time Jimmy Carter took the oath of office, Somoza had lost the support of virtually every important group inside the country, including business leaders, educators, labor, and the church. He was fighting for his life in a bitterly contested civil war. Moreover, his troops were guilty of gross violations of human rights, including indiscriminate murder and torture, behavior that prompted Archbishop Miguel Obando y Bravo to issue a pastoral letter denouncing his atrocities.

In spite of all these violations of human rights, the administration preferred to look the other way. In fact, the government was torn by conflicting purposes. On the one hand human rights advocates, especially Assistant Secretary of State for Human Rights Patricia Derian, made the case for sanctions against Somoza. Others, however, pointed with equal fervor to the administration's commitment to a non-interventionist policy. But what finally tipped the scale against action was the fact that the rebels, who had taken Augusto Sandino's name for their own, were being supported by Fidel Castro, a fact that raised the specter of a second communist state on America's doorstep.

Caught between the fear of communist expansion in Central America, his desire to avoid intervention in Nicaragua's internal affairs, and his commitment to human rights, Carter vacillated between threatening Somoza with a cutoff in aid and congratulating him whenever he gave the slightest indication that he was easing the repression.

The problem, as Carter saw it, was how to establish democracy and constitutional government in Nicaragua. This, of course, was absurd. The civil war in Nicaragua was not about democracy. It was about repression, murder, and the vastly unequal distribution of wealth produced by two grafting dictators who had since 1936 systematically looted the national economy.

The year 1978 opened violently in Nicaragua. On the morning of January 10, while driving to work, Pedro Joaquín Chamorro, the editor and publisher of *La Prensa* and a leading opponent of the government, was gunned down by two unidentified assailants. Somoza denied any involvement in the murder. And there is reason to believe he was telling the truth. Chamorro alive had been an irritation but not a threat to the regime. Dead he became a martyr. Thousands turned out for his funeral. Worse, in the aftermath of the killing a number of labor unions joined with opposition political parties to organize the FAO (The Broad Coalition Front) which, supported by the Nicaraguan Chamber of Commerce, called a successful general strike. At the same time the Sandinistas escalated their war against the regime.

Somoza responded to the growing opposition by increasing the level of violence and by even greater human rights abuses. According to Amnesty International and an OAS investigating team, the National Guard massacred entire villages and methodically murdered boys over the age of fourteen to prevent them from joining the rebels. The result of this, of course, was to convince increasing numbers of Nicaraguans to join in the insurrection.

By the summer of 1978, all factions inside the Carter administration agreed that Somoza would have to go. The President could have brought him down then and there but at considerable political cost in Congress where many conservatives supported Somoza. Moreover, the president had other problems competing for his attention. There was a crisis in Iran to be dealt with. And the administration was preparing for a major legislative battle over the SALT II treaty. Carter therefore attempted to convince a group of Central American nations led by Costa Rica to "mediate Somoza out of office." It was, according to Anthony Lake, the State Department's director of policy planning at the time, the "Let's have our cake and eat it too" approach to the Nicaraguan problem.[23] Hope for this idea soon faded, however, when it became clear that the Central Americans were unprepared to front for Washington.

Unwilling to act unilaterally and unable to convince the Central Americans to act for him, Carter remained on the sidelines during the remainder of 1978 while the situation in Nicaragua continued to deteriorate. Bishop Obando y Bravo, many of Nicaragua's business leaders, and the FAO leadership all called on the United States to intervene. At the same time, Somoza became increasingly hostile, even to the point of charging that the Carter administration was controlled by "leftists and communists."[24]

By the spring of 1979 it was clear that something would have to be done. Somoza's grip on power was slipping. His National Guardsmen were deserting in droves while the Sandinistas, now supported by Costa Rica, Panama, and Venezuela, were growing stronger by the day. In June, spurred on by the fear that a Sandinista victory would have disastrous domestic political repercussions, the administration finally responded with a scheme to remove Somoza and at the same time head off a Sandinista victory.

The Carter State Department approached the Organization of American States with a plan that called for a cease-fire in Nicaragua, the creation of an "interim government of national reconciliation," and an OAS peacekeeping force "to help establish a climate of peace and security and to assist the interim government in establishing its authority."[25] The plan died aborning. No other Latin American country wanted to join in what was obviously a blatant attempt to deny the Sandinistas the fruits of their victory.

At that point the administration was left with no choice but to face the music. A new American ambassador, Lawrence Pezzullo, was sent to Managua to secure Somoza's resignation. Since it was clear that the Sandinistas, now on the verge of total military victory, could not be denied, Pezzullo was to see that Somoza was replaced by a caretaker who would in turn transfer power to a recently organized five-person junta made up of Daniel Ortega Saavedra, Moises Hassan Morales, and Sergio Ramirez Mercado, all Sandinistas; Alfonso Robelo, a businessman, and Violetta Chamorro, the widow of the slain newspaperman, Pedro Joaquín Chamorro.

Pezzullo got off to a good start. Somoza went into exile and the Sandinistas agreed to a cease-fire and the transfer of power to the junta. Then, however, disaster struck. Francisco Urcuyo Malianos, the interim president, refused to transfer power to "a communist" junta. Unable to influence Urcuyo and unwilling to sanction his behavior or leave the Sandinistas with the impression that he was repudiating their agreement, Pezzullo left Managua.

It is not at all clear what, if anything, was going on in Urcuyo's mind. He appears to have been suffering from a completely unjustified case of hubris. In any event his behavior proved to be hopelessly unrealistic. The Sandinistas rejected his absurd demand that they lay down their arms, refused to consider a cease-fire, and insisted that since he had broken the agreement for the transfer of power they would accept nothing short of unconditional surrender. Government power collapsed almost immediately and Urcuyo fled.

On July 19, 1979, the victorious Sandinista forces entered Managua. Five days later the Carter administration recognized the new regime and began providing it with a limited amount of emergency aid.

The period that followed was marked by deep and mutual suspicion. The Nicaraguans could not forget that for forty years the United States had given aid and comfort to the Somozas or that Washington had done a great deal to keep the Sandinistas from achieving power. The Carter administration was equally suspicious, fearing that the Marxists in Sandinista ranks would drive out moderate elements in the coalition, proclaim a Marxist state, and develop close ties with Moscow and Havana.

But if each side was wary of the other, they both recognized a mutual interest in maintaining good relations. Managua was in desperate need of financial aid that could only come from Washington. It was also clear that lacking American approval, the World Bank and other international lending institutions were unlikely to provide loans. For its part the Carter administration believed that the best way "to keep the Sandinistas from turning to Cuba and the Soviet Union" was to adopt a conciliatory attitude and hope for the best.[26]

These mutual needs produced some rather surprising results. The Carter administration invested approximately $100 million in humanitarian aid to Nicaragua. And Managua, while it did turn to the left, was careful not to go too far. The private economic sector continued to function side by side with government controlled operations in a mixed Nicaraguan economy.

And while the junta did develop close relations with Cuba, it was careful not to push things. Thus it accepted thousands of Cuban teachers and health workers to help in its literacy and public health campaigns, but limited the number of Cuban and East bloc military advisers it would accept. Almost in spite of himself Carter had achieved something of a success in Nicaragua.

## REVOLUTION IN EL SALVADOR

Nicaragua was not the only hot spot in Central America during the Carter years. In February 1977, only a month after the Georgian entered the White House, General Carlos Humberto Romero stole the presidency of El Salvador in an utterly fraudulent election. A creature of the alliance between the army and the conservative oligarchy that had ruled El Salvador for generations, Romero had been instrumental in organizing right-wing death squads, which in the early 1970s hunted down and murdered students, teachers, labor leaders, priests, and campesinos suspected of opposing the government.

The Romero regime was, of course, anathema to the Carter administration because of its indifference to human rights and because policy makers feared that its repressive tactics might produce a Nicaragua-style revolution and yet another leftist government in the hemisphere. In Washington, policy makers debated how best to civilize the terrorists who controlled the Salvadoran government. The human rights advocates in the State Department wanted to cut off all aid unless reforms were immediately forthcoming. Others saw economic and military aid programs as providing leverage and for that reason recommended selective pressure.

For a time the human rights advocates had their way. But following the Sandinista victory in Nicaragua, the administration altered course, promising General Romero that it would restore its aid programs if only he would make some gesture indicating a changed attitude toward human rights in his country. Before Romero could respond, he was overthrown by a junta of reform-minded junior officers in the Salvadoran military. Washington policy makers saw in this sudden change (which they may or may not have engineered) the answer to their prayers, the solution that had escaped them in Nicaragua. Said Deputy Secretary of State Warren Christopher, "El Salvador has a new government pledged to open the political system, to pursue urgently needed economic reforms, and to respect human rights."[27]

Washington did not celebrate for long, however. The new government was quickly overthrown and replaced by another right-wing dictatorship. After that no critic of the army or the oligarchy was safe. When Archbishop Oscar Romero spoke out against them, he was shot dead while celebrating mass in San Salvador's cathedral. The archbishop was just one of some ten thousand persons murdered by death squads and the military during 1980 alone.

President Carter, wholly preoccupied with the Iranian hostage crisis and the Soviet invasion of Afghanistan, as well as with his bid for reelection, had little time and less inclination to add El Salvador to the list of issues he was prepared to deal with personally. In December, however, the rape and murder of four American women—a Catholic lay worker and three nuns—by members of the Salvadoran military led the president to send a special mission to San Salvador. A portion of the commission's report serves as a depressing final commentary on the failure of Jimmy Carter's Salvadoran policy. On their return the commission members told him that "hand grenades and automatic rifles" were to be heard "all during the night as people were killed. They don't have anybody in the jails," the commissioners noted, "they're all dead."[28]

## CARTER AND IRAN: THE UNMAKING OF A PRESIDENT

Human rights considerations notwithstanding, it was business as usual in 1977 between President Carter and Mohammad Reza Pahlavi, the shah of Iran. The president was aware that SAVAK, the monarch's ruthless security agency, routinely tortured and murdered those it considered enemies of the regime and that Iran's jails were filled with political prisoners. But conventional wisdom held that the national security interests of the United States required a warm and friendly relationship with the shah.

Though this had been the case since the original 1953 coup, it took on new meaning in 1969 when Richard Nixon first announced the Nixon Doctrine. In the wake of the Vietnam entanglement, Nixon stated that in future the United States would undertake no new unilateral interventions to check communist expansion. Washington would provide aid and military advice but would depend on nations more immediately threatened to confront the danger.

In the Persian Gulf region, Nixon and Kissinger relied upon Iran to be the guardian of stability and guarantor of the continued flow of oil to Japan and the West. They turned a blind eye toward the shah's dismal human rights record while doing everything possible to satisfy his astonishing craving for high-technology military equipment.

Nothing changed when Jimmy Carter moved into the White House. If the shah wanted advanced fighter aircraft, he got them in spite of the president's stated opposition to the international traffic in arms. And when he wanted AWACS (airborne warning and control system) aircraft and Congress objected, fearing that the supersecret technology on these planes would find its way from Iran into Soviet hands, the president fought the shah's battle and won in Congress.

By 1977 serious internal problems had already begun to erode the shah's power. Iran's agricultural economy was in a shambles. Moreover, the shah's program of modernization failed to produce jobs for the hundreds of thousands of peasants who migrated to the cities in hopes of finding even a meager living.

At the same time, Iran's middle class was showing signs of restiveness

In late 1977 the Carters visited the shah of Iran, who hosted a gala dinner for them on New Year's Eve. Here the president lifts his glass in a toast.

in the face of the shah's continued absolutist rule. Some lawyers and intellectuals were even demanding that SAVAK be disbanded. In November 1977, the first of what developed into a series of antigovernment demonstrations was put down by the police. And the shah's visit to Washington that month was marred by a demonstration outside the White House in which four thousand Iranian students chanted, "Down with the fascist shah."

None of this opposition had the least impact on the Carter White House, which seemed oblivious to developments inside Iran. In December 1977, the president visited Tehran, where he was greeted enthusiastically by a number of old Mossadegh liberals, who urged him to raise the question of human rights with the shah. But the president stayed with the old script. At a New Year's Eve banquet given in his honor, Carter applauded the shah for having established Iran "as an island of stability in one of the more troubled areas of the world." "This," he said, "is a great tribute to you, Your Majesty, and to your leadership and to the respect, admiration and love which your people give to you."[29]

Six days after the president left Iran—that "island of stability"— police fired into a crowd of demonstrators in the holy city of Qom, killing a dozen or more people. All through the spring and summer the rioting continued, culminating on September 8, "Black Friday," when somewhere between two hundred and two thousand antigovernment demonstrators (there is no exact figure) were killed by the army in Tehran's central square. Wealthy Iranians removed their money to the safety of foreign countries. And increasingly, as the crisis deepened, they followed it. The economy, never strong, ground to a halt. And the army, the basis of the shah's power, grew increasingly unreliable.

Iran's growing revolutionary movement was made up of an amalgam of groups. Old progressive nationalists of the Mossadegh era were joined by Marxists, students, and intellectuals, as well as merchants and businesspeople fed up with the regime's corruption and its mismanagement of the economy. But the most powerful group were the mullahs (Muslim teachers), 180,000 strong, who had enormous influence over the peasantry and who hoped to replace the shah with a true Islamic republic. The charismatic leader of this revolutionary group was the seventy-eight-year-old Ayatollah Ruhollah Khomeini, who was then living in exile.

During the spring and summer, as the shah's end drew near, the Carter administration continued to believe that he would be able to ride out the storm. America's much-vaunted intelligence-gathering apparatus failed completely to predict the collapse. As late as September 1978, the CIA was still saying that "Iran is not in a revolutionary or even a pre-revolutionary situation."[30] And the president clung to what had clearly become an outmoded policy, reiterating the importance of the alliance with Iran, expressing his strong support for the shah, and praising his commitment to "political liberalization and economic reform."

In November 1978, the administration at last awakened to the fact that it had a problem in Iran. But there was no consensus about what might be done. From Tehran, Ambassador William H. Sullivan urged the president to prepare for a transition by establishing contacts with the Ayatollah Khomeini. But more powerful voices urged all-out support for the shah. Brzezinski even proposed using military force to prop up the tottering monarch.

Secretary Vance argued only somewhat more realistically than Brzezinski that the shah, who was finished, should be encouraged to abdicate in favor of an interim government made up of reform-minded politicians who might be able to establish a viable, pro-Western government. Vance may not have realized it, but there was a good deal of irony in what he proposed. He was suggesting that what the United States needed in Iran was exactly what Mohammad Mossadegh had offered a quarter-century before. What he failed to understand was that it was far too late for a liberal solution to Iran's problems. Radicalism was in the saddle.

While policy makers in Washington carried on their futile debate, the shah gave up the struggle. He handed the government over to Shapour Bakhtiar, an aging reformer whose political roots went back to the days of Mossadegh, and went into exile. The shah really had no choice. Tehran was in chaos, with armed bands roaming the city. Stores and shops were for the most part closed as their owners attempted to protect inventories from looters. Virtually all public services had ceased to function. Because of antigovernment strikes in the oil fields, a country rich in petroleum had no fuel for cars, buses, or power plants.

The shah left Iran for the last time in January, 1979. Not long after his departure, the Ayatollah Khomeini returned and made short work of Shapour Bakhtiar, who quickly fled the country.

The first objective of the Iranian revolution had been achieved. The shah had been deposed. But a major issue remained to be resolved. Who would rule at home? Would it be men such as Ibrahim Yazdi, Mehdi Bazargan, and Abol-Hassan Bani-Sadr, reformers whose commitment to the Islamic revolution was tempered by their belief that Iran would have to come to terms with the modern world? Or would it be the Ayatollah Khomeini's more radical followers, who welcomed isolation from a corrupt world and hoped to create a true Islamic society? American policy makers were betting on the pragmatists. It was one in a series of misjudgments they made.

The Carter administration tried to make the best of a bad situation by adopting a conciliatory attitude toward revolutionary Iran. Policy makers were aware that a strong current of anti-Americanism was prevalent there. But banking on the good sense of the new prime minister, Mehdi Bazargan, as well as Iran's need to market its oil in the West and begin the reconstruction of its damaged economy, they expected relations to improve gradually. Unhappily, they underestimated the importance of Islamic fundamentalism in Iranian affairs and failed to assess correctly either the depth of anti-American sentiment in Iran or the power of the Ayatollah Khomeini, whom they wrongly viewed as little more than a symbol, a rallying point for opposition to the shah.

The ayatollah, whose power was decisive, focused his people's hatred on the United States, "the great Satan" that was responsible for all of Iran's past and present ills. To many Iranians, the evidence was compelling. The CIA had helped overthrow the Mossadegh government in 1953 and establish the shah's power at that time. Afterward, American oil interests profited from the exploitation of Iranian oil. And when the shah became a major arms purchaser, the United States again profited.

"The oil revenues," Khomeini charged, "have at no time been spent to serve the people's interests." Oil policy had been made to serve "the interests of the oil companies and the rich consumer countries . . . who plunder our resources, impose on us the purchase of weapons and then set up on our lands military bases to defend their interests and their policies." Through the shah, he charged, "they have turned us into the area's policeman. At the same time, they have sabotaged our agriculture so that they may become the source supplying us with wheat, rice and other food supplies."[31]

Following the shah's ouster, virtually every negative happening in the country was blamed on Washington. Delays in reconstruction, disappointing agricultural production, and restiveness among Kurds, Azerbaijanis, and other outlying tribes—these and other problems were all blamed on the United States.

## THE HOSTAGE CRISIS

In January 1979, when the shah first decided to go into exile, he intended to settle in the United States. But in February, after a group of young militants temporarily seized the American embassy in Tehran, Ambassador Sullivan warned that if the shah was allowed to travel to the United States the embassy would surely be taken again. At that point the shah was informed he would not be welcome in America.

Months later the president came under pressure from Henry Kissinger and David Rockefeller to let the shah come to the United States. Both men argued that the administration could not turn its back on a longtime ally without suffering serious repercussions elsewhere. They also pointed out that the shah was suffering from cancer and could not receive the therapy he required in Mexico, where he was staying at the time.

The White House asked the embassy in Tehran what to expect if the shah came to the United States. The chargé, Bruce Laingen, told the State Department point blank that the embassy would surely be seized. He thought "the danger of hostages being taken" was quite real.[32]

Laingen's warning went unheeded. The president, succumbing to the pleas of Kissinger and Rockefeller, allowed the shah to come to the United States for medical treatment. Not two weeks later a group of militant Iranian students seized the American embassy, taking all Americans on the premises hostage. Fifty-three of these remained in captivity for 444 days.

The Carter administration was once again badly divided, this time over how to react to the embassy takeover. Secretary of State Vance urged caution and advocated using only peaceful means in attempting to secure freedom for the hostages. Brzezinski, on the other hand, urged military action and headed up a task force that considered a variety of options that might be used to free the hostages. But nothing came of it. "The problem with all of the military options," the president told the White House chief of staff, Hamilton Jordan, "is that we could use them and feel good for a few hours—until we found they had killed our people. And once we start killing people in Iran, where will it end?"[33]

If the military approach seemed unfeasible, diplomacy proved ineffective. Vance and the State Department tried every avenue at their disposal to free the hostages. They sent former Attorney General Ramsey Clark, known for his sympathy to the Iranian revolution, to negotiate directly with Tehran. But Clark was not permitted to enter the country. They tried to work through third countries. They took the question to the World Court. The president, meanwhile, exerted economic pressure on Iran, forbidding the importation of Iranian petroleum products and freezing billions of dollars in Iranian assets. Nothing worked.

The American embassy was seized by militant Iranian "students" on November 4, 1979.
Some of the embassy employees who were taken hostage are here shown being
paraded in the streets of Teheran.

In April, after six months of frustration and with the presidential
campaigning season almost upon him, Jimmy Carter authorized a rescue
attempt. When Vance, who had not been consulted prior to the decision,
learned of this plan, he urged the president to reconsider. The secretary
was convinced that the attempt had little or no chance of succeeding; that it
would result in the death of many Iranians and Americans, including the
hostages; that it would produce a wave of anti-American sentiment that
would sweep the Islamic world; and that it would further diminish chances
of reestablishing normal relations with Iran. But nothing Vance could say
or do moved the president. When that became clear, Vance told Carter that
following the rescue attempt, regardless of whether it succeeded, he would
resign.

The rescue attempt failed in its earliest stages when three of the
eight helicopters that were to be used to evacuate the hostages developed
mechanical problems. At a desert base inside Iran, the mission was scrubbed.

But during a refueling operation prior to returning to their bases, a tanker plane and a helicopter collided. Both burst into flames and eight men were killed. Since the Iranians were certain to report the incident, a humiliated Carter had no choice save to announce the debacle himself.

Following this latest catastrophe, the hostage crisis more or less receded into the background. The media, which had followed the story unrelentingly for months, found other things to report. First there was an unsuccessful challenge to Carter prior to the Democratic national convention by John F. Kennedy's younger brother, Senator Edward Kennedy. Then there was the nomination of Ronald Reagan as the Republican presidential candidate and the political campaign itself.

In September 1980, the Iranians finally gave a clear signal that they were interested in resolving the hostage crisis. There were, no doubt, a number of reasons for this shift. First, the shah died early in that month, ending the possibility that the United States would seek his restoration to the Peacock throne. More important, however, was the fact that on September 4 Iraqi forces attacked Iran, beginning a war that would drag on for years and cost hundreds of thousands of lives. Considering the military needs brought on by the war and the dreadful shape of the Iranian economy at the time, Tehran no doubt viewed it as essential to unfreeze at least some of the billions of dollars then being held in American banks.

Actual negotiations began on November 2, 1980. Two days later, Ronald Reagan trounced Carter in the presidential election. Carter, of course, remained in office until January 20. During the interregnum he and his staff worked tirelessly to free the hostages prior to the transition. The going, however, was difficult. At the start Tehran demanded the transfer of $24 billion, including $10 billion in the shah's personal assets that it claimed belonged to the state. The two sides finally agreed that $7.955 billion in Iranian assets (by no means all of the funds then being held in American banks) would be placed in the Bank of England, to be turned over to Iran as soon as the hostages were surrendered.

Jimmy Carter waited up through his last night in the White House hoping that the hostages would be freed before he officially retired from office. But it didn't work out that way. Only a few minutes into Ronald Reagan's first term, the hostages started the long journey home.

The one time chair of the Democratic National Committee, Robert Strauss, who was serving as the administration's trade representative, offered this epitaph to Jimmy Carter's presidency. "Poor bastard," he said, "he used up all his luck in getting here. We've had our share of victories and defeats, but we've not had a single piece of good luck in the past three years."[34]

## ENDNOTES

1. Zbignieu Brzezinski, quoted in Gaddis Smith, *Morality, Reason, and Power: American Diplomacy in the Carter Years* (New York: Hill and Wang, 1986), p. 37.

2. Jimmy Carter and James Fallows, both quoted in Joshua Muravchik, *The Uncertain Crusade:*

*Jimmy Carter and the Dilemmas of Human Rights Policy* (Lanham, Md.: Hamilton Press, 1986), p. 1.

3. Patrick Caddell, quoted in ibid., p. 3.

4. Leonid Brezhnev, quoted in ibid., p. 30.

5. Arthur Schlesinger, Jr., quoted in ibid., p. 115.

6. Brzezinski aide, quoted in Strobe Talbot, *Endgame: The Inside Story of SALT II* (New York: Harper and Row, 1979), p. 49.

7. Anonymous strategist, quoted in ibid., p. 61.

8. Andrei Gromyko and Brezhnev, quoted in ibid., p. 74.

9. Carter and Anatoly Dobrynin, quoted in Gerald Clarfield and William Wiecek, *Nuclear America: Military and Civilian Nuclear Power in the United States, 1940–1980* (New York: Harper and Row, 1984), p. 415.

10. Jimmy Carter, *Keeping Faith: The Memoirs of a President* (New York: Bantam Books, 1982), p. 62.

11. Raymond Garthoff, quoted in Arthur Macy Cox, *Russian Roulette: The Superpower Game* (New York: Times Books, 1982), p. 118.

12. American Security Council report, quoted in ibid., pp. 84–85.

13. Cyrus Vance, *Hard Choices: Critical Years in America's Foreign Policy* (New York: Simon and Schuster, 1983), p. 361.

14. Carter, quoted in Smith, *Morality, Reason, and Power,* pp. 223–24.

15. Carter, annual address to Congress, January 23, 1980, *Public Papers of the Presidents: Jimmy Carter, 1980* (Washington, D.C., 1981), p. 197.

16. Carter, quoted in *Peace-making in the Middle East* (New York: Facts in File, 1980), pp. 132–42.

17. Carter, address to Congress, September 18, 1978, *Public Papers of the Presidents: Jimmy Carter, 1978* (Washington, D.C., 1979), II, 1537.

18. Carter, remarks at the National Arts Theater, April 1, 1978, *Public Papers of the Presidents: Jimmy Carter, 1978* (Washington, D.C., 1979), p. 647.

19. Andrew Young, quoted in Henry F. Jackson, *From the Congo to Soweto: U.S. Foreign Policy toward Africa since 1960* (New York: William Morrow, 1982), pp. 78–79.

20. Walter Mondale, quoted in Gwendolyn M. Carter, "United States Policies toward South Africa and Namibia," in *Beyond Constructive Engagement*, ed. Elliott P. Skinner (New York: Paragon House, 1986), p. 225.

21. Judgment by the Permanent Court of International Justice, quoted in ibid., p. 226.

22. Ronald Reagan and Jimmy Carter, both quoted in Smith, *Morality, Reason, and Power*, p. 112.

23. Anthony Lake, *Somoza Falling* (Boston: Houghton Mifflin, 1989), p. 136.

24. Anastasio Somoza, quoted in ibid., p. 137.

25. Carter proposal for Nicaragua, quoted in Peter Kornbluh, *Nicaragua: the Price of Intervention* (Washington, D.C.: Institute for Policy Studies, 1987), p. 15. See also Walter LaFeber, *Inevitable Revolutions: The United States in Central America* (New York: W. W. Norton, 1984), p. 234.

26. Carter, *Keeping Faith*, p. 585.

27. Warren Christopher, quoted in Smith, *Morality, Reason, and Power*, p. 123.

28. Commissioner's report, recalled in Carter, *Keeping Faith*, p. 585.

29. Carter, quoted in Barry Rubin, *Paved with Good Intentions: The American Experience in Iran* (New York: Penguin Books, 1980), p. 201.

30. CIA estimate, quoted in Gary Sick, *All Fall Down: America's Tragic Encounter with Iran* (New York: Random House, 1985), p. 92.

31. Ayatollah Ruhollah Khomeini, quoted in Rubin, *Paved with Good Intentions*, p. 279.

32. Bruce Laingen, quoted in James A. Bill, *The Eagle and the Lion: The Tragedy of American-Iranian Relations* (New Haven, Conn.: Yale University Press, 1988), p. 324.

33. Carter, quoted in Hamilton Jordan, *Crisis: The Last Year of the Carter Presidency* (New York: Putnam's, 1982), p. 52.

34. Robert Strauss, quoted in ibid., p. 60.

# 35

# *REAGAN AND THE FOCUS OF EVIL, 1981–1989*

In 1983, as part of the effort to intimidate the Sandinistas, American forces invaded the tiny Caribbean island of Grenada and overthrew the leftist government there.

Ronald Reagan began his career in 1932 as a sportscaster for a local radio station in Davenport, Iowa. Shortly afterward he moved to a larger Des Moines station, where he broadcast Chicago Cubs' baseball games. In 1937 he followed the Cubs to California for spring training and while there took a screen test. Jack Warner of Warner Brother's Studios liked what he saw and signed the young man to a movie contract.

Reagan, who once described himself as "the Errol Flynn of the B's," was not much of an actor.[1] But he had staying power, making more than fifty films before his career began to fade in the early 1950s. With his movie career winding down, Reagan moved to television, hosting the "General Electric Theater" and later "Death Valley Days." He also toured as a public relations spokesperson for the General Electric Corporation.

Given his good looks, charm, quick sense of humor, and interest in politics, it is not surprising that Reagan became a professional politician. During Barry Goldwater's 1964 run for the presidency he emerged as the one bright spot in the Republicans' otherwise dismal outing that year. He was so good, in fact, that in 1966 the Republicans drafted him to run for governor of California. He won handily and went on to become an increasingly prominent voice for conservative Republicanism.

Reagan's supporters began grooming him for the presidency in 1968.

But it was not until 1980, with the country moving steadily to the right, that he won the GOP nomination. A skillful campaigner, Reagan, who went on to an overwhelming victory in November, told the people what they wanted to hear. "There *are* simple answers," he said. "There just aren't easy ones." He told his supporters: "At the heart of our message should be five simple familiar words. No big economic theories. No sermons on political philosophy. Just five short words: family, work, neighborhood, freedom, peace."[2]

Like so many others, Reagan felt that in recent years America had allowed itself to be pushed around too much, that it was time to start pushing back, to "stand tall." The imagery, right out of a western movie, was perfect. In westerns there are no complexities: Right and wrong are easily perceived; the righteous always prevail; justice is always served.

## THE COLD WAR GOES FRIGID

In the conservative lexicon of the early 1980s, "making America great again" was almost a euphemism for getting tough with the Soviets. And when it came to that, Ronald Reagan had few peers. In one speech after another he subjected the Soviets to a barrage of invective. At his initial press conference he charged "The only morality they [the Soviet leaders] recognize is what will further their cause: meaning they reserve unto themselves the right to commit any crime, to lie, to cheat." It was a message he never tired of sending. Later he told a convention of evangelical Christians that the Soviet Union was the "focus of evil in the modern world . . . an evil empire."[3]

Suddenly there was more talk of rolling back the communist tide coming out of Washington than anyone had heard since the days of John Foster Dulles. Reagan elevated the struggle against communism to the level of a presidential doctrine, promising to aid "freedom fighters" in the struggle against totalitarian communism anywhere in the world. "The march of freedom and democracy," he said, "will leave Marxism-Leninism on the ash heap of history as it has left other tyrannies which stifle the freedom and muzzle the self-expression of people." Again he remarked: "The West won't contain Communism. . . . It won't bother to denounce it; it will dismiss it as some bizarre chapter in human history whose last pages are even now being written."[4]

The Soviets were used to harsh rhetoric from American leaders. In their minds it did not count for much. They were more interested in the policies the new president would implement. And Moscow saw Reagan as another potential Richard Nixon, a conservative who might also turn out to be a pragmatist and a supporter of détente. Said one hopeful Soviet observer, "Maybe Reagan will promise less, but I think he will be able to deliver more."[5]

The Soviets had many reasons for seeking a return to the palmy days of détente. Improved relations implied increased trade, greater access to Western technology, and, most important, a slowing of the nuclear arms race. Moscow's leaders were not prepared to let nuclear parity slip through their fingers. But neither did they want the arms race to escalate further. They were stretched to the limit. Their foreign commitments in Cuba, Africa, Kampuchea (formerly Cambodia), Vietnam, and Afghanistan placed extreme stress on an already weak economy.

For decades Moscow had diverted resources needed by the domestic economy to maintain a massive military machine and subsidize the weak economies of the satellites. By the early 1980s the problems this misallocation of resources created were coming home to roost. Even if the Soviets had been able to match Western technological achievements in an expanded nuclear arms race (something they very much doubted), the added economic stress would have been murderous. A better, less costly way to maintain parity was to restrict the race through negotiations.

Reagan, a longtime critic of détente, proved a bitter disappointment to the Soviets. If one of the key ingredients in his foreign policy was an extreme form of anticommunism, the other was his commitment to a major increase in defense spending. It was an article of faith in conservative circles that the Soviets had achieved military superiority over the United States. Though this was simply not true, Reagan engineered a 50 percent increase in defense spending during his first five years in office.

The president's condemnation of détente, his lack of interest in arms control, and the emphasis he placed on reestablishing American nuclear superiority all contributed to growing popular fears. Many, both in the United States and in Western Europe, came to believe that this administration had abandoned deterrence in favor of a "win" strategy. On several occasions Secretary of Defense Caspar Weinberger said as much by insisting that the United States must be prepared to "prevail" in a nuclear war.

One result of these changed policies, unanticipated by the administration, was the revival of the American antinuclear movement, which had been relatively moribund for at least fifteen years. The Union of Concerned Scientists, the World Council of Churches, the American Conference of Catholic Bishops, the American Medical Association, and Physicians for Social Responsibility, a group organized by the Australian pediatrician and antinuclear activist Helen Caldicott, were only some of the groups calling on the superpowers to end "the madness."

Many scientists, including the highly respected Carl Sagan, joined in the call for an end to the arms race while speculating on the possibility that in the event of a nuclear exchange the cloud of smoke, dust, and debris thrown up by thousands of nuclear explosions would form a cloud so thick that it would block out the sun and produce a "nuclear winter," ending all life on the planet. *The Day After*, a television film starring Jason Robards, threw a further scare into the public with its depiction of what the aftermath of a nuclear war might be like for those unlucky enough to survive.

Towns and cities nationwide responded to this growing concern with antinuclear demonstrations. On June 12, 1982, more than 500,000 people assembled in New York City for what may have been the largest single such demonstration ever held. Antinuclear activists, not satisfied with mere demonstrations, advocated as an initial step that the superpowers enter into an agreement for a mutual and verifiable freeze on the further testing, production, and deployment of nuclear weapons. Voters across the nation lent strength to the freeze movement by supporting ballot resolutions favoring the idea.

The antinuclear movement was especially powerful in Europe, where opposition to the deployment of two new American weapon systems— Tomahawk cruise missiles and Pershing II ballistic missiles—was intense. These "Euro-missiles" first became an issue early in the Carter administration. At that time the Soviets began deploying the first of 240 SS-20 mobile intermediate-range missiles as well as the medium-range Backfire bomber, systems designed for use in the European theater. West Germany's Chancellor Helmut Schmidt, who feared that the SALT talks would eliminate systems that could be used to counter these new Soviet weapons, wanted NATO to begin at once modernizing its Europe-based nuclear forces.

A bitter debate ensued between those who supported Schmidt and those who hoped that the SS-20s could be removed through negotiation. In the end a compromise was struck. The Allies agreed that the United States should negotiate with the Soviets for the purpose of removing the SS-20s from Europe. If the Soviets refused, the United States would then add to NATO's nuclear strength by deploying 464 Tomahawk cruise missiles and 108 Pershing II missiles.

This so-called dual track approach to the problem of Euro-missile modernization was acceptable to most Europeans because they believed the Carter administration was serious about arms control. The Reagan administration's extremist rhetoric shattered that assumption. One public opinion survey published in *SIFO Indikator*, a Swedish publication, demonstrated how much things had changed. A 1982 survey indicated that 78 percent of the respondents feared a nuclear war. That was up from 55 percent in 1973, the year in which SALT I was approved. The results of another poll, published in the *International Herald Tribune*, indicated that while most Western Europeans viewed the Soviets as primarily responsible for the insecurity they felt, "US aggressive policies towards the Soviet Union" or "superpower activities in the Third World" were not far behind.[6] In other words, the most significant reason for this increased fear of war was a sense that *both* superpowers were more or less out of control.

One result of this distrust was the emergence of a powerful opposition to the deployment of the Pershing and Tomahawk missiles. In November 1981, more than 400,000 demonstrators gathered in Amsterdam to protest the deployment of these weapons. Similar demonstrations took place in London, Rome, and other major European cities. "Somewhere, at some time, some people have got to decide that they will say no," wrote the eminent historian and antinuclear activist E. P. Thompson. "We in the European peace movement have decided that the place is Europe and the time is now and that the people will have to be us. Europe is the no-man's-land between the superpowers where at last the nuclear arms race might be stopped."[7]

## THE INF AND START TALKS

The widespread opposition to the deployment of the American missiles forced both superpowers to the bargaining table. In fact, however, neither side was genuinely interested in negotiating. The Reagan administration only feigned an interest to pacify its critics. The Soviets, meanwhile, thought that Western European opposition to deployment of the new American systems might force the NATO Allies to reject them without any quid pro quo.

Ten months after taking office, with less than a year before the Tomahawks and Pershings were scheduled to be deployed, Reagan announced "the zero option," an idea that was designed to be unacceptable in Moscow. The proposal called on the Soviets to dismantle all their SS-4, SS-5, and SS-20 missiles. In return, the United States would agree not to deploy its Tomahawks and Pershings. The Soviet news agency Tass immediately pointed out the plan's inequity. In the first place, the Soviets were again being asked to dismantle existing systems in exchange for promises from the United States. Moreover, while Reagan was asking Moscow to eliminate its "defense potential in Europe . . . the American forward based systems and submarine based missile complexes and nuclear bombers [and missiles] of Britain and France" would "be preserved."[8]

The Soviets, who had danced this minuet many times in the past, responded with a proposal that was at once equally plausible and completely unacceptable to the West. They suggested that both NATO and the Warsaw Pact eliminate all nuclear weapons aimed at European targets. Europe would thus become a nuclear-free zone. The Soviet proposal no doubt had a certain appeal to many Europeans, especially the Germans, whose towns, according to the American military's calculations, were no more than "a kiloton apart." At the same time, it was completely unacceptable to Washington, for it would have left the Warsaw Pact powers with vast superiority in conventional weaponry.

From November 1981 until the autumn of 1983 the intermediate-range force reduction talks (INF) continued at Vienna with both sides trading unacceptable proposals. Not until Reagan's second term, when a new Soviet leader, Mikhail Gorbachev, surprised everyone by accepting Reagan's zero-option proposal, would the Euro-missile question be set to rest.

The Reagan administration, which was required for political reasons to appear interested in a negotiated solution to the Euro-missile question, had a similar problem regarding long-range strategic missiles. The American public supported efforts to reduce the threat of nuclear war. And Reagan could not afford to ignore that fact. The arms control lobby in Congress added to the pressure by threatening to cut off funds for the MX missile—

a system the president wanted and the Soviets feared—unless he began serious negotiations. Even so, it took the administration eighteen months to assemble a negotiating team and establish a bargaining position.

General Edward Rowny headed the American delegation to the first round of the Strategic Arms Reduction Talks (START) in Geneva. General Rowny was knowledgeable on the subject of strategy and nuclear weaponry. But what truly qualified him for the job as far as the administration was concerned was the fact that he had opposed SALT II.

At the outset of the talks, Rowny's delegation tabled a proposal calling for a ceiling on the total number of strategic missile warheads each side could retain and a much lower ceiling on the number of warheads that could be deployed on land-based missiles. Since more than 80 percent of the Soviet missiles were land based while the United States was far more heavily invested in submarine-launched missiles, the plan would have required the Soviets to reduce their existing systems below SALT II levels while leaving the United States free to keep all its sea-based missiles and add to its land-based forces. The United States also asked for certain "collateral restraints" designed to limit the number of "heavy" SS-18 missiles the Soviets could deploy and further demanded that the number of undeployed ICBMs be strictly limited. To ensure against cheating, Washington also called for the virtually unrestricted right to on-site inspection. Nor would Washington consider altering its plans to develop and deploy an entirely new generation of weapon systems, including the MX, Trident II, and cruise missiles, even though the technological innovations they represented were certain to have a major impact on the strategic balance.

Moscow viewed the Reagan position, which emphasized more weapons for the United States and fewer for the Soviet Union, as an attack on parity. Not surprisingly, then, the START talks deadlocked. But that was no problem for Washington, where there was little inclination to negotiate in any case.

In November 1983, at the end of that fall's START negotiating session, Moscow announced an indefinite suspension to all arms control negotiations. Foreign Minister Andrei Gromyko railed against Reagan's "pathological obsession" for more weaponry, and Yuri Andropov, the ailing general secretary of the Soviet Communist party, who had only recently replaced the deceased Brezhnev, denounced the president for "torpedoing" the talks.[9] Since Moscow and Washington were not talking about anything else, this session ended all contact between the superpowers. Soviet-American relations had practically never been worse.

## THE STAR WARS INITIATIVE

In a major television address on March 23, 1983, Ronald Reagan made a startling break with the past, proposing the abandonment of the strategy of nuclear deterrence and the development instead of a missile defense system that "would intercept and destroy strategic ballistic missiles before they reached our own soil or that of our allies." He called on "the scientific community who gave us nuclear weapons . . . to give us the means of rendering these nuclear weapons impotent and obsolete."[10]

It was perhaps inevitable, since filmmakers Steven Spielberg and George Lucas were then making their famous trilogy, that the press should dub the president's proposal "Star Wars." The administration, preferring something less connected with fantasy, called it the Strategic Defense Initiative (SDI). But whatever it was called, the plan soon became highly politicized. Support for SDI became a sort of litmus test of true conservatism. And inevitably, the question of whether such a defense was practical was lost in the ideological combat it spawned.

Looking past the absurd political debate surrounding SDI, it is clear that the vast majority of knowledgeable scientists thought the idea scientifically unworkable and strategically dangerous. Hans A. Bethe, who had worked with J. Robert Oppenheimer on the Manhattan Project, pointed out that a Star Wars system would have to do a job of "staggering" proportions, "destroying thousand of ICBMs, SLBMs, cruise missiles and bombers within minutes or even seconds" and do this in the "face of an imposing array of counter-measures available to the attacker." At best, he pointed out, current technologies would be able to provide only a "partial defense."[11]

Bethe further believed that if a superpower confrontation did occur, a partially effective defense would create an incentive for each side to strike first. The American military, possessing a semieffective missile defense system, would, he assumed, calculate that an attack on Soviet missile installations would reduce the number of Soviet missiles SDI would have to contend with and therefore urge the president to act preemptively. Soviet planners, aware of this, would be anxious to strike early before their weapons could be attacked.[12]

Other opponents of SDI pointed to a confusion in popular thinking introduced by Reagan himself. The president had spoken of making nuclear weapons obsolete. But even if perfected—a dubious assumption— SDI would make only ballistic missiles obsolete. It would have no effect on strategic bombers, cruise missiles, low-trajectory missiles, or "suitcase bombs" planted around the United States. They also pointed out that the SDI program would sooner or later come into conflict with the 1972 ABM Treaty, which banned the testing (outside the laboratory) and deployment of defensive systems. Few scientists opposed continued research in the field as "a hedge" against the possibility of a Soviet breakthrough. But there was strong opposition to abandoning the ABM Treaty, the only obstacle to a potentially endless, destabilizing race in defensive technology.

Not even the defenders of SDI, such as Dr. Gerald Yonas, at one time the chief scientist for the SDI organization, believed it would be possible to develop the sort of perfect defensive shield that President Reagan described in his speech. Yonas thought that scientists ought to aim at creating a system sufficient "to make a first strike of no military significance." In this way, he argued, SDI would "enhance crisis stability" and create motives for policy makers to "move toward substantial reductions in armaments." George A. Keyworth III, the president's science adviser, saw no chance of protecting large civilian populations from missile attack, since if even "a fraction" of the Soviet Union's missiles reached their target American civilization would be turned to ashes. In Keyworth's view, SDI ought to be used to protect America's retaliatory missiles force. In that way it could contribute to stability and indirectly to arms control efforts. By removing the possibility of a successful preemptive attack, Keyworth argued, SDI could produce "an opportunity to negotiate major arms reductions that would leave each side with a strong retaliatory deterrent."[13]

Scientists on both sides of this debate had one thing in common. They were not on the president's wavelength. Reagan rejected the premise that a deterrent strategy such as mutually assured destruction and a stable nuclear balance were the best that could be hoped for. He wanted out of the nuclear conundrum. The scientists, on the other hand, knew there was no way out. The best the defenders of SDI could do was to argue that a partial defensive system would strengthen deterrence. Its opponents argued more persuasively that it would be a destabilizing factor that would increase the likelihood of an exchange.

Whatever the technical merits of Reagan's SDI proposal, it was a political masterstroke. The nuclear freeze movement's power was based on the fact that the president was indifferent to the nuclear threat and disinterested in arms control. Reagan's commitment to SDI changed all that. The freeze movement promised increased security in small increments as a result of painful negotiation. Reagan, who proposed instead a quick technological fix, stopped the freeze movement in its tracks.

Reagan's unwavering commitment to SDI had another significant effect as well. It paralyzed the START talks. The logical reaction to the development of a missile defense system by one side, all agreed, was for the other side to increase its offensive capabilities to overwhelm the defense. SDI, therefore, made it impossible for Moscow to consider significant cuts in its offensive missile forces.

## NEW DIRECTIONS IN SOVIET–AMERICAN RELATIONS

Influenced by Secretary of State George Shultz, who replaced Alexander Haig in mid-1982, as well as his own sound political instincts (there was an election coming), Ronald Reagan began softening his anti-Soviet rhetoric in 1984 and called for "a dialogue as serious and constructive as possible."[14]

The Soviets were also ready to resume discussions. Moscow may have believed that after three tense years Reagan was at last serious about negotiating. But more to the point, the Soviets realized that if he went ahead with "Star Wars," they would have no choice save to expand their offensive capabilities while attempting to develop a defensive shield of their own.

These would be costly ventures, too costly for an economy that was already in deep trouble. Moreover, the Soviets knew they did not have the technology to make a space-based defense system work but worried that Washington might. All things considered, they deemed it vital to eliminate SDI through diplomacy before its destabilizing effects could be felt.

When the START negotiations began again in Geneva early in 1985, it appeared to many including the Soviets that a "grand compromise" in which the United States traded "Star Wars" for reductions in the Soviet missile force was on the horizon. But the president was adamant. SDI was not on the trading block. Not surprisingly, then, the talks quickly deadlocked, and accusations of bad faith flew back and forth across the Atlantic.

It was at this point that Konstantin Chernenko, the latest septuagenarian caretaker of the Soviet state, died. He was replaced by Mikhail Gorbachev, a fifty-four-year old attorney and agricultural expert. Younger, more dynamic, and certainly more imaginative than his three predecessors, Gorbachev realized that something drastic had to be done to save the Soviet economy and state. Productivity was down, worker absenteeism was an endemic problem, and widespread substance abuse (in this case pervasive drunkenness) was a matter of serious concern. For decades the Soviet leadership had drained capital from the domestic economy to maintain huge military forces. Now, somehow, that trend had to be reversed.

The new Soviet leader was convinced that mere reforms would have little effect. Only a basic restructuring of the economy (*perestroika*) would do. Toward that end Gorbachev sought true détente with the West. Détente would provide greater access to modern technologies as well as increased trade while opening the door to foreign investment. It also meant reductions in East-West tensions and the establishment of an international environment in which Soviet military forces could be reduced, thus freeing capital for economic development.

Not surprisingly, Gorbachev was disappointed by the lack of progress at the Geneva START talks and Washington's refusal to abandon SDI. The implementation of "U.S. plans to militarize space," he said in May 1985, would both "thwart disarmament talks" and "increase the threat of a truly global, all destroying military conflict. Anyone capable of an unbiased analysis of the situation and sincerely wishing to safeguard peace can not help opposing 'star wars.'"[15]

In January 1986, Gorbachev tried to break the deadlock with a new omnibus arms control proposal. He called for a nuclear test ban treaty and new initiatives to limit chemical weapons and reduce conventional forces in Europe. But the centerpiece of his plan was a call for the total elimination of nuclear weapons by the year 2000.

The history of the nuclear arms race is studded with similarly grand proposals. Gorbachev's differed, however, in that he included a more or less detailed plan to implement the proposal and a schedule for its completion. He also offered two major concessions. First, contrary to the prediction of every hawk in or near the White House, he accepted President Reagan's zero option with regard to Euro-missiles. He also adopted the long-held Western view that on-site inspection was essential to verify that all sides fulfilled their commitments. The price Gorbachev asked for these concessions was the abandonment of SDI. "Instead of wasting the next ten to 15 years by developing new weapons in space, allegedly designed to make nuclear arms useless, would it not be more sensible to eliminate those arms?" he asked.[16]

Gorbachev's initiative took the administration by surprise. There was much to be said in its favor. The Soviet leader was offering major concessions. At the same time there were dangers. The abolition of all nuclear weapons without conventional force reductions would leave the Warsaw Pact far superior to NATO forces. Moreover, the American nuclear umbrella was the cement that held the Western alliance together. Was this merely another Soviet attempt to divide the alliance? Was it a propaganda ploy intended to put the administration on the defensive? Whether Gorbachev intended to do so, his initiative certainly had that effect.

Following months of waffling, during which Soviet-American relations remained in a state of uncertainty, Reagan and Gorbachev agreed to an informal two-day meeting at Reykjavik, Iceland. Presidential spokespersons, including White House Chief of Staff Donald Regan and Max Kampelman, the new head of the START delegation, went out of their way to dampen hopes. This meeting was to be a mere warm-up for a really important Washington summit to come later, they said.

The Reykjavik meeting turned out to be far more than that. Between them Reagan and Gorbachev broke all the rules. Working swiftly and with the aid of only a few experts who hammered out compromises on some issues while the two leaders worked on others, they achieved what armies of arms controllers had failed to accomplish in more than two decades—a tentative agreement calling for a 50 percent reduction in strategic missiles over five years.

On the last afternoon of the conference, Reagan went for more, proposing the total elimination of ballistic missiles at the end of ten years. Gorbachev quickly rejected that proposal, which would have left the United States with an unacceptable advantage in bombers and cruise missiles. He proposed instead an even more grandiose idea, the elimination of all nuclear weapons in ten years. The president, who was no longer young and was weary after two days of unaccustomed work, made a serious mistake. He agreed. But such an agreement unaccompanied by limits on conventional military forces would have left the Warsaw Pact with a huge advantage in Europe and gone a long way toward fragmenting the NATO alliance.

Later, in an attempt at damage control, the White House denied that the president had made such an obvious error, claiming the Soviets were misrepresenting him. But when Moscow took the extraordinary step of making the transcripts of the meeting public, an unnamed senior White House official was forced to admit that the president had indeed made a serious error. All he could do was point out that no final agreement had been reached at Reykjavik.

The angry debate over what President Reagan did or did not say obscured the fact that for a brief moment he and Gorbachev were on the brink of a major achievement, an agreement to reduce by 50 percent the number of strategic missiles in both arsenals. Unhappily, this agreement did not survive the conference itself. During the two-day summit, Gorbachev's strategy was to lay out his concessions one at a time while leaving veiled the concession he wanted in return. A year earlier he would have called on the United States to abandon SDI. Now, however, he softened his position, asking instead that, for a period of ten years, work on the system be confined to the laboratory.

Many on the American side thought the president should accept Gorbachev's offer, especially considering SDI's very debatable value. But the president was adamant. Convinced that attempts to limit development of SDI were in reality meant to kill it, he left the bargaining table angry, abandoning the tentative agreement for a 50 percent cut in strategic systems.

## SECOND PRIZE: THE INF TREATY

From the moment that Gorbachev first unveiled his omnibus arms control proposal, Western policy makers wondered whether his apparent willingness to accept Reagan's zero option regarding Euro-missiles was tied to Moscow's wishes regarding SDI. It was not. Viktor Karpov, the head of the Soviet START delegation, said so at the time. Gorbachev himself reiterated that point to Senator Edward Kennedy when the senator visited Moscow. Even as recriminations over the failure of the Reykjavik summit flew between Washington and Moscow, Karpov again made the same point. If the West wanted a zero option for Europe, it was there for the taking.

In a matter of a few months an INF Treaty eliminating all intermediate- and short-range missiles from Europe was made ready. At a Washington summit meeting held in December 1987, Reagan and Gorbachev signed the agreement.

Both sides made much of the treaty, and with justification. It was the first time that an entire class of launch vehicles had been eliminated. It was also path-breaking in that each side agreed to an elaborate program of on-site inspections to verify that the agreement was carried out.

Still, when one considers what might have been, the INF Treaty pales into insignificance. At Reykjavik, for the first time since the beginning of the nuclear age, the leaders of the two superpowers had tentatively agreed on massive cuts in nuclear firepower and even shown the moral courage to consider general nuclear disarmament. That they failed to bring even part of this vision to fruition was a tragedy, especially since the single obstacle dividing the two leaders was SDI, a system that at this writing seems unlikely to ever get beyond the research stage.

Here Ronald Reagan and Mikhail Gorbachev are seen on a walk through Red Square in Moscow.

## THE CENTRAL AMERICAN CRISIS

When Ronald Reagan took office in January 1981, he inherited a chaotic situation in Central America. The Sandinista government in Nicaragua was moving rapidly leftward. In El Salvador the civil war continued between the right-wing oligarchy supported by the army, and the Farabundo Marti National Liberation Front (FMLN). And another guerrilla movement was alive and active in Guatemala.

Reagan and Secretary of State Alexander Haig ignored the indigenous causes of Central America's growing instability, offering instead a cold-war analysis. The president, who remarked during the 1980 election campaign that if the Russians "weren't engaged in this game of dominoes there wouldn't be any hot spots in the world," claimed that the Central American revolution was being "exported from the Soviet Union and from Cuba." In February 1981, Haig's State Department issued a White Paper that warned of a "Moscow-Havana axis" that "could well bring more Cubas: totalitarian regimes so linked to the Soviet Union that they became factors in the military balance." The paper even claimed to provide "definitive evidence" of a "textbook case of indirect armed aggression by Communist powers" [Cuba and Nicaragua] against El Salvador.[17]

A construct of distortions and fabrications, the White Paper was soon debunked in the press. An embarrassed administration was even forced to repudiate it. Nevertheless, Washington continued to insist that the Central American revolutions posed a direct threat to national security. The president argued that "the political and strategic stakes" in the region were "the same" as those that had produced the 1947 Truman Doctrine. Unless the United States took action, he said, "the region's freedom will be lost and our security damaged in ways that can hardly be calculated." America had to respond to this Soviet challenge, Reagan continued, or face serious problems elsewhere. Using the well-worn credibility argument, he asked: "If the United States cannot respond to a threat near our own borders why should Europeans or Asians believe we are seriously concerned about threats to them? If the Soviets can assume that nothing short of an actual attack on the United States will provoke an American response, which ally, which friend will trust us then?" "Our credibility," he continued, "would collapse, our alliances would crumble."[18]

In 1981, not long after Reagan took office, a so-called "final offensive" by the FMLN in El Salvador failed miserably. The moment seemed right for talks between the contending sides. Some believe that if at this time Washington had offered to mediate between the government and the FMLN, a settlement might have been achieved. But the administration never gave the possibility of a negotiated peace the slightest consideration. A successful negotiation could only have resulted in some form of power sharing. Rather than accept that, the Reagan administration decided to throw its full support behind the Salvadoran government in hopes of achieving a total military victory.

Not long before, President Carter had responded to continued death squad activity and the rape and murder of three American nuns and a Catholic lay worker by cutting off all "lethal" aid to El Salvador. Now the Reagan administration announced that military aid would be resumed. At the same time, because it was difficult to win congressional support for aid to a government that was so obviously involved in the indiscriminate murder of thousands of its own citizens, Washington pressured San Salvador into holding national elections.

Bowing to American demands, the Salvadorans elected delegates to a Constituent Assembly in 1982. José Napoleón Duarte's Christian Democrats, resurrected for the occasion with a helping hand from the CIA, were opposed by the right-wing Arena party. The leader of Arena, Roberto D'Aubuisson, was involved in the 1980 murder of Archbishop Oscar Romero, and has been described by Robert White, the former ambassador to El Salvador, as "a pathological killer."[19]

The CIA provided Duarte and the Christian Democrats with more than $1 million and helped with the political campaign that preceded the election. Not to be outdone, D'Aubuisson and Arena hired a Madison Avenue

U.S. advisers entered El Salvador in 1981 to aid the Salvadoran military in the war against the FMLN. Here an American has a guerrilla fighter pinioned while Salvadoran troops look on.

firm to manage their campaign. When the smoke cleared, the CIA and the Reagan administration had been humiliated. Arena won a large majority of the seats in the new assembly and blocked all efforts at reform.

In 1984, El Salvador held presidential elections. This time, with even greater CIA involvement, the Salvadorans got it right. Duarte was elected president. Unhappily, however, he either did not wish to or could not control the army; the death squads continued their terrible work; and El Salvador remained mired in a seemingly endless war, which at this writing goes on.

## REAGAN AND THE SANDINISTAS

From 1981 on, the clear but unstated purpose of the Reagan administration was the overthrow of the Sandinista government in Nicaragua. Toward that end the president and his advisers gave some thought to military intervention but had to give up the idea, primarily because they failed to sell the public on the notion that the Sandinistas posed a threat to America's national security. Their best efforts notwithstanding, polls consistently showed that up to 70 percent of the American people disapproved of attempts to overthrow the Sandinistas.

Nor were the Joint Chiefs of Staff ready to support an intervention.

Recalling the Vietnam experience, the Joint Chiefs opposed any action the people and Congress would not support. Moreover, the military feared that another unpopular war so soon after Vietnam might lead Congress to reconsider its recent decision to fund large increases in defense spending.

With the military option closed to them, policy makers subjected the Sandinistas to economic pressures designed to paralyze the Nicaraguan economy. Their first move, which came early in 1981, was to cut off all forms of aid to Managua. The administration also used its influence with various international lending institutions, including the World Bank and the Inter-American Development Bank, to block loans from those sources. Nicaragua's sugar quota was cut. Later, the president banned all trade with Nicaragua.

Economic pressure was complemented by covert warfare against the Sandinista regime. In December 1981, the president signed National Security Directive 17 (NSD17) giving the CIA a free hand and an initial $19 million to organize a paramilitary force of five hundred Nicaraguan counterrevolutionaries, or contras, to work with foreign governments as appropriate for the purpose of destabilizing the Sandinista government.

The force that the CIA organized, which was made up in large part of the remnants of Anastasio Somoza's hated National Guard, onetime supporters of the revolution who were dissatisfied with the leftward movement of the Sandinistas, and about two thousand Miskito Indians, grew to number twelve thousand by 1984. Counting the family members, camp followers, and various hangers-on who lived in the Contra camps, at the height of the effort the CIA was supporting a Contra community of thirty-two thousand persons.

Operating from bases in Honduras, the Contras kept the border areas in flames but never achieved their fundamental purpose, which was to take and hold territory inside Nicaragua and win the support of Nicaragua's people. Their identification with Somoza and the United States as well as the terrorist tactics that they often employed evidently made them appear an unattractive alternative to the Sandinistas.

As pressure from Washington mounted, the Nicaraguan government declared a state of emergency and sharply restricted political freedom. Opposition to Sandinista policies was barely tolerated. People's committees, organized at the grass-roots level, disciplined those critical of the government. In 1985 the country's only opposition newspaper, *La Prensa*, and Nicaragua's Catholic radio station were both shut down for criticizing the regime. While it is difficult to judge how many persons the Sandinistas held as political prisoners at any one time, in 1989, when President Daniel Ortega authorized their release, Nicaraguan jails held more than three thousand such persons.

As United States–Nicaraguan relations soured, Managua turned increasingly for support to the Soviet bloc. Cuba sent some six thousand advisers, most of them nurses and teachers, to Nicaragua. And while the Soviets were not prepared to provide the kind of massive aid that kept Cuba afloat, they were reasonably generous according to Nicaraguan government figures. Between 1981 and 1989, they provided $2.9 billion in nonmilitary aid. They also sent approximately one hundred military advisers to Nicaragua and spent roughly $4 billion over eight years, arming and equipping the Sandinista army (which the International Institute for Strategic Studies estimated at roughly forty thousand troops and twelve thousand reservists) with AK-47 rifles, a number of T-55 tanks, artillery, and about fifty attack helicopters. Soviet, East German, and Cuban advisers also helped the Sandinistas establish an efficient intelligence-gathering and internal security apparatus.

East-bloc aid notwithstanding, by 1985, as a result of Washington's pressure and Sandinista mismanagement, Nicaragua was experiencing virtually every economic problem imaginable. There were serious food shortages. Basic medicines, even aspirin, were in short supply. Small businesses and large firms alike found it difficult to function. And unemployment was endemic. The Sandinistas railed against a flourishing black market that grew up amid the ashes of Nicaragua's economy. But there was nothing they could do about it. The black market was the only source of many basic commodities. In 1987 inflation was running at an annual rate of 1,350 percent. Before the end of the next year it had risen to 36,000 percent.

## THE CONTADORA PEACE PLAN

With the polls showing low approval ratings for the president's Central American policies, administration leaders felt constrained to disguise the fact that their real purpose was to overthrow the Nicaraguan government. Thus they justified the pressure they were exerting on Nicaragua by claiming that the Sandinistas were cooperating with Moscow and Havana in funneling arms to the FMLN rebels in El Salvador. Nor did they ever admit to their lack of interest in a negotiated settlement with Managua. But a secret 1982 National Security Council policy paper, which was leaked to the press, made it clear that serious talks were never part of the administration's agenda. The paper called for efforts "to co-opt negotiations issue to avoid Congressionally mandated negotiations which would work against our interests." Washington had "to keep the pressure on" the Sandinistas, who were "clearly feeling the heat." "They could hurt worse," the document continued. "They are not on the ropes."[20]

Several times during the early 1980s the State Department made what appeared to be attempts to negotiate with the Sandinistas. But these gestures were offered for domestic consumption and not with any serious thought of improving relations. Washington's terms, including a demand that Nicaragua expel all foreign advisers and return the military aid it had received from Cuba and the Soviets, were designed to be unacceptable to the Sandinistas.

In 1983 the Sandinistas, who were plainly in deep trouble, tried to resolve their differences with Washington. Managua offered to stop all arms coming through Nicaragua for El Salvador if in exchange the United States would stop supporting the Contras. This proposal should have had some appeal for Washington, since the arms traffic was supposedly the reason for the crisis. But the administration showed no interest in the Nicaraguan offer. Nor was it pleased when Mexico, Venezuela, Colombia, and Panama—the Contadora group, so called from the island where early conferences on the Central American crisis took place—came up with a peace proposal of their own in September 1983.

Convinced that the Reagan policy was in fact fueling revolutionary fires throughout the Caribbean rather than quenching them, the Contadora countries called for the removal of all foreign military advisers from Central America; sharp reductions in troop strength all around; an agreement on the part of all Central American countries to improve their human rights record; and greater political democracy.

The Contadora proposal proved a serious embarrassment for the Reagan administration, especially after Nicaragua approved it. Policy makers, therefore, played for time, hoping to prolong debate while neither accepting nor rejecting the plan. At the same time they increased economic and military pressures on Nicaragua. Leaked documents also show that the National Security Council decided in October 1983 to mobilize the governments of Costa Rica, El Salvador, Guatemala, and Honduras to block implementation of the Contadora plan. Washington's efforts bore fruit. An NSC document that leaked sometime later expressed satisfaction at "having trumped the latest Nicaraguan/Mexican effort to rush signature of an unsatisfactory contadora agreement."[21]

## CONGRESS TAKES A HAND

The administration kept a steady though limited flow of funds moving into Contra hands until 1984. But it was never easy. Congressional opponents of aid to the Contras argued that using former Somosistas to overthrow the Sandinistas was counterproductive and that Somoza's National Guard had been the most hated institution in prerevolutionary Nicaragua. The Contras' use of terrorist tactics against helpless campesinos, as well as their failure to take and hold a single foot of territory after years of fighting, stood as evidence, the critics said, of their failure to win popular support. The critics also argued—with increasing persuasiveness—that Reagan's policies were in fact strengthening the Sandinistas. The very existence of the Contras and the obvious pressure the United States was placing on Nicaragua gave Daniel Ortega's government an excuse to consolidate its power while restricting civil and political rights.

In 1984 the administration's problems with Congress became more acute as a result of several significant revelations. First, Congress learned that the CIA had been directly involved in attacks on Nicaragua's oil storage facilities and had mined Nicaraguan harbors. When Managua took its case against the United States to the International Court of Justice, the administration made matters worse by announcing in advance that it would not be bound by the court's action. In a decision that left the United States (once a major supporter of the effort to establish the law of nations) with an international black eye, the court held "that the United States of America, by training, arming, equipping, financing and supplying the Contra forces . . . has acted, against the Republic of Nicaragua, in breach of its obligation under customary international law not to intervene in the affairs of another state."[22]

As the Contra war against Nicaragua intensified, some congressional Democrats became increasingly concerned. At length, in August 1982, Congress enacted the Boland Amendment to that year's Defense Appropriations Bill, prohibiting the government from supporting paramilitary groups whose purpose it was to overthrow the Sandinistas. Still the administration persisted in its policy, in 1983 even stepping up the pressure. The CIA expanded the Contra force to 15,000 persons and the American military undertook a seven-month-long Central American military exercise called Big Pine II that involved thousands of troops as well as sailors and marines deployed on board two carrier groups that operated in Nicaraguan waters.

Congress monitored these developments with increasing skepticism and concern. All the polls showed that the public was strongly opposed to administration policy, America's European allies were sharply critical of the policy, and the country stood in obvious violation of a phalanx of international agreements including the United Nations Charter.

As though things were not bad enough, a manual published for the Contras by the CIA entitled *Psychological Operations in Guerrilla Warfare* then surfaced. Among other things, the manual advised that it might occasionally be necessary to "neutralize [murder] carefully selected and planned targets such as court judges . . . police and state security officials." Other sections of this "how-to" manual on murder and the other covert arts dealt with kidnapping and political blackmail.[23]

Governments sometimes resort to covert action and even on occasion to political assassination. But none wish to have it advertised. At this writing, even the Soviet KGB is trying to improve its image. It is, therefore, not surprising that Congress took a dim view of what it learned about American activities in Nicaragua during 1984 and prohibited further Contra aid.

For two years following the cutoff in aid, Congress believed the United States was out of the Contra-funding business. It learned differently when the "Iran-Contra" scandal broke. On November 3, 1986, a Lebanese weekly, *Al Shirra*, ran a story claiming that the Reagan administration had secretly sold large quantities of arms to Iran, hoping that in return the Ayatollah Khomeini's government would use its influence to free American hostages then being held by Shiite terrorists in Lebanon. The administration, which had time and again insisted that it would never do business with terrorists, at first flatly denied the report. But by mid-November so much corroborating evidence had surfaced that there was no longer any denying the fact. Then, on November 25, came an equally devastating admission. Attorney General Edwin Meese III informed the press that funds from the arms sale to Iran had been illegally "diverted" to the Contras.

The general public was less disturbed by this latest revelation than it had been by the Iranian arms sale. But Congress, which had prohibited all aid to the Contras, was outraged. The Reagan administration had clearly lost its respect for congressional prerogatives, the Constitution, and the law.

Before the scandal had run its course the nation was repeatedly rocked by new revelations. The president admitted that when Congress cut off aid to the Contras, he conceived the idea of soliciting funds and support from private contributors and was himself involved in an effort that not only tapped private donors but led to the solicitation of funds and other forms of support from foreign governments. Costa Rica and Guatemala were pressured into providing bases from which the secret, illegal effort to resupply the Contras was carried out. South Korea and Taiwan donated cash, as did the sultan of Brunei who, at the request of Assistant Secretary of State Elliot Abrams, gave $10 million to the cause. No one knows exactly how much Saudi Arabia contributed; one estimate ran as high as $1 billion. The Saudis began funneling secret funds to the Reagan administration for its various covert wars in 1981 and continued to do so until the scandal broke. In return the administration used its leverage in Congress to support Riyadh's repeated requests to purchase first-line, high-technology weapons.

## THE ARIAS PEACE PLAN

The Iran-Contra affair, which set the administration back on its heels, gave President Oscar Arias Sánchez of Costa Rica an opportunity he may have been waiting for. He presented a plan calling for negotiations between governments and guerrilla movements (with special reference to Nicaragua and El Salvador), a regional cease-fire, an end to both American aid for the Contras and East-bloc support for El Salvador's FMLN, and a commitment on the part of all five Central American republics (Costa Rica, El Salvador, Guatemala, Honduras, Nicaragua) to move toward greater political democracy. Six months later, in August 1987, the presidents of the five Central American states, including Nicaragua's Daniel Ortega, met in Guatemala City and signed an agreement paralleling the Arias plan.

Arias's peace plan was widely applauded both in the United States and abroad. The House and Senate passed resolutions endorsing the proposal, as did the American Conference of Catholic Bishops. Presidents Duarte of El Salvador and José Azcona of Honduras not only endorsed the Arias plan but urged Congress to withhold future aid from the Contras at least until the peace proposal had been given a chance to work. Finally, much to Washington's regret, Arias won the Nobel peace prize for his efforts.

Policy makers in the Reagan administration, of course, opposed the Arias plan because it would have left the Sandinistas in power. But support for a peace settlement in Central America was too powerful to be openly opposed. That being the case, the administration went after Arias himself. During Costa Rica's 1986 national election campaign the Republican party's Institute for International Affairs provided the opposition party in Costa Rica, the Social Christian party, with a $.5 million campaign contribution. General Manuel Noriega of Panama, who had not yet been exposed as an international drug dealer and was still working closely with the administration, contributed an equal amount. During the campaign the Social Christian candidate, Raphael Calderón, dutifully opposed the Arias plan. Despite administration efforts, Calderón lost.

In the spring of 1987 the president wanted another $105 million to finance Contra operations. But with Iran-Contra still front-page news and the Arias plan yet to be tested, there was no chance that Congress would enact a Contra aid package. Bowing to the inevitable, the White House put the issue on the back burner until September, hoping that by that time the political storm would have blown itself out.

Managua, no doubt aware that one false step could trigger a backlash in the United States, indicated a willingness to live up to its commitments under the Arias plan. The government allowed *La Prensa* to resume publication. Nicaragua's Catholic radio station resumed broadcasting at the same time. President Ortega also offered a general amnesty and full political rights for those Contras who laid down their arms and promised to free all thirty-three hundred political prisoners, providing some other country (the United States) would take them. Ortega also undertook peace talks with Contra leaders. In an open letter to President Reagan he even promised that if defeated in the scheduled 1990 elections he would surrender power.

President Reagan belittled the Arias peace plan and continued to campaign for Contra funding. The showdown between the administration and supporters of the Arias plan came in the House of Representatives, where a vote on Contra aid was scheduled for early February 1988. Prior to the vote, administration leaders abandoned hopes for large-scale funding. They did not have the votes. Instead, the bill the House voted upon called for a mere $36 million in aid, only 10 percent of which was to be used for arms and ammunition. Even so, the administration lost, 219–211.

Though Congress subsequently appropriated small sums for "non-lethal" or "humanitarian" aid for the Contras, the handwriting was clearly on the wall. In March, the Contra leadership agreed to a cease-fire. Though the peace talks, which continued off and on for the remainder of 1988, produced no significant breakthrough, it was evident that the Contra movement was in decline. Some of the resistance leaders, as for example Brooklyn Rivera, a Miskito Indian leader who had spent eight years in exile, returned to Nicaragua to join in the political dialogue that developed there prior to the 1990 elections. Others chose exile in the United States. A Contra force remained in Honduras living off small congressional handouts. But its offensive capability had been sharply reduced. Ronald Reagan had lost his bid to overthrow the Nicaraguan government by force.

In February 1989, the five Central American presidents met and handed the new administration of George Bush a major surprise. Nicaragua's Daniel Ortega reiterated his commitment to free elections in early 1990 and promised unconditionally to release all political prisoners prior to that time. At the same time, all five countries, increasingly edgy over the presence of a large armed force in their midst, agreed that the Contras should be disarmed, that their bases in Honduras should be closed, and that they should return as private citizens to Nicaragua.

The Contras were not disarmed and disbanded as the Central American leaders wished. President George Bush, who was in no hurry to see them go prior to the Nicaraguan elections, convinced Congress to vote $49 million in "humanitarian" aid for the purpose of keeping them in Honduras.

The Bush administration saw the upcoming 1990 elections as an opportunity not to be missed. The National Endowment for Democracy (NED), a supposedly private nonpartisan organization that Congress established in 1983, became deeply involved in the Nicaraguan electoral process. NED helped organize the fourteen party anti-Sandinista coalition known as the National Opposition Union (UNO) with Violeta Chamorro (wife of the slain editor of *La Prensa*) as its leader, and funded that group lavishly. According to news reports, the CIA also provided UNO with somewhere between $5 and $12 million, and Congress added another $9 million to UNO's coffers.

As election day approached, most observers predicted a Sandinista victory. But the effect of America's financial intervention on a war-weary population proved decisive. Chamorro won with more than 54 percent of the vote. Not long afterward President Bush lifted the economic sanctions that had so weakened the Sandinista government, urged Congress to pass an aid package for Nicaragua, and joined Chamorro in calling on the Contras to lay down their arms. Outgoing President Daniel Ortega did his part by declaring a unilateral cease-fire and urging the Contras to follow suit.

A few days prior to Chamorro's April 25 inauguration, all sides formally agreed to a cease-fire. Even after that, however, the Chamorro government had to do more than its share of maneuvering to convince the Contras to lay down their arms. As always in Nicaraguan politics, the issue boiled down to who would control the army and the security forces. To pacify the Sandinistas, Chamorro agreed to retain Humberto Ortega, the former president's brother, at the head of the military. That infuriated not only the Contras but many in UNO, who threatened to abandon her only days after she took the oath of office. To pacify the rightists in her coalition, Chamorro then decided to cut the size of the army in half. This action, when added to the fact that Washington was no longer supplying them, finally convinced the Contras to come in from the cold.

And so in mid-1990 an uneasy peace descended on Nicaragua. But at this writing it is not at all clear how long peace can last. The condition of the national economy has improved only marginally since the fighting ended, and the country remains politically divided. The Sandinistas retain widespread support, control powerful labor unions, and are the largest party in the national legislature. UNO, which was bound together only by a desire to bring down the Sandinistas, is a highly unstable coalition. Chamorro has her work cut out for her.

## REAGAN IN THE MIDDLE EAST

The Reagan administration's approach to Middle East affairs was quite different from that taken by President Carter, who lavished his attentions on the Arab-Israeli dispute. The focus of Secretary of State Alexander Haig's concern was the Persian Gulf and the threat that he believed the Soviet Union posed in the region. Nixon and Kissinger as well as Jimmy Carter had relied on the shah to provide stability there. Now the shah was gone and the Iranian revolution had destabilized the entire area. Soviet activities in the Horn of Africa and the war in Afghanistan led Haig to the conclusion that Moscow was about to pounce.

Haig and Reagan intended to deal with what they imagined to be this Soviet threat in two ways. First, they envisioned an alliance system that would directly tie Washington to Saudi Arabia and other "moderate" Arab states. In order to further discourage Soviet adventurism, they also intended to project American military power directly into the region.

The Reagan State Department believed that the Carter administration's failure to deal decisively with the Iranian revolution, especially the humiliations heaped upon the United States during the hostage crisis, had cost America the respect of the Arab states and Moscow as well. They intended to rectify this by expanding the Rapid Deployment Force (originally created under Carter) to 400,000 troops and at least two aircraft carrier battle groups. Operating from bases which Washington assumed its Arab allies would willingly provide, the RDF would be in a position to discourage both Soviet aggression and the spread of internal revolution as well.

The Reagan administration's Gulf policy never really got off the ground. This was true in large measure because key policy makers entertained certain basic misperceptions about the world in which they operated. Haig and Reagan focused their attention on a supposed Soviet threat to the Persian Gulf region at a time when Moscow's influence there was already in decline. Much more importantly, Washington's fixation with the Soviets, its conviction that revolution or instability anywhere could somehow be traced back to Moscow, blinded it to the real forces at work in the Middle East, radical Islamic fundamentalism and Arab nationalism.

Arab leaders, who did not share Washington's concerns about the Soviets, wanted no part of an alliance with the United States. Nor would they agree to the establishment of military and naval bases on their soil. To have done otherwise would have opened these regimes to attack from within.

And few in the Arab world believed that American forces would be proof against the power of a revolution sweeping up from below.

The lesson of the Iranian revolution was that radical social change brought about by uncontrolled economic growth could produce an Islamic backlash and internal revolution. Governments such as those in Saudi Arabia and the other Gulf states, which were already feeling such pressures, were hardly in a position to enter into an intimate military and political relationship with the United States, the "Great Satan" of the radical Islamic world. It took a direct threat to their sovereignty not by Moscow but by Iraq, an Arab state, to convince the Saudis and the other Gulf States to reconsider this policy.

Reagan and Haig agreed at the start of the administration that they would not become involved in the Arab-Israeli dispute. The problem appeared to be intractable. It seemed foolish, therefore, to waste political capital by launching a diplomatic initiative that was bound to fail. After all, the object of the Reagan policy was to appear strong, not weak or ineffective. Moreover, at that time administration leaders could not envision a settlement that did not involve the creation of a Palestinian state controlled by the Palestine Liberation Organization. Since Haig and Reagan viewed the PLO along with Lybia, Syria, and South Yemen as Soviet surrogates, this was an outcome to be avoided.

Though administration leaders wished devoutly to steer clear of the Arab-Israeli dispute, events conspired to entrap them. The escalating conflict between Israel and the PLO made involvement inevitable.

Following their expulsion from Jordan in 1970 the leaders of the PLO found a new home in Lebanon, a small internally divided country (one-third Christian, two-thirds Muslim with a large population of Palestinian refugees) that shared one border with Israel and another with Syria. During the next several years, while the Lebanese government discreetly looked the other way, PLO guerrillas regularly crossed the border to raid Israel. The Syrians too became involved in Lebanon, stationing troops and Soviet-made surface-to-air missiles in the Bekáa Valley.

During the 1970's the Israelis responded to the raids with artillery attacks against PLO positions in southern Lebanon and occasional retaliatory air assaults. But in 1981 the government of Menachem Begin began behaving more aggressively toward its Arab adversaries. Before mid-year, the Israelis had launched one air strike that destroyed Iraq's budding nuclear capability and another that hit PLO headquarters in the Lebanese capital of Beirut. They also consolidated their control over the Golan Heights, which they had taken from Syria during the 1967 war, and aggressively pursued their settlement policy in the West Bank territory, taken from Jordan in the same war.

In 1982 the Israeli government, perhaps provoked by the assassination of Israel's ambassador to Great Britain, decided that the time had come to destroy the PLO, drive the Syrians from the Bekáa Valley, and establish a friendly Maronite Christian government in Lebanon, thus securing its northern border. The Reagan administration's regular denunciations of terrorism as well as its often-stated conviction that the PLO and Syria were both Soviet surrogates, led Begin to the conclusion that at the very least Washington would not react negatively to such an operation. To make certain of this, Ariel Sharon, the Israeli defense minister, travelled to the United States in May 1982 for a meeting with Alexander Haig. Sharon probably did not share with Haig all that Israel intended to accomplish in Lebanon. But he returned to Israel satisfied that the Reagan administration would not object to a Lebanese incursion.

A month later, Israeli forces invaded Lebanon and decimated PLO forces there. But the Israelis failed in their political mission. Lebanon collapsed into feuding Christian, Shiite, and Druze factions, each with its own well-armed militia. Soon, a civil war was under way that devastated Beirut and continued for years to come.

The Israelis, who drove all the way to the outskirts of Beirut, now needed help in withdrawing from what had become an untenable position. The United States, aided by other Western countries, arranged a cease-fire and the Israeli army pulled back.

In the aftermath of Israel's ill-fated Lebanese incursion, State Department experts calculated that the moment might be right for a new initiative to settle the Arab-Israeli dispute. Certainly the Arab states would have been chastened by the power of the Israeli advance. Perhaps a gesture in their direction, a call for a fair settlement, would win some converts. And so in early September, 1982, the president proposed the creation of a new Jordanian-Palestinian state to include the occupied territories but to be ruled not by the PLO but by King Hussein of Jordan. The plan also called for an immediate stop to the construction of Israeli settlements on the West Bank and modifications in Israel's borders as a guarantee for its increased security in the future.

The State Department, which had made this proposal without consulting either Jerusalem or the Arab states, was wasting its time. This initiative, like all that had preceded it, went nowhere. Neither side would budge.

Israel's Lebanese incursion left Washington with a new Middle East concern, the possibility that Syria would take control of Lebanon. To head off that possibility, the administration decided to return a large contingent of marines to Lebanon. The stated reason for this was to keep the peace. But Washington's real purpose was to strengthen the Maronite Christian "government" of Amin Gemayel, an Israeli ally.

In the months that followed, the Reagan administration became increasingly involved in Lebanon's civil war. American military advisers trained the Maronite Christian army to use weaponry provided by Washington. American planes flew reconnaissance missions for Christian forces, while warships occasionally lobbed shells into Muslim villages near Beirut.

The Shiite and Druze forces retaliated as best they could. In April 1983 a bomb destroyed the American embassy in Beirut. Forty-six people—

sixteen of them Americans—were killed. On October 23, a car bomb exploded outside the marine barracks near Beirut, killing 241 servicemen.

Reagan denounced these attacks and stated that the United States would not be intimidated. But Congress was growing restive. Eighteen months before it had approved the president's decision to send troops to Lebanon. But in early 1984 a movement was afoot to rescind that authorization. Before Congress could act the president did, withdrawing the now-decimated force. The American involvement in Lebanon was a damaging blow to American credibility in the Middle East. After that it was pointless to attempt to play the role of mediator there. Arab confidence in American "evenhandedness," so ardently cultivated by Henry Kissinger and Jimmy Carter, had been squandered by Haig and Reagan.

## REVOLUTION IN AFRICA

Jimmy Carter was the first president to focus national attention on the plight of the exploited peoples of Africa. His human rights rhetoric and his frequent denunciations of white minority rule in South Africa aroused the feelings of many Americans for whom these issues had abiding significance.

Carter was also the first president to criticize in a serious and prolonged way the system of apartheid first imposed on black South Africans in 1948. The segregated and unequal public schools, recreational facilities, and hospitals provided for blacks in South Africa, and the fact that they had no political rights, were only elements in an elaborate social system designed to keep blacks and whites separate, black tribes separated from one another, and all blacks as a permanent underclass.

Ronald Reagan said little about Africa or apartheid during the 1980 presidential campaign. He knew nothing of African affairs and showed no interest in learning. Nevertheless, his administration did develop an African policy, largely due to the efforts of Assistant Secretary of State Chester Crocker. Crocker, a knowledgeable Africanist, tended to view the world in terms of the cold war conflict. He was also keenly aware that American banks and corporations had in excess of $15 billion in outstanding loans and investments in South Africa that needed protection.

Crocker believed that because "southern Africa" was "a region of unquestioned importance to U.S. and Western economic and strategic interests," the United States ought to make "a substantial effort . . . to forestall heightened conflict and polarization." He thought it "imperative" that the United States play a role "in fostering regional security, countering Soviet influence, and bolstering a climate that makes peaceful change possible."[24]

Toward this end, Crocker became the principal architect of a policy dubbed "constructive engagement." This new approach to southern Africa had two components. First, Crocker advocated working with more moderate elements inside South Africa's white power structure to implement reforms that would lead to the abolition of apartheid and some form of power sharing between the races. A second aspect of his strategy was to end the warfare on South Africa's borders. A country under siege, Crocker believed, was not likely to implement reforms at home.

The United States had considerable success in encouraging the latter of these two objectives. Under terms of the 1984 Nkomati accord, brokered by the United States, Mozambique and South Africa agreed to end their support for insurgent groups attempting to overthrow each other's government. More significant was a 1984 agreement between South Africa and Angola (the Lusaka accord) that established a cease-fire in what had been a long-drawn-out, low-intensity war.

The future of Namibia posed a particularly difficult problem for the Reagan administration. Crocker wanted to "bring about conditions that would make it possible for South Africa to relinquish control of" Namibia. The principal "condition" that had to be changed was the presence of Cuban troops in neighboring Angola. "From our standpoint," he said, "we don't see any reason why there ought to be communist forces in Africa, none whatsoever." Namibian independence, he believed, should be held in abeyance until the Cubans left Angola.[25]

In the end the administration got what it wanted for Namibia. The pacification of the border between Angola and Namibia established a basis for negotiations that led to the staged withdrawal of Cuban troops from Angola. Complete independence for Namibia followed in early 1990.

The real test of constructive engagement came in South Africa itself, where it was a complete failure. The Nationalist party of President P. W. Botha proved either unwilling or unable to implement significant domestic reforms. The administration worked hard to convince Pretoria that change was essential. And when in 1983 a majority of white South Africans voted in favor of a new constitution, it appeared for a brief moment that change was in the wind. An exultant Secretary Crocker even called the vote a "milestone in the modern history of South Africa." But the new Constitution fell far short of that, extending only limited political rights to Asians and people of mixed racial backgrounds and none at all to blacks, who made up 74 percent of the population. Moreover, the new Constitution left apartheid as vigorous and strong as before.

A black protest movement, which began prior to the 1984 parliamentary elections, escalated sharply thereafter. Blacks organized economic boycotts against white-owned businesses. Perhaps as many as a quarter-million black students boycotted their schools. And in the shantytowns where they lived, blacks created informal governments to make rules and to discipline those who cooperated with the white power structure.

Archbishop Desmond Tutu, the head of South Africa's Anglican church and a leader in the protest movement, won the Nobel peace prize in 1984 for his leadership and his commitment to nonviolent resistance. But Bishop Tutu was unsuccessful in restricting black anger to peaceful protest. Bomb blasts periodically rocked Durban and Johannesburg. Demonstrations sometimes turned to riots. And more often than not confrontations between

An anti-apartheid demonstration in Durban, South Africa.

the police and unarmed demonstrators resulted in the shooting down of black protesters. Hundreds were killed, and thousands (many of them children) were imprisoned without trial. Blacks who collaborated with the white minority government ran grave risks. A number of black policemen, for example, were hacked to death or burned alive by angry blacks.

## AMERICA AND APARTHEID

The American antiapartheid movement grew with each new report of arrests and killings in South Africa. Students, writers and intellectuals, church and labor leaders, as well as a growing number of ordinary citizens believed that something should be done to end apartheid. The World Council of Churches spoke out against it, as did Pope Paul II. On occasion antiapartheid sentiment took extreme turns, as in New York City where the American Museum of Natural History inadvertently landed in trouble when a city councilman from the Bronx learned that one of its exhibits included fossils that had been discovered in South Africa. The museum directors narrowly averted a fight over future city funding by agreeing to post signs in the museum denouncing apartheid and not to publish any more South African tourist advertisements in their magazine, *Natural History*.

Sitting-in in front of the South African embassy in Washington and being carted off in a paddy wagon become almost faddish. Before mid-July, 1985, some twenty-nine hundred persons had been arrested for blocking the entrance to the embassy. The feminist leader Gloria Steinem, Jimmy Carter's daughter Amy, the Reverend Jesse Jackson and two of his sons, leaders of the American Jewish Congress, and a number of well-known members of Congress including Ron Dellums of California, John Conyers of Michigan, Walter E. Fauntroy of the District of Columbia, and the maverick Republican, Lowell Weicker of Connecticut, were among them.

A number of student groups had for some time been arguing that universities should divest themselves of stock holdings in companies doing business in South Africa. They encountered stiff resistance at first. But as the crisis in South Africa escalated, a number of universities did begin to divest. Those that did not, including the University of California, Rutgers, and Columbia, had to deal with mass student demonstrations.

The idea of applying economic sanctions moved quickly from the campus to the legislature. Several state governments, among them Connecticut, Iowa, Maryland, Massachusetts, Michigan, Nebraska, and Wisconsin, voted for some form of divestment before the end of 1984. In 1985 New Jersey took similar action. Its divestment of $2 billion was the most impressive move of the sort undertaken to that time.

Some American businesses, perhaps sensitive to the pressure, began eliminating their South African operations. General Motors, Bell and Howell, Eastman Kodak, and IBM were only a few of those that left. Before the end of June 1985, more than fifty companies had pulled out. Frequently, however, there was less to this action than met the eye. Through licensing agreements, franchising, and trademark agreements, many of these companies left their capital behind and continued to do business under a non-American name.

By mid-1985, economic pressures were having an effect on the South African economy. The national currency, the Rand, lost more than half its value. The national government found itself temporarily unable to make payments on its short-term loans and shut down both its stock and currency exchanges. The looming financial crisis prompted some foreign bankers to take a long, hard look at what was evidently becoming a serious situation. Many followed the lead of the Morgan Guarantee Trust Company, which announced in the spring of 1985 that it would make no future loans to South Africa or its state-owned companies.

## REAGAN STANDS PAT

The idea of applying economic sanctions against South Africa became a national political issue after representatives Stephen Solarz and William Gray, both Democrats, introduced legislation banning new investments in or loans to South Africa and forbidding the importation of gold Kruggerands. There was an avalanche of bipartisan support for the idea. By the spring of 1985,

Many Americans believed that the best way to end apartheid in South Africa was through economic sanctions against the South African government. This demonstration calling on Citibank to leave South Africa took place in downtown Manhattan.

forty-one bills were pending in the House and Senate calling for economic sanctions against Pretoria.

The movement for sanctions gained momentum as a result of the increasing level of violence in South Africa. On March 21, 1985, South African police opened fire on four thousand unarmed black protesters. The official report put the death toll at seventeen, but unofficial estimates ran much higher. In July the South African government declared a state of emergency, suspended most civil rights, and carried out a sweeping crackdown on antiapartheid activists. No one knows how many blacks were actually rounded up. But a year later it was estimated that as many as twelve thousand black political prisoners were still being detained indefinitely without trial.

Amid the most serious wave of sustained violence in South Africa's history and confronted by a groundswell of support for economic sanctions, President Reagan stood pat. He deplored the March massacre but foolishly tried to exonerate the South African government by pointing out that many policemen were themselves black. He also insisted that the government of P. W. Botha had implemented major reforms and, in one of the more bizarre miscues of his administration, claimed that most public accommodations in South Africa had been desegregated. Constructive engagement, he argued, was producing results.

The Reverend Jerry Falwell, a television evangelist and the head of the Moral Majority, a religious pressure group committed to conservative causes, supported the president. After a trip to South Africa and a visit with President Botha, Falwell praised Botha and denounced Archbishop Tutu as a fraud. Interesting to note, both Reagan and Falwell felt compelled by the fierce public reaction to their remarks to retract their statements.

Some criticized the Reagan administration for being completely out of touch with developments in South Africa. Others, less charitable, saw the president's stubborn commitment to constructive engagement as his way of supporting Botha and South Africa's white minority regime. Whatever the case, by the middle of 1985 the administration had become isolated from much of the rest of the international community. Only days after Pretoria declared what amounted to martial law, the United Nations Security Council passed a resolution by a vote of 14–0 (the United States and Britain abstained) calling on governments everywhere to suspend all new investment in South Africa and take whatever other steps were appropriate to force an end to apartheid. Canada, Sweden, and Denmark subsequently suspended all trade with South Africa, while the Common Market countries, Margaret Thatcher's Britain excepted, also imposed sanctions.

At last the president realized he had to make some sort of gesture. He called his ambassador to South Africa home "for consultations" and for the first time publicly encouraged the South African government to abandon apartheid. Simultaneously, however, he made it clear that he would veto any bill Congress passed calling for economic sanctions. Reagan should have known better than to make such a threat. He did not have the votes. Even Senator Richard Lugar, the ranking Republican on the Senate Foreign Relations Committee, was on record indicating that he would vote to override a veto on a sanctions measure.

In an attempt to head off what senior White House officials themselves described as a potential humiliation, Reagan quickly reversed himself, issuing an executive order applying partial economic sanctions against South Africa. These sanctions, riddled with loopholes and designed to have the least possible effect on Pretoria, were intended to co-opt congressional supporters of more effective measures. And to some extent they had the desired effect.

In the summer of 1986, however, Reagan lost control of the situation. By that time the South African government had imposed what amounted to a news blackout, prohibiting reporters—especially television journalists—from covering antiapartheid demonstrations. Nevertheless, the outside world learned enough to know that the situation in South Africa had grown worse. In May an estimated 1.5 million black workers staged a one-day walkout to dramatize their grievances, and in June millions stayed off the job on the tenth anniversary of the 1976 massacre of black schoolchildren by the police in Soweto township. When a car bomb exploded in Durban, killing two whites, injuring fifteen other persons, and causing widespread damage, the government responded with a new crackdown in which at least three thousand blacks were arrested. President Reagan described the situation as "bordering on civil war" and urged all sides to act with restraint.

But Congress felt it had been restrained long enough. In July, after the administration made the astonishing admission that it had actually agreed to increase South African textile imports by 4 percent, Congress took matters in its own hands, enacting limited economic sanctions against South Africa. The president vetoed the legislation. But Congress brushed the veto aside by a vote of 78–21 in the Senate and 313–83 in the House.

Not long after this the president resorted to a time-honored tradition by appointing a presidential commission headed by former Transportation Secretary William Coleman and the former chair of IBM, Frank T. Cary, to make policy recommendations regarding South Africa. In February 1987, the commission pronounced constructive engagement a failure; recommended that the administration make every effort to establish good relations with South Africa's black leaders, who were, the commission believed, the future leaders of South Africa; and urged a full-scale effort to isolate Pretoria economically in order to force a quick end to apartheid. Seldom has a presidential commission more completely repudiated the policies of the president who created it.

In another time-honored tradition, President Reagan reacted by ignoring the commission's recommendations. In fact from that point on he did his best to ignore the South African crisis, which continued unresolved and unabated to the end of his term.

## REFORM OR REVOLUTION?

In mid-1989 the economic sanctions and global isolation imposed on South Africa began to have a political effect. The first signs of change came within South Africa's ruling Nationalist party in the form of a struggle for control that pitted the ailing President P. W. Botha against more reform-minded elements led by F. W. De Klerk. In August, following statements by both De Klerk and Foreign Minister Roelof F. Botha calling for a new political system free from either white *or* black domination, President Botha resigned. De Klerk was then sworn in as interim president, a post he won outright in national elections held in September.

During the next several months the De Klerk government, acting against a backdrop that featured continued antiapartheid demonstrations both inside South Africa and abroad, police violence, death squad activities, and growing internecine strife among blacks, moved cautiously in a reformist direction. First "whites only" beaches were eliminated. Then, a few months later, Parliament repealed legislation establishing racial segregation in most public places as well as on buses and trains and in hotels and restaurants.

No doubt the most dramatic decision taken by the new government was to release a number of exceptionally important political prisoners, among them Nelson Mandela, the head of the African National Congress (ANC), who had been in confinement for twenty-eight years. Subsequent to Mandela's release, De Klerk lifted the ban on the ANC and opened negotiations with Mandela, ostensibly for the purpose of creating a system of power sharing. Despite these promising developments, the situation in South Africa remains far from resolved. In the first place, the ANC and the De Klerk government are far apart on the basic issue of political representation. The ANC insists on "one person, one vote." But as far as De Klerk is concerned, that amounts to black domination and is therefore unacceptable. It is also important to note that De Klerk is having the greatest difficulty controlling white extremists, who have begun to perpetrate acts of violence against blacks and who promise a "holy war" if he persists in seeking reform. Nor is he in complete control of the police and security forces. The recent revelation that a nationwide network of death squads exists made up of police and security people has stunned the nation.

If De Klerk has his problems so do South Africa's black leaders. Fighting between supporters of the ANC and followers of the Zulu chieftain, Gatsha Buthelezi, has taken hundreds of lives. At this writing the situation in Natal Province is simply out of control. As the year 1990 moves toward its conclusion then, South Africa's future—whether there is to be a blood bath or not—remains unclear.

## ENDNOTES

1. Ronald Reagan, quoted in Paul Boller, *Presidential Anecdotes* (New York: Oxford University Press, 1981), p. 348.
2. Reagan, quoted in ibid., p. 350.
3. Reagan, remarks at the National Convention of the National Association of Evangelicals, March 8, 1983, *Public Papers of the Presidents: Ronald Reagan, 1983* (Washington, D.C., 1984), I, p. 363.
4. Reagan, speech to the members of Parliament, June 8, 1982, *Public Papers of the President: Ronald Reagan, 1982* (Washington, D.C., 1983), p. 747.
5. Soviet diplomat, quoted in Strobe Talbot, *Reagan and the Russians* (New York: Random House, 1984), p. 26.
6. Poll results, quoted in Jeffrey Porro et al., *The Nuclear Age Reader* (New York: Alfred A. Knopf, 1989), pp. 361–62.
7. E. P. Thompson, quoted in ibid., p. 363–64.
8. Tass, quoted in Strobe Talbot, *Deadly Gambits* (New York: Random House, 1985), pp. 84–85.
9. Yuri Andropov, quoted in Talbot, *Reagan and the Russians*, p. 6.
10. Reagan television address, March 23, 1983, *Public Papers of the Presidents: Ronald Reagan, 1983*, I, 442.
11. Hans A. Bethe, quoted in Porro et al., *Nuclear Age Reader*, p. 441.
12. Ibid.
13. Gerald Yonas and George A. Keyworth III, quoted in ibid., pp. 436–39.

14. Reagan, presidential statement, January 16, 1984, *Public Papers of the Presidents: Ronald Reagan, 1984* (Washington, D.C., 1985), p. 41.

15. Mikhail Gorbachev, quoted in Porro et al., *Nuclear Age Reader*, p. 450.

16. Ibid., pp. 466–67.

17. Reagan, quoted in James Chace, *Solvency: An Essay on American Foreign Policy* (New York: Random House, 1981), p. 47; "Communist Interference in El Salvador," quoted in Peter Kornbluh, *Nicaragua: The Price of Intervention* (Washington, D.C.: Institute for Policy Studies, 1987), pp. 166–67.

18. Reagan, quoted in Chace, *Solvency*, p. 47; also quoted in Eldon Kenworthy, "Central America: Beyond the Credibility Trap," in *The Central American Crisis: Sources of Conflict and the Failure of U.S. Policy*, ed. Kenneth M. Coleman and George C. Herring (Wilmington, Del.: Scholarly Resources, 1985), pp. 112, 127–28.

19. Robert White, quoted in Jeff McMahan, *Reagan and the World: Imperial Policy in the New Cold War* (New York: Monthly Review Press, 1985), p. 134.

20. National Security Council paper, April 1982, quoted in Mary B. Vanderlaan, *Revolution and Foreign Policy in Nicaragua* (Boulder, Colo.: Westview Press, 1986), p. 142.

21. National Security Council briefing paper, quoted in McMahan, *Reagan and the World*, p. 187.

22. Permanent Court of International Justice decision, quoted in Kornbluh, *Nicaragua*, p. 52.

23. *Psychological Operations in Guerrilla Warfare*, quoted in William I. Robinson and Kent Norsworthy, *David and Goliath: The U.S. War against Nicaragua* (New York: Monthly Review Press, 1987), p. 116.

24. Chester Crocker, quoted in Ann Seidman, *The Roots of Crisis in Southern Africa* (Trenton, N. J.: Africa World Press, 1984), p. 7.

25. Ibid., pp. 91–92.

# SUPPLEMENTARY READING

The most recent and most complete bibliography of works dealing with American foreign relations is Richard Dean Burns, ed., *Guide to American Foreign Relations Since 1700* (Santa Barbara, California, Clio Associates, 1982). This work is carefully annotated and amazingly complete for works written before 1980. The five volume series *Foreign Affairs Bibliography* published by the Council on Foreign Relations, is also carefully annotated. The first of these volumes was published in 1933, the last in 1976. Though dated, Samuel F. Bemis and Grace G. Griffin, eds., *Guide to the Diplomatic History of the United States, 1775-1921* (Washington, 1935) is still useful. See also Frank Friedel, ed., *Harvard Guide to American History* (Cambridge, Mass., Belknap Press of Harvard University Press, 1974). Numerous historical journals are likely to include articles dealing with American foreign relations. See especially *The American Historical Review, Diplomatic History, The International History Review, International Security,* and *The Journal of American History.*

## THE AGE OF EMPIRE, 1899-1917

There are many fine studies of American imperialism in the late nineteenth century. Aside from those noted in the preceding section see Julius W. Pratt, *Expansionists of 1898: The Acquisition of Hawaii and the Spanish Islands* (Baltimore, Md., Johns Hopkins

University Press, 1936); Ernest R. May's two fine books, *Imperial Democracy: The Emergence of America as a Great Power* (N.Y., Harcourt Brace and World, 1961) and *American Imperialism: A Speculative Essay* (N.Y., Atheneum, 1968); H. Wayne Morgan, *America's Road to Empire: The War With Spain and Overseas Expansion* (N.Y., John Wiley and Sons, 1965); Richard Hofstadter, *The Paranoid Style in American Politics and Other Essays* (N.Y., Alfred A. Knopf, 1966); David Healy, *U.S. Expansionism: The Imperialist Urge in the 1890's* (Madison, Wis., University of Wisconsin Press, 1970). See also Lewis Gould's excellent *The Presidency of William McKinley* (Lawrence Kansas, University of Kansas Press, 1980).

The anti-imperialist movement is discussed in Robert L. Beisner, *Twelve Against Empire: The Anti-Imperialists, 1898-1900* (N.Y., McGraw-Hill, 1968); Daniel B. Schirmer, *Republic or Empire: American Resistance to the Philippine War* (Cambridge Mass., Schenkman Pub. Co., 1972); Hans L. Trefousse, *Carl Schurz* (Knoxville, Tenn., University of Tennessee Press, 1982); and Kendrick Clements, *William Jennings Bryan, Missionary Isolationist* (Knoxville, Tenn., University of Tennessee Press, 1983).

Anglo-American relations in the period have attracted the attention of many scholars. Among the best books on the subject are A. E. Campbell, *Great Britain and the United States, 1895-1903* (London, Longman's, 1960); R. G. Neale, *Great Britain and United States Expansion: 1898-1900* (East Lansing, Mich., Michigan State University Press, 1966); Bradford Perkins, *The Great Rapprochement: England and the United States, 1895-1914* (N.Y., Atheneum, 1968); and Edward P. Crapol, *America For Americans: Economic Nationalism and Anglophobia in the Late Nineteenth Century* (Westport, Conn., Greenwood, 1973).

Policy makers of this period, pre-eminently Theodore Roosevelt, have received a great deal of attention from historians. Some of the best are Howard K. Beale, *Theodore Roosevelt and the Rise of America to World Power* (Baltimore, Md., Johns Hopkins University Press, 1956); David H. Burton, *Theodore Roosevelt, Confident Imperialist* (N.Y., Farrar, Straus, Cudahy, 1968); Raymond A. Esthus, *Theodore Roosevelt and the International Rivalries* (Seattle, University of Washington Press, 1970); John Milton Cooper Jr., *The Warrier and the Priest: Woodrow Wilson and Theodore Roosevelt* (Cambridge, Mass., Belknap Press of Harvard University Press, 1983). See also Richard Leopold, *Elihu Root and the Conservative Tradition* (Boston, Little, Brown and Co., 1954); K.J. Clymer, *John Hay: The Gentleman as Diplomat* (Ann Arbor, Mich., University of Michigan Press, 1975); Henry F. Pringle, *The Life and Times of William Howard Taft* (N.Y., Farrar and Rinehart, 1939); Walter V. and Marie V. Scholes, *The Foreign Policies of the Taft Administration* (Columbia, Missouri, University of Missouri Press, 1970).

China policy has a vast literature. See for example Paul A. Varg's *The Making of a Myth: The United States and China, 1897-1912* (East Lansing, Mich., Michigan State University Press, 1968); Jerry Israel, *Progressivism and the Open Door: America and China, 1905-1921* (Pittsburgh, Pa., University of Pittsburgh Press, 1971); Michael Hunt's two studies, *Frontier Defense and the Open Door: Manchuria in Chinese-American Relations, 1895-1911* (New Haven, Conn., Yale University Press, 1973); and *The Making of a Special Relationship* (N.Y., Columbia University Press, 1983); Delber L. McKee, *Chinese Exclusion versus the Open Door Policy, 1900-1906: Clashes Over China Policy in the Roosevelt Era* (Detroit, Wayne State University Press, 1976); Charles Vevier, *The United States and China, 1906-1913: A Study of Finance and Diplomacy* (New Brunswick, N.J., Rutgers University Press, 1955). See also Thomas J. McCormick, *China Market: America's Quest for Informal Empire* (Chicago, University of Chicago Press, 1967); and Marilyn B. Young, *The Rhetoric of Empire: American China Policy, 1895-1901* (Cambridge, Mass., Harvard University Press, 1968).

Japanese-American relations are discussed in Fred H. Harrington, *God, Mammon, and the Japanese: Dr. Horace N. Allen and Korean American Relations, 1884-1905* (Madison, Wis., University of Wisconsin Press, 1944); Roger Daniels, *The Politics of Prejudice: The Anti-Japanese Movement in California and the Struggle for Japanese Exclusion* (Berkeley, California, University of California Press, 1962); Charles E. Neu, *An Uncertain Friendship: Theodore Roosevelt and Japan, 1906-1909* (1965); Akira Iriye, *Pacific Estrangement: Japanese and American Expansion, 1897-1911* (Cambridge, Mass., Harvard University Press, 1972).

For Caribbean and Panama policy see Dana G. Munro, *Intervention and Dollar Diplomacy in the Caribbean, 1900-1921* (Princeton, N.J., Princeton University Press, 1964); Sheldon B. Liss, *The Canal: Aspects of United States-Panamanian Relations* (Notre Dame, Ind., Notre Dame University Press, 1967); Lester Langley, *The Cuban Policy of the United States: A Brief History* (N.Y., John Wiley and Sons, 1968); David G. Mc-Cullough, *The Path Between The Seas: The Creation of the Panama Canal 1870-1914* (N.Y., Simon and Schuster, 1977). See also Warren G. Kneer, *Great Britain and the Caribbean, 1901-1913: A Study in Anglo-American Relations* (East Lansing, Mich., Michigan State University Press, 1975). The United States role in Cuba is discussed in David F. Healy, *The United States in Cuba, 1898-1902* (Madison, Wis., University of Wisconsin Press, 1963); James H. Hitchman, *Leonard Wood and Cuban Independence, 1898-1902* (The Hague, the Netherlands, Nijhoff, 1971) and Louis A. Perez Jr., *Cuba Between Empires, 1878-1902* (Pittsburgh, Pa., Pittsburgh University Press, 1983).

The place to begin any study of Woodrow Wilson's interventionist policies is with three works by Arthur Link. See his *Woodrow Wilson and the Progressive Era* (N.Y., Harper and Row, 1954); *Wilson the Diplomatist* (Princeton, N.J., Princeton University Press, 1957); and *Wilson, The Struggle for Neutrality, 1914-1915* (Princeton, N.J., Princeton University Press, 1960).

In addition to many of the titles listed above that deal with Wilson's Far Eastern policy, see Tien-yi Li, *Woodrow Wilson's China Policy, 1913-1917* (Kansas City, Mo., University of Kansas City Press, 1952); Roy W. Curry, *Woodrow Wilson and Far Eastern Policy, 1913-1921* (N.Y., Bookman Associates, 1957); and Burton F. Beers, *Vain Endeavor: Robert Lansing's Attempt to End the American-Japanese Rivalry* (Durham, N.C., Duke University Press, 1962).

For Caribbean affairs see Hans Schmidt, *The United States Occupation of Haiti, 1915-1921* (New Brunswick, N.J., Rutgers University Press, 1971); David Healy, *Gunboat Diplomacy in the Wilson Era: The U.S. Navy in Haiti, 1915-1916* (Madison, Wis., University of Wisconsin Press, 1976); and Lester D. Langley, *Struggle for the American Mediterranean: United States-European Rivalry in the Gulf-Caribbean, 1776-1904* (Athens, Ga., University of Georgia Press, 1976).

There is an extensive literature dealing with U.S.-Mexican relations during this period. See especially Howard F. Cline, *The United States and Mexico* (N.Y., Atheneum, 1963); R. E. Quirk, *An Affair of Honor: Woodrow Wilson and the Occupation of Veracruz* (Lexington, Kty, University of Kentucky Press, 1962); Kenneth Grieb, *The United States and Huerta* (Lincoln, Neb., University of Nebraska Press, 1969); P. Edward Haley, *Revolution and Intervention: The Diplomacy of Taft and Wilson With Mexico, 1910-1917* (Cambridge, Mass., Massachusetts Institute of Technology Press, 1970); Larry

D. Hill, *Emissaries to a Revolution: Woodrow Wilson's Executive Agents in Mexico* (Baton Rouge, La., Louisiana State University Press, 1973); Jules Davids, *American Political and Economic Penetration of Mexico, 1877-1920* (N.Y., Arno Press, 1976); Friedrich Katz, *The Secret War in Mexico: Europe and the U.S. and the Mexican Revolution* (Chicago, University of Chicago Press, 1981).

## WORLD WAR I AND ITS AFTERMATH

There are many fine analyses of the origins of World War I. See especially Denna F. Fleming, *The Origins and Legacies of World War I* (Garden City, N.Y.: Doubleday, 1968); Fritz Fischer, *Germany's Aims in the First World War*, English transl. (New York: W. W. Norton, 1967); Sidney B. Fay, *Origins of the War* (New York: Macmillan, 1929).

The question of American neutrality during the war has spawned a vast literature. Among the most recent are John W. Coogan, *The End of Neutrality: The U.S., Britain, and Maritime Rights, 1899–1915* (Ithaca, N.Y.: Cornell University Press, 1981); Patrick Devlin, *Too Proud to Fight: Woodrow Wilson's Neutrality* (New York: Oxford University Press, 1975); Burton I. Kaufman, *Efficiency and Expansion: Foreign Trade Organization in the Wilson Administration* (Westport, Conn.: Greenwood Press, 1974); Ross Gregory, *The Origins of American Intervention in the First World War* (New York, W. W. Norton, 1971); John M. Cooper, *The Vanity of Power: American Isolationism and World War I, 1914–1917* (Westport, Conn.: Greenwood Press, 1969). Older studies that remain pertinent include Daniel Smith, *The Great Departure: The United States and World War I, 1914–1920* (New York: John Wiley and Sons, 1965), and his *Robert Lansing and American Neutrality* (Berkeley, Calif.: University of California Press, 1958). The best study of American neutrality policy continues to be Ernest R. May, *The World War and American Isolation, 1914–1917* (Cambridge, Mass.: Harvard University Press, 1959). Barbara Tuchman, *The Zimmerman Telegram* (New York: Macmillan, 1958), is also interesting reading.

Biographical studies of this era include Arthur S. Link's multi-volume biography, *Wilson* (Princeton, N.J.: Princeton University Press, 1947–65); Kendrick A. Clements, *William Jennings Bryan: Missionary Isolationist* (Knoxville, Tenn.: University of Tennessee Press, 1982); Ross Gregory, *Walter Hines Page: Ambassador to the Court of St. James* (Lexington, Ky.: University of Kentucky Press, 1970); Arthur C. Walworth, *Woodrow Wilson* (Boston: Houghton Mifflin, 1958); Arthur Link, *Wilson the Diplomatist* (Baltimore: Johns Hopkins University Press, 1957); Alexander L. George and Juliette L. George, *Woodrow Wilson and Colonel House: A Personality Study* (New York: J. Day, 1956).

The Russian intervention is admirably covered in John Silverlight, *The Victor's Dilemma* (New York: Weybright and Talley, 1970); George F. Kennan, *Russia Leaves the War* (Princeton, N.J.: Princeton University Press, 1956), and his *The Decision to Intervene* (Princeton, N.J.: Princeton University Press, 1958). For the Bullitt mission to Russia, see Beatrice Farnsworth, *William C. Bullitt and the Soviet Union* (Bloomington, Ind.: Indiana University Press, 1967).

For Wilson's peacemaking efforts and the Paris negotiations, see Arthur J. Walworth, *Wilson and His Peacemakers* (New York: W. W. Norton, 1986); Klaus Schwabe, *Woodrow Wilson: Revolutionary Germany and Peacemaking, 1918–1919* (Chapel

Hill, N.C.: University of North Carolina Press, 1985); Manfred Jonas, *The United States and Germany: A Diplomatic History* (Ithaca, N.Y.: Cornell University Press, 1984); Arthur C. Walworth, *America's Moment, 1918: American Diplomacy at the End of World War I* (New York: W. W. Norton, 1977); Keith L. Nelson, *Victors Divided: America and the Allies in Germany, 1918–1923* (Berkeley, Calif.: University of California Press, 1975); Arno J. Mayer, *Politics and Diplomacy of Peacemaking: Containment and Counter-revolution at Versailles, 1918–1919* (New York: Alfred A. Knopf, 1967); N. Gordon Levin, Jr., *Woodrow Wilson and World Politics: America's Response to War and Revolution* (New York: Oxford University Press, 1968); Seth P. Tillman, *Anglo-American Relations at the Paris Peace Conference of 1919* (Princeton, N.J.: Princeton University Press, 1961).

The debate over the League of Nations has received intensive coverage. See Lloyd E. Ambrosius, *Woodrow Wilson and the American Diplomatic Tradition: The Treaty Fight in Perspective* (New York: Cambridge University Press, 1987); William C. Widenor, *Henry Cabot Lodge and the Search for American Foreign Policy* (Berkeley, Calif.: University of California Press, 1980); Ralph A. Stone, *The Irreconcilables: The Fight against the League of Nations* (Lexington, Ky.: University of Kentucky Press, 1970); Robert J. Maddox, *William E. Borah and American Foreign Policy* (Baton Rouge, La.: Louisiana State University Press, 1969); Warren F. Kuehl, *Seeking World Order: The United States and World Organization to 1920* (Nashville, Tenn.: Vanderbilt University Press, 1969); John Chalmers Vinson, *Referendum for Isolation: Defeat of Article Ten of the League of Nations Covenant* (Athens, Ga.: University of Georgia Press, 1961); Thomas A. Bailey, *Woodrow Wilson and the Great Betrayal* (Chicago: Quadrangle Books, 1963); Paul Birdsall, *Versailles Twenty Years After* (New York: Reynal and Hitchcock, 1941); John M. Keynes, *The Economic Consequences of the Peace* (New York: Macmillan, 1920).

## BETWEEN THE WARS: 1921–1939

An overview of Republican foreign policy may be found in Warren I. Cohen, *Empire Without Tears: America's Foreign Relations, 1921–1933* (New York: Alfred A. Knopf, 1987); Frank Costigliola, *Awkward Dominion: American Political, Economic and Cultural Relations with Europe, 1919–1933* (Ithaca, N.Y.: Cornell University Press, 1985); L. Ethan Ellis, *Republican Foreign Policy, 1921–1933* (New Brunswick, N.J.: Rutgers University Press, 1968). Economic affairs have received a good deal of notice. See, for example, Mark Trachtenberg, *Reparations in World Politics* (New York: Columbia University Press, 1980); Melvyn P. Leffler, *The Elusive Quest: America's Pursuit of European Stability and French Security, 1919–1933* (Chapel Hill, N.C.: University of North Carolina Press, 1979); Michael J. Hogan, *Informal Entente: The Private Structure of Cooperation in Anglo-American Economic Diplomacy, 1919–1928* (Columbia, Mo.: University of Missouri Press, 1977); Joan Hoff Wilson, *American Business and Foreign Policy, 1920–1933* (Lexington, Ky.: University of Kentucky Press, 1971); Charles Kindleberger, *The World in Depression* (London: Allen Lane, 1974); and Joseph Brandes, *Herbert Hoover and Economic Diplomacy: Department of Commerce Policy, 1921–1928* (Pittsburgh, Pa.: University of Pittsburgh Press, 1966).

Other important works include Neal Pease, *Poland: The United States and the Stabilization of Europe, 1919–1933* (New York: Oxford University Press, 1986); Robert D. Schulzinger, *The Wise Men of Foreign Affairs: The History of the Council on Foreign Relations* (New York: Columbia University Press, 1984); Peter H. Buckingham, *International Normalcy: The Open Door Peace with the Former Central Powers, 1921–1929*

(Wilmington Del.: Scholarly Resources, 1983); Michael G. Fry, *Illusions of Security: North Atlantic Diplomacy, 1918–1922* (Toronto: University of Toronto Press, 1972); Betty Glad, *Charles Evans Hughes and the Illusion of Innocence: A Study in American Diplomacy* (Urbana, Ill.: University of Illinois Press, 1966); Elting Morison, *Turmoil and Tradition: A Study of the Life and Times of Henry L. Stimson* (New York: Atheneum, 1964).

General studies of America's Far Eastern policy include Akira Iriye, *After Imperialism: The Search for a New Order in the Far East, 1921–1931* (New York: Atheneum, 1973), and his *Across the Pacific: An Inner History of American-East Asian Relations* (New York: Harcourt, Brace, and World, 1967). Other important studies include Charles E. Neu, *The Troubled Encounter: The United States and Japan* (New York: John Wiley and Sons, 1975); William L. Neumann, *America Encounters Japan: From Perry to MacArthur* (Baltimore: Johns Hopkins University Press, 1963); Dorothy Borg, *American Policy and the Chinese Revolution, 1925–1928* (New York: American Institute of Pacific Relations, 1947).

The Manchurian incident is carefully discussed in Christopher Thorne, *The Limits of Foreign Policy: The West, the League and the Far Eastern Crisis of 1931–33* (London: Hamilton, 1972); Sadako N. Ogata, *Defiance in Manchuria: The Making of Japanese Foreign Policy, 1931–1932* (Berkeley, Calif.: University of California Press, 1964); Armin Rappaport, *Henry L. Stimson and Japan, 1931–1933* (Chicago: University of Chicago Press, 1963). See also James B. Crowley, *Japan's Quest for Autonomy: National Security and Foreign Policy, 1930–1938* (Princeton, N.J.: Princeton University Press, 1966).

On the naval armaments race and the Washington conference, see Roger Dingman, *Power in the Pacific: The Origins of Naval Arms Limitation, 1914–1922* (Chicago: University of Chicago Press, 1974); William R. Braisted, *The United States Navy in the Pacific, 1909–1922* (Austin, Tex.: University of Texas Press, 1971); Thomas H. Buckley, *The United States and the Washington Conference, 1921–1922* (Knoxville, Tenn.: University of Tennessee Press, 1970).

Latin American themes are covered in Lorenzo Meyer, *Mexico and the United States in the Oil Controversy, 1917–1942*, English trans. (Austin, Tex.: University of Texas Press, 1977); Cole Blasier, *The Hovering Giant: U.S. Responses to Revolutionary Change in Latin America* (Pittsburgh, Pa.: University of Pittsburgh Press, 1976); Kenneth J. Grieb, *The Latin American Policy of Warren G. Harding* (Fort Worth, Tex.: Texas Christian University Press, 1976); Dana G. Munro, *The United States and the Caribbean Republics in the 1920's* (Princeton, N.J.: Princeton University Press, 1972); Joseph S. Tulchin, *Aftermath of War: World War I and U.S. Policy Toward Latin America* (New York: New York University Press, 1971); William Kamman, *A Search for Stability: United States Diplomacy toward Nicaragua, 1925–1933* (Notre Dame, Ind.: Notre Dame University Press, 1968).

For Roosevelt's Latin American policies, start with Bryce Wood, *The Making of the Good Neighbor Policy* (New York: Columbia University Press, 1961). See also Dick Steward, *Trade and Hemisphere: The Good Neighbor Policy and Reciprocal Trade* (Columbia, Mo.: University of Missouri Press, 1976); Irwin F. Gellman, *Good Neighbor Diplomacy* (Baltimore: Johns Hopkins University Press, 1979), and his *Roosevelt and Batista: Good Neighbor Diplomacy in Cuba, 1933–1945* (Albuquerque, N.M.: University of New Mexico Press, 1972).

On the issue of Soviet recognition, see Joan Hoff Wilson, *Ideology and*

*Economics: U.S. Relations with the Soviet Union, 1918–1933* (Columbia, Mo.: University of Missouri Press, 1974); Edward Bennett, *Recognition of Russia: An American Foreign Policy Dilemma* (Waltham, Mass.: Blaisdell, 1969); Farnsworth, *Bullitt.*

On isolationism and foreign policy before 1940, see Wayne S. Cole, *Roosevelt and the Isolationists, 1932–1945* (Lincoln, Nebr.: University of Nebraska Press, 1983); William R. Rock, *Chamberlain and Roosevelt* (Columbus, Ohio: Ohio State University Press, 1988); David Reynolds, *The Creation of the Anglo-American Alliance, 1937–1941* (Chapel Hill, N.C.: University of North Carolina Press, 1982); Betty Glad, *Key Pittman: The Tragedy of a Senate Insider* (New York: Columbia University Press, 1986); Telford Taylor, *Munich: The Price of Peace* (New York: Random House, 1979); Robert Dallek, *Franklin D. Roosevelt and American Foreign Policy, 1932–1945* (New York: Oxford University Press, 1979); Arnold A. Offner, *The Origins of the Second World War: American Foreign Policy and World Politics, 1917–1941* (New York: Praeger, 1975); George W. Baer, *Test Case: Italy, Ethiopia, and the League of Nations* (Stanford, Calif.: Hoover Institute Press, 1976); Frank Hardie, *The Abyssinian Crisis* (Hamden, Conn.: Archon Books, 1974); Arnold A. Offner, *American Appeasement: United States Foreign Policy and Germany, 1933–1938* (Cambridge, Mass.: Belknap Press of Harvard University Press, 1969); Richard P. Traina, *American Diplomacy and the Spanish Civil War* (Bloomington, Ind.: Indiana University Press, 1968); Manfred Jonas, *Isolationism in America, 1935–1941* (Ithaca, N.Y.: Cornell University Press, 1966); Allen Guttman, *The Wound in the Heart: America and the Spanish Civil War* (New York: Free Press of Glencoe, 1962); Wayne S. Cole, *Senator Gerald P. Nye and American Foreign Relations* (Minneapolis: University of Minnesota Press, 1962); Robert A. Divine, *The Illusion of Neutrality* (Chicago: University of Chicago Press, 1962). See also William E. Leuchtenburg, *Franklin D. Roosevelt and the New Deal* (New York: Harper and Row, 1963); and James MacGregor Burns, *Roosevelt: The Lion and the Fox* (New York: Harcourt, Brace, and World, 1956).

## WORLD WAR II

There is a voluminous literature dealing with American involvement in the European aspect of World War II. Beyond the studies of the Roosevelt leadership mentioned earlier, see, for example, Waldo Heinrichs, *Threshold of War: Franklin D. Roosevelt and American Entry into World War II* (New York: Oxford University Press, 1988); Patrick J. Hearden, *Roosevelt Confronts Hitler: America's Entry into World War II* (De Kalb, Ill.: Northern Illinois University Press, 1987); Joseph P. Lash, *Roosevelt and Churchill, 1939–1941: The Partnership That Saved the West* (New York: W. W. Norton, 1976); Adolph A. Hoehling, *America's Road to War, 1939–1941* (New York: Abelard-Schuman, 1970); Theodore A. Wilson, *The First Summit: Roosevelt and Churchill at Placentia Bay, 1941* (Boston: Houghton Mifflin, 1969); James V. Compton, *The Swastika and the Eagle: Hitler, the United States and the Origins of World War II* (Boston: Houghton Mifflin, 1967); T. R. Fehrenbach, *F.D.R.'s Undeclared War, 1939–1941* (New York: D. McKay, 1967); Saul Friedlander, *Prelude to Downfall: Hitler and the United States, 1939–1941* (New York: Alfred A. Knopf, 1967); Robert A. Divine, *The Reluctant Belligerent: American Entry into World War II*, 2d ed. (New York: John Wiley and Sons, 1979); Warren F. Kimball, *The Most Unsordid Act: Lend-Lease, 1934–1941* (Baltimore: Johns Hopkins University Press, 1969); Philip Goodhart, *Fifty Ships That Saved the World: The Foundation of the Anglo-American Alliance* (New York: Doubleday, 1965);

William Langer and S. Everett Gleason, *The Undeclared War, 1940–1941* (New York: Harper and Row, 1964).

The literature dealing with U.S. policy toward East Asia in the early 1930s is rather thin. One study that stands out, however, is Dorothy Borg, *The United States and the Far Eastern Crisis of 1933–1938: From the Manchurian Incident through the Initial Stage of the Undeclared Sino-Japanese War* (Cambridge, Mass.: Harvard University Press, 1964). Other studies of note include James Herzog, *Closing the Door: American-Japanese Diplomatic Relations, 1936–1941* (Annapolis, Md.: Naval Institute Press, 1973); and Hamilton D. Perry, *The Panay Incident: Prelude to Pearl Harbor* (New York: Macmillan, 1969).

America's involvement in the Asian aspect of World War II has been a subject of great interest to scholars. Among the best studies are Akira Iriye, *The Origins of The Second World War in Asia and the Pacific* (New York: Longman, 1987); Ronald H. Spector, *Eagle against the Sun: The American War with Japan* (New York: Free Press, 1985); Gordon W. Prange, *At Dawn We Slept: The Untold Story of Pearl Harbor* (New York: Penguin Books, 1981); Robert J. C. Butow, *The John Doe Associates: Backdoor Diplomacy for Peace, 1941* (Stanford, Calif.: Stanford University Press, 1974); Dorothy Borg and Shumpei Okamota, eds., *Pearl Harbor as History: Japanese-American Relations, 1931–1941* (New York: Columbia University Press, 1973); Waldo Heinrichs, *American Ambassador: Joseph C. Grew and the Development of the American Diplomatic Tradition* (Boston: Little, Brown, 1966); Roberta Wohlstetter, *Pearl Harbor: Warning and Decision* (Stanford, Calif.: Stanford University Press, 1962); Robert J. C. Butow, *Tojo and the Coming of the War* (Stanford, Calif.: Stanford University Press, 1961); David J. Lu, *From the Marco Polo Bridge to Pearl Harbor: Japan's Entry into World War II* (Washington, D.C.: Public Affairs Press, 1961); Herbert Feis, *The Road to Pearl Harbor: The Coming of the War between the United States and Japan* (New York: Atheneum, 1962).

For American-Chinese relations during World War II, see Michael Schaller, *The U.S. Crusade in China, 1938–1945* (New York: Columbia University Press, 1979); Russell D. Buhite, *Patrick J. Hurley and American Foreign Policy* (Ithaca, N.Y.: Cornell University Press, 1973); Paul A. Varg, *The Closing of the Door: Sino-American Relations, 1936–1946* (East Lansing, Mich.: Michigan State University Press, 1973); E. J. Kahn, Jr., *The China Hands: America's Foreign Service Officers and What Befell Them* (New York: Penguin Books, 1972); Barbara Tuchman, *Stilwell and the American Experience in China, 1911–1945* (New York; Macmillan, 1971); Tang Tsou, *America's Failure in China, 1941–1950* (Chicago: University of Chicago Press, 1963); Herbert Feis, *The China Tangle: The American Effort in China from Pearl Harbor to the Marshall Mission* (New York: Atheneum, 1965).

On the wartime relationship between Churchill, Roosevelt, and Stalin, see Russell D. Buhite, *Decision at Yalta* (Wilmington, Del.: Scholarly Resources, 1986); Eric Larrabee, *Commander in Chief, Franklin Delano Roosevelt, His Lieutenants and Their War* (New York: Harper and Row, 1986); Gaddis Smith, *American Diplomacy during the Second World War, 1941–1945* (New York: John Wiley and Sons, 1985); Terry H. Anderson, *The United States, Great Britain and the Cold War, 1944–1947* (Columbia, Mo.: University of Missouri Press, 1981); Robert M. Hathaway, *Ambiguous Partnership: Britain and America, 1944–1947* (New York: Columbia University Press, 1981); Mark Stoler, *The Politics of the Second Front: American Military Planning in Coalition Warfare, 1941–1943* (Westport, Conn.: Greenwood Press, 1977); George C. Herring, *Aid to Russia, 1941–1946: Strategy, Diplomacy, and the Origins of the Cold War* (New York: Columbia University Press, 1976); Warren F. Kimball, *Swords or Ploughshares: The*

*Morganthau Plan for Defeated Nazi Germany, 1943–1946* (Philadelphia: Lippincott, 1976); Robert Beitzell, *The Uneasy Alliance: America, Britain and Russia, 1941–1943* (New York: Alfred A. Knopf, 1973); Raymond G. O'Connor, *Diplomacy for Victory: F.D.R. and Unconditional Surrender* (New York: W. W. Norton, 1971); Diane Shaver Clemens, *Yalta* (New York: Oxford University Press, 1970); William L. Neumann, *After Victory: Churchill, Roosevelt, Stalin and the Making of the Peace* (New York: Harper and Row, 1967); Herbert Feis, *Churchill, Roosevelt and Stalin* (Princeton, N.J.: Princeton University Press, 1957).

See the following on the decision to build and use the atomic bomb: Christopher Thorne, *Allies of a Kind: The United States, Britain, and the War against Japan, 1941–1945* (New York: Oxford University Press, 1977); Martin F. Sherwin, *A World Destroyed: The Atomic Bomb and the Grand Alliance* (New York: Random House, 1975); Walter S. Schoenberger, *Decision of Destiny* (Athens, Ohio: Ohio University Press, 1969); Herbert Feis, *The Atomic Bomb and the End of World War II: Contest over Japan* (Princeton, N.J.: Princeton University Press, 1967); Gar Alperovitz, *Atomic Diplomacy: Hiroshima and Potsdam—the Use of the Atomic Bomb and the American Confrontation with Soviet Power* (New York: Simon and Schuster, 1965); Robert J. C. Butow, *Japan's Decision to Surrender* (Stanford, Calif.: Stanford University Press, 1954).

## THE COLD WAR, 1945–1961

The cold war has generated an enormous literature. The following are among the more influential studies of this issue. Walter LaFeber, *America, Russia and the Cold War, 1945–1984*, 5th ed. (New York: Alfred A. Knopf, 1985); John Lewis Gaddis, *Strategies of Containment* (New York: Oxford University Press, 1982), and his *The United States and the Origins of the Cold War 1941–1947* (New York: Columbia University Press, 1972); Robert C. Donovan, *The Presidency of Harry Truman*, 2 vols. (New York: W. W. Norton, 1977–82); Thomas G. Paterson, *On Every Front: The Making of the Cold War* (New York: W. W. Norton, 1979); Richard Freeland, *The Truman Doctrine and the Origins of McCarthyism* (New York: Alfred A. Knopf, 1977); Daniel Yergin, *Shattered Peace: Origins of the Cold War and the National Security State* (New York: Houghton Mifflin, 1977); Thomas G. Paterson, *Soviet-American Confrontation: Postwar Reconstruction and the Origins of the Cold War* (Baltimore: Johns Hopkins University Press, 1973); Lisle A. Rose, *After Yalta* (New York: Scribner's, 1973); Barton J. Bernstein, ed., *Politics and Policies of the Truman Administration* (Chicago: Quadrangle Books, 1970); Lloyd C. Gardner, *Architects of Illusion: Men and Ideas in American Foreign Policy, 1941–1949* (Chicago: Quadrangle Books, 1970).

For the nuclear question in the Truman era, see Joseph Lieberman, *Scorpion and Tarantula: The Struggle to Control Atomic Weapons, 1945–1949* (Boston: Houghton Mifflin, 1970); Gregg Herkin, *The Winning Weapon: The Atomic Bomb in the Cold War, 1945–1950* (New York: Random House, 1982); Paul Boyer, *By the Bomb's Early Light: American Thought and Culture at the Dawn of the Atomic Age* (New York: Pantheon Books, 1985).

See also Michael J. Hogan, *The Marshall Plan: American, Britain and the Reconstruction of Western Europe, 1947–1952* (New York: Cambridge University Press, 1987); Robert A. Pollard, *Economic Security and the Origins of the Cold War* (New York: Columbia University Press, 1985); G. M. Alexander, *The Prelude to the Truman Doctrine: British Policy in Greece, 1944–1947* (New York: Oxford University Press, 1984); Lawrence Kaplan, *The United States and the Origins of NATO: The Formative Years* (Lexington, Ky.: University of Kentucky Press, 1984); Timothy P. Ireland, *Creating the Entangling Alliance: The United States and NATO* (Westport, Conn.: Greenwood Press, 1984); Theodore A. Couloumbis, *The United States, Greece and Turkey* (New York: Praeger, 1983); Avi Shlaim, *The United States and the Berlin Blockade, 1948–1949* (Berkeley, Calif.: University of California Press, 1983); Lawrence Wittner, *American Intervention in Greece, 1943–1949* (New York: Columbia University Press, 1982); Bruce Kuniholm, *The Origins of the Cold War in the Near East* (Princeton, N.J.: Princeton University Press, 1980); Barry Rubin, *Paved With Good Intentions: The American Experience in Iran* (New York: Penguin Books, 1980). George Kennan, *Memoirs: 1925 to 1950* (New York: Bantam Books, 1967); and Dean Acheson, *Present at the Creation: My Years in the State Department* (New York: W. W. Norton, 1969), are also invaluable.

For postwar China policy, consult books listed above as well as the following: Nancy Bernkopf Tucker, *Patterns in the Dust: Chinese-American Relations and the Recognition Controversy, 1949–1951* (New York: Columbia University Press, 1983); William Stueck, *The Road to Confrontation: American Policy toward China and Korea* (Chapel Hill, N.C.: University of North Carolina Press, 1982); Joseph Camilleri, *Chinese Foreign Policy: The Maoist Era and Its Aftermath* (Seattle, Wash.: University of Washington Press, 1980); Gary May, *China Skapegoat: The Diplomatic Ordeal of John Carter Vincent* (Washington D.C.: New Republic Books, 1979); Lisle A. Rose, *Roots of Tragedy: The United States and the Struggle for Asia, 1945–1953* (Westport, Conn.: Greenwood Press, 1976); Akira Iriye, *The Cold War in Asia: A Historical Introduction* (Englewood Cliffs, N.J.: Prentice Hall, 1974); Lewis M. Purifoy, *Harry Truman's China Policy: McCarthyism and the Diplomacy of Hysteria, 1947–1951* (New York: New Viewpoints Press, 1976); Foster Rhea Dulles, *American Foreign Policy toward Communist China, 1949–1969* (New York: Thomas Crowell, 1972); Warren I. Cohen, *America's Response to China: An Interpretive History of Sino-American Relations* (New York: Columbia University Press, 1990); Herbert Feis, *The China Tangle: The American Effort in China from Pearl Harbor to the Marshall Mission* (New York: Atheneum, 1965).

The Japanese occupation is well covered in Michael Schaller, *The American Occupation of Japan* (New York: Oxford University Press, 1985). See also William S. Borden, *The Pacific Alliance: U.S. Foreign Economic Policy and Japanese Trade Recovery, 1947–1953* (Madison, Wis.: University of Wisconsin Press, 1984); Kazuo Kawai, *Japan's American Interlude* (Chicago: University of Chicago Press, 1960).

On America's early Southeast Asian policy, see Lloyd C. Gardner, *Approaching Vietnam: From World War II through Dienbienphu, 1941–1954* (New York: W. W. Norton, 1988); Andrew J. Rotter, *The Path to Vietnam: Origins of the American Commitment to Southeast Asia* (Ithaca, N.Y.: Cornell University Press, 1987).

For the Korean entanglement see sources listed previously as well as Burton I. Kaufman, *The Korean War: Challenges in Crisis, Credibility and Command* (New York: Alfred A. Knopf, 1986); Rosemary Foot, *The Wrong War: American Policy and the Dimensions of the Korean Conflict, 1950–1953* (Ithaca, N.Y.: Cornell University Press, 1985); Bruce Cumings, *The Origins of the Korean War* (Princeton N.J.: Princeton University Press, 1981); Frank Baldwin, ed., *Without Parallel: The American-Korean Relationship since 1945* (New York: Pantheon Books, 1974); Richard H. Rovere and Arthur Schlesinger, Jr., *The MacArthur Controversy and American Foreign Policy* (New York: Farrar, Straus, Giroux, 1965); Allen S. Whiting, *China Crosses the Yalu* (Stanford, Calif.: Stanford University Press, 1960); I. F. Stone, *The Hidden History of the Korean War* (New York: Monthly Review Press, 1952).

A number of fine studies of Eisenhower and his administration have appeared in recent years. See, for example, H. William Brands, Jr., *Cold Warriors: Eisenhower's Generation and American Foreign Policy* (New York: Columbia University Press, 1988); Stephen E. Ambrose, *Eisenhower*, 2 vols. (New York: Simon and Schuster, 1983–84); Robert A. Divine, *Eisenhower and the Cold War* (New York: Oxford University Press, 1981); Charles Alexander, *Holding the Line: The Eisenhower Administration* (Bloomington, Ind.: Indiana University Press, 1975). For U.S. relations with Europe, see Robert Rhodes, *Anthony Eden: A Biography* (London: A. Lane, 1987); George W. Breslauer, *Khrushchev and Brezhnev as Leaders* (Boston: Allen and Unwin, 1982); Alfred Grosser, *The Western Alliance: European-American Relations since 1945* (New York: Random House, 1982); Emmet John Hughes, *Ordeal of Power* (New York: Atheneum, 1963).

On massive retaliation and the nuclear arms race, see Walter A. McDougall, *The Heavens and the Earth: A Political History of the Space Age* (New York: Basic Books, 1985); Gerard Clarfield and William Wiecek, *Nuclear America: Military and Civilian Nuclear Power in the United States, 1940–1980* (New York: Harper and Row, 1984); Robert Divine, *Blowing on the Wind: The Nuclear Test Ban Debate, 1954–1960* (New York: Oxford University Press, 1979); James R. Killian, *Sputnik, Scientists and Eisenhower* (Cambridge, Mass.: Massachusetts Institute of Technology Press, 1977); Richard Aliano, *American Defense Policy from Eisenhower to Kennedy* (Athens, Ohio: Ohio University Press, 1975); Jerome H. Kahan, *Security in the Nuclear Age: Developing U.S. Strategic Arms Policy* (Washington, D.C.: Brookings Institution, 1975); Warner Schilling, Paul Hammond, and Glenn Snyder, *Strategy, Politics, and Defense Budgets* (New York: Columbia University Press, 1962).

For coverage of U.S. policy in the Middle East during Eisenhower's eight years, see Chester Cooper, *The Lion's Last Roar: Suez, 1956* (New York: Harper and Row, 1978); Selwyn Lloyd, *Suez* (New York: Mayflower Books, 1978); Howard M. Sachar, *A History of Israel: From the Rise of Zionism to Our Time* (New York: Alfred A. Knopf, 1976); William R. Polk, *The United States and the Arab World*, 3d ed. (Cambridge, Mass.: Harvard University Press, 1975); Walter Laqueur, *Confrontation: The Middle East and World Politics* (New York: Quadrangle/New York Times Books, 1974); Kenneth Love, *Suez: The Twice-Fought War* (New York: McGraw Hill, 1969).

For Eisenhower's handling of Third World problems, see Jonathan Kwitny, *Endless Enemies: The Making of an Unfriendly World* (New York: Penguin Books, 1986); Martin Meredith, *The First Dance of Freedom: Black Africa in the Postwar Era* (New York: Harper and Row, 1985); Peter Duignan and L. H. Gann, *The United States and Africa: A History* (New York: Cambridge University Press, 1984); Richard H. Immerman, *The CIA in Guatamala: The Foreign Policy of Intervention* (Austin, Tex.: University of Texas Press, 1982); Madeline Kalb, *The Congo Cables: The Cold War in Africa from Eisenhower to Kennedy* (New York: Macmillan, 1982). For American activities in Iran and Guatamala, see Stephen G. Rabe, *Eisenhower and Latin America: The Foreign Policy of Anticommunism* (Chapel Hill, N.C.: University of North Carolina Press, 1987); Walter LaFeber, *Inevitable Revolutions: The United States in Central America* (New York: W. W. Norton, 1984); Rubin, *Paved with Good Intentions: The American Experience in Iran*.

For the Eisenhower policy in Southeast Asia, see George C. Herring, *America's Longest War: The United States and Vietnam, 1950–1975* (New York: Alfred A. Knopf, 1979); George McT. Kahin, *Intervention: How America Became Involved in Vietnam* (New York: Alfred A. Knopf, 1986); Stanley Karnow, *Vietnam: A History* (New York: Viking, 1983); Robert F. Randle, *Geneva, 1954* (Princeton, N.J.: Princeton University Press, 1969).

## YEARS OF CRISIS, 1961–1976

For the Kennedy-Johnson years, see David Burner, *John F. Kennedy and a New Generation* (Boston: Little, Brown, 1988); Herbert S. Parmet, *JFK: The Presidency of John F. Kennedy* (New York: Dial, 1984); Vaughn D. Bornet, *The Presidency of Lyndon B. Johnson* (Lawrence, Kans.: University of Kansas Press, 1983); George Ball, *The Past Has Another Pattern* (New York: W. W. Norton and Co., 1982); Warren I. Cohen, *Dean Rusk* (Totowa, N.J.: Cooper Square, 1980); David Halberstam, *The Best and the Brightest* (New York: Random House, 1972); Arthur M. Schlesinger, Jr., *A Thousand Days: John F. Kennedy in the White House* (Boston: Houghton Mifflin, 1965); Theodore Sorensen, *Kennedy* (New York: Harper and Row, 1965).

For the nuclear arms race, see Desmond Ball, *Politics and Force Levels: The Strategic Missile Program of the Kennedy Administration* (Berkeley, Calif.: University of California Press, 1981); Glenn Seaborg, *Kennedy, Khrushchev, and the Test Ban* (Berkeley, Calif.: University of California Press, 1981); Michael Mandlebaum, *The Nuclear Question: The United States and Nuclear Weapons, 1946–1976* (New York: Cambridge University Press, 1979); Ernest Yanarella, *The Missile Defense Controversy: Strategy, Technology, and Politics, 1955–1972* (Lexington, Ky.: University of Kentucky Press, 1977); John Newhouse, *Cold Dawn: The Story of SALT* (New York: Holt, Rinehart and Winston, 1973); Henry Trewhitt, *McNamara* (New York: Harper and Row, 1971); George H. Quester, *Nuclear Diplomacy: The First Twenty Five Years* (New York: Dunellan, 1970); William W. Kaufmann, *The McNamara Strategy* (New York: Harper and Row, 1964).

For Cuban relations, see Morris Morley, *Imperial State and Revolution: The United States and Cuba, 1952–1986* (New York: Cambridge University Press, 1988); Richard E. Welch, *Response to Revolution: The United States and the Cuban Revolution, 1959–1961* (Chapel Hill, N.C.: University of North Carolina Press, 1985).

For the Cuban missile crisis, see Raymond Garthoff, *Reflections on the Cuban Missile Crisis* (Washington, D.C.: Brookings Institution, 1987); Abram Chayes, *The Cuban Missile Crisis* (New York: Oxford University Press, 1974); Graham T. Allison, *Essence of Decision: Explaining the Cuban Missile Crisis* (Boston: Little, Brown, 1971); Herbert S. Dinerstein, *The Making of a Missile Crisis* (Baltimore: Johns Hopkins University Press, 1969).

For the American involvement in Vietnam, see sources listed in earlier chapters as well as Neil Sheehan, *A Bright Shining Lie: John Paul Vann and America in Vietnam* (New York: Random House, 1988); Larry Berman, *Planning a Tragedy: The Americanization of the War in Vietnam* (New York: W. W. Norton, 1983); Harry Summers, Jr., *On Strategy: A Critical Analysis of the Vietnam War* (Novato, Calif.: Presedio, 1981); Herbert Y. Schandler, *The Unmaking of a President: Lyndon Johnson and Vietnam* (Princeton, N.J.: Princeton University Press, 1977); Alexander Kendrick, *The Wound Within: America in the Vietnam Years, 1945–1974* (Boston: Little, Brown, 1974); Frances FitzGerald, *Fire in the Lake: The Vietnamese and the Americans in Vietnam* (Boston: Little, Brown, 1972); Chester L. Cooper, *The Lost Crusade: America in Vietnam* (New York: Dodd, Mead, 1970); Townsend Hoopes, *The Limits of Intervention: An Inside Account of How the Johnson Policy of Escalation in Vietnam Was Reversed* (New York: D. McKay, 1969).

The literature on the Nixon administration is growing rapidly. On Soviet-American relations and détente, see Robert D. Schulzinger, *Henry Kissinger: Doctor of*

*Diplomacy* (New York: Columbia University Press, 1989); William Hyland, *Rivals: Superpower Relations from Nixon to Reagan* (New York: Random House, 1987); Raymond Garthoff, *Detente and Confrontation: American-Soviet Relations from Nixon to Reagan* (Washington, D.C.: Brookings Institution, 1985); Seymour M. Hersh, *The Price of Power: Kissinger in the Nixon White House* (New York: Summit Books, 1983); Henry Kissinger, *The White House Years* (Boston: Little, Brown, 1979), and his *Years of Upheaval* (Boston: Little, Brown, 1982); Tad Szulc, *The Illusion of Peace* (New York: Viking, 1978).

Peacemaking is discussed in many of the titles cited previously. See also Arnold R. Isaacs, *Without Honor: Defeat in Vietnam and Cambodia* (Baltimore: Johns Hopkins University Press, 1983); Nguyen Tien Hung and Jerrold Schechter, *The Palace File* (New York: Harper and Row, 1986); Truong Nhu Tang, with David Chanoff and Doan Van Toai, *A Vietcong Memoir* (San Diego, Calif.: Harcourt Brace Jovanovich, 1985).

On Middle East affairs, see the titles listed earlier as well as William Quandt, *Decade of Decision* (Berkeley, Calif.: University of California Press, 1978); Noam Chomsky, *The Fateful Triangle: The U.S., Israel, and the Palestinians* (Garden City, N.Y.: Doubleday, 1984).

For SALT I, see titles listed earlier and Garthoff, *Detente and Confrontation*, and Gerard Smith, *Doubletalk: The Story of the First Strategic Arms Limitation Talks* (Garden City, N.Y.: Doubleday, 1980).

## TO THE PRESENT: CARTER AND REAGAN

The literature dealing with the Carter administration is not yet as rich as it surely will become. First try Gaddis Smith, *Morality, Reason, and Power: American Diplomacy in the Carter Years* (New York: Hill and Wang, 1986). See also David S. McLellan, *Cyrus Vance* (Totowa, N.J.: Cooper Square, 1985); Joshua Muravchik, *The Uncertain Crusade: Jimmy Carter and the Dilemmas of Human Rights Policy* (Lanham, Md.: Hamilton Press, 1986); Zbignieu Brzezinski, *Power and Principle: Memoirs of the National Security Adviser* (New York: Simon and Schuster, 1983); Cyrus Vance, *Hard Choices: Critical Years in America's Foreign Policy* (New York: Simon and Schuster, 1983); Jimmy Carter, *Keeping Faith: The Memoirs of a President* (New York: Bantam Books, 1982). On Ronald Reagan, see Jeff McMahon, *Reagan and the World* (New York: Monthly Review Press, 1985); Strobe Talbot, *The Russians and Reagan* (New York: Random House, 1984); I. M. Destler et al., *Our Own Worst Enemy: The Unmaking of American Foreign Policy* (New York: Simon and Schuster, 1984); Laurence I. Barrett, *Gambling with History* (Garden City, N.Y.: Doubleday, 1983).

For material on the nuclear question and SDI, see Diana Johnstone, *The Politics of Euromissiles* (London: Verso, 1985); Strobe Talbot, *Endgame: The Inside Story of SALT II* (New York: Harper and Row, 1979), *Deadly Gambits* (New York: Random House, 1985); Solly Zukerman, *Nuclear Illusion and Reality* (New York: Random House, 1982); W. K. H. Panofsky, *Arms Control and SALT II* (Seattle, Wash.: University of Washington Press, 1979).

For African policy, see Study Commission on U.S. Policy toward Southern Africa, *South Africa: Time Running Out* (Berkeley, Calif.: University of California Press, 1986); Gerald J. Bender et al., *African Crisis Areas and U.S. Foreign Policy* (Berkeley,

Calif.: University of California Press, 1985); Ann Seidman, *The Roots of Crisis in Southern Africa* (Trenton, N.J.: Africa World Press, 1984); Sanford J. Ungar, *Africa* (New York: Simon and Schuster, 1985); Devin Danaher, *In Whose Interest? A Guide to U.S.-South Africa Relations* (Washington, D.C.: Institute for Policy Studies, 1984); Anthony Lake, *The "Tar Baby" Option: American Policy toward Southern Rhodesia* (New York: Columbia University Press, 1976).

On the Central American crisis, see titles listed earlier and Thomas W. Walker, ed., *Reagan versus the Sandinistas* (Boulder, Colo.: Westview Press, 1987); Mary B. Vanderlaan, *Revolution and Foreign Policy in Nicaragua* (Boulder, Colo.: Westview Press, 1986); John Booth, *The End and the Beginning* (Boulder, Colo.: Westview Press, 1985); Kenneth Coleman and George Herring, eds., *The Central American Crisis* (Wilmington, Del.: Scholarly Resources, 1985); LaFeber, *Inevitable Revolutions*; Marvin Gittleman et al., eds., *El Salvador: Central America in the New Cold War* (New York: Grove Press, 1982); Tommie Sue Montgomery, *Revolution in El Salvador* (Boulder, Colo.: Westview Press, 1982).

On the Middle East and Southwest Asia, see titles listed above and William B. Quandt, *Camp David: Peacemaking and Politics* (Washington, D.C.: Brookings Institution, 1986); Itamar Rabinovich, *The War for Lebanon, 1970–1983* (Ithaca, N.Y.: Cornell University Press, 1984); R. K. Ramazani, *The U.S. and Iran* (New York: Praeger, 1982); Michael Ledeen and William Lewis, *Debacle: The American Failure in Iran* (New York: Alfred A. Knopf, 1981); Gary Sick, *All Fall Down: America's Tragic Encounter with Iran* (New York: Random House, 1985).

## ILLUSTRATION CREDITS

# INDEX

troubles with Mexico, 396–98
wants a naval disarmament agreement, 387–88
at Washington conference, 389–90
Hughes, Emmet John, 556
Hukuang railroad loan, 307
Hull, Cordell:
    agrees to attend Brussels conference, 442
    blocks aid to the Spanish republic, 421–22
    on Cuban Chaos, 405
    on the Ethiopian crisis, 418
    at the London economic conference, 412–13
    and Mexican oil crisis, 409–10
    negotiates with Admiral Nomura, 445
    on the Nye committee, 416
    opposes Morgenthau plan, 474
    and political-noninterference, 408
    on recognizing the Soviet Union, 413
    rejects last Japanese peace proposals, 448
    and repeal of the arms embargo, 426
    on sanctions against Japan, 444–45
Humphrey, Hubert, 647
Hungary:
    chaos in, 357
    1956 uprising in, 566
Hurley, Patrick:
    and China policy, 515–16
    his plan for China, 462–63
Hussein, Ahmed, 563–64
Hussein, King, 671–72

Ickes, Harold:
    denigrates the Japanese threat, 451
    and the Munich crisis, 424
    and sanctions against Japan, 445
    on the Spanish Civil War, 422
Indochina:
    Japanese advance into, 446
    U.S. role in French war for, 526–28
Indonesia, 589
Intermediate Nuclear Force Reduction treaty, 726
International Court of Justice, 733
Iran:
    hostage crisis in, 711–13
    Mossadegh overthrown in, 575–77
    revolution in, 707–11
    Soviet occupation of, 493–95
Iran-Contra scandal, 733–34
Iriye, Akira, 448
Ishii, Viscount Kikujiro, 317
Israel:
    and the Camp David accords, 694–96
    invades Lebanon, 738–39
    and the 1970 Jordanian crisis, 671–72
    and the Six Days' War, 640–41
Italy:
    Allied invasion of, 470–71
    claims at Versailles, 364
    invades Ethiopia, 416–18

Jackson, Henry, 691
Jackson, Jesse, 743
Japan:
    China policy of, 315

expansionist goals, 286, 443–44
    in Indochina, 446
    intervenes in Siberia, 354–55
    in Manchuria, 277, 392–95
    occupation of, 522–25
    and Russia, 278, 284–85
    and the Sino-Japanese war, 277
    surrenders, 484
    at the Versailles conference, 364–65
Jarring, Gunnar, 641
Jenner, William, 551
Johnson, Hiram, 369
Johnson, Lyndon Baines:
    agrees to Paris peace talks, 647–48
    in Berlin, 606
    decides against a second term, 647
    deploys an ABM system, 633
    and the Dominican crisis, 638–39
    on Gerald Ford, 677
    and the Six Days' War, 640–43
    sketch, 625–26
    and Sputnik, 580
    and the Tonkin Gulf affair, 629–30
Jordan, 671–72
Jordan, David Starr, 334
Judd, Walter, 518
Jusserand, Jules:
    urges compromise on the League, 372
    and Wilson, 358

Kaganovich, Lazar, 496
Kampelman, Max, 725
Karmal, Babrak, 692
Karnow, Stanley, 626
Károlyi, Mihály, 357
Karpov, Viktor, 726
Kasavubu, Joseph:
    and the Congo crisis, 590–91
    and Lumumba, 600
Katsura Taro:
    and the Great White Fleet, 289
    on the Russo-Japanese war, 284
Katyn Forest massacre, 472
Kaufmann, William, 560
Kawai, Kazuo, 487
Keating, Kenneth, 612
Kellogg, Frank B:
    China policy of, 391–92
    on Bolshevism in Latin America, 398
Kellogg-Briand Pact, 375
Kennan, George:
    critical of Truman Doctrine, 501
    criticizes Roosevelt, 465
    disagrees with Acheson's Indochina policy, 530
    Dulles purges, 556
    on the Marshall Plan, 501–2
    on NSC-68, 511
    opposes Korean policy, 541
    opposes Vietnam war, 643
    on Soviet purposes, 496–98
Kennedy, Edward, 713
Kennedy, John F.:
    and the Bay of Pigs invasion, 598–99
    and the Berlin crisis, 603–7
    and the Congo, 618–22
    and the Cuban missile crisis, 611–17

on flexible response, 608
    and the Laotian question, 601–3
    on massive retaliation, 607
    meets Khrushchev in Vienna, 604–5
    and the partial test ban treaty, 617–18
    reacts to the Berlin wall, 606–7
    sketch, 595–96
    on Sputnik, 580
    and Vietnam, 618–22
Kennedy, Joseph P., 501
Kennedy, Robert:
    challenges Johnson in the primaries, 644
    and the Cuban missile crisis, 615, 617
Kent State University, 656
Keynes, John M., 413
Keyworth, George A. III, 723
Khomeini, Ayatollah Ruhollah, 709–11
Khrushchev, Nikita:
    and Berlin, 581–83, 606–7
    and Castro, 588–89
    and the Cuban missile crisis, 612–13, 615–17
    crushes the Hungarian uprising, 566
    cultivates West Germany, 562
    meets Kennedy in Vienna, 604–5
    and the partial test ban, 617–18
    sends arms to Egypt, 563
    and the Suez crisis, 568
    and the U-2 affair, 584–85
    visits the U.S., 583
Kim il Sung, 537–38
Kim Koo, 533
Kimmel, Husband E., 449–51
King, Coretta Scott, 653
King, Ernest J., 487
King, Martin Luther, Jr., 643
King, William, 398
Kirkland, Lane, 691
Kissinger, Henry:
    and Africa, 679–82
    and Angola, 681
    and detente, 682–83
    and the Middle East, 670–75
    during the 1972 Paris peace talks, 658–61
    and Nixon, 651–52
    puts pressure on Carter, 711
    and SALT I, 667–68
    his secret China mission, 664–65
    on South America, 701
Knowland, William, 518
Knox, Frank, 431
Knox, Philander:
    and dollar diplomacy, 304–7
    and Japan, 304–7
Kolchak, Aleksandr V., 362–63
Konoye, Fumimaro:
    East Asian ambitions of, 444
    and the petroleum freeze, 446–47
    and the war in China, 442–43
Korea:
    divided and occupied, 532–34
    war in, 537–49
Korean Democratic party, 533
Korean People's Republic, 533
Korean truce talks, 556–58
Kosygin, Alexsei:
    and the ABM question, 631–32
    as Soviet leader, 630